THE TRUE IMAGE

". . . every man perfect in Christ Jesus"
(Col. 1:28)

THE TRUE IMAGE

The Origin and Destiny of Man in Christ

PHILIP EDGCUMBE HUGHES

WILLIAM B. EERDMANS PUBLISHING COMPANY
GRAND RAPIDS, MICHIGAN

INTER-VARSITY PRESS
LEICESTER, ENGLAND

Copyright © 1989 by William B. Eerdmans Publishing Company
255 Jefferson Ave. S.E., Grand Rapids, Mich. 49503

First British edition 1989 by Inter-Varsity Press
38 De Montfort Street, Leicester LE1 7GP, England

Library of Congress Cataloging-in-Publication Data

Hughes, Philip Edgcumbe.

    The true image: The origin and destiny of man in Christ / Philip Edgcumbe Hughes
        p.   cm.
    Includes bibliographical references and indexes.
    ISBN 0-8028-0314-8
    1. Man (Theology) 2. Jesus Christ—Person and offices. 3. Image of God. I. Title.
BT702.H82   1988
233'.5—dc19

                                        88-25843
                                              CIP

British Library Cataloguing-in-Publication Data

Hughes, Philip Edgcumbe, *1915-*
    The true image
    I. 1. Christology
    I. Title
    232

Inter-Varsity Press ISBN 0 85110 680 3

Inter-Varsity Press is the book-publishing division of the Universities and Colleges
Christian Fellowship.

Contents

Preface   viii

I. CREATION IN THE IMAGE OF GOD: INTEGRATION   1

  1. The Meaning of Creation in the Image of God   3
  2. Is There a Bodily Aspect of the Image?   10
  3. Man and the Divine Image Not Identical   15
  4. The Image of God in the New Testament   24
    Image   26
    Son   29
    Firstborn   35
    Word   40
    Glory   42
    Stamp   45
    Note on "Form" (morphē) in Philippians 2:6   47
  5. The Imprint of the Image in Man   51
    Personality   51
    Spirituality   55
    Rationality   57
    Morality   59
    Authority   61
    Creativity   62
  6. The Image in Fallen Man   65

II. THE IMAGE REJECTED: DISINTEGRATION   71

  7. The Origin of Evil   73
    Dualism   83
    The Privation of Good   86
    A Prenatal or Transcendental Fall   88
    Inherent Imperfection   93
    A Beneficial Necessity   96
    The Evolutionary Explanation   99
    Nothingness   101

Neoorthodoxy   107
8. The Perfection of the Creature   112
9. The Biblical Account of the Fall   115
10. The Meaning of Death   119
11. Original Sin   125
Romans 5:12-21   128
Evidences of the Fall   135
12. The Freedom of the Will   143
13. The Freedom of God   148
Foreknowledge and Foreordination   152
Election   158
The Primacy of Grace   163
The Response of Faith   167
The Free Offer of the Gospel   172
Election in Christ   178
Election and Christian Security   182
14. The Effect of the Fall   185
The Semi-Pelagian Synthesis   193
The Terminus of Synergism   200

III. THE IMAGE RESTORED: REINTEGRATION   211

15. The Word Becomes Flesh   213
16. The Evolutionistic Interpretation   224
17. The Self-Humbling of the Image   232
18. The Theanthropic Person of Christ   235
19. Docetic Christology   237
20. The Early Unitarians   249
21. Origen's Christology   260
22. Arianism   266
23. The Christology of Athanasius   276
24. The "Deification" of Man in Christ   281
25. The Christology of Apollinaris   287
26. Nestorius and Nestorianism   294
27. On to Chalcedon   307
28. The Importance of Orthodoxy   317
29. The Life of Jesus   328
30. The Death of Jesus   335
31. Understanding the Atonement   342
32. The Continuing Debate   355
33. The Glorification of Christ   363
34. Christology and History   375
35. Between the Comings   386

36. Between Death and Resurrection   393
37. Is the Soul Immortal?   398
38. The Kingdom   408
    Indexes   415
      Names and Subjects   415
      Biblical References   421

Preface

The standpoint of the author of this study is that of the Christian faith. In conformity with the position of classical Christianity from apostolic times onward the Bible is accepted as the authentic, divinely revealed source of knowledge concerning both God and man. The theme of this work is developed in the spirit of faith seeking understanding--a principle attributed by Augustine, late in the fourth century, to the prophet Isaiah,[1] and appropriated by Anselm seven hundred years later. Anselm's attitude was one of prayer, which expresses total dependence on God to whom we owe the grace that redeems our life and renews our mind.

> Lord, I acknowledge and I thank thee [he wrote] that thou hast created thine image in me in order that I may be mindful of thee, may conceive of thee, and love thee; but that image has been so consumed and wasted away by vices, and obscured by the smoke of wrong-doing, that it cannot achieve that for which it was made, except thou renew it and form it anew. I do not endeavor, O Lord, to penetrate thy sublimity, for in no wise do I compare my understanding with it; but I long to understand in some degree thy truth, which my heart believes and loves. For I do not seek to understand in order that I may believe, but I believe in order that I may understand. For this also I believe: that unless I believe I shall not understand.[2]

Our governing premise is that the doctrine of man (anthropology) can be truly apprehended only in the light of the doctrine of Christ (christology). Not only the destiny but also the origin of man involves a profound relationship with the Second Person of the Holy Trinity. Indeed, mankind's destiny in Christ is precisely the fruition of mankind's origin in Christ. This means, among

---

1. Augustine, *On Free Will* i.4. The reference is to Isa. 7:9, for which (in line with the Greek rendering of the Septuagint) Augustine read *nisi credideritis, non intelligetis.* "May God grant his aid," he wrote, "and give us to understand what we have first believed. The steps are laid down by the prophet who says, 'Unless you believe, you will not understand'. We know well that we must hold fast to that." See also Tract. XXVII on the Gospel of John, at 6:34, where, citing the same passage from Isaiah, he comments: "They do not understand because they do not believe."

2. Anselm, *Proslogion* 1. The last clause appears to be virtually a quotation, perhaps following Augustine, of Isa. 7:9.

other things, that redemption, which is the fulfilment of all God's purposes in creation, loses its proper force if it is considered in isolation from creation. "Christology," as Karl Rahner has remarked, "is at once the beginning and the end of anthropology."[3]

Of fundamental importance in the exploration of our subject is the understanding of *the Image of God* as itself designating, ontologically, the eternal Son, and the understanding of man as by creation constituted in or after that image, by sin fallen away from that image, and by redemption reconstituted in that image. Thus perceived, the divine purpose of creation is grounded in the Son, and what was begun in the Son is also completed in the Son. It follows that conformity to the image of God is essentially Christiformity.[4] Man's destiny, implicit in his origin, is the attainment of "the complete knowledge of the Son of God," which coincides with his becoming "the perfect man," his arrival at "the measure of the stature of the fulness of Christ" (Eph. 4:13). Christ, accordingly, is the True Image in which man was formed at creation and into which by the reconciling grace of re-creation fallen man is being transformed.

PHILIP E. HUGHES

3. Karl Rahner, *Current Problems in Christology: Theological Investigations*, Vol. I (London and Baltimore, 1961), p. 185. Of course, Rahner is not the first or only theologian to have perceived this truth.

4. On the dynamic concept of Christiformity see my *Lefèvre: Pioneer of Ecclesiastical Renewal in France* (Grand Rapids, 1984), pp. 192ff.

For Marion

PART I

Creation in the Image of God: Integration

CHAPTER 1

The Meaning of Creation in the Image of God

The question regarding the significance of man's creation in the divine image is raised on the opening page of the Bible, but it is not clearly resolved until we come to the revelation in the New Testament that Christ himself, the Son, is the Image of God (2 Cor. 4:4; Col. 1:15). This disclosure is indisputably of immense consequence if we wish to establish a right understanding of the nature of man; for it points us to the truth that the authentic identity of man can be grasped only through the knowledge of man's relationship to Christ—a relationship which, far from having its beginning with the incarnation of the Son of God at Bethlehem, extends right back to the creation itself, and even beyond that to the eternal distinction within the unity of the Godhead between the persons of Father, Son, and Holy Spirit. As we shall see,[1] the designation "son" is itself consistent with the concept of "image"—a fact that is recognized in the old saying "like father, like son." Hence we are prepared to affirm that he who is eternally the Son of God is also eternally the Image of God.

Before we seek to elaborate this theme, however, we must examine the account of man's creation as given in Genesis 1:26f., where we read:

> Then God said, "Let us make man in our image, after our likeness; and let them have dominion over the fish of the sea, and over the birds of the air, and over the cattle, and over all the earth. . . ." So God created man in his own image, in the image of God he created him; male and female he created them.

Three things are plain from this passage: (1) man is the last of God's creatures to be brought into existence and the crown or peak of creation; (2) man alone is created in the image of God and in this crucial respect is unique among God's creatures; and (3) man's creaturely supremacy and uniqueness find expression in the dominion which he alone is given, and which he alone is fitted to exercise, "over all the earth."

Only of man is it said that God created him in his image. It is in this charter of his constitution that man's uniqueness is specifically affirmed as a creature radically distinguished from all other creatures. In this respect a line

---

1. See pp. 29ff. below.

is defined which links man directly and responsibly to God in a way that is un-known to any other creature. Nothing is more basic than the recognition that being constituted in the image of God is of the very essence of and absolutely central to the humanness of man. It is the key that unlocks the meaning of his authentic humanity. Apart from this reality he cannot exist truly as man, since for man to deny God and the divine image stamped upon his being and to assert his own independent self-sufficiency is to deny his own constitution and thus to dehumanize himself. That this is so is confirmed by the appalling inhuman-ity of ungodly men in every age of human history.

This radical difference between man and all other creatures is indicated, further, by the manner in which man is spoken of as a *special* creation of God. It is true that, physically, human life is animal life, as distinct from vegetable life and the realm of inanimate entities, and that it is recorded that, like man, animals (with the exception of fish and birds, which appeared on the fifth day) were brought into existence on the sixth day of creation. But that there is the postulation of a basic distinction is shown by the fact that of the animals God had said, "Let the earth bring forth . . ." (Gen. 1:24), whereas of man God said, "Let us make man in our image. . . ," indicating that this was a divine decision and act of a different order from what had preceded.

The plural "Let us make . . ." should not be understood, as some have wished to explain it, as a plural of royalty or majesty, which in any case is a literary form that is foreign to the language of the Bible. Nor does the plural-ity of persons implied both in the plural noun *Elohim* ("God") and in the plu-ral verb, "Let us make," justify the conclusion that angels, who are sometimes designated by the term *elohim* ("exalted ones"), were responsible for the cre-ation of man, as is supposed in some of the gnostic writings,[2] or that a council or conference of God and angels for the same purpose is intended—a com-monplace of Jewish interpretation approved from time to time by Christian scholars. Creation belongs to the Creator and cannot be taken out of his hands or shared with creatures, no matter how exalted the latter may be.

The patristic authors, together with many other Christian expositors in the succeeding centuries, were on surer ground in discerning in the grammar of these verses a pointer to the truth that within the unity of the Godhead there is a plurality. This plurality is indicated by the plural Hebrew noun *Elohim* and the plural pronouns of the utterance, "Let *us* make man in *our* image, after *our* likeness"; the unity by the use of the singular pronoun in conjunction with the plural *Elohim:* "Elohim created man in *his* own image, in the image of Elohim *he* created him." The implication of plurality in unity is found also in the way in which the plural *Elohim* is construed with a singular verb: "*Elohim* [plural] said [singular]" and "*Elohim* [plural] created [singular]." Moreover, the plu-rality-in-unity of the divine existence rules out any suggestion that God made

2. See, e.g., Irenaeus, *Against Heresies* I.xxiv.1; Hippolytus, *Refutation of All Here-sies* vii.16.

man because he was lonely or to make good some deficiency in the divine experience.

The postulation of the divine plurality-in-unity is no mere theoretical abstraction or speculation. On the contrary it attests the truth, so important for our understanding of man's creation in the divine image, that God, being tri-une, is a *personal* God. God's decision to create man is an *interpersonal* decision, confirming to us that God is not some impersonal numinous force or world spirit or the construction of philosophical thought, but one whose self-existence is in the fullest sense personal precisely by reason of his essential plurality-in-unity. An isolated or lone unit cannot be or know personality. To be personal, otherness must be present together with oneness, the one must be confronted and must interact with another, for personhood is a reality only within the sphere of person-to-person relationship. To be solitary is to lack identity. Only this personal distinction within the unity of the Godhead makes it possible to say, "Let *us* make man." Furthermore, it is this distinction which enables us to identify the Second Person of the Holy Trinity as the eternal Son who is the Image of God and through whom man's person-to-Person relationship with God is made a vital reality.

The knowledge that the being of God is essentially and eternally personal is, indeed, of particular moment for our theme, because in creating man God was creating a *personal* being who, in a manner impossible for other animate creatures, is capable of personal fellowship with and personal response to his personal Creator. The personhood of the creature man cannot be derived from an impersonal Creator, for it is as inconceivable that an impersonal power could bring personal beings into existence as it is that irrationality could be the source of rationality. The fact that man is person from Person explains his ability to interact as person to Person. Thus the divine decision to create man the personal creature is the culminating "moment" in the sequence of creative fiats. The disclosure that man, in a way that makes him distinct from all other earthly creatures, is a personal being leads us to the very heart of a correct comprehension of the meaning of his being created in the image of God.

The special place of man in the created order is seen, further, in the manner in which the affirmation that "God created the heavens and the earth" at the beginning of the account of creation is balanced and completed by the affirmation that "God created man in his own image" at the end; for only at these two points is the Hebrew verb *bara* ("created") used. This marks out man not merely as the last act of God's creation but also and in particular as the summit of creation. It is the creation of man that gives proportion and meaning to the whole divine work of creation; for it is in and through God's personal creature man, who has been given dominion over all the earth, that the created order as a whole relates to God and achieves the purpose of its creation. The preeminent position of man in God's creation is more than ontological; it is also inherently functional. That is the significance of the *dominion* with which he was entrusted.

The dividing line which separates man from the animals is demarcated conclusively by the fact that man is made in the image of God, so that animals, not being made in the divine image, are subservient to man in his exercise of dominion. The superiority of man is signified by the narrative of the *naming* of the birds and beasts by Adam (Gen. 2:19f.). Their naming is itself a mark of man's dominion. The ability to name them involves also the ability to train and organize them, so that as man's servants they may effectively contribute to his administration of the earth in accordance with the will and purpose of the Creator who is Lord of all. Man's naming of the animals is also a recognition and grateful acknowledgment of the *orderliness* of creation—an orderliness that is already there, bearing testimony to the order and purpose of the Creator's mind, not an orderliness that is achieved through human initiative. The naming is a *taxonomy,* an act of which no animal is capable.

This naming indicates that man is much more than a fellow animal, or even a higher animal—something that is further emphasized by the assertion that among all the animals "there was not found a helper fit for him." The fundamental incompatibility, again, resides entirely in this, that, in contrast to them, man's formation is in the image of God and thus is radically different from theirs. No single one of them, nor all of them in their totality, is competent to be man's fellow or his true partner.

It is this same distinction, deriving from the image of God in which man alone has been created, that explains the difference posited between manslaughter and the killing of animals. By reason of his unique constitution in the divine image, man is invested with a special sanctity which may not be violated. This is the clear import of the admonition of Genesis 9:6: "Whoever sheds the blood of man, by man shall his blood be shed; for God made man in his own image"—while in the same passage Noah is told that "every moving thing that lives shall be food for you" (Gen. 9:3). Unlike human life, animal life is not personal and sacrosanct. It subserves human life without being answerable to God. Only man who bears the divine image stands in a position of responsibility before God; and because of this special personal relationship of accountability to the Creator the life of man has a holy value. The prohibition of the sixth commandment, accordingly, is a prohibition against manslaughter, not against the killing of brute beasts.

According to the biblical perspective, then, man cannot be classified as no more than an intelligent animal whose provenance is evolutionistically attributed to an animal origin from below and whose difference from the brute beasts is merely a matter of degree. To explain man in this way is actually to brutalize him and to open the door for the ungodly conclusion that man is after all but an animal and therefore virtually as dispensable as any other animal— that first-degree homicide is not deserving of the death penalty, and that for the improvement of society the lives of unwanted or disadvantaged babies may benevolently be extinguished by abortion and infanticide, and euthanasia administered to the aged, the handicapped, and the unproductive members of the race. As we know only too well from the history of this twentieth century, it is a view of man which has encouraged even the justification of genocide for the sake of purifying the human stock. Such are some of the evil consequences of subverting the truth that man, whatever his affinities with the animal realm, is radically distinguished from all other earthly creatures by the fact that he alone has been created in the divine image and is intended by constitution to be a godly creature.

There has long been an opinion that in the terminology of Genesis 1:26, "Let us make man in our image, after our likeness," a distinction of meaning or nuance is intended between the nouns "image" and "likeness."[3] Etymological considerations, however, are not necessarily related to semantic reality, as the history of language shows over and over again. In general, those who postulate a distinction between the two terms have tended to understand "image" as referring to the natural or physical and "likeness" as referring to the spiritual or ethical aspect of man's constitution, or, more philosophically expressed, as differentiating between "form" and "matter" in the being of humanity. Some have even convinced themselves that the use of different prepositions in this verse—"*in* our image" and "*after* our likeness"—confirms the rightness of making a distinction between the import of the nouns. But the precarious character of these judgments is demonstrated by the following considerations. For one thing, the statement in verse 27, which announces the fulfilment of the decision of verse 26, that "God created man in his own image," without the addition of "after his own likeness," suggests that the combination of "image" and "likeness" in the earlier verse is designed to convey but one notion, not two. For another, in the broader context of these opening chapters of Genesis precisely the same nouns and prepositions are treated as interchangeable. Thus in Genesis 5:1 we read that man was created "*in* the *likeness* of God*,*" and in verse 3 of the same chapter that Adam "became the father of a son *in* his own *likeness, after* his *image* ": the reordering and recombination of the terms at issue could not be more complete. It follows that to say "in or after the image" is the same as saying "in or after the likeness." The terms are employed here synonymously, and the form of expression is better explained, as, for example, Martin Luther and Emil Brunner explain it, as a case of Hebrew parallelism.[4]

---

3. "Image" in Gen. 1:26 corresponds to the Hebrew *tselem,* which in the Greek (LXX) is rendered *eikōn* and in the Latin (Vg) *imago;* and "likeness" to the Hebrew *d^{e}muth,* which in the Greek (LXX) is rendered *homoiōsis* and in the Latin (Vg) *similitudo.*

4. James Barr, in an article entitled "The Image of God in the Book of Genesis—a Study of Terminology" (*Bulletin of the John Rylands Library,* Vol. 51 [1968-69], pp. 11ff.), suggested the reason for the use of two words, and not one only, as follows: "The probability is that, though *tselem* is the more important word, it is also the more novel and the more ambiguous. *D^{e}muth* is added in order to define and limit its meaning, by indicating that the sense intended for *tselem* must lie within the part of its range which overlaps with the range of *d^{e}muth.* This purpose having been accomplished when both words are used

The distinction, in fact, occurs early on in the patristic writings. In the second century we find Irenaeus asserting that only the man who is "made perfect and spiritual by reason of the outpouring of the Spirit" is made "both in the image and in the likeness of God," whereas the man who is without the Spirit is psychical, carnal, and imperfect, since, though "in his formation he has the image of God, he has not yet received the likeness which is given by the Spirit."[5] To the same effect Clement of Alexandria held that "Adam was perfect in regard to his formation," since "none of the distinctive characteristics of the idea and form of man were wanting to him," but posited a difference between creation and development that corresponded to a difference between "image" and "likeness." In his view "a pious Christian alone" possessed not only the image but also the likeness of God.[6]

It is an interpretation which is more fully expounded by Origen, who, like others of the fathers and apologists, contended that the teaching of the ancient philosophers, that the highest good was to become as nearly as possible like God, had been borrowed by them from the biblical writings, and especially from the Mosaic account of the creation of man in the divine image and likeness. In differentiating between the two terms, Origen drew attention to the fact that the word "likeness" occurs in conjunction with the word "image" in verse 26 of Genesis 1, but is omitted in verse 27. This, he maintained, carried an eschatological significance. According to him, the silence of Moses concerning the "likeness" in verse 27 "points to nothing else but this, that man received the honour of God's image in the first creation, whereas the perfection of God's likeness was reserved for him at the consummation." The "likeness," then, was something for man to acquire for himself "by his own earnest efforts to imitate God"—an interpretation which, in Origen's view, was confirmed by the teaching of 1 John 3:2 that when Christ appears at the end of the age we, who do not yet experience what we shall be, will then be like him.[7]

---

together at the first mention, it now becomes possible to use one of the two alone subsequently without risk of confusion. In later exegesis the loss of sense for this literary device caused interpreters to suppose that the 'image' might be one thing and the 'likeness' something quite other" (p. 24).

5. Irenaeus, *Against Heresies* V.vi.1. A similar, but somewhat gnosticized, notion may perhaps be detected in Tatian, *Address to the Greeks* 15.

6. Clement of Alexandria, *Miscellanies* iv.23; *Exhortation to the Gentiles* 12.

7. Origen, *On First Principles* III.vi.1. Similarly, in his work against the philosopher Celsus, Origen complained that Celsus had failed to grasp "the difference between man being made in God's image and being made in his likeness," for at creation "God only made man in the image of God, but not as yet in his likeness" (*Against Celsus* iv.30); and, in his commentary on the Epistle to the Romans, he observed that "those who worship the true God and trust in him become like him," adding that this was "probably because in the beginning man, when it was decided that he should be made according to the image and likeness of God, was made according to the image, whereas the likeness was deferred in order that he might first trust in God and thus become like him" (Epistle to the Romans, at iv.5).

This understanding of the separation of "image" from "likeness" became widely prevalent during the centuries that followed and provided a starting point for a variety of theological conclusions. Most noticeably, it was pressed into use as a basis for what became a distinctive doctrine of "catholic" Christianity, the doctrine, namely, that original sin and the fall of man resulted in the loss of original righteousness, conceived of as a superadded gift (the "likeness"), without, however, involving the loss or deterioration of man's constitution in the "image." Thus interpreted, man was seen as being, though fallen, in a purely natural state, and the ground was laid for the construction of the Semi-Pelagian anthropology that has for so long been a distinctive component of Roman Catholicism. The theological consequences of this supposition are very considerable: influenced by Greek, and most of all Aristotelian, philosophical concepts, the unimpaired "image" is identified with the rational soul of man; human reason is competent to understand and analyze the realities of God and the universe; the human will is free to choose good and reject evil; good works can be performed without dependence on divine grace; and redemption, which is the recovery or the achievement of the lost "likeness," is effected by the cooperation of divine grace with human works.

The Reformation of the sixteenth century signalized the return to and the reaffirmation of the biblical doctrine of the abject depravity of sinful man, whose reasoning is perverted and will enslaved and supposed good works displeasing to God because of the ungodliness by which his life is darkened and deadened, and whose only hope of redemption is total dependence on the grace of Almighty God. The clear voice of Augustine was heard again after a thousand years and, even more important, of St. Paul after fifteen hundred.

Irenaeus, however, must not be held responsible for the aberrations of Semi-Pelagianism. His exegesis of Genesis 1:26 may be questionable, but the theology inherent in his interpretation is governed by a sound scriptural instinct. We refer especially to his perception that man as created was not what he finally would be, that his destiny was to advance from glory to glory, and that, even if there had been no fall, the end was designed to be even more splendid than the beginning. An interesting appearance of the same line of exposition took place in the sixteenth century and in a context that was very definitely not Semi-Pelagian, that, namely, of the third part of the Elizabethan Homily "Against Peril of Idolatry," which is attributed to the pen of the Anglican divine John Jewel, Bishop of Salisbury: "The image of God," we read, "is in every man, but the likeness of God is not in every one, but in those only which have a godly heart and pure mind."[8]

---

8. *Certain Sermons or Homilies* (London, 1899 edn.), p. 280.

CHAPTER 2

Is There a Bodily Aspect of the Image?

There has been speculation from time to time, in both Jewish and Christian circles, that the divine image in which man was created is in some way represented in the actual physical form or appearance of the human body. The upright stance of man has been regarded by some as particularly significant in this connection. Disapproval of any such corporeal understanding of Genesis 1:26, while in the main associated with Christian orthodoxy, was in some cases influenced by inappropriate preconceptions, such as the anti-matter prejudice of philosophical dualism. Origen, for example, objected that the human body, however much it might be spiritually purified, was incapable of displaying the likeness of God, not only on the ground that God himself is incorporeal, but also because bodies, being formed of matter, and corruption belong together and therefore man is destined for an incorporeal consummation.[1] Impelled by a comparable predilection for Platonic anthropology, the first-century Jewish philosopher Philo of Alexandria declared no less emphatically (with reference to Gen. 1:26) that "no one should represent the likeness as relating to bodily form," since "neither is God in human form nor is the human body God-like."[2] Even so, Philo was not unwilling to admit that man's physical constitution was fittingly ordered to manifest the unique dignity of his position in creation—a concept, incidentally, that was not foreign to pagan thought. He remarked that, in contrast to other living creatures whose eyes are turned earthward, God set man's eyes "high up, that he might gaze on heaven." In his judgment, it was "a natural consequence of man's soul having been made after the image of the Archetype, the Word of the First Cause, that his body also was made erect and could lift up its eyes to heaven, the purest portion of our universe, that by means of that which he could see man might clearly apprehend that which he could not see."[3] Thus, in Philo's view, the divine image was located in the soul and reflected in the physical frame of man.

Opinions similar to this are found in the writings of Christian scholars.

1. Origen, *On First Principles* III.vi.1.
2. Philo, *On the Creation of the World* 69.
3. Philo, *On Husbandry* 17, 20.

Gregory of Nyssa, for instance, held that man's upright form and upward glance were "marks of sovereignty which show his royal dignity" derived from his constitution in the divine image.[4] Augustine, too, though he taught that man's creation in the image of God "refers to the inner man where his reason and intellect are," and that this was the source of his power over all the earth's other creatures, and though he maintained that "we should understand man's formation in the image of God not to refer to the body, but to that power by which he is superior to all beasts," since "all other animals are subject to man not because of the body but because of the intellect, which we have and they do not have," was willing to grant that "even our body has been so structured that we are superior to the beasts and therefore like God," which in turn he took to signify "that our soul should be erect in celestial, that is, in eternal and spiritual things."[5]

The position expounded by Calvin was essentially the same; indeed, it is interesting to find him quoting lines from the Roman poet Ovid in corroboration of his opinion that, while the proper seat of the divine image is the soul of man, yet the glory of God is also exhibited in his external form. The passage from Ovid is rendered by Dryden as follows:

> . . . while mute creation downward bend
> Their sight and to their earthly mother tend,
> Man looks aloft, and with erected eyes
> Beholds his own hereditary skies.[6]

Calvin in fact might with equal effect have cited the rhetorician and philosopher Cicero, who, a generation before Ovid, wrote that nature had providentially "raised men from the ground to stand tall and upright, so that they might be able to behold the sky and so gain a knowledge of the gods," explaining further that "men are sprung from the earth not as its inhabitants and denizens, but to be as it were the spectators of things supernal and heavenly, in the contemplation whereof no other species of animals participates."[7] The concept, however, has a venerable ancestry and there is no need to pursue it further here.

Calvin dismissed those who wished to draw subtle semantic distinctions from the terms "image" and "likeness" as ridiculous. The image of God in which man was created, he declared, "is evident in the whole excellence by which the nature of man surpasses all the animal species," and he added that "there was no part of man, not even the body, in which some rays of its glory did not shine." He rebuked Andreas Osiander, however, for "indiscriminately extending God's image both to the body and to the soul" and thus "commingling heaven and earth," and also for his opinion that the consequent dignity

---

4. Gregory of Nyssa, *On the Creation of Man* iv.1; viii.1.
5. Augustine, *On Genesis against the Manicheans* ii.27; cf. *On Various Questions*, Q. 51.
6. Ovid, *Metamorphoses* I.84ff.
7. Cicero, *De natura deorum* (Loeb edn.) II.lvi.140.

of man was such that, even if Adam had preserved his integrity, Christ would still have become man.[8]

This notion, that the dignity of man was so great that the incarnation would have taken place even if man had not sinned, had been confidently propounded in the preceding century by Renaissance scholars who entertained an exaggerated view of man as the microcosmic focal point of the universe. Pico della Mirandola, for example, had asserted in one of the celebrated Nine Hundred Theses which he had offered to defend against all comers that, "had Adam not sinned, God would have been incarnate but not crucified";[9] and others before him, such as Nicholas of Cusa, Marsilio Ficino, Bartolomeo Fazio, and Bartolomeo Manetti, had been favorably disposed to this opinion.

In the thirteenth century, Thomas Aquinas had been prepared to grant that if there had been no sin God *could* have become incarnate, though he judged that it was more appropriate to say that if man had not sinned the incarnation would not have taken place, "since everywhere in Holy Scripture the reason for the incarnation is attributed to the sin of the first man."[10] With respect to the image in which man was formed, Osiander had affirmed that Christ was the prototype only in connection with his bodily existence as incarnate, and from this premise had argued the necessity of the incarnation without regard to sin and redemption. Calvin rejoined that it was in a far different sense that Scripture teaches that man was created in the image of God.[11]

In our own day, Gerhard von Rad has maintained, with reference to the Genesis account of man's creation, not only that "the marvel of man's bodily appearance is not at all to be excepted from the realm of God's image" but also that this was "the original notion" as opposed to "a spiritualizing and intellectualizing tendency."[12] But this is a questionable judgment, for the Old Testament affords no evidence that Genesis 1:26 was understood in this manner or that its anthropomorphisms were intended in a literal rather than a metaphorical sense. It was alien philosophical concepts, syncretistically adopted by the Hebrew mystics of a later age, which promoted the conclusion that what are commonly regarded as anthropomorphisms are in fact *theo*morphisms. The cabalistic scholars maintained that references in the Old Testament to the arm of the Lord, for example, meant that God actually has an arm, the true and original arm, since, in their perspective, the human body with its members is but

8. John Calvin, *Institutes of the Christian Religion* I.xv.3. In 1550 Osiander had published two treatises jointly on *Whether the Son of God would have had to become incarnate if sin had not entered the world* and on *What the Image of God is.*

9. Pico's *Nine Hundred Theses* were published in Rome near the end of 1486. The one mentioned was number 15 of "conclusiones in theologia XXIX secundum opinionem propriam a communi modo dicendi theologorum satis diversae." See the text edited "avec l'introduction et les annotations critiques" by Bohdan Kieszkowski (Geneva, 1973), p. 66.

10. Thomas Aquinas, *Summa Theologica*, pt. III, q. 1, art. 3.

11. Calvin, *Institutes* I.xv.3.

12. G. von Rad, *Genesis* (Philadelphia, 1961), p. 56.

the copy or temporal projection of the reality which is the divine archetype. Even the most sacred divine name, the tetragrammaton JHVH, was held to disclose the human form of God when its four Hebrew letters were written vertically, from the top down.[13]

It is the linking of the incarnation to creation rather than to redemption or re-creation (though because of the universal incidence of sin none would wish to dissociate it from the latter) that has led to the postulation that it would have taken place, and was predestined to take place, without taking the possibility of sin into account. The eternal Son is seen, quite rightly, as not only the archetype but also the fulfilment of man's being. Does this justify the conclusion that, sin or no sin, the incarnation was a necessity as the crown of creation? Bishop B. F. Westcott is among those who gave an affirmative answer. "In this august declaration of God's purpose and God's work," he said, referring to Genesis 1:26f., "we have set before us, clear beyond controversy, the primal endowment and the final goal of humanity. We are taught that man received, received inalienably as man, a fitness for gaining, through growth and discipline and continuous benediction, union with God. God's image was given to him that he might gain God's likeness"—a distinct echo, this, of the voice of Irenaeus. This was the basis on which Westcott rested his declaration that "the fitness and the necessity of the incarnation" existed "from the moment when man was made," or, otherwise stated, that the incarnation "corresponds with the perfection of man as he was constituted at first, and not merely with the restoration of man who had missed his end." And so he postulated "the predestined humanity of the Eternal Word, the Son of God, as the archetype of humanity," and stated his conviction that by "looking to the incarnation as the crown of creation we have found the true center of the system in which we are set to work."[14]

The nobility of these sentiments and the sincerity with which they are expressed cannot be questioned, but it must be objected that it is not in accordance with the biblical perspective to regard the incarnation as the crown of creation. With the creation of man the work of creation was completed and God rested from his creative labors (Gen. 1:31–2:2). It is true that the Son is the Image in which man was made and to which he must conform, that the whole created order coheres or holds together in the Son (Col. 1:17), and that the incarnate Son actualizes the perfection of the manhood which we have sinfully perverted. But the whole thrust and purpose of the incarnation was not to complete or consummate creation, which was already complete at the beginning, though with the prospect of a glorious future; its design was that of re-

13. See my article "The Jewish Cabala and the Secret Names of God," in *Philosophia Reformata* (Kampen, 1956), p. 86. The concept of *Adam Kadmon,* primordial man, in theosophical speculation is of special interest. *"Adam Ha-Rishon,* the Adam of the Bible, corresponds on the anthropological plane to *Adam Kadmon,* the ontological primary man" (Gershom G. Scholem, *Major Trends in Jewish Mysticism* [New York, 1941], p. 279).

14. B. F. Westcott, *Christus Consummator* (London, 1886), pp. 104-6, 109.

creation, restoration, and reconciliation. The incarnation was not the capping or crowning of an incomplete structure; it was a rescue operation. The Son's coming was to save the world (Jn. 3:17; 12:47). He came to live the perfect human life indeed; but this was but preparatory to the achievement of the primary purpose of his coming, which was to die, the righteous for the unrighteous, and thus to destroy the power of the devil (Mk. 10:45; 1 Pet. 3:18; Heb. 2:9, 14f.). And, his redeeming work accomplished, his coming was to bring us to the participation in his glory for which mankind was from the beginning destined. Redemption is not isolated from creation, for it is the establishment of the purpose of creation. But the incarnation was a mediatorial mission, not a necessity in itself; a self-humbling, not a crowning. These are themes, however, to which we shall return in due course and which will receive, as they deserve, much fuller discussion.

CHAPTER 3

Man and the Divine Image
Not Identical

It is not without significance that man is described as having been created *in* the image of God, and not as being himself that image; for if he were himself the image it would be pointless to speak of him as a creature constituted in or according to the divine image. Within the limits of his platonizing Logos philosophy Philo understood this distinction, as is shown by his identification of the Logos or archetypal Reason as the image of God (though not of course in any trinitarian sense) and man as the cast of that image, specifically with regard to his intellectual or rational faculty. He rightly drew attention to the fact that Moses did not say that the Creator made man the image of God but "after the image," and drew the conclusion that "the mind in each of us, which in the true and full sense is the 'man,' is an expression at third hand from the Maker, while between them is the model of our reason and the representation of God."[1] (Philo, it will be noticed, assigned the Logos an intermediate position somewhere between God and man—a pattern that would recur later on in church controversy, particularly in the christology of Arianism.) Philo envisaged the rational soul of man as bearing and indeed as being the stamp of the Logos who is the divine image, in such a manner that he was willing to describe man as "the image of the Image."[2]

The Christian theologians of Alexandria naturally identified the Logos with the eternal Son who, far from being some median entity, is himself true God, though the expression of their thought is not always entirely free from the philosophical influences of their culture. Clement, for example, associates the image of man's creation closely with the faculty of intellection or rationality, even speaking of the Divine Word as "the genuine Son of Mind." "The image of God," he says, "is his Word, . . . and the image of the Word is the true man, the mind which is in man, who is therefore said to have been made 'in

1. Philo, *Who is the Heir of Divine Realities?* 231. The noun "representation" renders the Greek *apeikonisma,* which can certainly be taken as synonymous with *eikōn,* "image." It is apparent, too, that Philo regarded *eikōn,* "image," and *charaktēr,* "stamp," as interchangeable terms by which the Logos was designated. See pp. 45ff. below.
2. Philo, *On the Creation of the World* 25: *eikōn eikonos.*

the image and likeness of God,' assimilated to the Divine Word in the affections of the soul, and therefore rational."[3] Origen makes the connection between creation and redemption that would, in the following century, be more fully expounded by Athanasius.[4] He explains that when "our Saviour, who is the Image of God," saw that man "who had been made according to his likeness" exchanged his own image for the image of the evil one, "moved with compassion he assumed the image of man and came to him."[5] Of Christian believers, who call upon God as their Father, he writes (in his treatise on prayer) that all their deeds and words and thoughts imitate "the image of the invisible God" (Col. 1:15) and take place "according to the image of the Creator" (Col. 3:10), "so that in them there is 'the image of the heavenly' (1 Cor. 15:49), who is himself 'the image of God.'" This being so, Origen, like Philo, is able to say that men, in particular the saints, are "an image of an image"[6] and to draw the conclusion that since the Son is the Image of which they are an image they accordingly acquire an impression of sonship.[7] The precise significance of the distinction that was thus recognized early on was not universally appreciated, however. In the medieval period, to give one instance, Peter Lombard agreed that "the Son is properly called the image of the Father" but, citing the support of St. Paul who in 1 Corinthians 11:7 calls man "the image and glory of God," rejected the implication that man is not himself the image.[8]

Lombard was not the first to offer this argument. Augustine had done so long before him, and at the same time had involved the discussion in a considerable amount of confusion. Though not wishing to deny that the Son is "the image equal to the Father," yet he contended that the image after which man was created was that of the Trinity. As his proof-text he cited the statement of Genesis 1:26, "Let us make man in *our* image, after *our* likeness," maintaining that, "since the Son is the image of the Father alone," the plural preposition *our* signifies the involvement of all three persons of the Trinity. Accordingly, Augustine did not scruple to call man "the image of the Trinity." Man is "not equal to the Trinity as the Son is equal to the Father," he explained, "but approaching to it . . . by a certain likeness, just as nearness may in a sense be signified by things distant from each other, not in respect of place, but in a sort

3. Clement of Alexandria, *Exhortation to the Heathen* 10.
4. See below, pp. 276ff.
5. Origen, Homily I on Genesis.
6. *Treatise on Prayer* xxii.4. *Eikōn eikonos.*
7. Ibid.
8. Peter Lombard, *Sentences,* lib. II, dist. XVI. The significance of St. Paul's terminology in 1 Cor. 11:7 is discussed below, pp. 22f. There is, incidentally, no justification for Lombard's interpretation of the term "likeness" in Gen. 1:26 as a reference to the Holy Spirit, "who," he says, "is the likeness of the Father and the Son," in contrast to the term "image," which, rightly, he relates to the Son (ibid.). In the sixteenth century Calvin rebuked Osiander, on the other hand, for speaking of Christ as the image of the Holy Spirit (*Inst.* I.xv.3).

of imitation."[9] The main problem with this attempt at equivocation is that *image* when used of man is different from *image* when used of the Son: the latter is *image* by equality, the former only by likeness understood as a kind of nearness which at the same time implies distance and inequality. This consideration should have caused Augustine to question the rightness of his interpretation of 1 Corinthians 11:7 and to respect the distinction between the Son who is the Image of God and man who is formed in the image of God.

The trinitarian image postulated by Augustine is manifested, as he thought, "not according to the shape of man's body, but according to his rational mind."[10] Indeed, he felt able to discern a number of trinitarian imprints: in that the mind remembers and understands and loves itself, and still more particularly in that it can remember and understand and love him by whom it was made; in the union experienced by the lover, the loved, and the love that unites them; in that the mind and the love of itself and the knowledge of itself are three things which are one; and in the threefold unities of memory, understanding, and will, of the object which we see, the act of seeing, and the will or attention of the mind which retains what is seen, and of will, memory, and recollection.[11] The rejoinder must be made, however, that these suggested unities, though threefold, are not properly trinitarian. They are but perceptions or notions in the consciousness of a single person; whereas the Holy Trinity is a unity of one God in three Persons, whose interpersonal being is absolutely unique. Consequently, the trinitarian images and vestiges that Augustine and others have professed to discover in man have no possibility of being what is claimed for them. True enough, it is the triune God who said, "Let us make man in our image," but the pronoun "our" does not necessarily imply plurality in that image. That this in fact is not the implication is made plain by the designation of the Son as the image of the invisible God (Col. 1:15; 2 Cor. 4:4). That is why the image in which man was made and to which he must conform is specifically the eternal Son, the Second Person of the Holy Trinity.

Thomas Aquinas pursued essentially the same method of argumentation as Augustine. Equality, he pointed out, does not belong to the essence of an image but is of the essence of a perfect image, "for in a perfect image nothing is wanting that is to be found in that of which it is a copy." Christ is the perfect image of God, and that is why "he is said to be *the Image,* and never *after the image.* . . . And since the perfect likeness of God cannot be except in an identical nature, the Image of God exists in his firstborn Son, as the image of the king is in his son, who is of the same nature as himself." Man, then, is an imperfect image and unequal to God. Aquinas went on to state his approval of Augustine's view of man as stamped with a trinitarian likeness.[12]

9. Augustine, *On the Trinity* vii.6; cf. xii.6.
10. Ibid. xii.7.
11. Ibid. xiv.8, 12; viii.10; ix.1, 4, 5, 12; x.11f.; xi.1ff., 7; see also *The City of God* xi.26.
12. Thomas Aquinas, *Summa Theologica,* pt. I, q. 93, arts. 1, 5-7.

A completely different line of interpretation is put forward by Karl Barth, who has asserted that the creation of man in the image of God refers to the formation of man as male and female. It is of some interest that in the fourth century Gregory of Nyssa had expressed the opposite view, maintaining that the statement "in the image of God he created him" marked the end of creation, while the declaration "male and female he created them" was, he held, something additional and subsequent to creation proper. "I presume that everyone knows that this is a departure from the Prototype," he said; "for 'in Christ Jesus,' as the Apostle says, 'there is neither male nor female.'" Thus he taught that "our nature is in a sense twofold: on the one hand like God, and on the other divided in accordance with this distinction." Gregory's supposition was that man was originally created equal with the angels and that God devised the male-female differentiation in anticipation of the fall—a differentiation "which has no reference to the divine Archetype," but "is an approximation to the less rational nature"; and he cited the words of Christ that in the age to come the children of the resurrection "neither marry nor are given in marriage, for they cannot die any more, because they are equal to angels" (Lk. 20:34-36). This, as Gregory saw it, would be a return to the sexless original of creation, "bringing back again to Paradise him who was cast out from it."[13]

The eccentric surgery performed by Gregory of Nyssa on Genesis 1:27 is altogether alien to Barth's explication of the text, according to which the clause "male and female he created them" explains and clarifies the preceding assertion that "God created man in his own image." "Could anything be more obvious," Barth asks, "than to conclude from this clear indication that the image and likeness of the being created by God signifies existence in confrontation, . . . in the juxtaposition and conjunction of man and woman which is that of male and female?"[14]—to which some might be disposed to answer that, yes, anything could be more obvious. Barth's confidence in this identification of the divine image and likeness of man's creation depends on the correctness of his conclusion that the statement "male and female he created them" elucidates the meaning of the antecedent declaration that God created man in his own image. But it is certainly no less possible that the statement, rather than being explanatory, is intended to give *additional* information: not only did God create man in his own image, but he also created man as male and female. If the statement is in fact additional and not explanatory (and this is the more natural way of taking it), then Barth's argument falls away.

Even though Barth is careful to warn the reader that he is postulating no more than an analogy—and no more than an analogy of relationship at that, definitely not an analogy of being or existence *(analogia entis)*—yet his hypothesis is open to serious objections. For one thing the interpersonal relation-

---

13. Gregory of Nyssa, *On the Creation of Man* 16f.
14. Karl Barth, *Church Dogmatics,* III/1, tr. G. W. Bromiley (Edinburgh, 1958), p. 195.

ship within the Godhead is in no sense a sexual relationship. For another, the interpersonal relationship in human society, while it is most intimately expressed in the sexual union of male and female, to which a special sanctity is attached (see, e.g., Gen. 2:24 and Mt. 19:4-6), is not dependent on sexuality; it is experienced in the bond of friendship, in the ties of the family between parents and children, and in the multiplicity of daily associations of human society in which sexual identity is of little, if any, importance. And of special significance in this connection is the teaching of Christ himself that hereafter, in the community of the redeemed, when the divine image in which they were created is restored and fulfilled, there will be no marrying or giving in marriage.

It would seem more reasonable to connect the statement "male and female he created them" with the divine command to "be fruitful and multiply" which follows rather than with the declaration of man's formation in the divine image which precedes, since sexual differentiation and reproduction or procreation belong together, the latter being a primary end to which the former is the means. Barth, however, contends that, in distinction from the beasts which are divided into "kinds" and classifications, man as originally created is one and undivided, that "the only real differentiation and relationship" in the case of man "is that of man to man, and in its original and most concrete form of man to woman and woman to man," and that this oneness and aloneness of man corresponds to the oneness and aloneness of God. "In this way," Barth says, "he is a copy and imitation of God"—apparently regarding "the duality of man and woman" as in some way answering to the distinction of persons within the trinitarian Godhead.[15] But this oneness and aloneness to which he draws attention might equally be predicated of each of the "kinds" of the animal creation. To them also a command was given to "be fruitful and multiply," and this command, too, is based on the fact of sexual differentiation or duality as male and female (Gen. 1:21ff.). Constitution as male and female is thus not a mark which distinguishes man from the beasts or which defines his uniqueness in the order of creation; on the contrary, it is an endowment he has in common with the world of animals.

The image of God in man cannot be demarcated by pointing to this particular "differentiation and relationship." It is the image of God in which man was created, rather, which pervades his existence in its totality and is the cause of his transcendence over the rest of God's creation. Man's life in every one of its modes, including the sexual duality of male and female, is enhanced and elevated by the central fact of his constitution in the divine image, which establishes him as a totally responsible personal being in relation to his Creator. And, as the New Testament clearly testifies, the image of God in which he is formed and to which it is the Creator's will that he should conform is the Son, the Second Person of the Holy Trinity. Though Christ was born a male child at Bethlehem, the duality of man and woman was in no way determinative of

15. Ibid., pp. 185f.

the incarnation and its purpose. All that is truly and fully human is revealed and defined in him who himself is the True Image. Creation that is so intimately related to the Second Person of the Trinity bestows on man the blessing of personhood which is denied to the animals below him; and thus this human personhood is derived from and linked to the personhood of God himself. This is indeed a remarkable witness to man's uniqueness. But to affirm, as Barth does, that the distinction of the sexes is "the only genuine distinction between man and man," which corresponds to "the fact that the I-Thou relationship is the only genuine distinction in the one divine being,"[16] is to beg rather than to answer the question.

Contrary to Karl Barth, then, we conclude that male and female duality does not provide the key to the understanding of the divine image in which man was formed. Man's person-to-Person relationship with his Maker, itself undoubtedly an indicator of that "image," is not determined by the fact of human sexuality. It exists independently of sexuality. Of this the perfect paradigm is the unclouded interpersonal harmony that informed the relationship between the incarnate Son and the heavenly Father, for in his incarnation the Son, who is himself the Image of God, expressed the fulness of life in that image, that is to say, as our fellow man, in a manner that was not in any way dictated by the issue of sexual duality.[17]

Mention may be made here of the fanciful notion that man as originally created was an androgynous being, that is, a creature in whom male and female sexuality coexisted at first in a potential sense. The concept has no place in the line of orthodox Christian theology, but belongs rather to the Platonic tradition of speculation. It is expounded in some detail by Aristophanes in Plato's *Symposium*. According to this account, "primeval man was round and had four hands and four feet, back and sides forming a circle, and one head with two faces looking opposite ways"; but human insolence was punished by Zeus by cutting these rotund units into two and shaping them as man and woman, in such a way that the one is incomplete without the other, with the result that in the quest for completion each seeks union with the other.[18] The notion seems to have found an echo in the writing of Philo in the first century of our era: "Love," he wrote, "brings together and fits into one the divided halves, as it were, of a single living creature, and sets up a desire for fellowship with the other with a view to the production of their like."[19] It appears again in some of the rabbinical interpretations of Genesis 1:27 based on a reading, "God created man in his own image; . . . male and female he created *him*" (instead of

16. Ibid., p. 196. Though he subsequently is disposed to define the "image" in a more general manner by extending it to interpersonal relationships in human society so that it is not absolutely determined by the male-female distinction and confrontation, Barth's starting point and main focus is that of the differentiation between male and female.
17. For further discussion of human personhood see pp. 51ff. below.
18. Plato, *Symposium* 189Cff.
19. Philo, *On the Creation of the World* 152.

"them"). Confirmation of this understanding was claimed from Psalm 139:5, "Thou dost beset me behind and before," which these rabbinists explained as meaning, "Thou createst me before and behind, that is, with two faces"; the sexual union of man and wife was regarded as in effect a rediscovery of the original oneness. At much the same time in some gnostic writings it was taught that spiritual or pneumatic man became androgynous man[20] in the image and likeness of God, with the implication that God himself is in some essential manner androgynous. Such speculations, however, are far removed from biblical reality, and are in any case invalidated, as those who opposed them pointed out, by the authentic text of Genesis 1:27, which reads, "male and female he created *them*"—that is, not as one male-female unit but as distinct male and female persons.

No doubt it is all too easy for theologians to speak loosely of man as being himself the image of God, without maintaining proper concern for the biblical teaching that his formation is not as but in the divine image. Karl Barth, for one, has rightly asserted that "man is not created to be the image of God but . . . he is created in correspondence with the image of God";[21] yet we find him calling man the image of God in disregard of the precision of this qualification.[22] Still more surprising is the statement of Herman Bavinck not only that "the distinctive being of man lies in this, that he is God's image," but even further, that "like the Son, so also man as such is fully and completely the image of God."[23] Admittedly, it is not altogether unacceptable for a general or inexact formulation to be employed when theological precision is not required (which is hardly the case where the context of Barth's and Bavinck's usage is concerned). An example of this is the effective manner in which William Tyndale sought to combat the cult of images and the neglect of the needy and the destitute, each of whom, he affirmed, is "the lively image of God," not an inanimate image, arguing that, "if we care more to clothe the dead image made by man and the price of silver than the lively image of God and the price of Christ's blood, then we dishonor the image of God and him that made him, and the price of Christ's blood and him that bought him."[24] Similarly Hugh Latimer, in a sermon preached in 1536, the year of Tyndale's martyrdom, denounced the setting up of images "covered with gold," "clad with silk garments," and "laden with precious gems and jewels," "whereas in the mean time we see Christ's faithful and lively images, bought with no less price than his

20. *Arsenothēlys anthrōpos*.

21. Barth, *Church Dogmatics*, III/1, p. 197.

22. Ibid., pp. 197, 184, etc.

23. Herman Bavinck, *Gereformeerde Dogmatiek*, Vol. II (Kampen, 2nd edn., 1908), pp. 491, 494. Notice also the title of a book on this theme by another distinguished Dutch theologian in the Reformed tradition, G. C. Berkouwer, *Man: The Image of God* (Grand Rapids, 1962)—in Dutch, *De Mens het Beeld Gods*.

24. William Tyndale, *Answer to Sir Thomas More's Dialogue*, in *Works*, Vol. III (Parker Society edn., Cambridge, 1850), p. 59.

most precious blood, alas, alas, to be an-hungered, a-thirst, a-cold, and to lie
in darkness, wrapped in all wretchedness, yea, to lie there till death take away
their miseries."[25]

Strictly speaking, however, as we have observed, man is not himself the
image of God, though his constitution is stamped at the very heart with that
image in which he has been created. Why then, it may be asked with Augustine
and Peter Lombard and others, does St. Paul call man "the image and glory of
God" in 1 Corinthians 11:7? Is the Apostle using language loosely or inaccu-
rately in this place? Not at all! For elsewhere he specifically states that *Christ*
is the image of God (2 Cor. 4:4; Col. 1:15; Rom. 8:29), and the context here
indicates that he is using the expression "image of God" in a different sense.
His primary purpose in this passage is to give instruction about marriage and
the relationship between husband and wife. This theme, it is true, is not unrelated to God's work of creation, as verses 8 and 9 show. But his concern here
is not with the creation of man but rather with the question of order and headship in both home and church. To fail to see that it is particularly the domestic
situation to which St. Paul is referring must lead to the unsatisfactory conclusion that, because he asserts that man "is the image and glory of God, but
woman is the glory of man," therefore only man, and not woman, as created
is God's image.

The connotation of the term "man" varies in Scripture according to the
context in which it occurs. In the Genesis account of creation "man" is used in
the generic or comprehensive sense. When we read, "God created man in his
own image, . . . male and female he created them," it is obvious that sexual differentiation is defined by "male and female," while "man" designates the
human being as either male or female. But when St. Paul says that man is "the
image and glory of God, but woman is the glory of man," he is clearly using
"man" in the limited sense of "male" as distinct from "female." As Calvin says,
"both sexes were created in the image of God and Paul exhorts women no less
than men to be formed anew according to that image."[26] In Christian marriage,
the Apostle is saying, there is a gradation of headship: God is over Christ the
incarnate Son, who is over man, who is over his wife. As head of the home the

25. Hugh Latimer, *Sermons,* Vol. I (Parker Society edn., Cambridge, 1844), pp. 36f.
It is a recurrent theme in Reformation writing and preaching; cf. the Elizabethan Homily
"Against Peril of Idolatry," of which John Jewel was the probable author: "For, if you will
truly honour the image of God, you should, by doing well to man, honour the true image
of God in him . . . refresh the hungry with meat, the thirsty with drink, the naked with
clothes, the sick with attendance, the stranger harbourless with lodging, the prisoners with
necessaries" (*Certain Sermons or Homilies* [London, 1899], p. 280). In *Institutes* II.viii.40
Calvin, who elsewhere repeatedly speaks of Christ as "the living image of God," follows
this pattern when, on the basis of his understanding of man as "both the image of God and
our flesh," he observes that "if we do not wish to violate the image of God, we ought to
hold our neighbor sacred," and that "if we do not wish to renounce all humanity we ought
to cherish him as our own flesh."

26. Calvin, *Commentary on 1 Corinthians,* ad loc.

husband is described in relation to the wife, not as *being* God, but as *imaging* God—something that, in this particular sequence, is not true of the wife. It is simply a relationship of order; it is an expression of the orderliness of creation. But not in a quasi-mechanical sense; for the "imaging" displayed by the husband is intended to be a manifestation or reflection of the self-sacrificial love and protection of the divine Redeemer for his bride the church—as Ephesians 5:22ff. shows, where St. Paul teaches that "the husband is the head of the wife as Christ is the head of the church, his body, and is himself its Savior," with the consequence that husbands should love their wives as their own bodies, as Christ loved the church and gave himself up for her. 1 Corinthians 11, then, is not a blueprint for male tyranny, nor is it at variance with what is consistently taught elsewhere in Scripture, namely, that man generically, whether male or female, has been created, not the image, but *in* the image of God.

CHAPTER 4

The Image of God in the
New Testament

Because a fuller light is thrown on the creation of man by the redemption of man, which is his re-creation, and the proper nature of the first Adam is more fully revealed by the person and work of the incarnate Son, who is the last Adam (1 Cor. 15:45), the significance of man's constitution in the image of God can most adequately be understood through the teaching of the New Testament in relation to this theme. If we are to have a right comprehension of the true being of man it is constantly important, as we have said before, to bear in mind that redemption and creation are indissolubly connected with each other. The explanation of the image in which man was created, as Calvin has observed, "cannot be better known from anything than from the reparation of his corrupted nature."[1] Our investigation of the New Testament doctrine will begin with those passages in which the expression "the image of God" actually occurs (with the exception of 1 Corinthians 11:7, which has been discussed above and shown to be unrelated to this theme), but will also take into consideration other passages where there is an equivalence or approximation of terminology. First of all, however, it is desirable to be informed of the import of the term "image" so that misunderstandings may be avoided.

In common usage the noun *image*[2] frequently signifies no more than a copy or reflection which is something other than the reality it represents, such as the head of a ruler imprinted on a coin—as in Luke 20:24, where Jesus asks concerning a denarius, "Whose image does it bear?"[3] The word, however, may stand for the reality, the true substance, as distinct from a copy or an insubstantial shadow. This is plainly seen in Hebrews 10:1, where we read that "the law has but a shadow of the good things to come instead of the true form of these realities" (RSV); for the rendering "the true form" gives the sense of "the image,"[4] which is the literal reading. "Image" here indisputably denotes the authentic and substantial actuality of the good things which, formerly prom-

1. Calvin, *Institutes* I.xv.4.
2. Greek, *eikōn*.
3. Greek, *tinos echei eikona*.
4. *Hē eikōn*.

24

ised, are now realities in Christ as the Mediator of the new covenant, in contrast to the shadow which, though cast as it were in advance by the reality, has no substantial existence of its own. The "image" in Hebrews 10:1 corresponds to the "body" in the parallel statement of Colossians 2:17, where, with reference to the ordinances of the old covenant, we are told that "they are only a shadow of what is to come, whereas the body[5] [i.e., the substantial reality] belongs to Christ." Thus in these two places "image" and "body," used in each case in contradistinction to "shadow," are interchangeable terms.[6]

In the linguistic usage of the first century, accordingly, the term "image" was semantically capable of standing as a designation of that reality which is authentic as distinct from a shadowy or unreal imitation; and from this the important consequence follows that when Christ is called "the image of God" it is not intended to mean that he is less or other than God, but to denote a dynamic identity of power and essence with God which is at the same time a revealing or manifestation of the divine reality. As Hermann Kleinknecht has asserted, it "is not to be understood as a magnitude which is alien to the reality. . . . It has a share in the reality. Indeed, it is the reality." And so it "does not imply a weakening or a feeble copy of something. It implies the illumination of its inner core and essence."[7] Likewise Gerhard Kittel insists that when Christ is called the image of God "all the emphasis is on the equality of the image with the original."[8] And A. M. Ramsey has declared that "Christ is 'the image of the invisible God' (Col. i.15) in that he shares in God's real being and hence can be a perfect manifestation of that being."[9] Clearly, then, in christological

---

5. *To sōma.*

6. Jacob Jervell maintains that the assertion of Col. 2:9 that in Christ "the whole fulness of deity dwells bodily *(sōmatikōs)*" could equally be rendered "in him the whole fulness of God dwells image-wise *(eikonikōs)*" (*Imago Dei: Gen. 1:26f. im Spätjudentum, in der Gnosis, und in den paulinischen Briefen* [Göttingen, 1960], p. 224). It is a not unattractive suggestion, but the context of Col. 2:9 makes its validity doubtful since St. Paul is evidently joining battle with a gnostic type of dualistic philosophy which denied the reality of the incarnation specifically because it affirmed the full deity of Christ in a genuine bodily existence. The Greek adverb, of which there seems to be no instance, may be legitimated by the attestation of the rare and late adjective *eikonikos.* But whether or not there is such an adverb does not affect the point Jervell is making, namely, that "image" and "body" can be interchangeable concepts.

7. H. Kleinknecht, *Theological Dictionary of the New Testament,* Vol. II, ed. G. Kittel, tr. G. W. Bromiley (Grand Rapids, 1964), *sub voc.,* p. 389.

8. Ibid., p. 395.

9. A. M. Ramsey, *The Glory of God and the Transfiguration of Christ* (London, 1949). Ceslas Spicq writes that "there is only one image of God that is adequate, namely, his Son, *eikōn tou theou aoratou.*" "The *eikōn* here," he says, "signifies less resemblance than derivation and participation. . . . The image of a being is its expression, the thing itself expressed." Thus in the case of Christ "the emphasis is in particular on the equality, if not the identity (the consubstantiality, as it will be called) of the *eikōn* with the original" (*Notes de Lexicographie Néo-Testamentaire,* Vol. III, Supplément [Göttingen, 1982], p. 208).

and anthropological studies the concept of "image," and especially its significance in the phrase "image of God," carries implications of exceptional moment for theological understanding. But far from being restricted to a single
term or concept, the scope of our comprehension is enriched and expanded by
the diversity of linguistic and intellectual perception which we find in the New
Testament. What follows is a consideration of some of the more important
terms and texts.

IMAGE

2 Corinthians 4:4. Christ is here specifically described as "the image of
God." St. Paul is not simply saying that Christ is like God or reflects the
character of God, or that through his incarnation he is the revealer of God to
the world, true though it may be that Christ represents God to us in these respects; for what is stated here is far more than a declaration of the function or
effect of the incarnation. It is in the profoundest sense a declaration concerning the essential being of Christ, that is to say, an ontological statement with
reference to the Second Person of the Holy Trinity. This conclusion is drawn
from the context—a context which speaks (3:7ff.) of the divine glory reflected
from the face of Moses but veiled from the people because of their unbelief,
and which declares that the divine glory now beams forth, unreflected and un-
veiled, from the face of Jesus Christ and in the gospel of God's grace, but with
transcendental brilliance. The glory of Christ is not a mere reflection or copy
of the glory of God; it is identical with it.

But the glory of the gospel which transcends the glory of the law is also
antecedent to the law, for it is the reflorescence of the glory of creation which
man in his fallenness has lost. St. Paul explains that through the malevolent
activity of Satan, "the god of this age," the minds of unbelievers have been
blinded so that they remain unenlightened by "the light of the gospel of the
glory of Christ, who is the image of God"; and then he links the light of redemption directly with the light of creation: "For," he writes, "it is God who
said, 'Let light shine out of darkness' [i.e., at creation, Gen. 1:3], who has shone
in our hearts [i.e., in the grace of re-creation] to give the light of the knowledge of the glory of God in the face of Christ" (4:4-6). The God who creates
is the God who redeems. This association of the image of God with the glory
of God points us to that reality which is both original and ultimate. The most
wicked and preposterous folly of man is his determination to "exchange the
glory of the immortal God," glory that is one with the image of God, "for the
likeness of the image of mortal man and birds and animals and reptiles," which
is precisely to deny the image and the glory in which he was created and to
substitute the creature for the Creator (Rom. 1:23-25). In Christ that original
glory is recovered and enhanced as, "beholding the glory of the Lord, we are
transformed into the same image from glory to glory" (2 Cor. 3:18)—being
conformed, that is, to him who is the Image of God in which we were created:

the more Christlike we become, the greater the glory. This is truly, in a word, Christiformity!

Romans 8:29. Here the same teaching is set by the Apostle in the light of God's eternal will: "Those whom God foreknew," he says, "he also predestined to be conformed to the image of his Son." Even before creation God ordained that man should be conformed to the image of his Son—the image, that is, which is his Son; for the Son himself is the Image of God. Accordingly, God created man in or after his own image. Conformity to the Son, purposed before the beginning, is there at the beginning, and for fallen man is redemptively achieved through that same Son who is the divine Image. The end is not only in the beginning but also before the beginning. Always it is in and through the Son. From eternity to eternity Christiformity is God's purpose for his creature, man. And because it is the end willed *by God* it cannot fail of fulfilment.

1 Corinthians 15:49. St. Paul teaches here that "just as we have borne the image of the man of dust, we shall also bear the image of the man of heaven." He is referring, as the context shows, to the resurrection of the body, which will no longer be a weak, frustrated, perishable, "psychical"[10] body but a powerful, glorious, imperishable, spiritual body. The man of dust whose image we have borne is "the first man Adam"; our bodies, like his since the fall, in death return "dust to dust" (see Gen. 3:19; 5:3). The man from heaven is "the last Adam," Christ; our bodies, like his since the resurrection, will bear the glory and exaltation that are his. Although St. Paul does not speak directly here of Christ as the Image of God, his usage of the term "image" is in itself significant, because the bearing of the image of "the man of heaven," to be experienced in the raising and transformation of our bodies into the likeness of his glorious body (Phil. 3:21), will bring to fulfilment the divine purpose for our conformity to him who is the True Image. The predestined end, moreover, is more than simply a return to the beginning. It is not just a starting again. It is the completion of creation. For from the beginning the destiny of God's people has been a heavenly destiny. Man, made to be "for a little while lower than the angels," was always destined to be "crowned with glory and honor" (Ps. 8:5; Heb. 2:5ff.), to be evermore exalted in and with Christ far above all angels and powers (Eph. 1:20ff.; Phil. 2:9ff.). To bear the image of the man of heaven, therefore, is nothing other than the completion of the age-long purpose that we should be conformed to the image of the Son of God (Rom. 8:29).

Colossians 3:10. Here, as in 2 Corinthians 3:18, St. Paul is writing of the renewal, the transformation, that is progressively taking place in the life of the Christian believer. He reminds the members of the Colossian church that they "have put off the old man with his practices," as in discarding an old garment, and "have put on the new man, which is being renewed in knowledge after the image of his Creator." Redemption is the re-creation of our humanity: in Christ

10. "Psychical" is the adjective used by St. Paul in v. 44 (where RSV renders it as "physical") in contrast to "spiritual."

each person is a new creation; the old ungodly alienation from the Creator has become a thing of the past (2 Cor. 5:17). The image marred by our fallenness is renewed in him who is the Image of God in which we were first formed. From the beginning he has been the key and the guarantee to a destiny more glorious than the beginning. The renewal of our humanity after the image of its Creator is already complete in the triumphant and glorious exaltation of the incarnate Son who is the Lord our Righteousness (Jer. 23:6; 1 Cor. 1:30), and during the course of this earthly pilgrimage it is progressively taking place within us as with the Holy Spirit's aid we increase in Christlikeness (2 Cor. 3:18; Eph. 4:12-16). Bishop Lightfoot comments that "the spiritual man in each believer's heart, like the primal man in the beginning of the world, was created after God's image," and then explains not only that "the new birth was a re-creation in Christ's image" but also that "the subsequent life must be a deepening of this image thus stamped upon the man."[11]

Colossians 1:15. Here St. Paul says of "God's beloved Son, in whom we have redemption, the forgiveness of sins" (preceding verse) that "he is the image of the invisible God." In the nature of the case, there can be no such thing as a pictorial copy of the invisible; consequently, the term "image" does not mean here simply a visible likeness other than the reality itself. Within the mystery of the infinite trinitarian being of God it is the Son who authentically reveals the divine nature and gives effect to the divine will. Certainly, he does this as the incarnate Son in the perfection of his life and his performance of the work of redemption. He is the image, however, not just temporally, during the time of his incarnate manifestation here on earth, but eternally; for, as St. Paul goes on to say in this same passage, it was through him and for him who is the image of the invisible God that all things were created (vv. 16f.). In the creation of the world, therefore, the Son was performing and fulfilling the Father's will, as he did and is doing also in the re-creative work of redemption. Origen, indeed, spoke of the Son as "the invisible image of the invisible God," maintaining that as the Father is invisible so also the eternally begotten Son who is his image is invisible by nature. The bodily form of the incarnation was not to be identified with that image, he insisted, for it is as the divine Word who is himself wisdom and light and truth that he reveals the Father, so that "there can be no suspicion of anything corporeal."[12] The underlying idea of the "image" is, as Lightfoot has observed, "the manifestation of the hidden."[13] The activity of him who is the image of the invisible God is revealed through its effects. This is true of the Son's work in creation and of his work of redemption, and also of his providential care and control of the universe, which is sus-

11. J. B. Lightfoot, *Saint Paul's Epistles to the Colossians and to Philemon* (London, 1892 edn.), ad loc.

12. Origen, *On First Principles* I.ii.6. Chrysostom, Homily III on Colossians, commenting on 1:15, says that "the image of the invisible is itself also invisible, and in like manner invisible, otherwise it would not be an image."

13. Lightfoot, *Colossians*, p. 143.

tained by the word of his power (Heb. 1:3). These effects are indeed visible effects, but their visibility must not be transferred to the Image through whom they are actualized.

It is true that St. John writes of the incarnate Son, the Word become flesh, that he dwelt among us "full of grace and truth," and that "we beheld his glory, glory as of the only Son from the Father" (Jn. 1:14); but the bodily aspect of the incarnation was not itself the image. That body, and this is only another way of saying that humanity, consubstantial with ours, was subject to fatigue and hunger and the other limitations of our present physical existence, and was also susceptible of death; in fact, the true purpose of the incarnation was that the humanity assumed by the Word might be offered up vicariously in death (Heb. 10:5, 10). Moreover, his was not the body as it were of some superman, so resplendent that none could mistake its uniqueness: "He had no form or comeliness that we should look at him," Isaiah prophetically declared, "and no beauty that we should desire him" (Is. 53:2). No! What St. John and his companions saw was the grace, the truth, and the glory emanating from the invisible Image—grace, truth, and glory that multitudes who saw the same bodily form failed to behold and comprehend.

We must understand that the incarnation of the Son is not the identification of us with him who *is* the Image but his identification with us who are made *in* the image. We may say that as man, living *in* or *according to* the image, the incarnate Son conformed to himself who, as God, *is* the eternal Image. In his incarnate existence on earth we see him as the only one who was perfect even as the heavenly Father is perfect and therefore with whom God is well pleased (Mt. 3:17; 5:48). Thus the Son, who *is* the Image, by becoming man became *in* the image, without however ceasing to *be* the Image. It is as consubstantial with God that he *is* the Image and as consubstantial with us that he identified himself with our human existence *in* the image; and thus he who is truly God revealed what it is to be truly man.

SON

It can readily be perceived that "son" and "image" are concepts which, within the purview of this study, have a close relationship. This association is well illustrated in the statement of Genesis 5:3 that Adam "became the father of a son in his own likeness, after his image." The "likeness" or "image" refers not to similarity in regard to external features, though it is true that a son may be like his father in this manner, but to identity of human nature or, in a word, consubstantiality—which included bearing the image of his fallenness (1 Cor. 15:49). The connotation, then, is not so much that of outward similarity as of equality and identity of nature. This consideration is of obvious significance for our understanding of the biblical designation of the Second Person of the Trinity as the Son.

There is an essential difference, of course, between human sonship and the sonship of the Second Person of the Holy Trinity, in that the former is temporal whereas the latter is eternal. Unlike the human relationship, there was no time before the Son came into existence and therefore before God could be designated as Father. The trinitarian distinction within the unity of the Godhead is a distinction which defines an eternal interpersonal relationship: just as the Second Person thus distinguished is eternally the Image of God, so also he is eternally the Son of God. The interpersonal unity of the Godhead is an eternal reality. It is a reality, moreover, which is in no way broken or interrupted by the incarnation of the Second Person; for, though at Bethlehem the Son of God becomes the Son of Man, he does not by doing so cease to be what he essentially is, namely, the Son of God. Hence the affirmation of the incarnate Son: "I and the Father are one" (Jn. 10:30). Before the creation of the world, indeed from eternity to eternity, the glory of the Son is one with the glory of the Father (Jn. 17:5). The function of the Son, whose nature and being are one with the nature and being of the Father, is to reveal, as the true Image, the character and will of God. As St. John says, "No one has seen God at any time; God the only-begotten, who is in the bosom of the Father, he it is who made God known" (Jn. 1:18).[14] No one else is in a position to "explain" God to us; he uniquely is able to do so. As the incarnate Son, he is still in the bosom of the Father. Appropriately, and necessarily, it is God who makes God known; for who else could possibly communicate the knowledge of God except God himself? Certainly no creature is competent to do so. Specifically, however, within the interpersonal relationship of the one God, it is the Son who, as the authentic Image, declares the truth about God.

The interpersonal relationship within the unity of the Godhead assures us, as we have previously mentioned,[15] that the existence of God is not one of loneliness. That is why the incarnate Son was able to affirm, in an absolute manner, "I am not alone, but I and the Father who sent me," and again, "He who sent me is with me; he has not left me alone" (Jn. 8:16, 29). Even though all his friends and disciples on earth should desert him, yet his position would not be that of loneliness: "You will leave me alone," he told his followers; "even so I am not alone, for the Father is with me" (Jn. 16:32). And the purpose of his coming into the world was that the love which eternally unites him

14. The term *monogenēs*, "only begotten," denotes sole and unique sonship, as in v. 14. The reading *monogenēs huios*, "only-begotten Son," is much less well attested than *monogenēs theos*, "only-begotten God," and is probably an assimilation to 3:16 and 18, where that expression is found. "Only-begotten God" accords well with the context, for *ho logos*, "the Word," has already been designated *theos*, "God," in the opening verse of the chapter, while *eis ton kolpon tou Patros*, "in the bosom of the Father," corresponds to *pros ton theon*, "with God," in the same place, but with the added implication, since the bosom is the place for one beloved, that the only-begotten is the beloved (cf. *agapētos*, "beloved," Mk. 1:11 and 9:7)—as is explicit in 3:35, "the Father loves the Son," and 17:24, where Jesus speaks of the Father as having loved the Son before the foundation of the world.

15. See pp. 4f. above.

and the Father in the one Godhead might also be in us as by redeeming grace we become united with him: "I made known to them thy name, and I will make it known," he says at the conclusion of his high-priestly prayer, "that the love with which thou hast loved me may be in them, and I in them" (Jn. 17:26). "This," C. H. Dodd has written, "is the ultimate mystery of Godhead which Jesus revealed to the world."[16]

But Christ is not only the Son of God: he frequently speaks of himself in the Gospels as the Son of Man—a designation the significance of which is more mysterious and difficult to fathom than might at first be expected. Assuredly, it is in effect a declaration of his authentic consubstantiality with mankind by virtue of the human nature which he took to himself from the Virgin Mary at Bethlehem. Yet it is more than a simple pointer to the reality of the incarnation; for in the New Testament the Son of Man emerges as a preexistent personage or being of more than merely human stature. The link that many have posited with the figure seen by Daniel in his vision is not unreasonable, even though that figure is described only as "one like the son of man," that is to say, one whose form or appearance was that of a human being. The vision in fact clearly portrays this manlike person as someone of unique importance. Daniel, we read, beheld "one like a son of man" coming "with the clouds of heaven" and being "presented before the Ancient of Days," a designation of Almighty God, and, further, as being "given dominion and glory and kingdom, that all peoples, nations, and languages should serve him," and as exercising "an everlasting dominion" through a kingdom "that shall not be destroyed" (Dan. 7:13f.). It is obvious that such a one who rules everlastingly transcends the powers of ordinary mortal man. We can hardly fail to be reminded of the messianic promise that God would raise up a son of David's line and "establish the throne of his kingdom for ever" (2 Sam. 7:12ff.; cf. Ps. 89:3f., 35-37) and of the prophecy of Isaiah concerning a child to be born and a son given, whose kingdom would be established with justice and righteousness forevermore, and whose names would include "Mighty God," thus testifying to one whose nature would be divine as well as human (Is. 9:6f.).

The self-understanding of Jesus in his capacity as the Son of Man is forthrightly disclosed in his teaching. As the Son of Man he is invested with authority: authority to forgive sins (Mt. 9:6; Mk. 2:10; Lk. 5:24), authority as Lord of the Sabbath (Mt. 12:8; Mk. 2:28; Lk. 6:5), authority to execute judgment (Jn. 5:27), and authority as the enthroned ruler of the eschatological kingdom (Mt. 19:28; Lk. 12:8f.; 21:36; 22:69). As the Son of Man, moreover, Christ proclaims his future coming (Mt. 10:23; Lk. 17:30; 18:8), which will be a coming in glory and majesty (Mt. 16:27f.; 24:37f.; 25:31; Mk. 8:38; Lk. 9:26) and also a coming on or with the clouds of heaven (Mt. 24:30; 26:64; Mk. 13:26; 14:62; Lk. 21:27f.). This dynamic perspective is more than merely reminiscent of the vision described in Daniel 7; the terminology used by Christ and the set-

16. C. H. Dodd, *The Interpretation of the Fourth Gospel* (Cambridge, 1955), p. 262.

ting in which he places it indicate his identification of himself with the mysterious figure "like a son of man" who comes in the clouds of heaven and is empowered with universal authority—only that figure is now given precise definition as *the Son of Man*. The identification is confirmed by the assertion of the risen Lord as he is about to ascend that "all authority in heaven and earth" has been given to him (Mt. 28:18; cf. 11:27; Lk. 10:22) and by the apostolic proclamation that the exalted and glorified Lord is now enthroned "far above all rule and authority and power and dominion" and that all things have been placed under his feet (Eph. 1:20-22; Phil. 2:9-11).

But the Son of Man's future coming in glory is preceded by a coming that involves humbling and nonrecognition. The glory that attends him in his present exaltation and future appearance is also the glory of his preexistence; for the glory to which he ascended is the glory from which he descended. This is the reality which lies behind Christ's saying that "no one has ascended into heaven but he who descended from heaven, the Son of Man" (Jn. 3:13). The incarnation, in other words, is not the beginning of the Son's existence but an event, so to speak, in his eternal existence. Accordingly, when speaking of "the food that endures to eternal life, which the Son of Man will give," Christ explains that he himself is "the living bread that came down from heaven" so that all who eat of it may live forever (Jn. 6:27, 33, 35, 38, 51). The initiative of that first coming fulfils the past and guarantees the future. But between the heights of glory that precede and follow his coming is the deep and dark valley of the shadow of death through which his coming causes him to pass. The purpose of the coming of the Son of Man was "to seek and to save the lost" (Lk. 19:10), and that purpose could be achieved only by the giving of his life as a ransom for many (Mt. 20:28; Mk. 10:45). Repeatedly he warned his disciples that the Son of Man must suffer betrayal, rejection, mockery, injustice, scourging, and execution (Mt. 16:21; 17:12, 22f.; 20:18f.; 26:2, 24, 45; Mk. 8:31; 9:31; 10:33f.; 14:21, 41; Lk. 9:22, 44, 58; 17:22-25; 18:31-33; 22:22, 48; 24:6f.). Yet the affliction and death of the Son of Man, far from spelling defeat and disaster (as at first the disciples uncomprehendingly imagined), betokened the Son of Man's victorious conquest; for, though apparently passive and helpless at last, he was actively fulfilling what he came to do. This is an important insight, to which we shall return.[17]

Had everything ended in the grave there would of course have been no conquest, but only defeat and failure. The Son of Man's foretelling of suffering and death, however, had been accompanied by the assurance that beyond the grave there would be resurrection and life, and that this would happen on the third day.[18] Thus everything from beginning to end was under control, notwithstanding the appearances to the contrary, and in due course the despair

17. See below, pp. 232f.
18. See the references given in the preceding paragraph; also Mt. 12:39f. and Lk. 11:30.

of the disciples was turned to joy as they witnessed for themselves the marvelous reality of the resurrection in their encounters with him who had indeed been dead but now was alive again. Even his bodily departure from this earthly scene when he ascended to the heavenly glory in no way cooled their ardor, for they knew that he was alive forevermore and they had his promise, soon fulfilled, of the outpouring of the Holy Spirit, who would make his presence not only universal but also more real and intimate than would have been the case had he remained physically here on earth (Jn. 14:16-18; Acts 1:8ff.). Thereafter Stephen, the first Christian martyr, testified in the hour of his ordeal that he saw "the heavens opened and the Son of Man standing at the right hand of God" (Acts 7:55f.). Finally, the glorious and awe-inspiring majesty of the exalted Son of Man was revealed to St. John in one of the visions given him on the island of Patmos: "one like a son of man," he wrote, ". . . his eyes were like a flame of fire . . . and his face was like the sun shining in full strength"; again, in another vision, he saw "a white cloud, and seated on the cloud one like a son of man, with a golden crown on his head and a sharp sickle in his hand" (Rev. 1:13-16; 14:14). The marks of affinity with the vision of Daniel are plain to see.

It is true that the expression "son of man" was a common Semitic idiom which simply denoted "man"—as, for example, in Psalm 8:4, "What is man that thou art mindful of him, and the son of man that thou dost care for him?", where "man" and "the son of man" are synonymous and interchangeable terms. Even though these words and those that follow in the psalm are applied to Christ in Hebrews 2:6ff., this is not done in such a way as to identify him as Son of Man in the special sense we have been discussing, but rather to demonstrate his total participation in our human nature by virtue of the incarnation. But there is an inner connection between his being the transcendental Son of Man and his becoming our fellow as "a son of man." The connection, indeed, applies to our creation as well as to our re-creation, and it links the two, since the Son is the Image in which we were formed and to which we are to be conformed. That the Son of God and the Son of Man are the same person is in itself a pointer to the inherent "possibility" of the Son's becoming our fellowman through incarnation, and to the reason why incarnation is never spoken of as a function of the First or Third Persons of the Triune God. This does not, however, cease to be a deep mystery, far beyond our limited powers of comprehension.

The identity of the Son as both Son of God and Son of Man is displayed in the New Testament as a perfectly natural fact. In St. Peter's historic confession at Caesarea Philippi, for instance, the response given to the twofold question of Jesus, "Who do men say that the *Son of Man* is? . . . But who do you say that I am?" is, "You are the Christ, *the Son of the living God*"—a truth Jesus applauded as revealed from above. The interchangeability of the titles is apparent also in the following passage from the teaching of Jesus: "Truly, truly, I say to you, the hour is coming, and now is, when the dead will hear the voice of *the Son of God,* and those who hear will live. For as the Father has life in himself, so he has granted *the Son* also to have life in himself, and has given him authority to execute judgment, because he is *the Son of Man*" (Jn. 5:25-27). And the connection between the Son of Man and the Son of God was made without hesitation by the members of the Jewish sanhedrin when Jesus was arraigned before them; for when he declared, "From now on *the Son of Man* shall be seated at the right hand of the power of God," they put the question, "Are you *the Son of God,* then?" (Lk. 22:69f.). Thus in the Son there is a certain mysterious linkage of God and man, a bond or affinity, associated with his being the Image in which man was created, that in a particular manner "qualifies" him to be the Mediator between God and men (1 Tim. 2:5).

In a certain sense, then, the Son of Man is the archetype of humanity, the Image to which humanity is conformed at first and at last, the Beginning and the End (Rev. 22:13). But this perception does not remove the absolute distinction between the divine and the human. The Son is not himself man; he is God. He *becomes* man for the restoration of mankind. Indeed, the verb "to become" is full of profound theological significance for our understanding of christology. The Word who is God *became* flesh (Jn. 1:1, 14); God sent forth his Son, who *became* of a woman (Gal. 4:4); he took the form of a servant, *having become* in the likeness of men (Phil. 2:7).[19] That he is the preexistent Son of Man does not mean that he is man before man, that there is a man in heaven before there is a man on earth, or that the Son is a human component within the Godhead.[20] Through the creation of man in the image of God the vital bond

19. The verb used in these places is *ginomai.*

20. The convoluted end-product of philosophical speculation is well illustrated in the thought of Philo, who postulated the creation of two men in the opening chapters of Genesis, maintaining that there is the greatest possible difference between the man of Gen. 2:7, whom God formed from the clay of the earth and into whose nostrils he breathed the breath of life, and the man of Gen. 1:27, who was an incorporeal "idea," neither male nor female (!), and imperishable by nature. This first man he designated the Word of God, the man after God's image (though elsewhere, as we have seen, he speaks more appropriately of him as himself the image after whom we are formed), and as God's first-begotten (*On the Confusion of Tongues* 146; cf. 62). By a surprising twist of exegesis he claimed Gen. 42:11, "We are all sons of one man," as support for his hypothesis that we are all "sons of God's invisible image, the most holy Word" (ibid., 147), who is "God's Man" (ibid., 41). The postulation of two different "Adams" in the opening chapters of Genesis is present also in the speculation of non-Philonic Jewish literature, both apocryphal and mystical; but the influence here is that of oriental religion and the Hermetic literature in which the notion of the "Primal Man" was prominent, rather than Greek philosophy. In this case the distinction was adapted to the supposition that the "first Adam" did not fall into sin but resolutely opposed the devil, and that it was the man of Gen. 2 who succumbed to the satanic temptation described in Gen. 3. Accordingly, it was possible to propound the identity of the Heavenly Man and the First Adam, who, himself perfect, would be the redeemer of fallen mankind (see *The Life of Adam* 12ff., 39). The development of a somewhat similar line appears in the type of early Jewish Christianity represented in the pseudo-Clementine document known as *The Preaching of Peter,* in which it is Eve, not Adam, who

between God's creature, man, and the Son of God who is also the Son of Man, the archetypal Image in which man was formed, is forged. In the incarnation, the becoming man of the Second Person of the Trinity for the renewal of creation, the "potential" inherent in his divine personhood is redemptively realized. As "all things were created in him, through him, and for him," the Image of God who is "before all things," and as "all things hold together" in him, so also it is through him that God reconciles to himself "all things, whether on earth or in heaven, having made peace by the blood of his cross" (Col. 1:15-20).

FIRSTBORN

There is the closest possible association of the designation "Son" with the designation "Firstborn," which in fact serves to define more precisely the significance of the appellation "Son" and to which, accordingly, the preceding discussion of the doctrine of sonship is fully relevant. In the Old Testament that which is firstborn has a special prominence. The firstborn males of both men and animals were holy to the Lord in the theocracy of the Israelites, as also were the firstfruits of the earth. The firstborn son was thus assigned a place of special dignity and sanctity and was in a special sense the heir to whom the birthright belonged.[21] As the recipient of the birthright the firstborn son was assured of a double portion of the paternal inheritance and of succession to the headship of the family. Thus the designation was readily transmuted into a title of exceptional dignity and preeminence. Israel, for example, is called God's firstborn son in Exodus 4:22, indicating that the Israelites were a people chosen by God and particularly dear to him; and, still more specifically, for this was the end toward which the choosing of Israel was directed, the promised messianic king of the line of David is prophetically described as "the firstborn, the highest of the kings of the earth" in Psalm 89:27—implicit in his being called firstborn was the concept of his supremacy as King of kings.

In the New Testament Jesus is spoken of as Mary's firstborn son in the literal sense (Lk. 2:7), but it is a statement from which the overtones of power

---

falls into sin; indeed, Christ, designated the True Prophet, is said to have first manifested himself as the Adam of the Genesis account, and as having repeatedly since then become incarnate in the identity of notable personages of Old Testament history, namely, Enoch, Noah, Abraham, Isaac, Jacob, and Moses, prior to his incarnation as Jesus of Nazareth. The description given by Irenaeus of the beliefs of the Sethian-Ophites illustrates the extremes to which gnostic speculation was carried. According to this mythology, "the Father of all" is called "the First Man," "the Thought" emitted by him is "the Son of Man" or "the Second Man," the Holy Spirit is "the First Woman," and "the Third Man" who is called "Christ" is the offspring of the First and Second Man and the Holy Spirit (*Against Heresies* i.30).

21. What Esau, Isaac's firstborn, bartered for momentary gratification was his birthright, his privileges of the firstborn, *ta prōtotokia autou* (Heb. 12:16).

and authority need not be excluded. Certainly, when the writer of the Epistle to the Hebrews says that Christ is the firstborn whom God brings into the world (Heb. 1:6) he is ascribing supreme eminence to him who in this context is denominated "Son," and who as the exalted heir of all things has inherited a name more excellent than that of the angels.[22] The description of Christ as "the firstborn of [or from] the dead" in Colossians 1:18 and Revelation 1:5 is more than merely temporal, for others had been restored to life prior to his own death and resurrection (cf. 1 Kings 17:17ff.; 2 Kings 4:18ff.; Heb. 11:35; Jn. 11:1ff.; Mk. 5:35ff.; Lk. 7:11ff.), only in course of time to die physically again. The unique character of the resurrection of Christ is that it is a resurrection to everlasting life and glory. Consequently as the firstborn of the dead he is both the first to be thus raised and the powerful guarantor of everlasting life and glory for all who through divine grace are dynamically united to him. To the same effect he is called "the firstfruits of those who have fallen asleep" (1 Cor. 15:20, 23), for the firstfruits are the assurance of the full harvest that is to follow. On the basis of this understanding the company of the redeemed is described as "the church of the firstborn" (Heb. 12:23), for, made one with him who is the Firstborn, they enter into the inheritance which belongs to the firstborn (Rom. 8:14-17).

Image and *firstborn* are brought together in Romans 8:29, where St. Paul writes that "those whom God foreknew he also predestined to be conformed to the image of his Son, in order that he might be the firstborn among many brethren." Conformity with the image of God's Son is, as we have earlier observed, conformity with the image of God in which man was originally created and into which, now through redeeming grace, it is his destiny to be re-created.[23] The destiny that was planned from the very beginning is fulfilled redemptively and re-creatively in the Son by God who proclaims: "Behold, I make all things new!" (Rev. 21:5). Our full and final likeness to the Son who is both the Image and the Firstborn will be an enduring reality at his appearing (1 Jn. 3:2); then we shall enter into the fulness of the inheritance of the firstborn that is ours in him, and we shall know the true meaning of that indescribable grace that made him not ashamed to call us brethren (Heb. 2:11ff.).

Another passage in which the Son is described as both *image* and *firstborn* requires more extended consideration. This is Colossians 1:15, where St. Paul declares that "the Son of God's love" (v. 13), which is a designation virtually synonymous with "firstborn," is "the image of the invisible God, the firstborn of all creation." The Arians in the fourth century seized on the phrase

---

22. The "heir of all things," *klēronomos pantōn* (v. 2), has "inherited," *keklēronomēken* (v. 4), a more excellent name. For a discussion of the terminology of this passage see my *Commentary on the Epistle to the Hebrews* (Grand Rapids, 1977), ad loc.

23. To be "conformed to the image of his Son" does not mean to be conformed to an image that is something other than or separate from the Son, but to be conformed to the image that *is* God's Son. In the Greek text, *symmorphous tēs eikonos tou huiou autou,* the second genitive is epexegetic of the first: "conformed to the image that is his Son."

"the firstborn of all creation,"[24] claiming that it meant that of every creature Christ was the first to be born or created, with the consequence that he was in some sense a creature and not the divine and eternal Son—though they carefully cloaked their teaching with cryptic terminology which implied that he was a unique being brought into existence intemporally before the creation described in Genesis 1. The patristic authors dealt effectively with this interpretation by demonstrating that the context in which the expression occurs taught something quite different; for St. Paul in the immediately following clause goes on to state that "in him all things were created, in heaven and on earth, visible and invisible, whether thrones or dominions or principalities or authorities— all things were created through him and for him" (v. 16). This affirmation is inclusive of every possible type of creature. There is no room for any exception, least of all for the Son himself to be an exception. Athanasius, for example, pointed out that the Arian position led to illogical and ridiculous conclusions, observing that "if he is a creature he will be the firstborn of himself" and must "exist before and after himself," then "one of the creatures must have created all the creatures," himself included, and "such notions are so full of absurdities and impossibilities that they at once confute our adversaries and establish the opposite truth."[25]

The heretical misinterpretation of this text made it necessary for the patristic scholars to wrestle with the question of the apparently built-in temporal element in the appellation "the firstborn of all creation." Chrysostom was among those who held that the term "firstborn" referred only to time and not to dignity and honor; to the Son indeed, but not the Son as preexistent, for "firstborn" would then seem to be in conflict with his uniqueness as the "only" or "only-begotten" Son, since "firstborn" was believed to imply the first of many. The solution, as Chrysostom saw it, was to take "the firstborn of all creation" as referring specifically to the incarnate Son and to the new creation in him, not to the original creation.[26] This explanation was widely accepted. Gregory of Nyssa, for instance, remarked that "we recognize a twofold creation of our nature, the first that whereby we were made, the second that whereby we were made anew," and asserted that it was with regard to the latter that Christ was called "the firstborn of all creation," adding that "the appellation 'only-begotten' testifies that the character of 'firstborn' does not apply to the Son in his pretemporal existence."[27] A similar judgment was expressed by Athanasius, who argued that "the same person cannot be only-begotten and firstborn except in different relations," and that "if all things were created by him he must necessarily be distinct from all created things."[28]

Others drew attention to the fact that St. Paul speaks of the Son as "first-

24. *Prōtotokos pasēs ktiseōs.*
25. Athanasius, *Orations against the Arians* ii.63.
26. John Chrysostom, Homily III on Colossians, ad loc.
27. Gregory of Nyssa, *Against Eunomius* iv.3.
28. Athanasius, *Orations against the Arians* ii.62.

born," not "first-created." The point was made by Ambrose, who, however, took the expression "firstborn of all creation" to signify the eternal preexistence of Christ: "born," he explained, refers to his nature as Son and "first" to his perpetuity.[29] In other words, the expression was treated as the equivalent of the eternal begetting or generation of the Son, who, as the firstborn of all creation, is the Son born, or generated, before all creation. This understanding is found as early as Justin Martyr in the second century: "We know him to be the firstborn of God and to be before all created things," Justin wrote;[30] and it found a permanent place in the credal tradition of the church. At the Council of Nicea in 325 Eusebius of Caesarea proposed the adoption of the creed of his own church, in which Jesus Christ was declared to be "God of God, . . . only-begotten Son, firstborn of all creation, begotten of the Father before all the ages, through whom also all things were made." Obviously, this christological statement is in the main an explication of the terms of Colossians 1:15; but a fuller statement was accepted at Nicea, emphasizing the full and authentic deity of the Son to ensure its effectiveness as an antidote to the errors of Arianism. The Son, it affirmed, is "of the substance of the Father, . . . true God of true God, begotten, not created, consubstantial with the Father." One of the implications of calling Christ "the firstborn of all creation" is, as Bishop Lightfoot has observed, that of "*priority* to all creation," in such a way that it declares "the absolute pre-existence of the Son."[31] This, in general, seems to have been well understood by the champions of orthodoxy in the early centuries.

But there is another implication, that, namely, of "the *sovereignty* over all creation,"[32] which, somewhat surprisingly, seemed to a large degree to escape the attention of the patristic authors. The reason for this oversight is, no doubt, that preoccupation with the christological controversies of their day induced them to argue on the level of the temporal interpretation presupposed by their opponents, and then to insist, as we have seen, on the reference being either to the eternal generation of the Son or to the new creation effected by the incarnate Son. But, as previously mentioned, the biblical concept of the firstborn involves a strong sense of preeminent dignity and authority, and this understanding belongs with the utmost appropriateness to Christ as "the firstborn of all creation." To quote Bishop Lightfoot again: "God's 'firstborn' is the natural ruler, the acknowledged head, of God's household. The right of primogeniture appertains to Messiah over all created things." As "the firstborn of all creation," then, the Son is "Sovereign Lord over all creation by virtue of primogeniture."[33] The conduct of Esau in despising the birthright which

29. Ambrose, *On Faith* 7; "Primogenitus, inquit, non primocreatus."
30. Justin Martyr, *Dialogue with Trypho* 100; cf. *The Second Apology* 6.
31. Lightfoot, *Colossians*, p. 144.
32. Ibid., p. 145.
33. Ibid. "In its Messianic reference," Lightfoot explains further, "this secondary idea of sovereignty predominated in the word *prōtotokos*." In classical literature the equivalent of *prōtotokos* in this elative sense is *prōtogonos*, "first-begotten," then "first in rank."

was his by reason of being the firstborn was ever thereafter remembered as a scandalous example of irreligious profanity (Gen. 25:29ff.; Heb. 12:16f.). The consequence of Esau's transaction was that the younger brother Jacob acquired for himself the blessing and the headship inherent in the status of the firstborn.[34]

Colossians 1:15-20 affirms, emphatically and categorically, the absolute supremacy of the Son, who as the agent of creation is not only *before* all things but also *over* all things, and as the agent of re-creation is "the head of the body, the church," and also "the beginning, the firstborn from the dead," and therefore the Lord of the future; and this means precisely this, that in everything, in creation, in providence, and in redemption, the preeminence belongs to him ("that in everything he might be pre-eminent," v. 18). This cannot be said of any creature, for there is no creature that is not finite and dependent and fallible; but it is true of him who is himself divine, the eternal Son of God, and in whom, when he became the incarnate Son, "all the fulness of God was pleased to dwell" (v. 19). In saying "all the fulness" the Apostle is expressing himself pleonastically, for *fulness* is a concept which does not allow of degrees; but he writes in this way in order to strike down the possibility of any suggestion that the Son, who is "the image of the invisible God, the firstborn of all creation," is less or other than God, or some kind of inferior God, or only partially God.

Perhaps the most balanced interpretation of the expression "the firstborn of all creation" that has come down to us from the patristic era is from the pen of Theodore of Mopsuestia, the great exponent of the sober Antiochene method of biblical exegesis, who wrote that "'firstborn' is used not only with reference to time, but also frequently in fact with reference to pre-eminence."[35] After proving his point by citing a number of passages (Ps. 89:26f.; Heb. 12:23; Exod. 4:22), he concludes: "So, too, here to say 'the firstborn of all creation' is the equivalent of saying 'honored above the whole creation.'"[36] And Theodoret, who succeeded Theodore as the leader of Antiochene exposition, commented that "the holy Apostle does not say 'first-created' but 'firstborn,'"

Still more recently K. L. Schmidt has shown himself to be of the same mind. The expression *prōtotokos pasēs ktiseōs* in Col. 1:15, he writes, "does not simply denote the priority of time of the pre-existent Lord," pointing out that "the -*tokos* is never emphasized in the New Testament passages which speak of Christ," and that consequently "the only remaining possibility is to take *prōtotokos* here hierarchically." This being so, "what is meant is the unique supremacy of Christ over all creatures as the Mediator of their creation" (*TDNT*, VI, pp. 878f.).

34. In this connection it is of interest that *prōtotokos* is the equivalent and the regular translation of the Hebrew word *b*^{e}*kor*, though the latter is not etymologically linked to notions of birth or begetting.

35. *Protimēsis*.

36. Theodore of Mopsuestia, Commentary on the Epistle to the Colossians (Migne, *PG*, LXVI, 928A).

that is, first," and that "the worthiness of persons is plainly shown by this designation, for the Only-Begotten is not the brother of creation but the maker of creation, as he teaches in what follows" (i.e., in the verses following Col. 1:15).[37]

WORD

Another designation of Christ closely related to the concept of the image of God is that of the Word in the prologue of St. John's Gospel. A word is a unit of language, and language is an essential phenomenon of personality as it fulfils its specific function of communication in interpersonal relationships. Both "image" and "word" serve a purpose that is revelatory. As the Image of God the Son is the authentic manifestation of the divine nature. As the Word of God he is the express declaration of the divine mind. "The Word" as a title of Christ denotes the Second Person of the Trinity in his capacity as the Revealer of the will and character of God. Verbal utterance discloses the thought and purpose of the speaker; but to be communication it must of course be addressed to a hearer in person-to-person relationship, for otherwise it is an empty utterance devoid of power and unproductive. The Son as the Word is God's utterance addressed to man. The fact that the Word proceeds from God carries the assurance that God himself is personal. That man can be addressed by God confirms not only the personality of man but also the reality of his creation in the image of God to whom he owes the personal character that is stamped upon his being. Man's formation in the divine Image is his formation in the divine Word.

A word, moreover, is necessarily rational, for language is the vehicle of rational communication between persons. Irrationality is the death of communication. The Greek term for *Word* in John 1:1, 14 is *Logos,* and it is not

37. Theodoret, Commentary on the Epistle to the Colossians (Migne, *PG*, LXXXII, 597CD, 600A).

Another exegetical possibility was suggested by Theodoret's contemporary, Isidore of Pelusium. Granting that he might seem to be cutting a new path of interpretation, Isidore proposed the shifting of the accent from the antepenult position to the penultimate syllable, so that instead of *prōtótokos,* which means "the first one to be born," the reading would be *prōtotókos,* which would make it an active epithet with the meaning "the one who first bears." In advocating this arrangement he claimed the support of Homer: "You who study Homer are well aware of this," he said; "for the woman who first bears is called *prōtotókos* by him; it is probable, therefore, or rather it is necessary to understand that St. Paul used it here in a similar sense" (*Epistolarum Lib. III,* Ep. 31 [Migne, *PG*, LXXVIII, 749C]). Plato in fact used the term in this way of women, and Homer and some other classical authors of different animals. The chief problem with this proposal is that the verbal part of the term when accented in this way, *-tókos,* is descriptive of the woman's function of childbearing and giving birth *(tiktein).* The conception of the Son as the mother of creation is not only farfetched and contrary to the solid tradition of interpretation but is also at variance with the sense of *prōtótokos* in the other passages, where it is descriptive of Christ.

without significance that *Logos* also means "reason."[38] That the Son is also the Logos assures us of the divine rationality, both in itself and as the source of human rationality, and informs us that the Son is God's disclosure and communication of himself to us. As the inescapable concomitant of our formation in the divine image this self-disclosure and self-communication was already a reality at creation; and it became a redemptive reality through the incarnation and saving work of the eternal Word, whereby the sheer irrationality of sin was overthrown.

Because of the association of word and reason implicit in the term *logos,* the intrinsic sense of *logos* is that of a word which is true as opposed to what is false and inauthentic.[39] The identification of word and truth is absolute in the case of the word of God, who is himself Truth and the source of all truth. Hence the acknowledgment of David: "O Lord God, thou art God, and thy words are true" (2 Sam. 7:28); and the declaration of Psalm 119:160: "The sum of thy word is truth," and similarly the assertion of the incarnate Son: "Thy word is truth" (Jn. 17:17). The same identification of word and truth is made in the person of the Logos in the Fourth Gospel, for the Logos himself is God (Jn. 1:1). The manifestation of the Logos as the incarnate Son is precisely a manifestation of the truth: "And the Word became flesh and dwelt among us, full of grace and truth," St. John testifies (Jn. 1:14). As the Word who is God Jesus categorically proclaimed himself to be *The Truth* (Jn. 14:6); and Christian believers are able confidently to assert: "We know that the Son of God has come and has given us understanding, to know him who is true; and we are in him who is true, in his Son Jesus Christ. This is the true God" (1 Jn. 5:20).

Truth is of course by definition the antithesis of what is false and inauthentic; indeed, the Greek word for truth, *alētheia,* means literally "unhiddenness," signifying the end of concealment and therefore the exposure or bringing to light of a thing in its genuine being.[40] From this the equation of truth with light readily follows. Falsehood darkens the understanding; truth enlightens the understanding. The Word who is the Truth shines in the darkness and dispels it (Jn. 1:5); for what can be said of God, that he "is light and in him is no darkness at all" (1 Jn. 1:5), can be said of the divine Word, who accordingly announced: "I am the light of the world; he who follows me will not walk in darkness, but will have the light of life" (Jn. 8:12). To come to Jesus is to come to the Word who is the Light; therefore "he who does what is true

---

38. Cf. the English derivatives "logic," "logical," etc. C. H. Dodd has observed that "it is only in Greek that a term is available which means both 'thought' and 'word'" (*The Interpretation of the Fourth Gospel,* p. 278).

39. This intrinsic sense is well brought out, for example, in Plato, *Timaeus* 26E, *to te mē plasthenta mython all' alēthinon logon einai pammega pou,* "the fact that it is no fabricated myth but a true logos is surely of great importance."

40. *Alētheia* is compounded of the alpha-privative and the stem of the verb *lanthanō* (*lēthō*), "to lie hidden"; cf. the definition of Heraclitus, *alēthes to mē lēthon,* "what is true is what is not hidden."

comes to the light, that it may be clearly seen that his deeds have been wrought in God" (Jn. 3:21).

The Son is both the preexistent Word of God and the final Word of God. As the preexistent Word he is the agent of creation; as the final Word he is the agent of redemption or re-creation. Thus St. John says of the Creator-Word that "all things were made through him, and without him was not anything made that was made" (Jn. 1:3); the author of the Epistle to the Hebrews writes that "the world was created by the Word of God" (Heb. 11:3); and St. Peter warns against scoffers "who deliberately ignore the fact that by the word of God heavens existed long ago" (2 Pet. 3:5; cf. Ps. 33:6, "by the word of the Lord the heavens were made"). The Creator-Word appears as the Redeemer-Word by becoming flesh and dwelling among us (Jn. 1:14). As the final Word, he is the Son by whom God has spoken in these last days (Heb. 1:2). The word of God is thus not simply verbalized Person-to-person communication (though it is that too, hence the proclamation of prophets and apostles); it is essentially the Word that is a Person, and that Person is himself God, the Second Person of the eternal trinitarian Deity. That is why, unlike the word of man which is vocal, transient, and evanescent, the Word of God abides forever (1 Pet. 1:23-25; Is. 40:8; Mt. 23:35). And that is why it is unfailingly active and dynamic, and never meaningless, purposeless, or powerless (Heb. 4:12). God's word is ever God's work; it does not return to him empty; it always accomplishes the purpose of its sending (Is. 55:11). As the creating and re-creating Word of God, therefore, the Son is not only the Revealer but also the Executive of the divine will. He, the Person-Word, not a fleeting vocable, is the true dynamic of both creation and redemption. And he is the Image of God stamped upon the very core of our constitution as human beings, the Truth of our being and the Light of our life, apart from whom we debase ourselves in falsehood, darkness, and death.

GLORY

The declaration,"We have beheld his glory, glory as of the only Son from the Father" (Jn. 1:14), plainly implies that the glory of Christ is nothing less than the divine glory itself; and this glory is therefore eternal glory—glory that from the standpoint of the Son's incarnation is preexistent glory (Jn. 17:5, 24), glory to which the ascended Redeemer has returned (Lk. 24:26; 1 Tim. 3:16), and glory in which all the redeemed will participate when he returns in majesty at the end of this age (Mt. 24:30; 25:31; Mk. 8:38; 13:26; Lk. 9:26; Rom. 5:2; 8:18; 2 Cor. 4:17; Col. 3:4; 2 Tim. 2:10; Tit. 3:13; 1 Pet. 4:13). Moreover, it is the transcendental glory of which Peter, James, and John were witnesses on the Mount of Transfiguration (Lk. 9:29, 32; 2 Pet. 1:16-18) and to which John 1:14 probably refers. This is absolute glory, the light which overcomes and destroys all darkness and untruth (Jn. 1:5; Rev. 22:3-5), "the glory of Christ, who is the image of God" (2 Cor. 4:4). Since he is the Image of God who is entitled by St. Peter "the Majestic Glory" (2 Pet. 1:17), it is not surprising that the aged Simeon should recognize in the infant Jesus "a light to lighten the Gentiles and the glory of thy people Israel" (Lk. 2:32), that the incarnate Son should declare himself to be "the Light of the world" (Jn. 8:12), or that the eternal city should have "no need of sun or moon to shine upon it," since "the glory of God is its light, and its lamp is the Lamb" (Rev. 21:23; cf. 22:5).

Nor is it surprising that St. James should in an absolute manner designate "our Lord Jesus Christ" as "the Glory" (Jas. 2:1). Numerous attempts have been made to obviate the need for treating "the glory" as an absolute title by connecting it with some other term in the sentence, some by adding "the Lord," which is not in the Greek text: "our Lord Jesus Christ, the Lord of glory," some by recombining the words as "the glory of our Lord Jesus Christ," some as "our Lord of glory, Jesus Christ," some as "our Lord Jesus, the Christ (Messiah) of glory," and some as "our glorious Lord Jesus Christ." But there is no more reason to feel embarrassment over the absolute designation of our Lord Jesus Christ as the Glory than there is over his absolute designation as the Word, the Way, the Truth, the Life, or the Light, or over the way in which the Father is called "the Majestic Glory" in 2 Peter 1:7.[41] It should also be seriously considered whether another example of the absolute usage of "the glory" as an appellation of Christ is to be found in Ephesians 1:17, where St. Paul writes of "the God of our Lord Jesus Christ, the Father of the glory."[42] The latter phrase may indeed be translated as "the Father of glory" or "the glorious Father"; but there is every justification for taking the two phrases as formally parallel, as follows: "the God of our Lord Jesus Christ, the Father of [him who is] the Glory."

Two other passages merit attention. First of all, Acts 7:55, where we read that Stephen "gazed into heaven and saw the glory of God, and Jesus standing at the right hand of God." This may well be more correctly rendered: "saw the Glory of God, even Jesus, standing at the right hand of God."[43] Secondly, Titus 2:13, where St. Paul speaks of our "awaiting the blessed hope and the appearing of the glory of the great God and our Savior Jesus Christ." A more apposite rendering would be: "awaiting the blessed hope, namely the appearing of the Glory of the great God, even our Savior Jesus Christ."[44] Christ, whom the rulers

41. J. B. Mayor, *The Epistle of St. James* (London, 1892), p. 75, approves the "perfectly natural and easy construction suggested by Bengel," namely, that "the glory" *(tēs doxēs)* is simply in apposition to the immediately preceding genitive, "our Lord Jesus Christ" *(tou kyriou hēmōn Iēsou Christou).* "The reason why the word *doxa* stands here alone, without *hēmōn* or *tou Patros*," Mayor comments, "is in order that it may be understood in its fullest and widest sense of Him who alone comprises all glory in Himself."

42. *Ho theos tou Kyriou hēmōn Iēsou Christou, ho Patēr tēs doxēs.*

43. *Eiden doxan theou kai Iēsoun.* . . . All that is done is to take *kai* here and in the passage that follows (Tit. 2:13) as meaning "even" instead of "and," a sense of which it is readily susceptible.

44. *Prosdechomenoi tēn makarian elpida kai epiphaneian tēs doxēs tou megalou theou kai sōtēros hēmōn Iēsou Christou.* The RSV and other modern translations treat the first *kai* as epexegetic; why not also the second *kai?* Our Savior Jesus Christ is himself the Glory of the great God.

of this age crucified, is in fact "the Lord of glory" (1 Cor. 2:8), and the reality of the indwelling of the Lord of glory in the hearts and lives of his people is the foretaste of future glory and the guarantee of ultimate participation in the fulness of that glory which is his who is the Glory—a reality summarized by St. Paul as "Christ in you, the hope of glory" (Col. 1:27).

In Hebrews 1:3 the Son is called "the radiance of God's glory" in a passage which also affirms, in the closest proximity to this designation, that the world was created through him and that he sustains all things by the word of his power. As the fathers of the early centuries persistently pointed out, there is no support or encouragement here for gnostics, Arians, and others who in their different ways taught that Christ was less and other than God. To maintain that the "radiance" is something substantially different from the "glory," as though Christ were but some kind of emanation and not himself God, was to place an interpretation on this text which was incompatible with and destructive of the plain christological teaching of Scripture. Radiance and glory, the orthodox theologians insisted, are inseparable from each other and therefore to assert that the Son is the radiance of God's glory is to testify to the consubstantiality and coeternity of the Son with the Father.[45] The radiance is the self-manifestation of the glory. Thus for the people of Israel the *Shekinah* glory was the radiance of God's presence dwelling in the midst of his people.[46] It was manifested in the pillar of fire by night and of cloud by day that accompanied them in the wilderness and in the glory that appeared between the cherubim in the inner sanctuary of tabernacle and temple; and in the New Testament it was displayed in the radiance on the Mount of Transfiguration and in the transcendental light that flashed around St. Paul in his encounter with the risen Lord on the road to Damascus. The Son who comes to us, and who is himself the Glory, is "Immanuel: God with us" (Is. 7:14; Mt. 1:23). He is the Word who became flesh and dwelt among us, the *Shekinah* radiance, whose glory the apostles beheld.[47]

The Christian believer has the certainty that he will at last enter into "the presence of his glory with great joy" (Jude 24). Then the resplendent fulness of the *Shekinah* will become for him an eternal reality as the covenant promise attains its ultimate completion: "Behold, the dwelling of God[48] is with men. He will dwell with them, and they shall be his people, and God himself will be

---

45. In the clause *hos ōn apaugasma tēs doxēs kai charaktēr tēs hypostaseōs autou* it seems most natural to take *autou* as defining both the preceding nouns, *apaugasma* and *charaktēr*, but *apaugasma tēs doxēs* can be construed independently of *autou*, "radiance of the glory"; cf. the Vulgate rendering *splendor gloriae*. If this is accepted, this is another instance of "glory" being used absolutely of the Son, especially if *tēs doxēs* is a subjective genitive.

46. *Shekinah* is a derivative from the Hebrew root *shachan*, "to dwell."

47. Jn. 1:14. It has often been suggested that the Greek verb *eskēnōsen*, "he dwelt," which has the same radical consonants S-K-N as *shachan*, may have been intended to imply a connection between the incarnate Son who dwelt among us and the *Shekinah* glory of God's dwelling among his people in the Old Testament.

48. *Hē skēnē tou theou*--the *Shekinah*.

with them" (Rev. 21:3). Meanwhile he is progressing "from glory to glory" as increasingly he is "transformed into the same image," that is to say, as his Christiformity advances (2 Cor. 3:18); for the glory of the Son is the glory of the Image. The bond of union between the Glory and the Image is plainly set forth also in Hebrews 1:3, where the Son is in the same breath designated "the radiance of God's glory" and "the very stamp of his nature." It is to the latter part of this definition that we now turn.

STAMP

In the description of the Son as "the very stamp" of the divine nature the Greek term so translated is *charaktēr*[49]—a term which was used of a stamp or impress made by a die or seal, though it also came to bear a variety of other significances. Any hermeneutical problem connected with this term as used in this place belongs no less to the interpretation of *image* as a designation of Christ. We must in fact treat the expression "the very stamp of God" as synonymous with "the image of God." Not to be disregarded is the evidence that the Jewish philosopher Philo, who was contemporary with the New Testament authors, treated "image" *(eikōn)* as interchangeable with "stamp" *(charaktēr)*, for he wrote of man as having at creation been "imprinted with the seal of which the stamp is the eternal Logos,"[50] and of "a certain imprint and stamp of divine power which Moses calls by the lordly name image."[51]

Clement of Rome, before the end of the first century, employs the term "stamp" in connection with the creation of man, but not as a synonym for the Son. "With his holy and faultless hands God formed man as the stamp of his own image,"[52] he writes. "For thus says God: 'Let us make man after our image and after our likeness.'" Here, interestingly, man is described as the stamp of God's image. This is an effective way of presenting the relationship between man and the image in which he is created, and it is virtually parallel to the arresting description of man as "the image of the image" found in Philo earlier and in Origen later.[53] "Stamp" *(charaktēr)* recurs, but with a different orientation, in Theodoret's version of the synodical letter regarding the Council of Ariminium (Rimini) sent to the Illyrians by Damasus and other western bishops in 369: "the Father and the Son are of one substance," they declare, "one

---

49. Heb. 1:3 is the only place in the New Testament where this term is used.

50. Philo, *On Noah's Work as a Planter* 18, *typōthen tina sphragidi theou, hēs ho charaktēr estin ho aidios logos.*

51. *The Worse attacks the Better* 83, *typon tina kai charaktēra theias dynameōs, hēn onomati kyriō Mōysēs eikona kalei.* Philo did not of course regard the Logos as fully divine, though he was willing to speak of him as "the second god" (*Questions and Answers on Genesis* i.62). For an extended discussion of Philo's use of *charaktēr* see Ronald Williamson, *Philo and the Epistle to the Hebrews* (Leiden, 1970), pp. 74ff.

52. Clement of Rome, *Epistle to the Corinthians* 33: *anthrōpon . . . eplasen tēs heautou eikonos charaktēra.*

53. See p. 16 above.

godhead, one virtue, one power, one stamp, and the Holy Spirit is of the same essence and substance."[54] Evidently, the term was regarded as appropriate for defining trinitarian identity as well as christological doctrine, which is a clear indication that for theological purposes "stamp" was accepted as implying authenticity, not inferiority, of being.

The discussion we have developed enables us to conclude that in the doctrine of the apostles and the understanding of the fathers the Image of God and the person of Christ were identified with each other in an absolute manner, that to designate him the Son, the Firstborn, the Word, the Glory, and the Stamp of God is entirely consonant with this conception, and that the import of man's creation in the image of God is that he should constantly endeavor to conform himself, in being and conduct, to the perfection of that image. Tertullian commented pleasingly on the response of Jesus to the question asked him about paying taxes to Caesar (Mt. 22:15-22; Mk. 12:13-17): "The Lord demanded that the coin should be shown to him, and inquired about the image, whose it was; and when he heard that it was Caesar's, he said, 'Render what is Caesar's to Caesar and what is God's to God'—that is, the image of Caesar which is on the coin, to Caesar, and the image of God which is on man, to God; and thus to render money to Caesar, to God yourself."[55]

We recall the perceptive judgment of James Orr that the nature of the divine image "lies in the doctrine of the Trinity that the Son of God is the Father's eternal image; but more, that He is the principle of revelation in the divine Being; more still, that the revelation in the creation of the world and of man takes place through the Son, and that, in a profound sense, He is the abiding ground, connecting point, and sustaining power in creation—nay, He is Himself the end of it." Orr affirmed two certainties in this connection: first of all, that "*without* this doctrine of the divine image in man the incarnation is an impossibility," and, secondly, that "*with* this doctrine the chief *a priori* objections to the incarnation disappear"; for with the incarnation of the Son "there is historically presented to us *the actual realization of the divine image* in man," while "in his archetypal character Jesus is the realization of the end or destiny of man."[56] In accord with this is the percipience of A. M. Ramsey, who has written that, "while Christ is the uncreated image of deity, man is *created* in the image of God," and "as such he possesses true affinity to his Creator, an affinity whereon the possibility of his redemption and knowledge of God rest"; and he added that "man, when he is raised up with Christ in glory, will be man as God created him to become . . . like unto Christ's perfect manhood," for "in Christ mankind is allowed to see not only the radiance of God's glory but also the true image of man."[57] In a word, man's being as created is *christomorphic*.

---

54. Theodoret, *Ecclesiastical History* ii.17.

55. Tertullian, *On Idolatry* 15.

56. James Orr, *God's Image in Man and its Defacement in the Light of Modern Denials* (New York and London, 1905), pp. 269, 271, 272.

57. Ramsey, *Glory of God,* p. 151.

It is this reality which above all distinguishes him from the beasts. Christiformity was the intention of God in the creation of man. As his origin is christomorphic, so also is his destiny. The end, however, as we shall see, will be more splendid than the beginning.

NOTE ON "FORM" *(MORPHĒ)* IN PHILIPPIANS 2:6

Philippians 2:5ff. is a passage of profound christological significance. It is necessary for us to consider some aspects of its teaching before we move on because some scholars hold that the terminology of verse 6 in particular propounds the concept of Christ as the Image of God or the Heavenly Man. Somewhat literally translated, the text reads: "Have this mind among yourselves which you have in Christ Jesus, who, though he was in the form of God, did not count equality with God a thing to be grasped, but by taking the form of a servant and becoming in the likeness of men emptied himself; and, being found in structure as a man, he humbled himself and became obedient unto death, even death on a cross." In discussing this passage the first thing to notice is the context in which it is placed. Far from being intended as an essay on ontology, the christological teaching given here is for the purpose of illustrating the first principle of Christian ethics, namely, the humility and selflessness of Christ. St. Paul is in the midst of exhorting the members of the Philippian church to be loving and of one mind. "Do nothing from selfishness or conceit, but in humility count others better than yourselves," he says. "Let each of you look not to his own interests but to the interests of others" (vv. 2-4). And the secret of this loving harmony is for them unitedly to be one with the mind of Christ, whose mind was displayed in his voluntary self-abnegation for the sake of others. The recognition of the ethical thrust of St. Paul's argument should remind us that, seen in its biblical perspective, Christian theology is never merely theoretical or academic, even when treating of the nature of God or the preexistence and incarnation of Christ, but inherently practical in its issues and implications. This fact should not be overlooked as we now isolate and examine a particular christological aspect of this passage.

Of primary interest for our present purpose is the meaning of the assertion that Christ was "in the form of God." In the christological conflict of the early centuries some of the heretical teachers attempted to interpret this as signifying that Christ was in some sense like God but was less than God and essentially other than God. Their arguments were firmly refuted by the champions of orthodoxy. Chrysostom, for example, pointed out that St. Paul speaks not only of "the form of God" but also of "the form of a servant" assumed by the incarnate Son, and that because it was agreed that "the form of a servant" signified man by nature so also "the form of God" signified God by nature. This conclusion is confirmed, he continued, by the information added by St. Paul that Christ enjoyed "equality with God," which can only mean that he is in no way inferior to the Father but consubstantial with him. To the objection that Christ must be less than God or a lesser god because the Apostle states that he did not grasp at equality with God, and one grasps at something more or greater than oneself, Chrysostom rejoined that, already being God, Christ did not grasp at being God, because no one grasps at what he already is, and that in any case there is only one God, not one God who is greater and another who is inferior. The scriptural quotations adduced by Chrysostom to establish the authentic deity of Christ are capped by Titus 2:13, where the "blessed hope" of Christians is defined as "the appearing of the glory of our great God, even our Savior Jesus Christ."[58] Calvin follows a similar line of argument in the sixteenth century when he asks: "Where is there equality with God without robbery except only where there is the essence of God?"[59] But to say that one does not grasp at what one already has hardly clarifies the issue under debate; it implies, rather, that St. Paul's statement is a statement without point to it.

We shall return to the discussion of this question, but first we must consider what signification is to be attached to the term "form" in verse 6. Undoubtedly, like some of the other terms that have been under consideration, the Greek noun *morphē* is susceptible of a variety of connotations, depending on the requirements of the context in which it occurs. Lightfoot has adduced ample evidence to show that both in the literature of classical Greece and in the thought of authors contemporary with St. Paul the term was invested with a sense that was not germane to other terms that could otherwise be regarded as synonymous, such as "image" *(eikōn),* "likeness" *(homoiōma),* and "appearance" *(schēma)*—the sense, namely, of "specific character"; though not itself the same as "nature" or "essence" yet it involved participation in the essence, for it "implies not the external accidents but the essential attributes."[60] "Being in the form of God" is, Lightfoot says, "an exact counterpart" to the opening statement of St. John's Gospel: "In the beginning was the Word, and the Word was with God, and the Word was God."[61] Thus understood, "being in the form of God" signifies the reality of divine coessentiality.[62]

58. Chrysostom, Homily 6 on the Epistle to the Philippians. It is obvious that Chrysostom understands *harpagmos* not as something to be grasped at *(res rapienda)* but as something to hold fast to *(res rapta);* and this is certainly a necessary interpretation if "in the form of God" denotes the deity of Christ.

59. Calvin, *Commentary on the Epistle to the Philippians,* ad loc.

60. J. B. Lightfoot, *St. Paul's Epistle to the Philippians* (London and Cambridge, 2nd ed., 1869), p. 108, and the excursus, "The synonyms *morphē* and *schēma,*" pp. 125ff.

61. Ibid., p. 108. Lightfoot observes, rightly in this context, that the verb *hyparchein* "denotes 'prior existence,' but not necessarily 'eternal existence,'" adding, however, that the idea of eternal existence "follows in the present instance from the conception of the divinity of Christ which the context supposes."

62. J. Behm, on *"morphē," TDNT,* IV, pp. 750-52, to the contrary insists that "there is no trace of Hellenistic philosophical understanding of *morphē* in this passage and certainly not of any supposed popular philosophical concept of *morphē theou* = *ousia* or *physis.*" Yet he seems to offer an understanding which is much the same as that of Lightfoot when he says that "the specific outward sign" of the humanity of Jesus is the *morphē*

Other scholars have drawn attention to the fact that there is evidence to show that "form" *(morphē)* can serve as a synonym of "image" *(eikōn),* and, more particularly, that there are instances of its use to translate the Hebrew nouns $d^e muth$ and *tselem,* the terms employed in Genesis 1:26 concerning the creation of man in the "image" and "likeness" of God.[63] This consideration has led some to postulate a direct relationship of the thought and terminology of Philippians 2:5ff. and the creation of man as narrated in Genesis 1:26f. Oscar Cullmann, for instance, contends that the Philippians passage "relates primarily to the Genesis story and can be understood only by reference to it," and his argument is largely based on the premise of the synonymity and interchangeability of "form" and "image." Accordingly, "the form of God" of Philippians 2:6 is seen as identical with "the image of God" of Genesis 1:26; and from this the conclusion is drawn that "by the 'form' of God in which Jesus Christ existed at the very beginning is meant precisely the form of the Heavenly Man, who alone is the true image of God," and that, "because Christ is the Son of Man, he is the pre-existent Heavenly Man, the pre-existent pure image of God, the God-man already in his pre-existence."[64] It is not Cullmann's christology but his interpretation of this text that we shall wish to question. He rightly rejects attempts that have been made to explain the passage as little better than a reproduction of hellenistic or oriental forms of the gnostic redeemer myth. As Ceslaus Spicq has tersely commented, St. Paul's thought "owes nothing to the gnostic redeemer myth, which had not yet been invented."[65]

It is not to be denied that in writing Philippians 2:5ff. St. Paul may at least have had Genesis 1:26f. in mind. There is, however, a serious obstacle to block the equating of "the form of God" in Philippians with "the image of God" in Genesis; and that obstacle is the presence of a preposition. We have already shown that the Son himself is the image in or according to which man was created: that is to say, the Son *is* the Image of God (which Cullmann also explicitly affirms); he is not *in* the image of God, for it is man the creature who is formed in that image. An exact correspondence between Philippians 2 and Genesis 1, therefore, would require St. Paul to declare that Christ's being was

---

doulou, and of his essential divine likeness the *morphē theou*"--except that what he means by "the specific outward sign" of Christ's essential divine likeness is not at all clear, even when he asserts that "the *morphē theou* in which the pre-existent Christ was is simply the divine *doxa.*"

63. In the Septuagint version of Dan. 3:19 the Aramaic form of *tselem* is rendered as *morphē* (referring to facial expression), and in gnostic literature there are instances in which *morphē* is found as equivalent or corresponding to $d^e muth$ as well as *tselem.* See, e.g., O. Cullmann, *The Christology of the New Testament* (London, 1959), p. 176; J. Jervell, *Imago Dei* (Göttingen, 1960), pp. 204f.; C. Spicq, *Notes de Lexicographie Néo-Testamentaire,* Tome II (Göttingen, 1978), pp. 568ff.

64. Cullmann, *Christology,* pp. 175, 177; and see R. P. Martin, *Carmen Christi* (Cambridge, 1967).

65. Spicq, *Notes,* p. 572.

"the form (= image) of God," without the preposition "in." The only possibility of circumventing this obstacle is to postulate that "being in the form of God" refers not to Christ's deity but to his incarnate existence; and some have interpreted it in this way. This understanding has, at first sight, a certain attractiveness, for it would enable one to explain St. Paul's argument as follows: "Being in the form or image of God as our fellowman Christ did not, like Adam the first man, grasp at equality with God." The difficulty with this, however, is twofold: first of all, in becoming man the Son did not cease to be God, and so, as previously remarked, could hardly be said to grasp at what he already essentially was; and, secondly, the meaning of his not grasping at or clinging to equality with God is elucidated by the act of incarnation, which involved, as St. Paul goes on to describe, his self-emptying and self-humiliation in taking the form of a servant and becoming in the likeness of a man and being obedient even to the death of the cross. The logical sequence in the recital of the Apostle's thought indicates that Christ's being in the form of God preceded his becoming man.

Certainly Adam, assured by Satan that disregard of God's word would place him on an equality with God (Gen. 3:5), did grasp at being equal with God; and certainly the incarnate Son in his existence as man did not copy Adam's sin but in a life of perfect obedience and harmony with the Father demonstrated what it was to be truly human. This is a legitimate contrast. But the main point seems to be rather that the Son, who eternally possesses what Adam grasped at, chose the way of self-abnegation by becoming man for the redemption of mankind, whereas Adam chose the way of self-exaltation with disastrous consequences for himself and the human race. There is good reason, too, to approve the suggestion that St. Paul had in mind the conception of Christ as the embodiment of the Suffering Servant of whom Isaiah wrote, as he depicted the Son taking the form of a servant and abasing himself even to the shameful death of the cross for our redemption (cf. Is. 53).

The coming of the Son to us not only contrasted radically with the way followed by Adam but also undid the evil and the curse which Adam brought into our world. By his act of total self-denial Christ, who is himself the Image of God, showed us what it means for man to live according to his constitution in the image of God, and he also procured for us the blessing of rebirth, so that by the bestowal of divine grace we might have the power to follow his example, in him gaining the victory where before, with Adam, we had suffered defeat. But a careful scrutiny of this passage compels us to conclude that the statement that Christ was "in the form of God" does not belong among those declarations of the New Testament which identify Christ, whether explicitly or implicitly, as the divine image.

CHAPTER 5

The Imprint of the Image in Man

Because he is made in the image of God, man differs in a radical manner from the rest of the animate creation. There are indeed numerous physical correspondences between human beings and animal life in its various forms, but man is unique in all creation because of the divine image that is imprinted on his being. The difference, it is important to remember, is a difference of creation, not development: it is a *constitutional* difference. The fact that he is created in the image of God is specifically the fact that constitutes man as man and distinguishes him from all other creatures. We are face to face here, not with hypothesis and speculation, but with reality which is fundamental to the right understanding of man and his nature. How, then, does this distinguishing reality in man manifest itself in his relationship to the rest of the created order? What are the marks or characteristics by which this image in which man is formed may be discerned? It may be said that, in general, the various answers that have been offered to such questions have been complementary rather than contradictory. The best summary answer was given long since by Augustine, who asserted that man's formation in the image of God refers to "that power by which he is superior to all the beasts,"[1] and reaffirmed more than a millennium later by Calvin, who declared that it displays itself "in the whole excellence in which the nature of man surpasses all the species of animals."[2] What follows is an attempt to expound the main respects in which this surpassing excellence of man is clearly discernible; and this will be considered under six heads, namely, personality, spirituality, rationality, morality, authority, and creativity.

PERSONALITY

Man, as we have noticed earlier, is a personal being because God in whose image he is created is a personal God; and God is personal because his unity

---

1. Augustine, *On Genesis against the Manicheans* ii.17. In *The City of God* xi.2 Augustine wrote somewhat similarly that, "since man is most properly understood . . . to be made in God's image, no doubt he is nearer to God above in that part of him by which he rises above those lower parts he has in common with the beasts."
2. J. Calvin, *Institutes* I.xv.3.

embraces the threefold interpersonal relationship of Father, Son, and Holy Spirit. Personal being is realized only in relation to the personal being of others. It is because his personal being is intrinsically plural, not singular, that God is self-sufficient in his personality. His oneness is not oneness in isolation. He is not dependent on a relationship with someone other than himself for the fulfilment of his potential as a person. Man, however, on his own is without self-sufficiency. The individual man does not possess personal being in the way in which God does. Man in isolation is without plurality. Nonetheless, man is a personal being, and, as we have said, he is so by virtue of his having been created in the image of God who is fully and absolutely personal. The stamp of the divine image upon man's constitution means that there is a vital and immediate, "built-in" relationship between man and his Creator. And this, inevitably, is a *personal* relationship by which man's being as person is established and fulfilled. The I-Thou relationship within the unity of the trinitarian Godhead is the ground and the source of human personality, through which man has knowledge of himself in an I-Thou relationship with his Creator.

The creation of man as male and female, together with the encouragement to "be fruitful and multiply," shows that man was intended to be a communal being enjoying personal fellowship with his fellow humans. Man, however, is not in principle dependent on the presence of other human beings for the realization of his being as a person, even though the companionship of others provides a context that is normally important for the expression of his personhood; for man in isolation from other men—for example, a captive in solitary confinement—does not cease to be truly a person. His segregation from human fellowship, it is true, diminishes his human potential within the created order. But he is not isolated from God. The imprint of the divine image at the core of his being, which is the true root of his personhood, cannot be assailed by man or devil. Accordingly, he is able to maintain, even in total separation from human company, that interpersonal relationship with God who formed him for fellowship with himself. Isolation does not destroy his personhood, for his I-Thou relationship with his Creator continues and is intensified by an experience of this kind. The survival, indeed the triumph, of personality in spite of persecution and solitariness is itself a witness to the reality of God, the self-personal God, who is the foundation and sustainer of the personhood of his creature, man. This truth was perceived by the expatriate philosopher Nicolas Berdyaev, who has written that "the existence of personality presupposes the existence of God."[3]

Thus constituted a personal being whose personhood is rooted in the reality of his I-Thou relationship with his Creator, man has also a person-to-person relationship with his fellowmen who share in his constitution in the image of God. It is not to be denied that human persons are also individuals, but it would be wrong to conclude that personality and individuality are the same

---

3. N. Berdyaev, *The Destiny of Man,* tr. Natalie Duddington (London, 1937), p. 72.

thing. Animals, too, are individuals; but they are not persons. They may live together in herds or flocks or as partners, and be related as parent and offspring and in other ways, but theirs is an impersonal existence, and this is so precisely for the reason that, unlike mankind, they have not been created in the image of God. Their behavior is governed by instinct, or it may be by training and conditioning, but not by forethought and compassion. They know no communion of minds and no response of gratitude to God. Such knowledge or awareness as they have is not self-knowledge. As John Donne put it, "the difference between the reason of man and the instinct of the beast is this, that the beast does but know, but the man knows that he knows."[4]

The dominance of man over animals is the dominance of personality over individuality. Animals may be domesticated as pets and harnessed for labor; their conduct may be controlled by training; their reflexes may be conditioned; they may be admired for their strength and beauty and give pleasure to man in a thousand different ways; but they live below the level of personal existence. It is for this reason that the killing of animals by man for food or for some other reasonable purpose is not a violation of the image of God[5] or of the sixth commandment. At the same time, however, the beasts and birds of the field and forest are God's creatures and in no way is their indiscriminate slaughter or ill-treatment justifiable.

Since, then, the seat of human personality is the image of the personal God with which his being is stamped, it is a natural consequence that man's personal I-Thou relationship with God is fulfilled in and through the Son, the Second Person of the Holy Trinity, who is himself the Image in which man has been created. The philosophy of humanism, which demands the elimination of God from the scene and postulates the animal origin of man, with the result that man is regarded as himself essentially an animal, albeit the highest of animals, can only lead to the depersonalization of man and therefore to his dehumanization and brutalization. The falling away of man into sin follows from his determination to deny God as the source of his personhood and to sever the I-Thou line that links him to his Creator. His rebellion is an act of wilful isolation and individualism. Because man cannot cease to be what by constitution he is, it is a stupid and a futile act; but nonetheless it is an act of mutinous self-assertion by which he vainly imagines he can establish himself as the autonomous source and center of his personhood.

It is easy enough, and certainly not wrong, to draw attention to the destructive dehumanization of society in those countries where, under the tyranny of enforced atheistic humanism, the citizens are treated as individuals rather than persons and their lives held to be hardly less common and dis-

4. John Donne, Sermon preached at St. Paul's, Easter Day, 13 April 1628. Cf. Augustine, *City of God* xi.26: "We both are and know that we are, and we delight in our being and our knowledge of it."
5. Gen. 9:3, 6.

pensable than the lives of animals. (Of this there is ample documentation in the writings of Aleksandr Solzhenitsyn and others.) But we must avoid the temptation to close our eyes to the deep penetration that has been made into the thought and conduct of our much vaunted "free world" by the humanistic principles and ideologies of educators and psychologists who are powerfully influencing the molding of Western society. In our culture the identity of the person is increasingly becoming equated with individualism, and as this continues personhood and its precious relations, first with God and then with our fellow humans, is being throttled—with the dire but predictable result that self-ism is becoming established as the fashionable religion of the Western world and its high priests, the humanistic mind-healers, who incessantly preach that self-fulfilment, self-gratification, and self-affirmation, achieved by any means and without regard to moral values (which are discounted as outmoded or non-existent), must be pursued if existence is to have meaning and satisfaction. Thus the self is being isolated and individuated, not only in irresponsible separation from those who are fellow human beings but also from God the Creator of personality, and our society is in danger of becoming depersonalized and enslaved by futility.[6] In a famous essay Martin Buber has written: "The more a man, humanity, is mastered by individuality, the deeper does the *I* sink into unreality";[7] and the reason for this is summed up in the assertion that "through the *Thou* a man becomes *I*."[8] But the essential and primary *Thou* is God and only thereafter one's fellowman—just as in Christ's summary of the law the love of God precedes and leads to the love of the neighbor.

The recovery of personhood that has been bent and choked by sinful individualism requires the reintegration of the image in which man was originally created. Because that image is in fact a Person, the Son who is the Image of God, it is in him that the vertical I-Thou, person-to-Person, relationship with God is restored, and also, as a necessary consequence, the horizontal I-thou, person-to-person, relationship with our fellow human beings. Hell, in at least one of its aspects, is to hear Christ's pronouncement "Depart from me!" (Mt. 7:23) and to suffer the intolerable condition of total introverted unconnectedness which is the end product of wilful self-separation from God, who is both the source and the fulfilment of our personhood. Self-obsession is not self-realization but self-destruction. That is the point of Christ's admonition: "Whoever would save his self will lose it, and whoever loses his self for my sake will find it" (Mt. 16:25).

6. See, e.g., Paul C. Vitz, *Religion as Psychology: The Cult of Self-Worship* (Grand Rapids, 1977); also my *Christian Ethics in Secular Society* (Grand Rapids, 1983), pp. 91ff.

7. Martin Buber, *I and Thou* (Edinburgh, 1937), p. 65.

8. Ibid., p. 28. To the same effect, Nicolas Berdyaev has said that "narrow self-centeredness ruins personality" (*Destiny of Man,* p. 75).

SPIRITUALITY

By virtue of his creation in the image of God man is also a religious being. The fact that he is a creature entirely dependent on God for his existence does not in itself invest his being with a spiritual dimension; for the animals also are creatures of God, but spirituality does not belong to their constitution: they do not occupy themselves with the worship of their Creator and they have no awareness of his infinite goodness and majesty. But man, the bearer of the imprint of the divine image, knows the truth of the "eternal power and deity" of his Creator and is conscious of his obligation to honor and worship him as God and to be thankful to him for his goodness (Rom. 1:19-21). Because God is spirit, man cannot escape from the fact that, sealed as he is at the heart of his being with the image of God, he is essentially a spiritual creature (for he cannot escape from himself or from his duty to worship God in spirit and truth [Jn. 4:24]). There is, however, absolutely no reason for man to presume that his innate spirituality places him on an equality with God and makes him spiritually self-adequate and independent.

Satan, who induced man to declare his own independence and equality, promising that by doing so he would be as God (Gen. 3:5), thereby usurped the place of God and gained the ascendancy over man. Yet, though a spirit, the devil is, and can never cease to be, a creature who, like man, owes his Creator spiritual worship and obedience. By giving heed to the word of Satan instead of to the word of God man "exchanged the truth about God for a lie and worshiped and served the creature rather than the Creator" (Rom. 1:25). He has substituted a created, finite spirit for the infinite and only God, who is absolute Spirit. One whose doom is fixed has been made the god of this age (2 Cor. 4:4; cf. Jn. 12:31; 14:30; 16:11; Eph. 2:2), and in transferring his allegiance to the devil man has become devilish, the very opposite of Godlike. The treacherous apostasy of the first Adam has been counteracted by the loyal spirituality of the incarnate Son, the last Adam, who totally rejected the false promise of Satan that by bowing down and worshiping him he would gain the whole world, and who drove him away with the biblical demand: "You shall worship the Lord your God and him only shall you serve" (Mt. 4:8-11; Dt. 6:13).

To God man owes worship and adoration as his beneficent Creator, gratitude for the blessing of his existence, obedience in honoring the word that lights his way, and constant prayerful dependence as, speaking and listening to his Creator, he commits himself to the religious performance of the divine will. Knowing that he has nothing that he has not received, he has no reason to be puffed up with pride and self-esteem (1 Cor. 4:6f.). As the bearer of the divine image, man is inescapably a religious being who, if he does not worship the true God, will idolatrously worship a false and finite "god" of his own imagination. By turning away from God, by professing even to be an atheist, man does not cease to be a spiritual creature. All he does is to pervert his spirituality and prostitute it to the insane worship of dumb, unhearing, and sightless idols made by himself, or of brute beasts, or of political parties, or sports, or leisure, or business, or wealth, or position, or even blatantly of the devil himself, who through all such idolatrous channels is the real recipient of man's degenerate adoration. For the glittering prospect of gaining the world man senselessly barters the soul of his being and in doing so dehumanizes himself (Mt. 16:26). The boasted independence of man is the degradation of his humanity, not his liberation but his destruction and the loss of everything.

Worship of God is essential to the self-fulfilment of man, who is by constitution a spiritual being. His worship comes to expression through the humble but joyful recognition of his own creatureliness and total indebtedness to God which causes him to ascribe all worthiness (worship=worthship) to God alone, and enables him to sing, in unison with the unceasing worship of the heavenly host: "Worthy art thou, our Lord and God, to receive glory and honor and power, for thou didst create all things, and by thy will they existed and were created" (Rev. 4:11). The image of God in which man is made draws and binds him to his Creator in a spiritual liaison which fulfils the deepest need of the human heart. It is the purpose of God in creation that gives purpose to the life of man as the head of creation, the love of God for his creatures that evokes the love of his spiritual creature, man, in return and stimulates him to love others as himself, and the providential care of God for what he has made that gives man complete security and trust in his total dependence on God. The wonderful potential of our humanity is realized only in unclouded worshipful communion with our Creator, for in the glorification of God we are being thoroughly human. Thus the praise of the psalmist should constantly be our praise: "O Lord, our Lord, how majestic is thy name in all the earth! . . . O Lord, my God, thou art very great! Thou art clothed with honor and majesty. . . . O Lord, how manifold are thy works! In wisdom hast thou made them all. . . . I will sing to the Lord as long as I live; I will sing praise to my God while I have being" (Ps. 8:1; 104:1, 24, 33).

Worship of the true God in spirit and in truth, then, is essential for the integrity of man as a religious being and an indispensable component of the lifeline which connects the spiritual creature to his spiritual Creator, who is the source not only of his existence but also of the harmony and goodness of his existence. For man to turn away from this spiritual communion with his Maker is for him to throw away the key to the understanding of his origin and his destiny. It is in effect the denial of the transcendental element of his nature which enables him to soar above and beyond himself in his finite and temporal existence to the sublime reality of harmonious fellowship with his infinite and eternal Creator and to admire the order and symmetry of the universe; and it is also the self-deprivation of the glorious future, far surpassing all that is at present known and seen, of which man's inherent spirituality is the seed and the promise—for "no eye has seen, nor ear heard, nor has the heart of man conceived what God has prepared for those who love him" (1 Cor. 2:9; Is. 64:4). To miss this is to miss the fulfilment of our humanity.

RATIONALITY

The excellence by which man is superior to the animals is seen, further, in the fact that he is by constitution a rational creature, and this too is an aspect of the image of God in which he is created. The animals are called dumb or brute beasts because of the irrationality of their nature. Man, in striking contrast, is not dumb and uncomprehending, but is endowed with a mental faculty that enables him to use language for the rational expression and communication of his thoughts and wishes, to pursue intellectual studies, to investigate the connection between things, and to appreciate the rationality of God's creation, of which he himself is a part. And man is not dumb because God is not dumb. God is a God who speaks, and his speaking is the declaration of his mind and his will. Creation itself is the effect of God's speaking: "God said, 'Let there be . . . and it was so'" (Gen. 1). Thus the creation is imprinted with the rationality of the Creator. As a part of the created order man too is a product of the speaking of God, but in a special sense, for "God said, 'Let us make man in our image,'" and "so God created man in his own image" (Gen. 1:26f.). Being exclusively formed in the divine image, man alone of earth's creatures is endowed with the faculty of rationality which enables him, as a reflector of the Creator's rationality, to think and to plan and to speak. His rationality is another strand in the bond that binds him to his Maker. The personal intercommunion between God and man is rational as well as spiritual.

The ordered system of the universe, itself the effect of the divine, and therefore dynamic, Logos, inescapably, though silently, bears witness to the supreme rationality of the Creator. David, contemplating from the vantage point of our little planet the immensity and yet the cosmic integrity of creation displayed in the night sky and in the regular sequence of times and seasons, was filled with wonder at this silent testimony to the mind of the Maker: "The heavens are telling the glory of God, and the firmament proclaims his handiwork," he sang. "Day to day pours forth speech, and night to night declares knowledge. There is no speech, nor are there words; their voice is not heard; yet their voice goes out through all the earth, and their words to the end of the world" (Ps. 19:1-4). The eloquence of this silent witness is not lost on man, because by the exercise of his rational faculty he is able to perceive and admire the ordered wholeness of the world to which he belongs, and to praise the Creator of all for his matchless power and wisdom.

The systematic rationality of creation provides an environment without which it would be impossible for man to function as a rational being. Man could not possibly live as a rational being in a world that was unordered and therefore incoherent; for man is not a being outside and independent of the world but is himself a component part of this created reality. A part cannot make sense unless the whole makes sense, and, by the same token, the whole is meaningless when its parts are disjointed. There is an interdependence between the logic of the whole and the logic of the parts. It is in fact natural for man, God's rational creature, to accept without questioning that the whole is a cosmos, not a chaos. He knows intuitively that the world, far from being a disunited jumble of unconnected bits and pieces, is a coherent unity which he need not hesitate to call the *universe;* for without a rational whole he would not be a reasoning part.

The scientist pursues his research precisely on the basis of the tacit assumption that there is no such thing as an isolated or brute fact which is unconnected with the rest of reality; he presupposes, necessarily and rightly, that one fact leads on to another because there is an interrelationship between all facts; and he can do this only because he is a rational person in a coherent universe. The philosopher constructs his logical system without stopping to prove the correctness of his silent premise that the whole of reality can be rationally investigated because if the whole does not have a meaning nothing makes sense. The astrophysicist who calculates the speed of light and the movements of the constellations is able to plan the exploration of outer space with minutely detailed precision because of the mathematically ordered orbits of our earth and of the heavenly bodies. His calculations and the predictability on which their application is based confirm the subconscious and unquestioned presupposition that the whole of physical reality is ordered and consistent. And this in turn testifies to the supremely rational purpose of the Creator of all things. Distinguished physicists of our age have expressed their admiration for the cosmic logic of the universe. Sir Edmund Whittaker, to take one example, has affirmed that "reality is an interrelated system, possessing a rational and coherent structure," that "the notion of reality involves the notion of predictability, the notion of predictability involves the notion of laws of nature, and the laws of nature form a rational structure underlying nature," and that essential to the promotion of the scientific enterprise is "the fundamental principle of the rational interconnectedness of reality."[9]

All the scientific and philosophical activities of man as an intelligent human person and all his abilities to formulate and convey to others his thought by means of the logical communication of language bear witness to the truth that he is formed in the image of his all-wise Creator, of whose perfect rationality his finite mind is in its finite way a reflection, and whose consummate logic he is privileged to contemplate in the majestic orderliness of the universe in all its parts, both small and great. This all-pervading logic is the logic of the Logos, the true Image of God, through whom and for whom all things were brought into being and by whom they are maintained in being (Col. 1:16f.; Heb. 1:3).

9. Edmund Whittaker, *The Modern Approach to Descartes' Problem,* the Herbert Spencer Lecture at the University of Oxford, 1948 (London, 1948), pp. 25, 26.

MORALITY

No less important for the appreciation of the essence of our humanness is the understanding that man's creation in the image of God means also that he is by constitution a moral being. God himself is absolutely holy and the image of God is inseparable from the holiness of God. Stamped in the heart of his being with the divine image, man is radically designed for holiness, which is the sum of all morality. Man is intended to be holy, holy in himself and holy in all his relationships, in conformity with the standard of God's own holiness. This standard is affirmed as a logical demand in the word of God addressed to his people: "You shall be holy; for I the Lord your God am holy" (Lev. 19:2; 20:7, 26; 11:44f.)—truly an image-of-God demand. The immorality of sin is evident in that it is defection into unholiness, and therefore into ungodliness. But in no way does it annul the divine demand for holiness as essential to the fulfilment of the potential of our humanity. The Christian believer finds that his incorporation into the Son, who is the holy Image of God, brings not only the restoration of right thinking but also the restoration of right living and the reestablishment in his heart of concern for the divine standard of holiness. Hence the reaffirmation of this standard by St. Peter: "As he who called you is holy, be holy yourselves in all your conduct; since it is written, 'You shall be holy, for I am holy'" (1 Pet. 1:15f.).

God's standard of holiness is not just an ideal, or an unattainable goal, toward which man is required to strive; it is the actual demand which man was created to meet. Only for man in his fallenness is it altogether impossible for him to achieve. But for man as originally created it was a goal within reach, for, constituted in the divine image, and placed in the perfect goodness of God's world, the way was clear before him to attain it. His obedience to the word of God should have been the expression of his love and gratitude to God. Only by honoring and meeting the divine standard of holiness can man live before God (Lev. 18:5; Neh. 9:29; Ezek. 20:11, 13, 21; Mt. 19:16f.; Rom. 10:5; Gal. 3:12). The trouble with man in his fallenness is not merely that he falls short of this standard but that he wilfully and rebelliously breaks the law of God, which then, instead of being the way of life, becomes an instrument of death, judging and condemning him as a law-breaker (Rom. 3:23; 6:23; 2 Cor. 3:7ff.). Not that the law is malign; it is sinful man who is at fault. St. Paul, indeed, praises the law as holy and just and good and spiritual (Rom. 7:12, 14). But by departing from the way of life man chooses the way of death. "Did that which is good [i.e., the law], then, bring death to me?" St. Paul asks; and he answers: "By no means! It was sin working death in me through what is good" (Rom. 7:13).

In his original state, however, there was no sin working in man, who was possessed of human nature in its unmarred potential. Since he knew only good and enjoyed personal communion with his Maker, it was altogether unthinkable for him to seek anything but the loving fulfilment of God's will. Yet even in the total goodness that he first knew man was a moral creature, answerable to the One in whose image he was formed for the privileged status which had been assigned to him in the order of creation. The condition of goodness in which he was created was not one of static goodness; he was not made to sit still in the world, to be passively good, but to be *actively* holy. In a very real sense he had to *establish* his holiness by faithful performance of the Creator's will. Doing this, he would have actualized the potential with which he was by nature endowed and have known what it is to be authentically human. Any test should have been a step up, not a step down, a victory, not a defeat, the affirmation, not the denial, of the image in which he was formed. But the first test ended in disastrous failure. The course man should have followed was demonstrated in person by Christ himself, the last Adam, in what was to all intents and purposes a recapitulation of this testing, when the devil tempted him, as he did the first Adam, to eat; but this testing, and every other testing, of the incarnate Son was an occasion of victory and a triumph of holiness, as, rather than seek self-gratification, he faithfully respected the divine word and will (Mt. 4:1ff.). It is this principle by which the first Adam and all men ought wholly to have been governed. Grateful obedience to the divine will would have been both honoring to God and enriching to man in his advance toward the attainment of his christomorphic destiny. Far, then, from being a passive state, conformity to the image in which man is created is an active responsibility. Otherwise the moment of creation would be the end point as well as the beginning of all things. The failure of Adam, however, was not the failure of God's purpose in creation. The divine will, that the end should be more glorious than the beginning, cannot fail of fulfilment.

Man, therefore, created in the divine image, has a moral obligation which at the same time is a moral incentive, namely, to promote the will of his Creator. Morally constituted, he is by nature morally responsible. His answerability to God is central to the authentic expression of his humanity; indeed, his very life depends on it. His conscience, which is the innate awareness at the deep root of his being that there is a distinction between right and wrong and between truth and falsehood, and which belongs to the imprint of the divine image on his nature, incessantly testifies that he is accountable to God for his life (Rom. 14:12; 1 Pet. 4:5; Heb. 4:13). From this witness to God's demand for holiness man cannot escape, because it is an internal witness, and he cannot escape from himself any more than he can escape from the ultimate reckoning in the presence of his Maker. A conscience at harmony with his Creator's will is the true pulse beat of his humanity.[10] Only when the human will is one with the divine will can man be his authentic self. Only in the living and dying of the incarnate Son has this perfect harmony been achieved and demonstrated in our midst. This demonstration would but tantalize us, and increase

10. For a fuller discussion of the human conscience see my *Christian Ethics in Secular Society*, pp. 27ff.

the weight of condemnation that lies heavily upon us, by throwing into relief
the enormity of our shortfall, were it not that its purpose is first and foremost
redemptive, and its effect the cancellation of our ungodliness, the restoration
of fellowship with our Creator, and the planting of our feet on the path of positive holiness under the power and guidance of the Holy Spirit—the recovery,
in a word, of our native morality.

AUTHORITY

The image of God in which man is formed is further displayed in the fact
that within the created order he is a being who exercises authority. The authority with which he is endowed is not absolute, of course, but derivative from
and subject to the supreme authority of the Creator who is sovereign over all.
The constitutional character of man's authority is disclosed in the divinely
given commission to subdue the earth and to have dominion over every living
thing (Gen. 1:28). It is a mandate received from a higher authority. Man exercises his authority over creation, therefore, as one who himself is under authority. The position of privilege and power thus granted to man is acknowledged
and reaffirmed by the psalmist who, addressing the Creator, says: "Thou hast
given him dominion over the works of thy hands; thou hast put all things under
his feet" (Ps. 8:6). An interesting example of the tendency for personal judgment to be influenced by reaction rather than by reason is seen in the manner
in which in times now past the minds of many became prejudiced against allowing the dominion of man any role at all in the manifestation of the divine
image in which he was formed, simply because advocates of Socinian heterodoxy held that it was in man's lordship over the created order that the image
found complete expression. Since, however, it is one of the distinguishing
marks which unquestionably elevates man above the rest of creation, there is
every justification for approving it as a genuine aspect of the divine image.

Man's authority over creation, even when perversely used for his selfish
designs, is clearly evident in his ability, noticed earlier, to domesticate the animals in all their variety and to subject their conduct to the dominance of his
will, in his power to cultivate the land and transform the wilderness into
pleasure parks and orchards, in his capacity as a scientist for investigating the
secrets of the universe and harnessing its energies, and in the artistic and technological competencies that he brings to the development of human civilization. God, in short, gave man the world to master, but to master to the glory of
the Creator, by whom man himself, to be truly human, must first be mastered.
Man, after all, in fulfilling this task of mastery is but exercising the ability he
has received, and in discovering and organizing the forces and harmonies of
the universe he is but discovering and organizing what God has first implanted
there. And so the glory and the gratitude belong to God, not to man.

As with all the other endowments that give him a unique status among
God's creatures, man has abused and prostituted the authority with which he

is invested, with the consequence that in this respect also he is in need of redemption. We will have more to say about this later on. It will suffice for us to observe here that man's perversion of the authority did not frustrate the purpose for which God brought the created order into being nor did it mean the defeat of God's sovereign dominion over all that he had made. The inviolability of the authority of God and the supremacy of his will are shown by the judgment he enforces and the redemption he provides. The key to unlocking these deep issues is, as always, the Son, who is the Image in which man is formed, and who is both before the first Adam as the True Image and after him as the last Adam. The failure of the first Adam to wield the authority given him to the glory of God is offset by the victory of the last Adam in the rehabilitation of that same authority. Man's origin is rooted in the Son, and his destiny is fulfilled in the Son, who, having taken to himself our humanity in the incarnation and redeemed it on the cross, raised it to the glory and the dominion which has all along been God's purpose for it (Heb. 2:6ff.). Thus the ascending Savior, still incarnate, declared that all authority in heaven and earth had been given to him (Mt. 28:18), and, since the destiny of the regenerate is one with his, St. Paul was able to assure the twice-born in Ephesus: "God has made us alive together with Christ (by grace you have been saved), and raised us up with him, and made us to sit with him in the heavenly places in Christ Jesus" (Eph. 2:4-6; cf. Col. 3:1-4). In the community of the redeemed the authority of the Lord is even now reestablished and reactivated; and hereafter, in the renewed creation, the dominion conferred on man by the divine mandate will be universally honored, and "the earth will be full of the knowledge of the Lord as the waters cover the sea" (Is. 11:9; Hab. 2:14).

CREATIVITY

All the aspects and manifestations of the divine image in which man is created and which we have been discussing are closely interlocked with each other; and the same is true of man's faculty of creativity. None exists in isolation from the others. Each in its own distinctive manner contributes to the rest and derives from the rest. And all belong to the wonderful unity that is man and testify to the unique position that he holds under God at the head of creation. The creativity of man may of course be discerned in the intellectual research and the technological inventiveness by which his command of the physical world is increased and the practical tasks of daily life are made less burdensome; but our concern here is with creativity as an expression of man's distinctive character as an aesthetic being. The supremely aesthetic creativity of God as the Designer as well as the Maker of all things is revealed in the beauty and harmony of the cosmos. We may justly say that the created order is the work not only of the supreme intellect but also of the supreme artist. It reflects the beauty of God himself and assures us that the Creator, far from being merely as it were an exalted pragmatist who constructed the world as a functional or utilitarian enterprise, is the source of all that is beautiful and elevating to the human spirit.

The creativity of man, it should be obvious, is not at all identical with the creativity of God. If as a rational being man's proper function is to think God's thoughts after him, and as a being with authority to exercise authority under authority, as a creative being man is endowed with the competence, not to bring something into being where before there was nothing, but creatively to bring into ever new relationships and combinations the inexhaustible aesthetic potential latent in the forms and colors and harmonies of creation. Though it is true that many animals and birds and insects exhibit an amazing competence for making elaborate and admirable structures, yet they do so in accordance with the dictates of an instinct that is innate and not spontaneously creative and that programs them always to follow the same pattern of behavior. Unlike such phenomena, which undoubtedly belong to the harmony of the whole, the creative masterpieces of art, music, literature, and architecture are all produced by man—and this is another indicator of man's superiority to the rest of the animate creation by virtue of the divine image in which he was made. Aesthetic creativity comes to expression in the composition of works that are original and masterly. (It must be allowed that there are degrees of mastery, and that the lesser do not approach the magnificence of the greater.) The person who merely copies what has already been done by someone else is at best an unimaginative plagiarist.

Of course not everybody is aesthetically creative; but virtually everyone has the capacity to be uplifted and enriched by the creativity of others. The life of any person can be enhanced by the appreciation and enjoyment of the masterworks of those who have been born with the rarest gifts. Each succeeding generation is inspired by the contemplation of the masterpieces created by Phidias, Michelangelo, Rembrandt, Monet, and many others, and by the serene symmetries of such structures as the Parthenon, the Taj Mahal, and the medieval cathedrals of Europe. The treasury of great literature, in all its wonderful variety, is more precious than mountains of money. And the undiminishing power of the music of genius to enthrall and elevate our spirits, the beauty of which is an echo or reflection of the unfathomed music of the universe—the joyful and devout logic of Bach, the irrepressible fountain of invention springing from the inner hearing of Mozart and Schubert, the imperial ardor and vision of Beethoven, the emotional and intellectual depths of Brahms: all this, and much more that ennobles the mind and heart of man, is the bountiful harvest of the seed of creativity that is implanted in our human nature. We are indeed indebted to a multitude of masterworkers whose creative genius has helped to open our eyes and ears and minds to rejoice in the elemental energies of beauty and nobility that permeate the universe. But we are indebted above all to the Creator himself, who has blessed mankind with the ability to perceive and work creatively with the sounds and colors and concepts which interpenetrate and make glorious his own creative work. Through this lesser creativity God invites us, as it were, to exult in the harmony of the whole and to take pleasure in all that is true, noble, just, pure, lovely, and gracious (Phil. 4:8), and in doing so to magnify him who has created us in his image. Yet this present pleasure is but a small foretaste and a flawed shadow of the superb vistas of beauty and the enrapturing music that we shall know in the undistorted perfection of the new heaven and the new earth.

Man in his fallenness has done much, alas, to debase the creativity of his constitution by perverting it to serve the cult of the ugly and the unclean and the ignoble, which may indeed be the reality of ungodliness and its consequences (and in this depraved sense realistic), but certainly is not the reality or the truth of God's creation. The noblest and most brilliant achievements of genius, even though they are not free from many imperfections, should remind us that man is not meant to live like the brute beasts, which live to themselves and are not blessed with powers of aesthetic sensibility, and that his creative capabilities are God-given. God's creation provides the environment and the material for man's creativity. Here and now, moreover, the divine handiwork is more lovely than anything beautiful we may compose. "Consider the lilies of the field," Christ said to his disciples; "they neither toil nor spin; yet I tell you, even Solomon in all his glory was not arrayed like one of these" (Mt. 6:28f.).

CHAPTER 6

The Image in Fallen Man

Did the fall cause the loss of the image in which man was created, or is the divine image still retained in the constitution of sinful mankind? This is a matter that has long been disputed by theologians, and it is a controversy to which we must give some attention before proceeding with the next part of this work. It should not be overlooked that the precise significance attached to particular terms may differ from one author to another, and that qualifications may be introduced in their usage. The same author may assert in one place that the image is obliterated in fallen man and in another place that it is retained, at least in certain respects, without necessarily being inconsistent with himself; but in such a case theological definition of the terms as they are used is important. Indeed, some authors have had a change of mind in their consideration of this issue. An interesting example of the need for theological explanation is found in the *Retractations* of Augustine, where he points out that the assertion that "by his sin Adam lost the image of God in which he was made," written by him in his work on the literal sense of Genesis,[1] "should not be taken to mean that none [of the image] remained in him, but that it was so deformed that it was in need of reformation."[2] This qualification brings it into line with his position as stated elsewhere. Thus, in the treatise *On the Spirit and the Letter*, Augustine says that "God's image has not been so completely erased in the soul of man by the stain of earthly affections as to have left absolutely no vestiges of it," and that "what was imprinted on men's hearts when they were created in the image of God has not been wholly blotted out";[3] and in his work *On the Trinity* he declares that "the image cannot reform itself as it could deform itself," and that "righteousness and true holiness were lost by sinning, through which that image became defaced and tarnished," but that it recovers that loss "when it is formed again and renewed."[4]

Calvin's sermons and commentaries include numerous references to the

---

1. Augustine, *De Genesi ad literam* (written in the early years of the fifth century) vi.27f.

2. *Retractations* ii.24. Augustine died (in 430) before this retrospective survey was completed.

3. *On the Spirit and the Letter* 48.

4. *On the Trinity* xiv.16.

65

image of God in which man was created. As often as Calvin speaks of the image as obliterated or effaced he speaks of it also as obscured or defaced, as not completely obliterated, by the sinfulness of man. The clarity and precision of his mind were such, however, that he was hardly susceptible to the charge of self-contradiction or slovenliness in expressing his thoughts. When he affirms the obliteration of the image in man he has in mind the deadening and alienating effect of sin which cuts the sinner off from God as the source of all life and meaning. The placing of God's image in us, he says, is "an inestimable blessing" which sets us as "rational creatures" apart from "oxen, asses and dogs"; but "because we are corrupted in Adam and are altogether accursed, sin dominates to such a degree that this image of God has been obliterated,[5] the understanding we imagine we have is but stupidity, our hearts are perverted, and all is rebellion"; and in view of this "we do not deserve to be regarded or accepted as people."[6] Man's fallenness, Calvin says elsewhere, has "separated him from his sense" and made him "like the brute beasts"; it is our own fault that we are "more like the beasts than the true men we ought to be"; and, instead of being spiritual, "man's image has been transformed into flesh."[7]

The devastating effect of sin on our human nature justifies, in Calvin's view, the conclusion that the image in which we have been created, and which is constitutive of our true humanness, has suffered extinction. From the spiritual standpoint, sinfulness has been lethal in its effect on our humanity. A more general survey of the overall scene, however, allows this radical judgment to be modified. Thus Calvin can also say that the image of God in man is "virtually obscured,"[8] "disfigured," "deformed," "marred," "soiled," and "almost entirely extinguished."[9] "It is true," he declares, "that we still bear some trace of the image of God in which Adam was created; but that image has been so disfigured that we are full of wickedness" and our spiritual condition is one of "blindness and ignorance."[10] Again: "We always carry some mark of this image of God that was imprinted on the first man"; but always with the qualification that "we have corrupted everything."[11] Likewise in the *Institutes* Calvin at times asserts that the image has been extinguished[12] and at other times that remnants of it are discernible in the gifts and abilities of mankind.[13] Within the limits of natural theology, then, Calvin did not hold that the divine image in

---

5. "Effacée" is the French term most commonly used by Calvin when he describes the image as "obliterated."

6. Sermon 183 on Deuteronomy (32:20ff.).

7. Commentary on Genesis (6:3).

8. "Quasi obscurcie"; Sermon 43 on Job.

9. "Défigurée," "difformée," "gâtée," "souillée," "quasi du tout éteinte" (*On the Divinity of Christ* [Calvini Opera 47], p. 481).

10. Sermon 55 on Job (14:14).

11. Sermon 164 on Deuteronomy (29:1ff.).

12. As in *Institutes* II.i.5 and III.ii.12.

13. *Institutes* II.ii.17; III.iii.19.

man was totally lost or extinguished; indeed, he maintained in answer to any objection that the image has been obliterated in us that "the solution was perfectly simple," namely, "that some remainder of it is always there to such a degree that the dignity and excellence of man are far from insignificant." And to this he added the important further consideration that, "however much man may be corrupted, the heavenly Creator always keeps before himself the goal of his creation."[14]

The persistence of the divine image in man even in his fallenness, moreover, has significant ethical implications, for it is a prime incentive for the practice of neighborly love. Calvin insists that "we are not to consider what men merit of themselves, but to look upon the image of God in all men, to which we owe all honor and love." Even if a person seems to us unworthy of any assistance we must remember that "the image of God, which we contemplate in him, is well worthy of our giving ourselves with all we possess." This goes against the grain of our fallen nature, but "we must not be hindered by the malice of men, but rather contemplate the image of God in them, which by its excellence and dignity moves and enables us to love them."[15] What is more, "because men bear the image of God engraved within themselves, God regards injustice and violence done to them as done to himself";[16] and to treat manslaughter lightly or as a kind of sport is "something detestable," for to kill a fellowman is "to destroy and obliterate the image of God which shines forth in his creatures, inasmuch as all men have been created in his image."[17]

Irenaeus, we have said,[18] was wrong in supposing *image* and *likeness* in Genesis 1:26 to mean two different things, though the theological significance he attached to this supposed distinction was controlled by a sound biblical instinct. Whether Irenaeus's dual interpretation implied or intended some kind of dichotomy is certainly questionable. Catholicism's later differentiation between nature and supernature is something quite other than he had in mind. The Reformers of the sixteenth century rightly insisted that "image" and "likeness" are not two things but one (hendiadys) and that man's sinfulness involved the depraving of his nature in every part, and therefore his utter need for and dependence on divine grace if the evil consequences of the fall were to be undone.

More recently, Emil Brunner has firmly rejected the separation of "likeness" from "image" and reaffirmed the essential unity of human nature, above all in its ineradicable relationship to God; and in doing so he has stated his approval of the Reformed understanding of man and his condition. At the same time, however, he has criticized the postulation of Calvin and others that there

14. Commentary on Genesis (9:6). There is a similar passage in the commentary on the Epistle of James (3:9).

15. *Institutes* III.vii.6.

16. Commentary on Genesis (9:6); cf. the commentary on Jonah (1:14).

17. Sermon 5 on 2 Samuel (2:14); cf. Sermon 6 (2:30f.).

18. See p. 8 above.

is a remnant or relic of the divine image discernible in sinful mankind as a "confused and dogmatically extremely doubtful concept."[19] But this formulation does not, as Brunner seems to imagine, imply a quantitative distinction, an isolation of a part from the whole, which disrupts the unity of man's nature. This criticism, moreover, is a boomerang which flies back to strike Brunner himself; for his own preference for defining the divine image in man in two senses, the one formal and the other material, is, in all essential respects, only another way of saying what the Reformers were saying—as he himself cannot deny.[20]

The real focus of Brunner's uneasiness with the position of the Reformers is located in their biblical-historical perspective of man and the fall. He asserts that "the whole historic picture of 'the first man' has been finally and absolutely destroyed for us today," because "the victory of the scientific view" has brought about the "inevitable decline of the ecclesiastical view."[21] "Primitive Man" is now said to have a connotation radically different from its meaning for the authors of the Bible and of the patristic period and of the Reformation. This being so, a new framework is required for the doctrine of man and his nature, and the solution offered by Brunner is that of a dialectical explanation of the human situation, which is virtually the same thing as the existentialization of man: Adam as a historic figure of the past is out; he is retained, however, by identifying him with everyman. Brunner's "new formulation" declares that "when we talk about the origin of man we are not speaking of a certain man called Adam, who lived so many thousand years ago, but of myself, and of yourself, and of everyone else in the world."[22] But "creation" and "fall" then are floating ideas without historical moorings. "Creation" becomes a click-sound betokening the "impassable gulf between the Creator and the creature" and at the same time the bond between the two—though now "Creator" and "creature" cannot have any more content than the vocable "creation."[23] And "fall," which is in conflict with the evolutionistic dogma of the rising and historical development of man, must be turned around to signify incompleteness and shortcoming not with reference to the past but with reference to the future and the goal toward which man's progress is leading him.

19. E. Brunner, *Man in Revolt,* tr. Olive Wyon (London, 1939), pp. 94f., 514.

20. Regarding the "formal element" Brunner says: "The Reformers expressed this truth in the rather dubious notion of the 'relic' of the *Imago;* and I, on the other hand, express this as a dialectical relation between the *Imago*-origin and the humanity-of-the-sinner" (ibid., p. 513). He goes on to say that he has "now renounced the use of this expression 'formal *Imago*' because of the way it had been misinterpreted by some persons" (ibid.). For the distinction between the formal and the material image see Brunner's *Natural Theology* (London, 1946), p. 24. For a discussion of the positions of Brunner and Barth and the controversy between the two see David Cairns, *The Image of God in Man* (London, revised edn., 1973), chs. 12 to 14.

21. Brunner, *Man in Revolt,* p. 85.

22. Ibid., p. 88.

23. Ibid., pp. 90f.

The retention of classical terms and doctrines such as "fall" and "resurrection"[24] but with different and sometimes contrary senses imposed on them is not only confusing, it is academically unethical. The confusion is compounded by the contradictory manner in which Brunner persists in referring to the fall as though it were some event of the past—not didactically, of course, but casually. What event or date is he pointing to when he states that "the life originally given to man is being in the love of God"?[25] or that man "was originally created to decide in accordance with the divine determination"?[26] The suitability of Brunner's distinction between "material" and "formal" senses of the image in which man is created is also questionable, even though sympathy may be felt for the point he is intent on making.[27] If the "matter" is lost, there is no content for the "form." The dangers of this differentiation are similar to those of the distinction between "substance" and "accidents" which has banefully influenced Roman Catholic eucharistic doctrine. Brunner rightly stresses the unity of man's being; but the duality of "matter" and "form" is inescapably divisive. The unity of man is seen in this, rather, that he cannot cease to be what he is by constitution, namely, a creature formed in the divine image. It is a truth that he may attempt to deny or to cover up, but even that he can attempt only because of the unique powers which set him above the rest of the animal creation. These powers, as we have previously observed, are evidence of the stamp of the divine image at the core of his being. The sinful perversion of his abilities, rational, scientific, artistic, and so on, for selfish and destructive ends can only be the perversion of the abilities with which he is endowed. The powers that are man-perverted are still God-given. In fighting against God he is also fighting against himself. He cannot possibly escape from what he is. And this perversion of his humanity, his refusal to conform to the true image of his being, his contradiction of himself, is also his judgment and his condemnation in the presence of his Creator.

24. On Brunner's view of the resurrection of Jesus see pp. 366, 369ff. below.

25. Brunner, *Man in Revolt*, p. 104.

26. Ibid., p. 118.

27. Despite his decision to renounce the use of the dual "material" and "formal" understanding of the image of God (see n. 20 above), Brunner returns to it in his later *Dogmatics;* see, e.g., Vol. II, *The Christian Doctrine of Creation and Redemption*, tr. Olive Wyon (London, 1952), pp. 59f.

PART II

The Image Rejected: Disintegration

CHAPTER 7

The Origin of Evil

Formed in the image of God, entrusted with authority over a domain divinely blessed and wholly good, and with the goal of an eternity of immortal glory set before him, man had a matchless opportunity to fulfil the wonderful potential implanted within him by the Creator. Everything was in his favor; there was nothing that he lacked. Yet by an act of incredible folly, by which he dishonored his Creator, debased his humanity, and failed to meet the challenge of the holy image in which he was constituted, he despised and turned away from the privileged purpose of his being under God. Through his God-defying declaration of independence he lost the true power and meaning of his existence. The inevitable disintegration of his personhood was self-induced, the consequence of his own sin, and that sin was introduced into the Edenic scene through the only door that could be opened to it, namely, the will of man who alone of this world's creatures is a morally responsible person. By opening his heart to sin man not only sought wilfully to suppress the image in which he was made and to separate himself from his Creator, but also, because of his position at the head of the created order, he dragged down the rest of creation with himself into depravity and frustration.

It is plain that man was by nature testable: that he could be tested to do what was right carried with it the possibility of his being tempted to do what was wrong. Temptation to do evil is not in itself evil (on the part of the one who is tempted); properly considered, it should be not a stumbling block but an opportunity for upward progress in godliness. The fault of man's fall does not lie in the fact of his temptability but in his ungodly response to the temptation by which he was tested. And it certainly does not lie with God, who had beneficently endowed him with power and dignity, bestowed nothing but good on him, placed him in an environment in which provision was made for his every need, and above all given him that greatest of all blessings, full and harmonious fellowship with himself. Who but the devil would have imagined that there was any chance of man's being enticed to turn elsewhere for satisfaction and in doing so to abandon the blessedness he so freely enjoyed? This question immediately raises the problem of the presence of the devil in the garden and the origin of evil.

In the account of the fall of man the problem of the source or origin of evil meets us even before the problem of man's fall, for in the goodness of the creation that has issued from God's hand a malign and alien force intrudes itself. Whence does this force and personification of evil come? What right does it have to be present in God's creation at all? Who is this enemy who works subversively against God and his goodness? In the New Testament "the serpent" is patently a designation of the devil, whose description as "that ancient serpent" identifies him with the original tempter; for he is depicted as "the dragon, that ancient serpent, who is the Devil and Satan, the deceiver of the whole world" (Rev. 12:9; 20:2). Accordingly the serpent in Genesis 3 is the representation of the devil, who menaces man with his evil subtlety and deception. The character of the devil is uncompromisingly portrayed by Christ's delineation of him as "a murderer from the beginning," who "has nothing to do with the truth because there is no truth in him" and who, "when he lies, speaks according to his own nature, since he is a liar and the father of lies" (Jn. 8:44). Death-dealing falsehood, then, has the devil as its source.

But who precisely is this devil who from the beginning is a liar and a murderer? No plain answer to this question is ready to hand in the Scriptures, though the reality of the devil's existence and the malignity of his activity are taught in the plainest terms. Such evidence as is available leads to the conclusion that the devil is both a personal and a spiritual, that is to say, an incorporeal, being belonging to the order of angels, and that he is the leader of those fallen angels who in their rebellion against God now seek demonically to pervert and nullify the divine power and purpose throughout creation. This is the understanding of both classical Judaism and classical Christianity. The New Testament depicts warfare in heaven between the archangel Michael and his angels on the one side and the devil and his angels on the other, resulting in the overthrow of the latter and their being cast down to the earth, where they persecute God's people (Rev. 12:7ff.). This passage clearly postulates a division of the angelic hosts into those who loyally serve God and those who mutinously align themselves behind the devil as their leader. Consonant with this is the teaching of Jesus, who explicitly described Beelzebul, whom he identified with Satan, as the prince or leader of the demons (Lk. 11:15ff. = Mt. 12:24ff.), and who responded, "I saw Satan fall like lightning from heaven," when the seventy he had sent forth returned and joyfully announced, "Lord, even the demons are subject to us in your name" (Lk. 10:17f.).

The proper function of angels is defined in Psalm 103:20f., where they are called "mighty ones who do God's will, hearkening to the voice of his word," and "his ministers who do his will." Similarly in Hebrews 1:14 they are spoken of as "ministering spirits sent forth to serve for the sake of those who are to obtain salvation."[1] While their mission is to execute the divine bidding with

---

1. This definition accords with the literal meaning of the term "angels," namely, "those who are sent" or "messengers"; the Greek *angeloi* and the Hebrew *mal'akim* both have this connotation.

elemental speed and efficiency (cf. Heb. 1:7), and especially, in this fallen world, with reference to the redemptive purpose of God, the objective of Satan and his angels is to overturn this purpose. Being incorporeal spirits, angels, both good and wicked, are ordinarily invisible to man. The army of demons, with whom Christians are in conflict, is composed, St. Paul says, of "principalities," "powers," "world-rulers of this present darkness," and "spiritual hosts of wickedness in the heavenly places" (Eph. 6:12). They are "world-rulers" only because of their sway over sinful men, who follow them instead of God. For the same reason Satan is described as "the ruler of this world" (Jn. 12:31; 14:30; 16:11) and "the god of this world" (2 Cor. 4:4; cf. Eph. 2:2). Such terminology, however, is in no sense absolute, but is related to the prevailing infidelity of man; for the devil is a mere creature whose pretensions exceed his grasp, whose "rule" is no threat to God's supreme sovereignty, and whose tyranny is overthrown and doom sealed through the conquest and the re-creation achieved by Christ's coming into the world (Heb. 2:14f.; Mk. 3:22-27; Rev. 20:10).

Some authors of the patristic period, and indeed others since then, have supposed that the angels were separately brought into being before the creation of this present world.[2] Support for this position was sometimes claimed from Job 38:4-7, where the sons of God, understood as denoting angels, are said to have shouted for joy when God laid the foundation of the earth. Others have attempted to find a place for the creation of angels on one of the days preceding the sixth day on which man was created. Augustine, for instance, maintained that the angels must have been created when God said, "Let there be light" (Gen. 1:3-5), and interpreted Job 38:7, "When the stars were made the angels praised me with a loud voice" (as he rendered it), as proof that the angels were made before the fourth day, when the stars were made.[3] There is in fact no mention in the Genesis account of the creation of angels; but Scripture hardly gives sufficient grounds for concluding that angels are not part of this creation, which throughout is evidently regarded as embracing all creatures. We would wish simply to affirm that, since the Apostle clearly states that *all things* were created in the Son, "in heaven and on earth, visible and invisible, whether thrones or dominions or principalities or authorities" (Col. 1:16; cf. Jn. 1:3), angels (to whom it is generally agreed that such terms as "thrones," "dominions," "principalities," and "authorities" refer, and who are evidently intended by the designations "in heaven" and "invisible") have their place within the universe that God brought into being as recounted in the first chapter of Genesis.[4]

2. See, e.g., Origen, Homily 1 on Genesis and Homily 4 on Isaiah; Basil, *Hexaemeron*, Homily 1; Gregory of Nazianzus, Oration 38; John of Damascus, *On the Orthodox Faith* ii.3.
3. Augustine, *On the City of God* xi.9ff. Augustine favored the view that the separation of the light from the darkness on the first day of creation signified, in addition to its literal sense, the separation of the good from the wicked angels (loc. cit., 33). The notion is also found in the *Confessions* xiii.3 and 8.
4. Thomas Aquinas was unwilling to categorize as erroneous the view of the Greek

Many biblical passages could be discussed with regard to the nature of angels and their operations, but one in particular demands our attention as we seek some understanding of the origin of evil, namely, the Lucifer passage in Isaiah (14:12-17), which since ancient times has been interpreted as descriptive of the rebellion and fall of Satan. This interpretation has not been without its critics, but it may well be taken as illustrative of all high-handed mutiny against God and therefore as justifiably applicable to Satan, the original insurrectionary of this kind. Certainly the immediate reference appears to be to the king of Babylon. His fall, however, is as it were a recapitulation in miniature of the fall of Satan. Moreover, in the New Testament Babylon has become a synonym for the realm or domain of the devil (Rev. 14:8; 16:19; 17:5; 18:2ff.; in these places the language strongly echoes that of the Old Testament prophets—cf. Is. 21:9; Jer. 51:6ff.). Isaiah 14:12ff., then, is not inappropriately related to the original rebellion led by Satan. It reads as follows:

> How are you fallen from heaven,
>   O Day Star [= Lucifer], son of Dawn!
> How are you cut down to the ground,
>   you who laid the nations low!
> You said in your heart,
>   "I will ascend to heaven;
> above the stars of God
>   I will set my throne on high;
> I will sit on the mount of assembly
>   in the far north;
> I will ascend above the heights of the clouds,
>   I will make myself like the Most High."
> But you are brought down to Sheol,
>   to the depths of the Pit.
> Those who see you will stare at you,
>   and ponder over you:
> "Is this the man who made the earth tremble,
>   who shook the kingdoms,
> who made the world like a desert
>   and overthrew its cities,
>   who did not let his prisoners go home?"

The self-vaunting lust for power and totalitarian domination of Babylon's king is a reflection of the egomania of the devil himself, and, as with the devil, it led to his downfall. Self-centered ambition leads to a condition opposite to what is intended: pride brings down, it does not exalt. "Before de-

---

fathers and Jerome that the angels were in existence prior to the creation of the world, but he himself held as "more probable" the opinion "that the angels were created at the same time as corporeal creatures," adding that "the angels are part of the universe" and "do not constitute a universe of themselves," but together with corporeal creatures "unite in constituting one universe" *(Summa Theologica,* pt. I, q. 61, art. 3).

struction a man's heart is haughty," the wise man wrote; "but humility goes before honor" (Prov. 18:12; cf. 15:33). Christ taught similarly that "whoever exalts himself will be humbled, and whoever humbles himself will be exalted" (Mt. 23:12; Lk. 14:11; 18:14). The reason for this paradoxical phenomenon, that humility exalts and pride brings down, is, as Augustine pointed out, that godly humility enables us to submit to him who is above us as the supremely exalted One, so that by making us subject to God it actually exalts us; whereas self-exaltation is a turning away from God who is exalted above all, and therefore a decline of the self toward the nonbeing of its origin. Thus perceived, the very lifting up of oneself in opposition to and denial of God is already a fall.[5]

The fall of man was his acquiescence in the evil to which he was tempted by another creature who had sinned previously. Yet in recognizing Satan as the originator of sin the origin or source of sin itself has still not been explained. What was it that caused Satan to commit the first sin of rebellion against God? The consideration of this question brings us face to face with what is probably the most difficult of all theological issues—difficult because of the virtual silence of Scripture regarding this problem and because, apart from divinely given revelation, man's finite and now fallen understanding is incompetent to resolve the mystery of the entry of evil into God's creation. How was it possible for a dark and sinister reality to intrude into and disrupt the perfection of the work of God? In the first place it must be insisted, and insisted with emphasis, that God is not the author of evil. His work is expressive of the perfection of his goodness, and the existence of good precedes the appearance of evil. Indeed, apart from the prior presence of good, evil would have had no entry at all. Good can exist without evil, as the absolute goodness of the divine existence shows and as it will be in the absolute perfection of the new heaven and the new earth when all evil will have been eliminated; but evil cannot exist without good, because, if we follow the argument of Augustine, evil presents itself only in natures which God has created good, and the fact that evil is an injury of such natures, angelic or human, demonstrates its character as a perversion of what is good and as a departure from God.[6]

God is indeed the Creator of all things, but sin, though now clearly a reality in the world, is not a created entity, nor is it an entity that has an independent existence of its own. Evil is in itself neither a corporeal nor an incorporeal creature. It is the creature's abuse or depravation of his own good nature that makes evil an actuality—that is to say, in man's case, the use of his humanness in a manner contrary to its proper nature. Still more specifically, it is the consequence of the action of a responsible personal being, whether man or angel, who behaves in a manner contrary to the divine will, which is the standard or norm for the expression of man's true humanness or the angel's true nature as an angel. For such a creature to function in a way that subverts the

5. Augustine, *On the City of God* xiv.13.
6. Ibid. xii.1; xiv.11.

purpose of his creation is to function unnaturally and to become a sinful creature. Sin therefore defines moral character, not a substance or quantity. For Augustine, indeed, evil has no positive nature, but is simply the loss of good; it has no efficient cause, but is evidence of a state of deficiency.[7] Man, who is part of God's entirely good creation, commits sins and becomes sinful when, contrary to his own nature and the true order of his being, which is gratefully to serve and glorify God, he defies the divine will, with disastrous consequences not only for himself but also for the rest of creation, also created very good, which he now despoils and misgoverns in a manner contrary to its true nature.

God, we repeat, is the author of good, not evil. All that he brings into existence is marked by the pure goodness of its Source. If there were any deviation from this absolute goodness he would not be God, for God by definition is holy and good and perfect (cf. Lev. 19:2; 20:7; Mt. 5:48; 1 Pet. 1:15f.), and he is the source only of good, and invariably so. Hence the assertion of St. James that "every good endowment and every perfect gift is from above, coming down from the Father of lights with whom there is no variation or shadow due to change" (Jas. 1:17). Goodness, indeed, can be predicated absolutely of God alone—as Christ himself said, "no one is good but God alone" (Mt. 10:18). All creaturely goodness is derived goodness. Moreover, that God, who is absolute goodness, should tempt his creatures to do what is evil is no less unthinkable than that he should be the source of sin. Of such temptation St. James says: "Let no man say when he is tempted, 'I am tempted by God'; for God cannot be tempted with evil and he himself tempts no one; but each person is tempted when he is lured and enticed by his own desire" (Jas. 1:13f.).

7. Ibid. xi.9; xii.7. Thomas Aquinas accepted the Augustinian definition of evil. Agreeing that "evil is the absence of the good which is natural and due to a thing," and that "good is the subject of evil," he asserted that evil has neither "a formal cause but is rather a privation of form" nor "a final cause but is rather a privation of order to a proper end," and, further, that "evil has a cause by way of an agent, not directly but accidentally," since "the fact itself that it is a deficient being is accidental to the good to which it belongs essentially to act"; hence "evil in no way has any but an accidental cause" (*Summa Theologica*, pt. I, q. 49, art. 1). Herman Bavinck wrote to the same effect that "sin is *anomia*, deformitas"; but his description of God as the "deficient cause" or "negative cause" of sin is highly questionable and can easily be misleading, not least after a strenuous denial that God is the cause of sin. Aquinas had written similarly, but with what seem to be more careful qualifications. Bavinck explained his position as follows: "Sin is *anomia*, deformitas, and thus has God not as causa efficiens, but at most as causa deficiens. Light cannot produce darkness out of itself; darkness arises alone as the light is taken away. God is thus at most the negative cause, the causa per accidens, of sin; its real positive cause is to be sought in man. Because, however, sin is only forma and not substantia, and is formaliter the act of man, in no single respect does it fall outside of the providence of God" (*Gereformeerde Dogmatiek*, Vol. III [Kampen, 2nd ed., 1910], p. 46). The adequacy of the medieval philosophical distinctions, and the appropriateness of retaining them, must also be questioned as divisive, however unintentionally, of the unitary nature of man.

This last affirmation, that "each person is tempted when he is lured and enticed by his own desire," offers a clue for our understanding of the origin of evil, for it indicates that the essence of sin is giving way to the temptation to indulge one's own selfish desire in disregard of the will of God. Though the biblical account of the fall narrates how the temptation to desire what was forbidden was aroused in man's heart by the alien agency of the devil, personal desire or lusting was clearly involved (Gen. 3:6). As for Satan, nothing suggests that he was originally tempted to do evil by some malign power outside of himself. It is apparent, rather, that sin had its source in the devil and that he is the original enemy of all that is good and in accordance with the divine will. As we have seen, Christ characterized the devil as a murderer from the beginning and the father of lies (Jn. 8:44). Similarly, St. John admonishes that "he who commits sin is of the devil, for the devil has sinned from the beginning," and that the purpose of Christ's coming into the world was to "destroy the works of the devil" (1 Jn. 3:8).

Sin and evil originated then with the devil; not, however, at or in but after his creation as an angelic being of eminence. The sin that he committed had its source in his own heart, that is to say, in the central core of his creaturely being. In this connection it is instructive to find St. Paul warning his son in the faith Timothy that to be "puffed up with conceit" is to "fall into the condemnation of the devil" (1 Tim. 3:6)—a warning that accords well with the self-aggrandizing ambition expressed in the Lucifer passage already cited: "I will ascend to heaven . . . I will set up my throne on high . . . I will make myself like the Most High" (Is. 14:12ff.). Driven by burning pride and conceit, Satan abused his proper nature as an exalted spiritual creature and presumed to imagine that he could enthrone himself as God—just as in a similar manner he later enticed man in the garden with the promise that by disregarding the word of God he could seize his independence and become as God (Gen. 3:5). Man, succumbing to the devil's assurance that he would be like God, in fact became like the devil! He debased his true nature, lost the purpose of his existence, and passed from life to death.

But how, it will still be asked, was it possible for egocentric ambition to arise within this angelic being whose setting was one of perfect goodness from the hand of the Creator? This indeed is a dark mystery. All that can be said is that, like man, created a responsible being whose life-principle is harmony with the will of God, he was brought into existence with the possibility of sinning— that is, of rebelliously asserting his own autonomy and self-sufficiency in defiance of his Creator. But the possibility of sinning does not at all imply the inevitability of sinning, as is evident from the fact that, though some of the angels attached themselves to Satan in his mutiny against God, others remained faithful and continued loyally and gratefully to honor the divine will. With the angels, therefore, the possibility of sinning was equally accompanied by the possibility of *not* sinning. Their responsibility was not unreal and hollow, but genuine. Wilfully to deny responsibility before God and indebtedness to him for the goodness of their being was to pervert the angelic nature and to sink into a state of degeneracy.

So also with the creation of man: the possibility of his sinning does not at all preclude the genuineness of the possibility of his not sinning. Nor does this dual or alternative possibility imply that God is in a reciprocal sense dependent on the responsible creatures he has brought into existence in such a way that he has to suspend his own planning and action while he waits to see whether or not these creatures will honor their responsibility. To have created responsible beings does not inhibit God or involve him in uncertainty and contingency in his control of all things. God could, no doubt, have programmed his creatures to function automatically and indefectibly in accordance with a prescribed or built-in routine; but then they would have been no better than mechanical robots or instinct-driven insects, not intelligent and responsive beings in person-to-Person relationship with their Maker. They could not then *spontaneously* have rendered worship and praise and gratitude to him. The world would have been a clockwork world enveloped in an atmosphere of unreality. As Christ said to the Samaritan woman, worship of God to be genuine must be "worship in spirit and truth" (Jn. 4:24). The will with which God endowed his personal and responsible creatures is a will that, as created, is truly free, but whose true and natural freedom is realized only as it operates in spontaneous harmony with the perfect and supreme will of its source. Real freedom is freedom to function in harmony with the purpose for which one has been brought into existence. Defiance of the divine will is destructive of the freedom of the human (or angelic) will. To live contrary to one's nature and constitution is to exchange freedom for bondage and futility.

Any supposition that in creating angels and men with the possibility of their falling into sin God was like a gambler taking a risk, or that he anxiously had to wait to see what would happen, betrays a defective understanding of who God is and how he acts. It is to impose on him the limitations of our human finitude. God's knowledge, like his will and his power, is comprehensive. The future that is hidden from us is controlled by him no less than the present. Far from being static, God's being is essentially dynamic, and his inexhaustible dynamism is the driving force of the universe. His absolute authority over all he has created is not threatened or diminished even to a minute degree by what appear to us to be unforeseen and unforeseeable eventualities. The restricted dimensions of our human existence cannot be superimposed on the limitless existence of God. Even an eventuality such as the fall, which to us seems to create a situation of crisis, does not create a necessity for God to deviate from his original purpose or to devise an emergency plan in order to cope with this development. His purpose in the creation of man, as we have seen, was the intensive conformity of man to the image in which he was made. That purpose, being *God's* purpose, cannot fail of fulfilment. Despite the fall of man into sin, which seemed to be disruptive of the divine intention, that purpose is indefectibly carried forward and brought to completion in and through him who is himself the Image and who, both Son of God and Son of Man, is "the same yesterday and today and forever" (Heb. 13:8).

Even within our confined human horizons the manner in which God sovereignly overrules evil for the promotion of what he purposes is not entirely hidden from us. The dynamic principle of the divine control of all that happens is clearly propounded in the assurance St. Paul gave to the Christians in Rome: "We know that in everything God works for good with those who love him, who are called according to his purpose. For those whom he foreknew he also predestined to be conformed to the image of his Son, in order that he might be the firstborn among many brethren. And those whom he predestined he also called; and those whom he called he also justified; and those whom he justified he also glorified" (Rom. 8:28-30). This encompasses the whole majestic and uninhibited mastery of all that happens. God is not the victim of events. The future is not the fairground of haphazard chance. God foreknows, not as some kind of exalted clairvoyant, but because the purpose of his will dynamically overrules the entirety of history and brings it to the end for which it was designed from the very beginning. Precisely because he is God and not man, what he predestines infallibly prevails; and no more can his calling fail as it leads to justification now and to the ultimate blessing of glorification hereafter.

The supreme authority of the divine will is a reality even, and most dramatically, in the course of events that has been set in motion by the evil will of the creature. This is well illustrated in the story of Joseph. The ill will of his brothers and their evil deed in selling him into slavery in Egypt were divinely overruled to become a means of blessing to Joseph and his kinsfolk and thereby to set forward God's purposes for the whole world. This did not render his brothers less culpable or their deed less evil. Yet as a man of faith Joseph discerned the hand of God guiding the course of events and was subsequently able to console his penitent brothers with the assurance: "God sent me before you to preserve for you a remnant on earth, and to keep alive for you many survivors; so it was not you who sent me here, but God." "You meant evil against me," he told them, "but God meant it for good" (Gen. 45:7f.; 50:20). The apparently intractable opposition of Pharaoh to God and his will actually served the purpose of showing to the world the absolute power of God as the deliverer of his people (Ex. 9:16; Rom. 9:17), as ultimately, despite the frenetic hostility of all the forces of evil, he is also the deliverer of the whole of his creation (Rom. 8:19-21). Thus even the wrath of man is turned to the praise of God (Ps. 76:10).

Above all else, God's sovereign overruling of the wickedness of man for the advancement of his purposes is seen in what took place on the hill of Calvary; for there the greatest wickedness in the whole history of mankind, the condemnation and murder of Jesus, the innocent incarnate Son of God who had done and spoken nothing but good, was absorbed into the divine purpose for the greatest blessing of man and creation. There the greatest evil is caused to coincide with the greatest good; the cross of shame is transmuted into the cross of glory, and through the will of God it becomes the pivot of all ages and the focal point that gives meaning to all history. Thus in the apostolic preaching it is emphatically affirmed that Jesus, though indeed "killed by the hands of lawless men," was nonetheless "delivered up according to the definite plan and foreknowledge of God" (Acts 2:23). All the earthly powers that defiantly arrayed themselves "against the Lord and his Anointed" (Ps. 2:1f.) by putting Jesus to death in fact did exactly "what God's hand and plan had predestined to take place" (Acts 4:24-28). We repeat that the sovereignty of God in setting forth his purposes not merely in spite of but even by means of those who are intent on doing evil in no way diminishes or excuses the evil character of evil-doers and their deeds. The important lesson to be learned is that the divine purpose cannot fail of attainment and that no rebellious creature, whether angel or man, can possibly overturn or frustrate the will of the Creator.

Though sin itself is not a created entity, its alien presence and reality are all too evident from its effects in the society of mankind. Sin or evil cannot be exhibited as a specimen in a display cabinet any more than thought can be dissected from the tissues of the brain or morality from good actions. Kindness and unkindness, love and hatred, are descriptive of the attitude and the deed. There is, however, and always will be, an intractable problem that is inseparable from every attempt to describe sin and its origin—a problem not present in describing other intangible realities such as love and justice and holiness, which, because they belong to the being of God and in man are reflective of the divine image in which he is formed, fit into the true scheme of things. Sin, to the contrary, does not fit. It is ungodly, and therefore obstructive of the divine image in man, and therefore, further, inhuman. It is unloving, unjust, and unholy. It is out of place in God's creation. And it is irrational; for as the expression of hostility to God, who is the source not only of all life but also of all reason, it is opposed to reason as well as to life. The rationality to which it pretends is radically irrational, and cannot be otherwise. Sin is the surd, the non-sense, which disrupts the vital relationship between man and his Creator and destroys the meaning and purpose of human existence. The problem, then, is this: how can it ever be possible to explain, that is, to give a rational account of, the origin of this irrational factor? Being irrational, evil is inexplicable, and its origin will remain a mystery until at last we know even as we are known (1 Cor. 13:12). Meanwhile man is required not to explain sin, but to acknowledge his own sinfulness and to repent of it, and also to receive gratefully the redemption and reconciliation freely offered him by his gracious Creator.

In considering some of the theories that have been offered to account for the disturbing presence of evil in the order of God's creation, as we now propose to do, and in our thinking about this problem, we must constantly be careful not to impose our creaturely limitation and incomprehension upon God or in any respect to reduce his ways to the dimensions of our restricted understanding.

DUALISM

By dualism we mean the theory that within and behind all reality there is the presence not of one but of two absolute and eternal principles which are irreconcilably opposed to each other. As such, dualism is intended as a resolution of the problem of the coexistence of both good and evil in the world. It was an important ingredient, for example, in the stream of philosophical speculation that flowed from Pythagoras and his school. Apart from the fact that he was a native of the island of Samos and flourished in the sixth century B.C., together with a few traditions to the effect that he strove after economy of words and practiced the severest simplicity of diet and life-style, the person of Pythagoras is shrouded in obscurity to a degree that has given his name an almost mystical luster. The thought of this fascinating but elusive figure made a lasting impression on the Greek mind, and not least that of Plato, during the succeeding centuries. Aristotle, writing in the fourth century B.C., tells us that according to the teaching of the Pythagoreans the principles of reality are opposites.[8] The antinomies mentioned by Aristotle include limit and the unlimited, good and evil, and light and darkness.[9] One problematical concept inherent in the dualistic theory is that the undesirable principle inevitably acts as a limiting factor on the desirable principle: the extent of the good is limited by the presence of evil, light is inhibited by darkness, and the unlimited is questionably so defined because of the frustrating concomitance of limit. In other words, there is no getting away, not even for the Supreme Being, from the irrational surd that is there like a wrench in the works.

There is, moreover, no place in the dualistic hypothesis for any genuine concept of creation. This became especially clear in the postulation of the antithesis between spirit and matter as essentially the antithesis of good and evil. There is, indeed, no creation of matter when matter is regarded as belonging to the eternal principle of evil; but the creation of matter in any sense could not be the work of a Supreme Being who is spirit, and as such radically opposed to matter, for this would involve a congenial connection between spirit and matter, and would imply in turn the inherent goodness rather than the inherent evil of matter. Accordingly, "creation," when it is spoken of in dualistic formulations, far from being the bringing of the world into existence from nothing, is no more than the organization or shaping of already existing matter from a state of chaotic formlessness to a state of functional order; and this "creative" work is then assigned to a secondary god or demiurge, who, while bringing good to bear on evil, at the same time keeps matter separate from spirit. By logically questionable accommodations it was hoped to protect the nature of the Supreme Good from the evil that supposedly clung to matter.

8. Aristotle, *Metaphysics* A5, 986^{b}3. The contemplation of opposites, and the question of the possibility or impossibility of their synthesis, has been a matter of perennial fascination in the history of philosophy.
9. Ibid., 986^{a}20ff.

Plainly, then, the dualistic interpretation of reality imposes inescapable limitations on God himself. And this constitutes an insoluble conflict at the very heart of dualism—a fact that is apparent in Plato's attempt to reconstruct a philosophical understanding of the universe. The generation, or "creation," of the world (the "cosmos" or ordered universe) through the agency of the demiurge, Plato maintained, was effected by a combination of necessity and reason in which reason could not operate without the limiting factor of necessity, described as the "errant cause."[10] The divine power to form what is good or to order things rationally is ever qualified by necessity, and it was with the desire that all things should *as far as possible* be good and free from evil that all that is visible (i.e., matter) was brought from disorder to order.[11] Necessity, even if it appears in this hypothesis to be to some degree tractable, can hardly by definition be treated as a force less than equal to reason—and it could well seem to be the greater force, since it is always there to act as a brake on the movement of the good and a curb on the achievement of its full potential. Necessity *(anankē)*, indeed, is but the ancient principle, familiar in nature religions, of Fate *(moira),* which inevitably, and most of all in the form of death, pressed down like a dark incubus on the life of all things and persons. How could it be overcome? How could it be eliminated from the stream and flow of life? This was the ever-nagging soteriological problem which dualism, by its very premises, was incompetent to solve.

For man, of course, conscious that he is both a spiritual and bodily being, this is, obviously, an existential problem of particular severity, as the Platonic philosophy well recognized. The downward drag of matter was seen as militating against the upward aspirations of spirit, and this implied that salvation was attainable only by the progressive liberation or disengagement of the soul from the confinement of the body. According to the Platonic Socrates the notion of the soul as divine in origin and of the body as the tomb or prisonhouse into which the soul was sent to endure punishment for sin committed prenatally was derived from the ancient Orphic cult.[12] Socrates himself, as we read in *The Symposium,* was to a remarkable degree an exponent of the belief that the more independent one is of the body the further advanced one is in the emancipation of the spirit, which, once set free, was destined to return to its source—a marriage of ethics and eschatology in line with Pythagorean orthodoxy. On the other hand, as the Platonic doctrine of metempsychosis or transmigration of the soul maintained, the debasement of the soul could be increased by preoccupation with materialistic pursuits and indulgence in bodily passions, with the consequence that in its next sojourn on earth the soul, instead of being ele-

10. Plato, *Timaeus* 47E, 48A.
11. Ibid. 30A. Cf. 69B, where Plato asserts that proportion was introduced among things "in as many ways as it was possible for them to be proportionate and harmonious."
12. Plato, *Cratylus* 400C, 492E. Socrates held that the incarceration of the soul in the body was for the purpose of its salvation, and even that the term *sōma* (body) was derived from *sōzein* (to save).

vated to a higher bodily residence, could reappear and be confined within the body of a brute beast as an intensification of the punishment designed to teach it to seek that which is spiritual.

Another ancient form of dualism, this time from the east, was a constituent of the Zoroastrian religion reputed to have been founded by the Persian sage Zoroaster about 1000 B.C. Here we encounter the postulation of the eternal existence and eternal antagonism of two gods, Ormuzd and Ahriman, the former good and the latter evil, who represented the ceaseless conflict between light and darkness. This type of dualism became a prominent element in the syncretistic philosophy of Manicheism, founded by a Persian named Mani (or Manes) in the third century of the Christian era, which strongly attracted Augustine before his conversion to the Christian faith.

There is undoubtedly a realistic ring to the conception of a cosmic conflict between good and evil, but the solution proposed by dualism, though it may promise an ill-defined and impersonal kind of salvation for those who are classified as "perfect" and "spiritual," is incompetent to deal in any radical manner with the problem of evil since evil is regarded as itself an eternal principle inseparable from the constitution of the world. Dualistic religion is religion without hope of the ultimate elimination of sin and triumph of good. Any attempt to wed dualism to Christianity can only lead to the ruination of the latter. The two are so totally incompatible with each other that there can be no vital affinity between them. This was a lesson that even the leaders of the apostolic church had to learn. Irenaeus, writing in the second century, informs us that St. John composed his Gospel in order to refute the false teaching of Cerinthus, a propagator of dualistic speculation whose presuppositions caused him to deny the reality of the incarnation. Simon Magus, who professed conversion and was baptized in the earliest period of the Christian church (Acts 8:9ff.), was, as the subapostolic authors tell us, another whose dualistic teachings subsequently gained for him a following.[13]

The doctrines of heresiarchs like Cerinthus and Simon were in effect but simpler anticipations of the much more elaborate doctrines of the gnostic teachers of the second century in which dualism continued to be a governing concept. Marcion, for example, was constrained by his dualistic premises to abandon monotheism and to posit the coexistence of two gods, an evil god of the Old Testament who was responsible for the creation of the material world and a good god of the New Testament who was the bringer of spiritual salvation; and this gave him sufficient cause not only for eliminating the Old Testament canon but also for mutilating and cutting away much of the New Testament in order to make it compatible with his preconceptions. But the question as to how good was to triumph over evil was not to be solved with a pair of scissors.

---

13. See pp. 237ff. below for a discussion of docetism, the heresy associated with Cerinthus and Simon Magus.

THE PRIVATION OF GOOD

We have already mentioned in passing the view of Augustine that evil is not something concrete in itself, and certainly not a created entity, since nothing made by God could fall short of goodness, but is rather the departure from and thus the deprivation of good. It was not that he regarded evil as unreal or nonexistent, as was the case with some expressions of neo-Platonic thought, but rather that he denied it any substantial or independent existence: the negation of good accounts for, and indeed is, the reality of evil. For Augustine, however, the creature's rejection of good did not betoken the impotence of God, who is himself the sum and the source of all good. Abjuring the dualism of the platonist and gnostic systems, he insisted on one Supreme Being, who is not only absolutely other than his creation but also absolutely good and sovereign over his creation. Augustine was not the first Christian theologian to formulate a theory of evil as the privation of good. Origen, for example, some two hundred years before him, had expressed the opinion that "to depart from good is nothing else than to be made bad" and that "to lack goodness is to be wicked," with this corollary, that "to the degree that one falls away from goodness to that same degree does one become involved in wickedness."[14]

Augustine propounded essentially the same view in his *Enchiridion*. "Since the Author of all natures without exception is supremely good, therefore all natures are good," he wrote; but, unlike their Author, created natures are not "supremely and unchangeably good," and consequently "the good in them can be both diminished and increased." Evil is the diminishment of good. But the goodness inherent in a particular nature as God's creation does not cease unless the nature itself is destroyed. If the good is not there to be corrupted, there is no corruption—so that "where there is no good there is nothing that can be called evil."[15] Both Origen and Augustine, moreover, assign the origin of evil to the will. The former affirmed that God bestowed on man "the power of free and voluntary action" by which man was able either to embrace goodness for himself and make it his own or to depart from goodness and decline into its opposite, namely, evil. And the latter charged Faustus the Manichean with "taking away the origin of evil from free will and placing it in a mythical nature of evil" which caused man under compulsion to commit sin. Augustine insisted, to the contrary, that if persons do not choose to do what is

14. Origen, *On First Principles* II.ix.2. There is no denying that the influence of Greek philosophical thought on Origen's mind is evident in many places in his copious writings.

15. Augustine, *Enchiridion* 12f. Origen's position regarding the nature of the creature was less satisfactory, for it was his opinion that any power possessed by rational natures is not in them by nature but is bestowed by God, and that "everything which is a gift may also be taken away and disappear" (*On First Principles* II.ix.2). Augustine rightly emphasized the innate goodness of the creaturely nature that has come from God's hand.

right "the fault is in their will, not in necessity," and that because "the origin of sin is in the will therefore the will also is the origin of evil."[16]

The position of Augustine had also been anticipated by some of the best-known fathers of the fourth century. Athanasius had spoken of the soul as "mobile by nature," that is to say, "made not merely to move, but to move in the right direction," but at the same time capable of moving away from good and thus choosing evil—a movement "toward what is not," for "good is, while evil is not." He vigorously opposed "certain of the Greeks" who "ascribed to evil a substantive and independent existence," observing that this implied either that God is not the Creator of all things, or, if he is, that he is the author of evil as well as good. He made known his displeasure, too, with the advocates of dualism, who "arbitrarily imagine another god besides the true one, the Father of our Lord Jesus Christ, and that he is the uncreated producer of evil and the source of wickedness as the artificer of creation."[17] Athanasius saw turning away from God as a turning away from life and a decline or reversion into nonexistence:

> If from a former state of non-being they were called into being by the presence of the Word and his love of man, it was a natural consequence that when men emptied themselves of the knowledge of God and turned back to what was not—for evil is what is not and good is what is—they should be everlastingly emptied even of being, seeing that they derive their being from God who is—in other words, that they should become disintegrated and remain in death and destruction. For by nature man is mortal, in view of the fact that he has come into being from nothing.[18]

Similarly Basil warned against the impiety of declaring that evil has its origin from God, pointing out that in Genesis like proceeds from like and that God cannot be held to generate what is contrary to himself. Evil, he explained, is not a "living animated essence" but "the condition of the soul opposed to virtue." "Do not then go beyond yourself to seek for evil," he admonished, "and imagine that there is an original nature of wickedness. Each of us, let us acknowledge it, is the first author of his own vice." Were evil involuntary, we should not be responsible for our sin and the law would not terrify us.[19] Basil's brother, Gregory of Nyssa, was another who affirmed the wrong exercise of free will to be the source of evil. He too advised his readers that "no growth of evil had its beginning in the divine will" and that "vice would have been blameless were it inscribed with the name of God as its maker and father." Vice should be recognized as "the absence of virtue," and "the distinctive difference between virtue and vice is not to be contemplated as that between two actually

16. Origen, *On First Principles* II.ix.2; Augustine, *Against Faustus the Manichean* xxii.22.

17. Athanasius, *Against the Heathen* 4-6.

18. Athanasius, *On the Incarnation* 4f.

19. Basil, *Hexaemeron,* Homily II.4f.

subsisting phenomena," but as between entity and nonentity. Like a man who voluntarily closes his eyes in the sunlight and sees only darkness, the sinner, "by his very unwillingness to perceive the good, became cognizant of the contrary of goodness."[20]

These examples are sufficient to show that the definition of evil as the privation of good, which is often described as the Augustinian position, was known and approved in the church well before the day of Augustine. Because, however, of the anthropological controversies in which he was involved, Augustine developed and defended this explanation of the origin of evil and human sinfulness more fully than had been done previously. A further point of interest in this respect is that, intent on establishing the full responsibility of man for his fall into sin, Augustine argued that the sin committed in the garden was not originated by the satanic intrusion but by a prior and spontaneous aversion of the human will which provided the opportunity for the devil to bring about man's defection.[21] But this is to carry the argument beyond the evidence afforded by the text.

A PRENATAL OR TRANSCENDENTAL FALL

Though Origen was (to speak anachronistically) an Augustinian in the respect we have indicated, he offered a theory regarding the origin of sin and its presence in human society which was far from being similar to the position later maintained by Augustine. Origen perceived that, for anyone attempting a theodicy, some explanation was demanded for the ubiquitously uneven diversity of status and condition in which, through no design of their own, the members of human society find themselves placed. Some persons are born with healthy bodies, others with bodies that are weak or deformed; some persons belong to polite and civilized communities, others to uncouth and barbaric nations. Such fortunes or misfortunes, which seem to be determined by the chance of birth, are not controlled by the exercise of the faculty of free will. Are they then just a matter of accident or chance? Or is God to be held responsible for the injustice or partiality that appears to prevail in such inequality? If the latter, people would no longer believe that the world was made by God or administered by his providence, Origen said, and would cease to regard the deeds of each individual as subject to divine judgment; how then could the teaching that "God, the Creator of all things, is good and just and omnipotent" be defended?

The answer given by Origen was, in the first place, that originally God, in whom there is no variation or change, created all rational natures equal and alike. The endowment of such natures with the power of free will meant that there was no rational creature that was not capable of evil as well as good, none unable either to fulfil or to decline from the rectitude of his nature. In other

20. Gregory of Nyssa, *The Great Catechism* 5f.
21. Augustine, *On the City of God* xiv.13.

words, the derivation of the imbalance and inequality that are evident in the world was to be sought not in the will or decision of the Creator but in the freedom of the creature's will. But, in the second place (for this consideration was plainly inadequate to resolve the problem Origen was addressing), he postulated the creation of all rational natures, including the souls of men, at a time prior to the birth of individual human beings and indeed prior to the creation of mankind, by propounding the hypothesis that all rational natures were originally angelic beings or spirits. Of these, the spirits that remained faithful were now, he explained, the good and holy angels constantly serving God, but those that were unfaithful were driven from their high estate and were subject to punishment; and of the latter some were punished by being confined within human bodies as the souls of men, while others, namely Satan and his retinue, had sunk even lower to become infernal or demonic spirits.

In this perspective, men, or their souls, are in a position intermediate between angels and demons. But Origen viewed the process as reversible; if angels had been degraded to become men or demons, it was possible for demons to rise to be men or angels. "Those who have been removed from their primal state of blessedness," Origen wrote, "have not been removed irrecoverably"; the debasement they now suffered was remedial as well as punitive, so that, "being remoulded by salutary principles and discipline, they may recover themselves and be restored to their condition of happiness."

As for the inequalities that belong to the present state of human society, they are, Origen argued, a consequence not of the injustice but of the justice of God, since it was according to their deserts that the fallen spirits that are the souls of men were confined within human bodies—those that had been the greater offenders being the more disadvantaged and those whose guilt was lesser being more happily placed. Origen even suggested that there was theological significance in a supposed etymological connection of the term *psychē*, the Greek noun for the soul, with the verb *psychein,* "to grow cold," indicating that the very word *soul* had implicit within itself the notion of something that had cooled off from the fire or warmth of its original being: as he put it, the soul was so called "because it has grown cold from the fervor of just things and from participation in the divine fire, and yet has not lost the power of restoring itself to the condition of fervor in which it was at the beginning." In support of this view he cited Psalm 116:7, "Return, O my soul, unto thy rest," and Romans 9:11-13, where, recalling the divine assertion concerning Jacob and Esau, "The elder will serve the younger" (Gen. 25:23), even "though they were not yet born and had done nothing either good or bad," and the declaration of Malachi 1:2, "Jacob I loved, but Esau I hated," St. Paul asks, "What shall we say then? Is there injustice on God's part?", and immediately responds with an emphatic negative. The Apostle's theme was divine sovereignty in election; but Origen supposed that the distinction made between Jacob and Esau while they were still in their mother's womb was attributable to the differing degrees of guilt incurred by the lapse of their souls in the transcendental realm prior to their birth as human beings, and that this distinction was, accordingly, an accurate indicator of divine justice and impartiality.[22]

That Origen's hypothesis accords with the mind of Plato rather than of the biblical authors hardly calls for demonstration. The notion of human bodies as places of punishment for errant spirits betrays a latent dualism that is destructive of the integrity of the human person. Man has become little more than a material body inhabited for the time being by a fallen spirit; and (however little this may have been Origen's intention) the soteriology implied is indistinguishable from Platonic self-liberation. Preoccupation with the saving of fallen spirits instead of fallen human beings has had the effect of driving the incarnation and the cross from the scene. Thus philosophy casts its shadow over revealed truth. But, this said, it is only fair to point out that Origen advanced this hypothesis "as a topic for discussion rather than as a dogmatic and well-defined proposition."[23] Augustine subsequently looked on this theory as culpably erroneous: "Origen," he wrote, "is justly blamed for holding this opinion." And he expressed his astonishment that "a man so erudite and well versed in ecclesiastical literature" should not have observed how contrary his theory was to the authoritative teaching of Scripture, and also how logically unsatisfactory it was to hold that "the world was created in order that souls might, for their sins, be accommodated with bodies in which they should be shut up as in houses of correction, the more venial sinners receiving lighter and more ethereal bodies, while the grosser and graver sinners received bodies more crass and groveling," and then to assert that "the devils, who are deepest in wickedness" and therefore ought to be incarcerated in the meanest bodies of all, are not restricted but continue to enjoy an ethereal existence free from bodies of clay.[24] We will only add that Origen's hypothesis opens the door for that other speculation for which he was censured, namely, the possibility of the ultimate salvation and restoration of all rational creatures, including the devil himself.

Among the authors of the modern era N. P. Williams has found Origen's theory of a prenatal fall attractive, though without approving all of its postulations. Williams judged "the essential function of the Fall-doctrine" to be "that of saving the infinite goodness of God by relieving him from direct responsibility for the creation of evil."[25] Despite protestations of concern for the preservation of Christian orthodoxy, the reconstruction proposed by Williams was governed by his unwillingness to accept the authenticity of the biblical doctrine of the fall as being the consequence of the sin of the first man. The reason for this was that the biblical doctrine could not be reconciled with his own acceptance of the evolutionary hypothesis of man's origin and development,

22. For the above see Origen, *On First Principles* i.5-8; ii.8-9.
23. Ibid. ii.4.
24. Augustine, *On the City of God* xi.23.
25. N. P. Williams, *The Ideas of the Fall and of Original Sin,* The Bampton Lectures for 1924 (London, 1927), p. 496.

which postulates the rise, not the fall, of man. Origen's view that the fall took place in the realm of the spirits before the creation of man, and that fallen spirits were now punitively imprisoned in human bodies, with the result that men are not fallen because they are men but are men because they, or the souls within them, are fallen, apparently appealed to Williams because it suggested a way of circumventing the scriptural view of the fall of mankind in Adam by going back to a still more primitive and distant event, that of the fall of Satan and his angels. Origen's theory that (in Williams's words) "this life is a purgatory and a tearful prison-house, in which the soul expiates a sin of which she no longer possesses even the bare memory," was a theory that he was unwilling to dismiss as "inherently impossible or directly unorthodox."[26] The radical disability in the case of the church fathers, it seems, and likewise the biblical authors, was that they were born before "the light of that Darwinian revolution in thought and knowledge" burst forth upon our world, revealing "that vast evolutionary panorama in which the history of this planet and our race has been depicted by the genius of modern science," and persuading us that "Augustinianism, with its theory of a Paradisal condition of original perfection, cannot possibly be dovetailed into the picture which is given us by geology and biology." Somewhat surprisingly, however, Williams favored "the conception of the collective fall of the race-soul in an indefinitely remote past."[27]

The first human sin, as envisaged by Williams, was a "stepping aside from the true line of upward progress" rather than "a fall from a high level of moral and intellectual endowment." He imagined a transition from "a time, doubtless to be counted by aeons, during which the moral consciousness had not dawned on this planet" to "an age of responsibility and conscious ethical obligation"—though with regard to the manner of this transition's occurrence he says, "we can only confess ourselves to be totally ignorant"! Nonetheless, he depicted "a period of twilight during which the lineaments of the animal slowly melted into the human" as "the gregarious impulse which had kept the ancient hunting-pack together gradually flowered in the idea of a communal law and in a rudimentary sense of ethical and tribal obligation."[28] Against this backdrop he designated the primeval sin of man as "the self-assertion of the individual against the herd," involving "selfishness, lovelessness, and hate."[29]

But this conjectural reconstruction hardly accounted satisfactorily for the pervasiveness of evil in the world; and the need for a resolution of this problem induced Williams to propose the notion of what he called "the ultimate fall," which he suggested had taken place "at a point before the differentiation of life into its present multiplicity of forms and the emergence of separate species." Accordingly, he propounded "a pre-cosmic vitiation of the whole Life Force,

26. Ibid., p. 512.
27. Ibid., p. 513.
28. Ibid., pp. 514, 515.
29. Ibid., p. 521.

when it was still one and simple," thus hoping to explain, "so far as explanation is possible, the continuity and homogeneity of evil throughout all ranks of organized life, from the bacillus up to Man."[30] This speculation, which must be said to require a rather prodigious leap of credulity, thus attributed responsibility for the impulse of the individual to revolt against the herd to a primordial corruption in the Life Force. The Life Force itself Williams identified with "the World-Soul" as a quasipersonal entity, which, he declared, was created good, but which, "at the beginning of Time, in some transcendental and incomprehensible manner, . . . turned away from God and in the direction of Self, thus shattering its own interior being." He regarded attempts to establish social and international harmony as symptomatic of "the instinctive strivings of the dissociated World-Soul to recover . . . the unitary self-consciousness that it had at the beginning."[31]

Thus Williams supposed the World Soul to be a created and more or less conscious Force struggling laboriously to recover what was lost in the "ultimate fall," and he suggested, further, that there was "a certain profound and intimate connection between the created Life-Force of the universe and the eternal Logos of God." The remnants of goodness in nature, according to his hypothesis, manifested even among the dumb beasts in tokens of gentleness, humility, and devotion, "may embolden us to believe that, long ages before man was, the Spirit of Christ was at work in the world, sustaining the blinded Life-Force, which otherwise would have lapsed into nothingness, fostering within it the potentialities of goodness and love, combating those elements which made for selfishness and cruelty, and leading it slowly and gently back towards the recovery of its original harmony, peace, and unified self-consciousness."[32] In this way Williams envisaged that mysterious and intangible something called the World Soul as driven by some kind of Pelagian impulse and as moving ever onward with evolutionary inevitability and the goodwill of the Logos to its destined goal of perfection which was also its beginning.

A conjecture of this kind displays little affinity with the realities of the biblical faith. It is very difficult to see the relevance of the incarnation, let alone the cross, for such a process, except as some sort of mystical stimulus urging us to recover that herd instinct which was fragmented by the original sin. We are apparently meant to hope that somehow (Williams does not explain exactly how, though he hints that it is by sacramental means) "the defect of love, of social feeling, of gregariousness, of 'herd-instinct'" can "be remedied through the direct transfusion into our souls of the Logos's own self-sacrificed life."[33] The World Soul, we are asked to believe, originally created personal, became a blind and impersonal force as a result of the transcendental fall, but grop-

30. Ibid., p. 523.
31. Ibid., pp. 526f.
32. Ibid., p. 529.
33. Ibid., p. 530.

ingly, thanks to the evolutionary urge within and the Logos, began to recover personality as man emerged in the age-long struggle, and will continue its purposeful ascent to the reunification of all things. It is a nice thought, but the state of human society today affords even less ground for confidence in the world process than it did when Williams delivered his Bampton Lectures.

Williams did not conceal the congruity of much of his speculation with the thought of Plato, whom, in Alexandrian fashion, he designated "the Attic Moses." "If our revised Fall-doctrine is to be intelligible at all," he said, "the 'Life-Force' becomes for us the World-Soul, the 'only-begotten Universe' of Plato's *Timaeus*, . . . replenished (with the potentiality of) all mortal and immortal creatures living and visible, containing all things that are visible, the image of its Maker, most mighty and good, most fair and perfect."[34] The divine image is thus attributed to "the collective Life-Force which was God's primal creature" and the self-perversion of which "would necessarily manifest itself in a development of organic life permeated through and through with the spirit of selfishness, manifested in ferocious competition and in a bloodthirsty struggle for existence."[35] Yet, strangely, the prehistoric fall of the World Spirit, despite its massively disastrous consequences, is described as a "fortunate fault" in view of the anticipated realization in Christ of "the redintegrated consciousness of the general Soul" and the consummation of "the Redemption which is the predestined sequel of the Fall"—in accordance with the medieval couplet which is sung in the Catholic mass on the eve of Easter, and the second line of which reads: "O fortunate fault, which deserved to have such and so great a Redeemer!" It was with this sentiment that Williams concluded his work.[36]

INHERENT IMPERFECTION

Some theorists have argued that because God is infinite and his creatures finite it follows axiomatically that metaphysical imperfection is inherent in the very constitution of the created order—or, otherwise stated, that as the world, in comparison with the absolute perfection of the Creator, possesses only a limited perfection, therefore evil, which is the deficiency of divine goodness, is inevitably built into the structure of things. G. W. Leibniz (1646-1716), whose theory of the origin and nature of sin is set forth in his *Theodicy*,[37] was a notable exponent of this viewpoint. To begin with, Leibniz mentioned two particular difficulties, the one arising from man's freedom, which appeared to him to be incompatible with the sovereignty of God, and yet which was necessary if man was to be a responsible creature; and the other concerning the

34. Ibid., p. 525. The language is that of the conclusion of the *Timaeus* (92C).
35. Ibid., p. 527.
36. Ibid., p. 530.
37. G. W. Leibniz, *Theodicy: Essays on the Goodness of God, the Freedom of Man, and the Origin of Evil*, tr. E. M. Huggard (London, 1951).

conduct of God as Creator which seemed to involve him in the existence of evil in a manner contrary to the divine holiness, justice, and goodness.[38] Leibniz sought to justify God by explaining that out of an infinite number of possible worlds which he might have created he was bound, in accordance with his nature, to have chosen the best. "As a lesser evil is a kind of good," he wrote, "even so a lesser good is a kind of evil if it stands in the way of a greater good; and there would be something to correct in the actions of God if it were possible to do better."[39] Leibniz argued that, even though one might imagine worlds without sin and unhappiness, those worlds would be inferior to ours in goodness, on the ground that "an evil often brings forth a good which would not be attained without that evil." That this is so was supremely demonstrated by the fact that but for the presence of sin Christ would not have come into our world. And here he quoted the *felix culpa* couplet to which we referred at the end of the preceding section:

> O truly necessary sin of Adam, which by Christ's death is cancelled!
> O fortunate fault, which deserved to have such and so great a Redeemer![40]

Thus the end was held to justify the means, at least where God was concerned. It is true that the Apostle refused to countenance the very idea of doing evil that good might result (Rom. 3:8; 6:1), but Leibniz contended that this did not apply to God, who "from permitting of sins derives greater goods than were present before the sins," pointing out, again, that "we have gained Jesus Christ himself by reason of sin."[41] But he appealed also to the experience of everyday life: a little acid sharpens the taste and bitterness is often more pleasing than sweetness; colors are enhanced by shadows and an appropriate dissonance heightens harmony; likewise it was necessary for a little evil to improve what is good and make it more discernible.[42] It must be objected, however, that man's sin did not *deserve* Christ nor did it *gain* his coming. What sin deserved and gained was the condemnation and judgment of the All-Holy God. Its effect was ruination, not redemption. Christ is not an afterthought or an emergency measure of whose presence, were it not for our sin, we would have been deprived; for, as we have seen, to know and to be like Christ has from the very beginning been the destiny of man's being.

Leibniz insisted, however, that, even though God chose to create a world in which evil is intermingled with good, evil must not be attributed to God; for God was doing his best with the options available to him and was bringing ulti-

---

38. Ibid., § 1.
39. Ibid., § 8.
40. Ibid., § 10.

> O certe necessarium Adae peccatum, quod Christi morte deletum est!
> O felix culpa, quae talem ac tantum meruit habere Redemptorem!

41. Ibid., § 11.
42. Ibid., § 12.

mate good out of it all. In fact evil, so he contended, arose from the nature of the creature, since "there is an original imperfection in the creature, even before the commission of sin, because the creature is limited in its essence." Moreover, he reproduced the so-called Augustinian doctrine that "properly speaking, the formal character of evil has no *efficient* cause, for it consists in privation." The necessary character of what is created meant only that God had been induced, not to cause, but to *permit* evil.[43] And the permission of God also involved the *will* of God; but in saying this Leibniz was careful to make a distinction between moral evil and physical evil. "God wills *antecedently* the good and *consequently* the best," he declared. "And as for evil, God wills moral evil not at all, and physical evil or suffering he does not will absolutely." Therefore "one may say of physical evil, that God wills it often as a penalty owing to guilt, and often also as a means to an end, that is, to prevent greater evils or to obtain greater good."[44] He maintained also, by way of analogy, that, as in human society there are incomparably more houses than prisons, so there is incomparably more good than evil in human society and in the universe.[45] To this it must be rejoined that the whole moral guilt of mankind is very far from being confined within prisons, nor is evil absent from the inhabitants of houses. In the final analysis, the logic of Leibniz was unable to protect God from being an accomplice in evil. This is apparent in the affirmation that, "even though the source of evil lies in the possible forms, anterior to the acts of God's will, it is nevertheless true that God cooperates in evil in the actual performance of introducing these forms into matter."[46]

The rationalizations of Leibniz's system tend to remove any absolute distinction between good and evil, so much so that evil is portrayed as even a kind of secondary or potential good, or at least as a justifiable means to the attainment of goodness, in a manner tantamount to saying, "Evil, be thou my good!" God is made the planner if not the source of evil. If God is absolutely good and his works are, as Scripture proclaims, entirely good, and if evil is the opposite of good and its corruption and privation, how can evil be held to belong to the will and purpose of God? If a creation with evil is more beneficial than a creation without evil, why does God take action to eliminate evil from his creation and to establish a new heaven and earth in which there is not a single trace of evil? This surely contradicts the notion that God was restricted to making the best of the choices, all imperfect, that were supposed to be open to him. By postulating evil as a given factor which God could not avoid Leibniz left himself the task of making the best of a bad case.

The suggestion that God had permitted the presence of evil in his creation as a means to an end that was good, or better than would otherwise have

43. Ibid., §§ 20, 21.
44. Ibid., § 23.
45. Ibid., §§148, 262.
46. Ibid., § 381.

been the case, had been made long before the time of Leibniz by authors as distinguished as Augustine and Aquinas,[47] who likewise were attempting to justify God's ways. But theologizing of this kind can hardly be said to escape the danger of involving God in responsibility for the existence of evil in the world. Moreover, the *felix culpa* mentality, or rather sentimentality, is a misguided distortion of theodicy which has the effect of condoning the sin of man and saddling God with complicity in the introduction of that which he hates into his creation. It would be just as reasonable to go back beyond the original sin of man and to sing "O felix culpa" of the primordial rebellion of Satan, for the Redeemer came into the world to destroy the devil as well as to set free his captives (Heb. 2:14f.); and let us not forget that this was at the cost of infinite suffering. Evil and God are in no way compatible. Hence the solemn admonition regarding the coming of Christ which St. John has given: "You know that he appeared to take away sins, and in him there is no sin. No one who abides in him sins. . . . Little children, let no one deceive you. He who does right is righteous, as he is righteous. He who commits sin is of the devil; for the devil has sinned from the beginning. The reason the Son of God appeared was to destroy the works of the devil. No one born of God commits sin; for God's nature abides in him, and he cannot sin because he is born of God. By this it may be seen who are the children of God, and who are the children of the devil" (1 Jn. 3:5-10).

A BENEFICIAL NECESSITY

A step beyond the view of those who regard man's fall into sin as an evil means leading to a good end is the hypothesis, which has had many advocates in the modern age, that the fall itself was intrinsically good rather than evil and a development necessary for the achievement by man of his authentic humanness. The most influential advocate of this theory was no doubt the philosopher G. W. F. Hegel (1770-1831), who held that man existed essentially as spirit and that it was central to the character of spirit to be self-conscious and free, with the ability to place the natural over against itself. Hegel contended that the familiar description of man's original state as a state of innocence was descriptive of a merely natural or animal condition. If man was to realize his existence as a spiritual being it was needful for him to "come out of the state of innocence and become guilty"; for, Hegel explained, the state of innocence was "the condition of animals, of unconsciousness, where man does not know either good or evil." Animals were not moral creatures, they were neither good nor evil; and man in an animal condition, man as he was by nature, was not as he ought to be. This line of argument led to the conclusion that man was evil

---

47. Cf., e.g., Augustine: "God judged it better to bring good out of evil than to suffer no evil to exist" (*Enchiridion* vii.27); Aquinas: "God allows evils to happen in order to bring a greater good from them" (*Summa Theologica*, pt. III, q. 1, art. 3).

by nature—that the state of innocence was for man an evil state. According to Hegel's reasoning, "it is the everlasting history of the freedom of man that he should come out of this state of dullness or torpor, in which he is in his earliest years, that he should come, in fact, to the light of consciousness, or, to put it more precisely, that both good and evil should exist for him." He even argued that the loss of the paradise of man's first state "proves that it is not absolutely essential as a state."[48]

Evil, then, as Hegel saw it, was attributable to man's original state of animal or infantile innocence. For man to free himself from this state was both good and necessary, and this, Hegel asserted, was precisely what man did in the biblical account of the fall, which has "a deep philosophical meaning." By eating the forbidden fruit man attained to the knowledge of good and evil, the knowledge which constitutes the character of spirit, and thus gained for himself consciousness and freedom. But why, if that was the case, was a divine prohibition attached to the taking of this fruit? Hegel's answer was that this knowledge was a dangerous gift: it had a negative side, the power of arbitrary choice to do what was evil, as well as an affirmative side, the freedom to do good. And yet this primitive state of innocence was declared to be also man's final destiny: "In the child there is no freedom, and yet it belongs to the essential character of man that he should once more reach innocence"—not absolutely, however, the original state as previously defined by Hegel, in which man had no knowledge of good or evil, but an ultimate state of "harmony between man and the Good." This transition, or return, was to be achieved in a typically dialectical fashion through the synthesis of the primal thesis and antithesis, involving, as Hegel put it, the reconciliation of the natural and the spiritual sundered by the self-liberation of the "fall." This reconciliation was not conceived as a return to the evil that supposedly consisted in resting in the natural state, but rather as the triumph of good over evil as man became righteous in the performance of the divine will.[49]

Thus Hegel supposed that both good and evil were necessary if man was to develop into the fulness of manhood, and that the attainment of synthesis was possible only by way of the confrontation of thesis and antithesis. Though Hegel affirmed man's natural condition to be evil, he also affirmed that man was by nature good, by which he meant that "his universal substantial essence is good," that "he is potentially spirit," and that "he has been created in the image of God." But if man were *solely* by nature good there would be no room for dialectic; there would be "no element of division," "no need of reconciliation," and no place for "the course of development" which was so integral an ingredient of Hegel's philosophical system. In Hegel's judgment, indeed, man as created was one-sided: he was entirely in the animal or infantile state

48. G. W. F. Hegel, *Lectures on the Philosophy of Religion*, tr. E. B. Speirs and J. B. Sanderson, Vol. I (London and New York, 1974 edn.), pp. 271ff.

49. Ibid., Vol. II, pp. 199ff.

of innocence; he was only *potentially* good, and "it is just in the very fact that Man is only potentially good that the defect of his nature lies." Knowledge, which came from eating the forbidden fruit, was what set man free to follow the road that leads to the development of his potential for good. Knowledge in fact appears to be the sum of Hegel's gospel: by this acquisition of knowledge man became equal to God, as the serpent had said he would. Knowledge was, for Hegel, the key to the dialectic of reconciliation: as "the principle of spiritual life" it was also "the principle of the healing of the injury caused by disunion"; and, further, it supplied "the principle of man's divineness, a principle which by a process of self-adjustment or elimination of difference must reach a condition of reconciliation or truth, or, in other words, it involves the promise and certainty of attaining once more the state in which Man is the image of God."[50]

It is obvious that Hegel, although he professed to be interpreting the biblical account of the fall of man, actually offered a hypothesis of the origin of evil which was completely at variance with the biblical perspective. Man, as the scriptural authors repeatedly affirm, was not placed at creation in a state of animal insensitivity, morally undetermined, and unaware of good or unwarned of evil. His state of innocence was one of positive goodness untouched and unspoiled by evil. His moral responsibility was displayed in his ability to receive a word of command from his Creator. For Hegel to have acknowledged this, however, would have destroyed his whole case, which depended on man's disobedience to the divine command in order to achieve freedom and spirituality for the fulfilment of his potential for good. In Hegel's eyes, therefore, the fall of man was not reprehensible but praiseworthy. It was a fall upward!

Also unsatisfactory is the inaccurate manner in which Hegel speaks of the forbidden tree, as he does at important points in his argument, as the tree of knowledge instead of the tree of the knowledge of good and evil. This opens the way for him to commend man's presumed desire for knowledge and, as we have seen, to elevate knowledge as the principle of salvation and reconciliation. But, as created, man already had knowledge, the only necessary knowledge, that of the goodness of God and of personal fellowship with his Creator. And his existence was one of freedom and spirituality. The one thing he did not need was the knowledge of evil which he acquired through his disobedience to the divine command. The consequent antithesis of good and evil in the history of mankind is not resolved by Hegel's dialectical form of synthesis, but by the atonement effected in the incarnate Son through which the disastrous results of the fall are annulled and sinful man is reconciled to his holy Creator. The contradiction in which Hegel's theorizing involved him has been well summarized by the Hegelian scholar J. McT. E. McTaggart: "The advance from Innocence to Virtue can only be through Sin. Sin is a necessary means to Virtue. . . . Hegel, while he considers that the story of the Fall embodies a great

50. Ibid., Vol. III, pp. 45ff.

truth, considers also that the Fall was in reality a rise."[51] The inconsistencies that beset Hegel's efforts at biblical interpretation distort his religious philosophizing as a whole. His problem throughout was precisely that of knowledge.

THE EVOLUTIONARY EXPLANATION

Another school of thought which is predisposed to speak of the rise rather than the fall of man is that of evolutionism. This position has had many exponents since the rise of Darwinism (including, in his own way, N. P. Williams, as we have seen above) and has been elaborated with numerous variations and embellishments. As its representative we take F. R. Tennant, who argued the case for an evolutionistic interpretation of the origin of evil in his Hulsean Lectures given at Cambridge at the beginning of this century.[52] While admitting the necessity "to move largely in the sphere of theory and speculation," Tennant assumed "as overwhelmingly probable that there is continuity between the physical constitution of man and that of the lower animals."[53] This presupposition provided a basis for the construction of a hypothesis which has a number of marks in common with the Hegelian theory.

Within this purview, the central question concerns the mode of transition from animality to humanity, from the nonmoral and nonresponsible being of the animal (the equivalent, *mutatis mutandis,* of Hegel's state of nature and innocence) to the moral and responsible being of the human person. "We are natural before we are moral beings," Tennant declared, adding that "the impulses of our nature are in full sway before the moral consciousness begins to dawn."[54] By "the impulses of our nature" he meant an inherited carryover from our supposed animal ancestry. Thus he explained that such "instincts, appetites, and impulses, with self-assertive tendencies" belonged to our physical or animal nature, which "contains abundance of raw material for the production of sin, as soon as these native propensities are brought into relation with any restraining or condemning influence." Though these propensities were formerly "useful or necessary to life and were therefore through countless ages intensified by natural selection," Tennant denied that there was any reason "for referring their clamorous importunity to an evil bias or a corrupted nature," affirming rather that they belong "to man as God made him."[55] We are assured, accordingly, that "fear and anger, envy and jealousy, self-centeredness and self-pleasing are qualities which form part of the birthright of the human being in virtue of his animal ancestry," and that "the 'ape and tiger' in our nature" are "natu-

51. J. McT. E. McTaggart, *Studies in Hegelian Cosmology* (Cambridge, 1918—first published in 1901), pp. 234, 235.

52. F. R. Tennant, *The Origin and Propagation of Sin* (Cambridge, 1908—first published in 1902).

53. Ibid., pp. 85f.

54. Ibid., p. 96.

55. Ibid., p. 95.

ral and normal and necessary" and indeed "nonmoral" or "*neutral* in character": they are to be regarded simply as "indifferent material waiting to be moralized."[56]

What Tennant called "the basal proposition" of his theory was this, that "until the will has emerged, and life begins to be self-conducted, no germ of evil can be said to exist in the individual"; the presence of sin is excluded "until moral sentiment appears."[57] The acquisition of conscience, he supposed, coincided with the ceasing to be innocent "with the innocence of ignorance of good and evil," so that it was at this moment that man, "the new-born moral agent," was confronted with "the task of moralizing his organic nature."[58] Tennant acknowledged that the evolutionary hypothesis of the origin of sin required the rejection of the factuality of the biblical account of the fall, though he contended that "in thus naturally accounting for the origin and universality of sin we neither excuse evil nor explain it away." He claimed that he had no wish to deny "man's crying need of grace" but, not surprisingly, the reformulation of the doctrine of sin demanded a reformulation of the doctrine of redemption. "The nature of redemption," he said, "would need to be defined in terms somewhat different from those to which we have long been used." This was particularly evident when Tennant insisted that the fact that "man's performance lags behind his aspiration" (as he put it) was attributable, "not to a defection from a sinless yet moral state, but to the fact that he is rising in moral culture."[59] Just what new form redemption must be given was not spelled out by Tennant, nor did he attempt to explain how the incarnation, which apparently he affirmed, could possibly be fitted into the evolutionistic process whose fundamental principle is that of gradual naturalistic and moralistic progress.[60] The doctrine of original sin as involving the whole of mankind in sinfulness and guilt (which Tennant, like Williams, viewed unfavorably as Augustinianism—why not Paulinism?) was replaced by the doctrine of the universal solidarity of mankind in respect of a common animal origin, with the consequence that man "inherits the tendencies of the stock" which provide the impulses to sin; but we are advised that as such this propensity is no more than "the product of the ordinary course of Nature, and ought not properly to be called original sin."[61]

In the ultimate issue, it seems that the redemptive resolution of the problem of sin which Tennant had in mind amounted to a combination of evolutionary progress and Pelagian self-help. The addition of grace would doubtless have been accepted as welcome, but it is difficult to see what need there is in this perspective for the intervention of divine grace. With regard to evolution-

56. Ibid., pp. 101f.
57. Ibid., p. 105.
58. Ibid., p. 109.
59. Ibid., pp. 112ff.
60. This question is discussed below in the section on evolutionism and incarnation, pp. 224ff.
61. Tennant, *Origin and Propagation of Sin*, p. 117.

ary progress, we have already noticed Tennant's persuasion that man, far from being a fallen creature, "is rising in moral culture" (though past and present history affords no evidence that this is so—it is a postulation inseparable from the hypothesis); and with regard to Pelagian self-help, Tennant held that man's natural position was one of ethical neutrality (though Scripture witnesses emphatically to the contrary). "Evil," he asserted, "is not the result of a transition from the good, but good and bad are alike the results of volitional reaction upon what is ethically neutral." It was his contention that introspection discloses "an internal conflict between nature and nurture," and that man is born to "the arduous task of subjugating and annexing his organic to his rational and moral nature."[62] On these premises, the solidarity of mankind is displayed in the *possibility* of sin which is derived from our common animal ancestry, whereas the *actuality* of sin, the actual commission of sins, derives "solely from the individual will influenced by its social environment" and therefore belongs to the sphere of human individuality and freedom. For this understanding Tennant duly gave credit to Pelagius, declaring that this "is the truth which Pelagius abstracted from its proper relation to the solidarity of mankind in the non-moral material of sin."[63]

In the evolutionistic scheme, then, not only does life come originally from nonlife and personality from nonpersonality, but also spirit comes from matter and morality from nonmorality, and the fall of man really means its opposite, the rise of man. Thus Scripture is distorted into a meaning that is contrary to what it clearly states and the authentic principles of logic and science are set aside by postulating that in some hypothetical manner the superior is generated by the inferior. From both the Christian and the scientific point of view this whole procedure is one of inversion.

NOTHINGNESS

A novel theoretical solution to the ancient question of the origin of evil was devised by Karl Barth, who posited the existence of "an alien factor," indeed, "an entire sinister system of elements," from which "opposition and resistance to God's world-dominion" proceeded.[64] This factor he called *nothingness,* while at the same time he boldly affirmed its "existence, presence, and operation."[65] A postulation of this kind, however, immediately involved Barth in a problem of language and semantics. Logical definition requires that "nothingness" can have no existence, presence, or operation. One may say that "nothingness is nonexistent," but that is no more than a tautological statement. On the other hand, to say that "nothingness is," that it exists, is a self-contra-

62. Ibid., pp. 118f.
63. Ibid., p. 120.
64. Karl Barth, *Church Dogmatics,* III/3, tr. G. W. Bromiley (Edinburgh, 1960), p. 289.
65. Ibid., p. 294.

dictory statement. This in turn raises the question: How can nothingness be the enemy of God and his creation, as Barth maintains it is? How can the identity of "thingness" be ascribed to nothingness? The problem is intensified, not alleviated, by the assurance that it is an alien third factor, an intangible *tertium quid,* which can be identified neither with the Creator nor with his work of creation. Barth's intention was not to remove the factor of nothingness from the sovereign lordship of God, but rather to explain the presence of evil within the world in a way that avoids, on the one hand, the Manichean error which compromises God by making him the cause of evil, and, on the other hand, the Pelagian error of putting man in control of evil in a way which challenges God's providential rule over all things.

Barth criticized Leibniz for degrading the Augustinian concept of evil as privation to that of negation, whereby the metaphysical imperfection of the creature was held to open the way to sin and suffering and death;[66] yet Barth himself seemed to move close to the position of Leibniz when he propounded a "negative aspect" of creation as existing alongside the positive: darkness as well as light, night as well as day, water as well as land. This negative aspect, he said, "is as it were the frontier of nothingness and oriented towards it." Though he saw this as a constant menace to creation, he insisted that it was not the same as the nothingness he had postulated and that there was no common ground between the two. Barth pointed out that as in creation "there is not only a Yes but also a No, not only a height but also an abyss," so also in creaturely existence we meet with "success and failure, laughter and tears, youth and age," and so on. He held, moreover, that such antitheses belong to the goodness of God's creation by implying that his creatures may "praise him more mightily in humility than in exaltation, in need than in plenty, in fear than in joy, in the frontier of nothingness than when wholly oriented to God."[67] But it must be questioned how this can possibly be an appropriate description of creation as it came from the hand of God, or, for that matter, as it will ultimately be when its ordained destiny is fulfilled. The valleys and the tears and the fears of our creaturely existence belong to the interim period of creation in its fallenness, during which it is the redeemed sinner who is enabled by the grace of God triumphantly to praise his Maker even and especially in the darkness of affliction. Furthermore, it is a constant theme of Scripture that man fully and most mightily praises God only when he is wholly oriented to him, as was originally the situation prior to the fall and as will everlastingly be the situation when all creation is renewed and glorified. At last, as at first, there will be no abyss, no need, no sorrow, no death, and no dark side of life (Rev. 21:1-4).

In explaining what, according to his conception, "nothingness" *is,* Barth admitted that "only God and his creature really and properly are"; but he strenuously rejected the conclusion that "nothingness" is therefore nothing or non-

66. Ibid., p. 318.
67. Ibid., pp. 296f.

existent. He argued that this alien factor "can have nothing in common with God and his creature," but that, since "nothingness is not nothing," it must be held that "in a third way of its own nothingness 'is'." Yet, even while contending that "nothingness" is, and thus is "certainly an objective reality for the creature," Barth asserted that it does not possess an existence which can be discovered by the creature, with whom it has no accessible relationship.[68] If this is so, one may be permitted to wonder how its existence was discovered by a creature called Karl Barth. Be that as it may, the key produced by Barth for unlocking the mystery of the lurking, undercover reality of "nothingness" is that of his understanding of divine election as the basis of God's activity, which as such necessarily implies the rejection of what is not elected. "Grounded always in election," he wrote, "the activity of God is invariably one of jealousy, wrath, and judgment." God's action takes place "in a definite opposition, in a real negation, both defensive and aggressive. . . . God wills, and therefore opposes what he does not will. He says Yes, and therefore says No to that to which he has not said Yes. . . . Both of these activities, grounded in his election and decision, are necessary elements in his sovereign action." "Nothingness," then, is what God willed not to create, and as such it stands "under his No, the object of his jealousy, wrath, and judgment." In a paradoxical manner "as inherent contradiction, as impossible possibility," it really "is."[69]

Referring to Genesis 1:2, Barth associated this "nothingness" with "the chaos which the Creator has already rejected, negated, passed over, and abandoned even before he utters his first creative word," that is to say, with "the unwilled and uncreated reality which constitutes as it were the periphery of his creation and creature." The correctness of this understanding, Barth claimed, is confirmed by the description of man's sin in Genesis 3, for sin, he stated, "is purely and simply what God did not, does not, and cannot will"; and it is by the sin of man that the real existence of "nothingness" is manifested. But, paradoxically again, sin, like "nothingness," has "the essence only of non-essence, and only as such can it exist." This aspect of reality, as he saw it, Barth described as God's *opus alienum* ("alien work"), which he does not will and which stands in contrast to the *opus proprium* ("proper work") of his election, creation, providence, and grace. As the enemy of divine grace "nothingness," he asserted, "is really privation, the attempt to defraud God of his honor and right and at the same time to rob the creature of its salvation and right."[70]

The mention of privation with its overtones of negativity must not be allowed to mislead us into imagining that Barth was but developing and refining the position of Augustine. That there is a world of difference between Barth and Augustine at this point should become apparent as we attempt to form an evaluation of Barth's hypothesis. It is a hypothesis which, though expounded

68. Ibid., pp. 349f.
69. Ibid., p. 351.
70. Ibid., pp. 352f.

with confidence, we believe to be defective for a number of reasons. In the first place, his concept of the reality of "nothingness" involved him in such irreconcilable contradictions that language, evacuated of its genuine sense, simply became nonsense. There is no need for us to add to the evidence that has already been given in this connection.

Secondly, within the perspective of Scripture the doctrine of divine election belongs to the sphere not of creation but of redemption, as also does the related doctrine of divine grace. Barth obliterated this distinction by his rejection of natural theology and his bringing together of creation and grace into one, so that creation was for him a work of divine grace which fell within the framework of God's covenant of grace.[71] Thus, as we have noticed, for Barth creation was effected through the operation of electing grace. Indeed, on the premises proposed by Barth there was an evident need for the activity of electing grace at creation and in the garden even before the occurrence of the fall of man, not only in electing what to create and what to pass over but also in supplying man with the grace to be safe from the dark and hostile force of that "nothingness" which had been rejected, and which constituted an ever present threat to man in particular as God's dominant creature formed in the divine image. But the biblical revelation betrays the presence of no menacing cloud, no hidden, sinister factor connected with the accomplishment of God's work of creation. On the contrary, "God saw everything that he had made, and behold, it was very good" (Gen. 1:31).

Thirdly, God's positive decision to create the world did not at all necessarily require from him the negative decision to reject what he had not willed to create. Any such notion is indicative rather of a defective doctrine of God, as though he were confronted, and to that extent limited, with an existentialist necessity for making a choice. It is quite unjustifiable to suppose that God's *opus proprium,* which he willed to do, involved him inevitably in an *opus alienum,* which he did not will to do (and which is not an *opus* at all!). Again, the Bible knows of no such division in the work of creation. A mechanical expert or inventor may choose or elect to make an airplane rather than a submarine, but his decision against the latter does not invest what he has rejected with a negative but real existence; nor is the submarine that he has elected not to make therefore the object of his jealousy, wrath, and judgment. His *opus proprium* does not involve him in the complication of an *opus alienum* by which his achievement is menaced. Much less is God subject to an inevitability of giving reality to a sinister entity of "nothingness" by choosing to assign a particular form to his creation.

Fourthly, it is impossible to acquiesce in Barth's identification of the formless and void condition of the earth spoken of in Genesis 1:2 with the chaos which, according to his hypothesis, God "rejected, negated, passed over,

---

71. Helmut Kuhn has spoken of Barth's "abysmal hatred of nature and natural man" (*Encounter with Nothingness* [London, 1951], p. 111).

and abandoned" before uttering his first creative word; for this interpretation leaves out of account the immediately preceding statement of Genesis 1:1 that in the beginning God created the earth. To identify it with primeval chaos gives the impression of reversion to Greek speculation rather than faithfulness to the biblical mind (far though this may have been from Barth's intention). In any case, the transformation of disorder into order implies the elimination of disorder, not its continuation as some kind of subversive entity that has suffered rejection.

Fifthly, Barth would seem to have argued himself to the frontier of dualism. To conceive of God's creation of the world in such a way that the positive reality of his creative work is automatically accompanied by the negative reality, brought into "being" by rejection, of a hostile force totally opposed to the divine will, is tantamount to saying that by electing to create God was fated to bring about a dualistic situation. If this does not make God the willing author of evil, it at least makes him the victim of his own action—and, still more strangely, the unwilling victim, in that, *ex hypothesi,* his choosing to create the world, which is wholly good, inescapably involved him in giving existence to what he had rejected, which is wholly evil. What sort of God is it who is trapped on the horns of such a dilemma? To imagine that God is unable to choose to do good without conferring reality on a negative, rejected power of evil is intolerable. The system of Scripture has no place for the idea that an antithetical negative lurks beneath the divine positive, plainly declaring that all that God does is good and perfect without any possibility of there being a dark and threatening underside, or a shadow realm that precedes and provides occasion for the fall.

Yet, as we have said, Barth had no desire to question the absolute goodness of God or the totality of his sovereign power over all things, including the "nothingness" that his creative election is supposed to have made a reality. "God," Barth remonstrated, "is indeed eternally holy, pure, distinct, and separate from the evil which is nothingness." But even so, he insisted that "God himself is primarily affected" by the "contradiction and opposition" of this nothingness. The assurance that "nothingness has no perpetuity" looks like an attempt to deny the dualistic implications of his hypothesis. Describing this "nothingness" as "insubstantial and empty," he asked: "How can it be anything but empty when it is only by God's non-willing that it is what it is?"; and he explained, further, that God's "alien work" (which is here something quite different from what Luther meant by the same expression) gave nothingness "only the truth of falsehood, the power of impotence, the sense of nonsense." But it may justly be objected again that for Barth to use language in this contrary way can only have the effect of giving his hypothesis the sense of nonsense. His whole development of this theme is more than paradoxical; it is so perversely couched in contradictions that it is dependent on the assassination of language. This should no doubt be an indication of the utter inscrutability of the mystery of evil, and the futility of claiming to fathom that mystery. Barth's argumentation, however, is of a piece with his dialectical method, which presupposed that the utterance of Yes, even by God, could not fail to be at the same time the utterance of No.

This dialectic, moreover, was implicated with a logic which Barth was unprepared to pursue to its conclusion; for, although he asserted the inevitability of this "alien work" as "the divine negation and rejection" which is "the obverse of the divine election and affirmation" in creation, yet he stressed that it was "of major importance . . . that we should not become involved in the logical dialectic that if God loves, elects, and affirms eternally he must also hate and therefore reject and negate eternally."[72] But why not? If God's election inevitably requires the evil reality of what he does not elect, to deny the ultimate inevitability of this "alien work" is to cut away the foundation on which the structure is supposed to stand. Perhaps this amounted to yet another addition to the contradictions already formulated, that, namely, of the evitability of the inevitability of nothingness resulting from God's proper work.

By applying the doctrine of election and reprobation to the act of creation Barth associated, whether intentionally or not, the origin of the reality of evil with the Creator's instead of the creature's decision. We can associate ourselves with his christological resolution of the antinomy of evil in our world, but this does not remove the confusion introduced by the postulation of an alien as well as a proper work of God in the creation of all things. Meontological theology[73] is self-destructive theology, if only because its basis is that of the irrationality of contradiction. Though it has a long and checkered history stretching from some of the early Greek philosophers up to some of the existentialists of our day,[74] meontology, which in one way or another affirms that concept of the reality of nothingness, turns out to be, as it has always been, an exercise in obfuscation rather than enlightenment.

Both Leibniz and Barth envisaged God in his role of Creator as being placed under the necessity of making a decision which simultaneously implicated him in an act of rejection or passing over. The former supposed that God had to weigh and select what was the best of an infinite number of possible worlds, all of them stamped with relative imperfection; the latter maintained that God's electing to create this world conferred negative and sinister reality on that which was disapproved. Both portrayed God as in a certain sense the victim of his own decision to create, and both in one way or another associated the origin of evil with this divine decision. Leibniz romanticized the hypothetical dark aspect of creation in the shape of the *felix culpa* notion; Barth, on the

72. Barth, *Church Dogmatics*, III/3, pp. 360f.
73. "Meontic" and "meontological" are terms formed from the Greek *to mē on,* meaning "that which is not," "the nonexistent." The use of the negative *mē*, not *ou*, was regarded theoretically as giving a paradoxical reality to nothingness in distinction from *to ouk on*, designating utter nonexistence or nonentity.
74. For example, in the writings of Jean-Paul Sartre and Martin Heidegger, whose thought Barth discussed at some length (pp. 334ff.).

other hand, came close to presenting a situation of dualistic antithesis. Apart from the fact that both accepted a christological solution, the philosophical constructions of both are logically incompatible with the biblical view of the eschatological consummation of all God's creative purposes in the new heaven and the new earth, in which, as at the beginning, there will be no imperfection, no menacing evil, and no hostile factor or power.

NEOORTHODOXY

Neoorthodoxy, which is not a sharply defined classification, is intended as a designation of the position of those theologians who, having turned away from the destructive liberalism of the past century-and-a-half, professed to listen attentively once again to what the Bible has to say, without, however, abandoning a critical attitude to the scriptural witness. It was thus no more than a partial reorientation to classical orthodoxy. Karl Barth and Emil Brunner have generally been regarded as the leading exponents of neoorthodoxy, though it would be mistaken to assume that they were always in theological agreement with each other. Brunner's understanding of evil and its origin, for example, differed from that of Barth (which we discussed in the preceding section), and it was also more truly representative of the neoorthodox attitude on this theme. As defined by Brunner, "sin is the desire for the autonomy of man; therefore, in the last resort, it is the denial of God and self-deification: it is getting rid of the Lord God and the proclamation of self-sovereignty."[75] Critical of "Augustine's unfortunate theory that evil is defect,"[76] Brunner affirmed that sin was not just a negative, a minus-sign indicating a subtraction, but something positive and definite. "To be a sinner," he wrote, "means to be engaged in rebellion against God. Sin never becomes a quality or even a substance. Sin is and remains an act."[77] He was, however, prepared to describe sin as "the one great negative mystery of our existence" and, paradoxically, as "a positive negation."[78]

This emphasis on the positive, aggressive character of sin is certainly a desirable corrective to any notion that sin is merely negation and privation. But Augustine's position was not at variance with that of Brunner in this respect. His thesis that evil is the defection of good was much less a capitulation to Greek philosophical thought than an attack on the dualistic aspect of Greek and Manichean speculation which accorded to evil an existence that was both substantial and eternal. Augustine was intent on maintaining the truth that only what God has brought into being has substantial existence and that, for the very

75. E. Brunner, *Dogmatics,* Vol. II, *The Christian Doctrine of Creation and Redemption,* tr. Olive Wyon (London, 1952), p. 93.
76. *Man in Revolt* (London, 1939), p. 131.
77. Ibid., p. 148.
78. Ibid., pp. 132, 129.

reason that it has been created by God, it is good and cannot be evil. Evil, there-fore, is not a concrete entity which poses a threat to the goodness and the exis-tence of God. And in stating that "sin never becomes a quality or even a sub-stance" Brunner would seem to have been saying exactly the same thing. Not that Brunner was unappreciative of the contribution made by Augustine to the understanding of this difficult subject; indeed, he praised him as "the real founder of the classical doctrine of Sin" (though others might wish to give that accolade to St. Paul or even to the Holy Spirit), observing that "it is significant that again and again, whenever the Biblical Gospel is rediscovered—as, above all, at the Reformation—this is due to the influence of Augustine." He referred in particular to Augustine's insistence on the universality and totality of sin, the inability of the unredeemed person not to sin, the incapacity of man to ac-quire merit or grace before God, and the perception of God's redeeming grace in Jesus Christ as intended first of all for the removal of guilt.[79]

Brunner could also be described as Augustinian in his affirmation that the responsibility for man's sin rested entirely upon man himself—that the blame for evil could not facilely be assigned to the intrusion of some outside force, or to inescapable fate or to a part of man, such as his flesh or the mate-rial aspect of his being. "The meaning of sin, by its very nature, affects the whole," Brunner wrote, "because it aims at making the whole man 'free'." Thus he stressed the involvement of the totality of man's being in the commission and the guilt of sin: "It is as a whole that the person *commits* sin; this is not due to some part of the personality. *I* am a sinner, not this or that aspect of my na-ture."[80] Sin, moreover, has brought contradiction into the being of man—"not simply 'something contradictory' in man, but . . . a contradiction of the whole man against the whole man, a division within man himself."[81]

Unlike Augustine, however, Brunner denied the factuality of the bibli-cal account of man's fall into sin, and he did so because of his claim to be scien-tifically enlightened in a way that was not possible in the age of Augustine. Thus he declared that "the whole historic picture of 'the first man' has been fi-nally and absolutely destroyed for us today." The conflict between science and Scripture has led, he held, to "the victory of the scientific view" and the "in-evitable decline of the ecclesiastical view," with the result that "no facts have been left which could support the Augustinian ecclesiastical view of the his-torical 'first man,' or which could prove that the empirical origin of the human race was to be sought on a specially elevated plane of spiritual existence."[82] It was Brunner's opinion, furthermore, that not only for scientific but also "for theological reasons the Adam narrative ought to be abandoned" as "a neces-sary purification of Christian doctrine." Adam, if we still use the term, could

79. *Dogmatics*, Vol. II, p. 114.
80. Ibid., p. 94.
81. *Man in Revolt*, p. 118.
82. Ibid., pp. 85f.

no longer mean the first man, he argued, but simply you and me, because now "when we talk about the origin of man we are not speaking of a certain man called Adam, who lived many thousand years ago, but of myself, and of yourself, and of everyone else in the world."[83]

The source of this new light was the evolutionary hypothesis with its principle of development and the "genetic thinking" it has promoted, which, while "quite alien to the thought of earlier generations," is "one of the chief characteristics of the modern mind."[84] And so the church became the loser: "What at first seemed to be hypothesis transformed itself more and more into stable knowledge, and made it increasingly evident that the Biblical narrative of Paradise and the Primitive State was untenable." Brunner contended, further, that historical science has confirmed the verdict of natural science, so much so that he spoke dogmatically of "the established truths of historical and natural science" in justification of his assertion that "there is no longer any room for the traditional view of the Church or the temporal beginning of the human race."[85] This cannot fail to raise the momentous question regarding the reality of the creation of man and his formation in the divine image. Brunner lifts the whole history of the origin and fall of man from history and replants it in the soil of empiricism. "The man who has been created by God as good," he wrote, "is not the Neanderthal man, nor the Heidelberg man, nor the Peking man, nor the *homo sapiens,* but simply 'man' in general." Abraham, for example, "is no nearer the good Creation and the event of the Fall than I am, because he lived at an earlier time."[86]

Nonetheless, in Brunner's reconstruction, modern man, so superior in power and knowledge, has to battle against his origins; his constitution is still not free from every vestige or relic of his primitive past; infantile and atavistic elements lurking in the background constantly threaten to break forth and interrupt his progress. Brunner supposed, indeed, that "in all sin there is something of atavism or archaism or 'infantilism,'" but with the qualification that the "infantile or atavistic tendencies" still present in the nature of man "only become sin when man in his moral decision, in his self-determination, makes room for them, or allows them to remain."[87] This notion provides a clue to Brunner's conception of the origin of evil: the remnants of man's primitive and less reputable ancestry provide the fuel for sinning; his volition ignites it.

Though he acknowledged the diminution of scientific confidence in Haeckel's theory that "ontogeny recapitulates phylogeny," that is, that the growth and organization of the human embryo from a single cell to a full-grown human being reenacts as it were in miniature the history of the age-long development of man from an original unicellular organism, yet this is the pattern

83. Ibid., p. 88.
84. Ibid., p. 390.
85. Ibid., pp. 393f.
86. Ibid., pp. 398, 399.
87. Ibid., pp. 400f.

Brunner adopted in his attempt to explain the facts of human personality and human sin. He applied it as a principle to every human being, arguing that each individual person was a development from a subhuman beginning in the womb. "The specifically human element in man," he affirmed, "is not there from the very outset—in the infant or even in the embryo, in the fertilized ovum—but it develops in connection with and in a certain parallel to bodily and psycho-physical development." It is a conclusion for which Brunner even claimed the support of the New Testament, contending on the basis of 1 Corinthians 15:45 that "man is first of all a *psychikos* and not a *pneumatikos,* that is, that the fully human element is not present from the outset but that it is added to that which first existed," and, on the basis of Matthew 18:3 and 19:14, that "it is beyond doubt that Jesus himself takes into consideration a relative innocence on the part of the child."[88]

But to grasp at these particular passages for support shows how hard-pressed Brunner was to find biblical confirmation of his theory. In the Pauline passage the Apostle is contrasting man's present earthly body with the future spiritual body with which the redeemed will be clothed at the eschatological moment of Christ's return. Though the latter is the glorious fulfilment of our humanity as God created it to be, St. Paul hardly intended to say that throughout the course of this present life and no matter how long we live we are less than fully human—which is what the logic of Brunner's argument would require if he showed concern for the context of St. Paul's statement. And in the Matthean passages Christ's blessing of little children demonstrates, it is true, his approval of their innocent trustfulness; but only the tyranny of a preconceived judgment could interpret his action to mean that "the specifically human element" was not yet present within them; on the contrary, he admonished his adult audience that of such little children is the kingdom of heaven, and that unless they became like little children they would never enter the kingdom of heaven. He was certainly not inviting them to return to infantilism.

By itself, Brunner's supposition that every man is his own Adam could not unjustly be thought to have Pelagian overtones; but his theory of inherent atavism made it possible for him to avoid the extremes of individualism and to postulate the solidarity of mankind in sinfulness, and even to affirm that "Adam is the unity of humanity." This recognition of sinfulness as the state of the whole of mankind, corporately, as well as of the whole man, individually, accounts for Brunner's willingness to postulate that "the solidarity of being involved in sin manifests itself also in 'inheritance.'"[89] In this connection Brunner had much in common with Kant's conception of radical evil in human nature. Sin was seen as not just the individualistic repetition of the sin of Adam (though, however "Adam" was understood, if each man is his own Adam this was certainly implied) but also as the consequence of a universal propensity

88. Ibid., p. 404; cf. p. 408.
89. *Dogmatics*, Vol. II, p. 82; *Man in Revolt*, p. 123.

to evil in the human constitution—a propensity by which man's innocence was compromised, but which was not itself sin, for if it were, Kant maintained it would nullify man's freedom. Kant expressed himself as follows: *"Mutato nomine de te fabula narratur.*[90] From all this it is clear that we daily act in the same way, and that therefore 'in Adam all sinned' and still sin; except that in us there is presupposed an innate propensity to transgression."[91]

Kant also anticipated Brunner in that, while acknowledging the presence of "an already innate wickedness in our nature," he postulated a recapitulation of the Adamic history in terms of an early infantile period in the existence of each individual, holding that "we must search for the causes of each deliberate transgression in a previous period of our lives, far back to that period wherein the use of reason had not yet developed, and thus back to a propensity to evil (as a natural ground) which is therefore called innate."[92] Brunner, understandably, was attracted by the opinion of Irenaeus that Adam when created was in a state of moral and intellectual infancy from which he was intended to develop into a state of maturity, and regarded this interpretation as "more correct than that of Augustine," who held that Adam had been created a fully mature person.[93] Brunner's theory of the evolutionary origin of man, however, and his notion of infantilism as a potentially evil substratum differed considerably from Irenaeus's concept of the infancy of man with its inherent potential for progressing toward maturity, from "image" to "likeness," but without implying any denial of the perfect goodness of man as God's creation.

90. "Just change the name: the story is about you," i.e., Adam is you! The line is quoted from Horace, *Satires* i.1.

91. Immanuel Kant, *Religion within the Limits of Reason Alone,* tr. T. M. Greene and H. H. Hudson (Chicago, 1934), p. 37. Original German edn., 1793.

92. Ibid., p. 38.

93. E. Brunner, *Dogmatics,* Vol. II, pp. 82, 113; *Man in Revolt,* p. 505; Irenaeus, *Against Heresies* iv.38f. The identical view is found in Theophilus of Antioch, writing c. 180, that is, about the same time as or perhaps a few years earlier than Irenaeus. Adam, according to Theophilus, was psychologically an infant at his creation and incompetent to receive knowledge in a worthy manner; hence the prohibition against eating fruit from the tree of knowledge (as he called it). A child is at first nourished with milk, Theophilus explained, and only as he grows up does he advance to solid food; and so "it is unseemly that children in infancy should be wise beyond their years, for as one increases in stature by orderly progress, so he does also in wisdom" (*To Autolycus* ii.25).

CHAPTER 8

The Perfection of the Creature

We have seen that the presence of evil in the world has been variously explained as inherent in the very nature of creaturely existence. The presupposition of the dualist was that matter itself is essentially evil and that therefore the universe in its material aspect is inescapably evil and in radical conflict with the goodness that is regarded as belonging to entities that are spiritual; but this in turn raised insoluble problems in connection with the nature of God and his association with the universe. Others, like Leibniz, have supposed that in deciding to create God had no option but to choose as a model for the world the best from a number of possible but imperfect worlds, and that, having created this best of all possible worlds, he then set to work to bring good out of the evil implicit in its imperfection. Others again, such as Hegel, have postulated that the power of evil in the world has actually been beneficial, and particularly that the fall of man was necessary for the attainment of his true humanness and its freedom in that it meant for him the transition from the animal-like condition of undiscriminating innocence to that of responsible personhood. Somewhat similarly, the evolutionist sees the existence of evil as a vestigial relic or remainder of man's brutish ancestry which either man or that mysteriously fictional *deus ex machina* known as natural selection is steadily purging from the system. Comparable is Brunner's notion of the inheritance of an entail of atavistic infantilism.

Others have even propounded the view that the fall was some kind of primeval and prehuman event, Origen, for one, maintaining that the souls of men are in fact fallen spirits now undergoing punishment by being confined within human bodies, and Williams, for another, speculating that there was a primordial, though undemonstrable, fall of the Race Soul (whatever that may be) or vitiation of the hypothetical Life Force. Barth placed the blame for the problem of evil on nothingness, that menacing, hostile *tertium quid* and real unreality which, supposedly, God passed over in his elective work of creation, and which, so to speak, is the hinterland of the created order of things. But such theorizings are fraught with difficulties no less intractable than the specific difficulty they are intended to resolve, and the implications they carry for the doctrine of God (theology) and the doctrine of man (anthropology) cannot be approved as compatible with the realities of the biblical revelation. Brunner, indeed, is far from being alone among modern scholars in assigning to natural science and historical science, now together crowned with canonical superiority, the right to pronounce for or against the acceptability of the doctrines of Scripture. The denial of the factuality of the fall of man in Adam undermines the doctrine of Christ as the second or last Adam and opens the way for the denial of any other doctrines that are judged to be incompatible with contemporary scientific orthodoxy, such as the preexistence of Christ and his virgin birth and resurrection and ascension. And this, as we shall see, is precisely the road that has been followed. The canon of Scripture as the Word of God can only be replaced by the canon of the subjective and shifting word of man.

The right understanding of the doctrine of man is impossible apart from the right understanding of the doctrine of God. Christianly comprehended, the latter affirms not only that God in himself is perfect but also that all his works are perfect. This affirmation, however, does not require us to deny that there is a distinction between the perfection of God's being and the perfection of his works. The perfection of the divine being is infinite and absolute, whereas the perfection of the divine works is finite and derived, but nonetheless perfection within its own sphere. The contingent character of the created realm is evident in its total dependence on God, from whom it derives its existence and by whom it is sustained in existence. The perfection demanded of man in particular, created as he is in the image of God and entrusted with dominion over the earth, is that of conformity to the perfection of the image in which he is created, which inevitably involves conformity to the perfection of the will of his sovereign Creator. The injunction of Christ, "You must be perfect as your heavenly Father is perfect" (Mt. 5:48), refers not to the perfection of God's absolute being but to the perfection of God in his holiness. The perfection was there at creation, when God saw all that he had made to be very good (Gen. 1:31), that is, to possess the excellence of creaturely perfection. In the case of man, then, it was not a question of advancing from imperfection to perfection, or from imbecility to knowledge, but of consolidating the perfection which was his at creation by grateful obedience to the revealed will of his Creator. Thus the great potential of his human nature would have been actualized and his holiness established, and the still greater glory for which he was destined would have been attained. Man in his fallenness has lost this perfection and this destiny; but all this loss is redemptively restored, and more than restored, in Christ, the true Image, in whom man's full stature is achieved and his eternal destiny secured, and to whose image the redeemed are being progressively conformed until at last they are brought to "the measure of the stature of the fulness of Christ," which is the perfection of their humanity (Eph. 4:12f.; 2 Cor. 3:18; Jude 24; 1 Jn. 3:2f.; 1 Pet. 5:10).

The perfection of the creature which was there at the beginning will be there at the end, only more gloriously so, as the new heaven and the new earth, the renewed creation in which there is no imperfection, is everlastingly established and the consummation so long desired becomes a joyful reality (Is.

65:17ff.; Rev. 21:1ff.). Man, as himself part of that excellence which dignified the whole of God's creation, was created perfect—created, however, for a destiny even more glorious than his beginning. His formation in the divine image capacitated him to enjoy personal communion with his Maker and to fulfil that distinctive function for which he was uniquely fitted of exercising dominion, under God, over the rest of the created order. His power was matched by his responsibility. His self-fulfilment and the freedom of his being belonged inseparably to the daily conduct of his life in harmony with the purpose for which he was created. Yet it was from this full expression of his humanness that man turned away when he opposed his will to the will of the Creator to whom he owed the total goodness and the total meaning of his existence.

CHAPTER 9

The Biblical Account of the Fall

The setting of Adam and Eve in the garden is descriptive of their blissful existence in an entirely congenial environment, and the walking of God in the garden depicts the reality of the free and uninhibited communion they enjoyed with their Creator. Their knowledge was knowledge only of good. The designation of the tree whose fruit they were forbidden to eat as the tree of the knowledge of good and evil reflects the nature of the command associated with that tree: obedience to the divinely expressed will would mean the continued experience of unclouded good, but disobedience would corrupt their good with evil. It was not that evil was inherent in this specific tree, as though it was in itself noxious and deadly, for it belonged to and shared in the excellence of God's creation. The evil effect derived not from the fruit but from man's action in defiantly eating the fruit in opposition to the divine command. Evil was engendered not by the fruit of the tree but by man's rebellious self-will in deciding to eat the fruit. Thenceforth man had knowledge not solely of good but of good *and evil*. "Sin," as St. Paul explains, "came into the world through one man and death through sin" (Rom. 5:12). The act of eating the forbidden fruit was a rejection of the Creator and his will, a turning away from life which could only be a turning to death, so that this good tree was made the tree of death, now standing in strong contrast over against the tree of life "in the midst of the garden," to which no prohibition had been attached and which symbolized the fulness of life that was freely accessible to man; but through the folly of his contempt for the divine will man chose the way of evil and death instead of the way of blessing and life. Despising his birthright and his destiny, he was expelled from the garden. Only through the redeeming work of the incarnate Son would access to the tree of life be restored (Rev. 22:2, 14).

The account of the original act of disobedience and its consequences plainly illustrates the nature of man's relationship to the divine law. To obey God's will revealed in his command is to know true life and freedom. The harmonious union of the human will with the divine will ensures free and unimpeded access to the tree of life. Disobedience leads to death and frustration. This is because God's command is always designed for man's good. It is not an oppressive instrument of authoritarian tyranny intended to keep man in a condition of bondage. Thus St. Paul insistently taught that the law, coming as it does from God, is holy, just, good, spiritual, and glorious (Rom. 7:12, 14; 2 Cor. 3:7-9); and Scripture repeatedly asserts that it is by keeping God's law that man shall live (Lev. 18:5; Neh. 9:29; Ezek. 20:11, 13, 21; Mt. 19:17; Rom. 10:5; Gal. 3:12). To disobey God is precisely to choose death instead of life. The statement that "the soul that sins shall die" formulates this obverse principle (Ezek. 18:4, 20; Rom. 6:23). And this is the very heart of the human predicament, namely, that man, every man, is a law-breaker (Rom. 3:9-12, 22f.), so that he is now condemned to death by that very law which was given as a way of life. Hence St. Paul's affirmation that "the very commandment which promised life proved to be death to me" (Rom. 7:10). The law, which is God's standard of holiness, has become a dispensation of condemnation and death in relation to the sinner (2 Cor. 3:7, 9). But the fault is in the sinner, not in the law. Fallen man's great need and only hope was for God's Holy One to keep the law perfectly and then to offer himself to death in the sinner's stead, the righteous for the unrighteous, thus annulling both the penalty and the power of man's sin and reopening the way for him to the tree of life, so that he might once again be able to live, and, more particularly, to *live to righteousness* (1 Pet. 2:24; 3:18).

The serpentine subtlety of the tempter's method is displayed in the Genesis narrative as he first put an apparently innocuous question to the woman: "Did God really say you were not to eat from any of the trees in the garden?" To this the woman answered that it was permitted to eat the fruit of all the trees except one, which they were not to touch, lest they die. But the devil's question sufficed to sow a seed of doubt and self-concern in the woman's mind: might this prohibition be an arbitrary restriction of man's freedom and the withholding of something good? And the suggestion of uncertainty regarding the divine motivation prepared the ground for the outright denial of the truth of God's word, for the devil then said: "You will not die. For God knows that when you eat of it your eyes will be opened, and you will be like God, knowing good and evil" (Gen. 3:1-5). The divine utterance was contradicted as a lie and made to appear like a hostile threat instead of a loving warning intended to preserve man in life, while the satanic assurance with its deadly purpose assumed the guise of a promise of blessing and self-fulfilment, indeed, of becoming godlike. The sin of man, however, did not lie in the ordeal of being tempted but in the act of yielding to temptation and choosing to believe the lie of the devil instead of relying on God and the truth of his word.

The devil's declaration that God knew that if man did what he had forbidden him to do his eyes would be opened and he would be like God implied that God was actually threatened by the existence of man, that the design of the prohibition was to prevent man from realizing that he is God's equal, and that this restriction was an intolerable violation of man's right of self-determination. The implication was not only that God was intent on cruelly keeping man in a state of subservience but also that the warning that death would follow disobedience was no more than a device for frightening man and perpetuating his servile existence. The prospect held before man of being God's equal was one with the satanic desire to be God's rival and thus of crowning the impulse of rebellion with the overthrow of God himself and becoming the possessor of all things. Throughout history Satan has continued to tempt man to imagine that he has it within his power to seize for himself the lordship over God's vineyard (cf. Mk. 12:11ff.). But to obey the malevolent adversary instead of the beneficent Creator, who is Lord of all, is folly of the most irresponsible and inexcusable kind; for man who is made in the divine image knows full well that he is a finite creature, that he owes his existence and all his faculties to his Creator, and that he is answerable to God for his conduct. The temptation of the devil in the garden was an incitement to obliterate the divine image in which we are created—an obliteration, however, that can never be achieved because that image with which we are stamped is constitutional to our being, indeed is the ineradicable root of our humanity.

To know evil was certainly a new experience for man, who had not known it hitherto; but it did not belong to his good to know evil (as some have supposed).[1] It is in his fallenness that man knows evil, and man's true good coincides with the entire absence of evil, as the consummation of all things will show, when at last, as at first, it is good alone that he will know. God, it is true, said, "Behold, the man has become like one of us, knowing good and evil" (Gen. 3:22), but this cannot mean that evil had after all turned out to be good, in that man by his disobedience had attained to equality with God in accordance with the assurance given by the devil. There is no way in which the finite can exalt itself to identity and rivalry with the infinite. Fallen man has become godlike in the sense that, now knowing both good and evil, he has to distinguish between them. But his godlikeness is a perverted godlikeness, for now that his life is based on the devil's lie he calls good evil and evil good. The perversion of his judgment is the evidence of his fallenness. Hence the woe pronounced by the prophet against "those who call evil good and good evil, who put darkness for light and light for darkness" (Is. 5:20), and the declaration in the gospel that men stand condemned by the fact that, though light has come into the world, they "loved darkness rather than light, because their deeds were evil"—with the further explanation that "every one who does evil hates the light and does not come to the light, lest his deeds should be exposed" (Jn. 3:19f.). Man knows good and evil in a manner altogether contrary to God's knowledge of good and evil. His discernment is inverted as well as perverted. Only by the renewal of his mind in Christ is he able again to distinguish rightly between good and evil (cf. Rom. 12:2). Unregenerate persons, as St. Paul told the Christians in Ephesus, are plagued by "the futility of their minds," because, "alienated from the life of God, they are darkened in their understanding." Consequently, there is a fundamental need for them to "be renewed in the spirit of

1. See, e.g., pp. 96ff. above.

their minds" and to "put on the new man, created after the likeness of God in true righteousness and holiness" (Eph. 4:17f., 23f.).

The tree of life in the midst of the garden stood as a symbol of God's purpose that man should live and not die. The banishment of fallen man from that tree did not betoken the failure of the divine purpose or the victory of death over life. Man's banishment, moreover, was more than a punitive measure on God's part; it was at the same time an act of mercy. For man evermore to live a life founded on falsehood would have been totally disastrous for man—as the devil intended it to be—and disastrous also for creation over which man had been placed. And God had no intention of abandoning his work to disaster, which would indeed have been the defeat of the divine will. The blocking of the way to the tree of life symbolized the unimpaired sovereignty of God over all he had made. God was not taken unawares or caught unprepared by the fall of man. Even before the ejection from the garden the promise of restoration and ultimate victory had been spoken: the seed of the woman, though bruised in his heel, would crush the serpent's head (Gen. 3:15). This promise and its outworking gave the assurance that provision had been made for redemption and for paradise to be regained, that the future, far from being without hope, was controlled by "him who accomplishes all things according to the counsel of his will" (Eph. 1:11), and that God's purposes for man and creation cannot possibly come to nothing or fail of fulfilment.

CHAPTER 10

The Meaning of Death

Death has meaning for man. Indeed, of all the experiences of the human being death may be said to be the one that most of all is fraught with meaning. Even when considered in its simplest terms, the death of a human person is the cancellation or nullification of the birth of that person into the world. Not only does it place a question mark against the whole term of his earthly existence; it is also the obliteration of his earthly existence. It is the annihilating surd that makes no sense. If it is objected that this applies with equal force to the death of animals and plants, we reply that this is quite clearly not the case. Death for man is not something merely natural, an inexorable phenomenon of the cycle of nature which is marked by the sequence of birth, life, and death. The death of an animal and even of a plant may cause regret and distress for one reason or another, but it is not, as with the death of a human being, the termination and disappearance of a life of transcendent potential and unique worth. The reason for this, as we have seen, is that man alone of God's creatures is constituted in the image of God and thus endowed with personhood which links him as a responsible and rational being to the person of his Creator. It is in this vertical relationship that man transcends the merely horizontal relationship of the brute beasts.

No person can genuinely believe that the meaning of death is simply that all the living with all the striving of mankind is after all meaningless, that death imprints the stamp of final absurdity on the whole. As the poet observed regarding man, "he thinks he was not made to die." It does not lie within the capacity of the brute beast to think, let alone to think about the meaning of life and death. But man, created in the image of God, is aware within himself that God's work of creation has purpose and therefore meaning, as it reaches out to fulfilment in "one far-off divine event, to which the whole creation moves."[1]

For the Christian believer, trusting the *risen* Lord, who assures him, "I am the living one; I died, and behold I am alive for evermore, and I have the keys of Death and Hades" (Rev. 1:18), death has been swallowed up in victory (1 Cor. 15:54) and the tomb has been deprived of its terror; but for the ungodly, who have not passed from death to life (Jn. 5:24), death and despair are insep-

---

1. Alfred Tennyson, *In Memoriam,* proem and cxxx.

arable companions. "Oh, weep for Adonais—he is dead!", Shelley lamented over the death of John Keats:

> For he is gone, where all things wise and fair
> Descend;—oh, dream not that the amorous Deep
> Will yet restore him to the vital air;
> Death feeds on his mute voice, and laughs at our despair.

And the death of a human person inevitably raises the question of the meaning of his and our existence:

> Whence are we, and why are we? of what scene
> The actors or spectators? Great and mean
> Meet massed in death, who lends what life must borrow.
> As long as skies are blue and fields are green,
> Evening must usher night, night urge the morrow,
> Month follow month with woe, and year wake year to sorrow.[2]

Yet even the God-denying poet cannot rest content with purposeless nihilism:

> Dust to dust! but the pure spirit shall flow
> Back to the burning fountain whence it came,
> A portion of the Eternal, which must glow
> Through time and change, unquenchably the same,
> Whilst thy cold embers choke the sordid hearth of shame.

In these and other euphemistic sentiments, such as "he hath awakened from the dream of life" and "'tis Death is dead, not he," Shelley groped for consolation.[3]

Thinkers and philosophers in every age have sought for words to express a vestigial awareness or recollection of an original state of blessedness that mankind has lost and longs to regain. Another poet wrote of "our instincts of immortality," declaring that "our birth is but a sleep and a forgetting," that "trailing clouds of glory do we come," and that "our Souls have sight of that immortal sea which brought us hither."[4] Reinhold Niebuhr maintained that "no man, however deeply involved in sin, is able to regard the misery of sin as normal," and that "some memory of a previous condition of blessedness seems to linger in his soul." In his judgment "the universal testimony of human experience is the most persuasive refutation of any theory of human depravity which denies that man has any knowledge of the good which sin has destroyed."[5] Niebuhr pointed to the fact that man's self-awareness of his own limitations in time and space indicated that in some sense he transcended these

---

2. One recalls the despairing line of the Roman poet Propertius: *Sunt apud infernos tot milia formosarum.*

3. Percy Bysshe Shelley, *Adonais,* iii, xxi, xxxviii, xxxix, xli.

4. William Wordsworth, *Intimations of Immortality,* proem, v, ix.

5. Reinhold Niebuhr, *The Nature and Destiny of Man,* Vol. I (London, 1941), pp. 281, 282.

limitations,[6] that "the self in the moment of transcending itself exercises the self's capacity for infinite regression," and that "it is in the moment of self-transcendence that the consciousness and memory of original perfection arise."[7] As, however, he treated the biblical narrative of the fall of man as mythology, it is not clear what Niebuhr meant when he spoke of "the Fall" and of "original perfection" or "a previous condition of blessedness." The uncertainties of his position are hardly resolved by his explanation that the concept "before the Fall" should be understood as indicating "not an historical period" but, for each individual person and also for all persons, the time before the act of sinning is committed. The account of Adam's fall is taken as a symbolical justification of this interpretation: "Adam," Niebuhr wrote, "was sinless before he acted and sinful in his first recorded action. His sinlessness, in other words, preceded his first significant action and his sinfulness came to light in that action."

This seems to be but another way of saying, like a dialectical theologian, that every man is his own Adam and, like Pelagius, that every man's sin is the imitation of Adam's sin. To place man's original righteousness and original sin outside of history, as Niebuhr did, and yet to wish to relate them to man's sin and fallenness within history is irrationally to confuse categories. The original state of blessedness and the event of the fall then become no better than floating notions unconnected to historical reality. Nonetheless, Niebuhr took the Genesis narrative of the garden and the fall as "a symbol for the whole of humanity." "The original righteousness of man," he continued, "stands, as it were, outside of history. Yet it is in the man who is in history, and when sin comes it actually borrows from this original righteousness. For the pretension of sin is that its act is not in history but an act of impartiality, a deed of eternity."[8]

One can but wonder how man has a memory of a state that does not belong to past history and how his activity "borrows" from a symbol that is without concrete reality. It is both more reasonable and more realistic to believe that this memory within man is in fact the remembrance of an original state *within history* to which he is therefore *radically* related, indeed that this recollection deep within himself is inherent in the divine image of his formation, which inescapably reminds him of the potential for a glorious immortality that was originally his and that, apart from the redeeming grace of the Creator, in his fallenness he has irrecoverably lost. Created in the image of God, who is Life, man was created to live. Hence the intuition of mankind that the death of a human person is something *unnatural,* a deplorable monstrosity contrary to and destructive of his true nature.

Denial of the reality of death is a desperate form of indulgence in self-

6. Ibid., p. 194.
7. Ibid., pp. 293f.
8. Ibid., pp. 293, 296.

deception. Death and the dissolution which accompanies it give incontrovertible proof of the falsity and futility of all pretensions to human indestructibility (such as those of Mary Baker Eddy and her followers). There is nothing, certainly, that the unregenerate person would find more welcome than the assurance that death is unreal and illusory. Death is so ungodlike, and there is nothing that more devastatingly demolishes the aspiration of rebellious man to be as God than the inexorable fact of death. Death is the irrefutable demonstration that man is not God. Death, by which even the ablest and most dominant of men are stripped of every faculty and power, is more than just the termination of human life; it is the failure of human life and the final frustration of every claim to self-adequacy.

These considerations indicate that human death cannot be described merely as the cessation of physical life, as is the case with the dying of brute beasts. The mystery of human death goes much deeper than that. It is sensed in man's inner knowledge that as the possessor of the distinctive qualities and competencies of personhood which flow from his constitution in the divine image he is born not to die but to live. The deep significance of human death therefore is spiritual before it is physical. The day of Adam's dying was the day of his disobedience to God, not the day of his bodily dissolution (Gen. 2:17). Death then may be understood as punishment or retribution, but it is punishment which man has brought upon himself. It is the wage he has earned as a sinner (Rom. 6:23). Every man is dead in his trespasses and sins before he experiences physical death (Eph. 2:1); and the latter bears testimony not only to the former but also to man's urgent need to be restored to life through spiritual regeneration. Man's death, spiritual and physical, moreover, is self-induced because the sin of which he is guilty is at root his own wilful turning away from God who is the Living God and the source of all life. Thus to turn one's back on God is to choose death instead of life. Man has only himself to blame, for his death is both the consequence and the judgment of his ungodly declaration of independence. Nothing more futile or stupid could be imagined than to seek one's own immortality apart from God, for to set up self-centeredness in place of God-centeredness is self-destructive. It is an act of suicide, because to reject God is to reject life. "God," as Christ told his critics, "is not the God of the dead but of the living" (Mk. 12:27).

Nothing, then, is more ungodlike than death, and nothing more conclusively negates the arrogant pretension of the ungodly person to godlike autonomy. The powerless and decaying corpse of such a person provides a shattering commentary on would-be godlike man. But the full horror of human death extends beyond the frustration of the grave to the deep-seated awareness that each man is answerable for the life he has lived, that the life ended by death is irrevocable, without the possibility of its being relived and corrected, that it is to the living God, before whom all things, including the innermost thoughts and intentions of the heart, are laid bare that the account has to be rendered, and that "it is a fearful thing to fall into the hands of the living God" (Heb.

4:12f.; 10:31). It is thus that the profound spiritual significance of the death of man is revealed. Man's death is the unmistakable demonstration of his fallenness and of the terrible judgment he has brought upon himself through his ungodly pretension to be godlike. "If our death were something other than a sign of divine judgment," Otto Weber observed, "then it could only be the sign of nothingness, and every decision would be made in relation to nothingness, that is, it would be either senseless or be the form of our own self-assertion or self-destruction. . . . Death can only have a revealing, an opening sense when it confronts us with the living God."[9] The distinctive significance of human death, moreover, confirms the reality of man's constitution in the image of God: that image with which he is stamped is the documentation of his accountability to the Creator whose image it is.

The problem of sin and of death, the consequence of sin, is resolved through the redeeming work of the incarnate Son of God, who "through death," his own death, destroyed "him who has the power of death, that is, the devil," in order to "deliver all those who through fear of death were subject to lifelong bondage" (Heb. 2:14f.), thus depriving death of its sting, which is sin, and the law of its power, which is the condemnation of the sinner, as "death is swallowed up in victory" (1 Cor. 15:54-57).

Having said this, however, we must remember that Scripture speaks of a *second death,* and that man's deep inner fear of death is related far more to this second death than to the event of the physical death of the body. This reality is summarily stated in Hebrews 9:27, where we read that after dying comes judgment. Final judgment that follows the first or physical death is the judgment of God that sentences the unregenerate to the second death. This is the import of the warning solemnly uttered by Christ: "You will die in your sins unless you believe that I am" (Jn. 8:24). Over those who through faith in Christ have been reborn to eternal life the second death has no claim (Rev. 20:6), and they are no longer plagued by the fear of death; but the ungodly who have rejected the gospel and whose names therefore are not written in the book of life receive the doom of the second death, which is the exact antithesis of life without end (Rev. 20:11-15). Herein is the real terror of the death of the ungodly, that of endless separation from God and thus of endless separation from life. In the death of Christ, the holy incarnate Son of God, on the cross of Calvary the immense and devastating seriousness of death has been made plain to the world; for there, in his sacrifice of himself, he endured not only the first but also the second death; there, in an awful mystery, he suffered physical dying and at the same time what is infinitely more dreadful, separation from the living God (Mt. 27:46); there he passed into our hell in order that we might enter his heaven (Jn. 5:24); there he who was without sin was made sin for us, so that in him we might become the righteousness of God (2 Cor. 5:21). For those who

---

9. Otto Weber, *Foundations of Dogmatics,* Vol. I, tr. D. L. Guder (Grand Rapids, 1981), p. 623.

are his the death of Christ was indeed the death of death; but for the rejecters of the divine grace that flows freely from the cross that cross has become the place of their final condemnation. The horror of the death of the incarnate Son, as the necessary means of our redemption, leaves us without any possible excuse for misunderstanding the true significance of human death.

CHAPTER 11

Original Sin

The doctrine of original sin postulates that the first sin of the first man, Adam, which was the occasion of the fall, is in a certain sense the sin of all mankind, and that accordingly human nature is infected by the corruption of that sin and the human race as a whole bears its guilt. It is a doctrine which never fails to raise a number of quite basic questions. How can the sin of one man be attributed to all men? Why should the responsibility and guilt of one man be a burden imposed on all men? Is not the very concept of original sin arbitrary and unjust? As we seek a right understanding of this difficult subject we can conveniently start with the consideration of two important realities which are commonly accepted as true: first, the fact of the universality of human sin, and, second, the fact that each person is answerable for his own sin, not for another's. Proof that these realities have a prominent place in biblical teaching is hardly necessary. In his letter to the Romans St. Paul draws attention to the scriptural emphasis on the worldwide sinfulness of mankind and insists that, regardless of race or culture, "all men, both Jews and Greeks, are under the power of sin." Among the passages he cites from the Old Testament is the opening section of Psalm 14: "None is righteous, no, not one; no one understands, no one seeks for God. All have turned aside, together they have gone wrong; no one does good, not even one." This necessarily means that "there is no distinction, since all have sinned and fall short of the glory of God" (Rom. 3:9-12, 19-20, 22f.).

The principle that each person is responsible for his own sin is also pervasively present in the doctrine of Scripture, repeatedly stressing as it does the need for personal repentance, personal faith, and personal holiness. It is unequivocally affirmed, for example, in the declaration of the prophet Ezekiel that "the soul [= person] that sins shall die," that "the son shall not suffer for the iniquity of the father, nor the father suffer for the iniquity of the son," and that "the righteousness of the righteous shall be upon himself, and the wickedness of the wicked shall be upon himself" (Ezek. 18:20). Guilt before God is personal and individual.

This principle, however, does not justify the conclusion that the evil effects of sin are limited to the individual who commits it. On the contrary, the sin of one has a corrupting influence on others and on society in general. The

125

Bible is perfectly clear regarding the social obligations of the individual and in no way sanctions the detached isolationism of the individualist. John Donne's perception that "no man is an island"[1] is a thoroughly biblical perception. This is the import of the admonition of the second commandment in the Decalogue, that God visits the iniquity of the fathers upon the children to the third and fourth generation of those who hate him, but shows steadfast love to the thousandth generation[2] of those who love him and keep his commandments (Ex. 20:5f.); for this teaches, not that children are punished for sins committed not by themselves but by their fathers, but that parents have a responsibility for the upbringing of their children and for the successive generations: by their instruction and example their children may learn to love God or to hate him; as lovers of God they will know his boundless goodness and mercy (to the thousandth generation), as haters of God they will bring judgment upon themselves. The principle of personal responsibility is thus not denied but expanded by this admonition.[3] Scripture has no wish to deny the interrelated solidarity of human society or to minimize the impact for good or ill that the conduct of the individual has on the lives of others.

It is not enough to explain, as, for example, Albrecht Ritschl attempted to do,[4] the universality of human sinfulness as simply the accumulation of the individual sinfulness of all persons—or, in other words, to say that just as everyone has physical limitations so it happens to be the case that everyone is a sinner. The biblical position is not merely that all men are sinful by their actions, but, further and primarily, that all men are sinful *by nature*. Thus St. Paul instructed the Ephesian believers that "we were by nature the children of wrath, like the rest of mankind" (Eph. 2:3). So also David, while acknowledging his personal guilt and accountability to God for his own sin—"I know my transgressions, and my sin is ever before me. Against thee, thee only, have I sinned, and done that which is evil in thy sight, so that thou art justified in thy sentence

1. John Donne, *Devotions upon Emergent Occasions* 17, written in 1623 and first published the following year.

2. God "shows mercy to the thousandths, *i.e.* to the thousandth generation. . . . The cardinal number is used here for the ordinal, for which there was no special form in the case of *eleph*" (C. F. Keil and F. Delitzsch, *Commentary on the Pentateuch*, Vol. II, tr. James Martin [Edinburgh, 1872], p. 116). Likewise the Hebrew is rendered "unto the thousandth generation" in *The Pentateuch and Haftorahs,* ed. J. H. Hertz, Vol. I, p. 296 (no date or place of publication given).

3. Cf. Calvin's comment: "When God declares that he will cast back the iniquity of the fathers into the bosom of the children, he does not mean that he will take vengeance on poor wretches who have never deserved anything of the sort, but that he is at liberty to punish the crimes of the fathers upon their children and descendants, with the proviso that they too may be justly punished, as being the imitators of their fathers" (*Harmony of the Four Last Books of Moses*, Vol. II, tr. C. W. Bingham [Edinburgh, 1853], p. 114).

4. See A. Ritschl, *The Christian Doctrine of Justification and Reconciliation,* first German edn. 1870-74, tr. H. R. Mackintosh and A. R. Macaulay (Edinburgh, 1900), ch. 5, §§ 40, 41 (pp. 327ff.).

and blameless in thy judgment"—declared, "Behold, I was brought forth in iniquity, and in sin did my mother conceive me" (Ps. 51:3-5). In saying this David certainly did not mean, as some of the church fathers imagined, that sexual relations between husband and wife are inseparable from sinful lust or that sin is transmitted by the act of procreation; but he did mean that even the newborn babe enters the world with a sinful nature which is conducive to the commission of sinful acts when he comes to years of discretion and responsibility.

The assertion that we are sinful *by nature,* however, must not be misunderstood. The nature of which the Apostle speaks is not man's nature as created but as fallen. The distinction is this (as Augustine explained long since): for man as created it was possible not to sin. The nature of man as created was such that he could live entirely to the glory of God; the nature of man as fallen is such that he cannot but fall short of the glory of God. In the biblical purview not only do all the sins of mankind stem from the original sin of the first man but the whole of mankind was involved in the commission of that first sin and is therefore afflicted by its consequences—consequences which flow from the perversion of man's true nature, so that now it is natural for him to be evil instead of good. Man's greatest need is to recover his truly natural state.[5] Unless and until he is created anew in Christ Jesus (2 Cor. 5:17; Eph. 2:10) the orientation of his being is so disturbed that the unnatural has become natural to him. He is at war with his true self.

In the Genesis account of the fall and its consequences it soon becomes evident that the curse which the first man brought upon himself because of his sin (Gen. 3:17ff.) applied to the human race of which he was the progenitor. Eve thereafter bore Cain, saying: "I have gotten a man with the help of the Lord" (Gen. 4:1)—an allusion to the meaning of Cain, which is "acquisition" ("getting"). This naming was an expression of hope that she had given birth to the Lord's man (cf. Gen. 3:15). But Cain, far from being the desired deliverer, grew up to be the first murderer. Well before the occurrence of this dreadful deed of fratricide, however, Eve had discerned Cain's depraved character and had expressed the disappointment of her hope in him by naming her second son Abel, which means "vanity." That Abel, though innocent of offense against Cain, was not without sin is indicated by his action in bringing the firstlings of his flock as an offering to the Lord God and, further, by the event of his dying (from whatever cause), death being the entail of sin. Eve's naming of her third son Seth, signifying "appointed," gave evidence of her confidence in the divine faithfulness and her trust that in the appearance of Seth there was a replacement for Abel ("she said, 'God has appointed for me another child instead of

5. "While we abide in the natural state we abide in virtue," John of Damascus wrote in the eighth century, "but when we deviate from the natural state, that is from virtue, we come into an unnatural state and dwell in wickedness. Repentance is the returning from the unnatural into the natural state" (*On the Orthodox Faith* ii.30).

Abel' ") and the restoration of the line of promise that in God's good time would lead to the advent of the woman's Seed, who would crush the serpent's head (Gen. 3:15; 4:25).

The bearing of these three sons and the unfolding history of hope and tragedy, of bitter disappointment and then revival of hope, plainly demonstrated to the first parents that their fallenness was the fallenness also of their children. The line of promise, restored in Seth, continued in the succeeding generations through Enosh, Kenan, Mahalalel, Jared, Enoch, Methuselah, Lamech, and Noah (Gen. 5:6-32). But meanwhile the sinful perversion of human behavior had become so intense that lust and violence threatened the devastation of all human society. "The Lord," we read, "saw that the wickedness of man was great in the earth, and every imagination of the thoughts of his heart was only evil continually" (Gen. 6:5). There followed the drastic judgment of the flood—an ordeal in which the line of promise was reduced to the single thread of Noah and his immediate family, who were brought safely through the terrors of this cataclysm. In this, as in all subsequent history, there is ample proof both that sin is a debasing and deadly poison in human nature and also that God sovereignly remains in control of his creation, visiting the wicked with condign judgment and at the same time preserving against all the forces of evil the line that leads to the fulfilment of his promise of redemption and the ultimate elimination of all unrighteousness. The flood of Noah's day is a warning, as is every other judgment throughout the course of human history, of the inevitability of final judgment. The lesson was driven home by St. Peter, who wrote that "if God did not spare the ancient world, but preserved Noah, a herald of righteousness, with seven other persons, when he brought a flood upon the world of the ungodly; if by turning the cities of Sodom and Gomorrah to ashes he condemned them to extinction and made them an example to those who were to be ungodly; and if he rescued righteous Lot, greatly distressed by the licentiousness of the wicked, . . . then the Lord knows how to rescue the godly from trial, and to keep the unrighteous under punishment until the day of judgment" (2 Pet. 2:4-9).

ROMANS 5:12-21

The apostolic doctrine of original sin is nowhere more carefully expounded than in this passage. The argument of Romans 5:12ff. is concentrated on a comparison of two individuals, Adam and Christ, and the manner in which the action of each had contrasting implications for the whole human race. Indeed, these two figures are presented as uniquely pivotal in the history of mankind in such a way that the destiny of every person is determined by reference to them. Karl Barth aligned himself with the modern liberal mind when, rejecting the historical perspective of the New Testament, he depicted Adam as no more than a notional foil for the formulation of christological truth; for in his comments on this passage he expressed the opinion that "Adam has no existence on the plane of history and of psychological analysis," that "he committed the invisible sin," and that "the Adam who did this is not Adam in his historical unrelatedness, but Adam in his non-historical relation to Christ." The first Adam became but the shadow cast by the light of the second Adam. The fall, then, was "not occasioned by the transgression of Adam," but, according to Barth, it "occurred with the emergence of human life."[6] To postulate the non-historicity of Adam and the nontemporal character of the fall may be convenient to a certain type of the modern mind, but historicity is one of the foundation stones of biblical doctrine. It is plainly central to the argument developed in Romans 5:12ff., in which the historicity of Christ and his act of obedience is balanced by the historicity of Adam and his act of disobedience—not by the invisible sin of someone who never existed.

"Sin," St. Paul writes, "entered into the world through one man and death through sin, and so death passed through into all men, by reason of the fact that all sinned" (v. 12).[7] This declaration concurs with the sequence of developments narrated in the Genesis account of the fall. Man was made to live, not to die; but he was warned that if he disobeyed God's word, that is to say, if he sinned, he would die. Thus death was the consequence of sin; and this, as we have previously explained, was inevitable, for to rebel against God is to reject life. The universal prevalence of death is itself proof of universal sinfulness. Hence St. Paul's statement that "death passed through into all men by reason of the fact that all sinned."

This, however, does not simply mean that all persons die because all are guilty of committing sins; for this condition would apply only to those who reach the age of discernment and answerability. But little children of tender years also die, even though they are not old enough to have committed deliberate sins in the way that adults do. The death of little children is the most troubling of all calamities. In a specially tragic manner it testifies to the fact that there is something radically wrong with human nature. The *reign of death* (v. 14; cf. v. 21) is a reality for all human beings, no matter how young or old they may be. St. Paul points out, moreover, that "death reigned from Adam to Moses." (The Apostle, we repeat, is speaking of history, not of some noumenal realm that is detached from the course of human events.) The period from Adam to Moses was a period without law in which sinners did not break a precisely communicated command of God, as Adam did, and were not law-breakers in the way that the Israelites were after the giving of the law to Moses on Mount Sinai. Yet these persons also died; death reigned no less over them. Why? Because, as St. Paul has explained earlier, being created in the image of God the

6. Karl Barth, *The Epistle to the Romans*, tr. E. C. Hoskyns (Oxford, 1933), pp. 170-73.

7. The rendering of the phrase *eph' hōi* by "reason of the fact that" gives its most natural sense; cf. RSV, JB, NIV, "because"; NEB, "inasmuch as"; KJV, "for that." Some of the patristic authors translated it "in whom," namely, in Adam (cf. Vg, *in quo*), influenced perhaps by theological rather than linguistic considerations.

divine law was written on their hearts, and the inner voice of that law is the voice of conscience, by which all know that they are ultimately answerable to the Creator of all (see Rom. 2:12-16).

But, again, in Romans 5 the Apostle is saying that this universal sinfulness is connected with the corruption of human nature, and that this corruption of human nature issues from the first sin of the first man. And it is this conception that provokes the crucial question: how and why should the first sin of the first man have this adverse effect on all other men? Questioning of this kind is understandable, but nonetheless it proceeds from an oversimplification of the human situation and a failure to grasp the profound reality on which the biblical teaching is founded. In Romans 5:12 the Apostle is in fact asserting that the sin of Adam was not merely an alien sin, the sin of someone else, but also our sin, the sin of all, and therefore that there is a definite sense in which we and all others were involved when the first sin was committed. He is saying that when the first man sinned all sinned. The use of the aorist tense in the Greek, when affirming that "all sinned,"[8] confirms this conclusion, for the aorist tense is customarily used to designate the commission of a particular deed in the past. The Apostle does not say that death is the lot of all men on the ground that all commit sins (which would require the use of the present tense), true in itself though this may be. He has already used the same verb and the same tense in 3:23, where he points out that, in respect of being sinful and in need of justification, there is no distinction between one person and another, "since all sinned [aorist] and fall short [present] of the glory of God." The Greek aorist tense here, as in 5:12, defines a specific act in the past which St. Paul's argument identifies with the original sin of Adam. Had he meant simply that all fall short of the glory of God because all commit sin he would have used two present tenses instead of an aorist and a present. In Romans 3:23 accordingly a double rather than a single reference should be discerned: all sinned (aorist) when Adam sinned and all fall short (present) of the glory of God in their own personal conduct.[9]

We find the critical contrast between Adam and Christ, and the involvement of the destiny of all men in the deeds of these two men, no less plainly affirmed in 1 Corinthians 15:21f., where St. Paul writes: "For as by a man came death, by a man has come also the resurrection of the dead; for as in Adam all die, so also in Christ shall all be made alive." There is, moreover, another significant aorist in 2 Corinthians 5:14, where St. Paul argues that "one [i.e., Christ] died for all, therefore all died [aorist]"[10]—that is to say, the death of Christ was the death of all, what happened to Christ happened to all. The death which Adam's sin brought upon all has been cancelled by the death which

8. *Pantes hēmarton.*

9. Rom. 3:23, *pantes gar hēmarton kai hysterountai tēs doxēs tou theou;* Rom. 5:12, *eis pantas anthrōpous ho thanatos diēlthen eph' hō pantes hēmarton.*

10. *Heis hyper pantōn apethanen, ara hoi pantes apethanon.*

Christ died for all, and Christ's resurrection is the resurrection of all to that life which was lost to all through the sin of Adam. The analogy between Adam and Christ is as radical as the contrast between them; but before discussing this relationship further we must give some consideration to the connotation of the term *all* within the context of this teaching.

St. Paul clearly teaches that the universal effect of the sin of Adam is offset and counteracted by the universal effect of the saving work of Christ. The death that flows from Adam to all is overcome by the life that flows from Christ to all. To believe in Christ is to pass from death to life (Jn. 5:24); to refuse to believe in him is to continue in death. Hence the admonition which applies to all: "He who believes in the Son has eternal life; he who does not obey the Son shall not see life, but the wrath of God rests upon him" (Jn. 3:36). Obviously, all cannot be both in Adam and in Christ at the same time. It follows therefore that all are either in Adam or in Christ, and that this distinction demarcates the radical and the ultimate line of division between man and man: mankind in its totality is either in Adam, dead, or in Christ, alive. As the Son is the Image of God, it is in him that mankind when first created was alive, and it is in him that all the redeemed, fully conformed at last to the Image of their creation in the new heaven and earth, which is the renewed creation, will have everlasting life. There will then no longer be mankind in Adam, for the first death will have worked its logic to completion in the judgment of the second death, which is the death of death.

In what sense, then, were all present and did all sin when Adam sinned? It will not do to say that all have descended from Adam and have inherited a sinful nature from him, for sin is not a genetic unit which is procreatively passed on from generation to generation, and in any case, as we have already observed, the children are not answerable for the fathers' sins. Nor will it do to explain that the solidarity of mankind is such that the sin of one man, and particularly of the first man, cannot fail to have an evil effect on the rest, for it is not the influence of one person on others but the perversion of human nature as a whole in that one person that is at issue. Nor does it suffice to say that Adam was our representative before God, for the Apostle is talking about identification, not representation.[11]

This much is evident from the biblical record, that the totality of human nature was at creation concentrated in Adam, who was the original human being. The original sin of Adam was the sin of the totality of human nature. This perspective does not remove Eve from the picture, for Eve was bone of Adam's bones and flesh of his flesh (Gen. 2:23), and Adam was guilty of the first sin not only because of his participation with Eve in committing it but also

11. The concept of Adam as the representative, and even the vicarious representative, of all mankind persists especially in a particular tradition of Reformed theology, which also generally presents Adam in the role of the federal head of the human race on the basis of a divinely imposed covenant. For a careful exposition of this view see John Murray, *The Imputation of Adam's Sin* (Grand Rapids, 1959).

because it followed from his permitting her to assume the initiative of head-ship that properly belonged to him. It should be stressed, further, that in assert-ing that the whole of human nature was concentrated in Adam, the original human being, we are speaking of human nature not as a quantity or a dimen-sion but as an existential reality. The sin of Adam and the corruption it intro-duced were the sin and corruption of our nature, our humanity, for our human nature is one with the human nature of the first man. The recognition of this truth enables us at least to touch the meaning of the affirmation that in Adam all die because when he sinned all sinned. All human nature was vitiated by that first sin because the whole of humanity was present at and took part in its commission. But while that first sin gave rise to the vitiation of human nature, it is the vitiation of human nature, commonly known as "original sin," which gives rise to all subsequent individual acts of sin.

There is something analogous even in the history of a single person who, in a full life span, passes through the successive stages of childhood, adult-hood, and old age. The elderly man of eighty is very different from what he was when he was a boy eight years old. He is different in appearance and in size; he is different in the ways and habits of his life; his thoughts, actions, and circumstances are all different. Even his body is different from what it formerly was; its tissues and fluids have been used up, eliminated, and replaced many times since the days of childhood. Is then the octogenarian responsible for his conduct when he was, say, a teenager—some offense or misdemeanor, it may be, which caused injury to other persons, or, on the other hand, some deed of kindness or courage which called forth the commendation of others? Are we talking about the same person? Assuredly, we reply, for it is the one continu-ous life of the one developing person, even though visibly, physically, and in-tellectually great changes have taken place in him since his boyhood.

The existence of the human person is indeed bodily existence; but the humanness of the person cannot simplistically be identified with or located in the brain or any other component of man's physique. When a man has died his dead body cannot be imprisoned or otherwise punished for crimes committed during his lifetime; for a corpse is not a man and cannot be treated as re-sponsible for deeds committed through the instrumentality of the body when the man was alive. It is the human being, not the body, who is responsible for these bodily acts. The burial of the corpse is not the burial of the human nature but of a residue that is no longer human. Though at death matter and dimen-sion remain unaltered in the corpse, there is no power of volition or energy of emotion; though the brain tissue is intact, there is no intellect. The mind and the will and the temperament of the human person cannot be anatomically dis-sected. The humanness of our nature, whether concentrated in one individual or distributed among many, is an intangible mystery. The possession, then, of human nature is not the possession of a material substance, and by the same token the corruption of human nature is not the corruption of a material sub-stance.

Let us ask what is an ancient question: At what stage does an acorn become an oak? When root and shoot are put forth? when it becomes a sapling? or when it has grown to a mighty tree? The answer is not to be found by isolating a single stage from all the other stages; for each stage is but a period in the total existence of the oak, and one period cannot be dissociated from the others if the concept of the oak is to be maintained in its integrity. The explanation of the oak tree is that of a progressive history or sequence of developments. The tree may realistically be conceived as already present in the acorn; but the acorn is only the beginning, not the end: its generic history as an oak tree extends beyond the phase of the acorn, and an adequate understanding of what is meant by an oak tree depends on the inclusion of every phase of development, from the insignificant acorn to the fulness of growth. Moreover, a defect in the acorn will lead to a defective tree. Thus the nature of the oak, its oakness, belongs indivisibly to the entirety of its history. So, too, a proper comprehension of the nature of man, our humanness, requires the understanding of the unity of that nature from its beginning onward. Human nature is one and indivisible; it cannot be isolated from its origin. Adam is the acorn; mankind is the tree produced from that acorn. Adam's defect is the defect of the tree of our humanity. Adam's fall is our fall, and it is so precisely because it is the cause and origin of the depravity of that intangible and indivisible reality which is human nature.

Let us listen to the inimitable John Donne preaching on Psalm 38:4, "For mine iniquities are gone over my head; as a heavy burden, they are too heavy for me": "Scarce any man considers the weight, the oppression of original sin. No man can say that an acorn weighs as much as an oak; yet in truth there is an oak in that acorn: no man considers that original sin weighs as much as actual or habitual, yet in truth all our actual and habitual sins are in original. . . . Thus sin is heavy in the *seed*, in the *grain*, in the *acorn*, how much more when it is a *field* of corn, a *barn* of grain, a *forest* of oaks in the multiplication and complication of sin in sin?"[12] And again, preaching before the king at Whitehall on 24 February 1625:

> How and how justly do we cry out against a man that hath sold a *town* or sold an *army*. And *Adam* sold the *world*. . . . And if *Christ* had not provided for himself by a *miraculous generation, Adam* had sold *him:* if *Christ* had been conceived in *original sin,* he must have died for *himself,* nay, he could not have died for *himself,* but must have needed another *Saviour.* . . . So the *Jews* were, and so were *we* sold by *Adam,* to *original sin,* very *cheap*; but in the *second sale,* as we are sold to *actual* and *habitual,* by *our selves, cheaper;* for so, says this prophet, *You have sold yourselves for nothing: our selves,* that is, *all our selves;* our *bodies* to intemperance and riot and licentiousness, and our

12. John Donne, Sermon preached at Lincoln's Inn, *The Sermons of John Donne,* ed. G. R. Potter and E. R. Simpson, Vol. II (Berkeley and Los Angeles, 1955), p. 121. I have modernized the spelling.

souls to a greediness of sin; and all this for *nothing,* for *sin* itself, for which we sell ourselves, is but a *privation,* and *privations* are *nothing.* . . . All the name of *substance* or *treasure* that *sin* takes is that in the Apostle, *Thesaurizastis iram Dei, You have treasured up the wrath of God, against the day of wrath:* and this is a fearful *privation,* of the grace of God here, and of the *Face* of *God* hereafter; a *privation* so much worse than *nothing,* as they upon whom it falls would fain be *nothing,* and cannot.[13]

By taking human nature to himself in the incarnation the Son of God gave it a new beginning. The human nature he assumed at Bethlehem was the same human nature Adam received at creation; that is to say, it was pure and unblemished human nature which, unfallen as was Adam's at first, had the possibility both of sinning and of not sinning. In order to redeem this human nature of ours it was necessary in the first place that Christ should gain the victory where Adam had suffered defeat. Accordingly, it was essential that the incarnate Son should submit himself to the temptation of the devil. This he did, and he did so triumphantly, and with this consequence, that, in contrast to our human nature in Adam which is fallen and defiled, human nature in Christ is godly and unblemished. It was essential, in the second place, that he should then offer up himself, in whom this victorious and godly human nature was concentrated, to endure the death of the cross (the profound implications of which will be discussed later) and thus bear and satisfy the penalty of death to which we in the ungodly fallenness of our Adamic nature are liable. And it was essential, in the third place, that he should rise from the dead and thereby confirm not only his total conquest of sin and death and the overthrow of their dread reign but also the rebirth of our race in himself, the last Adam.

Thus, as St. Paul explains in Romans 5:15ff., there is both a radical likeness and a radical contrast between Adam and Christ. Each is the recipient of our human nature in its primal authenticity. Each is our fellowman, Adam by creation, Christ by incarnation. The action of each has consequences which are determinative of the destiny of mankind. Adam by his unconcern for the will of God is the pioneer of our fallenness, Christ by his perfect fulfilment of the Father's will is the pioneer of our salvation. Both Adam and Christ experienced death; but Adam died for his own sin which is also ours, whereas Christ, being without sin, died for the sins of others. The condemnation of Adam's sin is not imputed to us as though it were the sin of someone other than ourselves, but by the grace of God the perfect righteousness of Christ is imputed to us who gratefully believe in him and receive that grace because we have no righteousness of our own. This is what St. Paul means when he declares that "God was in Christ reconciling the world to himself, not counting their trespasses unto them," and that "God made Christ to be sin who knew no sin, so that in him we might become the righteousness of God" (2 Cor. 5:19, 21). And so the

13. *John Donne: Complete Poetry and Selected Prose,* ed. John Hayward (London, 1929), pp. 556f. The biblical passages cited are Is. 52:3 and Rom. 2:5.

way was opened for us to pass from the defeat and corruption of our nature in Adam to the victory and gloriousness of our nature in Christ; and this is nothing less than the renewal of the image of our creation. The eternal Son is the agent of our new creation as he was of our original creation. In short, the Christian life of sanctification is characterized as the putting off of Adam and the putting on of Christ (cf. Rom. 13:14). "Put off *the old man* which belongs to your former manner of life and is corrupt through deceitful lusts," the Apostle exhorts, ". . . and put on *the new man* which after the likeness of God has been *created in true righteousness and holiness*"—that is, the restoration of the divine image in which man was at first created; again: "Do not lie to one another"—the lie of the arch-liar is at the root of our fallenness—"seeing that you have put off *the old man* with his practices, and have put on *the new man, which is being renewed in knowledge *after the image of his Creator*" (Eph. 4:22-24; Col. 3:9f.). Christiformity is the completion of our creation in the image of God.

> We think that Paradise and Calvary,
>   Christ's Cross and Adam's tree, stood in one place;
> Look, Lord, and find both Adams met in me;
>   As the first Adam's sweat surrounds my face,
>   May the last Adam's blood my soul embrace.
>
> So, in his purple wrapped, receive me, Lord,
>   By these his thorns give me his other crown;
> And as to others' souls I preached thy word,
>   Be this my text, my sermon to mine own,
>   Therefore that he may raise the Lord throws down.[14]

EVIDENCES OF THE FALL

The dire consequences of the fall of man stand out with unmistakable plainness throughout the history of human society. The evidence not only surrounds us on all sides, it also is present within ourselves. The turmoil of the individual heart is but a microcosmic indicator of the turmoil that afflicts the community of mankind. Disharmony and disorientation prevail so obviously that it is folly to deny that the human race is plagued with problems of the most serious nature—problems, moreover, which, even when frankly acknowledged, man has shown himself signally unsuccessful in solving. Among contemporary sociologists some wishfully profess optimism for future improvement and others are gripped by the despair of disillusionment, but it is generally agreed that as things are, man is not man as he should be. The advances of science and technology have failed to produce the ethical amelioration of society and the spread of human brotherhood that had been confidently predicted. In some quarters, indeed, the disappointments that have attended the

14. John Donne, *Hymn to God my God, in my Sickness.*

so-called progress of civilization have given rise to a vain nostalgia for a mode of existence that is regarded as simple and satisfying because it is primitive and unsophisticated. The trouble is that progress, which is not evil in itself, is invariably accompanied or overtaken by a sort of nemesis which blights the achievements of man, so that he almost invariably puts these achievements to uses which are harmful as well as to uses which are beneficial to his fellow-man.

The bright promise of the remarkable potential inherent in human nature seems to be darkened by a curse, and this is particularly frustrating for the humanist who, having no time for the Christian doctrine of the fall, must do all he can to persuade himself that man is the master of his destiny. One such has written admiringly of the "new world" which man has created by his scientific discoveries and inventions, but admits regretfully that man has not succeeded in being god over himself. He speaks frankly of "a sense of futility with regard to all his activities" which man experiences, and he acknowledges that "while we have created wonderful things we have failed to make ourselves beings for whom this tremendous effort would seem worthwhile," and that "ours is a life not of brotherliness, happiness, contentment but of spiritual chaos and bewilderment close to a state of madness."[15]

The biblical account does of course portray the fall as having placed man under a curse; for a curse was pronounced not only against Satan who had enticed man to distrust and disobey his Creator but also against the sinner and the earth over which he had been given dominion, with the result that man's work was turned into toilsome labor and levelled him at last with the dust of his origin (Gen. 3:14-19). His personal communion with God shattered, man guiltily attempts to hide himself from his Maker (Gen. 8:8ff.); and this is also the shattering of the meaning of his existence. Driven, through his own folly, from the tree of life, his existence has become rooted in contradiction because it is now existence with death at its heart. There is conflict and disintegration at the very core of his being. He has robbed himself of harmony with his Creator, harmony within himself, and harmony with his fellow human beings. This is the source and explanation of all that is wrong with man and the world he inhabits. It is the sickness unto death from which man in his fallenness inescapably suffers.

Even a general familiarity with the ills that have been endemic in human society from generation to generation is sufficient to correct the notion that the history of mankind consists of little more than the dates of kings and the conquests of armies—though there is no denying that rulers and soldiers have contributed vastly to the corruption and violence that belong to the unhappiness of the human race. It is society as a whole that is sick and disoriented, not just those who dominate it in one way or another. That even the authority of good

15. Erich Fromm, *Man for Himself: An Inquiry into the Psychology of Ethics* (n.p., 1947), p. 4. See my *Christian Ethics in Secular Society* (Grand Rapids, 1983), pp. 91ff.

leaders is powerless to expunge the mark of Cain from the community of men is dramatically illustrated by the annals of the chosen nation of the Israelites when Moses was their head. Their recalcitrance was such that the whole of that ungrateful and rebellious generation led by him out of Egypt perished in the wilderness and forfeited the privilege of entering the land of promise (Heb. 3:17-19).

The genius of the Romans for governing a great empire did not enable the executants of imperial authority to govern either their own passions or those of the populace at large. "It was the most frightful feature of the corruption of ancient Rome that it extended through every class of the community," W. E. H. Lecky wrote.[16] He observed that "the pages of Suetonius remain as an eternal witness of the abysses of depravity, the hideous, intolerable cruelty, the hitherto unimagined extravagances of nameless lust . . . manifested on the Palatine" and "cast a fearful light upon the moral chaos into which pagan society had sunk."[17] The members of a society supported by a foundation of abject slavery easily learned to regard all labor as degrading and were content in their lethargy to allow the government to fill their stomachs with free corn and their hours with free entertainment. Gross immodesty and perversion, the abortion of the unborn, and the abandonment of the newborn were practiced with complacency. Add to this the pleasure with which, to the point of addiction, they thronged to spectacles of human carnage provided in the gladiatorial contests and in the bloody agonies of unfortunate human victims as they were savaged to death by ravenous wild beasts, and the total picture is horrifying indeed. "It is well for us to look steadily on such facts as these," Lecky remarked. "They display more vividly than any mere philosophical disquisition the abyss of depravity into which it is possible for human nature to sink."[18]

To the evidence of pagan authors like Suetonius may be added that of Christians. Tertullian, for example, the son of a Roman officer, had himself been immersed in many of the excesses mentioned above prior to his conversion to the Christian faith, and toward the close of the second century he wrote a treatise to warn Christians that attendance at the popular entertainments could only be harmful to their spiritual integrity. It would not do, he said, to argue that all created things are good because they come from God and therefore can be enjoyed uninhibitedly; for, he admonished, "we must not consider merely by whom all things were made, but by whom they have been perverted," and "there is a vast difference between the corrupted state and that of primal purity."[19] Regarding the theatrical exhibitions, he reminded his readers that "Venus and Bacchus are close allies" as "the patrons of drunkenness and lust." Immodesty is forbidden to Christians, he explained, and therefore "we are ex-

16. W. E. H. Lecky, *History of European Morals from Augustus to Charlemagne*, Vol. I (5th edn.; London, 1882), p. 262.
17. Ibid., p. 261.
18. Ibid., p. 282.
19. Tertullian, *On the Spectacles* 2.

cluded from the theatre, which is immodesty's own peculiar abode, where nothing is in repute but what elsewhere is disreputable."[20] The frequenters of the amphitheatre and its spectacles Tertullian described as "human wild beasts" who "could not find pleasure exquisite enough save in the spectacle of men torn to pieces by wild beasts." Only "if we can maintain that it is right to indulge in the cruel and the impious and the fierce, let us go there" to "regale ourselves with human blood," he challenged.[21] He insisted that as Christians "we should have no connection with the things which we abjure, whether in deed or word," and, indeed, that it was a sign and a witness to the unbelieving world that Christians did not participate in such amusements. "How monstrous it is to go from God's church to the devil's," he exclaimed, "—from the sky to the sty, as they say!"[22]

When the profession of Christianity became respectable following its imperial approval in the fourth century there was a moderation of the worst public excesses, but indolence and luxury continued to be the cherished ambition of the average Roman citizen. The ethical standards of the Christian faith were not pleasing to most, and even the warnings of "noble pagans" who saw state and empire heading for disaster went unheeded. In the early part of the fifth century, when the army of the Goths captured and sacked Rome the Christian religion was widely blamed for this calamity, and Augustine took up his pen to compose his famous work *The City of God*. He averred that the true cause of the downfall of the Romans was the ungodly depravity of their lives. "Why in your calamities do you complain of Christianity," he addressed the pagans rhetorically, "unless because you desire to enjoy your luxurious licence unrestrained, and to lead an abandoned and profligate life without the interruption of any uneasiness of disaster?" He charged that not even the terrible catastrophe that had come upon them had brought them to their senses.

> Depraved by good fortune, and not chastened by adversity, what do you desire in the restoration of a peaceful and secure state but the impunity of your own vicious luxury? Scipio wished you to be hard pressed by an enemy, that you might not abandon yourselves to luxurious manners; but so abandoned are you that not even when crushed by the enemy is your luxury repressed. You have missed the profit of your calamity; you have been made most wretched, and yet have remained most profligate.[23]

At the same time the Christian church had proved singularly unsuccessful in keeping its own ranks free from contamination. Even in the apostolic church it had been necessary for St. Paul to censure the toleration of gross immorality and scenes of gluttony and drunkenness, coupled with neglect of the needy, that preceded the celebration of the sacrament at Corinth (1 Cor. 5:1ff.;

20. Ibid., 11, 17.
21. Ibid., 12, 19.
22. Ibid., 24, 25.
23. Augustine, *On the City of God,* tr. Marcus Dods (Edinburgh, 1871), i.30, 33.

11:17ff.). Indeed, the purity of the church was under constant threat. The temptations of the flesh, the lust for power, and unscrupulous charlatanism, so foreign to the authentic standards of Christian conduct, continued, like an evil leaven, to menace the integrity of the church at every stage of its history. At the very time when Augustine was writing his *City of God* and deploring the profligacy of pagan manners the African bishops at the Council of Carthage in 419 promulgated canons enjoining continence and chastity on the clergy, denouncing the cupidity of avarice, forbidding the administration of baptism and the eucharist to corpses, the frequenting of taverns by clergy, the observance of heathen feasts, attendance at theatrical spectacles on Sundays and other sacred days of the Christian year, and condemning pastoral neglect.[24]

The corruption that had infiltrated the confines of organized Christianity has been vividly described by Lecky.

> The Agapae, or love feasts, which formed one of the most touching symbols of Christian unity, had become scenes of drunkenness and of riot. Denounced by the Fathers, condemned by the Council of Laodicea in the fourth century, and afterwards by the Council of Carthage, they lingered as a scandal and an offence till they were finally suppressed by the Council of Trullo, at the end of the seventh century. The commemoration of the martyrs soon degenerated into scandalous dissipation.

Lecky goes on to speak of the immoral lives of many of the clergy, the wanton breaking of vows of celibacy, the cohabitation of virgins and monks, and the surrounding of rich widows by swarms of clerical sycophants. "Great multitudes entered the Church to avoid municipal offices; the deserts were crowded with men whose sole object was to escape from honest labour." The behavior of pilgrims, who became virtually as numerous as modern tourists, and as irresponsible, did nothing to enhance the good name of the church.

> Palestine, which was soon crowded with pilgrims, had become, in the time of St. Gregory of Nyssa, a hotbed of debauchery. The evil reputation of pilgrimages long continued; and in the eighth century we find St. Boniface writing to the Archbishop of Canterbury, imploring the bishops to take some measures to restrain or regulate the pilgrimages of their fellow-countrywomen; for there were few towns in central Europe on the way to Rome, where English ladies, who started as pilgrims, were not living in open prostitution. The luxury and ambition of the higher prelates, and the passion for amusements of the inferior priests, were bitterly acknowledged.[25]

The degenerative sickness of the church during the medieval centuries has received ample documentation,[26] and there is no necessity for us to expatiate on it here. There were, of course, many good Christian men and women

24. The Council of Carthage, canons 3, 5, 18, 40, 60, 61, 71.
25. Lecky, *History of European Morals,* Vol. II, pp. 150-52.
26. See, e.g., G. G. Coulton, *Five Centuries of Religion,* 4 vols. (Cambridge, 1923-50).

by whose devotion the faith and practice taught by the apostles was maintained and whose light shone all the more brightly in dark places, but these were precisely the persons who saw and pleaded for the restoration of the church to a healthy state, perceiving that the very survival of genuine Christianity was imperilled by the unspiritual excesses of worldliness, carnality, and indolence. The Reformation of the sixteenth century injected a transfusion of the living faith of the New Testament into the tired body of the church, but even so its leaders had to struggle persistently against obstinacy and opposition of the most daunting kind. In England, for example, the revival of evangelical preaching and biblical exposition, the giving of the Scriptures to the people in their own mother tongue, and the reform of traditional worship in accordance with the doctrine of Christ and his apostles ushered in a new era of vital Christianity which, despite conflicts both political and ecclesiastical, was carried through into the next century. But a developing movement which laid stress, to begin with, on the partial competence of man, with the partial incompetence of God as its corollary, in the matter of achieving salvation, and then on the supremacy of human reason and the sufficiency of natural law, began to erode the foundations of the faith as increasingly it assured men of their own adequacy and banished God to an irrelevant deistic position at the circumference of the sphere of everyday reality.

The road thus followed led step by step to the atheistic humanism of the Enlightenment as its terminus. It did not take England long to sink again into a morass of moral and religious decay. The degradation of society at every level in this period, which became known as "the gin age," was so catastrophic that to call it brutish would be an injustice to the animal kingdom. Wesley Bready has given a graphic account of the vicious sports of the time, which "were characteristic of a rum-inflamed mentality, cruelty, gambling, and coarseness being their outstanding marks, and the ruthless torture of animals their pivotal allurement,"[27] the "appalling bestialities" practiced on friendless children,[28] and the shameless flaunting of promiscuous immorality in public places under the pretext of the worship of nature received from the hands of a remote Supreme Being.[29] Dramatic performances were debased to the same impure level, so that "the profligacy of the theatre during the generation that followed the Restoration can hardly be exaggerated."[30] It was only the heroic preaching of Whitefield and the Wesleys that saved England from being plunged into a catastrophic revolution of the kind that destroyed the complacency of the French nation.

Though much more could be written, there is little need for further evidence of the perversity of the human heart, which can so rapidly deprave the

27. J. Wesley Bready, *England before and after Wesley* (London, 1938), p. 152.
28. Ibid., p. 145.
29. Ibid., pp. 158ff.
30. W. E. H. Lecky, *History of England in the Eighteenth Century,* Vol. I (London, 1878), p. 538.

life not only of an individual but of a community and a nation. It is a regrettable fact that the story of mankind is in large measure one of tyranny, brutality, lasciviousness, and superstition. The annals of the human race bear massive testimony to man's sinful fallenness and his need for divine grace and redemption. But we are not dependent on the records of the past for illustrations of human depravity, for our own age affords unmistakable proof of the same thing. Indeed, because of the almost inconceivable massiveness of its ferocity our age may well be judged to surpass all others in deeds of inhumanity, perpetrated often enough by those who profess adherence to humanitarian philosophical principles. The horrors of the sack of Rome and the French Revolution dwindle in size beside the extermination in our day of tens of millions of inoffensive persons by the Marxist overlords of the Soviet Union and its satellites, the holocaust of six million Jews in Hitler's Germany, and the savage massacres of populations by the despots of new nationalisms who rule by terror instead of justice and whose thirst for blood seems to be as impenitent as it is insatiable. Apart from the uncounted number of men and women who have been torn from homes and families and are suffering cruel tortures and indignities in dark prisons and labor camps and psychiatric wards, whole nations are confined and enslaved by the élite few who dominate the lives of the masses.

Such things bear witness in our own day to the terrible reality of evil and the fallenness of human nature. It will not do, however, merely to point the finger at others, for what we like to call the free world is certainly not free from the depravity of human wickedness. The rabid materialism and mindless pursuit of pleasure of the free societies go hand in glove with unscrupulous rivalries in the building of financial empires, the promotion of the big business of pornographic and other means of sexual excess and perversion, the exploitation, indeed the ruthless destruction, of young children to the same end, the termination of the lives of millions of unborn babes, the addiction to gambling and other expressions of the greed of man, and in general the self-seeking and godless existence of the multitudes—all these things and much more provide a mountain of evidence of the reality of original sin and the fall.

There is a pathetic element of tragedy, too, in the existence of so many who, without being offensive to others, live their lives aimlessly from day to day, uninspired by any lofty ideal and unconcerned with anything more than the routine of survival and the restricted interest of small-mindedness. John Henry Newman wrote of the troubling experience of "looking into this living busy world and seeing no reflection of its Creator."

> To consider the world in its length and breadth, its various history, the many races of man, their starts, their fortunes, their mutual alienation, their conflicts; and then their ways, habits, governments, forms of worship; their enterprises, their aimless courses, their random achievements and acquirements, . . . the greatness and littleness of man, his far-reaching aims, his short duration, the curtain hung over his futurity, the disappointments of life, the defeat of good, the success of evil, physical pain, mental anguish, the prevalence and inten-

sity of sin, the pervading idolatries, the corruptions, the dreary hopeless irreligion, that condition of the whole race, so fearfully yet exactly described in the Apostle's words, "having no hope and without God in the world"—all this is a vision to dizzy and appal, and inflicts upon the mind the sense of a profound mystery, which is absolutely beyond human solution.

Newman pictured an encounter with a boy "of good make and mind, with the tokens on him of a refined nature, cast upon the world without provision, unable to say whence he came," which would lead one to conclude that "there was some mystery connected with his history" and that for some reason he had lost touch with his parentage. "Thus only," Newman suggested, "should I be able to account for the contrast between the promise and the condition of his being. And so," he continued,

> I argue about the world: *if* there be a God, *since* there is a God, the human race is implicated in some terrible aboriginal calamity. It is out of joint with the purposes of its Creator. This is a fact, a fact as true as the fact of its existence; and thus the doctrine of what is theologically called original sin becomes to me almost as certain as that the world exists and as the existence of God.[31]

Another factor to which we have already alluded is symptomatic of a contradictory disorientation within the nature of man, namely, the failure that amounts almost to a chronic inability to apply scientific discoveries and technological constructions to uses that are solely beneficial to human society. The greatest advances are darkened with a menace of the greatest disasters for mankind. What promises the best forebodes the worst. Modern media of global communication disseminate lies as well as truth. The airplane is a machine of destruction as well as an instrument of neighborly goodwill. The conquest of outer space is opening up secrets of the universe, but it is also extending the scope of the deadliest forms of warfare. Even advances in medicine and psychiatry for assuaging the ills of men and women are iniquitously perverted to the invention of ever more diabolical methods for tormenting persons with inconvenient views and destroying their minds. The United Nations Organization, for all its good intentions, has become a hotbed of dissent and intrigue. Man himself is man's most intractable problem.

---

31. J. H. Newman, *History of My Religious Opinions (Apologia pro vita sua)*, first published in 1864. See *Newman: Prose and Poetry*, selected by Geoffrey Tillotson (London, 1957), pp. 757f.

CHAPTER 12

The Freedom of the Will

The first sin was committed when by the determination of his will the first man disobeyed the plainly expressed will of his Creator. Does this personal decision, this choosing to be disobedient, prove that he was free either to please God or to please himself? Many, as we have already noticed, have praised this original act of disobedience as an escape or advance on man's part from restricted to total freedom, or else as evidence that man is a completely free agent in the exercise of his will. The question at issue is essentially that of sovereignty. Is man in himself sovereign in the exercise of his will? Or is he in the constitution of his humanness, which includes his faculty of volition, subject to a sovereignty outside of himself? Are freedom of the will and self-determination necessarily synonymous concepts?

In seeking an answer to these questions it is important to realize that the commonly approved equation of the freedom of man's will with sovereign self-determination is actually self-destructive. The outcome of the original temptation makes this very plain. Before God man was free to enjoy the blessings of his environment to the full, with this provision, however, that he was not free to do what was forbidden. His decision to be disobedient was indeed a wilful act, but it was an act by which he determined himself against the freedom that was his under God. The prohibition itself was a reminder to man that his freedom is freedom under authority. What the tempter did, in effect, was to present this prohibition to man as a denial of his freedom to choose, an infringement of his rights, and a diminution of his humanness. The implication was that to be really free man must be sovereign in his determination, without interference or dictation from elsewhere, and at liberty to choose for himself what course he will follow. He was induced to believe that his self-sovereignty could be established specifically by the determination of his will to choose what had been forbidden. The assertion of self-will would demonstrate that he was after all free to do what under God he was not free to do. It is a line of argument that sounds logical and convincing. But it led directly to the fall of man. What is the flaw in the argument?

The flaw lies in the fact that man is not in himself sufficient. He is not and cannot be sovereign in an absolute sense. Even the sovereignty he has over the created order is a sovereignty *given* from above. It is a vice-sovereignty,

143

deputed to him under the supreme sovereignty of Almighty God, that is to say, it is God's sovereignty exercised through the mediation of man, not man's own exclusive sovereignty. The reason why man does not have absolute sovereignty over the world or over himself is simply that he is a finite creature who for life and logic is totally dependent on the power and the will of his infinite Creator. This inevitably means that the freedom with which man is endowed is dependent on the sovereign will of his Creator, and thus that man's will is properly free only when it is in harmonious unity with the will of God. As he functions in accordance with the purpose of his creation, so, and only so, does he function freely. (Even in secular society man's freedom is achieved under sovereignty, the sovereignty of the law of the land. He is not free to break the law, say, by committing murder, and yet he is able by his own wilful decision to break the law, say, by murdering someone; but then he must endure the unpleasant consequences of his law-breaking. Freedom to murder would mean freedom to be murdered, which all would find intolerable. The sovereignty of the law, therefore, is not in itself a threat to the citizen's freedom and self-fulfilment.)

That the freedom of the creature consists in conforming to the purpose of its creation is a principle we have already mentioned. A fish is truly free when swimming in the water and a bird when flying in the air. A fish is not free to fly nor a bird to live under water, but their freedom is not thereby violated; indeed, a reversal of roles would be lethal for both and therefore the end of their freedom. So also for man to seek to conduct his life in a manner that is contrary to the purpose of his creation is destructive of his freedom. The determination to be as God, to ignore or deny the existence of God, and to absolutize his own finite being is incapacitating and deadly. The will of man is free only when it is one with the will of his Creator. It is then that man knows freedom which is true and full. But when man arrogantly determines to exert his will in a manner contrary to the will of his Creator, it is then that his will ceases to be free. Instead of being free in the performance of God's will, in accordance with the purpose of his creation, his will becomes enslaved to the ungodly and unnatural determination to live his life without concern for the will of his Creator. Like a fish out of water he is separated from the true element of his existence, which is conformity to the will of God. And this proves deadly, because sin, which is self-willed opposition to the divine will, always brings bondage instead of freedom and death instead of life.

Thus St. Paul declares that unregenerate persons who "follow the evil ways of this present age" and "the spirit now at work among God's rebel subjects" are "dead in sins and wickedness"; and he adds that "we all lived our lives in sensuality, and obeyed the promptings of our own instincts and notions," with the result that "in our natural condition we, like the rest, lay under the dreadful judgment of God." The true freedom of life that is lived in harmony with the will of the Creator is restored in Christ, so that Christian believers can testify that "God, rich in mercy, for the great love he bore us, brought us to life with Christ even when we were dead in our sins" (Eph. 2:1-5, NEB). Only he who does the will of God abides forever (1 Jn. 2:17; cf. Mt. 7:21).

It is true that man as created had within himself a power of self-determination—a power, however, implanted in him, not self-generated. That power of self-determination, made clear in the communication of the divine prohibition, designated man as a responsible being who was answerable to God for his actions. It indicated the possibility not only of obedience but also of disobedience to the will of God. But the word God spoke did not confront man with an option, as though God were saying, "You are free either to obey me or to disobey me." On the contrary, it ruled out an option, for, by forbidding a particular action, it left only one way open for man to follow. Moreover, far from placing a restriction on the free exercise of man's will, it made perfectly plain to him the only line along which his will could be freely exercised, that, namely, of conformity to the will of God as revealed in the word he had spoken; and at the same time it warned him unambiguously of the dire consequence of disobedience to that word. In no way was that word dictatorial or restricting, for it set before man the way of life and the way of death and showed him how to shun the latter. Thus it was a caring word, a word of love and goodwill.

There is no justification, then, for imagining that man as created was in a neutral position, placed centrally between the choice of good on the one hand and evil on the other; for his feet were already firmly planted on the way of life and blessing. He already enjoyed beatific communion with his Maker. Warned against the disaster of disobedience, his only sensible course was to continue along the road of the fulfilment of his humanness on which he was already walking. But the devil twisted that gracious word into a tyrannical imposition designed to inhibit and cripple the freedom of the human will and advocated disobedience as the means of achieving absolute freedom and self-fulfilment. And so man passed from freedom to bondage as he sinfully turned away from the purpose of his creation and denied the divine image with which his being was stamped.

Therefore man is now no more neutrally placed between good and evil since the fall than he was before the fall. Before, he knew only life and blessing; now, he is under the curse with its sentence of death. Before, he was free in the performance and enjoyment of good; now, he is enslaved under the tyranny of evil. He has subjected himself to lifelong bondage (Heb. 2:15). How can it be otherwise when he has turned his back on God who is the source of all life and all good? Men in their fallenness are *slaves of sin* (Rom. 6:20). As Christ himself taught, "every one who commits sin is a slave to sin" (Jn. 8:34). Like their master the devil, ungodly persons promise freedom to others, and in the same old way, "but they themselves are slaves of corruption; for whatever overcomes a man, to that he is enslaved" (2 Pet. 2:19). By exchanging the truth about God for a lie and worshipping and serving the creature rather than the Creator (Rom. 1:25) they have set themselves to overturn the whole of reality. The fixation of the unregenerate will on falsehood is such that spiritual truth becomes incomprehensible to fallen man and is judged by him to be foolishness (1 Cor. 2:14). It is a fixation of the will before it is a fixation of the mind. The mind-set is determined by the will-set. Man's mind with all its amazing power is misdirected by his perverted will. The enslavement of the will which comes first leads inescapably to the enslavement of the understanding. The resulting incapacitation is so radical that fallen man, who has cut himself off from his Creator, is quite unable of himself to return to God. His alienation has separated him from the sole source both of his life and of the meaning and purpose of his existence. Apart from the undeserved mercy of God, he is entirely without hope of restoration. Hence the admonition of Christ: "No one can come to me unless the Father who sent me draws him" (Jn. 6:44).

God's work of redemption in Christ is essentially a rescue operation for the purpose of setting free those whose sin has placed them in hopeless bondage to the devil (Heb. 2:14f.). This setting free or liberation comes with the assurance that "if the Son makes you free, you will be free indeed" (Jn. 8:36)— not free, however, in the humanistic sense that being free means being indeterminately placed in a position of neutrality between good and evil, but free in the biblical sense that in Christ one is both free from bondage to sin and free to serve God, "whose service is perfect freedom." In this salvation there is no place for neutrality, for, as we have seen, true freedom is to be experienced only as man walks in accordance with the will of God and thus achieves fulfilment of the purpose for which he was created. Total submission to the will of the Creator is the key to total freedom. This is the authentic bondage which at the same time is the authentic freedom. It is the way of the fulness of life which releases the wonderful potential of our humanity as we conform our whole existence to the divine image in which we have been created. All persons without exception, St. Paul insists, are slaves—slaves "either of sin, which leads to death, or of obedience, which leads to righteousness." Those who have been set free from bondage to sin and its end, which is death, have become "slaves of righteousness"; and "now that you have been set free from sin," the Apostle instructs the believers in Rome, "and have become *slaves of God,* the harvest you get is sanctification and its end, eternal life" (Rom. 6:22).

Where the human will is concerned there is no such thing in the whole world as neutrality: every person is bound either to sin and death or to godliness and life. Only in the latter bondage is there genuine freedom, as the will of man gratefully accords with the will of God. It would therefore be more appropriate, with Augustine, to speak of the bound will rather than the free will of man, since the only will that is absolutely free is the will of God and it is only by the binding of his will to the divine will that man enters into and enjoys true freedom. This submission to, which is at the same time unification with, the will of God is the key to the perfect freedom of the incarnate Son in whom the psalmist's prophetic words, "Lo, I have come to do thy will, O God," have their fulfilment (Heb. 10:7-10; Ps. 40:7f.). For him who could truly say, "I seek not my own will but the will of him who sent me," it was meat and drink to do the Father's will (Jn. 4:34; 5:30; 6:38). This explains precisely why the Son is able to make us *free indeed* (Jn. 8:31-36). In the first Adam we are enslaved to sin, in the last Adam we are rescued from this slavery, and at root it is a matter of the will: "the former has ruined us in himself," Augustine wrote, "by doing his own will instead of his who created him; whereas the latter has saved us in himself by not doing his own will but the will of him who sent him."[1] Hence St. Paul's affirmation of "the glorious liberty of the children of God" in conjunction with which the whole creation will be "set free from its bondage to decay" (Rom. 8:21).

What is at issue here is the whole orientation of a person's life. There is of course a general everyday sense in which the choice between alternatives is indifferent. Eternal consequences are not involved in choosing to eat fish instead of beef, in deciding to plant roses rather than azaleas in one's garden, or in voting for a particular candidate in an election. In such things a person's will is exercised a hundred times every day. The important question concerns the principle of bondage by which one's life is governed, whether it is self-centered bondage to ungodliness or God-centered bondage to sanctification. It matters not how respectable a neighbor or reputable a citizen a person may be, his life is either directed not at all to the glory of God or it is directed in its totality to the glory of God. The person who has been regenerated in Christ is therefore enjoined, in contrast to the thrust of his former way of life: "Whether you eat or drink, or whatever you do, do all to the glory of God" (1 Cor. 10:31).

---

1. Augustine, *On the Grace of Christ and on Original Sin* 11.28.

CHAPTER 13

The Freedom of God

The true freedom of man, we have said, is possible only through harmonious accord with the freedom of God, and it is solely in submission to the free will of God that the will of man can attain to genuine freedom. But how free is God? Does he not, like man, have to wait on the development of events? Are not the apostasy of Satan and the fall of man contingent events outside of God's control? Can the entry of sin into God's world really be accepted as compatible with the will of God? Are such eventualities at all compatible with the doctrine of the absolute freedom and sovereignty of the divine will? These are indeed very difficult questions, especially as our own comprehension of ultimate reality is in the nature of things restricted by the limited sphere of our finiteness. There is transcendental truth beyond the grasp of our understanding. Even the apostle who had been give revelations of surpassing wonder and greatness (2 Cor. 12:7) frankly admitted that his present knowledge was but partial (1 Cor. 13:12). There was for him, as there is for all, a profound mystery surrounding the purposes of God and their outworking—mystery, however, which led him, as it should lead us, not to doubt but to doxology: "O the depth of the riches and wisdom and knowledge of God!" he exclaimed. "How unsearchable are his judgments and how inscrutable his ways! 'For who has known the mind of the Lord, or who has been his counsellor? Or who has given a gift to him that he might be repaid?' For from him and through him and to him are all things. To him be glory for ever and ever! Amen" (Rom. 11:33-36; Is. 40:13; Job 35:7; 41:11).

God is not to be reduced to the limited dimensions of our humanity. Between God and man there is an absolute difference, so that as it must be said that God is not man so also it must be said that man is not God (Hos. 11:9; Ezek. 28:2). God's thoughts and God's ways are other and higher than man's thoughts and man's ways (Is. 55:8f.); all the nations are as nothing before God (Is. 40:17); and what is impossible with men is possible with God (Mt. 19:26; Jer. 32:17, 27). Though this should go without saying, it is necessary today to emphasize afresh that when we are speaking of God we are not speaking of man, or even of superman, but of him who in being and power and goodness is wholly beyond and other than man. This truth we can only begin to express by the use of negatives and superlatives, by describing God, for example, as *infinite* in contrast to the finite existence of man and *omnipotent* in contrast to the limited ability of man; and to speak in this way is right, because the partiality of our knowledge and comprehension provides no excuse for not speaking about God. Speak about God, indeed, we must, for we cannot begin to speak truly about man unless we speak of him in relation to God his Maker. What is more, God has not left us to grope blindly in the dark but has graciously spoken about himself to man, and it is sheer folly for us to ignore the revelation which God has given us concerning himself through his prophets and apostles in the record of Holy Scripture.

In speaking of God we must keep in mind not only the limitations of our finitude but also the inadequacies of human language. The language we use itself shares in the restricted competence of our finite existence. It is no more able to express the unrestricted and absolute fulness of God's infinite being than we are able to comprehend it. Like Job, who said, "I lay my hand on my mouth" (Job 40:4), we must acknowledge that whatever we may say about God is not fully said and that, as his ways and purposes are so largely hidden from us, so we have no competence to be critical of God and to pass judgment on him. This, however, does not mean that it is impossible for us to speak truly about God or for God in communicating with us to speak truly about himself. Even though in the very nature of things the creature cannot fully comprehend the Creator, God's revelation of himself is both true and sufficient, so that there is no justification for pleading ignorance on the ground of innate incompetence on our part. God's word spoken through his servants and incarnate in the person of his Son is the light that dispels the darkness of our wilful ignorance (Ps. 119:105; Jn. 3:19-21). He who believes that word joins with the psalmist in saying: "The testimony of the Lord is sure, making wise the simple; . . . the commandment of the Lord is pure, enlightening the eyes" (Ps. 19:7f.).

In speaking of God, then, we may speak rightly about the freedom of God, even though the boundlessness of the divine freedom immeasurably exceeds all that we as men know and experience. We may speak rightly about it because it is declared to us by God in his self-manifestation, and also because we are, through union with Christ, caught up into the reality of that freedom which is freedom indeed (Jn. 8:35). Only God, infinite and omnipotent, is absolutely free; were it not so, he would not be God. God, we may say, must of necessity be absolutely free. Should it be objected that this conjunction of necessity and freedom has the appearance of a contradiction, the response must be made that we are struggling again with the inevitable limitations of human language as we endeavor to explain the character of God's infinite being. Any necessity postulated of the divine being is not an external necessity but an internal necessity arising from the very nature of God. This means simply that God must be true to himself and thus truly himself, that he cannot be what by nature he is not, he cannot cease to be what he is. The divine nature, unlike the nature of the creature, is not given from outside or from above. God's name,

"I AM WHO I AM" (Ex. 3:14), is the name of absolute sovereign existence. God is of necessity absolutely free, holy, just, loving, and sovereign over all; but he is not *under* necessity: the necessity is within himself, *it is himself*. He is not "free" to be unholy, unjust, unloving, or subject to some force outside of himself, for, again, to be "free" in this sense would mean that we were talking of someone other than God. It is with this understanding that we may speak of absolute freedom as necessarily belonging to God.

The freedom of God is such that "he does according to his will in the host of heaven and among the inhabitants of the earth, and none can stay his hand or say to him, 'What doest thou?'" (Dan. 4:35). Because it is absolute God's freedom involves freedom from contingency. His freedom and the infallibility of what he purposes belong together. In his unrestricted freedom the future is as clear to him as the past and the end as certain as the beginning. His word, which is the expression of his purpose, never returns to him empty and unfulfilled (Is. 55:11); for the word of God is the work of God; it is dynamic in redemption as at creation, and it abides forever (Heb. 4:12; Is. 40:8; 1 Pet. 1:25). "Remember this and consider," God says through his prophet; "for I am God, and there is no other; I am God, and there is none like me, declaring the end from the beginning and from ancient times things not yet done, saying, 'My counsel shall stand, and I will accomplish all my purpose.' . . . I have spoken, and I will bring it to pass; I have purposed, and I will do it" (Is. 46:8-11; cf. 44:6-8).

The self-designation of the Lord God as the First and the Last, the Alpha and the Omega (Rev. 1:8; 22:13) is both the promise and the guarantee of the absoluteness of his freedom and the indefectibility of his purposes. In his omniscient and omnipotent cognition the beginning and the end are united. What he starts he brings to completion (cf. Phil. 1:6), for the beginning ensures the end and the end fulfils the beginning.

It is in this freedom that God controls the course of human history in accordance with the sovereign determination of his will. To this truth the whole sweep of the biblical revelation bears witness, attesting by typology and through prophecies and promises God's overruling care and control of his creation and the establishment of his purposes in his Son (2 Cor. 1:20). In the remarkable recital concerning the righteous sovereignty of God over the history of his people, set down in Nehemiah 9, those who returned from captivity to the land of promise, chastened and repentant, unitedly acknowledged the faithfulness of God and the truth of his word which previously they had despised. The keynote of their affirmation was: "Thou hast fulfilled thy promise, for thou art righteous" (Neh. 9:8). This, in effect, was a reaffirmation of the declaration made long before when the Israelites had first taken possession of the land: "Not one of all the good promises which the Lord had made to the house of Israel had failed; all came to pass" (Josh. 21:45).

This principle of the freedom of God in his government of human affairs rests on his sovereign control of all things, which in turn follows from the fundamental fact that he is the Creator of all things. Moreover, because the Son is the divine agent of creation, the dynamic Word through whom all things were brought into being (Jn. 1:1-3) and for whom all things were created (Col. 1:16), he is the focus of the created order. His also is the sustaining energy of creation; in him all things hold together (Col. 1:17) and it is by his word of power that all things are borne onward in fulfilment of the purpose for which they were created (Heb. 1:2f.). That is why the Son is also the focus of re-creation through whom God reconciles all things to himself (Col. 1:20; 2 Cor. 5:18f.; Acts 3:21). Thus the Apostle speaks of the divine purpose in the fulness of times "to head up all things both in heaven and on earth in Christ" (Eph. 1:9f.). And since God "accomplishes all things according to the counsel of his will" (Eph. 1:11), it follows that for those who love him and are called according to his purpose all things work together for good (Rom. 8:28). Such are assured that in giving them Christ God gives them all things (Rom. 8:32). Because "you are Christ's, and Christ is God's," they are told, "all things are yours" (1 Cor. 3:21-23).

The coming of the Son into our world to reconcile sinful men to their Maker and to bring the work of creation to its destined consummation is the supreme demonstration of God's control of the course of human history; and in the light of the gospel this is most apparent where otherwise it seems least obvious, that is, at the cross of Calvary. There, we have said, the greatest concentration of the forces of evil, the fiercest defiance of divine truth and justice, and the perpetration of the most iniquitous act in all the annals of mankind took place; yet at the same time we see this depth of wickedness overruled by God in such a way that it becomes the high point, the actual moment, of the achievement of his plan for our eternal redemption. The perpetrators of Christ's crucifixion were not for this reason any less responsible for what they did. Their determination to eliminate the Holy One of God, however, posed no threat to the will and purpose of God which that Holy One had come to fulfil; quite the contrary, for their evil will was directed by God to the achievement of his good will. It was not that there was a coincidence of wills, for the will of the devil and the will of God are radically opposed to each other, but rather that the satanic will, contrary to its design, proved to be instrumental in setting forward the divine will. In his sovereignty God used the work of the Enemy to effectuate, ironically, his own foreordained work of redemption, so that what appeared to be the defeat of God as the incarnate Son's dead body was taken down from the cross and placed in the tomb was in fact the defeat of Satan; what appeared to be the crushing of the head of the seed of the woman was in fact the crushing of the serpent's head. Calvary had all along been the purpose of Bethlehem. The objective of the coming of the Good Shepherd was specifically that he should lay down his life for the sheep (Jn. 10:11; 15:17f.). And what took place at Calvary was in accordance with the Scriptures, that is to say, in accordance with the predetermined will of God. Of this Jesus was fully aware: "Behold, we are going up to Jerusalem," he told his disciples, "and everything that is written of the Son of Man by the prophets will be accomplished" (Lk. 18:31; cf. Mt. 26:24, 54, 56).

So also, after his resurrection, the living Lord opened the minds of the apostles to understand the Scriptures and especially their teaching "that the Messiah should suffer and on the third day rise from the dead" (Lk. 24:45f.); and the apostles, in turn, filled with the Holy Spirit, proclaimed that Jesus was "delivered up according to the definite plan and foreknowledge of God," and that the paradoxical outcome of the concentration of hostile powers against God's Holy Servant was that they did exactly what God's hand and God's plan had predestined to take place (Acts 2:23; 4:27f.). God is never bound by ignorance of future eventualities or by the development of contingencies over which he has no control. There can never be any frustration of the purpose of him "who accomplishes all things according to the counsel of his will" (Eph. 1:11). God's freedom is never less than absolute.

FOREKNOWLEDGE AND FOREORDINATION

It is in the light of this truth concerning God's sovereign supervision of all things that those who through union with Christ have entered into the divine freedom should have the assurance, in the face of all the changes and perplexities of this present existence, that "for those who love God, who are called according to his purpose, all things work together for good" (Rom. 8:28). They know and affirm this precisely because in Christ they have been brought into the midstream of God's purpose and their lives are under the control of his sure hand. Their security, indeed, reaches back into the past as well as forward into the future. It is founded in eternity. As conceived in the divine mind and in accordance with the divine will the structure of our salvation transcends the limited dimensions of our present temporality. This is explained by St. Paul in the declaration which follows in connection with the assurance we have cited above: "For those whom God foreknew," he writes, "he also predestined to be conformed to the image of his Son; . . . and those whom he predestined he also called; and those whom he called he also justified; and those whom he justified he also glorified" (Rom. 8:29f.). Even though glorification is still future, its certainty is indicated by the use of the past tense, which implies that it is as good as done. The glorification of those who have been called and justified rests on the firm foundation of God's foreknowledge and predestination; and this in turn is the basis of the Apostle's unshakable confidence that nothing in the whole universe, whether tribulation or powers both seen and unseen or death itself, can possibly separate us from the love of God in Christ Jesus our Lord (Rom. 8:31-39; also v. 18).

The explanation which some offer that because God foresees the future he is able to foretell the future, or, in other words, that his foreordination is dependent on his foreknowledge, is particularly inept, for it empties foreordination of all meaning. It would be mere clairvoyance. Any charlatan can claim to foreordain what he happens to know beforehand. It would make more sense to explain what God foreknows in terms of what he foreordains. Though they are simultaneous, God's foreknowledge and foreordination are not coterminous, and care must also be taken not to oversimplify matters by postulating the dependence of divine foreknowledge on divine foreordination. To do this can lead to problems of a different sort, especially if it is maintained that human history in its entirety happens exactly as God has predestined it should (and therefore foreknows it will) happen; for we have then to ask whether we have not stepped across the border into the territory of determinism in which man does only what he is programmed to do. The sovereignty of God is indeed absolute and his will cannot fail of fulfilment; but to conceive of the divine sovereignty in such a way that nothing whatsoever can happen that is not in accord with the will of God (rather than holding that nothing whatsoever can happen that can defeat the will of God) means, if it is taken to its logical conclusion (as some in fact wish to take it), that even the closing or opening of a door and all the moves in a game of chess are predetermined by God. History in all its details and developments becomes like the printout of a piece of solid-state circuitry. God becomes not only the Prime and Unmoved Mover of Greek philosophy but also the Sole Mover. Moreover, it is difficult to see how such a view does not leave us with a God who is the author of sin, or at least who is responsible for the presence of sin in the world inasmuch as he is regarded as having sanctioned and decreed it for the promotion of his own purposes.

Predestination is beyond all question an important biblical doctrine. But we must never forget that to us the ways of God are profoundly and inscrutably mysterious. The mind of God cannot be measured by the mind of man. God's judgments are "like the great deep" (Ps. 36:6); his thoughts are "very deep" (Ps. 92:5); "his understanding is beyond measure" and "unsearchable" (Ps. 147:5; Is. 40:28). The Creator of all is infinitely above and beyond all. Thus, at the conclusion of his discussion of the theme of divine election, the Apostle does not pretend to understand, but simply, by exclamation, marvels at the unfathomable riches of God's wisdom and knowledge and the unsearchability of his ways (Rom. 11:33). Much less, then, can we presume to comprehend the mind of God. We can but affirm what is plainly taught and by comparing scripture with scripture seek to guard against misrepresentation of so lofty a theme as the sovereign purpose of God.

The Augustinian position on the subject of divine foreordination is so called because it was first extensively formulated by Augustine in his writings refuting the Pelagian heresy during the early part of the fifth century. It will be convenient for us to consider it here as it was restated by Calvin, with his customary force and clarity, in the sixteenth century. ("If I wanted to weave a whole volume from Augustine," Calvin wrote, "I could readily show my readers that I need no other language than his";[1] and again: "Augustine is so wholly

1. John Calvin, *Institutes* III.xxii.8.

with me that if I wished to write a confession of my faith I could do so with all fulness and satisfaction to myself out of his writings."[2] Calvin rightly warned against the danger of approaching the question of predestination in a careless manner. To inquire into it, he cautioned, is to "penetrate the sacred precincts of divine wisdom," and "the moment we exceed the bounds of the Word our course is outside the pathway and in darkness."[3] He described "God's eternal ordination" as "that deep abyss" which is "a bottomless whirlpool" whose depths swallow up those who imagine that "the stupidity of human reason" is competent to investigate "God's eternal plan apart from his Word."[4] A degree of ignorance in regard to this matter was nothing to be ashamed of, Calvin contended; indeed, using an expression which he may perhaps have borrowed from Augustine, he commended the cultivation of "a certain learned ignorance."[5] At the same time, however, he insisted that "we must guard against depriving believers of anything disclosed about predestination in Scripture."[6]

All this is admirably said and needs to be said. But Calvin went on to propound, as Augustine had done before him, the dark thesis of what is known as "double predestination," that is to say, the doctrine that those who are not from eternity foreordained to life are from eternity foreordained to destruction. Defining predestination as "God's eternal decree, by which he compacted with himself what he willed to become of each man," so that "eternal life is foreordained for some, eternal damnation for others,"[7] he asserted that "God once established by his eternal and unchangeable plan those whom he long before determined once for all to receive into salvation and those whom, on the other hand, he would devote to destruction," and that it was "by his just and irreprehensible but incomprehensible judgment" that "he has barred the door of life to those whom he has given over to damnation."[8] God's preterition or reprobation of that portion of the human race which has not been predestined to eternal life takes place, Calvin affirmed, "for no other reason than that he wills to exclude them from the inheritance which he predestines for his own children."[9] "With Augustine I say," he declared, "the Lord has created those whom he unquestionably foreknew would go to destruction. This has happened because he

2. *The Eternal Predestination of God*, tr. Henry Cole in the volume entitled *Calvin's Calvinism* (London, 1927), p. 38.
    3. *Institutes* III.xxi.1, 2.
    4. Ibid. III.xxiv.3, 4.
    5. Ibid. III.xxi.2. The expression "learned ignorance" occurs in Augustine's letter (no. 130) to Proba; but it was also well known from Nicholas of Cusa's use of it as the title of his work on mystical theology, *De docta ignorantia*, which was completed in 1440. Cf. *Institutes* III.xxiii.8, where Calvin says that "of those things which it is neither given nor lawful to know ignorance is learned."
    6. Ibid. III.xxi.3.
    7. Ibid. III.xxi.5.
    8. Ibid. III.xxi.7.
    9. Ibid. III.xxiii.1.

so willed it."[10] Calvin frankly acknowledged that "the decree is dreadful"; but he added that "no one can deny that God foreknew what end man was to have before he created him, and consequently foreknew because he so ordained by his decree."[11] He held, further, that this predetermination applied also to the fall of man: "God not only foresaw the fall of the first man, and in him the ruin of his descendants, but also meted it out in accordance with his own decision."[12] The reprobate, he wrote, God "created for dishonor in life and destruction in death, to become the instruments of his wrath and examples of his severity,"[13] and this is their lot "because his immutable decree had once for all destined them to destruction."[14] The fall, accordingly, which "the Lord had judged to be expedient"[15] and which was preordained by "the remote secret counsel of God," was pronounced by Calvin to have been "most certainly . . . not contrary to, but according to, his divine will."[16]

It must be questioned, however, whether Calvin's powerful logical drive did not lead him to be overdogmatic and overrational in postulating the inevitability of the fall of man and the reprobation of many by reason of a divine determination made prior to creation. The basis of this postulation is the premise that should anything take place which is not in accordance with the will of God it would be a contradiction of the absolute sovereignty of the divine will. Man, it is true, is responsible for his fallenness because of his sinful disobedience to the divine command; but this disobedience is precisely contrariety to the revealed will of God. How can what is contrary to the divine will be presented as in accordance with the divine will? To respect the mysterious unsearchability of the mind of God is one thing, but to involve God in self-contradiction is altogether unacceptable. One must ask, also, how all responsibility for the fall and for the sin that occasioned it can be removed from God, if the fall was foreordained by the immutable will of God. Calvin, of course, could but insist that the responsibility for the entry of sin into the world rested solely on man. "Even though by God's eternal providence man has been created to undergo that calamity to which he is subject," he wrote, "it still takes its occasion from man himself, not from God, since the only reason for his ruin is that he has degenerated from God's pure creation into vicious and impure perversity."[17] But this qualification does not extricate him from inconsistency, for to say that "the only reason" for man's ruin is the perversity of his own defection ill accords with the assertion that God's condemnation of the nonelect takes place "for no other reason than that he wills to exclude them."

10. Ibid. III.xxiii.5.
11. Ibid. III.xxiii.7.
12. Ibid.
13. Ibid. III.xxiv.12.
14. Ibid. III.xxiv.14.
15. Ibid. III.xxiii.8.
16. *Calvin's Calvinism,* pp. 91, 92.
17. *Institutes* III.xxiii.9.

The problem with the Augustinian argument at this point is that it requires God to decree what is contrary to his command—indeed, to will what is directly opposed to his will. The line of logic (with its commendable concern for the protection of God) has been carried too far, so that necessity is created to explain, where the fall of man into sin is concerned, that God is not the cause of what he has ordained beforehand, even though in the very nature of the case what he has ordained cannot fail to come to pass. It is surely preposterous for us to imagine that God should ordain the entry into the world of that which it is his unremitting purpose to eliminate from the world. It is because the essence of sin is opposition to God and his will that God is the implacable enemy of sin. Sin evokes God's curse, not his indulgence. God wages war against sin (Rev. 12:7ff.; 16:14; 19:11). The ways of the wicked, indeed their very thoughts, are an abomination to the Lord (Prov. 15:9, 26; 12:22; Dt. 25:16, etc.). As there was no sin in the world when it came forth from the Maker's hand, so there is no place for it in the new heaven and the new earth, which constitute creation brought to its destined consummation. The renewed creation will be thoroughly purged of all those things that now disfigure the community of mankind, all injustice, homicidal violence, impurity, perversion, idolatry, and lying: "nothing unclean shall enter it, nor any one who practices abomination or falsehood, but only those who are written in the Lamb's book of life" (Rev. 21:8, 27). Sinfulness is simply ungodliness, and in the consummation of all things there will be a total abolition of all that is ungodly.

In the meantime Christ's disciples are charged to follow the example of their Master, not only by abstaining from the practice of sin because they are "born of God" and know that "he appeared to take away sins" and that "in him there is no sin" (1 Jn. 2:29; 3:5, 9), but also by engaging in warfare against sin (Eph. 6:10ff.) as good soldiers of Jesus Christ, who "fight the good fight of faith" and resist their adversary the devil (1 Tim. 1:18; 6:12; 2 Tim. 2:3f.; Jas. 4:7; 1 Pet. 5:8f.).

For God then to will, and to foreordain in line with that will, the fall of man and the entry of sin into the world would be directly contrary to both the character and the intention of God as plainly revealed in the Scriptures. If, moreover, the sin of man took place in accordance with the antecedent determination of God, the original temptation is enveloped in unreality, for there is then no way in which the state of man's innocence could have been preserved. Adam's probation is presented in Scripture as a real probation, and its outcome is not declared to have been predetermined; and if the probationary testing of the First Adam was unreal in that his defeat was willed beforehand by God (even though man is held to be solely responsible for his lapse), this cannot fail to call in question the reality of the probationary testing of the Last Adam and the counteracting power of the victory that is claimed for him. There is no denying that the entry of evil into the perfection of God's creation remains a deep mystery. Our own limited understanding must be controlled by what is plainly declared, namely, that man, formed in the image of God, at first enjoyed the blessing of harmonious fellowship with his Creator and was entrusted with the responsible task of governing himself and the world in accordance with the divine will, that this situation displays the true purpose of God in creation, and that this same purpose will most surely be attained, and is even now being attained, in and through the mediation of the incarnate Son, in whom, as the True Image, from before the foundation of the world and to all eternity the destiny of man is concentrated.

Though, however, we cannot maintain that God ordains what he opposes and approves what he abhors, we can and must unhesitatingly affirm the absolute indefectibility of his purposes. Constantly we see throughout the course of history that the forces of evil which threaten to overwhelm God's people are powerless to thwart his will, indeed that God overrules and harnesses them in such a way that they set forward rather than hinder his purposes. The consequences of sin and ungodliness are certainly disastrous for human society, but sin, as we have argued earlier, is not an entity in itself: it is not something that God created nor is it a foreign body that came from some alien source. It is the disobedient and corrupting use of faculties and potencies which as they were received from the hand of God are themselves entirely good. It is self-will in defiance of the divine will. It is the suppression of the truth about God, and therefore also of the truth about ourselves. Yet, granted that it is no threat to God and his purposes, God does not view with complacency the perversion of his handiwork. The sin of man is an affront to the holiness of his Creator, and the righteousness of God is manifested in the judgment he pronounces on the sinner. But judgment alone, which necessarily must fall upon the whole of humanity, inasmuch as all are sinful, does not restore what has been corrupted. Hence the need for redemption; and the seriousness with which God regards sin is shown not merely by the severity of his judgment but also by the immense length to which he went to provide atonement for sinners.

It is out of sheer love that God has provided redemption for his creation (Jn. 3:16; Rom. 5:8; 1 Jn. 4:9f.). Many, Augustine and Calvin among them, have asserted that because of man's universal sinfulness God could with perfect justice have condemned all persons to perdition, and this is no doubt true if we are considering the deserts of mankind at God's hands. But it was certainly not God's intention that his work should come to nothing. All are indeed, without exception, under divine judgment because of their sinfulness; but universal perdition, though it would have testified to the absolute justice of God, would also have signified the defeat of God's purposes in creation. It would have meant that the world planned and brought into being by God had failed to work, and so had been destroyed as a failure; and this in turn would have called in question the infallibility of all that God designs to do. The justice of God, however, does not exist in isolation from the love of God. His justice and his love are not mutually exclusive, nor does the one minimize the other. God, because he loves what he has made, had no thought of casting away his creation, least of all man who is made in his image so that he may be blessed with direct personal fellowship and communion with his Creator. Not only the destiny of creation but the doctrine of God itself is at issue.

What was God to do, Athanasius asked, confronted with the devastating effect of sin on man and the world? (The question is prompted by faith seeking understanding; it is not intended to suggest that God was in a quandary.) For God to have done nothing was unthinkable because the worth of making man in his image would then have been nullified as man sank from so noble an origin to the level of the brute beasts. The solution is the reintegration of man by God's renewal of his image within us, and this renewal was achieved by the coming of the True Image himself, so that by his redemptive work on our behalf we might be re-created according to the image of our constitution.[18] The key to our perception of the divine mind and will in the work both of creation and of re-creation is to be found not in conflicting speculations regarding supralapsarianism and infralapsarianism but in none other than the eternal Son, who as the personal Word is the agent of the divine mind and will and as the divine Image in which man was formed is the focus and also the locus of the destiny ordained for man before as well as after the fall. As all things hold together in him, in whom all the fulness of deity dwells, so also it is God's pleasure "through him to reconcile to himself all things, whether on earth or in heaven, having made peace by the blood of his cross" (Col. 1:17, 19, 20). Thus it is in the Son that all God's purposes for mankind and the world are gloriously realized, since in him their fulfilment is unfailingly assured from eternity to eternity, as he through whom all things were created is also the one through whom all things are reconciled.

ELECTION

The doctrine of election, according to which those who are regenerated by God's grace through faith in Jesus Christ have been chosen or elected by God to be blessed with eternal life, is so clearly taught in Holy Scripture that there is no excuse for disregarding its importance. It is essential to remember that this doctrine speaks of God's dealings with man, not man's dealings with God, and that consequently every attempt to define and explain it in a way that brings it within the limited dimensions of our human understanding ends up as a rationalization and distortion of a profound truth. Even though the election of some seems to imply the reprobation of others, we must beware of resorting to rationalizing simplifications; for this is not just a matter of simple arithmetic, or of love for some and hatred for others, or of favoritism and arbitrary choice. God is no respecter of persons (Acts 10:34; Rom. 2:11; Eph. 6:9); but he always treats us as persons, not as mere ciphers to be counted and categorized—as persons, moreover, of dignity and value to him since we bear the imprint of his own image. As such we were created for life, not for death;

18. Athanasius, *On the Incarnation* 13.

hence the purpose of divine redemption is to bring men back from death to life and thus to fulfil the purpose of their creation. And the work of redemption is the proof of God's *compassion* for his human creatures. Wickedness is not pleasing to God (Ps. 5:4) and the death of the ungodly gives him no pleasure: "Have I any pleasure in the death of the wicked, says the Lord God, and not rather that he should turn from his way and live?" (Ezek. 18:23; cf. v. 32; 33:11).

Jesus Christ is the incarnation of the divine compassion. He, the Image of the divine being, is the actualization of God's compassion for us who are created in that image. His pure life was a life of compassion and his atoning death was a death of compassion. Repeatedly we read that he was moved with compassion as he encountered the afflicted and the distressed and at the sight of the multitudes who were as sheep without a shepherd (Mt. 9:36; 14:14; 20:34; Mk. 1:41, etc.). Calvin was surely at fault in declaring that Christ in his lamentation over Jerusalem—"O Jerusalem, Jerusalem, killing the prophets and stoning those who are sent to you! How often would I have gathered your children together as a hen gathers her brood under her wings, and you would not!"—was speaking simply "in his character as a man,"[19] instead of acknowledging that this, as in the many other places where God pleads with men to turn and believe, was the expression of love and longing that the Creator has for his creatures. Concern to safeguard the absolute sovereignty of Almighty God can itself become so obsessive that it develops into rationalization. In the assertion, "I would . . . but you would not," the "I would" then becomes emptied of meaning for fear that it is incompatible with the authority of God, whose "would," it is argued, cannot be met by man's "would not." This is rationalizing at the one extreme just as Arminianism, which holds that God's purpose can be nullified by man's "would not," is rationalizing at the other.

God is indeed supreme, and not man; but his sovereignty is exercised in relation to persons, human persons, and the Person-to-person relationship between God and man flows from the formation of man in his Creator's image. This essential relationship does not in any way diminish or threaten the sovereignty of God; it establishes it. God's sovereignty is not a timeless impersonal abstraction or a metaphysical attribute. He is not sovereign in a vacuum. His sovereignty is displayed by being exercised, and it is exercised in relation to man who was given dominion over the created order. The sequence of events within the sphere of human history provides the setting for the display of divine sovereignty. Sin is the denial and defiance of God's sovereignty, but its entry into the world was no defeat for his sovereignty, which in relation to sinners is exercised in judgment and redemption. To argue that because God is sovereign therefore the entry of sin into his creation must be in accordance with the decree of his will is a rationalization which in effect removes divine sovereignty from history to prehistory and robs it of its essen-

19. John Calvin, *Institutes* III.xxiv.17; cf. *Calvin's Calvinism*, p. 254. Mt. 23:37.

tially dynamic character. In the biblical perspective, God's sovereignty is not dependent on the predetermination of all that comes to pass. It is confirmed by entering into engagement with the evil will that is arrayed against the divine will and overthrowing it, by actively demonstrating that there is absolutely no hostile force or power that can frustrate the sovereign purpose of the Creator, and indeed by effectively overruling the schemes of his enemies in such a way that they promote rather than hinder the fulfilment of what he has ordained to take place.

To postulate, as Calvin does, a distinction between remote and proximate causes is legitimate enough in the general affairs of everyday life; but to apply this distinction to the presence of sin in God's creation leads to conclusions that are highly questionable. If God is the remote cause of man's fall into sin, he is still a cause, no matter how strongly it is contended that it is not God but Adam, as the one who commits the sin, who is to blame for the fall as the proximate cause. As we have observed, the earnest desire to safeguard the ark of divine sovereignty has been thought to require the thesis that nothing, not even sin which is opposition to God's will, can happen which is not in accordance with God's will. We have shown that this was emphatically the position of Calvin, who insisted that "it could not be otherwise: Adam could not but fall, according to the foreknowledge and will of God," and declared his "solemn confession that whatever happened to or befell Adam was so ordained of God."[20] Given these premises, there was no way in which Adam could have gained the victory when he was tempted to sin against God. The only possibility on this understanding is that by reason of the divine predetermination he should fall into sin. But then, again, God is presented as having predetermined that what is contrary to his will is according to his will.[21] How is this to be distinguished from static determinism? Is it not tantamount to affirming that God has pleasure in that which causes him no pleasure, namely, "the death of any one" (Ezek. 18:33)?

God is love. Scripture does not set before us a God who is motivated by ill will or hatred for his creatures. Sin, certainly, which is opposition to his will and contempt for his love, is hateful to God and brings its own retribution of judgment on those who persist in it. If it is supposed that election and reprobation are invested with a certain balancing necessity, the former as necessary for the display of God's loving mercy and the latter for the display of his justice, this is to create a false dichotomy, for, as we have said, the divine love and the divine justice belong together and are not antithetical to each other. Nor does the divine love wait for our love; it is active for us even when we are without love for God, so that "while we were enemies we were reconciled to God by the death of his Son" (Rom. 5:10). The fact, moreover, that final judgment is not immediate but delayed is due, St. Peter tells us, to the Lord's forbearance, "not wishing that any should perish, but that all should reach re-

20. *Calvin's Calvinism*, pp. 90-93, 127, 267.
21. Ibid., pp. 290, 308.

pentance" (2 Pet. 3:9). The union of God's love and justice is of course pre-eminently displayed in the cross of Calvary where the Son's sacrifice of himself is both the supreme enactment of God's love and at the same time the complete satisfaction of the demands of his justice (Rom. 3:26; 5:8). The plain message of the cross is that each person must at last meet God either as his Savior or as his Judge. It is worthy of consideration, further, that even ultimate judgment is not something separate from or alien to God's love, for to acquiesce in the perpetual presence of evil in his creation would be incompatible with love for his handiwork and the eternal welfare of his people. Thus the elimination of evil from the world which final judgment will ensure also gives proof of his loving concern for what he has brought into being.

To speak, then, of "God's hating of the reprobate," as, for example, William Perkins did, is objectionable, even when it is explained that "this hatred of God is whereby he detesteth and abhorreth the reprobate when he is fallen into sin," and is postulated therefore as hatred that comes after, not before, the fall. It is nonetheless a scheme which makes rejection antecedent to the fall, for it is held that there was a decree of reprobation prior to the creation, "whereby God according to the most free and just purpose of his will hath determined to reject certain men unto eternal destruction and misery, and that to the praise of his justice." It makes little difference to protest that this is not "any absolute decree of damnation, as though we should think that any were condemned by the mere and alone will of God, without any causes inherent in such as are to be condemned," and that "all the fault and desert of condemnation" remains in those who suffer rejection;[22] for, as previously remarked, the notion of a predestinating decree of reprobation is founded on the postulation of a prevenient determination of God which is antecedent to creation and the fall and which requires that even the entry of sin into the world belongs to the same secret will of God in eternity.

If it is objected that the assertion of the Lord spoken through the prophet Malachi, "Jacob I loved, but Esau I hated," and cited by St. Paul when discussing the doctrine of election, shows that God does in fact hate some and love others (Mal. 1:2f.; Rom. 9:13), we respond that this is a manner of speaking in accordance with Hebrew idiomatic usage. A parallel is found in the saying of Jesus that no man can be his disciple who "does not hate his own father and mother and wife and children and brothers and sisters" (Lk. 14:26). This assuredly is not a demand for the hatred, the negation of love, of those who by nature are one's nearest and dearest and whom elsewhere in Scripture one is enjoined to love and honor. The issue is quite simply one of priorities: the love of Christ comes before, but does not rule out, the love even of those to whom we are most intimately attached, as is evident from Christ's analogous decla-

---

22. William Perkins, *A Golden Chain* (1590), in *The Work of William Perkins,* introduced and edited by Ian Breward (Appleford, England: Sutton Courtenay Press, 1970), p. 169; see the table or chart annexed to this work.

ration that anyone who loves father or mother or son or daughter more than him is not worthy of him (Mt. 10:37). And so it is not a matter of loving some and hating others, or of not loving any but Christ. "God is love," St. John writes, "and he who abides in love abides in God, and God abides in him" (1 Jn. 4:16); in other words, the Christian believer, as St. Paul says, is one into whose heart the love of God has been poured (Rom. 5:5). The basis of this teaching is the admonition of Christ himself that we should not hate even our enemies but love them, because in doing so we show ourselves to be the children of our Heavenly Father and reflect the perfection of his being (Mt. 5:43-48).

To interpret the affirmation, "Jacob I loved, but Esau I hated," to mean that God's attitude to Esau was that of hatred understood as unloving hostility would be to contradict this teaching. The passage is cited by St. Paul, as the context indicates, to confirm the principle of election that he is propounding, and in particular the election of the people of Israel, and, still more particularly, the inner election within that people of "the children of the promise"— the line that leads from Abraham through Isaac (not Ishmael) and from Isaac through Jacob (not Esau) to the One in whom the promise finds its focus and its fulfilment (Rom. 9:6ff.; 2 Cor. 1:20; Gal. 3:16). The Apostle, then, is not saying that God was animated by hatred toward Esau, but that in line with his elective purpose it is Jacob, not Esau, who has a place. God's sovereign activity in election is apparent from the way in which Rebekah was told, even while the twin children Esau and Jacob were still within her womb, that the elder would serve the younger. St. Paul explains that the fact that this word was spoken when "they were not yet born and had done nothing either good or bad" demonstrates that God's purpose of election functions "not because of works but because of his call," and that consequently "it depends not upon man's will or exertion, but upon God's mercy" (Gen. 25:23; Rom. 9:11, 16). His electing grace is neither influenced by nor dependent on human merit or demerit. The mind of God in his work of election remains an inscrutable mystery to the mind of man. It is sufficient for us to know that the divine activity in election is an activity of mercy and grace.

Yet the divine counsel has depths that are still more impenetrable. The choice of the Israelites did not mean, as many mistakenly took it to mean, the exclusion of the Gentiles from God's purposes of grace. Indeed, the election of their forefather Abraham signalized not the restriction of blessing but its expansion to mankind, for the covenant promise included the assurance that in his seed all the nations of the earth would be blessed (Gen. 12:3; 18:18; 22:18). St. Paul is careful to emphasize the worldwide scope of God's purposes of blessing in his discussion of the doctrine of election. He reminds the believers in Rome that God has chosen "even us whom he has called, not from the Jews only but from the Gentiles," and that this is the fulfilment of the promises given through the prophets of old. Thus he quotes from the prophecy of Hosea: "Those who were not my people I will call 'my people,' and her who was not beloved I will call 'my beloved'; and in the very place where it was said to

them, 'You are not my people,' they will be called 'sons of the living God'"
(Hos. 1:10; 2:23; Rom. 9:24-26; cf. 15:7-12).

The choosing of the nation of Israel was therefore designed for the blessing of all earth's nations. But within this framework there is also an election within the election, as has in fact already been implied in the choosing of Jacob but not Esau. For confirmation that this is so St. Paul turns to the prophet Isaiah, who speaks of the salvation of a remnant: "Isaiah cries out concerning Israel: 'Though the number of the sons of Israel be as the sands of the sea, only a remnant of them will be saved; for the Lord will execute his sentence upon the earth with rigor and dispatch'" (Is. 10:22; Rom. 9:27f.). Why only a remnant of Israel the chosen people? Because they failed to pursue righteousness by faith, vainly imagining that it could be achieved by the supposed merits of their works and allowing the warning that only "he who believes in him will not be put to shame" to go unheeded (Rom. 9:30-33; Is. 28:16). The remnant then consists of those who have no faith at all in themselves and their own works but solely in God as their Redeemer. It is because of unbelief that Jews are broken off as branches from God's olive tree, and it is through faith that the Gentiles are grafted in as branches. Just as faith unites the branches, both Jewish and Gentile, to the living stem of divine grace, so also unbelief severs from it (Rom. 11:17-23). Faith, however, does not exist apart from grace. Hence St. Paul describes the remnant as the "remnant according to the election of grace" and explains that "if it is by grace, it is no longer on the basis of works," for "otherwise grace would no longer be grace" (Rom. 11:5f.). Faith and grace are the two facets of election. Faith is man's response to God's bestowal of grace; but faith is not meritorious, as though it in some way made the believer worthy of grace, for that would be equivalent to the reckoning of faith as a deserving work, which in turn would be the contradiction of grace, since grace is the free communication of unmerited favor and mercy. It would also imply, contrary to the consistent teaching of Scripture, that faith comes before grace and man before God.

THE PRIMACY OF GRACE

The question naturally arises: What is the relationship between faith and election? Does not the doctrine of election make the demand for faith meaningless? Only if election is a synonym for determinism, which is an equation explicitly rejected by Augustine and the theologians of the Reformation. No less firmly rejected was any notion that divine grace can become effective only as a response to human faith. Determinism reduces man to the condition of an impersonal puppet. On the other hand, to give priority to faith reduces God to the state of a helpless spectator, who has to wait to see which persons will take the initiative of faith, and which persons, having taken the initiative, will subsequently lose or abandon the faith they have professed to have—to wait and see, indeed, whether *any* persons will believe. In the light of biblical realism, we may actually go further and affirm that, if divine grace were dependent on human faith, God would not even be an uncertain onlooker, since by reason of fallen man's ungodly self-deification the failure of any to take the initiative of faith would be more than a possibility and more even than a probability; it would be a certainty. The grace of God would then fail entirely of its purpose, and this can only mean that the doctrine of God that leads to such a conclusion is seriously at fault. Only if God is not after all God is it possible to conceive that his will and his work can be frustrated and come to nothing. As God comes before man, so grace comes before faith. As with creation, so with re-creation, the initiative belongs to God. It is grace which creates the occasion for faith, not faith the occasion for grace. Grace does not obliterate faith; it brings it into being. The dynamic force of God's elective grace is such that it unfailingly effects the miracle of bringing life out of death.

As St. Paul told the Corinthian Christians, God "is the source of your life in Christ Jesus." Every blessing that is ours is freely bestowed in Christ Jesus. Consequently, there is no place for human self-glorying in the presence of God: our glorying must be glorying only in the Lord (1 Cor. 1:29-31; Jer. 9:23f.). Abraham, the recipient of the covenant promise of blessing which finds its eternal fulfilment in Christ, is set before us as an eminent example of the principle that it is God "who gives life to the dead and calls into existence the things that do not exist" (Rom. 4:17). The only road open to Abraham was that of faith, for the promise that he would be the father of many nations and through this fatherhood a blessing to the world, was a promise which in himself he was completely powerless to fulfil. God had promised him what was humanly speaking an impossibility, both because of his and his wife Sarah's advanced age and because of the barrenness of Sarah's womb. But he believed God's word, and these apparently insuperable obstacles to its fulfilment did not cause his faith to weaken; on the contrary, "in hope he believed against hope," and "no distrust made him waver concerning the promise of God, but he grew strong in his faith and gave glory to God, fully convinced that God was able to do what he had promised." Thus, unable to contribute even in the slightest degree to the achievement of what was promised, and wholly dependent on the power and grace of God, Abraham was justified before God by his faith, which was reckoned to him as righteousness (Rom. 4:16-22; Gen. 15:6). Nothing could demonstrate more clearly the priority of divine grace and the initiative of divine power; for the impossible thing that God had promised, life from what was dead, was in due course made real by the birth of Isaac and thereafter by the great posterity whose existence was derived from this one divine work of grace.

The firmness of Abraham's faith was further demonstrated by his triumphant endurance of a trial that was, if anything, still more severe, his obedience, namely, to the command, at a time when Isaac had grown to young manhood, to take this son of the promise and offer him up in sacrifice. No action more incomprehensible and self-defeating could have been imagined, for the killing of Isaac could only mean the cutting of the line leading to the advent of the Savior, whose day Abraham greeted joyfully as it were from afar (Jn. 8:56; Heb. 11:13). By every human reckoning the death of Isaac would proclaim the falsification of his faith and the dashing to pieces of all his hopes. But there was no diminishment of Abraham's confidence in the power of God to perform what he had promised. Was not Isaac himself all the proof necessary for him to know and believe that God brings life out of death? God who had done this once could and would do it again and again! God cannot be against his own covenant and promise! And so we read that "by faith Abraham, when he was tested, offered up Isaac, and he who had received the promise was ready to offer up his only son, of whom it was said, 'Through Isaac shall your seed be called'"; for, it is significantly added, "he considered that God was able to raise him even from the dead," and in a figurative sense he did receive him back from the dead, though in the end another victim was offered up in his place (Heb. 11:17-19; Gen. 22:1-19).

When we come to the fulfilment of the promise in its most profound significance, the coming, that is, of him who is in a unique sense the seed of Abraham and the affirmation of all God's gracious promises (Gal. 3:16; 2 Cor. 1:20), the initiative still rested entirely with God. Yet once again, at this absolutely decisive and pivotal moment of human history, God showed himself to be the author of life by an act which is altogether beyond all human capacity. The promised seed of Abraham, which had come down through Isaac, Jacob, and David, was born of a virgin mother. The annunciation to Mary that she was to be the mother of Jesus was at the same time an annunciation that in him the covenant promises of God would achieve realization: "Behold," she was informed, "you will conceive in your womb and bear a child, and you shall call his name Jesus. He will be great and will be called the Son of the Most High; and the Lord God will give him the throne of his father David, and he will reign over the house of Jacob for ever; and of his kingdom there will be no end." Mary, being a virgin, was understandably perplexed: "How can this be, since I know no man?" she asked. And the answer was given that this birth would take place through the power of God the Holy Spirit, together with the assurance that with God nothing is impossible (Lk. 1:31-35, 37). The divine omnipotence that was demonstrated in the birth of Jesus was again manifested in his resurrection when yet once more God brought life out of death. As St. Paul says, Jesus Christ was "designated Son of God in power by his resurrection from the dead" (Rom. 1:4).

It should not surprise us to discover the same principle whereby God brings deadness to life effectively working in the application of divine grace to the heart of the sinner which is called the new birth or regeneration. What sinful man desperately needs is precisely life from the dead, and this is provided by the grace of God which is always life-giving grace, and it is provided in Christ who himself is alive from the dead. Hence the admonition that "the wages of sin is death" is balanced by the good news that "the free gift of God is eternal life in Christ Jesus our Lord" (Rom. 6:23). Those who have been transformed by this regenerating power bear witness that "God, who is rich in mercy, out of the great love with which he loved us, even when we were dead through our trespasses, made us alive together with Christ" (Eph. 2:4f.). Now, once more, it is obvious that that which is dead has no power whatsoever to bring itself to life, and that there is no possibility of life from the dead unless this is the work of God, and entirely the work of God. That is why St. Paul insists that our salvation by grace through faith is "not our own doing" but is "the gift of God," who not only initiates our salvation but also brings it to completion in Christ (Eph. 2:8f.; Phil. 1:6; cf. Heb. 12:2). It follows that we who are one with Christ know and rejoice in "the immeasurable greatness of God's power in us who believe, according to the working of his great might which he accomplished in Christ when he raised him from the dead" (Eph. 1:19f.).

In the light of this teaching it is evident that in our fallen state we are incompetent to contribute to our own salvation, and therefore that unless the priority of grace is a reality there can be no hope of redemption for mankind. Thus "while we were yet helpless . . . Christ died for the ungodly" (Rom. 5:6), and God's love reached out to us even though we were without love for God (1 Jn. 4:9f.). Grace therefore comes first, and it does so by the merciful initiative of God.

But it is surely unjustifiable to conclude from this principle that the fall of man was decreed to the end that he might come to a realization of his utter weakness in separation from God and that there might be an opportunity for God to exercise his grace. Calvin indeed asked, with reference to the devil and man, how it was that God, who could have preserved them, permitted their ruin if he had not decreed their destruction, and, further, "why he did not furnish each with at least some small degree of ability to stand"; and he actually came surprisingly close to propounding a variation of the *felix culpa* argument when he sought to explain that, "although man was created weak and liable to fall, yet this weakness contained in it a great blessing, because man's fall immediately afterwards taught him that nothing out of God is safe or secure or enduring."[23] This begs the question whether man was in fact created weak and by a divine decree bound for ruination. The type of theodicy offered by Calvin here casts a shadow over the goodness of God's creation. Moreover, the conception of man as destined to fall into sin and thereafter as incapable of turning back to God can hardly imply that the resultant knowledge of weakness and insecurity was of any practical avail to him; and consequently the attempt to present the fall in a favorable light as beneficial in this respect seems strangely incongruous. Otherwise, of course, Calvin maintains with the greatest plainness that the deadening effect of sin is counteracted by the life-giving power of divine grace. Through the same Word by whom life was created where before there

23. *Calvin's Calvinism*, pp. 272f.

was no life, life is also re-created where now there is death. It is his breathing forth of the Spirit of Holiness that causes those slain by sin to live again (cf. Ezek. 37:9f.; Jn. 20:22; Acts 2:32f.).

THE RESPONSE OF FAITH

Granted that it is God alone who raises the dead to life, it may well be asked how faith can be demanded of the sinner as a condition of his salvation. How can the dead be expected to make any response at all? What use was it, in answer to the Philippian jailer's inquiry "What must I do to be saved?" to tell him, "Believe in the Lord Jesus, and you will be saved" (Acts 16:30f.)? What sense was there in St. John's telling the readers of his Gospel, "These things are written that you may believe that Jesus is the Christ, the Son of God, and that believing you may have life in his name" (Jn. 20:31)? Certainly, it is well for us to remember that by our own wisdom and logic and powers of persuasion we will not succeed in convincing a single unbeliever of the truth of the gospel. Yet Christians have the command of the risen Lord to evangelize and bear witness to all persons throughout the length and breadth of the world (Mt. 28:19f.; Acts 1:8; Mk. 16:16). We cannot ignore the amazing zeal of the apostles as they expend themselves in the fulfilment of this commission. We see St. Paul driven by the determination to preach, to plead, to persuade, and to win for Christ those who have not yet heard the Good News and the call to reconciliation. What purpose was served by his appealing to those who were dead in their sins? Was it not futile for him to proclaim that "the same Lord is Lord of all and bestows his riches upon all who call upon him," without distinction, and even to confirm this declaration with the promise given through the prophet Joel that "whosoever calls upon the name of the Lord will be saved" (Rom. 10:12f.; Joel 2:32)? Not only this, but St. Paul explains further that to call upon God for salvation persons must first believe, and to believe they must first hear, and to hear there must first be a preacher, and the preacher, if he is to be heard, must first be sent (Rom. 10:14).

In other words, the ungodly, though dead in their sins, are not treated as totally impercipient and incapable of response. Looked on with compassion as being urgently in need of the gospel, they are appealed to and reasoned with as responsible individuals. And Romans 10, which so clearly shows this, is centrally placed within the setting of the Apostle's firm exposition of the doctrine of divine election and predestination in Romans 9 and 11. Indeed, it is abundantly plain throughout the New Testament that the apostles' practice in their work of evangelism was to offer the gospel freely to all without discrimination. The principle governing this practice is twofold, namely, that there is no distinction between one person and another, or between one nationality and another, first of all, because all are sinners who come short of the glory of God, and, secondly, because the grace of God is bestowed on all who call upon him for salvation (Rom. 3:22f.; 10:12f.).

Nonetheless, Scripture postulates a radical antithesis between belief and unbelief. The unbeliever is under the power of sin, indeed enslaved and deadened by it, whereas the believer is liberated from the dominion of sin and is alive to God in Christ Jesus (Rom. 3:9; 6:6-11, 17-19). The unbeliever makes himself the center of all things; starting from himself, as though he were the judge of the meaning of all existence, he is inescapably limited by his finiteness from comprehending more than a minute fragment of the whole of reality and by his fallenness from interpreting even that fragment correctly; whereas the believer knows that all things derive both their existence and their meaning from God and that the fear of the Lord is the beginning of wisdom and knowledge (Ps. 111:10; Prov. 1:7). It is the actuality of an antithesis as radical as that between life and death which poses acutely the problem of the possibility of spiritual communication between the believer and the unbeliever. Can the attempt to evangelize or bear witness to those who are spiritually dead be anything but an empty exercise? The apostles quite obviously did not think so. What then is the point of contact between the believer and the unbeliever? How can the Christian "get through to" and penetrate the defense, indeed the deadness, of the skeptic, the agnostic, the unconcerned, the self-righteous, or the professed atheist? This is undeniably a question of fundamental importance for the evangelistic and apologetic task of the church as its members seek to give effect to the injunction always to "be prepared to make a defense to any one who calls you to account for the hope that is in you" (1 Pet. 3:15).

The solution to the problem regarding the point of contact is present in the heart and center of the being of man, every man, namely his constitution in the image of God. Man cannot escape from his own nature; he cannot obliterate the divine image with which his being is stamped. He may close his eyes to or even isolate himself from the evidence of the divine power and deity of the Creator which surrounds him on all sides, but he cannot get away from himself. He may vehemently deny this central fact of his constitution in the image of God, but he is still, and will never cease to be, what he is by the very nature of his being. Despite the unbeliever's self-centeredness and hard-heartedness, despite his determination to suppress the truth about God and therefore about himself, the very fact that he is rebellious and wishes to be rid of this truth concerning his creaturehood indicates that he knows the truth. It is this truth that, foolishly, he wishes not to know. The believer, likewise, is God's creature made in the divine image, but one who now gladly acknowledges this truth and in whom the integrity of that image is by the grace of God being restored. The truth about God which the believer affirms the unbeliever denies; but it is nonetheless truth that, in this antagonistic manner, is common to both.

The point of conflict is the point of contact. If it ceases to be the point of conflict (as it does if the believer, by a misconceived strategy, imagines that he can gain the victory by taking his stand on the same ground as the unbeliever and accepting his presuppositions) it ceases to be the point of contact.[24] The believer who ignores the antithesis between the two positions can do so only by surrendering his own position.

No matter how much the unbeliever has sought to smother the image in which he is created, no matter how drastically he has abused and perverted it, that image is not destroyed. He does not cease to be a fellow human being. Even though he sinfully argues from wrong presuppositions, he still retains his rational faculty (if this collapses he is placed in a lunatic asylum!). Even though he is egotistically turned in upon himself, he is still a being with feelings and emotions and a will of his own. Even though he worships the creature instead of the Creator, he is still a religious being who worships. Even though he disregards the standards and obligations of morality, he still has a conscience. Even though he pollutes his environment and gives himself to deeds of violence, he is still in his twisted way exercising dominion over the earth. In a word, he is still a person, and that again means that he cannot escape from the image of God that is impressed upon the heart and core of his being or from the word of God that is addressed to him as a person. The believer, therefore, in desiring to win the unbeliever, must relate to him as person to person, on the basis of the humanity which they have in common; but in doing so he must never forget that his own position is diametrically contrary to that of the unbeliever, whose mind and will are exalted against the knowledge of God and need to be made captive to the obedience of Christ (2 Cor. 10:4f.).

In appealing to the unbeliever to respond with repentance and faith to the loving and merciful grace of God freely offered in Christ Jesus, the believer himself should be motivated by love and compassion; for, remembering his own state before regeneration, he will be aware that the unbeliever, because he is suppressing what he knows to be the truth about God, has an evil conscience, and, because of the resulting disintegration in the depth of his being, is lost and disoriented as he vainly struggles to recover the meaning of his existence. He will know, none more clearly, that alienation from God brings in its train alienation deep down within oneself which darkens the mind and cripples the will, because there is self-contradiction at the heart of fallen man's being. The believer knows that it is only by the power of the gospel that this self-stultifying antithesis which is the root of the human tragedy can be remedied. The believer knows full well the reality of the antithesis from his own experience and sees it clearly by reason of the enlightenment he has received; hence he is able to testify: "One thing I know, that whereas I was blind now I see" (Jn. 9:25). To the unbeliever he can say with full compassion, "What you still are I once was," because he has proof within himself that the grace of God in Christ

24. "The Christian," Herman Dooyeweerd warned, "must never absorb the ground motive of an apostate culture into his life and thought," or "strive to synthesize or bridge the gap between an apostate ground motive and the ground motive of the Christian religion," or "deny that the antithesis, from out of the religious root, cuts directly through the issues of temporal life" (*Roots of Western Culture*, tr. John Kraay [Toronto, 1979], p. 39).

Jesus is the answer to the radical unrest of the unredeemed heart. To every sinner, the ungodly, the immoral, the idolatrous, the dishonest, the drunkard, the blasphemer, he can truthfully bear witness: "Such was I; but I was washed, I was sanctified, I was justified in the name of the Lord Jesus Christ and in the Spirit of our God" (1 Cor. 6:9-11).[25]

The miracle of the new birth is indeed something that God alone can perform, for the unregenerate person not only rejects the truth of the gospel as folly but is also incapable of understanding it because it is spiritually discerned (1 Cor. 2:14). Yet the finding of new life in Christ is not unconnected with the faculties and longings of the human personality. The Apostle Paul's sudden and dramatic conversion, for example, did not take place in a spiritual vacuum. In St. Paul's own personal history we can speak of a *praeparatio evangelica,* a preparation of his disposition for the gospel. Fierce anti-Christian persecutor though he was, he was not free from the painful stirrings and spurrings of his conscience: "It hurts you to kick against the goads," he heard the Lord saying to him at the time of his conversion (Acts 26:14). He had witnessed the dying of the first Christian martyr and perhaps had listened to the powerful testimony to the truth that preceded it (Acts 7:58). His frenetic obsession with the persecution of the Christian church which followed could not erase that

---

25. "The point of contact for the gospel," Cornelius Van Til has said, "must be sought within the natural man. Deep down in his mind every man knows that he is the creature of God and responsible to God. Every man, at bottom, knows that he is a covenant-breaker. But every man acts and talks as though this were not so. . . . The truly Biblical view . . . is assured of a point of contact in the fact that every man is made in the image of God and has impressed upon him the law of God" (*The Defense of the Faith* [Philadelphia, 1955], p. 111). To the same effect Emil Brunner wrote that "even as a sinner man can only be understood in the light of the original Image of God, namely, as one who is living in opposition to it," and that "the very same point which is the real 'point of contact' is also the point of the greatest contradiction" (*Man in Revolt* [London, 1939], pp. 105, 539). For the controversy between Emil Brunner and Karl Barth regarding natural theology and, as one of the matters at issue within the debate, the image of God, see *Natural Theology* (London, 1946), which contains Brunner's contribution on "Nature and Grace" and Barth's response "No!" Barth had contended that the image of God in man was entirely obliterated by the fall and that there remained no point of contact (see *Church Dogmatics,* I/1). Brunner offered the following rejoinder: "No one who agrees that only human subjects but not stocks and stones can receive the Word of God and the Holy Spirit can deny that there is such a thing as a point of contact for the divine grace of redemption. This point of contact is the formal *imago Dei,* which not even the sinner has lost, the fact that man is man. . . . Not even sin has done away with the fact that man is receptive of words, that he and he alone is receptive of the Word of God. But this 'receptivity' must not be understood in the material sense. This receptivity says nothing as to his acceptance or rejection of the Word of God. It is the purely formal possibility of his being addressed" (*Natural Theology,* pp. 20, 21, 31). Barth in turn attacked this position, including the distinction posited by Brunner between "formal" and "material" concepts or senses of the image of God in relation to the being of man (ibid., pp. 78ff.). Subsequently, however, Barth seemed to come close to the position defined by Brunner concerning the association of the image of God in man with the point of contact for evangelism (see *Church Dogmatics,* III/1, pp. 183f.).

memory or quiet the accusations of his conscience—indeed, the joyful constancy of Christ's followers under suffering and affliction must have increased the disquiet within his breast. Though all appearances were to the contrary, the witness in life and in death of Stephen and these others moved even the heart of Saul of Tarsus and prepared the way for his being transformed by the grace of God into Paul the Apostle.

And so it is with all Christian witness: it is directed to the heart of the unbeliever by engaging his interest, persuading his mind, and arousing his conscience, to the end that he may call upon the name of the Lord for mercy. Its purpose is salvific, not condemnatory, in line with Christ's declaration regarding the purpose of his advent and incarnation: "I have come as light into the world, that whoever believes in me may not remain in darkness. . . . I did not come to judge the world but to save the world" (Jn. 12:46f.). He came in love and compassion to seek and to save the lost (Lk. 19:10). His mission to us was a mission of reconciliation; and to those who have been found by him he has entrusted the message of reconciliation. Through them as his ambassadors God makes his appeal to the rest of mankind: "We beseech you on behalf of Christ, be reconciled to God" (2 Cor. 5:18ff.).

It is true, of course, that condemnation enters into the picture, for to reject salvation automatically means to choose condemnation. Thus to his assertion that he had not come to judge the world but to save it Christ added: "He who rejects me and does not receive my sayings has a judge; the word that I have spoken will be his judge on the last day" (Jn. 12:48). Christ is either the Redeemer or the Judge of all. His cross is the place either of our salvation or of our condemnation. The sharp two-edged sword that proceeds from his mouth will not fail to cut us either with the edge of his merciful grace or with the edge of his wrathful judgment (Rev. 1:16; 2:12, 16). Inseparable therefore from the gospel declaration that "God sent the Son into the world, not to condemn the world, but that the world might be saved through him" is the warning that, while "he who believes in him is not condemned," at the same time "he who does not believe is condemned already, because he has not believed in the name of the only Son of God" (Jn. 3:17f.). But the motivation of Christ's coming is love and the primary purpose of the cross is salvation. Moreover, that saving love reaches out to *whoever* believes in him (Jn. 3:16). Saving grace is freely and fully offered to every person, without discrimination, who calls upon the name of the Lord (Rom. 10:12f.). This is the good news that the apostles confidently and constantly proclaimed in every place and to every audience.

The "whoever" of the gospel invitation presupposed a point of contact. It is not an empty word that has no force for those who are supposedly predestined to perdition. The genuineness and sincerity of the open invitation on the lips of Christ and his apostles is not to be questioned. If the final destiny of every single person is immutably fixed prior to creation, then to invite people to choose between salvation and judgment becomes a meaningless mockery. And God does set before us the challenge of an alternative: the way of life and blessing or the way of death and perdition. His attitude, however, is not the casual "take it or leave it" attitude of one to whom it matters little whether the response is positive or negative: he *urges* and *pleads* with us to choose the way of life. This is further evidence that God's disposition toward his creatures in their fallenness is one of love and grace and indeed longing. He really wants them to return to him. Thus through his mouthpiece Moses the challenge was issued to the Israelites: "See, I have set before you this day life and good, death and evil. If you obey the commandments of the Lord your God, . . . the Lord your God will bless you. . . . But if your heart turns away and you will not hear, . . . I declare to you this day, that you shall perish." That this is no dispassionate address is evident from the manner in which he then appealed to them to choose life and blessing: "I call heaven and earth to witness against you this day, that I have set before you life and death, blessing and curse; therefore choose life, that you and your descendants may live, loving the Lord your God, obeying his voice, and cleaving to him" (Dt. 30:15-20). God again entreated the people through the prophet Ezekiel to choose life instead of death by turning back to him: "Repent and turn from all your transgressions, lest iniquity be your ruin. Cast away from you all the transgressions which you have committed against me, and get yourselves a new heart and a new spirit! Why will you die, O house of Israel? For I have no pleasure in the death of any one, says the Lord God; so turn, and live" (Ezek. 18:30-32). And the divine pleading is movingly repeated in Ezekiel 33:11: "As I live, says the Lord God, I have no pleasure in the death of the wicked, but that the wicked may turn from his way and live; turn back, turn back from your evil ways; for why will you die, O house of Israel?"

In the New Testament, similarly, the apostolic preaching is a plea to the hearers to turn in repentance from sin and to commit themselves in faith to Christ as their Redeemer and Lord. Indeed, on one occasion when St. Paul is addressing an audience of philosophers in Athens the plea is presented as a command: "God commands all men everywhere to repent"; and the command is expressed in the light of the approaching day of judgment when God will judge the world in righteousness by Jesus Christ, the risen and reigning Lord (Acts 17:30f.). The command is issued to *all men;* it would be evacuated of its force if it were predetermined that a multitude of mankind would have no capacity for heeding it. The question at issue is this: Does God wish all or does he wish only some to repent? Is the gospel intended for all or only for some? Is the "all" of evangelism an inclusive or in some particular sense an exclusive term? Does "whosoever" mean less than it appears to mean?

THE FREE OFFER OF THE GOSPEL

Though it is plain that in the apostolic ministry of the New Testament the gospel was universally preached and freely offered to all, and that this was done constantly and sincerely, there are some who hold that to invite all to receive new life in Christ is an objectionable practice. They argue that the gospel invitation is intended for the elect alone, whose number and identity have been decreed beforehand, that the saving grace of the gospel is sufficient only for the elect, since, were it sufficient for more than the elect, there would be an excess of grace which would be wasted and ineffective, and that the offer of salvation is heard by the nonelect only for the purpose that they should reject it. It is an attitude that is governed by a strangely quantitative view of divine grace; whereas we are assured that "it is not by measure that God gives the Spirit" (Jn. 3:34). The grace of God is as boundless as his love. It cannot be weighed or computed. While the day of grace continues, so also does the report, "Still there is room," and so also does the command, "Compel them to come in, that my house may by filled" (Lk. 14:22f.). Was the invitation at first extended to those who for worldly reasons excused themselves from accepting it and thus excluded themselves from the banquet of divine grace a hollow invitation? Was St. Paul's incessant preaching of the gospel and his becoming all things to all men that by all means he might save some misguided (1 Cor. 9:16, 22)? Was he wrong in his conviction that where sin is abundant grace is superabundant (Rom. 5:20)?

The intense urgency with which the apostles applied themselves to the task of evangelization is explained both by the commission they had received from the Lord to preach the gospel throughout the world and by their awareness that the present period between the two comings of Christ is the period of *the last days,* which will be terminated by *the last day,* the day of final judgment for the unrepentant. The mainspring of the gospel is that God is the source of life, life indeed from the dead, and that no person is brought into being for the purpose of perishing. Accordingly, the prolongation of this final age is explained by St. Peter as the prolongation of the day of opportunity for sinners to repent and return to God through faith in Jesus Christ. He assures his fellow believers that, though the day of Christ's return may seem to be long delayed, "the Lord is not slow about his promise as some count slowness, but is forbearing toward you, not wishing that any should perish, but that all should reach repentance" (2 Pet. 3:9). It was because "*now* is the day of salvation" that St. Paul willingly endured "afflictions, hardships, calamities, beatings, imprisonments, tumults, labors, watchings, hunger" as with single-minded dedication he proclaimed the Good News to all people (2 Cor. 6:1-10; 11:23-29), and, further, that he urged that prayers should be made "for all men," adding that to do this was "good and acceptable in the sight of God our Savior, who desires all men to be saved and to come to the knowledge of the truth" (1 Tim. 2:1-4).

Why should Christians be exhorted to pray for all men, and how can it be said that God desires all men to be saved, if by a fixed decree many are destined never to be saved and cannot therefore be helped by our prayers? It only confuses the issue to argue (as, e.g., Calvin does)[26] that the Apostle does

---

26. Calvin, *Institutes* III.xxiv.16.

not mean all men as individuals but all orders or classes of men; nor is this contention confirmed by the specific mention of "kings and all who are in high positions," as though this were intended as an illustration of one class of men, since the purpose of this particular specification is "that we may lead a quiet and peaceable life," which is a condition that is desirable precisely because it is conducive to the free declaration of the gospel and thus to the salvation of all men. Thus St. Paul asserts later in this same epistle: "For to this end we toil and strive, because we have our hope set on the living God, who is the Savior of all men, especially of those who believe" (1 Tim. 4:10). This indicates that God reaches out redemptively to all men, but that only those who believe actually experience his redemption. If "all men" here means all classes of men, then "those who believe" must mean those classes of men who believe; but this is inadmissible since believing is the response of persons as individuals, not as classes. The obligation placed on Christians to be Christ's witnesses to the uttermost parts of the earth follows from the fact that the propitiation achieved at the cross is cosmic in its amplitude (1 Jn. 2:2).

St. Paul leads us to the same conclusion in the comparison between Adam and Christ which he develops in Romans 5:12ff. (a passage to which we have already given some consideration),[27] where he asserts that "as one man's trespass led to condemnation for all men, so one man's act of righteousness leads to acquittal and life for all men" (v. 18). The argument rests upon the exact numerical correspondence between the "one man" Adam and the "one man" Christ and between the "all men" affected by the sin of the former and the "all men" affected by the righteousness of the latter. In both cases the action of one man has consequences that determine the destiny of all men. That "all men" means the entire human race, not just all the elect or all the nonelect or all classes of men, is evident from the declaration that "as sin came into the world through one man and death through sin, so death spread to all men because all men sinned" (v. 12), where "all men" indisputably signifies the whole of mankind. In Adam, therefore, there is perdition for the whole of mankind, and in Christ there is reconciliation for the whole of mankind. This being so, St. Paul is able, as we have seen, to speak of God as the Savior of all men and as wishing all men to be saved, to encourage the offering up of prayers for all men, and to require the proclamation of the gospel to all men.

In actuality, of course, all men cannot simultaneously be perishing in Adam and alive in Christ: the two conditions are mutually exclusive. As a matter of logic it would be possible for the whole of mankind whose status in Adam is one of perdition to be brought to the new status of redemption in Christ; but such universalism is unknown to Scripture, even though the potential may be said to be there. The reality is that the gospel which is offered to all for acceptance is rejected by many, and to reject Christ is to remain in Adam. The ultimate dividing line for the whole of mankind, then, is the line which separates

27. See pp. 128ff. above.

those who are in Christ from those who are in Adam. Hence the offer of salvation is accompanied by the warning of judgment which gives it its true urgency, as is apparent from the frequency of admonitions such as the following: "He who believes in the Son has eternal life; but he who does not obey the Son shall not see life, but the wrath of God rests upon him" (Jn. 3:36). Those who thrust the word of grace from them judge themselves unworthy of eternal life (Acts 13:46)—a conclusion that is also taught in Romans 5:17, where St. Paul writes: "If, because of one man's trespass, death reigned through that one man, much more will those who receive the abundance of grace and the free gift of righteousness reign in life through the one man Jesus Christ." Only the reception of God's abundant grace and the acceptance of the free gift of righteousness can ensure the transition from death to life.

Within this perspective the gospel is freely offered to all persons throughout the world as the provision of divine grace for the rescuing of mankind from the predicament in which through their sin they have placed themselves; and it is offered in all seriousness as "the power of God for salvation for every one who believes" (Rom. 1:16). Through his gospellers God genuinely appeals to mankind to be reconciled to him (2 Cor. 5:20). To those rejecters of his grace on whom his judgment inescapably falls he still says: "I was ready to be sought by those who did not ask for me; I was ready to be found by those who did not seek me. I said, 'Here am I, here am I,' to a nation that did not call on my name. I spread out my hand all the day to a rebellious people, who walk in a way that is not good, following their own devices, a people who provoke me to my face continually" (Is. 65:1-3). Divine expostulation of this kind clearly indicates that there is on man's part responsibility for accepting God's grace as well as for rejecting it. Always the damning sin is the turning away from the grace and goodness of God which are there to be freely received. "What wrong did your fathers find in me that they went far from me?", the Lord asked through his prophet Jeremiah; and then he accused the people of committing two evils: "They have forsaken me, the fountain of living waters, and hewed out cisterns for themselves, broken cisterns, that can hold no water." It was not that God had abandoned them, but that they had abandoned God: "Have you not brought this upon yourself by forsaking the Lord your God, when he led you in the way? . . . Know and see that it is evil and bitter for you to forsake the Lord your God" (Jer. 2:5, 11, 13, 17, 19). Thus they were chided, but without pleasure on God's part. Even so, God pleaded with his people to turn back to him: "Return, faithless Israel, says the Lord. I will not look on you in anger, for I am merciful, says the Lord. I will not be angry for ever. Only acknowledge your guilt, that you rebelled against the Lord your God. . . . Return, O faithless sons. I will heal your faithlessness." It is the cry of a father's heart as he hopes and waits for the response: "Behold, we come to thee; for thou art the Lord our God" (Jer. 3:12, 13, 22). The appeal then made by God to Israel is now extended to all. God is at hand to do us good, chiding us with the reminder: "Your sins have kept good from you" (Jer. 5:25).

Throughout Scripture God compassionately promises blessing to those who love and serve him according to his will, warns that those who rebelliously persist in ungodliness will bring judgment upon themselves, and entreats those who have wandered out of the way to repent and return to him. It is his grace manifested in and through the incarnate Son that creates the possibility for sinful men to make a positive response to his appeal.

The manner of God's dealings with his human creatures is well illustrated by the account of Jonah and his mission to the city of Nineveh. Jonah had been commanded by the word of the Lord: "Arise, go to Nineveh, that great city, and cry against it; for their wickedness has come up before me" (Jonah 1:1f.). When at length, after being frustrated in his attempt to escape from this assignment, Jonah arrived in Nineveh, he announced the impending judgment of God: "Yet forty days, and Nineveh shall be overthrown!" The effect of this declaration was, contrary to what Jonah had expected, the proclamation of a fast and the putting on of sackcloth by the entire population, from the king down. "Let every one turn from his evil way and from the violence which is in his hands," the king said. "Who knows, God may yet repent and turn from his fierce anger, so that we perish not?" And the consequence of this change of heart, we read, was that "when God saw what they did, how they turned from their evil way, God repented of the evil which he had said he would do to them, and he did not do it" (Jonah 3:4-10). Jonah, however, was intensely displeased with the outcome of his mission, for he had desired to see the destruction, not the sparing of Nineveh—which shows how wrongheaded and lacking in compassion even a chosen servant of God can at times be. It was not as though Jonah did not know that God was a God of grace and mercy. "I pray thee, Lord," he protested, "is not this what I said when I was yet in my country? That is why I made haste to flee to Tarshish; for I knew that thou art a gracious God and merciful, slow to anger, and abounding in steadfast love, and repentest of evil" (Jonah 4:1f.).

From this and many other places in Scripture we learn that God is not sternly inflexible in his dealings with mankind, that even in his denunciation of judgment there is room for mercy, and that he is not, so to speak, self-imprisoned in a sequence of events that has been imprinted on all history prior to creation. The absolute sovereignty of Almighty God does not have to be maintained by him or safeguarded by us by as it were casting it in concrete. His sovereignty is dynamic, not static, and it is not less real for being sensitive to the fluctuations among his creatures between rebellion and repentance. He is a *personal* God, and in dealing with *personal* creatures formed after his own image how should he not take pleasure in showing mercy where his warning of judgment has caused men and women to cry to him for salvation?

That so excellent a servant of God as Calvin should have found it possible to assert that "God declared to the Ninevites . . . that he would do that which, in reality, he did not intend to do" is indeed surprising, for such an assertion posits (however unintentionally) a dichotomy between the word of God and the deed of God. It empties God's warning of judgment, in this case, of all content. Nor is the problem eased by the postulation that the supposed incongruity between what God said and what God did is attributable to the controlling factor of his hidden or unrevealed intention, which is a type of rationalization quite foreign to the whole account. If the repentance of the Ninevites was fixed beforehand as the predetermined consequence of the announcement of imminent punishment, which, however, God secretly had no intention of executing, how can it be said that "God repented him of the evil which he had said he would do to them"? (Such language, of course, means simply that God was moved by their change of heart to show them mercy instead of punishment. It is a human way of speaking about God: there was no wrongdoing for God to repent of; his "repenting" is descriptive of his sensitivity to the human situation; and certainly his judgment, when executed, is only holy and righteous, though, as it is experienced by man, evil in that it is the opposite of blessing.) Moreover, the qualification "yet forty days" indicated a period of opportunity for repentance, a time of grace, as the judgment was delayed. Thus the warning of judgment was not incompatible with the manifestation of mercy.

Calvin, in his controversy with Pighius, appeared to be unwilling to admit the possibility of any change of attitude on God's part. His explanation that the punishment denounced against the Ninevites was *conditional* on their response might at first seem to undermine the position he was maintaining, until it is seen that in Calvin's argument not even the condition offered a genuine option for those to whom it was addressed. The conditional promises which invite all men to salvation do not reveal, Calvin said, "what God has decreed in his secret counsel, but declare only what God is ready to do to all those who are brought to faith and repentance," and "he brings to eternal life those whom he willed according to his eternal purpose."[28] It is gratifying to find Calvin expounding this same passage without resorting to speculation regarding a twofold purpose or intention of God, one open and the other hidden and contradictory, and altogether in a manner that accords with the context, in his commentary on the book of Jonah, in the writing of which he was not preoccupied with the polemics of controversy. The following quotation is from his exposition of Jonah 3:10:

> Jonah now says that the Ninevites obtained pardon through their repentance; and this is an example worthy of being observed, for we hence learn for what purpose God daily urges us to repentance, and that is because he desires to be reconciled to us and that we should be reconciled to him. The reason then why so many reproofs and threatenings resound in our ears, whenever we come to hear the word of God, is this, that as God seeks to recover us from destruction he speaks sharply to us: in short, whatever the Scripture contains on repentance and the judgment of God ought to be wholly applied for this purpose, to induce us to return into favour with him; for he is ready to be reconciled and

28. *Calvin's Calvinism*, pp. 99f.

is ever prepared to embrace those who without dissimulation turn to him. We then understand by this example that God has no other object in view, whenever he sharply constrains us, than that he may be reconciled to us. . . . It is certain that God was freely pacified towards the Ninevites, as he freely restores his favour daily to us.[29]

ELECTION IN CHRIST

There is a constant temptation, even for those who have experienced the grace of divine election, to explain the mystery of election by a method of rationalization, that is to say, by reducing it to the dimension of our finite human understanding. This, even though it is not intended to be so, is a form of reductionism which is given expression in one of two ways: either by emphasizing the human aspect of the gospel invitation in such a way as to exclude the sovereignty of God, or by so concentrating on the divine aspect as to eliminate the responsibility of man. In much the same way there have always been those who stress the deity of the incarnate Son at the expense of the humanity or the humanity at the expense of the deity. The paradoxes of the Christian faith are there precisely because we are confronted with truths which surpass the abilities of our finite comprehension. If there were no mystery, we would not be talking about the infinite being of God and the transcendent ways and purposes of the Creator, but only about man. It is possible to dissolve any paradox of the Christian faith by putting the weight only on the one limb of the paradox to the neglect of the other; but this is to destroy the balance of the doctrine by resorting to human reason in an attempt to contain all truth concerning God and the universe within the confines of man's understanding. Thus to assign everything, in the consideration of the doctrine of election, to the sovereignty of God in such a way that all that happens in human history is seen as inexorably determined beforehand is rationalistic. No doubt it conduces to a nicely logical system purified of all loopholes and contingencies; but it does so by devaluing the personhood of man who, formed in the divine image, has a person-to-Person relationship with his Creator. It constructs a static conception of God and his being, as though he were unmoved and unmovable. It makes God's pleading and reasoning with sinful man meaningless, except as a mechanism for the effective calling of the elect and reprobation of the nonelect. But God has a history as well as man—though admittedly in a manner that transcends all human history and all human experience. Do not Creation, the Fall, the

---

29. John Calvin, *Commentaries on the Twelve Minor Prophets,* tr. John Owen, Vol. III (Edinburgh, 1847), pp. 113f. See also, e.g., his *Commentary on the Epistle of Paul the Apostle to the Romans,* where, on 10:12, "there is no difference, . . . for the same Lord over all is rich unto all who call upon him," he says that "since he who is the Creator and Maker of the whole world is the God of all men, he will show himself kind to all who will acknowledge and call on him as their God, for as his mercy is infinite it cannot be but that it will extend itself to all by whom it shall be sought."

Promises, the Incarnation, the Crucifixion, the Resurrection, the Ascension, and, yet to come, the Second Advent and the Consummation of the new heaven and the new earth constitute a history for God? So also God has a dynamic history in relation to the persons and peoples of the human race, whom he loves and addresses and invites to repent and believe and warns of judgment.

On the other hand, to make everything rest on the decision of man provides a neat logical package which, free from any suspicion of determinism, brings man fully into the picture, but at the cost of making nonsense of the sovereignty of God. In the sphere of redemption, indeed, it reverses the right order of things by assigning sovereignty to man and leaving God in a dependent role. Everything then lapses into a state of total uncertainty as God must wait, passively, to see who, if any, will respond with faith to his offer of saving grace, and who, of those who have thus responded, will continue to the end without falling away from grace. This, too, is a rationalization which, in this case, places the weight on the human side of the paradox and by doing so drains the doctrine of election of significance.

The two limbs of this paradox are the sovereignty of God and the answerability of man, and a balanced theology is achieved only if the balance of the paradox is preserved. The rationalizing method appropriates one limb and to all intents and purposes ignores the other, and the resulting explanation is in principle, though not in design, humanistic because it is a procedure by which the issue is reduced to the measure of the human understanding. At the one end of the paradox God beseeches man, "Turn back, turn back from your evil ways, for why will you die?", and gives him the assurance that "whosoever calls on the name of the Lord will be saved" (Ezek. 33:11; Joel 2:32; Rom. 10:13), together with the gracious invitation, "He who will, let him take the water of life freely" (Rev. 22:17). At the other end of the paradox Jesus declares, "All that the Father gives me will come to me," and "No one can come to me unless the Father who sent me draws him" (Jn. 6:37, 44); and we learn that God in his love destined believers "to be his sons through Jesus Christ according to the purpose of his will" (Eph. 1:5), and, further, that it is the Lord, not man, who through the preaching of the gospel adds to the number of believers those who are being saved (Acts 2:47).

That this is a deep mystery is not to be denied; and the mystery is in the paradox whose two arms balance each other and belong together. If it is asked how they can possibly be brought together, the answer is that they find their meeting point in Christ. Only in Christ do we experience the truth of this mystery. In the incarnate Son the two arms of the paradox meet and are dynamically united. As the eternal Son, Christ is one with Almighty God; as the incarnate Son he is one also with our humanity. As the divine Word, he reveals and brings to pass the will of the Father; as the Word made flesh he obeys and fulfils that will. As the Image of God in which man is created, he is the true bond between God and man. As the one Mediator between God and men, himself truly God and, through the incarnation, truly man, he reconnects the lifeline that has been severed by the sin of our ungodliness, and he does this by the incorporation of redeemed humanity into himself, thus renewing our creation in the divine image. As God, the incarnate Son is the dynamic expression of the divine sovereignty, and as man he is the perfect manifestation of human responsibility in free and joyful harmony with the divine will. Thus it is in the incarnate Son, and in those who through faith have become one with him, that the meaning of the mystery is known and its power experienced.

It is in the incarnate Son, then, in whom divine sovereignty and human responsibility are perfectly combined, that the harmony of the paradox is displayed; and, just as it was meat and drink for him of his own free will to do the will of the Father who sent him, so also the will of man soars aloft as it becomes one with the will of his Creator and thus restores the meaning and purpose of his existence. The summit of human fulfilment is the ability to affirm with spontaneous elation, "I delight to do thy will, O my God" (Ps. 143:10); and the deepest satisfaction of the human heart flows from the knowledge that "God is at work in us, both to will and to work for his good pleasure" (Phil. 2:13)—that is, from the confluence of the divine and human wills, first of all in Christ, and then in the believer, whose whole being before God is his being in Christ.

The being of the unbeliever, by contrast, is not in Christ but in the Evil One (1 Jn. 5:19). But he is not for this reason any the less bound to give an answer to the divine appeal which comes to him, whether it be the response of faith or the response of disobedience. As deep calls to deep, so the appeal of God penetrates to and the response rises from the heart of man's being on which the divine image is stamped. It is truly a matter of heart to heart; for the image of God in which man is created is the meeting place of appeal and response. Sin is indeed lethal in its effects, with the result that man is totally incapable of saving himself or of making even the least contribution to his salvation. But he is still man, and no matter how much the divine image in which he is constituted has been shrouded and perverted it is not destroyed. To this fact and to the fact of his answerability the guilty conscience at the core of man's being steadily bears witness. And the meeting of the sovereignty of God and the responsibility of man in this deep seat of our humanity takes place *in Christ,* both for the believer and for the unbeliever, as in the one case belief meets with Christ as Redeemer, and in the other unbelief meets with Christ as Judge (Jn. 3:16-19, 36; Acts 17:31; Rom. 2:16; 8:1).

It is because the incarnate Son is at the same time God sovereignly in action (2 Cor. 5:19) and man responsibly conforming himself to the divine will (Jn. 4:34; Heb. 10:7) that the sovereignty of God and the responsibility of man exist in perfect communion in Christ. With Christ, and with no one else, God is well pleased (Mt. 3:17; 17:5), and it is specifically Christ who is designated as God's Elect One. He is so as the faithful Servant of whom Isaiah's prophecy spoke: "Behold, my Servant, whom I uphold, my Elect One, in whom my soul delights; I have put my Spirit upon him; he will bring forth justice to the nations" (Is. 42:1); and as the one on whom the Lord's Spirit rests he is God's Anointed One. Thus Jesus applied to himself the definition of Isaiah 61:1f.: "The Spirit of the Lord is upon me, because he has anointed me to preach good news to the poor; he has sent me to proclaim release to the captives and recovering of sight to the blind, to set at liberty those who are oppressed, to proclaim the acceptable year of the Lord," telling his audience, "Today this scripture has been fulfilled in your hearing" (Lk. 4:16-21). The rulers of the Jews were well acquainted with the identification of their long-expected Messiah or Anointed One as God's Elect One, as we see from the mockery with which they taunted Jesus as he was hanging on the cross: "He saved others; let him save himself; if he is the Messiah of God, his Elect One" (Lk. 23:35). St. Peter also declared the fulfilment in Jesus Christ of another of Isaiah's prophecies: "Behold, I am laying in Zion a stone, a cornerstone elect and precious, and he who believes in him will not be put to shame" (1 Pet. 2:6; Is. 28:16). Since, then, Christ is the Elect One, all others who are spoken of as elect are necessarily "elect in the Lord" (Rom. 16:13).

These considerations point to the truth that the election of the Christian believer is not at all in himself but solely *in Christ,* who is uniquely God's Elect One. The election of believers, who in themselves are totally unworthy and undeserving of God's favor, can only be in Christ, that is to say, through being made one with him, so that God welcomes us in him who alone is his Beloved and his Elect, and is well pleased with us and calls us his sons only because we are incorporated into him who is his only Son and the only one with whom he is well pleased. Accordingly, St. Paul blesses "the God and Father of our Lord Jesus Christ, who has blessed us *in Christ*" and "elected us *in him*" and destined us "to be his sons through Jesus Christ," so that all is "to the praise of his glorious grace which he freely bestowed on us *in the Beloved*" (Eph. 1:3-5). "If we seek God's fatherly mercy and kindly heart, we should turn our eyes to Christ on whom alone God's Spirit rests," Calvin wrote in an admirable passage. "If we seek salvation, life, and the immortality of the Heavenly Kingdom, then there is no other to whom we may flee, seeing that he alone is the fountain of life, the anchor of salvation, and the heir of the Kingdom of Heaven." The purpose of election, Calvin explained, is "that we, adopted as sons by our Heavenly Father, may obtain salvation and immortality by his favor"; and, he added, "those whom God has adopted as his sons are said to have been elected not in themselves but in Christ." It follows that, "if we have been elected in him, we shall not find assurance of our election in ourselves," and thus that "Christ is the mirror wherein we must, and without self-deception may, contemplate our own election."[30]

The biblical teaching on this theme may be summarized then in the following propositions: (1) all God's purposes from eternity to eternity have their focus and their fulfilment in Christ, the only-begotten Son and the dynamic

30. John Calvin, *Institutes* III.xxiv.5.

Word, including the election of sinners to life and their adoption as sons; (2) the initiative of redemption rests entirely with God and divine grace is always prior to human faith; (3) the call to repent and believe is a genuine summons on the basis of God's action in Christ for the redemption of the world; (4) the response of faith is an authentic human response and not just a predetermined reflex; (5) the meeting point of divine sovereignty and human response is the constitution of man in the divine image, which, however much it may be ignored or denied, has not been annihilated by sin; (6) the harmonious union of divine sovereignty and human answerability is achieved and manifested in the divine-human person of the incarnate Son, in whom the whole of our redemption, from beginning to consummation, is established; (7) God is dynamically, not statically, sovereign in his control of the history of mankind, his attitude to all who are formed in his image is one of love, not love to some and hatred to the rest, and the prolongation of the present age of grace is indicative that God in his forbearance takes no pleasure in the death of the wicked and offers his salvation to all; (8) the paradox of the absolute sovereignty of God and the answerability of man incapacitated by sin remains, however, and it is not for us to offer logical, and therefore humanly finite, explanations of this mystery by virtually disregarding either its human or its divine side; (9) the relationship between God and his fallen creatures is still essentially personal, but always in such a manner that human answerability does not diminish or nullify divine sovereignty; (10) even though the response of faith is a genuine human response, yet this response is itself owed to God by reason of the primacy of his grace, so that God is the sole author of man's salvation and all the glory without exception belongs to God, who not only begins but also brings to completion the work of grace in his believing creatures (Eph. 2:4-10; Rom. 8:28-30; 1 Cor. 1:26-31; 2 Cor. 5:18-21; Phil. 1:6).

ELECTION AND CHRISTIAN SECURITY

The doctrine of election in Christ should be a source of great strength to the Christian believer, since it places his security entirely in Christ and not at all in himself. The biblical insistence on man's total inability to save himself and, therefore, his total dependence on the grace of God if he is to be saved at all removes the work of salvation altogether from the arena of human effort, which even at its best is beset by weakness and fallibility, and ascribes it solely to God, whose power is indefectible and grace inexhaustible. As has previously been noted, even saving faith is God's gift, and the works of man, no matter how good and pious they may seem to be, are completely excluded as in any sense a meritorious means or contribution to the justification of the sinner before God—though good works and holy living should be the fruit that springs from the root of justifying grace (Eph. 2:8-10; Tit. 2:13f.; 3:4-6; 2 Tim. 1:9; Rom. 3:19-28). Furthermore, the doctrine of election should be a strong inducement to the unbeliever, whose whole existence in ungodliness is one of insecurity and hopelessness, to seek and find the security of forgiveness and eternal life in Christ. It is a doctrine, moreover, which gives the believer confidence that God's act of reconciliation in Christ and the preaching of the gospel to the ends of the earth will not be in vain, that no force of evil can possibly overthrow God's purposes for his creation, and that the company of the redeemed who are brought to glory will be an innumerable multitude (Rev. 7:9ff.).

Since our salvation in its totality—its beginning, its continuation, and its consummation—is in Christ Jesus and all the glory belongs to God who in Christ has redeemed and reconciled us to himself (2 Cor. 5:18-21), it follows that no human being may presume to boast or indulge in self-glorification before God. God, as St. Paul told the members of the Corinthian church, "is the source of your life in Christ Jesus," and that is the reason for the admonition, "Let him who glories glory in the Lord" (1 Cor. 1:28-31; Jer. 9:23f.; 1 Cor. 3:21; 2 Cor. 10:17). If there is one conclusion that plainly flows from this teaching it is this, that the doctrine of man cannot properly be formed and discussed in isolation from the doctrine of God. Because God is the source not only of man's existence and of the meaning of his existence but also of his redemption and restoration, there can be no true understanding of man apart from his relationship to God. Even as in his fallenness he suppresses and denies the truth about God and proclaims his own self-adequacy, man cannot disconnect himself from his Creator; when not under divine grace he is under divine judgment, and the lostness, the emptiness, the meaninglessness at the heart of his being are the consequence of his turning away from God, from whom all life and light and meaning proceed; for, turned away, he is still related to and dependent on God, though negatively instead of positively.

Fortunately for us, God is not as man: his power, his wisdom, and his love are constant; his word and purpose do not fail, and his work cannot come to nothing. The doctrine of predestination gives us the assurance that not merely salvation history but all history at every stage is under his sovereign control, manifesting his power and wisdom and love and, in accordance with his purpose, fulfilling the word of his promise. God's will, moreover, is from eternity to eternity, even though it is enacted in the temporal sequence and the finite circumstances of our human history. Hence the apostolic affirmation that "those whom God foreknew he also predestined to be conformed to the image of his Son, . . . and those whom he predestined he also called, and those whom he called he also justified, and those whom he justified he also glorified" (Rom. 8:29f.)—a passage that assures us that our whole salvation is already complete in Christ in accordance with God's immutable purpose. We should not fail to notice how St. Paul regarded predestination and all that it involves as a foundation of everlasting security for the Christian believer, not as an excuse for uncertainty or an incentive to anxious speculation concerning one's spiritual state. Set free from the shifting sands of self-trust, the Christian believer has absolute security in God, who is the Rock of his salvation (Mt. 7:24-27; Dt. 32:4, 15; 1 Sam. 2:2; 2 Sam. 22:2, 3, 32, 47).

The predestination of Holy Scripture is not the expression of an inexorable determinism which robs man of any genuine power of response by rendering him the victim or the beneficiary of a destiny that has been inescapably fixed for him. Nor does the responsibility with which man is invested rob God of his sovereign power to control all that comes to pass in his creation in accordance with the wisdom and purpose of his will. Far from filling us with doubts concerning our standing before God and driving us to engage in anguished soul-searching to discover whether we belong to the number of God's elect, or in moralistic self-discipline to convince ourselves that we do, the doctrine of predestination should encourage us to place our whole trust and confidence in Christ and the promises of the gospel. The reason for God's acceptance of us is not found in ourselves; for Christ, the True Image, is in a unique sense God's Elect One from all eternity; he alone is the beloved Son with whom the Father is well pleased (Lk. 9:35); therefore, our sonship, our election, and our privilege as heirs of eternal glory are real only in Christ (Rom. 8:15-17).

The faith God gives to the stricken one who out of the depths cries, simply and blindly, for help (Mt. 15:25) is, because it is *God's* gift, indefectible faith. The cry itself is the reaching out from the heart of one's being for reintegration with him who is the Image in whom we were created; and the faith bestowed is the reconnection of the person-to-Person lifeline as the heart in its self-induced darkness longingly inquires, "Who art thou, Lord?" and receives the response, "I am Jesus" (Acts 9:5)—Jesus who saves his people from their sins (Mt. 1:21).

How can we doubt for one moment that God, "who did not spare his own Son but gave him up for us all," does not give us all things freely with him (Rom. 8:32)? How can we imagine that self-righteousness or the supposed merit of our own works can serve to justify us in the light of this truth? How can we not see that to trust at all in ourselves for acceptance with God is not to trust fully in Christ, and is indeed to question the perfect adequacy of his redeeming work for us and the sufficiency of divine grace? We owe everything to God and his goodness. We have nothing that we have not received (1 Cor. 4:7). "So let no one boast of men," St. Paul writes. "For all things are yours, whether Paul or Apollos or Cephas or the world or life or death or the present or the future, all are yours, and you are Christ's, and Christ is God's" (1 Cor. 3:21).

CHAPTER 14

The Effect of the Fall

A right understanding of what is implied by the fallenness of human nature is important not only for defining the condition of man in his sinful state but also for judging the ability of man in the appropriation of redemption. That the subject is not without difficulty is apparent from the divergence of opinion that has persisted throughout the history of the church. The two main historical forms of this divergence may, for the sake of convenience, be called Semi-Pelagianism and Augustinianism. But the designation Semi-Pelagianism immediately indicates the existence of a third form, namely Pelagianism, the salient features of which must be described before entering into the discussion of the other two. Pelagianism takes its name from Pelagius, a British monk and eloquent preacher who at the beginning of the fifth century propounded views regarding the fall and its consequences which Augustine stringently opposed. Pelagius, with the support of Celestius, another Britisher, and Julian of Eclanum, taught that Adam's lapse had consequences only for himself and not for mankind as a whole, and that the sins committed by his descendants were committed in imitation of the first sin. This position was based on the supposition that all men come into this world as Adam originally did, in a state of purity and innocence and with a completely free will, that Christ's requirement of perfection of life (Mt. 5:48) implied an inherent ability on the part of all persons to attain such perfection, and indeed that this perfection had been achieved by numbers of saintly persons from generation to generation. It was, in short, a doctrine of total human ability.

The Pelagian denial of original sin and of the universal depravity of human nature was at the same time a denial of the absolute necessity of the gospel; for if each person has the innate capacity to live a life of perfection, then those who succeed in doing so have no need of redemption, and those who fail to do so have not fulfilled their own potential. Even though the latter may be said to need saving grace, there is no intrinsic necessity for a redeemer of mankind that is self-competent and unfallen. Disturbed, it is said, by the low state of morals he found in the church at Rome, Pelagius seems to some extent to have been motivated in his teaching of natural ability by a desire to promote a worthy level of ethical conduct. His opinions were condemned and anathematized as heretical at the Council of Ephesus in 431, but in specific association with the name of Celestius.

In his work *On the Gift of Perseverance,* written in 428 or 429 near the close of his life, Augustine mentioned that his words addressed to God, "Give what thou commandest and command what thou wilt," which were published in his *Confessions* before the rise of the Pelagian heresy, had been quoted to Pelagius "by a certain brother and fellow bishop of ours," and that Pelagius, finding them unendurable, had strongly objected to them.[1] In another book, *On Heresies,* written at about the same time, Augustine said that the disciples of Pelagius and Celestius were such opponents of the grace of God that they maintained the ability of man to perform all the commandments of God apart from his grace. "If this were true," he rejoined, "God would evidently have said in vain, 'Without me you can do nothing.'"[2] Elsewhere, referring to Ezekiel 18:31, where God says, "Make you a new heart and a new spirit," and to the promise of God later in the same prophecy (36:26), "A new heart I will give you, and a new spirit I will put within you," Augustine asked: "How is it, then, that he who says 'Make you' also says 'I will give you'? Why does he command, if he himself means to give? Why does he give if man is to make, except it be that he gives what he commands when he helps him to obey upon whom he lays his command?"[3] It was along these lines that he argued the correctness of the passage in the *Confessions* to which Pelagius had taken exception. Supporting himself with an array of scriptural quotations, he insisted, contrary to the Pelagian contention that human nature, since it comes from God, cannot be infected with original sin, "that man is born in sin and under the curse."[4]

The assertion made, for example, by Charles Hodge, that Augustine held the loss of the divine image to be a consequence of original sin is not strictly correct. It is true, as we have seen, that Augustine wrote, when commenting on Genesis, that because of his sin Adam lost the image of God in which he had been created; but Hodge failed to notice that in his *Retractations* Augustine explained that he did not mean that none of the image remained in man, but, rather, that it was so cripplingly deformed by sin that it was in need of being reformed.[5] This, moreover, is evident from the position defined in others of his works, where he asserted clearly that the image of God has not been so completely expunged from the heart of man as to leave no traces of its presence,[6] and, again, that the loss was not of the image as such, but of man's original righteousness and holiness, with the result that it is now marred and de-

1. Augustine, *Confessions* X.xxix.40; *On the Gift of Perseverance* 53.
2. *On Heresies* 88.
3. *On Grace and Free Will* 15.
4. *On Marriage and Concupiscence* ii.29.
5. Charles Hodge, *Systematic Theology,* Vol. II (London, 1960; 1st edn.; Princeton, 1872), p. 161; Augustine, *Retractations* 11.24. See p. 65 above.
6. Augustine, *On the Spirit and the Letter* 48.

faced. Augustine held that the image could be reformed only by God who had first formed it, since it was unable to form itself again by the ability with which it had deformed itself.[7] This would become essentially the position of Calvin and of Reformed theology in general (though Calvin, as we have seen, was not at all consistent in his manner of expression). The point is that while sinful man is totally unable to redeem and reintegrate himself, yet he has not ceased to be God's creature formed in the divine image, though he denies this truth and his nature is perverted.

Semi-Pelagianism, as the designation suggests, is a position intermediate between Pelagianism and Augustinianism, though its inherent inclination is toward the former rather than the latter. In important respects it is similar to Arminianism, which arose in the seventeenth century and has been widely accepted ever since in the world of Protestant Christianity. The Council of Trent in the sixteenth century formally approved the synergistic principle of Semi-Pelagianism as part of the official teaching of the Roman Catholic Church. During the centuries that intervened between the patristic period and the Reformation a diversity of emphasis continued, the line of division being, in the main, between those who favored and those who opposed the Augustinian doctrines of sin and grace.[8]

Augustine himself was involved in friendly controversy with Semi-Pelagian Christians during the last years of his life. In 426 he sent two letters to Valentinus and the monks of Hadrumetum in North Africa and also two treatises, the first *On Grace and Free Will* and the second (the following year) *On Rebuke and Grace,* for the purpose of reaffirming and at the same time removing misunderstandings regarding his doctrine. Referring, in the first letter, to passages such as John 3:17 and Romans 3:6, which speak of salvation and of judgment, he asked: "If there is no grace of God, how does he save the world? and if there is no free will, how does he judge the world?"[9]—though he also warned his readers that they should "neither deny God's grace nor uphold free will in such a way as to separate the latter from the grace of God, as if without it we could by any means either think or do anything in God's way, since this

7. *On the Trinity* xiv.16.
8. Despite Adolf Harnack's denunciation of the designation "Semi-Pelagianism" as "a malicious heretical term" (*History of Dogma,* Vol. V [Edinburgh, 1897], p. 245), it is a serviceable label which, in any case, has now been too long in use to be easily replaced. Owen Chadwick's preference for the designation "Anti-Augustinianism" perhaps reflects more accurately the historical climate, but as a portmanteau designation it obscures the fact that opposition to the emphasis of Augustine was in significant respects partial rather than total. The Semi-Pelagian denied both the total ability of man to justify himself (Pelagius) and the total inability of man to do so (Augustine). As Chadwick says, "the semi-Pelagians professed homage to Augustine and all his works except in the matter of predestination and irresistible grace" (*John Cassian* [Cambridge, 1950], p. 113).
9. This may well be a source of the celebrated dictum of Bernard of Clairvaux, seven hundred years later: *Tolle liberum arbitrium, et non est quod salvetur; tolle gratiam, et non est a quo salvetur.*

is an achievement quite beyond our power." He admonished them that it was "a most erroneous opinion" for any man to say "that it is by the merit of his own works, or owing to his own prayers, or by virtue of his own faith, that God's grace has been conferred upon him," or to suppose "that the doctrine which those heretics hold is true that the grace of God is given to us in proportion to our deservings." The question of grace and free will, he granted, is "a very difficult one and intelligible to few"; for, faced as we are with the divine precepts and injunctions, "we could exercise no obedience without liberty of will," and yet we must believe "that both man's will is free and that there is also God's grace, without whose help man's free will can neither be turned towards God nor make any progress in God."[10]

The treatise *On Grace and Free Will* opened with expressions of disapproval not only of those who emphasize the freedom of the human will in an attempt to do away with the grace of God but also of those who, to the contrary, "so defend God's grace as to deny man's free will, or else suppose that free will is denied when grace is defended." Augustine counselled his readers not to be disturbed by the obscurity of this question and to thank God for such things as they understood. He affirmed, once more, that "God has revealed to us, through his Holy Scriptures, that there is in man's will a liberty of choice," pointing out that "God's precepts themselves would be of no use to a man unless his will were at full liberty to choose, so that by its assent he might obtain the promised reward as he obeys the precepts." Adducing numerous texts where a response is demanded, Augustine asked: "What is the import of the fact that in so many passages God requests his commandments to be kept and fulfilled, and of the way in which he makes this request, if the will is not free? ... And what do they all show us but the liberty of man's will in its preferences and choice?" To this he added the important instruction that "it does not detract at all from man's own freedom of will when he performs any act in accordance with the will of God."[11] He was careful to stress that the justification of the sinner before God was due entirely to divine grace and not at all to human merit or deserving, without, however, wishing to draw the conclusion that "men themselves in this matter do nothing by their free will," since the contrary was evident from appeals such as "Harden not your hearts," "Make you a new heart," and "Turn yourselves and live"—though such appeals did not render unnecessary the promise "I will give you a new heart" or the response "Turn us again, O Lord."[12]

Augustine's description of the unregenerate will as a will without power[13] and his denial of any prevenient merit—for "otherwise grace would be no longer grace"[14]—certainly accord with the teaching of Scripture; but his

10. Augustine, Letter I to Valentinus and the Monks of Adrumetum 2-7.
11. *On Grace and Free Will* 1, 2, and 4.
12. Ibid. 31f.
13. Ibid.
14. Ibid. 44.

willingness to speak of the unregenerate person as possessing a free will is confusing rather than enlightening. It would have been preferable to describe man in his fallenness as responsible, not merely in the sense of his being responsible for his sinful state, but in the sense also that he is able to respond to the appeals of his Maker with the response that comes from impotence and from the desire itself to be turned—the response, that is, which cries out to God to do for him what he cannot do for himself and to set even his will free by bringing it into conformity with the divine will. The fundamental reality and utter simplicity of this response are strikingly illustrated by the prayer *de profundis* that arose from the desperate need and resourcelessness of the Canaanite woman: "Lord, help me!" (Mt. 15:25). It was a cry from the root of her being.

In the treatise *On Rebuke and Grace* Augustine postulated that the number of the elect was fixed in such a way that it could be neither increased nor diminished, though the identity of the elect was hidden. This led him to conclude that no one could be sure of his own salvation: "for who of the multitude of believers can presume," he asked, "so long as he is living in this mortal state, that he is in the number of the predestinated?"[15] This inference is somewhat surprising, if only because uncertainty regarding salvation and final perseverance has always been characteristic of and is indeed inherent in the perspective of Semi-Pelagianism. Yet, given a rigid interpretation of the doctrine of predestination, perhaps uncertainty is a consequence to be expected, as is seen, for example, in the anxious introspection and self-examination for the purpose of determining, if possible, whether one could regard oneself as numbered among the elect which occupied the Puritan mind in the post-Reformation decades. As we have already observed, one of the benefits of the doctrine of election in Christ, rightly understood, is that it is conducive to assurance of salvation and eternal security in the beloved Son. Also questionable is the distinction that Augustine proposed between a will that is free and a will that is freed. What sort of argument is it that attempts to persuade us that the assertion that "there is always within us a free will" means that the will is either free from righteousness when it serves sin, in which case it is not good or freed, or free from sin when it is the servant of righteousness, in which case it is good and freed?[16] By this logic it might equally be argued that as one who is alive is free from death so one who is dead is free from life. It is a logic, moreover, which takes away what previously Augustine had granted.

Semi-Pelagianism was at first in large measure a reaction to the extreme rigidity of Augustine's formulations of the doctrine of predestination and reprobation. It was feared that what looked very much like fatalism would encourage church members to abandon the Christian struggle and to relapse into idleness as they awaited the outcome of their lives, over which, supposedly, they had no ultimate control. The mouthpiece of the opposition was Augus-

15. *On Rebuke and Grace* 39f.
16. *On Rebuke and Grace* 42; *On Grace and Free Will* 31.

tine's contemporary John Cassian, the leader of monasticism in Marseilles, who, busy at that time writing a volume of *Conferences* or conversations, purportedly with distinguished monks of the desert, devoted the thirteenth of these to what was in effect a rejoinder to Augustine's treatise *On Rebuke and Grace*. It is a guarded and in places a somewhat ambivalent statement. Acknowledgment is made that human pride should never try to put itself on a level with the grace of God or to imagine that divine blessing is merited by human works, and also that "the initiative not only of our actions but also of good thoughts comes from God, who inspires us with a good will to begin with."[17] Cassian, however, went on to propound a position that is plainly synergistic. He assured those who might object that the teaching referred to above seemed to be destructive of the freedom of the will not only that God's will was not death but life for his creatures, but also that the grace of God cooperated with the good will of man, which itself might be the consequence either of divine or of human initiative: "When God sees in us some beginnings of a good will, he at once enlightens it and strengthens it and urges it on towards salvation, increasing that which he himself implanted or which he sees to have arisen from our own efforts."[18] He maintained, nevertheless, that "the completion of our salvation is assigned to our own will."[19]

The sovereignty of God and the priority of his grace were not denied by Cassian; indeed, they were asserted to be manifest in his dealings with some persons. But the effect of the position held by Cassian was to subjugate the will of God and his grace to the will of man. Thus he contended that "the will always remains free in man, and can either neglect or delight in the grace of God," while at the same time granting that man has need of divine aid in the attainment of salvation.[20] Moreover, a will that is free and good and leads to human effort can hardly fail to bring in the notion of human merit, in such a way that divine grace, in return for human effort, small in comparison though the latter may be, bestows the reward of immortality and eternal bliss. Cassian held up the centurion who was commended by Jesus as an example: "For there would have been no ground for praise or merit if Christ had only preferred in him what he himself had given" (a palpably anti-Augustinian thrust!).[21] The grace of God is granted, said Cassian, "according to the measure of the faith which he finds in each one, or as he himself has imparted it to each one."[22] And even this careful statement is guarded by the further qualification, which strains Cassian's self-consistency, that there is no intention to suggest "that the chief share in our salvation rests with our faith, according to the profane notion of

17. John Cassian, *Conferences* xiii.3.
18. Ibid. xiii.4, 7, 8.
19. Ibid. xiii.9.
20. Ibid. xiii.12.
21. Ibid. xiii.13, 14. See Mt. 8:5ff.
22. Ibid. xiii.15.

some who attribute everything to free will and lay down that the grace of God is dispensed in accordance with the desert of each man."[23]

The position defined by John Cassian could hardly have failed to be influenced by the presuppositions of his own monastic asceticism. It reflects the confusion between justification and sanctification historically characteristic of the ascetic mind, which almost inevitably was girded with the hope that the rigors of monastic self-discipline and self-isolation, of chastity, poverty, and obedience, must count toward salvation when God makes his reckoning. But, as Owen Chadwick has said, "Cassian was certainly in error. Christianity demands that the human personality shall be wholly surrendered into the hands of God, that there be no reserve. Not the least of Augustine's services to the Church is the framing of this truth. Even if a tiny portion, an *ortus bonae voluntatis,* is kept out of the sphere of God, men may be encouraged to place ultimate reliance upon human nature instead of God."[24]

Antipathy to the Augustinian doctrine of a more vehement nature came from Vincent of Lérins, also in Gaul, who composed a number of *Objections* in which the teaching of Augustine was viciously caricatured—charging, for example, that he held God to be the author of sin and responsible by his decrees for adulteries and murders, and that to pray "Thy will be done" was in the case of the majority of Christians to pray for their own damnation.[25] In the *Commonitory,*[26] a work written some four years after the death of Augustine, Vincent denounced Augustine's doctrine (without mentioning him by name) as heretical, wildly accusing him of "casting away the universal and ancient faith of the Catholic Church," and of presuming to do so by producing "a thousand testimonies, a thousand examples, a thousand authorities" from the Scriptures, and by means of false interpretations precipitating unhappy souls "from the height of catholic truth to the lowest abyss of heresy." But Vincent himself was guilty of false interpretation as he complained acrimoniously that the Augustinians "dare to teach and promise that in their church, that is, in the conventicle of their communion, there is a certain great and special and altogether personal grace of God, so that whosoever pertain to their number, without any labor, without any effort, without any industry," are assured of eternal salvation.[27]

Vincent's bitterness is understandable, as was John Cassian's reaction,

23. Ibid. xiii.16.

24. Chadwick, *John Cassian,* p. 137.

25. The *Objectiones Vincentianae* are in substance preserved in a communication of Prosper of Aquitaine to Augustine (Migne, *PL,* LI, 177ff.). Owen Chadwick calls the composition "a scurrilous document . . . portraying as the teaching of Augustine the most unpleasant deductions which could be drawn from the doctrines in question" (*John Cassian,* p. 111).

26. *Commonitorium* in the sense of "remembrancer" or "aide-mémoire," as Vincent himself explains, "to aid my memory, or rather, provide against my forgetfulness, with particular reference to the teachings of the fathers of the universal church" (p. 3).

27. Vincent of Lérins, *Commonitory,* § 69.

to the extent that Augustine's doctrine of grace appeared to be the negation of the security he had sought in the solitude of a monastic cell. He wrote of himself as "avoiding the concourse of crowds and cities" by "dwelling in the seclusion of a monastery." There, he said, "I have cast anchor in the harbor of religion, a harbor to all always most safe, in order that, having been there freed from the blasts of vanity and pride, and propitiating God by the sacrifice of Christian humility, I may be able to escape not only the shipwrecks of the present life, but also the flames of the world to come."[28] Though we may assume that Vincent professed belief in divine grace and the necessity of faith, it is obvious that he was preoccupied with ideas of self-salvation and regarded his seclusion and self-abnegation as a road leading to acceptance with God. What could be more unevangelical, and therefore more remote from the heart of Christianity, than the expectation of "propitiating God by the sacrifice of Christian humility"? What could be more foreign to the apostolic proclamation that by his sacrifice of himself for sinners Jesus Christ the righteous is the propitiation for our sins (1 Jn. 2:2; 4:10)? The deep incompatibility between Vincent's theology and that of Augustine goes far to explain the hostility of the monk of Lérins.

Vincent died before the middle of the century and his mantle fell upon Faustus, who, after serving as abbot of Lérins, became bishop of Riez in Provence in 458 and whose works included two volumes on the grace of God and the free will of the human mind, composed about 474, in which the Augustinian doctrine of the priest Lucidus was opposed and Augustinianism was depicted as no different from pagan fatalism. A determination which affirmed the orthodoxy of Augustinianism was subsequently made at the Second Council of Orange (Arausiacum) in 529, over which Caesarius, archbishop of Arles and an able advocate of Augustinian theology, presided. Augustinianism was cleared of the charges of uncatholic novelty and pagan fatalism and declared to be consonant with the position of the Scriptures and the fathers of the church. The absolute necessity of prevenient grace for salvation and the inability of the human will to initiate faith received repeated emphasis. The issue of predestination, however, was passed over in silence, except for a repudiation of any notion of predestination to evil. The doctrinal statement appended to the 25 canons promulgated by the council declared plainly that "in every good work it is not we who take the initiative and are then assisted through the mercy of God, but God himself first inspires in us faith in him and love for him without any previous good works of our own that deserve reward."[29] Confirmed by papal approval, the judgment of the Council of Orange looked like the victory of Augustinian theology, albeit in a somewhat modified form. But the victory,

---

28. Ibid., § 2.

29. An English translation of the canons issued by the Council of Orange and of the concluding statement is given in *Creeds of the Churches,* ed. John H. Leith (New York, 1963), pp. 38-45.

if such it was, was little more than academic. Differing opinions regarding the effects of the fall on the freedom and power of the will continued to be advocated, and Semi-Pelagianism in particular, far from being extinguished, succeeded in establishing itself as the generally accepted form of interpretation during the medieval centuries and beyond.

THE SEMI-PELAGIAN SYNTHESIS

Although the anthropology of Greek philosophy is radically incompatible with the anthropology of the New Testament, the medieval period was not free from attempts to effect an accommodation between them. This compromising propensity, which had long had a strong attraction for some, was attributable to a residue, mainly unsuspected, of Greek conceptual premises in the mind-set of a number of the church's leading thinkers rather than to any intentional departure from the emphases of apostolic doctrine. The Greek dualism of matter and spirit, so threatening in the patristic era, was to all intents and purposes replaced by an ecclesiastical dualism of nature and grace. The canons published by the Council of Orange were so expressed that they were in some respects susceptible of constructions of which Augustine would hardly have approved. While the priority of divine grace was insisted on as a *sine qua non,* even so the free will of man was described as but impaired and weakened, and the way was not expressly closed against the cooperation of good works subsequent to the reception of prevenient grace for man to be acceptable to God. Of course, almost any statement can be lifted from its context and given an interpretation that is unintended by its author, and there were undoubtedly places in the writings of Augustine which, when isolated, were open to misconstruction, notwithstanding his insistence on the total inability of man in his fallenness to contribute to his justification before God. He could, for example, speak of human nature as sick and in need of healing, without intending, however, to suggest that man was only partially disabled and accordingly capable of self-help in conjunction with the healing power of the Physician. What he did mean was that human nature, though fallen, was still human nature, that sinful man has not ceased to be man who is God's creature formed in the divine image. Thus he affirmed that all the good qualities which human nature "still possesses in its constitution, its life, its senses, its intellect, it has from the Most High God, its Creator and Maker," and that "the flaw, which darkens and weakens all those natural goods, has not been contracted from its blameless Creator . . . but from that original sin, which it committed of its own free will."[30]

A good tree that degenerates into a corrupt tree does not cease to be a tree. "Man makes the tree corrupt when he corrupts his own self, when he falls away from him who is the unchanging good," Augustine wrote. This, certainly,

30. Augustine, *On Nature and Grace,* § 3.

is devastating for man, but it is not the obliteration of man. Hence Augustine's assurance to his readers that "this decline does not initiate some other nature in a corrupt state, but it vitiates that which has been already created good." The nature which has been vitiated is still there to be healed. Thus we may speak of the vitiation of human nature, but not of human nature as itself essentially vicious.[31] To the same effect Augustine maintained that, no matter what sins a person commits, "these defects of character do not eliminate his manhood from man," for "God's good workmanship continues still, however evil be the deeds of the impious." True though it is that man in his ungodliness is compared to a brute beast (cf. Ps. 49:12; 73:22), "yet the resemblance is not so absolute that he becomes a beast": the comparison is not by reason of nature, but because of the degrading and stupefying effect of vice in man. "God, therefore, condemns man because of the fault by which his nature is disgraced, and not because of his nature, which is not removed out of existence in consequence of its fault."[32]

In contrast to this teaching of Augustine on the depraving effect of original sin on human nature Semi-Pelagianism represented human nature as in itself unimpaired by the fall, though not free from creaturely weakness and in need of divine assistance. The original sin was held to have brought about the loss of original righteousness, which was regarded as a supernatural gift added on to man's nature, with the result that its loss left man in a purely natural state—that is to say, in a state in which his nature was unvitiated, a state of neutrality, as it were, poised between good and evil, and not, therefore, a state of incapacitation. This was certainly not what Augustine meant when he spoke of the continuity of human nature as God's handiwork following the fall. Nor was Semi-Pelagianism a reversion to the Pelagian notion of the total ability of man apart from the grace of God. Its adherents did not deny the universality of human sinfulness and the necessity accordingly of the grace of God for salvation; but they did affirm the ability of man, which implied also his responsibility, to contribute to his own redemption, and thus a partition of sovereignty between God and man in the experience of salvation—though in fact it could not avoid leaving the final word with man, since whether he received or rejected the salvation offered, and whether he persevered in or defected from the faith, once he had professed belief, rested not with God but with man and left man's sovereignty as the ultimate deciding factor.

The subsoil in which this distinction between the additional grace of original righteousness and the purely natural state of man found rootage was the separation between the image of God and the likeness of God which was postulated in the interpretation of Genesis 1:26 before the end of the second century,[33] and which had continued to be influential in the theological thought of

31. *On the Grace of Christ and Original Sin*, § 19.
32. Ibid., § 40.
33. See pp. 7ff. above.

the church. In accordance with this interpretation the "image" represented man's natural state at creation, whereas the "likeness" represented his assimilation to the holiness of God, and the achievement of the latter required not only reliance on help given by God but also the concentration of man's own serious efforts. As we have previously pointed out, this exegetical differentiation between "image" and "likeness" is unacceptable; nor is it proper to regard it as justifiable on the ground that it could lend itself to sound as well as to unsound conclusions. Its application to the sphere of ontology was especially mischievous. Human nature remained human nature, it is true, but there was a radical change from good to bad, from blessing to curse, a change not of ontology but of direction: man, seeking to suppress the image in which he was made, which is the mark of God's lordship over him, turned away from his Creator and, paying attention to the lie of the tempter, made the devil his father and his god (Jn. 8:38, 41, 44; 2 Cor. 4:4; Jn. 12:31; 14:30; 16:11) and in doing so perverted and debased his nature. Far from being neutral by nature and able to merit divine favor, man is now a child of wrath (Eph. 2:3)—which means, since that wrath is the wrath of divine judgment, that he has escaped not one inch from the total sovereignty of God over him.

Now it is clearly not incompatible with the biblical perspective to speak of the original righteousness of man; but this state of original righteousness consisted in the perfection of man's creation as a moral personal being, in the harmony of his relationship to his Creator, and in his conformity to the divine will—in short, in the integrity of his constitution in the divine image. This is the structure of man's nature as he is meant to be and the necessary condition for the fulfilment of the wonderful potential of his God-given personhood. Original righteousness was not an extra superadded to man's natural state. On the contrary, man's natural state was precisely that of original righteousness.

There were, however, other influences than a point of exegesis proposed by Irenaeus to be taken into account, influences traceable to pagan philosophy rather than to the interpretation of a particular biblical text. From the earliest times the church had to do battle with the threat posed to Christian orthodoxy by certain modes and notions especially of Greek philosophical thought, and most of all with the Pythagorean and neo-Platonic spirit-matter dualism inherent in the docetic and then the gnostic heresies, in their various formulations, which assailed not only the reality of the incarnation, the very foundation of christological and soteriological truth,[34] but also the integrity of human nature itself. In the medieval period the reappearance of Aristotle's philosophy made a considerable impact on the ecclesiastical mind, thanks in the main to the endeavor of Albert the Great and Thomas Aquinas to "baptize" it into the Christian faith. The God of Aristotle was defined as pure or absolute Mind, the "Thought of Thought,"[35] who as such was pure form completely separated from

34. See pp. 237ff. below.
35. *Noēsis noēseōs*.

matter, while in man the soul was viewed as the form of the body, the former being immortal and the latter perishable. Moreover, the affinity between God who is absolute mind or reason required the human soul to be identified with man's rational or intellective faculty. Thus, though he modified and reshaped the concepts of his master Plato and forged his own distinctive theory of reality, Aristotle retained the central dualistic principle of the Platonic system.

In the work of Thomas Aquinas, composed in the thirteenth century, neo-Platonic and Stoic as well as Aristotelian influences are discernible and in places controlled his theological thought. Characteristically Aristotelian was his concept of the dichotomy of rationality and matter. Thus he assigned the corruptible or perishable aspect of man to the material part of his nature and excluded it from the rational soul, which, he maintained, had an immaterial operation of its own and was alone able to achieve perpetuity.[36] Man, according to him, as originally constituted, could know the truth in all things without the addition of any new illumination to the natural light of his reason; it was only in the things that surpassed his natural knowledge that he needed the assistance of supernatural enlightenment. Deprived, however, of supernatural power, human nature after the fall was left in a weakened state, unable completely to fulfil its own potential. Aquinas explained that "in the state of the integrity of nature" man needed "a gratuitous strength superadded to natural strength" to enable him "to do and will supernatural good," while "in the state of corrupted nature" there was "a necessity of grace," both so that he might be healed and to enable him "to carry out works of supernatural virtue, which are meritorious."[37] Aquinas held the loss or privation of original righteousness to be the formal element in original sin, and the consequent disorder of the human faculties, which manifested itself in concupiscence or lust, the material element.[38]

The introduction of the concept of human merit, even in conjunction with the need for divine grace, inevitably involves the notion of human ability and desert in the procuring of salvation, and this is of the very fabric of Roman Catholic Semi-Pelagianism. The desire to produce a synthesis of merit and grace, or of nature and supernature, was nothing new; but grace and merit cannot be synthesized; they are antithetical the one to the other: grace is free and unearned, merit is earned and is owed a reward. Total grace corresponds to total demerit. To the extent that man is supposed to merit the favor of God, to that extent he has no need of grace. The issue is confused, further, by concepts of merit deserving grace and grace stimulating merit. And this is the confusion at the heart of Semi-Pelagianism. It is apparent in Aquinas's qualification of his assertion that "man, by his will, does works meritorious of everlasting life" (which by itself would be bare Pelagianism) with the proviso that "for this it

36. Thomas Aquinas, *Summa Theologica,* pt. II, q. 85, art. 6.
37. Ibid., pt. II, q. 109, arts. i, 2.
38. Ibid., pt. II, q. 82, art. 3.

is necessary that the will of man should be prepared by the grace of God."[39] The idea of man as in any sense meriting his own salvation cannot fail to call in question the full sufficiency of the redemption freely provided through the atoning work of Christ. Moreover, for man's salvation to depend to however small a degree on his own meritorious works throws his ultimate salvation into complete uncertainty: if he is able to deserve eternal life by his good works, he is equally able to deserve eternal death and the loss of grace by subsequent evil works. His final perseverance is something about which he can never be sure. This, too, is characteristic of Semi-Pelagianism, and it should not surprise us to find Thomas Aquinas stating that "grace is given to many to whom perseverance in grace is not given."[40]

It is worth noting here that in interpreting Genesis 1:26 Aquinas made a distinction between "image" and "likeness" in such a way that "likeness" could be explained either as falling short of "image" or as perfecting "image."[41] He evidently regarded either construction as acceptable, presumably because either was adaptable to his dialectic of nature and supernature. But this dialectic, because of its division of human nature into a rational soul (eternal spirit) and a human body (perishable matter), destroyed the radical unity of man as God's creature, dissolved the radical character of the fall and its consequences, and obviated the radical depth of our redemption in Christ.

The position of Aquinas is essentially that adopted officially by the Papal Church at the Council of Trent in the sixteenth century. There is a plain rejection of the doctrine of Pelagius. Original sin, it is held, involved the loss of original righteousness and is transmitted by physical generation.[42] The inability of man to liberate himself from enslavement to sin is acknowledged, but the will, though "attenuated and bent down in its powers," is treated as still free and "by no means extinguished."[43] The necessity of "the prevenient grace of God, through Jesus Christ," is affirmed, because man "is not able, without the grace of God, by his own free will to move himself unto righteousness in his sight," though his power of "cooperating with that grace" is maintained.[44] It is stated, moreover, that "faith cooperating with good works" produces an "increase in the justification received through the grace of Christ," so that one can become "still more justified"[45] (a concept which well illustrates the long-standing confusion of justification and sanctification in Catholic theology, which is virtually inseparable from the belief that good works contribute to a person's justification; justification in Christ does not allow of degrees; if it is not total it is not possessed at all, whereas it is sanctification that is progres-

39. Ibid., pt. II, q. 109, art. 5.
40. Ibid., pt. II, q. 109, art. 10.
41. Ibid., pt. I, q. 93, art. 9.
42. Council of Trent, Session 5, Decree concerning Original Sin.
43. Session 6, Decree concerning Justification, ch. 1.
44. Ibid., ch. 5.
45. Ibid., ch. 10.

sive, from glory to glory; cf. Rom. 3:28; 5:1; 2 Cor. 3:18). Contrariwise, justification which can be deserved and increased may also be lost through failure of faith or the commission of mortal sin; but, again, if lost, it may be regained through sacramental confession, sacerdotal absolution, and the sacrament of penance, with "satisfaction by fasts, almsgivings, prayers, and other pious exercises of spiritual life."[46]

Within the Semi-Pelagian scheme, therefore, the disposition of man becomes really determinative of the state of grace or of reprobation of each person, and that state is as changeable as is the disposition. This situation obviously leaves the ultimate state of the church member in complete uncertainty, without any possibility of assurance regarding final salvation (apart from the unlikely miracle of a divine communication). Accordingly, it was decreed by Trent that "each one, when he regards himself and his own peculiar weakness and indisposition, may entertain fear and apprehension concerning his own grace, inasmuch as no one can know with a certainty of faith, which cannot be subject to mistake, that he has obtained the grace of God," or "that he is assuredly in the number of the predestinated, . . . for, except by a special revelation, it cannot be known whom God hath chosen unto himself."[47]

The dogmatic stand of Rome on these matters was fortified by the pronunciation of anathemas against specific teachings which the Reformers contended were true to Scripture and the gospel, notably that the free will of man "in no way cooperates to the end that it should dispose and prepare itself for obtaining the grace of justification," or that all works done before justification are without merit and displeasing to God, or that the sinner is justified by faith alone, or that assurance of salvation and of final perseverance may be had by believers, or that the grace of justification may not be preserved and also increased by good works, or that justification may not be lost by those who fall after baptism and regained through the sacrament of penance, or that the guilt and penalty of sin are so blotted out by the grace of justification "that there remains not any penalty of temporal punishment to be discharged either in this world or in the next in purgatory, before the entrance to the kingdom of heaven can be laid open."[48] These definitions and condemnations give clear expression to the Semi-Pelagian emphasis on the necessity of human cooperation for divine grace to become effective. The priority of grace is indeed asserted, but not in such a way that it is sovereign and indefectible. Rather, it is seen as generally dependent on the mood of man, whose cooperating good will and good works are regarded as rendering him deserving of grace, either in gaining or in increasing it, and who by a change of mind may forfeit grace and possibly receive it again. What this amounts to, in the determination of the ultimate state of salvation or reprobation of each person, is the superiority of the

46. Ibid., ch. 14.
47. Ibid., chs. 10, 12.
48. Ibid., Canons 4, 7, 9, 16, 17, 24, 29, 30.

human will over the divine will, as the latter waits upon the decision of the former with all its fickle variability.

The dialectic of nature and grace on which Semi-Pelagianism rests with its confidence in the natural ability of fallen man as a rational being with freedom of will to cooperate with the grace of God, and its dichotomy of man as mortal flesh and immortal soul, gives rather clear evidence of ancestral linkage with the dialectic of matter and spirit in Greek philosophy that agitated the church in earlier centuries. Thomism was in reality an attempt to adjust and accommodate the one to the other, and it was followed by other attempts to do the same thing under a variety of guises and permutations. The incongruity of such dialectical endeavors is apparent, as we have mentioned, in the way in which the divine will is left hanging upon the human will and the essential unity of human nature is disrupted. Yet it is a dialectic that has been and continues to be widespread not only in the Semi-Pelagian teaching of Roman Catholicism but also in the Arminian mentality of much of Protestant Christianity. The virtual, though unintended, dualism of this perspective can hardly fail to give rise to an intractable dilemma. The Thomistic dichotomy of man and emphasis on the inherent immortality of man's rational soul as the seat of knowledge and center of human nature carried with it uncomfortable gnostic overtones. So also did the attempt to deal with the dilemma by divorcing the events of human history from the realities of divine grace and eternal truth that is associated with the thesis of Hermann Reimarus and Gotthold Lessing, who, in the eighteenth century, declared that the facts of history, held to be accidental, contingent, and temporal, could never become the proof of or be identified with those truths of reason that are regarded as necessary and eternal. This of course trivialized the great cardinal events of the New Testament gospel, since, even if they were true, they were *ex hypothesi* void of abiding significance, let alone indicative of the activity of God in and through our history. In the later years of the same century Immanuel Kant taught to much the same effect that there could be no connection between the external events of history and the speaking of God who is known to us subjectively through our faculty of reason.

Because there was no possibility of effecting a Hegelian synthesis of the thesis of pagan philosophy and the antithesis of Christian truth, the principle of the one which made man and the principle of the other which made God the center of reference being irreconcilable, either they had to be compartmentalized and kept in separation from each other or the one had to be stressed to the virtual exclusion of the other. Semi-Pelagianism, as we have remarked, is an attempt to produce the impossible synthesis. The alternative course was followed, for example, by Karl Barth, who so filled the scene with grace that there was no room for nature, even placing creation prior to the fall under the umbrella of grace and covenant. This showed that he had not freed his thinking from the old dichotomy of nature and grace, as also did his separation of *Historie,* that is, natural or secular history, from *Geschichte,* that is, supernatural history, involving in particular the events of Christ's saving work, which were thus, in a manner unknown to the New Testament, removed from the sphere and the level of the human continuum. The other route, that of reducing everything to the natural dimension by eliminating the supernatural, has been followed by the radical liberal theologians of the nineteenth and twentieth centuries with their programs of demythologization and deabsolutization and evolutionary development. There has been a failure, or an unwillingness, to acknowledge that the true heart of man is not his reason or his emotion or his will but his constitution in the image of God, which is the source of the identity and unity of his whole being. It is not the mind but man that reasons, not the breast but man that is moved, not the will but man that decides. The deep disharmony of man's being is due not to his constitution but to the sin of his ungodliness, which is the denial of his being in the image of God and therefore the rejection of the true heart of his humanity.

Seen in this biblical perspective, man's only desert is the wrath of God. Dead in sins, his sole hope is in God, who raises the dead to life (Eph. 2:1-5; 2 Cor. 1:9). Since he is blinded by Satan, the darkness of his faculties can be dispelled only by his Creator, who is the source of all light and understanding (2 Cor. 4:4-6; Jn. 1:4f., 9; Eph. 5:14; Rom. 1:21f.). Nor is the sinner's state one merely of helplessness in himself but also one of enmity and hostility toward God (Rom. 5:6, 10; Col. 1:21). His evil conscience is in desperate need of being purified from dead works (Heb. 9:14; 10:22). The one question to be asked is the question put to Jesus by his disciples: "Who then can be saved?" And the only answer to be given is the response of Jesus: "With men this is impossible, but with God all things are possible" (Mt. 19:25f.). It is in relation to this situation of the total inability of man to initiate or achieve his own salvation and the total ability of God to do so, from beginning to end, that the doctrine of predestination comes into its own.

THE TERMINUS OF SYNERGISM

Synergism (a term which signifies collaboration or working together), when used in connection with the doctrine of redemption and justification, refers to the opinion that man contributes to and thus cooperates with God in the work of his salvation. Though the principle of Semi-Pelagianism is similar to that of Arminianism (named after the sixteenth-century Dutch scholar Jacobus Arminius), for both affirm the necessity of divine grace for salvation and the power of man freely to cooperate with that grace and thus to dispose himself favorably toward the reception and the retention of salvation, it is convenient to use the former term to designate the synergism associated with Roman Catholic theology and the latter that associated with Protestant theology. The logical tendency of synergism, with its concept of God and man as co-workers, is toward the equation of God and man, even though this may be far from the intention of what may be called decent everyday synergistic teaching and worship. The historical evidence indicates, however, that this equation is reached as a terminus by different routes: synergistic Catholicism with its emphasis on human merit tended to elevate man to the height of union with God, whereas synergistic Protestantism with its persuasion of human competence tended to reduce God to the level of human relationships. Though different routes are followed, these can be perceived as adjacent platforms of the same destination.

The terminus to which Semi-Pelagian synergism leads is exemplified in the development of mariology in the Roman Catholic Church. In the devotional and dogmatic life of Catholicism the Virgin Mary is revered as the one who ideally illustrates the cooperation of man in the work of redemption. As early as the second century a comparison had been drawn between Eve and Mary: both were virgins visited by angelic beings, but whereas Eve disobeyed the word of God and brought evil upon mankind Mary welcomed the word of the Lord and became the mother of the Savior of mankind.[49] This comparison, innocent enough in itself, was subsequently elaborated by the postulation of a parallel between Christ as the Second Adam and Mary as the Second Eve, which has continued to be popular in Catholic thought. Given a distinctive role in counteracting the mischief of Eve's disobedience, Mary is viewed as sharing in the reconciling work of Christ. Indeed, her function is seen as being antecedent to the coming of Christ in such a way that apart from it his coming would not have been possible. This conception of Mary as the one who actually enabled God to proceed with the incarnation is dependent on a particular interpretation of the account of the Annunciation: her response to the angel Gabriel, "Behold, I am the handmaid of the Lord; let it be to me according to your word" (Lk. 1:38), is explained as showing her willingness to cooperate with God, without which the incarnation would not have taken place. And so Mary was assigned the status of mediatrix, initiating, contributing to, and uniting herself with the mediatorship of the Son to whom she gave birth.

This conclusion was fortified by taking the words with which Gabriel greeted Mary to mean that she was full of grace[50] and therefore the dispenser of grace. Her designation as "Mother of God" (*Theotokos*) at the Councils of Ephesus and Chalcedon (in 431 and 451 respectively) was intended to safeguard the authentic deity of Jesus, as opposed to false notions to the effect that Jesus was a mere man (psilanthropism) or some kind of unique creature whose being was less than that of God (Arianism). The title Mother of God, however, encouraged some to conclude that a person of such dignity must have been free from sin, and the idea gained currency that Mary herself was conceived and born untainted by sin—despite the fact that this was inconsistent

49. See, e.g., Justin Martyr, *Dialogue with Trypho* 100; Irenaeus, *Against Heresies* iii.22; and, early in the third century, Tertullian, *On the Flesh of Christ* 17.

50. This understanding relied on the Latin rendering *Ave, gratia plena;* but the Greek of Lk. 1:28, *Chaire, kecharitōmenē*, which RSV translates "Hail, O favored one," clearly implies that she is the recipient, not the dispenser, of grace.

both with the view of Mary, who addressed God as her Savior (Lk. 1:47), and of the New Testament as a whole with its insistence that the incarnate Son alone was without sin (Heb. 4:15; 7:26; 1 Pet. 2:22; 3:18; 2 Cor. 5:21; 1 Jn. 3:5; cf. Rom. 3:9ff., 23). Little though the advocates of the doctrine of Mary's immaculate conception intended to make concessions to the Pelagian heresy, for Mary to have been born in a state of innocent sinlessness could hardly imply other than that hers was a distinctly Pelagian start to life. Moreover, the doctrine should have raised the question of the sinfulness of her parents, who, if the argument were logically pursued, should in turn have been immaculately conceived, and so on back in a regress that would ultimately have extended right back to Adam and Eve, thus eliminating original sin altogether and, if anything, establishing the correctness of the Pelagian hypothesis.

The question was in fact hotly disputed for centuries, especially between the Scotists, who approved the conclusion that Mary was born free from sin, and the Thomists, who rejected it. Such leading schoolmen as Bernard, Albert the Great, Bonaventure, and Thomas Aquinas contended that since, as they held, original sin is transmitted by natural generation, and Mary's birth was by natural generation, she could not have been born sinless. Nevertheless, in 1854, Pope Pius IX proclaimed *ex cathedra* that the Immaculate Conception of the Blessed Virgin Mary was a dogma binding on the faithful.[51] This served to make the cult of Mary an imperatively credal fixture. The remaining step, to raise Mary as it were from earth to heaven, was taken officially in 1950 when Pope Pius XII promulgated *ex cathedra* the dogma of her bodily assumption into heaven and subsequently designated the date 31 May for the annual celebration of the Feast of Mary Queen of Heaven.

In the interval between the dogmatic definitions of 1854 and 1950 the Marian cult was energetically promoted, not least by a number of papal pronouncements which elevated the mother of Jesus to the supreme level of equality with God. In 1891 Leo XIII declared that, "as no one can come to the Most High Father except through the Son, so, generally, no one can come to Christ except through Mary";[52] in 1904 Pius X described Mary as the restorer of a fallen world and the dispenser of all the gifts of grace won for us by the death of Christ;[53] in 1918 Benedict XV affirmed that Mary had redeemed the human race in cooperation with Christ;[54] in 1923 Pius XI expressed his approval of addressing Mary as Co-Redeemer;[55] and in 1946, on the occasion of the crowning of the statue of the Virgin at Fatima, Pius XII proclaimed that "Mary is

51. The dogma was promulgated in the papal bull *Ineffabilis* as having been revealed by God. It declared that "the most holy Virgin Mary was, in the first moment of her conception, by a unique gift of grace and privilege of Almighty God, in view of the merits of Jesus Christ, the Redeemer of mankind, preserved free from all stain of original sin."

52. Encyclical *Octobri mense*.

53. Encyclical *Ad diem*.

54. Encyclical *Inter sodalicia*.

55. Encyclical *Explorata res est*.

indeed worthy to receive honor and might and glory," that "she is exalted to hypostatic union with the Blessed Trinity," and that "her kingdom is as great as her Son's and God's."[56] That indeed set a terminus beyond which it is impossible to go. The deification of Mary is the *ne plus ultra* in the outworking of Semi-Pelagianism and the logical destination of the *analogia entis* adopted from the philosophy of the Greeks. Notwithstanding certain qualifications which issued from the Second Vatican Council (1962-65),[57] the absolute distinction between the Creator and the creature has been dissolved in the worship of Mary, revealing the end to which the tide of Semi-Pelagianism flows. The particular blessedness of Mary as the mother of the Redeemer is not to be questioned, but the development of mariolatry involves a radical digression from the apostolic doctrine and worship of the New Testament, according to which the exaltation of human nature has taken place not in Mary but in Christ the incarnate Son, who, having made our nature his own, having kept it pure by the perfection of his holiness, and having redeemed it by his vicarious sacrifice of himself on the cross, has also raised it to glory in his resurrection and ascension.

If Semi-Pelagianism in Roman Catholic devotion is conducive to the worship of the creature rather than the Creator (Rom. 1:25), the same is true of the tendency of Arminianism in Protestant circles, for, as we have mentioned, its logical conclusion is, through proceeding seemingly in the reverse direction, to attribute to men equality with God by bringing God down to the level of equality with man. This may be far from the desire and intention of many, indeed most, of those whose minds are controlled by Arminian presuppositions; but the fact is that synergism, whatever form it takes, assigns to man the power by the determination of his will to frustrate or nullify the work of God's grace, and thereby invests him with a sovereignty which in this respect is superior to the divine sovereignty, primary though the latter may by definition be. Any diminution of the absolute distinction between the Creator and the creature leads either to a false aggrandizement of human nature and its

56. For a discussion of these developments see W. von Loewenich, *Modern Catholicism* (London, 1959); also Giovanni Miegge, *The Virgin Mary: Roman Catholic Marian Doctrine* (London, 1955).

57. In Chapter VIII, on the role of the Blessed Virgin Mary, of the *Dogmatic Constitution on the Church* theologians and preachers are instructed that "in treating of the unique dignity of the Mother of God" they should "carefully and equally avoid the falsity of exaggeration on the one hand and the excess of narrow-mindedness on the other." The assurance that because Mary "belongs to the offspring of Adam" she is "one with all human beings in their need for salvation" is strangely incongruous with the affirmation that Mary was "entirely holy and free from all stain of sin," being "adorned from the first instant of her conception with the splendors of an entirely unique holiness," and in all her deeds was "impeded by no sin," which can only imply that she was not in need of salvation. Equally unsatisfactory is the assurance that "the maternal duty of Mary toward men in no way obscures or diminishes" the "unique mediation of Christ." See *The Documents of Vatican II* (New York, 1966), pp. 86, 90, 93, 95.

potentiality or to a reductionist view of the Deity, which in the end amounts to the same thing.

The degenerative effect of Arminian doctrine is quite dramatically exemplified in the vicissitudes suffered by English Christianity after the death of Elizabeth I in 1603. In the sixteenth century the structure of the Church of England had been carefully assembled on a foundation of solidly reformed theology and worship, enshrined in the Book of Common Prayer and the Thirty-Nine Articles of Religion and attested by the sermons and writings of its leading minds. Notions of synergism were resolutely opposed and excluded from the doctrine of justification, and there was a quite remarkable coherence of theological conviction from Cranmer to Hooker in the periods that preceded and followed the reactionary interlude of the reign of Mary Tudor.[58] But thereafter the theological climate began to change. Richard Bancroft, who became archbishop of Canterbury in 1604, showed no enthusiasm for the "calvinistic" persuasion of his predecessors. James I, though he had expressed dislike of the Arminian tenets that had come across from the Netherlands, evinced no scruples about appointing men of Arminian inclination to the episcopal bench, and his son Charles I pursued this policy with increased vigor and openness. The dominant position to which Arminianism was brought under the latter's rule signalized a substantial departure from the consistent emphasis of the reformers of the previous century. The manipulation of theology for political ends even played a part in stirring up the unrest that led to civil war;[59] and the advance of Arminianism was certainly not discouraged by what Bishop Fitz-Simons Allison has called "the rise of moralism" in the Church of England in the seventeenth century.[60]

The state of religion in England during the years of the civil war helped, if anything, to facilitate the propagation of moralistic opinions in connection with the doctrine of justification which were to all appearances synergistic, without necessarily having any intentional link with Arminianism. Richard

---

58. See my *Faith and Works: Cranmer and Hooker on Justification* (Wilton, Connecticut, 1982), which includes the text of Cranmer's *Homily of the Salvation of Mankind* and Hooker's *Learned Discourse of Justification,* together with an introductory essay.

59. In a perceptive study of the implications and effects of these theological developments Dewey Wallace has expressed the judgment that "Arminianism in England represented an utterly radical theological innovation," that "it isolated Calvinist Episcopalians who had hitherto represented the mainstream of Anglicanism," that "it broke the main unity between Puritan and conformist, leaving the Puritans as a whole more bitterly opposed to the established church than they had ever been," and that "this theological division was significant enough to be a factor in the coming of civil war" (*Puritans and Predestination: Grace in English Protestant Theology, 1525-1695* [Chapel Hill, North Carolina, 1982], p. 220, where he affirms "the strongest possible agreement" with the conclusions of Nicholas Tyack, "Puritanism, Arminianism, and Counter-Revolution," in *The Origins of the English Civil War,* ed. Conrad Russell [London, 1973], pp. 199ff.).

60. C. FitzSimons Allison, *The Rise of Moralism: The Proclamation of the Gospel from Hooker to Baxter* (New York, 1966).

Baxter, for example, was disturbed by the antinomian character of much of the religious instruction being received by the soldiery when he was a young army chaplain, and also by the antinomian proclivities of the hypercalvinistic faction, and it was this that inclined him to postulate the need for ethical preparation for justification and for "evangelical" works to make a person a fit recipient of justifying grace. His espousal of these views made it hardly surprising that some of his contemporaries accused him of teaching Roman Catholic synergism. John Owen for one complained that he made works "to be meritorious causes of justification and salvation" in no other sense than that asserted by the papists.[61]

Bishop Jeremy Taylor, whose writings, like Baxter's, were widely influential far beyond the period of his life, was another seventeenth-century divine who propounded moralistic notions which emphasized obedience as a necessary way into the Christian covenant and held that there was no quick and easy forgiveness for our sins. So insistent was he on the importance of *Holy Living* and *Holy Dying* (the titles of two of his best-known works) for justification that he even likened deathbed repentance to the washing of a corpse, since it allowed no opportunity for living the holy life that is demanded of us and that he held to be the right preparative for a holy death. This laid him open to the criticism that he was requiring a standard of godly conduct from the unregenerate that was possible only in those who had first been justified by divine grace. Taylor's position in fact seemed to be indistinguishable from Semi-Pelagianism, and even in places to be Pelagian without modification.[62] Thus he not only propounded a fundamental dichotomy between nature and grace—maintaining that Adam's fall involved the loss of the "supernatural endowments" bestowed on him in his state of innocence, with the result that he "was reduced to the condition of his own nature," that is to say, that God did not take "from him or us any of our natural perfections, but his graces only"—but also held that Adam started the sinning of mankind by setting a bad example, but was not the cause of that universal sinfulness—"sin propagated upon that root and vicious example, or rather from that beginning, not from that cause"—a statement that would have pleased Pelagius.[63]

Underprivileged because of Adam's lapse and loss, man was regarded by Taylor as having actually "sinned less than Adam" and as being relatively

61. John Owen, in his preface to William Eyre's tract *Vindiciae justificationis gratuitae* (London, 1654).

62. See the sermon on "The Invalidity of a Late or Death-Bed Repentance," in *The Whole Works of the Right Reverend Jeremy Taylor,* Vol. I (London, 1853), pp. 782ff. It is a subject that crops up elsewhere in Taylor's writings. On the doctrine of original sin see chapters 6 and 7 of *Unum Necessarium or the Doctrine and Practice of Repentance, describing the Necessities and Measures of a Strict, a Holy, and a Christian Life* (ibid., Vol. II, pp. 531ff.).

63. Ibid., Vol. II, p. 532.

or "imperfectly righteous," in that he falls short of the perfection of Christ.[64] Taylor insisted, then, that "the sin of Adam neither made us heirs of damnation nor naturally and necessarily vicious";[65] but he did not teach that justification before God was in man's power apart from the redeeming grace of God. As he saw it, mankind's state since Adam was an "animal" or natural state, and his position one of neutrality, midway between heaven and hell. This "animal" state, he wrote, was "not a state of enmity, or direct opposition to God, but a state insufficient and imperfect"; for in the state of "animality" man "cannot go to heaven, but neither will that alone bear him to hell."[66]

Taylor even contended that there was a beneficial aspect to the fall of man, not, however, in line with the *felix culpa* tradition, but because of his supposition that the fall resulted in an increase of human knowledge, and therefore also in an increase of his wisdom and his ability to choose right and reject evil. Maintaining that man's will-power, or power of election, as he also called it, was unimpaired and that he was "not naturally sinful," he declared that "it is so far from being true that man after his fall did forfeit his natural power of election, that it seems rather to be increased." The reason given for this conclusion was that man now has the benefit of knowing the difference between right and wrong, the danger of disobeying God, and the disturbance of a guilty conscience; and we are advised, further, that "God was pleased" to eject man from paradise in consequence of this advance in knowledge—as though the ejection were a gain rather than a loss.[67] Yet this natural competence was accompanied, according to Taylor, by "a natural impotency"; because "natural agents can effect but natural ends, by natural instruments," it was necessary to understand that "our natural state is not a state in which we can hope for heaven," that to be "born in pure naturals" is not enough, and that therefore we "must be born again."[68] The suspicion of latent dualistic presuppositions is strengthened by his further assertion not only that "the state of the body is a state not at all fitted for heaven," but also that "even in innocent persons, in Christ himself it was a hindrance or a state of present exclusion from heaven."[69]

64. Ibid., p. 533.
65. Ibid., p. 535.
66. Ibid., p. 543.
67. Ibid., p. 548.
68. Ibid., pp. 552, 553.
69. Ibid., p. 560. Such vestiges in Taylor's thought of body/spirit dualism are subsumed under the nature/grace antithesis. Taylor had no wish to deny the sinlessness of Christ, but he was prepared to argue that sin could in a metonymous manner be attributed to him because, in his view, the condition of the mortal body he took to himself in the incarnation was by nature "a state of misery and of distance from heaven." He was, indeed, guilty of an altogether extraordinary lapse when he put forward the explanation that "thus in the epistle to the Hebrews it is said that our blessed Lord, who is compared to the high priest among the Jews, did 'offer first for his own sins,' whereas it is the exact opposite which is affirmed, namely, that, being sinless, Christ had no need, like the levitical high priests, to offer sacrifice first for himself (Heb. 7:27)" (ibid., p. 534).

Taylor in particular disapproved of what he called "the usual doctrines about original sin" because he regarded them as false for the moralistic reason that, "as they are commonly believed, they are no friends to piety, but pretences of idleness."[70] Christians, freed from the notion that original sin was properly sin for anyone (other than for Adam), and assured that the human nature that was theirs was not depraved but only deprived of an original supernatural gift of righteousness, would now, it was hoped, do battle with the concupiscence that was inseparable from human nature and strive to advance heavenwards assisted by the strengthening grace of God. Jeremy Taylor was no romanizer,[71] but he had traveled some not inconsiderable distance along the road that led, little though he desired it, to the declaration of man's complete self-adequacy in the determination of his eternal destiny. Bishop Allison has justly called his ethical concern a "rootless moralism" of a type which has had ungodly consequences for later generations. Morality that "is deprived of its roots" and "is disastrously separated from orthodox Christian dogma" was, he says, "the origin and the curse of the moralism which now is ascendant in the West."

> It exhorts a power of freedom that fallen man does not possess; it is a religion of control (called "self-control") and not redemption, and it ends inevitably in despair rather than in hope. The moral imperatives exacted of men are predicated on a definition of sin that is only wilful and deliberate, thereby implying that the problem of sin is essentially superficial, a misconception that culminates in a false hope of self-justification.[72]

The domestic violence which obviated the subjugation of England to the alien domination of Spain and Rome did not put an end to the progress of Arminianism with its confidence in the natural ability of man, especially in relation to the freedom of his will and the power of his reason. A still more theologically radical tributary to this humanizing movement was that of Socinianism, which, like Arminianism, came to England from across the Channel.[73] The Socinian system was compounded of humanistic, rationalistic, latitudinarian, and antitrinitarian elements, and as such it was fundamentally incompatible with historic Christian orthodoxy and, so far as the Church of England was concerned, with the Thirty-Nine Articles and the Book of Common Prayer. Socinianism and Arminianism could, however, be described as traveling companions, though the former was somewhat in advance of the latter, and it is not altogether surprising that at times the terms were treated almost interchangeably, since both emphasized the competence of man as a moral and rational

70. Ibid., p. 574.
71. See his *Dissuasive from Popery* (ibid., pp. 761ff.).
72. Allison, *The Rise of Moralism*, pp. 207f.
73. Socinianism was so named after Fausto Sozzini (Faustus Socinus, 1539-1604), an Italian artistocrat whose thought was influenced by his uncle Lelio Sozini (1525-1562), and who after leaving his homeland and visiting numerous countries, including England, finally settled in Poland.

agent. The attempts of Archbishop Laud, himself an ardent Arminian, to bring in measures for the suppression of the "antichristian rabble of Socinians" met with limited success;[74] and John Owen, the leader of Reformed orthodoxy, who in 1642 had published *A Display of Arminianism,* was one of the scholars moved by the spread of unitarianism in England to write against Socinianism.[75]

In *The Liberty of Prophesying* (1647) Jeremy Taylor pleaded not only for religious toleration but also for the right of every man to be guided by the dictates of his reason in deciding what he wished to believe. The single requirement of an authoritative nature Taylor made was that of adherence to the articles of the Apostles' Creed (which by themselves could hardly be regarded as an infallible safeguard against Socinianism). Otherwise the judgment of a man's reason, coupled with the morality of his conduct, was propounded as sufficient to validate his profession of faith, even though he had embraced erroneous teaching: "because he leads a good life he is a good man, and, therefore, no heretic."[76] Though he acknowledged that the Church Fathers were unanimous in their acceptance of the canonical Scriptures as the rule and standard of Christian belief, Taylor disallowed the appeal to Scripture for the determination of orthodoxy (on the premise of difficulties and obscurities in the text and conflicts of interpretation); he also disallowed the appeal to tradition and ecclesiastical councils and papal pronouncements (on the ground that they were incapacitated throughout their history by uncertainties and contradictions). And so his great principle was the guidance of the individual's own reason: "Herein I consider that no man may be trusted to judge for all others," he wrote, ". . . yet every man may be trusted to judge for himself." His assertion that "no man speaks more unreasonably than he that denies to men the use of their reason in choice of their religion" plainly reveals the rationalistic propensity of his mind.[77] Taylor, of course, was no unitarian, but his rejection of the inherent guilt of original sin and his belief in the unimpaired integrity of man's natural faculties subsequent to the fall were otherwise consonant with the perspective of Socinianism.[78]

74. "'Arminianism,'" Hugh Trevor-Roper has observed, "in England as in Holland, was intellectually a liberal movement: it joined hands with the 'Socinianism' which it officially repudiated" *(Archbishop Laud, 1573-1645* [2nd edn.; London, 1962], p. x).

75. See his *Vindiciae Evangelicae, or the Mystery of the Gospel Vindicated and Socinianism Examined,* which came out in 1655.

76. Taylor, *The Whole Works,* Vol. II, p. 314.

77. Ibid., pp. 365-67.

78. H. John McLachlan has supposed that during the time that he was a fellow at All Souls Taylor was impressed by the broad and liberal principles of the Oxford school of rational theologians. "It can hardly be an accident," he says, "that they are also those of Hales and Chillingworth. Moreover, they are also the principles of Socinus and his school, of whose writings the Oxford men were students" *(Socinianism in Seventeenth-Century England* [Oxford, 1951], p. 89). Mention may appropriately be made, too, of the so-called Cambridge Platonists at the other English university, who cultivated a similar mind-set—antidogmatic, rationalistic, and latitudinarian. As McLachlan remarks, "there is no deny-

Certainly many others could effectively be cited as exponents of this growing rationalistic temper, but for our purposes Jeremy Taylor, a man of high repute as a churchman and a scholar, adequately exemplifies the new trend in religious thought. The magnification of man's ability must be expected to lead to the depreciation of the need for divine grace. The weakening of biblical theism prepared the way for philosophical deism, which banished God from the sphere of human affairs and made him little more than a spectator from afar; but deism, having rendered God irrelevant, was but a stage on the road that terminated in atheism. The declension was hastened, if anything, by the distaste felt by many for the rigid tenets of hypercalvinism, which was a reaction in the opposite direction to the growing laxity of belief among those who called themselves Christians.[79] Samuel Taylor Coleridge went so far as to describe Jeremy Taylor as an unconfessed Pelagian,[80] and asserted that Socinianism was "as inevitable a deduction from Taylor's scheme as Deism or Atheism is from Socinianism."[81] It is a judgment with which Allison concurs. He charges that the moralizing divines of seventeenth-century England "postulated a freedom of will in sinners that was of Pelagian proportions," and that, as the sequence of history shows, starting from such assumptions "soteriological thought, by an implacable logic, moved inexorably through an exemplarist atonement to an adoptionist christology, to a Socinian deity, and finally from deism to atheism."[82]

The end product of this exaltation of man and his competence was rapidly enough displayed in the moral degradation and religious bankruptcy at every level of society during the first decades of the eighteenth century, to which attention has been drawn earlier.[83] In our own day we have witnessed the resurgence of a reductionist theology that demands the diminution or demotion of God to the merely human level. The identification of God with man, or man with God, is the destination to which the logic of synergism is a station on the way. In the call for the demythologization of the Bible by the removal of all that is supernatural God becomes the ultimate myth to be got rid of. The ap-

---

ing the striking similarity of temper and viewpoint between the Cambridge men and Socinian and Arminian writers" (ibid., p. 101).

79. See Peter Toon, *The Emergence of Hyper-Calvinism in English Nonconformity, 1689-1765* (London, 1967).

80. S. T. Coleridge, *Notes on English Divines*, Vol. I (London, 1853), p. 275.

81. Ibid., p. 278. It is interesting that Coleridge had Jeremy Taylor to thank for convincing him of the superiority of Calvinism to Arminianism. His reading of Taylor's work on repentance *(The Doctrine and Practice of Repentance)*, which he described as a book "calculated to drive men to despair," "first opened my eyes to Arminianism," he wrote, "and that Calvinism is *practically* a far, far more soothing and consoling system" (ibid., Vol. II, p. 38).

82. Allision, *The Rise of Moralism*, p. 192. See also J. I. Packer's valuable essay "Arminianisms," in *Through Christ's Word*, ed. W. Robert Godfrey and Jesse L. Boyd (Phillipsburg, New Jersey, 1985), pp. 121ff.

83. See pp. 140f. above.

peal for the deabsolutization of Christian doctrine perforce includes the de-absolutization of the doctrine of God, who, we are now assured, is not supremely and transcendentally other than man but is no more than the depth of man's own being. In the sphere of soteriology synergism is a stage *en route* to humanistic monergism—the postulation of man's total ability to save himself, and then the notion that man, precisely because of his self-adequacy, is after all in need neither of salvation nor of God.[84] This humanistic terminus, however, is foreign to the Christianity of the New Testament, and it is now to the theme of the reintegration of our humanity by its restoration to the likeness of him who is the Image of God in which man was created that we must turn.

84. See, e.g., the essays in *The Myth of God Incarnate,* ed. John Hick (London, 1977). Cf. also J. A. T. Robinson, who cites with approval the assertion of the atheist Julian Huxley that "the sense of spiritual relief which comes from rejecting the idea of God as a supernatural being is enormous," and likewise the admonition of Paul Tillich that "you must forget everything traditional that you have learned about God, perhaps even that word itself." In calling for "a radically new mould, or *meta-morphosis,* of Christian belief and practice" and for preparedness "for *everything* to go into the melting," Robinson demands that "the first thing we must be ready to let go is our image of God himself" *(Honest to God* [London, 1963], pp. 41, 47, 124). Robinson also agrees with "men like Feuerbach and Nietzsche" who "saw such a supreme Person in heaven as the great enemy of man's coming of age" (ibid., p. 47).

PART III
The Image Restored: Reintegration

CHAPTER 15

The Word Becomes Flesh

The Son of God, who as the divine Word is the expression of the will and power of God, is not only the agent of creation by whom all things were brought into being and the providential sustainer of the universe as a historical continuum (Col. 1:15-17; Heb. 1:2f.) but also the redeemer in and through whom all God's purposes in creation are established and brought to fulfilment. Within the order of creation, however, man is the focal point of redemption. Having been formed in the divine image and given dominion over the earth, man by falling into sin perverted his own nature and at the same time dragged the rest of creation down with himself by his selfish and ungodly abuse of the dominion entrusted to him. Accordingly, the reconciliation of man to his Creator means also the restoration of the whole creation and the realization of the destiny for which he and it were always intended. The fundamental requirement for the achievement of this end is the reintegration within man of the image of God at the heart of his being, and this is necessarily effected through the Second Person of the Holy Trinity for the reason that he himself is the Image after whom man was created. There is, as we have shown earlier, a special line of affinity that links the Son of God to our humanity—a line which, though it in no way nullifies the absolute ontological transcendence of the Creator over the creature, does establish an association that is unique to man in the ontological sphere of creation, and that points to the "possibility" of the incarnation, the becoming man, of the Image himself in whom man has been formed. The nature of this linkage between the Image and man who is formed in the image remains, of course, a profound mystery that surpasses our comprehension, but it is assuredly a reality constitutive of man's being and his unique position at the head of creation. The supremacy of man in relation to the rest of creation reflects the supremacy of God in relation to the whole of creation, including man. Man alone has had affinities that reach both downward within the world over which he has been placed and upward to the Creator who is the Lord of all being. The truth that lies behind this double linkage is, first of all, that man is God's *creature;* secondly, that man alone of God's creatures is formed *in the image of God;* and, thirdly, that the eternal Son is *the Image* in accordance with which man was formed. The deeply intimate bond that binds man to the Second Person of the Godhead is thus constitutional to the very being of man and its restoration is essential for the rehabilitation not merely of man but also of the whole order of creation.

The doctrine of the Image of God is the key to the factuality of the incarnation no less than to the understanding of the true nature of man. The problem, arising from the limitation of our being and horizon, is: How can God become what he is not? How can God become one with his creature for the purpose of restoring all things? The answer to this problem is present, as we have indicated, in the line that connects man to the Second Person of the Holy Trinity, that links image to Image, that is, the image of God at the center of man's being to the Image who is God the Son. But it must be understood that in becoming flesh the Word does not cease, even temporarily (if that were possible), to be the eternal Word. In becoming man the Son does not cease to be God. The Son was under no necessity to leave off being God if he was to start being man. The provision for the coexistence of the divine nature and human nature in one theanthropic person was there all along thanks to the wisdom by which man was created in the divine image. In any case, God cannot cease to be what he essentially is. It is readily conceivable that a creature which comes from nonbeing may return to nonbeing. But for God to change from being to nonbeing, or to cease being God in order to enter into being man, is inconceivable, since God himself is eternally Life and Being and the source of all life and being other than himself. For God the Son to cease being God by becoming man in the incarnation would be a contradictory concept. The Son would then not be God in action but God out of action, because out of existence; and this would inevitably mean not the restoration but the collapse and dissolution of all things, since, as we have said, the Son is both the agent of creation and the one through whose power the universe is sustained in existence. The incarnation is God the Son actively taking to himself our human nature without in any sense ceasing to be God. And this assumption of human nature was not the assuming of a role as in play-acting or the donning of a different guise, as the old heresy of modalism imagined, or the use for a time of a separate human being, as the docetists taught,[1] which robbed the incarnation of reality and degraded it to the realm of make-believe, but the Son truly and historically becoming man. At Bethlehem the ever present "possibility" of the incarnation of the Second Person of the Trinity was actualized, without doing violence either to the Son's divine nature or to our human nature.

There is, however, a further problem which presents itself: seeing that ours is a fallen nature under the cloud of divine judgment, how is it possible for the Son to avoid the fallenness of our nature in his act of becoming man? How can he escape bringing himself under the same cloud of judgment that casts its shadow over our humanity? The "solution" to this problem is the virgin birth. In the Son's birth the divine meets with the human. In the ordinary course of events birth is a distinctly human occurrence, even in those cases

1. On docetism and modalism see pp. 237ff. and p. 254 below.

where there is an interposition of divine enabling, as in the birth of Isaac and of John the Baptist. These births were not without particular significance, but the children so born were by nature not instances of God becoming man; their persons were solely human; moreover, the human nature that was theirs was human nature in its fallenness and in need of redemption. The conception of Jesus in the womb of Mary was, as St. Luke carefully explains in his account of the nativity (which he doubtless received from Mary herself), effected by the same almighty power of God, indeed, but yet was quite different from the conceptions of Isaac and John the Baptist. The incarnation was a unique event for a unique purpose. In this case it is the power of God enabling Mary to conceive a child without first receiving the seed of a human father. From Mary our Lord took to himself our humanity, but through the operation of the Holy Spirit he did so without in any way compromising the full reality of his deity as the eternal Son. Hence the assurance given to Mary by Gabriel: "The Holy Spirit will come upon you, and the power of the Most High will overshadow you; therefore the child to be born will be called holy, the Son of God" (Lk. 1:35).

The circumstances of the birth of Isaac are illustrative of the way in which God fulfils the purposes of his will. God, when he chose for himself a people through whom his design for the redemption of mankind was to be promoted, chose a people not yet in existence; and as the progenitor of this people he chose Abraham, whose wife Sarah was not only aged but also barren, and gave him the humanly speaking laughable promise that he was to be the father of many nations.[2] How could Abraham possibly expect to gain a posterity through infertile Sarah, who in any case was long past the age of childbearing? To add to the impossibility, he was kept waiting another twenty-five years before Isaac, the child of the promise, was born. This was a wonder indeed! Not, however, where God, the source of all life, was concerned. To bring life out of deadness is for man as inconceivable as it is impossible; but not for God, who has brought all things into being out of nothing. The human impossibility of quickening Sarah's womb was therefore no problem at all for God. The conception and birth of Isaac instruct us that the achievement of God's purposes is not dependent on man and is not hindered by human impossibilities. God's power is supreme, and in that power his purposes are secure and indefectible. God's purpose in choosing Abraham and his seed, as also in the birth of Isaac, was fulfilled in the still more marvelous event of the birth of Jesus at Bethlehem, which involved the still more marvelous miracle of the childbearing of the virgin Mary.

God's great overarching purposes start from what to the human mind are intractable situations, indeed from situations in which there is apparently nothing to start with at all, such as the creation of the world from nothing, the choice of a nonexistent nation, and the birth of the Redeemer of mankind from the

---

2. The name Isaac means "laughter" and is evidently connected with the laughter with which both Abraham and Sarah reacted to the promise of a son (Gen. 17:17; 18:9-15).

womb of a pure and untouched virgin. This (and much else) is indicative of the sovereign power of Almighty God, which prevails in the midst of the impotence and hopelessness of our fallen condition to raise and restore us according to his mercy and grace. God chooses what the wise of this world count foolish and what the strong of this age count weak and what by the worldly mind is despised and passed by, and even "things that are not, to bring to nothing things that are" (1 Cor. 1:27ff.). Truly the birth of Jesus from a virgin mother was like the growth of a plant in infertile ground (Is. 53:2). Thus the ancient promise of the protevangel that Satan would be destroyed by the seed of the woman (Gen. 3:15) was fulfilled as God's hour struck, for, as St. Paul testifies, "when the time had fully come, God sent forth his Son, born of a woman" (Gal. 4:4).[3]

It was by means of the virgin birth that the Son of God took our human nature to himself. Few things would seem to be more passive and confined than an embryo in a woman's womb, but the conception and birth of Jesus were not mere passivities to which the eternal Son submitted; they belonged, rather, to his own activities. It is true that he was *sent* by the Father (see, e.g., Jn. 5:23, 24, 30, 37), but it is also true that he *came* of his own accord to perform the Father's will (see, e.g., Mk. 10:45; Jn. 6:38, 51; 1 Tim. 1:15; Heb. 10:7, 9). The virgin birth is inseparable from his active coming. The nativity was not the beginning of the Son's existence, but an event, a *becoming,* in his eternal existence. That is why it is said that the Word, who is God, *became* flesh (Jn. 1:1, 14), that he *became* in the likeness of man (Phil. 2:7, Greek), and that he *became* of or from a woman (Gal. 4:4, Greek).[4] The virgin birth of Jesus, then, is God in action uniting the human and the divine in the one theanthropic person of the incarnate Son. Accordingly, Ignatius, writing early in the second century, spoke of Jesus Christ as Son of Mary and Son of God, as generate and ingenerate.[5]

The uniqueness of the virgin birth in the history of mankind should not be a hindrance to faith; on the contrary, it should confirm the expectation that when God intervenes in a decisive manner in the affairs of men the event will be altogether out of the ordinary. The incarnation, as God's unique central act in human history, relates back to and interprets the original unique act of creation and relates forward to and interprets the ultimate unique act of the last judgment and the fulfilment in the new heaven and the new earth of all God's purposes in creation. Creation, which had been dragged down by the fall of the first Adam, was in need of a new Adam who by his perfect harmony with the

3. Literally, "having become of a woman" *(genomenon ex gynaikos).* See the next note.

4. In such passages the verb *ginesthai* is theologically significant because it designates a becoming in the eternal life of the Son and is therefore something other than a somewhat unusual way of designating the birth of Christ. In Gal. 4:4 *genomenos ek gynaikos* is not identical with the Hebraistic expression *gennētos gynaikōn,* one born of women, meaning simply a human person. Notice how, in Gal. 4, where *ginesthai* is used of Christ, *gennasthai* is used when speaking of Ishmael and Isaac (vv. 4, 23, 24, 29).

5. Ignatius, *Letter to the Ephesians* 7.

will of the Creator would raise it with himself to the glorious heights of its ever intended destiny. For this to be achieved it was necessary for Jesus Christ, the last Adam, to enter this world like the first Adam, innocent, God-centered, unstained by sin, and unburdened by guilt. God could actually have *created* a second Adam in the same way as he created the first Adam; but that unique event was not to be repeated because it would have meant an entirely new start and the abandonment of the original creation, whereas it was precisely to redeem and restore the original creation that the incarnation of the Son took place. Disconnection and discontinuity could not have effected this. The problem, then (though not for God), was how to do what was necessarily unique without sacrificing vital contact with man and the world—for vital contact was essential for the saving of creation.

There was, it may be suggested, the possibility at the other extreme of choosing to do what was ordinary and not at all unique—that is to say, the appointing of one born in the usual manner from the conjugal union of husband and wife. This would have ensured continuity, but continuity incapable of achieving the objective of salvation, since it would have been continuity with man *in his fallenness,* with the incapacitating consequence that anyone entering the world in this way would himself be in need of salvation and not its dispenser.

It was the birth of Jesus from a virgin mother, our fellow human being, that preserved the vital connectedness with our human nature, and it was the power of God active in his conception in the womb of Mary that guaranteed and made real his holiness as the new Adam under whose headship the regeneration of all things would be effected. Through the virgin birth the Word not only became flesh but also started his human life in a state of perfect integrity. In this latter respect he started as the first Adam had started; and this was important because it was necessary that the new Adam should do what the old Adam had failed to do—that he should retain and consolidate his integrity by gaining the victory where the first Adam had suffered defeat. Only thus could the way become clear for him to offer up himself for our redemption.

There is, however, no justification for concluding, as did some of the patristic authors, that the virginity of Mary was the source of the sinlessness of Jesus. This notion was bolstered by the view that the intimacy of marriage was inescapably defiling, even though not forbidden, and that accordingly Mary thanks to her virginity was free from any defilement in her conception of Jesus.[6] The biblical account of the nativity clearly attributes the holiness of

---

6. Support for this opinion was not infrequently claimed from the statement of David in Ps. 51:5, "Behold, I was brought forth in iniquity, and in sin did my mother conceive me," which, however, is not a statement affirming that sin is inherent in the generation of children but a declaration of the inherent sinfulness of all human nature in its fallenness. Ambrose in the fourth century, for instance, cited this text as confirming the viewpoint referred to above (*On Penitence* i.3), and he also adduced the saying of Jesus that in the heavenly state there will be no marriage but the redeemed will be like the angels (Mk. 12:25), drawing the conclusion that virginity was an anticipation of existence in heaven

the child borne by Mary not to her virginity but to the sanctifying operation of the Holy Spirit (Lk. 1:35)—though it is far from unimportant that as the one chosen to be the mother of the Messiah Mary was a pure maiden; but, as we have said, this did not mean that she had no need of salvation (cf. Lk. 1:47).

While it is the Second Person of the Godhead who becomes incarnate, his mission to us is perceived throughout the New Testament as a trinitarian operation. There is, indeed, no place in unitarian theology for incarnation. The life of the Christ of the Gospels is spent in doing the Father's will and in intimate fellowship, through prayer, with the Father who has sent him and anointed him with the Holy Spirit. Such interpersonal communion and collaboration cannot be postulated of a unitarian God. Hence by the inner logic of its system unitarianism is forced to devise some form of modalism or to deny the deity of Christ (and therefore also the incarnation). But to be an authentic mediator between God and man the Redeemer must bring both God and man together in his own person, thus himself constituting the bridge, so to speak, that spans and thereby joins both sides of the gulf that otherwise separates man from his Creator. Jesus Christ is precisely such a mediator. In the virgin birth there is, as we have seen, the union of the divine and the human. The incarnate Son is truly God: his work is the saving work of God for us sinners who cannot save ourselves (Jn. 1:1, 14; Col. 2:9; 2 Cor. 5:19). And he is truly man: his incarnation is his participation in the flesh and blood of our human nature (Heb. 2:14; Gal. 4:4; Rom. 1:3).

The Lord from above is accordingly one with God in his divine nature and one with man in his human nature, and both natures are brought together in the unity of his theanthropic person. At Bethlehem he who is the eternal Image of God took to himself our human nature which is created in the image of God—that is to say, created in him—and in doing so he conformed our human nature to that image in which it was created—that is to say, conformed it to himself, thus fulfilling the wonderful potential of that nature in its true integrity and making actual the purpose for which it was created.

The supernatural birth of Jesus gives us the assurance not only that he is the Son of God (Mk. 1:1; Lk. 1:35) but also that he is the seed of Abraham and the son of David (Mt. 1:1). As the seed of Abraham he is in the truest and en-

---

and the way of angelic purity. Indeed, of the incarnation he asserted that "virginity has brought from heaven that which it may imitate on earth" (*On Virgins, to his sister Marcellina* i.3). This line of interpretation was approved and adopted by Augustine (*Against two letters of the Pelagians* IV.xi.29) and Jerome. All three protested that it was not their intention to condemn marriage, though they regarded the married state as inferior to the excellence of virginity. Jerome, in fact, in a backhanded way, extolled marriage because it was productive of virgins: "I praise wedlock, I praise marriage," he wrote, "but it is because they give me virgins. I gather the rose from the thorns, the gold from the earth, the pearl from the shell"; and he assured any mother who had a daughter pledged to virginity that this meant that she (the mother) was thereby privileged to be "the mother-in-law of God" (Letter 22, to Eustochium, 18-20; *Against Helvidius* 22f.; *Against Jovinianus* i.36ff.)!

tirely unique sense the fulfilment of the promise given to Abraham that in his seed all the nations of the earth would be blessed (Gen. 22:18; Gal. 3:8, 16). His coming at Bethlehem is proof that God has remembered the mercy of which he spoke "to Abraham and to his seed for ever." It is the honoring and the performance of "the oath which he swore to our father Abraham, to grant us that we, being delivered from the hand of our enemies, might serve him without fear, in holiness and righteousness before him all the days of our life" (Lk. 1:54f., 73-75). As the son of David he is the promised personage who rules on David's throne and whose kingdom of peace and justice is without end (Lk. 1:32f., 69f.; 2 Sam. 7:12ff.; Ps. 89:3f., 20, 28f.; Is. 9:6f.). Only by supernatural provision from above could such a king be a reality and such a kingdom established, for no mere mortal king or earthly kingdom is perfect and everlasting. And this supernatural provision took place in Mary's virginal conception and his birth at Bethlehem, in the midstream of human history.

But Bethlehem is not the whole story. The birth that took place there was not an end in itself but a means to an end. The end to which Bethlehem was a means was Calvary, and unless Bethlehem is seen in direct relationship to Calvary its true purpose and significance are missed. The cradle was the start of the road that led to the cross; and the purpose of Christ's coming was achieved not in the cradle but on the cross. The purpose of the incarnation, in other words, was not ontological but soteriological. Thus Jesus declared of himself that "the Son of Man came . . . *to give his life as a ransom for many*" (Mk. 10:45), and St. Paul proclaimed that "Christ Jesus came into the world *to save sinners*" (1 Tim. 1:15). As Athanasius observed, it was not the Son's wish merely to become incarnate or to make himself visible, but rather by taking our nature to himself to offer himself up bodily to death in the place of all.[7]

In the modern age of much vaunted scientific sufficiency the mentality of deistic naturalism and humanistic rationalism is predisposed to treat the supernatural elements of Christianity as dispensable on the ground that they are either unnecessary or unacceptable, or both. It is hardly surprising that belief in the virgin birth of Jesus has been subjected to persistent attack. Friedrich Schleiermacher, for instance, writing more than a hundred and fifty years ago, denied any need for Christian sentiment to be tied to the dogmas of Scripture and argued that in any case the original Christian in the apostolic church did not hold the virgin birth of Jesus to be of dogmatic weight or worth. The accounts given by Matthew and Luke in their Gospels could not have been regarded as doctrinally important, and perhaps not even historically factual, Schleiermacher maintained, because the virgin birth has no mention anywhere else in the New Testament. Besides, he regarded it as a further disadvantage that "anyone who takes the stories of a virgin birth as literally exact has of course one miracle more to stand for." Nor did the fact that belief in the virgin birth of Jesus is affirmed in the ancient and also not so ancient creeds and con-

---

7. Athanasius, *On the Incarnation* 8, 10.

fessions cause Schleiermacher to modify his opinion, for he blandly brushed this consideration aside by assuring his readers that the passages expressing this article of belief "betray virtually no trace of a dogmatic purpose."[8]

It is certainly very remarkable to be told that any article of the historic creeds of the church betrays virtually no trace of a dogmatic purpose, if only because the primary purpose of credal summaries of the faith is essentially dogmatic. On this basis any part of the creed or the creed in its entirety may be dismissed as void of dogmatic purpose. Schleiermacher's pattern of criticism, however, has been embraced and developed with elaborations by many others who are predisposed to relegate what is supernatural in the biblical record, and not least the virgin birth as narrated in the First and Third Gospels, to the museum of fiction and legend. It has become almost commonplace for it to be asserted that what an author does not mention is *not known* by that author. Emil Brunner, for one, argued tortuously that "Matthew and Luke do not mention an Eternal Son of God who became man," but "simply tell us how the Son of God, Jesus Christ, was begotten." The reason for this, he supposed, was that they "still knew nothing of an Eternal Son," and so, in an attempt to explain the origin of Jesus, proposed "their idea of a parthenogenesis." Brunner contended, further, that this was "a clear contradiction" of the teaching of the Gospel of John that the Word was God and became flesh (something unperceived by the fathers and doctors of the church for 1800 years!); and this in turn brought him to the conclusion that "it is therefore not wholly improbable that the Johannine Prologue was deliberately placed where it is, in opposition to the doctrine of the Virgin Birth."[9] By tendentious reasoning of this kind, in which one hypothesis is made to stand on the shoulders of another, Brunner could hardly expect to persuade any except those who shared his presuppositions.

Like Schleiermacher before him, Brunner propounded the opinion that, since it is not mentioned in the other writings of the New Testament or in the preaching of the apostles, "the doctrine of the Virgin Birth does not belong to the *Kerygma* of the Church of the New Testament," and that "we must assume, either, that the Apostles were unaware of this view, or, that they considered it unimportant, or even mistaken."[10] The supernatural aspect was summarily dealt with by denying the historicity of the nativity stories in Matthew and Luke. Brunner explained that, together with other "negative indications," "the fact that this incident occurs exclusively in the two introductory sections of the Gospels which contain legendary features to a larger extent than anywhere else in the New Testament" made it "difficult for the conscientious historian to maintain the historical credibility of this tradition."[11]

To the same effect, Wolfhart Pannenberg has dismissed the account of the virgin birth of Jesus as a "legend" which "probably emerged relatively late in

8. Friedrich Schleiermacher, *The Christian Faith* (Edinburgh, 1928), pp. 403f.
9. Emil Brunner, *Dogmatics,* Vol. II (Philadelphia, 1952), pp. 352f.
10. Ibid., p. 354.
11. Ibid., p. 356.

circles of the Hellenistic Jewish community," though what the grounds are for this probability he does not say. He adds that "Paul and Mark were as little familiar with it as was John,"[12] and he categorically asserts that, "in its content, the legend of Jesus' virgin birth stands in an irreconcilable contradiction to the christology of the incarnation of the preexistent Son of God found in Paul and John," giving as his reason for this judgment that, "according to this legend, Jesus first *became* God's Son through Mary's conception."[13] This can only be described as a particularly tendentious piece of argumentation which imposes an alien construction on the text and is totally in conflict with the historic understanding of the church. The supposition that "an irreconcilable contradiction" remained for so many centuries undetected is but the creation of a modern legend.

Pannenberg does, however, permit us to affirm our belief in the virgin birth of Jesus when reciting the creed, provided we do so corporately, and also provided we bear in mind the "antidocetic" and the "antiadoptionistic" intention of the credal formulations. (The latter is an extremely problematic proviso for the ordinary congregation.) On the basis of these conditions we are assured that the article concerning the miraculous birth of Jesus "can be confessed in worship without abandoning truthfulness," since "the repetition of the confession of the church is certainly something different from the statement of faith of an individual."[14] In other words, we can say "we believe" but not "I believe." But it must be objected that this introduces an intolerable schizophrenia, for the congregation is compounded of individuals, and there is no way in which it can make sense for an individual who is a member of the church to affirm the belief of the church which is not his own personal belief. This is a prescription for confusion and insanity. It is but another indication of the hubristic mentality of modern man. "In the age of technology can we speak seriously of the descent and ascent of a heavenly divine being?" Pannenberg asks;[15] and he answers that "the figure of a Logos mediating between the transcendent God and the world no longer belongs to today's scientific perception of the world."[16] And so the unbelief of the individual is an uncomfortable bedfellow with the faith of the church.

In effect, these and similar critical spirits[17] propose a criterion which con-

---

12. Wolfhart Pannenberg, *Jesus—God and Man,* tr. L. L. Wilkins and D. A. Priebe (Philadelphia, 1968), p. 142.

13. Ibid., p. 143.

14. Ibid., p. 150.

15. Ibid., p. 154.

16. Ibid., p. 166.

17. Cf. Hans von Campenhausen, *The Virgin Birth in the Theology of the Ancient Church,* tr. Frank Clarke (London, 1964), for similar and fuller lines of argumentation and speculation. St. Paul's silence, he says, "can hardly fail to lead to the conclusion that he knew of no such theological doctrine." Likewise he asserts that the Apostolic Fathers "do not seem to know of the virgin birth"—with, however, the considerable and incapacitating (for his thesis) exception of Ignatius, who, he admits, "lays great theological stress on the virgin birth, and already regards it as an indispensable doctrine that has been handed down, and to which he refers in formal, almost confessional, language" (pp. 18, 19). What

veniently stipulates that an event or narrative recorded by only two authors (and presumably all the more so if only by one) may be held to have been unknown to the other authors of the New Testament, or if not unknown to them then rejected by them. It is a strange sort of reasoning that concludes that because the account of the virgin birth is given only by Matthew and Luke therefore "the Apostles were unaware" of such a birth, or "considered it unimportant, or even mistaken." In view of the fact that Matthew was one of the Twelve and Luke a companion of the apostles, the sensible conclusion is that apostles were well aware of the virgin birth of Jesus and did not consider it unimportant or mistaken. Moreover, it is improbable in the extreme that an article of belief unknown to the apostles or disapproved by them should have been accepted as apostolic and credally binding in the postapostolic church. It is antisupernatural bias that is betrayed by the rejection of the virgin birth on the ground that it is a legendary invention or "one miracle more" to be swallowed. Nothing should be less unexpected than that, when God is acting in a new way for his world, he should do so in a manner that is demonstrative of the dynamism of his transcendental power. As B. B. Warfield has stated, "no one can doubt that the Christianity of the New Testament is supernaturalistic through and through," and, as he further observes, the supernatural birth of Jesus "is already given . . . in his supernatural life and his supernatural work, and forms an indispensable element in the supernatural religion which he founded."[18]

The type of scholarship that attempts to explain passages like the nativity accounts of the First and Third Gospels by giving them a meaning that is obviously incompatible with the sense intended by the authors, or by presenting the apostles as though they were at variance among themselves, or by equating silence with ignorance, cannot expect to escape the suspicion of being devious and disingenuous. The writings that make up the canon of the New Testament are all comparatively brief compositions, and not one of the authors sets out to give a full biography of Jesus or a complete system of theology. There were no doubt many more things that were taught and believed in common by the leaders of the apostolic church which, if a record of them had been preserved, would show that the range of their knowledge extended far beyond the brevities we possess. It is unrealistic to think otherwise. To suppose, for example, that because St. Mark opens his Gospel with the words, "The beginning of the gospel of Jesus Christ, the Son of God," and immediately recounts

---

possible sense is there then in declaring that the Apostolic Fathers do not seem to know of the virgin birth? Still more sweepingly dogmatic is the extraordinary assertion of Rudolf Bultmann that "the legend of Jesus' birth from the virgin is unknown to it (the earliest church) as also to Paul" (*Theology of the New Testament*, Vol. I, tr. Kendrick Grobel [London, 1952], p. 50). The most thorough recent study is that of Raymond E. Brown, whose two volumes *The Virginal Conception and Bodily Resurrection of Jesus* (New York, 1973) and *The Birth of the Messiah* (New York, 1979) are discreetly skeptical and inconclusive in their findings.

18. B. B. Warfield, *Christology and Criticism* (New York, 1929), p. 451.

the work of John the Baptist and the appearance of Jesus to commence his public ministry, he therefore had no knowledge of the miraculous birth of Jesus or else was signalizing his disbelief in it, would convince only those whose preconceptions demand an entirely natural form of religion. Apart from the obvious fact that St. Mark's purpose was to compose a gospel with the ministry, not the birth, of Jesus as its starting point, it would be much more reasonable to take his description of Jesus as the Son of God as an indication that he was aware of and accepted the factuality of the virgin birth. The same may be said of the opening of the Fourth Gospel, where the Apostle John affirms that the Word who is God became flesh and dwelt among us. J. Gresham Machen had much justification for describing as "abysmal" "the intellectual morass into which we have been flung by the modern business of 'interpreting' perfectly plain language in a sense utterly different from the sense in which it has always hitherto been used."[19]

Leaving aside the nativity passages in Matthew and Luke, the New Testament authors do not in fact write about Jesus in a way that is incompatible with his supernatural birth of the Virgin Mary. That the coming of Jesus into the world was a supernatural coming is implied in both Matthew and Mark, where he is the messianic Son of Man *who has come* (Mt. 20:28; Mk. 10:45); and similarly in John he is the one *who has come down from heaven* or *from above* (Jn. 3:31; 6:38, 51, etc.), and who being God has *become* man (Jn. 1:1, 14).[20] The retort of the Jews who boasted that Abraham was their father, pointedly addressed to Jesus, "We were not born of fornication," strongly suggests that they were aware of a report that his had been an unusual birth; and this implication is, if anything, confirmed by the response of Jesus: "I proceeded and came forth from God" (Jn. 8:41f.),[21] and by his magisterial affirmation: "Truly, truly, I say to you, before Abraham was, I am" (Jn. 8:58). These and many other statements in St. John's Gospel point to a supernatural origin which fully accords with the belief in his miraculous conception by a virgin mother. To the same effect in both St. John and St. Paul we read that Christ who has ascended into heaven is he who first descended from heaven (Jn. 3:13; Eph. 4:9f.). But even if these considerations are left out of account, the witness of the First and Third Gospels to the historical fact of the virgin birth of Jesus sufficiently testifies to the acceptance of this belief in the apostolic church.

19. J. Gresham Machen, *The Virgin Birth of Christ* (London, 1930), p. 389.

20. On the significance of the verb *become* in relation to the Son's advent see p. 216 above and nn. 3 and 4 there.

21. C. K. Barrett comments as follows on Jn. 8:41, *hēmeis ek porneias ouk egennēthēmen:* "The Jews find a fresh way of turning the argument against Jesus. The implication (especially of the emphatic *hēmeis*) is that Jesus was born of *porneia*. . . . It is probable that John is subtly bringing out by implication what he believes to be the truth regarding the birth of Jesus, who, though the circumstances might to the uninitiated suggest fornication, was in fact born of no human act but of God" *(The Gospel according to St. John* [London, 1955], p. 288).

CHAPTER 16

The Evolutionistic Interpretation

Mention has already been made[1] of the speculation which was not infrequent in the late medieval period as to whether the incarnation of the Son would have taken place even if man had not sinned, and which proved particularly attractive to the philosophical mind of the Renaissance when so much emphasis was placed on the unique dignity of man in the order of creation—a dignity altogether worthy, many thought, to be acclaimed by the crowning honor of the incarnation. In the sixteenth century this notion was put forward again by the Lutheran scholar Osiander and evoked a refutation from Calvin.[2] More recently, with the development of the evolutionary theory of the progressive and upward surge of life from the humblest beginnings, the view has enjoyed a revival in a suitably revised formulation which postulates the incarnation as the proper culmination of the evolutionary process. The idea was propounded toward the end of the last century by some Anglican scholars who favored the "liberalizing" of Christian belief and its accommodation to the evolutionary hypothesis that was then becoming widely accepted. The publication in 1889 of the volume of essays entitled *Lux Mundi* which was edited by Charles Gore, with the subtitle "A series of studies in the religion of the Incarnation," marked a departure, on the part of its Anglo-Catholic contributors, from the conservative position of the Tractarian leaders who had preceded them. In his preface to the volume Gore spoke of the need for "disencumbering" and "reinterpreting" the faith and described the essays of which it was composed as an endeavor "to put the Catholic faith into its right relation to modern intellectual and moral problems."[3] There was a strong emphasis on "development," which accorded well with the dogma of evolutionary progress then fashionable, but which was doubtless also to some degree indebted to

---

1. See p. 12 above.
2. *Whether the Son of God would have had to become incarnate if sin had not entered the world* was the title of a treatise published by Andreas Osiander in 1550. Osiander claimed that his view had been held by Pico della Mirandola (see p. 12 above and also n. 9 there), and before that by Duns Scotus and Alexander of Hales. Another of Calvin's contemporaries, the antitrinitarian Michael Servetus, held the same opinion (in his *Christianismi restitutio*).
3. *Lux Mundi* (London, 1889), p. vii.

Newman's thesis on the development of Christian doctrine. Theology, Gore wrote, "must take a new development," and he stressed that "the real development of theology" involved entering "into the apprehension of the new social and intellectual movements of each age" and the ability "to assimilate all new material."[4]

The fifth essay in *Lux Mundi*, on "The Incarnation and Development," was written by J. R. Illingworth, who made "the Theory of Evolution" his starting point because he saw "the law of evolution" as "the category of the age."[5] He regarded with approval the idea of those scholastic theologians who suggested that the incarnation was "the predestined climax of creation, independently of human sin," though at the same time acknowledging that "the thought is of course a mere speculation, 'beyond that which is written.'"[6] The introduction of the evolutionistic factor, however, led by intrinsic necessity to the relativizing of the faith of Christianity, for the evolutionary hypothesis if it is true must apply not merely to the biological but also to the religious realm: the physical development of man cannot be isolated from his intellectual and spiritual development. Christianity, then, can but be the climax of the religious development of the race, and all other movements and systems of religion must be viewed as relatively true tributaries that flow together in this climax. As Illingworth saw it, all in greater or lesser degree were reflections of the divine light which enlightened "the primaeval hunter, the shepherd chieftain, the poets of the Vedas and the Gathas, the Chaldaean astronomer, the Egyptian priest," "artists and ascetics," and Greeks and Jews, ever in an ascending order of intensity, and all leading to the apex of the incarnation. "The pre-Christian religions were the age-long prayer," Illingworth averred. "The Incarnation was the answer." Duly advised that "the history of the pre-Christian religion is like that of pre-Christian philosophy, a long preparation for the Gospel,"[7] room must now be made in the new pantheon for the cults of heathendom alongside the speculations of the Greeks. The seductive powers of the latter had long been felt and at times submitted to by the ecclesiastical mind.

In the evolutionary perspective the lower species of life were viewed not only as persisting in their specific individuality but also as contributing to and being incorporated into the higher species produced from them. (It should be remarked again that the notion that the higher form is a product of the lower, the greater power of the lesser, the animate of the inanimate, is contrary both to scientific common knowledge and to scientific common sense.) So also the incarnation is presented as the production of a new species. "Now in scientific language," Illingworth explained, "the Incarnation may be said to have introduced a new species into the world—a Divine man transcending past human-

4. Ibid., p. ix.
5. Ibid., p. 181.
6. Ibid., p. 186.
7. Ibid., pp. 205, 206.

ity, as humanity transcended the rest of the animal creation."[8] The theme was taken up by Gore in his 1891 Bampton Lectures on the Incarnation. He, too, accommodated the person of Christ to the evolutionistic scheme: "What," he asked, "is the testimony of nature in regard to the supernatural Christ?" It is the testimony, he answered, of interconnection and advance. In the natural sphere "development from the inorganic to the organic, from the animal to the rational," which is "progressive evolution of life," corresponded, he maintained, to "a progressive revelation of God," and "this revelation of God, this unfolding of divine qualities, reaches a climax in Christ." Christ, moreover, was supernatural "only in the sense of transcending, or advancing upon, what nature exhibits apart from him, while at the same time he appears in fundamental harmony with the whole, and as incorporating its previous record."[9] And, like Illingworth again, Gore held that "Christianity unifies the truths which appeal to Jew and to Greek, to Mohammedan and Buddhist and Brahman," that it supersedes "all other religions, not by excluding but by including the elements of truth which each contains," and that the incarnation can accordingly be described as "the crown of natural development in the universe."[10]

It is a vain hope that relativities can be absolutized in this or any other way; but, this consideration apart, the type of incarnational theology advocated by Gore is inconsistent where it can least afford to be: Christ, who is presented as the goal or climax to which the evolutionary process moves, is not himself a part or product of that process. For those who, like Gore, believe in the factuality of the Son's incarnation, he did not come from below up, but from above down. This is a reversal of the upward movement which is the essence of the evolutionary hypothesis and, therefore, a failure in principle at its most vital stage. The incarnation is seen as completing through intervention from above, like the *deus ex machina* device of ancient Greek drama, the inherent incompletion of the whole process. The adoption of this perspective goes far to explain why the proponents of this kind of christology see redemption in terms of incarnation rather than in terms of propitiation and view Calvary in the light of Bethlehem rather than Bethlehem in the light of Calvary. The importance of the cross is not denied, but its reference to the need of mankind is recast. Gore, in fact, had faced himself with the impossible task of fusing the natural with the supernatural, of fitting the action from above into compliance with the upward sequence from below. He described "the world without Christ" as "nothing else than an imperfect fragment." The whole trend of his argument is to equate soteriology with ontology, and this required the relativizing of the supernatural heart of the incarnation. Gore's answer to the question whether Christ is supernatural was this: "The term supernatural is purely relative to what at any particular stage of thought we mean by nature. Nature is a progressive development of

8. Ibid., p. 207.
9. Charles Gore, *The Incarnation of the Son of God* (London, 1896), pp. 32, 33.
10. Ibid., p. 43.

life, and each new stage of life appears supernatural from the point of view of what lies below it. . . . In the same sense Christ is supernatural from the point of view of mere man." As "the crown of nature" Christ "is thus profoundly natural."[11] The deflation of christology was the price Gore had to pay for the accommodation of the old to the new that he wished to bring about.

The developmental concepts of recapitulation and consummation received further philosophical exploration in the writings of Lionel Thornton, who acknowledged that Jesus Christ, while standing within the succession of history, "entered it from beyond," maintaining that "in him the absolute actuality of God was incorporated into the historical process."[12] For Thornton the evolutionary principle of upward progress by struggle and change was important also in the unfolding history of morality. He regarded tension as a symptom of ontological incompleteness or imperfection, declaring that "degeneration, disharmony, and non-attainment are aspects under which tension remains unresolved in the advancing series" and indicative of "the unfinished character of the series on its various levels." At the level of human morality, "through the experience of ethical non-attainment we apprehend these forms of unresolved tension as stages in the manifestation of the problem of evil." Not that tension itself is evil; it is, rather, a catalyst inducing progress to the higher and more refined levels of reality. "Evil," Thornton said, "is manifested in an arrest of the movement towards resolution of tension by transformation towards higher forms of harmony."[13]

Morality, on this basis, is improvement by self-effort; but, being an incarnationist, Thornton contended that the desired resolution was achieved, or made a realistic possibility, through the incarnation, perceived of course within an evolutionary setting. "The relative unities of nature, of history and of man's individual experience mounting up in an ascending series demand a culmination," Thornton wrote. "Such a culmination was bestowed by the Creator in the event of the Incarnation." As with Gore, the cross then becomes not so much the purpose of the incarnation as simply a part of it; incarnation and redemption become virtually synonymous. In Christ "there is not simply a completed cosmology, but a new creation through which the old creation is redeemed. Creation is brought to its goal through redemption. . . . In the Incarnate Lord the whole time-series is taken up through man into a new order where it has a transformed history."[14] Personal redemption is attained through the imitation of the life and suffering of Christ. "Under the historical conditions of the Incarnation," according to Thornton, "and in face of human sinfulness the

11. Ibid., p. 34. Lewis B. Smedes has remarked that "for Gore the cross is the incarnation set on a hill" (*The Incarnation: Trends in Modern Anglican Thought* [Kampen, 1953], p. 79).

12. L. S. Thornton, *The Incarnate Lord: An Essay concerning the Doctrine of the Incarnation in its Relation to Organic Conceptions* (London, 1928), p. 164.

13. Ibid., pp. 138f.

14. Ibid., p. 430.

way of the Kingdom became the way of the cross, the way which our Lord followed to its uttermost fulfilment in his death. Thus Christianity came into the world as a way of life with a specific doctrine of life. Man attains his true self through the principle of self-sacrifice or dying to self."[15] Thus perceived, at the human level the tension of ontological incompleteness is extended by the experience of moral deficiency and finds resolution through the new principle of harmony between God and man which has been introduced by the incarnation. The governing concept is that of the rise of man as consummated by the ontological and morally inspiring event of the incarnation, not that of the fall of man as counteracted by the soteriological event of the atoning death of the incarnate Son.

This line of theological inquiry has been carried on by Eric Mascall, who has expounded "the doctrine of the Incarnation as being the re-creation of human nature by its elevation into union with the pre-existent Son and Word of God."[16] Mascall's attempt to restore in some measure the balance between Bethlehem and Calvary is welcome. "The question is," he says, "whether the re-creation of human nature, which is the *leitmotiv* of the Gospel, is to be located in the union of human nature with the Person of the Word in the womb of Mary the Virgin or in the death of the Lord Jesus upon the Cross. Is it, in short, Lady Day or Good Friday that is the supreme commemoration of our redemption?" And he wisely answers this question by affirming that the one cannot be held in isolation from the other.[17] Mascall's evolutionistic preconceptions, however, are still conducive to the supposition that the incarnation would in any case have been a necessity for the removal of man's ontological incompleteness even if sin had not entered the scene;[18] and his soteriological formulation seems to posit redemption as involving the hypostatic union of the believer with Christ in a manner comparable to the union of the divine and human natures in the person of the incarnate Son, which has the appearance of a relapse of soteriology into ontology.

It is not for us to pursue the ramifications of Mascall's incarnational theory here, except to observe that the logic of his argument leads to the opening up of incarnation as a possibility for the whole world. Mascall thus envisages "the effects of the Incarnation in a gradual supernaturalization of the whole created order," on the supposition that "the Incarnation was not only something happening to Christ" but also "something happening to the world itself."[19] Incarnation, however, is "becoming flesh," "becoming man," and this applies only to the Second Person of the Holy Trinity, who, being God, took our humanity to himself at Bethlehem. Man, because he is already man, does

15. Ibid., pp. 431f.
16. E. L. Mascall, *Christ, the Christian, and the Church: A Study of the Incarnation and its Consequences* (London, 1946), p. 68.
17. Ibid., pp. 69, 76.
18. Cf. ibid., p. 70.
19. Ibid., p. 150.

not become incarnate, and the other creatures of this world do not become incarnate because they are what they are. In its *literal* meaning incarnation has
reference only to the person of Christ. The *effects* of the incarnation are indeed
ultimately universal, but as the consequence only of the redemption and reconciliation achieved by the incarnate Son of Calvary, not of the act of incarnation by itself.

To discern any necessary connection between Bethlehem and Calvary in
the thought of Pierre Teilhard de Chardin is particularly difficult. Driven by a
romantic conception of the universe and its destiny, Teilhard also propounded
a belief in the gradual supernaturalization of the entire created order. In his
view, the incarnation was a decisive and restorative moment in the historical
progress of the universe. He held that God "cannot in any way blend or be
mingled with the creation which he sustains and animates and binds together,"
but that he "is nonetheless present in the birth, the growth and the consummation of all things." At the same time, however, he was willing to speak of the
"physical incorporation of the faithful into Christ and therefore into God" as
"the earthly undertaking which is beyond all parallel," adding that "this supreme work is carried out with the *exactitude and harmony of a natural process
of evolution.*"[20] Perhaps here, as elsewhere, poetic license was permitted to
keep logical consistency at arm's length; in any case he went on to explain that
"there had to be a transcendent act which, in accordance with mysterious but
physically regulated conditions, should graft the person of a God into the
human cosmos." This transcendent act was identified as the incarnation, defined in terms of grace by which our human potential is expanded: "And from
this first, basic contact of God with our human race, and precisely by virtue of
this penetration of the divine into our human nature, a new life was born: that
unforeseeable aggrandizement and 'obediential' extension of our natural
capacities which we call 'grace.'" But because "the Incarnation means the renewal, the restoration, of all the energies and powers of the universe," the penetration proclaimed by Teilhard is more than human, it is cosmic.[21]

Teilhard was intensely dogmatic in his belief in "the continuation of the
evolutionary movement at the heart of Humanity,"[22] and he clung tenaciously
to "the idea of a general trend of Man towards some state of super-humanity,"[23]
which also involved, in a manner now conscious within man, "the evolution
of the world towards spirit." We are urged to promote this process not just for
ourselves or even for this earth of ours, but "for the salvation and success of
the Universe itself";[24] and we can do this, Teilhard asserted, because of the

20. P. Teilhard de Chardin, *Hymn of the Universe,* tr. Simon Bartholomew (New
York, 1965), pp. 143f. The emphasis is Teilhard's, here and in the quotations that follow.
21. Ibid., p. 144.
22. *L'Energie Humaine* (Paris, 1962), p. 155. Translations from this work are my
own.
23. Ibid., p. 153.
24. Ibid., pp. 155, 156.

great potential of the Energy of Humanity, because there is "no essential difference" between physical energy and moral force, and because the stuff of the cosmos is spiritual. The Energy of Humanity is in fact described as "physicomoral."[25] Man, accordingly, is now challenged to raise the order of creation from the Biosphere, or world of physical life, to the level of the Noosphere, or world of thought and intellection—to "the ultimate formation, over and above each personal element, of *a common human soul.*"[26] This will mean, Teilhard hoped, the consummation of evolution in a universal Personality to be realized through the "ultra-concentration" of the personal human elements in a higher consciousness, the attainment of the "cosmic point omega" or "total synthesis."[27]

Thus we are advised that evolution's achievement of man, "hominization," must now lead on to the formation of the next stage of reality, the "noosphere," and that the energy essential to the achievement of this "spiritual totalization" is, in a single word, Love. It is here that we encounter what may be called Teilhard's conception of irresistible grace, for he insisted that "the Energy of Humanity cannot be hindered by any obstacle from freely attaining the natural term of its evolution," which is "the totalization, in a total love, of the total Energy of Humanity."[28] It is energy, moreover, that flows from the incarnation. And this is apparently the gospel according to Teilhard. "The essential message of Christ," he stated, "is not to be sought in the Sermon on the Mount, nor even in what took place on the cross; it is completely contained in the announcement of a 'divine fatherhood' . . . in the affirmation that God, personal being, presents himself to men as the goal of a personal *union.*"[29] This involved the defining of a third decisive stage in the evolutionary ascent, beyond the biosphere and the noosphere: "the final metamorphosis," "the passage of the circles to their common center: *the appearance of the Theosphere*" in which God is the self-fulfilment of all reality.[30]

This looks very much like the ultimate triumph and consecration of the *analogia entis* by the divinization of all things. The function of Christ and his incarnation seems to be hardly more than that of a catalyst which speeds up and helps forward what is already and inevitably taking place, namely, "the evolution of the world towards spirit," or, as Teilhard also expressed it, "the general 'drift' of matter towards spirit." "This movement," Teilhard explained, "must have its term: one day the whole divinizable substance of matter will have passed into the souls of men; all the chosen dynamisms will have been recovered; and then our world will be ready for the Parousia."[31] We have been

25. Ibid., pp. 157f.
26. Ibid., p. 171.
27. Ibid., pp. 178ff.
28. Ibid., pp. 181ff., 189ff.
29. Ibid., pp. 192f.
30. Ibid., pp. 197f.
31. *Le Milieu Divin* (London, 1960), p. 94.

brought back, it seems, to the old dualistic conflict between matter and spirit, though now with the optimistic notion of the eschatological conquest of the former by the latter. Revelation has been surpassed by evolution. Within the perspective of the unimaginably prolonged transition from biosphere via noosphere to theosphere, from matter to spirit, the apostolic emphasis on the cross has been mislaid. In George Bernard Shaw's play *Back to Methuselah* the cosmic pilgrimage of Man and Woman is described by Lilith in the following terms: "After passing a million goals they press on to the goal of redemption from the flesh, to the vortex freed from matter, to the whirlpool in pure intelligence that, when the world began, was a whirlpool in pure force."[32] As a proof-text it would have served Teilhard de Chardin better than anything from the New Testament. Teilhard, however, was no agnostic.

That all things are moving toward a climactic *dénouement* was undoubtedly the conviction of the apostles, whose teaching had been received from Christ himself. But this destined consummation is not presented in the New Testament as attributable to the thrust of an inbuilt energy belonging to creation or even to the dynamism of the church's faith, but to God's sovereign control of the course of history. Far from any notion of the divinization of matter and humanity as the ultimate achievement of an age-long evolutionary process, Christ taught plainly that at his return the world in general would be anything but "divinized" and ready for his appearance, and that the climax of his parousia would be catastrophic as well as restorative—a day of cataclysmic judgment for the ungodly as well as joyful salvation and fulfilment for those who love his appearing (Lk. 17:24ff.). St. Paul similarly foretold not an improvement but a deterioration of human society in "the last days." People, he said, "will be lovers of self, lovers of money, proud, arrogant, abusive, disobedient to their parents, ungrateful, unholy, inhuman, implacable, slanderers, profligates, fierce, haters of good, treacherous, reckless, swollen with conceit, lovers of pleasure rather than lovers of God," adding that "all who desire to live a godly life in Christ will be persecuted, while evil men and impostors will go on from bad to worse, deceivers and deceived" (2 Tim. 3:1-4, 12f.). The moment of climax will come by the mighty intervention of God as he acts in holiness, executing final judgment for the elimination of evil from his creation and establishing his everlasting kingdom of peace and justice (2 Thess. 1:7-10; 2 Pet. 3:13; Rev. 21:1). This conclusive event will be from above, not from below.

32. G. B. Shaw, *The Complete Plays* (London, n.d.), p. 962.

CHAPTER 17

The Self-Humbling of the Image

In the biblical perspective the purpose of the incarnation is to raise man, not from a lower to a higher level of ontology, but from the degradation of his sinful fallenness to the fulfilment in Christ of the immense potential implanted in him at creation. The reason for the Word's becoming flesh is, as we have said, redemptive. The saving action of the incarnate Son in fact achieves even more than the restoration of man to the integrity of existence that was lost through the fall, for it brings him, at last and again in Christ, to that destiny of glory for which he was created in the first place. Consequently, even more is gained in Christ than was lost in Adam. This redemption that leads to glory is brought about by the *coming down* of the Son from glory, not by the going up of man to a higher level of being—by the Son's stepping down to the level of our humanity, not by our humanity stepping up to the level of his deity. The incarnation as it affects our humanity is not just one more stage in an incredibly long sequence of stages from inanimate matter to biological organization, from animality to intellectuality, and thence on to spirituality and divinization. It is the grace of God intervening to lift man out of the pit which he has dug for himself and to restore him to the wholeness of his creation, so that once again he may function freely in accordance with the purpose of his being and his high calling under God. In the incarnation God stoops down in order to pull man up—something that man is powerless to do for himself. Through the saving work of the incarnate Son the believer recovers both the integrity of his being and also the purpose and the power and the ultimate glory that belong to his constitution in the image of God.

But what about the incarnate Son? Does not his coming down, his condescension, imply an ontological change in *his* being? Can it be denied that his becoming man meant his sharing in the reality of our human ontology? What effect, then, did this have on his deity? Did it involve a diminution of his deity, or the exchange of one ontology for another? We have acknowledged that the incarnation is a mystery beyond our finite capacity to fathom or explain. This, however, does not excuse us from trying to understand it to the extent that we are able, and perhaps especially to guard as best we can against errors and misconceptions of its nature and purpose. We have already set up one fence by insisting that for the Son to become man does not and cannot require his ceasing to be God. Nonetheless, it is still necessary to inquire what St. Paul meant when he said of Christ that, though he was rich, yet for our sakes he became poor (2 Cor. 8:9) and that he emptied himself and humbled himself (Phil. 2:7f.). If the Son cannot cease to be what he essentially and eternally is, what room is there for poverty, humbling, and emptying? What exactly was the *kenōsis* he experienced?[1]

It is evident from the passages in which they occur that the statements "he became poor," "he emptied himself," and "he humbled himself" refer to the Son's act of incarnation. Those who have propounded kenotic theories have supposed that he emptied himself of his deity when he became man, or that he divested himself of certain of his powers or attributes, such as his omniscience and his omnipotence. But their conclusions are based on a wrong starting point: they have argued that something must have been subtracted or taken away from him; whereas, on the contrary, the Apostle associates his becoming poor, his humbling and emptying of himself, with the adding or taking to himself of something, namely, our human nature. A king who leaves his palace to live *incognito* among his poverty-stricken subjects for a while and to distribute his wealth to them does not cease to be the king who exercises authority over them. So also (though the action of this hypothetical king does not correspond to incarnation) the incarnate Son is still the rich Lord who comes to us in our poverty in order to make his riches available to us. His humbling and his emptying are related to his assuming of our human nature and dwelling among us in order that we may share in his glorious fulness. His divine nature remains what it always was and is, even though his dwelling among us as the Word made flesh is also a concealing of his divine nature. Living in poverty in Palestine and dying in shame on the cross, he was still, and above all else, God powerfully at work in our midst. His apparent weakness is actually the effect of his almighty power, for everything is his doing: it is he who *comes down,* he who *becomes* flesh, he who *empties himself,* he who *humbles himself* even to the death of the cross, which is the purpose of his coming, and is *glorified,* not shamed, although it is shame he endured, as he is lifted up for us (Jn. 12:23, 27f.). All along the power is his, to lay down his life and to take it again (Jn. 10:17f.). Even in his death-throes on the cross and when his lifeless body is laid in the tomb he is upholding the universe by his word of power (Heb. 1:3). For the incarnate Son is *God in action,* and all-powerfully so, not God stripped and impotent. The amazing truth is that in Christ, our seemingly weak, poor, despised, fellow, God was reconciling the world to himself (2 Cor. 5:19).

So the incarnation is not a subtracting but an adding. Hence St. Paul's declaration that Christ "emptied himself, having taken the form of a servant," that is, his self-emptying is explained by his taking our humanity to himself

---

1. *Kenōsis* is the transliteration of a Greek noun meaning, "emptying." Kenotic theories of the incarnation are based on the assertion of Phil. 2:7, *heauton ekenōsen,* "he emptied himself."

for the purpose of serving—just as he himself announced that "the Son of Man came not to be served but to serve, and to give his life as a ransom for many" (Mk. 10:45). His emptying is his *taking*. He who has become fully human through the incarnation has not ceased to be fully God; otherwise all this could never have taken place. As Aloys Grillmeier has said: "Because this kenosis is a 'taking,' or better an 'adding,' the first kind of being is not done away with. He who is on an equality with God adds something to his divinity, the form of a servant."[2] This, again, is a mystery which human language is inadequate to define. But if some are disposed to ask how anything can be added to him who, as the divine Son, is the fulness of all things (Eph. 1:23; Col. 2:9f.), let them consider what it is that is added; for this adding is not an increase in power and glory (since fulness cannot be increased) but a humbling; it is marked not by lordship but by servanthood; it is an identification with us in our need, not a withdrawal from us; it is the condescension of the transcendent; it is the acceptance for his own of human frailty and suffering, the absorption of sorrow and scorn and rejection and of death itself; it is the pathetic isolation of this human figure, who at the same moment is God with us (Mt. 1:22f.), as he is falsely condemned and spat upon and nailed to the wooden cross. That appalling addition is the true kenosis, the self-emptying and self-humbling, of the eternal Son.

In a word, the incarnation is the kenosis. And the lowest point of this kenosis is the Son's self-offering on the cross of Calvary. There is no depth deeper than that, no descent beyond it, for it is the suffering of the hell that is our due. There, as he endured the death of the lowest criminal, the innocent Son took upon himself the sin of mankind, all the hatred and violence and foulness of our ungodly depravity, and paid its penalty. That is what St. Paul means when he says that Christ Jesus "humbled himself by becoming obedient unto death, even death on a cross" (Phil. 2:8), and St. Peter when he says that Christ "himself bore our sins in his body on the tree, that we might die to sin and live to righteousness," and that he "died for sins once for all, the righteous for the unrighteous, that he might bring us to God" (1 Pet. 2:24; 3:18). There is no descent, no condescension, no kenosis to compare with that! No wonder the Apostle extolled not only the breadth, length, and height but also the depth of "the love of Christ which surpasses knowledge" (Eph. 3:18f.)!

2. A. Grillmeier, *Christ in Christian Tradition:* Vol. I, *From the Apostolic Age to Chalcedon (451),* 2nd revised edn., tr. John Bowden (Atlanta, 1975), p. 21. Grillmeier observes also that the christology of Phil. 2:5-11 is "a 'katagogic' christology, which makes any 'anagogic' christology such as the adoptionist spirit-christology impossible" (pp. 22f.).

CHAPTER **18**

The Theanthropic Person of Christ

We have seen that the incarnation was the action of him who is himself God, that in becoming man the Son did not cease to be God, and that the very "possibility" of the incarnation resides in the special link that connects man, who is constituted in the image of God, to the Second Person of the Trinity, who is the Image of God in which man was created. In becoming man the Son maintained his identity as the Image of God, but he now also, as our fellow-man, identified himself with us who are formed in the divine image. Thus as the eternal Son he is the Image, and as the incarnate Son he is in the image. This brings us face to face with the deep mystery of the twofold character of the person of Christ. Because it is beyond the ability of man to describe the manner of the union of the two natures, divine and human, in the single person of the incarnate Son, faith can but seek understanding, or rather some partial degree of understanding, of this profound truth. It is a mystery which the church even in its earliest days had to defend and define, to a large extent negatively by declaring what it does not mean in the refutation of erroneous hypotheses and speculations.

The reality which is at the same time the mystery of the theanthropic person of Christ repeatedly presents itself in the record of his ministry given by the writers of the four Gospels. St. John testifies that the Word who is God, and through whom all things were made, "became flesh and dwelt among us, full of grace and truth," adding that "we have beheld his glory, glory as of the only Son from the Father" (Jn. 1:1, 14). In what ways was Christ's divine glory manifested for men to behold it? His humanity was obvious to all, for he lived as a man among men, traveling from place to place, speaking the languages of Palestine, experiencing hunger and thirst and fatigue, eating, drinking, sleeping, and sharing in the joys and sorrows of others, meeting with slander and hostility, and finally suffering the abominated death of crucifixion. In all such respects he was thoroughly and obviously our fellow human being.

But there are other facts of his life and ministry to which the apostolic authors bear witness. His ability to heal the sick and afflicted, to raise the dead, and to still tempests, and all by a simple word of command, revealed his possession of powers that were more than human. It was entirely appropriate for St. John in his Gospel to designate the miraculous deeds of Jesus as *signs,* for to those who saw them they signified that the power of God was at work among them. Thus St. John says that the changing of water into wine at the wedding in Cana of Galilee was "the first of his signs" and that in performing it Jesus "manifested his glory" (Jn. 2:11). His calming of the storm on the Sea of Galilee evoked the astonished response from his disciples, "What sort of person is this, that even winds and sea obey him?" (Mt. 8:27; Mk. 4:41); and when he stilled a tempest on a second occasion the significance of his power was grasped, for they then worshipped him and professed, "Truly you are the Son of God!" (Mt. 14:33). The casting out of demons provided further evidence of his divine glory, so much so, that he charged those who attempted to discredit him with blasphemy against the Holy Spirit and advised them, "If it is by the Spirit of God that I cast out demons, then the kingdom of God has come upon you" (Mt. 12:28, 31). But most memorable and resplendent of all the manifestations of Christ's glory must have been the transcendental radiance which suffused his person at the time of the transfiguration in the presence of Peter, James, and John (Mt. 17:1ff.; Mk. 9:2ff.; Lk. 9:28ff.). No doubt this event was in the forefront of St. John's mind when he wrote "we have beheld his glory," and it was certainly an unforgettable experience for St. Peter, who testified as the day of his martyrdom drew near: "We were eye-witnesses of his majesty; for when he received honor and glory from God the Father and the voice was borne to him by the Majestic Glory, 'This is my beloved Son, with whom I am well pleased,' we heard this voice borne from heaven, for we were with him on the holy mountain" (2 Pet. 1:16-18). It was indeed a display for a brief while of that glory which the Son had with the Father before the world was made (Jn. 17:5).

In the person of the incarnate Son, then, there is a meeting of the eternal with the temporal, of the infinite with the finite, and of the heavenly with the earthly. But it is precisely in this union of the divine and the human that the "offense" of the incarnation resides. It was offensive to the philosophical mind of the early centuries and it is offensive to the humanistic mind of our day. In battling against denials and distortions of the doctrine of the incarnation the apostolic and patristic church was battling for the survival of the Christian faith. The formulation of orthodox christological belief was the outcome of the conviction that opposition to the doctrine of the incarnation was not opposition to an optional ontological construct or theological speculation but to a truth that belongs to the heart of the Christian gospel.

CHAPTER 19

Docetic Christology

Just as the Greek language had become virtually the international medium of communication in the time of Christ, so also Greek culture and philosophical thought formed a major part of the social and intellectual environment of the Christian church as it spread outward from Jerusalem. A distinctive feature of the prevalent Greek cosmology was the dualistic concept of reality, which (as we have explained earlier)[1] postulated the existence of two eternal and irreconcilable opposing principles, the one good and the other evil. More specifically, good was associated with spirit and evil with matter. The presupposition of this antithesis led to the conclusion that God who is spirit and therefore good could not have contact with the world, which, being composed of matter, is evil. A cosmological preconception of this kind could not fail to strike at the very root both of the biblical doctrine of creation, which teaches that the material universe is the work of God and therefore good, and also of the biblical doctrine of incarnation, which teaches that God has entered this world in order to redeem it. No dualist could have approved the assertion that in Christ "the whole fulness of deity dwells bodily" (Col. 2:9). Yet there was a sequence of determined attempts to accommodate the christology of Scripture to a dualistic conception of reality which the church was bound to resist if the gospel was to be preserved.

Docetism was the earliest manifestation of this strange endeavor to wed Christianity and dualism. The term *docetism* comes from a Greek word which means "to seem,"[2] for the "solution" to the offense of the incarnation proposed by the docetists was that Christ had only *seemed* to become man—that the incarnation had taken place in appearance only, not in reality. Docetism was an early form of gnosticism, which in the second century developed into an elaborate theosophical system. Irenaeus, writing in the latter part of that century, set forth the origin and the teaching characteristic of the gnostic heresy in an extensive work with the title *Refutation and Overthrow of the Falsely-Called Knowledge*.[3] He informs us that its first exponent was Simon

1. See pp. 83ff. above.
2. *Dokeō*.
3. "Knowledge" here is the English for the Greek noun *gnōsis*, from which the term "gnosticism" is derived. The work is commonly known as *Against Heresies*, from the title of the Latin translation that has come down to us.

Magus,[4] who first appears in the pages of the New Testament in the account of the remarkable response of the Samaritan people to the evangelistic preaching of Philip the Deacon (Acts 8:5ff.). Prior to the coming of Philip, Simon had practiced sorcery with spectacular success in Samaria, claiming that his presence was the presence of the supreme deity on earth.[5] When, however, the people turned from him to Philip, and he saw the transforming power of the Holy Spirit in those on whom St. Peter had laid his hands, Simon himself professed belief in the Christian gospel and submitted to baptism. Subsequently he offered the Apostle money, thinking that he could purchase the ability to confer on others the Holy Spirit together with the accompanying manifestations of divine power.[6] This called forth a severe rebuke from St. Peter: "Your silver perish with you, because you thought you could obtain the gift of God with money! You have neither part nor lot in this matter, for your heart is not right with God." Urged to repent and seek God's forgiveness, Simon then requested St. Peter to pray for him (vv. 18-24).

It is on this seemingly hopeful note that Simon Magus disappears from the annals of the New Testament. But there is plenty of evidence from the writings of the next century that he remained unrepentant and faithless, and, reverting to the practice of sorcery, not only set himself against the apostles but also wished by his magical displays and rhetorical powers to convince the world that he was the Redeemer God. In this he seems to have enjoyed no small degree of success. Irenaeus relates that many glorified him as God and that he claimed to have appeared among the Jews as the Son, descended in Samaria as the Father, and visited other nations as the Holy Spirit, asserting, moreover, that though he seemed among men to be a man yet he was not a man, and though he was thought to have suffered in Judea yet in fact he had not suffered.[7] It was from his followers, according to Irenaeus, that the designation "knowledge [or *gnōsis*], falsely so called" (1 Tim. 6:20) received its beginning.[8]

From this information it is apparent that Simon Magus attempted to adapt and assimilate Christian teaching and terminology to his own theosophical theory, no doubt reckoning that with the spread of Christianity this would increase his own acceptability. His docetic notions are discernible in his affirmation that the incarnation and the crucifixion only seemed to have taken place.[9]

4. "Magus" here = sorcerer, one who practices the art of magic.
5. This is the significance of his pretension to be "someone Great" and of the people's acclamation of his as "the power of God which is called Great" (vv. 9, 10), as is confirmed by the patristic understanding of his claims.
6. Hence *simony,* the purchasing of spiritual positions and preferments with cash.
7. Irenaeus, *Against Heresies* i.23.
8. Ibid.
9. Irenaeus may have been indebted to a work of Justin Martyr, "Against All Heresies," written in the middle of the second century but now lost, for his information about Simon Magus and other early gnostic heresiarchs. Justin does mention Simon a couple of times in his *First Apology* (chs. 26 and 56) as having gone to Rome and done "mighty acts of magic" there "by virtue of the art of the devils operating in him."

Early in the third century Tertullian wrote somewhat briefly of Simon's aberrations;[10] but Simon's theoretical constructions were discussed in much more detail by Hippolytus not long afterward. These abstruse imaginations need not detain us here, except to say that Simon was apparently accustomed to describe himself as "he who stood, who stands, and who will stand," intending by this appellation to demarcate himself as the supreme and imperishable deity, and that his teaching (which had affinities with Zoroastrianism), provided a starting point, so Hippolytus says, for the gnostic doctrine of Valentinus.[11] A useful summary of the origin and arrogance of Simon Magus is found in the *Pseudo-Clementine Recognitions,* a composition of the same period, which states that he was a native of Samaria, from the village of Gitta, and was "exceedingly well trained in the Greek literature";[12] and in a similar passage in the *Pseudo-Clementine Homilies* it is said that Simon received academic training in Alexandria,[13] which, if correct, may be taken to indicate that there he received his schooling in the philosophy of the Greeks.

Simon Magus may very well have become acquainted with Zoroastrianism in his native Samaria. He would also almost certainly have encountered its exponents in Alexandria, which in his day was the leading center of learning and sophistication, the intellectual capital, indeed, of the world's wisdom, not only for Egyptians and Greeks and pagans of other nationalities but also for the Jews of the dispersion, who formed a considerable proportion of that city's population. It was there that the Old Testament Scriptures had been translated into Greek and that Philo and other Jewish philosophers lived and pursued their studies. Egypt had long enjoyed a reputation for the wisdom of its seers and mathematicians. Moses, who led the Israelites out of Egypt, was "instructed in all the wisdom of the Egyptians" (Acts 7:22). The fame of Egyptian learning is reputed to have attracted the intellectual pioneers of Hellas's golden age. Pythagoras, for example, is said to have spent no less than twenty-two years studying in Egypt and to have derived his numerological philosophy from the sages of that country, and thereafter to have traveled to Persia where he was instructed by Zoroaster concerning the original causes of things;[14] and Democritus is said to have conferred with "many gymnosophists among the Indians and with priests in Egypt and with astrologers and magi in Babylon."[15] The patristic authors not infrequently contended that Plato was indebted to the Egyptians and

10. Tertullian, *On the Soul* 34; *Against All Heresies* 1.

11. Hippolytus, *Philosophoumena,* usually referred to by the title *Refutation of All Heresies* iv.51; vi.4 and 15.

12. *Pseudo-Clementine Recognitions* ii.7.

13. *Pseudo-Clementine Homilies* ii.22.

14. The possibility of the meeting of Pythagoras and Zoroaster depends of course on their being contemporaries. There is notorious disagreement among scholars, involving centuries of difference, about the time when Zoroaster lived.

15. Iamblichus, *Life of Pythagoras* iii.13; Isocrates, *Encomium* 11; Hippolytus, *Refutation* i.2 and 9.

Babylonians for his wisdom and to the Hebrews for such theological truth as he possessed.[16] Be these things as they may, in the apostolic period no place could compete with the city of Alexandria as the meeting point and in many respects the melting pot of religious cults and theories, modern as well as ancient. There the various theosophical systems jostled with each other either as rivals or as equals, there by the eclectic alchemy of syncretism new synthetic formulations were compounded, and from there these notions and speculations circulated freely through the territories of the Roman Empire.

Simon Magus was as much a charlatan as a heretic, always ready to appropriate any term or idea that might serve to promote his pretension to be a divine visitant to this earth.[17] More dangerous because more philosophically subtle than Simon's egotistical abuse of Christian concepts for his own personal aggrandizement was the attempt of Cerinthus, still in the first century, to reconstruct christology in accordance with the premises of gnostic dualism. We know little about Cerinthus. Irenaeus tells us that after spending a long time in Egypt he traveled on to Asia, where he came into conflict with St. John, and that St. John wrote his Gospel for the purpose of refuting the error that Cerinthus was disseminating. Irenaeus's primary source of information was evidently the venerable martyr Polycarp, whom he had known in his youth, and who in turn had known the Apostle John in Asia, where by apostolic appointment he was bishop of Smyrna.[18] In his summary of the teaching of Cerinthus, Irenaeus attributed the following positions to him: that the world was not made by the primary God but by a certain power separate from him; that Jesus was not born of a virgin but was the son by ordinary generation of Joseph and Mary, more righteous, however, and wiser than other men; that after the baptism of Jesus, Christ descended from the Supreme Ruler in the form of a dove upon him, and then proclaimed the unknown Father and performed miracles; and that before the crucifixion Christ departed from Jesus, leaving him to suffer and rise again, since Christ, a spiritual being, was incapable of suffering.[19]

16. See, e.g., Clement of Alexandria, *Exhortation to the Gentiles* 6. Augustine at first accepted and reproduced with some enthusiasm Ambrose's anachronistic "discovery" that Plato had met and been instructed by Jeremiah in Egypt, but subsequently, realizing that this was an impossibility because Jeremiah and Plato had lived in different centuries, retracted this opinion. See *Christian Doctrine* ii.43; *City of God* viii.11; *Retractations* II.iv.2.

17. According to Hippolytus (*Refutation* vi.15) Simon went to Rome, where he set himself up as a teacher, was opposed by St. Peter, and finally, promising that if he were buried alive he would rise on the third day, persuaded his followers to dig a grave and bury him in it. And "there," Hippolytus comments laconically, "he remains until this day, for he was not the Christ."

18. Irenaeus, *Against Heresies* iii.3, where he also recounts the incident, heard through Polycarp, of St. John's precipitate departure from a bathhouse in Ephesus when he saw Cerinthus within, exclaiming as he left, "Let us flee, lest the bathhouse collapse, because Cerinthus the enemy of the truth is inside."

19. Irenaeus, *Against Heresies* i.26. This account is reproduced by Hippolytus, *Refutation* vii.21.

The dualistic standpoint of Cerinthus is readily discernible in this summary. There is the distinction between the primary God, who as spirit can have no contact with matter, and the secondary god or power to whom, as the creator or organizer of the world of matter, this contact is assigned. There is the clear-cut separation of Jesus from Christ, the former regarded as an ordinary though exceptionally virtuous human being, the latter as an immaterial spiritual being or emanation from the supreme spiritual being. The christology is thoroughly docetic. There only *seems* to be an incarnation. The supernatural birth is denied. The miracles performed by Christ only *appear* to be performed by Jesus. Only Jesus, not Christ and not Jesus Christ, is crucified. One may comment that it would seem to be a fundamental inconsistency for matter and spirit to be brought into close, even if temporary, association with each other while Jesus acts as the receptacle of Christ. It is also surprising to find the resurrection of Jesus allowed, but presumably in the Cerinthian scheme of things this was an unimportant concession since it involved no more than the resurrection of a material being.

This, then, was the form of early gnostic heresy which threatened to destroy the evangelical message of the apostolic church. By informing us that St. John wrote his Gospel as an antidote to the false teaching of Cerinthus, Irenaeus has provided us with a key for the accurate understanding of particular emphases and formulations in the Fourth Gospel, and also, as we shall see, in the Johannine Epistles. St. John, in fact, tells us plainly the purpose which led to the composition of his Gospel: "These things are written," he says in John 20:31, "that you may believe that Jesus is the Christ, the Son of God, and that believing you may have life in his name." Applying the key, we see that where Cerinthus separates between Jesus and Christ as two incompatible entities St. John insists that *Jesus is the Christ,* one and undivided, and, further, that *Jesus,* or Jesus Christ, *is the Son of God,* in conformity with the doctrine of the incarnation propounded in the earlier part of his Gospel.

This door of comprehension that is unlocked and opened for us enables us to appreciate the significance of numerous other statements. Thus the Word who was in the beginning is God, not, as in contemporary Alexandrian *logos* speculation, some power separate from the Supreme Being; and it was through this Word who is God that this world was brought into being, for "all things were made through him, and without him was not anything made that was made" (Jn. 1:1-3)—an affirmation that strikes at the root of the theory that the creation or ordering of the material universe was the work of an inferior and sinister demiurge. If anything, still more repugnant to the dualist is the declaration that the Word who is God "became flesh and dwelt among us" (Jn. 1:14)—the doctrine, in a word, of the incarnation. In this Gospel the identity of Jesus as the Messiah, the Christ, is unequivocally asserted (1:41f.; 4:25; 11:27). Jesus is revealed not only as the Son of Man but also as the Son of God (1:34, 49, 51; 6:69; 11:27). Jesus declares himself to be one with the Father (10:30); he says, as no mere man could say, "Before Abraham was, I AM"

(8:58); and he speaks of the glory which he had with the Father before the world was made (17:5). Because the incarnation is real and not a mere appearance St. John can confidently testify that "grace and truth came through Jesus Christ" (1:17). There is no foothold for docetism in his Gospel.

The First Epistle of John is more openly polemical in the denunciation of teaching that is recognizably docetic. The whole point of the introduction is the tangible factuality of the incarnation. As in the prologue to the Gospel, the Word of life is from the beginning and has now been heard, seen, looked upon, touched, and is substantial in a way that rules out any possibility of a phantom appearance. "Our fellowship," St. John writes, "is with the Father and with his Son Jesus Christ" (1:1-3). It is plain that Jesus Christ is a personal unity: it is he, Jesus Christ, who is the Son; it is Jesus Christ the righteous who is our advocate with the Father and the propitiation for our sins (2:1f.). To deny that *Jesus is the Christ,* as the docetists did, is to be a liar and an antichrist (2:18, 22). Still more specifically, the teaching that confesses that *Jesus Christ has come in the flesh* is of God; the teaching that denies it is the spirit of antichrist (4:1-3). Only the person who confesses that Jesus is the Son of God and that Jesus is the Christ is a child of God (4:15; 5:1).

The same key opens for us the otherwise cryptic assertion: "This is he who came by water and blood, not with the water only, but with the water and the blood" (5:6). Cerinthus, as we have seen, taught that Christ descended on Jesus at the baptism in the river Jordan, but departed from him before the crucifixion at Calvary, because his presuppositions dictated that it was impossible for Christ who, according to him, is spirit to suffer and die. It was acceptable to the docetist, therefore, to affirm the baptism but not the crucifixion. By his insistence that Jesus Christ came by *both water and blood* the Apostle is attesting the genuine incarnational unity of Jesus Christ not only in baptism but also in crucifixion. Belief in the reality of the incarnation and the crucifixion is not something optional or dispensable. Of this St. John is absolutely certain. "We know that the Son of God has come and has given us understanding, to know him who is true," he testifies further; "and we are in him who is true, in his Son Jesus Christ. This is the true God and eternal life" (5:20). This knowing is the true *gnōsis*. Again, in his Second Epistle, St. John leaves us in no doubt that the denial of the incarnation is the negation of Christianity: "Many deceivers have gone out into the world," he warns, "men who will not acknowledge the coming of Jesus Christ in the flesh; such a one is the deceiver and the antichrist" (2 Jn. 7).

The Johannine writings provide ample evidence that docetic doctrine was an aberration with which the apostolic church had to wrestle, and indeed that some who were spreading it had at first moved in orthodox circles (1 Jn. 2:19). Simon Magus appeared early on the scene, before the conversion of St. Paul, and Cerinthus followed close on his heels. To expect to find at least some trace of conflict with this early form of gnosticism in the Pauline letters, which constitute a major part of the New Testament, is not unreasonable. In his work entitled *Panarion*,[20] written about 375, Epiphanius, bishop of Constantia in Salamis, represented Cerinthus as an opponent of St. Paul (and St. Peter).[21] Such evidence as is available indicates that Cerinthus was an Alexandrian Jew by birth who reformulated christological teaching in an attempt to make it compatible with his own philosophical preconceptions, and that he was active in promoting his theories in places where the apostles were active. We have previously noticed Irenaeus's assertion that St. Paul's warning to Timothy to avoid "contradictions of what is falsely called knowledge *(gnōsis)*"[22] referred in particular to the gnostic notions that the followers of Simon Magus were disseminating. But this is not the only indication of conflict with gnostic dualism in St. Paul's letters.

Knowledge is of course of fundamental importance for the Christian. It is not knowledge in itself but what is falsely called knowledge or gnosis that the Apostle rejects. Salvation and coming to *the knowledge of the truth* are inseparably connected (1 Tim. 2:4), and throughout the New Testament the message is plain that true and authentic gnosis is the knowledge of God through faith in Jesus Christ by the inward working of the Holy Spirit. Hence St. Paul's emphasis on "the surpassing worth of knowing Christ Jesus my Lord" (Phil. 3:8). In the first of his canonical letters to the Corinthian church St. Paul addressed some who arrogantly claimed to have "knowledge," and the context suggests that they had come under the influence of gnostic teaching and in doing so had pushed aside the graces of love and compassion, so that their apostle found it necessary to admonish them that "knowledge" puffs up, whereas love builds up (1 Cor. 8:1-3).[23] St. Paul was careful to insist that there is no place for gnostic self-esteem: "Even if I should have all knowledge," he said, "and have not love, I am nothing" (1 Cor. 13:2). The "all knowledge" some boasted of having was not the "all knowledge" for which he had given thanks at the beginning of the letter (1 Cor. 1:5). Certainly he himself made no pretension to the possession of all knowledge in the sense intended by these troublemakers; and it was as much a reprimand to them as his own profession when he wrote: "Now I know in part, but then [i.e., in the hereafter] I shall know fully, even as also I am fully known [i.e., by God]" (1 Cor. 13:12). Such fulness of knowledge

20. That is, "Medicine Chest," for the healing of those infected with heretical venom. The work is generally cited with the title *Against Heresies*.

21. Epiphanius, *Against Heresies* 28.

22. The rendering given is that of the RSV. The English translation of the Jerusalem Bible conveys the sense effectively: "antagonistic beliefs of the 'knowledge' which is no knowledge at all."

23. In the gnostic system the possessor of gnosis claimed to be immune to defilement, no matter what he did, and the issue at this point in St. Paul's letter is that of the spiritual defilement that may be contracted as a result of eating meat that had previously been offered in heathen temples to idols. There is an interesting connection with gnostic claims, for Irenaeus informs us (*Against Heresies* i.6) that the Valentinian gnostics in the next century "make no scruple about eating meats offered in sacrifice to idols, imagining that in this way they can contract no defilement."

belongs to God alone, and it is enough for the Christian believer to be fully known by God, which at the same time means to know God truly.

There is, in fact, a radical opposition between the gnostic wisdom of this fallen world and the wisdom of God. That is why the message of the cross is weakness and foolishness to those who are perishing, though to those who are being saved it is the power of God and the wisdom of God (1 Cor. 1:18ff.). The unregenerate mind, because of its ungodliness, has got things completely wrong. That is the point of Isaiah 29:14, which St. Paul cites, "I will destroy the wisdom of the wise, and the cleverness of the clever I will thwart," for, as is said in Romans 1:22 of those who suppress the truth about God, "claiming to be wise, they became fools." Vaunting themselves as self-sufficient they dismiss divine wisdom and divine strength as foolishness and weakness. But, as St. Paul penetratingly asserts, "the foolishness of God is wiser than men, and the weakness of God is stronger than men" (1 Cor. 1:25).

In brief, the true gnosis is "the knowledge of God's mystery, even Christ, in whom are hid all the treasures of wisdom and knowledge" (Col. 2:2f.)— wisdom and knowledge which are for all believers, without exception or differentiation. Thus St. Paul taught "every man in all wisdom" in order that he might "present every man perfect in Christ" (Col. 1:28). The one ultimate and decisive distinction is between belief and unbelief, between salvation in Christ and perdition without Christ (Jn. 3:36), and it is a distinction that in no way conforms to the values and classifications of this present age. The antithesis, indeed, on which the Apostle insists is entirely beyond and alien to the thinking of the unregenerate person, simply because the truth of the gospel is "not in words taught by human wisdom, but taught by the Spirit." The world's hostility and incomprehension are explained by the fact that "the unregenerate man does not receive the things of the Spirit of God, for they are foolishness to him, and he is not able to understand them because they are spiritually discerned." The spiritual man, on the other hand, is in a position to judge all things (1 Cor. 2:12-15). There is, moreover, no superior knowledge or spirituality that lifts a person, so to speak, out of this present world and away from its responsibilities. The New Testament makes it abundantly clear that Christian theology is always intended to translate into Christian conduct. Right belief demands right action. That is why St. Paul found it necessary to chide the members of the Corinthian church, who had been endowed with many gifts, because of the jealousy and strife and disorderliness by which their Christian unity was being disrupted. They were gifted, but not fruitful. Their lives, to be plain, were, inconsistently with their profession, productive of "works of the flesh" rather than "the fruit of the Spirit" (Gal. 5:19-24). Their lack of love was a symptom of stunted spiritual growth, and so St. Paul regretfully wrote, "I, brethren, could not address you as spiritual, but as carnal, as babes in Christ" (1 Cor. 3:1-3).

Certain terms used by St. Paul in this and some other places, in particular "perfect," "unregenerate," "spiritual," "carnal," though part of the common stock of religious language, were readily recognizable because of their distinctive usage in gnostic circles. Those who claimed to be the possessors of gnosis designated themselves as perfect and spiritual, while the unenlightened remainder of humanity were described as carnal or fleshly, for whom there was no redemption. The adjective we have rendered "unregenerate" in quoting 1 Corinthians 1:14 is used there in contrast to those who are "spiritual."[24] In the Valentinian gnosticism of the next century this term "psychic" denoted an intermediate category between the "pneumatic" (spiritual) and the "sarcic" (carnal) of those who had the expectation of an inferior degree of salvation. To retain this status the "psychics" were required to conduct themselves with ascetic discipline, whereas the "spirituals" at the top level held themselves to be incapable of contamination from any excess of immorality or self-indulgence, and therefore free to live without restraint. St. Paul's application of the terms is, naturally, quite different, and, even though they are not unusual in themselves, there is no reason to doubt that in his use of these and other words, including *gnōsis,* he was not only using them rightly but also contending against their use in a false and heretical manner.[25]

Another term that was prominent in the vocabulary of gnosticism was "fulness" (Greek, *plērōma*). The gnostic *plērōma* was the wholeness of spiritual or immaterial reality comprising the eons or emanations sent forth from the Supreme Spirit. The spiritual totality was both the expression of divine power and a zone, so to speak, preserving the divine being from contact with the material world. St. Paul's use of the word *fulness* is striking. In his doctrine the incarnate Son is the focus of God's fulness. "In him," he says, "all the fulness of God was pleased to dwell," and indeed to dwell bodily (Col. 1:19; 2:9)— a declaration that can hardly be regarded as other than polemically antignostic and antidualistic as well as a positive affirmation of the reality of the incarnation. It is fulness in which the believer is privileged to participate; thus St. John testifies, "from his fulness have we all received, grace upon grace" (Jn. 1:16). The constant desire of those who have experienced the grace of re-creation in Christ (2 Cor. 5:17) is to "be filled with all the fulness of God" as they press on to the consummating attainment of "the measure of the stature of the fulness of Christ," which is the climactic perfection of our manhood (Eph. 3:19; 4:13).

24. The word *psychikos* is difficult to translate directly in this context. It is obvious, however, that it is the opposite of what St. Paul means by *pneumatikos*. A negative form seems most suited to convey the sense; hence "unspiritual" (RSV, NEB, Jerusalem Bible) and "without the Spirit" (NIV). "Natural" (KJV) is imprecise and could be misleading.

25. As J. B. Lightfoot said, with reference to the term *teleios,* "perfect": "While employing the favourite Gnostic term, the Apostle strikes at the root of the Gnostic doctrine" (*St. Paul's Epistles to the Colossians and Philemon* [London, 1892 edn.], p. 169). Irenaeus protested that "the 'most perfect' among them practise recklessly every kind of forbidden deed of which the Scriptures assure us that 'those who do such things shall not inherit the kingdom of God' [Gal. 5:21] . . . and practising many other abominable and ungodly things, they deride us, who through fear of God avoid sinning even in thought or word, as stupid and contemptible persons, while they exalt themselves to the sky, claiming to be perfect and the seed of God's elect" (*Against Heresies* i.6).

This, the true *plērōma,* will also signalize the full conformity of our human personhood to that Image of God, the Second Person of the Holy Trinity, in whom we were created. Thus we will become what we were destined to be.

We see, then, that the warfare against error was already being waged in the apostolic church and that the New Testament writings were in large measure an expression of that warfare. The unfolding of history shows us, further, that the conflict in the first century was but the beginning of a warfare that continues right up to the present time. The engagement with the dualistic theory of docetic/gnostic religion was indeed a battle over christology, but, as we have observed, it was the gospel itself, the heart of Christianity, that was at stake. If we are wrong on christology, we will be wrong on soteriology; and we will be wrong also on anthropology, because an erroneous understanding of the Son, who is the Image, inevitably leaves us with an erroneous understanding of man, whose creation is in that image. Thus we keep on coming back to these fixed points: that the truth about man cannot be isolated from the truth about the Son, that the work of Christ cannot be isolated from the person of Christ, and that redemption cannot be isolated from creation. Our fulness, before as well as since the fall, has always been in Christ. And so it is in Christ that the church will enter into "the fulness of him who fills all in all" (Eph. 1:23).

The dualistic presuppositions, which accounted for the docetic denial of the incarnation, continued to be an important ingredient of the elaborate gnostic systems that were formulated in the second century. The theorizings of Simon Magus continued in the teaching of his pupil Menander, a fellow Samaritan, and then in turn were propounded by Menander's disciple Saturninus, a Syrian who taught in Antioch. According to them, the formation of the world and of man was the work not of God but of angels, and Saturninus was reputed to have claimed to be an angelic being, but the enemy of those by whom the world was created and especially of the God of the Jews (declared in the Old Testament to be the creator of the material universe), whom, they taught, Christ came to destroy. Though by appearance a visible man, Christ was declared by Saturninus to be "without birth, without body, and without figure."[26]

Basilides, also probably from Syria, advocated his particular form of gnostic teaching in Alexandria during the reign of Hadrian (117-138). Irenaeus says that he developed his ideas at immense length as he postulated a vast sequence of angels and emanations and the formation of 365 heavens, the lowest of which was occupied by those angels who formed the world, of whom the God of the Jews was chief. The Supreme Father, "without birth and without name," sent Christ, "his first-begotten Nous (Mind)," to rescue believers from those who formed the world. Christ's appearance on earth was that of a man, but, being "an incorporeal power," he transfigured himself as he pleased. Nor was it he who suffered death but Simon the Cyrenean who had been made to carry the cross for him and who, after being transformed into the likeness of

26. Irenaeus, *Against Heresies* i.23.

Jesus, was then crucified, while Jesus assumed the appearance of Simon and stood by laughing at what was taking place. This meant that there was no necessity to confess the one who was crucified, but only the one who, sent by the Father, looked like a man and was thought to have been crucified.[27] In this form of docetism the distinction posited by Simon Magus between Jesus and Christ has apparently disappeared; Jesus himself is the purely phantom appearance of Christ from above.

In the middle years of the second century Marcion, a native of Pontus on the coast of the Black Sea, was proclaiming gnostic heresy in Rome. Marcion is said to have adopted and developed the teachings of Cerdo, a Syrian who received instruction from the followers of Simon Magus and had also made his way to Rome. We learn from Irenaeus that Marcion advanced "the most daring blasphemies" against the God of the Old Testament, whom he asserted to be the author of evil. Teaching that Jesus came in the guise of a man to abolish the works of this God, together with the writings of the law and the prophets, Marcion excised from the canon not only the Old Testament but also much of the New Testament, mutilating the Gospels by removing Luke's account of the virgin birth and all the passages where Jesus spoke of the Creator of the universe as his Father, and likewise deleting from St. Paul's epistles everything that was uncongenial to his dualistic preconceptions. Polycarp did not hesitate to denounce Marcion to his face as "the firstborn of Satan." Irenaeus was insistent that the originator of the gnostic error propounded by Marcion and others was Simon Magus.

> All who in any way pervert the truth and do damage to the church's message are the disciples and successors of the Samaritan Simon Magus. Even though they may not admit to the name of their master for the purpose of seducing others, yet they teach his doctrine. Indeed, they put forward the name of Christ Jesus as an enticement, but by various means introduce the impiety of Simon and thus destroy many as under cover of a good name they wickedly disseminate their own notions, and by the sweetness and dignity of that name manage to infect them with the bitter and malignant poison of the serpent, who is the author of apostasy.[28]

The gnostic heresiarch who attracted the greatest following was Valentinus, a contemporary of Marcion who had grown up and studied in Alexandria, but who, like Marcion (and Simon Magus and others earlier), set himself up as a teacher in Rome. The system he constructed was so labyrinthine and cumbersome that it is surprising that he should have had so many disciples and

---

27. Irenaeus, loc. cit.
28. Irenaeus, *Against Heresies* i.27; iii.4. See also Tertullian, *Against Marcion*, passim, the most thorough and extensive refutation of Marcionism; Hippolytus, *Refutation* vii.17-19, who contended that the origin of Marcion's system should be traced back to the Greek philosopher Empedocles of Agrigentum (5th century B.C.); and Epiphanius, *Against Heresies* 42.

imitators. Eusebius spoke feelingly of "the unfathomable abyss of Valentinus's errors."[29] Hippolytus stated that the Valentinian heresy owed a large debt to Pythagorean and Platonic theory (as was true of all these dualistic fabrications) and that accordingly Valentinus could "justly be reckoned a Pythagorean and Platonist, not a Christian."[30] A man of outstanding ability, it was when his hopes of becoming a bishop were disappointed that Valentinus deviated from the truth and, as Tertullian tells us, gained a multitude of disciples "who had a propensity for fables." Tertullian explained that the complexity of the philosophy he propounded made it easy for this heresy "to fashion itself into as many various shapes as a courtesan, who usually changes and adjusts her dress every day."[31]

According to the Valentinian christological theory there could be no union of Christ, who as the Only-Begotten *(Monogenēs)* and Mind *(Nous)* was spiritual, with the material, which was irredeemable and doomed to perish. An association with the intermediate category of being, the psychical, which could incline either to good or evil, was, however, considered possible—especially as the tendency of the psychical was held to be on the right hand rather than on the left, light rather than heavy, and upward rather than downward. A psychical nature was provided for Christ by propagation from the Demiurge, who was depicted as the power responsible for the formation of all material and psychical entities. This special, psychical, "body," which was visible to men and capable of suffering, passed through Mary like water flowing through a channel, but did so without partaking of her substance. The spiritual Savior, who belonged to and was formed by the Pleroma, descended upon the psychical being at the baptism in the river Jordan, and was taken away when the trial before Pilate took place, with the consequence that it was not the spiritual being, who was incapable of suffering, but the psychical being that suffered and was crucified.[32] The devisers of this christological theory were already traveling along the road that leads to the Arian Christ who is neither truly divine nor truly human but some kind of intermediate being.

Even though the differentiation between Jesus and Christ made by the early docetists is not retained in the Valentinian construction, the dualistic principle still plainly prevails. It is simply a refinement that has taken place, for now not just Christ but also Jesus is docetic: his is not a material but a psychical body, which only *seems* to be a material body. It is a device that enables Christ to avoid contact with matter. This may be an advance in subtlety, but it created rather than solved christological problems. We see again that the dualistic presuppositions of the gnostic mind ruled out the tenability of a genuine incarnation and a genuine crucifixion. The elimination of Bethlehem and Calvary was a severing of the taproot of Christianity. The church could not disregard this and survive.

29. Eusebius, *Ecclesiastical History* iv.11.
30. Hippolytus, *Refutation* vi.16, 24.
31. Tertullian, *Against the Valentinians* 1.4.
32. Irenaeus, *Against Heresies* i.1-7.

CHAPTER 20

The Early Unitarians

A different christological "explanation" was offered by those who taught what is called *adoptionism.* The thesis in this case rested on the premise that Jesus was a mere man[1] who, because of the perfection of his life, was adopted into the Godhead. The earliest indication of this notion is found in *"The Shepherd" of Hermas,* a work belonging to the first half of the second century which enjoyed considerable popularity largely because of the belief that its author was the Hermas mentioned by St. Paul in Romans 16:14.[2] Since, however, the adoptionist idea appears only in one place and is imprecisely expressed, it does not follow that those who had a high opinion of this work were adoptionists; indeed, the brevity and lack of clarity should make us cautious to build too much on what is said. The "incarnation" is apparently regarded as analogous with the indwelling of the believer by the Holy Spirit, who is equated with the Son. The reward for cooperating with and not defiling the Holy Spirit was the elevation of the man into divine partnership.[3]

Later in the same century a leather merchant from Byzantium named Theodotus brought his christological speculations to Rome, where in due course he was excommunicated by the bishop (Victor, 189-198); but, undeterred, he set up his own sect and attracted a following. Theodotus, a man of intellectual vigor, had been influenced, it was said, by the gnostic theories of Cerinthus and Valentinus and by the judaizing sect known as the Ebionites. He taught that Jesus was simply a man,[4] who had no power to perform miracles

---

1. The opinion that Jesus was a mere man is known as *psilanthropism,* from the Greek *psilos anthrōpos* = mere man.

2. *"The Shepherd"* is quoted by Irenaeus, Tertullian, Clement of Alexandria, and Origen. Origen said that it was "a book which was despised by some," but plainly not by him (*On First Principles* IV.i.11). With regard to the ascription of the authorship to St. Paul's friend Hermas Eusebius writes: "It should be observed that this too has been disputed by some, and on their account cannot be placed among the acknowledged books; while by others it is considered quite indispensable, especially to those who need instruction in the elements of the faith. Hence, as we know, it has been publicly read in churches, and I have found that some of the most ancient writers used it" (*Ecclesiastical History* iii.3).

3. *"The Shepherd" of Hermas,* Similitudes v.6f.; ix.1.

4. The heretical description of Jesus as "a mere man" *(psilos anthrōpos)* is recorded

before Christ descended upon him in the form of a dove at his baptism in the river Jordan. The separation of Jesus from Christ is distinctly Cerinthian, as is the interpretation of the descent at the baptism. (The descent of the Spirit understood as the descent of Christ on the occasion of Jesus' baptism may also have contributed to the confusion of the Holy Spirit and the Son in the *"Shepherd" of Hermas.*) The concept of the mere manhood of Jesus would coincide with both Cerinthian and Ebionite notions, the former being dualistic and the latter unitarian in line with the judaistic view of monotheism. Some, though not all, of the disciples of Theodotus believed that Jesus was raised from the dead and adopted into the Godhead.[5]

Epiphanius has described how Theodotus manipulated Scripture to support his claim that Jesus was a mere man. Theodotus argued that it was not God but man whom he denied—that is to say, it was not the existence of God but the deity of the man Jesus that he rejected. Among the passages he cited were the following: John 8:40, the words of Jesus to his critics, "You now seek to kill me, a man who has told you the truth"—to which Epiphanius rejoined that he had failed to complete Jesus' statement, ". . . the truth which I heard from God"; Deuteronomy 18:15, the prophetic utterance of Moses, "The Lord will raise up a prophet from among your brethren like me," as indicating that the Messiah would be a man just as Moses was a man—to which Epiphanius rejoined that the human likeness of Jesus was the human nature born of the Virgin Mary in fulfilment of the prophecy of Isaiah 7:14, as attested in Matthew 1:23, "Behold, a virgin shall conceive and bear a son, and his name shall be called Immanuel, which means 'God with us,'" showing that Jesus is both God from the Father and man through Mary."[6]

Another heretical faction comprising a group which broke away from the following of Theodotus was led by a banker of the same name. This Theodotus, like his namesake, was condemned by the bishop of Rome (Zephyrinus, 198-217, Victor's successor). He too proclaimed that Jesus was a mere man. The particular distinguishing mark of his teaching was the position of supremacy he assigned to Melchizedek. He maintained that the declaration of Psalm 110:4, "You are a priest for ever after the order of Melchizedek," meant that Christ, to whom it was applied by the author of the Epistle to the Hebrews, must be inferior to Melchizedek. Epiphanius refuted this contention of the Mel-

---

by Eusebius, who found it in a work called *The Little Labyrinth* (see Theodoret, *Compendium of Heretical Fables* ii.15), possibly written by Hippolytus, in which Theodotus was denounced as "the leader and father of this God-denying apostasy and the first to declare that Christ is mere man" (*Ecclesiastical History* v.28). The expression is used by Hippolytus in his treatise *Against the Heresy of Noetus* 3, with reference to the teaching of Theodotus.

5. See Hippolytus, *Refutation of All Heresies* vii.23; Tertullian, *On the 'Prescription' of Heretics* 53; Clement of Alexandria, *Excerpts from the Writings of Theodotus;* Epiphanius, *Against Heresies* liv.1; Theodoret, *Compendium of Heretical Fables* ii.5.

6. Epiphanius, *Against Heresies* liv.

chizedekians, as they were known, by a careful examination and exposition of the passages involved.[7] This conception of the exalted position of Melchizedek was doubtless taken over from a Jewish source, though the precise path of its transmission is unknown to us. We do know, however, that in first-century Palestine the Qumran community, a branch of the Essene sect, accorded a position of the highest dignity to Melchizedek, and apparently identified him with the archangel Michael, who in the hierarchy of the eschatological kingdom they were awaiting was to wield the supreme authority, above even that of the messianic personage.[8]

This view of Melchizedek may perhaps have come to the Theodotians by way of the Ebionites, whose doctrine was an unstable compound of Jewish and Christian ideas. Thus they insisted on the observance of the Mosaic law, they regarded St. Paul as an apostate from the law and therefore rejected him and his writings, and they accepted only St. Matthew's Gospel. The name "Ebionite" is formed from a Hebrew word meaning "poor" and was descriptive, almost certainly, of the voluntary poverty of their style of life. Some of the patristic authors, however, took advantage of the designation to refer to the poverty of the understanding of the Ebionites, particularly with regard to their conception of the person of Jesus, whom, like the Theodotians, they held to be a mere man.[9]

Before we discuss certain other developments in the early history of unitarianism some consideration must be given to the cult of Montanism, which appeared on the scene during the latter part of the second century. The cult took its name from Montanus, a priest of Cybele from Phrygia in Asia Minor, who declared himself to be the promised Paraclete (see John 14:16, 26; 15:26; 16:7, 13), either as an incarnation of the Holy Spirit or as the chosen vessel of the Spirit's indwelling. In close association with him were two supposedly Spirit-inspired prophetesses, Maximilla and Priscilla, whose activities promoted a charismatic fanaticism. Montanus promised the establishment of the new Jerusalem on Phrygian soil and preached the imminence of the millennial reign, and in preparation for these eventualities he imposed on his followers a discipline of rigorous asceticism. The Montanists, in fact, regarded themselves as

7. Ibid. lv. Hippolytus (*Refutation* vii.23) would seem to be wrong in saying that the first Theodotus accepted the virgin birth, though this may be true of the second Theodotus (see Tertullian, loc. cit.).

8. Or personages: the Qumranians evidently expected the appearance of two messiahs, one priestly and the other kingly. On this and on the history of speculation regarding the significance of Melchizedek see my *Commentary on the Epistle to the Hebrews* (Grand Rapids, 1977), pp. 12ff., 237ff.

9. See Origen, *On First Principles* iv.22; *Against Celsus* ii.1; also Eusebius, who said that they were properly called Ebionites "because they held poor and mean opinions concerning Christ," whom they considered "a plain and common man," the natural son of Mary and a human father. In their view, Eusebius explained further, Christ was justified by his superior virtue and the observance of the ceremonial law was essential to salvation (*Ecclesiastical History* iii.27).

"spiritual" in distinction from all other Christians, whom they held to be "carnal." No place for penitence and restoration was permitted to disciples who had lapsed into sin. Celibacy was required and martyrdom was welcomed. Even two centuries later Jerome needed to dissuade one of his correspondents from becoming a Montanist, pointing out that the promise of the sending of the Holy Spirit was fulfilled on the Day of Pentecost, as narrated in Acts 2, and that there was no place for any other fulfilment. "We do not so much reject prophecy," he wrote, "as refuse to receive prophets whose utterances fail to accord with the Scriptures old and new." He criticized the Montanists for "closing the doors of the church to almost every fault," while they themselves, blinded by their self-righteousness, were not free from serious sins. Their error was further summarized by Jerome as follows:

> I must confute the open blasphemy of men who say that God first determined in the Old Testament to save the world by Moses and the prophets, but that finding himself unable to fulfil his purpose he took to himself the body of the Virgin and, preaching under the form of the Son in Christ, underwent death for our salvation. Moreover, that when by these two steps he was unable to save the world he last of all descended by the Holy Spirit upon Montanus and those demented women Prisca and Maximilla; and that thus the mutilated and emasculate[10] Montanus possessed a fulness of knowledge such as was never claimed by Paul.[11]

Jerome actually accused the Montanists of unitarianism: "adhering to the doctrine of Sabellius,"[12] he wrote, "they force the Trinity into the narrow limits of a single personality."[13] This may have been to some extent true of some Montanists in Jerome's day, or it may have been an inference on his part. The judgment of Epiphanius, Jerome's contemporary, was, however, quite different, for although he stated that the Montanists had turned away from the right road, having embraced erroneous theories and doctrines of demons, he asserted that "regarding the Father, the Son, and the Holy Spirit their beliefs are similar to those of the holy catholic church."[14] It seems improbable that Tertullian would have aligned himself, as he did in his later years, with a sect that was unorthodox in the sense indicated by Jerome. It was its dogmatic and ascetic rigor that attracted him, and the Montanism he committed himself to in North Africa early in the third century was probably shorn of the excesses associated with it in Phrygia, which included extreme forms of ecstatic excitement acclaimed as manifestations of the Spirit's power. The pretensions of the Mon-

10. This description was presumably based on the tradition that Montanus was a priest of Cybele.
11. Jerome, Letter 41, to Marcella. He went on to quote St. Paul's words in 1 Cor. 13:9, 12, "We know in part and we prophesy in part," and, "Now we see through a glass darkly."
12. See below, p. 257.
13. Loc. cit.
14. Epiphanius, *Against Heresies* 48.

tanists to be the recipients of continuing revelation and the failure of their extravagant prophetic utterances helped to impress on the patristic leaders the necessity of defining and insisting on the authoritative finality of the canon of Holy Scripture. Montanism, it may be remarked, represents a type of phenomenon which recurs during the history of the church as a reaction against the numbing effects of stagnant traditionalism, as, for example, in the case of the more flamboyant of the Anabaptists of the sixteenth century, such as the Zwickau Prophets who claimed to have received immediate revelation and apocalyptic visions.

Opposition to the Montanists came from heterodox as well as orthodox quarters. An instance of the former was the sect of the *Alogi,* whose name was derived from their rejection of the Logos doctrine of the Fourth Gospel—they in fact rejected St. John's Gospel in its entirety, mainly because of its teaching on the Paraclete to which the excesses of the Montanists were linked. They charged, further, that gnostic bias was betrayed by the identification of the Logos with the Son of God, by the absence of any account of the nativity, and by the abrupt transition from the prologue to the baptism and ministry of Jesus. They even affirmed that the Fourth Gospel and also the Revelation, with its apocalyptic visions and prophecies, were the work of Cerinthus, whose heresy St. John's writings so strenuously opposed![15] As might have been expected, the Alogi overemphasized the humanity of Christ and reduced his stature to little more than that of a mere man.[16]

Another assailant of Montanism was the unitarian Praxeas, who was mainly responsible for persuading the bishop of Rome to condemn Montanus and his teachings. Somewhat ironically, he was in turn denounced by Tertullian for his antitrinitarianism. In a celebrated aphorism Tertullian declared that "Praxeas did a twofold service for the devil at Rome: he drove away prophecy and he brought in heresy; he put to flight the Paraclete and he crucified the Father."[17] Of these two "services" the first refers to Praxeas's opposition to the Montanist notions concerning prophecy and the Holy Spirit's activity, and the second to Praxeas's own error of patripassianism, which postulated that it was the Father who suffered and died on the cross. Tertullian described the position of Praxeas with regard to the incarnation as follows: "He says that the Father himself came down into the Virgin, was himself born of her, himself suffered, indeed was himself Jesus Christ"; and he accused Praxeas of being "the first to import into Rome from Asia this kind of depravity."[18] The theory offered by Praxeas was developed from his denial of the tripersonality of God. Unlike the docetists and other dualists, however, he did not deny the reality of the incarnation, but envisaged the unipersonal God as fulfilling different roles,

15. See pp. 240f. above.
16. Epiphanius actually charged the Alogi with psilanthropism, using as a source the *Syntagma* of Hippolytus, now lost (*Against Heresies* 51).
17. Tertullian, *Against Praxeas* 1.
18. Ibid.

like an actor assuming different guises for different impersonations: that of the Father before the incarnation, that of the Son during the incarnate existence, and that of the Holy Spirit at Pentecost. In this respect there was some resemblance to the claim of Simon Magus to have appeared in one place as the Father, in another as the Son, and again in another as the Holy Spirit.[19] The unitarianism associated with Praxeas and certain others became known as *monarchianism* (from the Greek, meaning the rule of one), and more particularly as *modalistic* monarchianism, because of the different modes of being that God was supposed to have assumed.

The term *monarchy* was actually used by Praxeas and others to describe their unitarian notion of the Godhead. In his treatise *Against Praxeas* Tertullian vigorously reaffirmed the orthodox doctrine of trinitarian monotheism, insisting that the monarchy of God was not invalidated by a proper understanding of the tripersonal Godhead.[20] Some of Tertullian's own formulations and analogies, however, were less than happy, even though he intended them in an orthodox sense. He was willing, for instance, to speak of the Son as a "projection" or "emanation"[21] from the Father, while acknowledging that the gnostic Valentinus had used this term in defining his theory of eons. "Truth," he explained, "must not refrain from the use of such a term and its reality and meaning simply because heresy also makes use of it."[22] This argument is sound enough, provided it is a fully appropriate or necessary term; but the suitability of this particular word is hard to justify. Tertullian interpreted his usage, as one would expect, in an orthodox manner: "The Son is a projection from the Father without being separated from him," he wrote, ". . . just as the root puts forth the tree, and the fountain the river, and the sun the ray. . . . The tree is not severed from the root, nor the river from the fountain, nor the ray from the sun; nor, indeed, is the Word separated from God." The Third Person of the Trinity was accommodated by extension of the analogy: the Holy Spirit is "third from God and the Son, just as the fruit of the tree is third from the root, or as the stream out of the river is third from the fountain, or as the apex of the ray is third from the sun"—the principle being that "nothing is alien from that original source whence it derives its own properties."[23] So much for unity; now for diversity, which Tertullian sought to demonstrate as follows: "I should give the name *sun* even to a sunbeam, considered in itself; but if I were mentioning the sun from which the ray emanates I certainly should at once withdraw the name of sun from the mere beam. For although I do not make two suns, still I shall reckon both the sun and its ray to be as much two things and

19. See p. 238 above.
20. *Against Praxeas* 24. It is here that the term "Trinity" *(Trinitas)* is first encountered. Tertullian would seem to have been responsible for its formation.
21. Tertullian of course wrote in Latin, but cited the Greek word *probolē,* which Valentinus had used.
22. *Against Praxeas* 8.
23. Ibid.

two forms of one undivided substance as God and his Word, and the Father and the Son."[24]

However, as we have remarked earlier, to propose any similitude or analogy of the Holy Trinity is extremely precarious and likely to confuse rather than enlighten the understanding. One can hardly deny that in the continuing controversy Tertullian's analogy was more serviceable to unitarian error than to trinitarian truth. Since the reality of the Trinity is absolutely unique and transcendental, there is no way in which it can be matched or paralleled in the finite world of creation. Yet the orthodox mind has tended to find the temptation to discover trinitarian analogies irresistible.

Because they are rationalizations that proceed from a heart of irrationality the speculations of heretical minds cannot be expected to escape from confusion and inconsistency (cf. Rom. 1:21f.). We see this exemplified again in the case of Praxeas, who, in a manner that conflicted with his unitarian conclusions, made a distinction between the Father and the Son and also between Jesus and Christ. Tertullian pointed out that Praxeas understood the Son to be flesh, that is, the man Jesus, and the Father to be Spirit, that is Christ, and he accordingly charged that he and his followers, "while contending that the Father and the Son are one and the same, do in fact begin by dividing them rather than uniting them." He supposed that they had picked up this separation between Jesus and Christ from the school of Valentinus, and this may well be so, for it is evident that the thinking of Praxeas was not free from dualistic presuppositions, and that he too was heading in the direction of the Arian heresy. It is interesting to find Tertullian accusing Praxeas, a century before the church's clash with Arius, of making the Redeemer a compound or mixture of flesh and spirit and thereby producing a *tertium quid* that cannot be God because in becoming flesh the Word has ceased to be the Word, and cannot be man since he is not properly flesh: "Being compounded therefore of both he actually is neither; he is rather some third substance, very different from either."[25] That person was blind, he said, who failed to perceive that to confuse Christ and the Father was to invent some other God, and he adduced passages from the New Testament to demonstrate the incompatibility of such theorizing with the teaching of the apostles.[26] Finally, after quoting 1 John 5:12, "He who has not the Son has not life," Tertullian commented, "And that man has not the Son who believes him to be anything other than the Son."[27]

Views similar to those of Praxeas were propounded by his contemporary Noetus, a native of Smyrna, whose unitarian teachings were transported to Rome by his disciple Epigonus. We learn from Hippolytus that Noetus affirmed that "the Son and the Father are the same," and that "when the Father had not been born he was rightly designed Father," but when it pleased him to be born

24. Ibid. 13. The analogy recurs in Athanasius (*Orations against the Arians* iii.3f.).
25. Ibid. 27.
26. Ibid. 28.
27. Ibid. 31.

"he himself became his own Son, not another's";[28] and, further, that he argued christologically in this way: "If I acknowledge Christ to be God he is the Father himself, if he is indeed God; and consequently the Father suffered, for he was the Father himself."[29] Hippolytus took exception to the manner in which Noetus manipulated Scripture by detaching verses from their context without regard to the teaching of the Bible as a whole—"following the same one-sided method used by Theodotus when he attempted to prove that Christ was a mere man."[30] Respect for the authority of Scripture and its right use was of primary importance:

> There is, brethren, one God, the knowledge of whom we gain from the Holy Scriptures, and from no other source. . . . All of us who wish to practice piety will be unable to learn its practice from any other quarter than the oracles of God. Whatever things, then, the Holy Scriptures declare, at these let us look; and whatever things they teach, these let us learn; and as the Father wills our belief to be, so let us believe; and as he wills the Son to be glorified, so let us glorify him; and as he wills the Holy Spirit to be bestowed, so let us receive him—not according to our own will, nor according to our own mind, nor yet doing violence to those things which are given by God, but even as he has chosen to teach them by the Holy Scriptures, so let us discern them.[31]

It is worthy of remark, because it is symptomatic of the internal problems and dissensions by which the church has been plagued from one century to another, that four successive bishops of Rome, Eleutherus, Victor, Zephyrinus, and Callistus (the middle two of whom had excommunicated the elder and younger Theodotus in turn), looked on modalistic monarchianism with approval. Hippolytus, who had been a pupil of Irenaeus and who settled and served the church as a presbyter in Rome, had no good word for Zephyrinus, calling him "an uninformed and shamefully corrupt man," influenced by the unscrupulous Callistus (who would be his successor).[32] Callistus he accused of actively promoting the heresy of Noetus, describing him as a man who was cunning in his wickedness, subtle in his deception, and "impelled by a restless ambition to mount the episcopal throne." Zephyrinus, "an ignorant and illiterate individual, unskilled in ecclesiastical definitions," whose covetous nature made him "accessible to bribes," was evidently easy prey for Callistus. On the accession of Callistus to the episcopate in 217 Hippolytus denounced him as a heretic and allowed himself to be set up as antipope by his followers. Callistus in turn accused Hippolytus of being the worshipper of two gods.[33] Though this was a baseless slander, it cannot be denied that the christology of Hippolytus was less

28. Hippolytus, *Against Noetus* 1; *Refutation of All Heresies* ix.2, 5.
29. *Against Noetus* 2.
30. Ibid. 3.
31. Ibid. 9.
32. *Refutation of All Heresies* ix.2.
33. Ibid. ix.6.

than satisfactory in its formulation, and especially his assertion that the Logos was brought forth by "the solitary and supreme Deity" as "a ratiocination of the universe" and alone "produced from existing things," since "the Father himself constituted existence." Thus stated, the Logos would seem to be no more than an expression or effect of the divine mind through which the creation of the world was accomplished; Hippolytus, however, contended that the Logos, being from God himself, was the substance of God, and therefore God. He also called him "the first begotten child of the Father," whom the Father sent forth to receive our humanity by being born of a virgin, and by his life and death to set us an example to emulate,[34] thereby implying, in a manner consonant with his own rigorist standards, justification through self-discipline rather than through faith in the merit of Christ's vicarious sacrifice on the cross.

Sabellius, a native of Libya, according to Basil,[35] was another modalistic unitarian who taught in Rome during the early part of the third century and was opposed by Hippolytus. After the end of this century Sabellianism became the common name for modalistic monarchianism in the east. Hippolytus makes it plain that he did not regard Sabellius as intractable and deaf to persuasion, but was convinced that he had been perverted instead of corrected by the malign Callistus,[36] by whom he was subsequently excommunicated. Athanasius says that in his time the advocacy of Sabellian views by some of the bishops in Libya was so effective that the Son of God was scarcely any longer preached in the churches there.[37] This fits in with the information that Sabellius even presumed to describe God as "Son-Father"[38]—an appellation that was not intended to signify that God was Father and Son (and Holy Spirit) at the same time, but rather that it was within his power to act by a succession of manifestations or "energies."[39] In contrast to Sabellius, who "said that the Son and the Father were the same, and did away with either, the Father when there is a Son, and the Son when there is a Father," Athanasius insisted that "when we say that the Father and the Son are two, we still confess one God, so that when we say that there is one God, let us consider Father and Son two, while they are one in the Godhead, and the Father's Word as indissoluble and indivisible and inseparable from him."[40]

The term *prosōpon*,[41] which in orthodox circles was used of each *person*

---

34. Ibid. x.29.

35. Basil, Letter 9, to Maximus, and Letter 207, to the clergy of Neocaesarea.

36. Hippolytus, *Refutation* ix.6.

37. Athanasius, *On the Opinion of Dionysius* 5.

38. The Greek neologism was *huiopatōr*.

39. See Athanasius, *On Synods* 16; *Exposition of the Faith* 2; Hilary, *On the Trinity* iv.12; Gregory of Nyssa, *Answer to Eunomius's Second Book* (near the beginning).

40. Athanasius, *Orations against the Arians* iv.9, 10. The fourth volume of this work was probably a compilation by a disciple of Athanasius.

41. A transliteration of the Greek noun meaning variously "face," "person," and actor's "mask," and hence a part or character in a drama.

of the trinitarian Godhead, was interpreted in a manner convenient to his own theological predilections by Sabellius, who turned it to mean "impersonation" in relation to each particular mode or role of his unitarian God.[42] Three quarters of the way through the fourth century Basil of Caesarea was constrained to issue a solemn warning against the recrudescence of Sabellianism, which he described as "Judaism imported into the preaching of the gospel under the guise of Christianity." "For," he wrote, "if a person calls Father, Son, and Holy Spirit one thing of many faces,[43] and makes the hypostasis[44] of the three one, what is this but to deny the everlasting pre-existence of the Only-Begotten? Denied too is the Lord's sojourn among men in the incarnation, the going down into hades, the resurrection, the judgment, and also the proper operations of the Spirit."[45]

Another form of unitarian speculation, known as dynamic (or dynamistic) monarchianism, had affinities with the teaching of the Alogi and Theodotians, who maintained that Jesus was a mere man. Its most noted exponent was Paul of Samosata, who became bishop of Antioch in the year 260 and was formally condemned and excommunicated by a synod which met in that city in 268. Eusebius recorded that "he held, contrary to the teachings of the church, low and degraded views of Christ, namely, that in his nature he was a common man,"[46] and quoted from a letter addressed by the synod of Antioch to the bishops of Rome and Alexandria and to the church at large in which Paul of Samosata was accused of "strutting about in the abominable heresy of Artemas."[47] The synodical letter depicted Paul as inordinately vain, arrogant, and tyrannical, exercising secular as well as ecclesiastical power, and living a life of luxury and licentiousness, and charged him with unwillingness "to acknowledge that the Son of God has come down from heaven" and with the declaration that "Jesus Christ is from below."[48]

While denying that Jesus Christ was from above, Paul of Samosata ap-

42. A meaning the term could certainly bear (see preceding note).
43. Or "one thing of many roles" (hen pragma polyprosōpon).
44. The Greek term hypostasis is the exact equivalent in its basic meaning of the Latin substantia, the underlying essence. As such it could serve to designate the essential being of God, which belongs to each of the three Persons of the Trinity. It was at times used of each of the natures, human and divine, of the incarnate Son. But in the development of christological definition it at length became synonymous with "person." This is an indication of the extreme difficulty of providing terminology adequate to define the mystery of the divine-human being of the incarnate Son.
45. Basil, Letter 210, to the Notables of Neocaesarea.
46. Eusebius, Ecclesiastical History vii.27.
47. Ibid. vii.30. Artemas was also known as Artemon. Eusebius mentions "a laborious work . . . against the heresy of Artemon, which Paul of Samosata attempted to revive," the heresy, namely, "which teaches that the Saviour was a mere man" (v. 28). The work mentioned, identified by Theodoret as The Little Labyrinth (Heretical Fables ii.5), has been questionably attributed to Hippolytus.
48. Eusebius, Ecclesiastical History vii.30.

parently did not deny the virgin birth. He contended that Mary's son was inspired by the divine Logos, just as the Logos had inspired the prophets of old, though not to the same degree. He admitted to a certain threefoldness in the unity of the Godhead, in that he distinguished the Son and the Spirit as Logos (Word) and Sophia (Wisdom), but only as qualities or powers,[49] not as persons. God was thus reduced from a tripersonal to a unipersonal being, and Jesus was simply a man, distinct from the Logos, who, anointed by the Holy Spirit at his baptism, manifested perfect obedience and conformity to the will of God and was enabled to perform miracles. And so he became the Savior of mankind and, dignified with the name that is above every name, was exalted to everlasting union with God (adoptionism). This being so, he could be called God and it was even permissible to speak of his preexistence inasmuch as he was the fulfilment of God's preexistent plan for the world's redemption. Paul objected, however, that to teach that Jesus was by nature the Son of God involved the postulation of two gods and therefore the subversion of monotheistic belief.[50]

49. *Dynameis*—hence the designation "dynamic" or "dynamistic."
50. Epiphanius, *Against Heresies* 65; Athanasius, *On Synods* 26 and 45.

CHAPTER 21

Origen's Christology

The intention of monarchianism was to safeguard the unity of the Godhead, but the dynamic form produced a Christ who was in effect mere man and the modalistic form a Christ who was in effect mere God, neither of whom was competent to mediate between God and man. The Arian attempt to close the gap devised a Christ who was neither truly God nor truly man; but the ground was to a considerable extent prepared for Arianism by the careless use of subordinationist terminology. In the theology of subordinationism the Father was conceived as the fountain or source of the Godhead, the Son, being derivative, even if eternally so, as subordinate to the Father, and the Holy Spirit as subordinate to the Son. Though the name of Origen is most readily associated with the concept of subordinationism in the early church, expressions of the doctrine can be traced in the writings of his teacher Clement of Alexandria and, still earlier, in Irenaeus and Justin Martyr. But it would be wrong to conclude that Origen inclined toward a unitarian view of the Deity. He did not regard the Son and the Spirit as intermediary emanations or powers flowing from a monarchical origin.[1] It is true that St. Paul spoke of Christ as "the power of God and the wisdom of God" (1 Cor. 1:24), but Origen warned that this implied, not a being without person or substance, but, to the contrary, one who is personal and substantial, that is, who exists "hypostatically"—the Father's only-begotten Son, indeed, who "derives from the Father what he is, but without any beginning."[2] This is the doctrine of the eternal generation of the Son, from which it follows that there never was "a time when" the Father was not Father and the Son not Son. With reference to the statement in Colossians 1:15 that the Son is "the image of the invisible God," Origen argued that since the Father was invisible he generated an image that was invisible, who as such was "the invisible image of the invisible God," and that "this image contains the unity of nature and substance belonging to Father and Son."[3] This coessentiality of the Son with the Father was a further reason for Origen to insist that "there never was (a time) when

1. Origen, *On First Principles* IV.i.28; also I.iii.3, 4, 7.
2. Ibid. I.ii.2.
3. Ibid. I.ii.6.

he did not exist"—which sounds like a refutation of Arianism at a time before Arius existed![4]

While, however, Origen affirmed the consubstantiality of the Son with the Father, he also saw the Son as subordinate to the Father in the same way as an effect is subordinate to its cause. There is no question that at times his speculative manner of expression was ill advised and rendered him liable to misinterpretation. To say, for example, that "there are three hypostases, the Father, the Son, and the Holy Spirit" and then to add that "at the same time we believe nothing to be uncreated but the Father," has every appearance of opening the door for the conclusion that the Son and the Holy Spirit are creatures of some kind. The problem is not eased by the further assertion "that all things were made by the Logos and that the Holy Spirit is the most excellent and first in order of all that was made by the Father through Christ."[5] Yet, as we have seen, Origen affirmed the coeternity of the Three Persons of the Trinity. Furthermore, to speak of Christ as a "second God," as he does in his work against Celsus, certainly gives the impression of splitting the Godhead into two—but this carelessness occurs in a place where he is contrasting the folly and impiety of those who worship crocodiles with the virtuous lives of Christians who worship, not a creature, but the Son of God.[6]

The same subordinationist perspective disposed Origen to postulate an ontological distinction in the assertion of John 1:1 that "the Word was God"[7]— not "the God" but "God" without the addition of the definite article. The Apostle, according to his explanation, "uses the article when the name of God refers to the uncreated cause of all things, and omits it when the Logos is named God"; and this Origen took to indicate that "the God who is God over all is God with the article." His purpose was to settle the minds of those who might be perplexed by this statement in the prologue of the Fourth Gospel, and who, for fear of proclaiming two Gods, might deny (in a unitarian manner) the dis-

---

4. Ibid. IV.i.28; I.ii.9. Origen's declaration *ouk estin hote ouk ēn,* "there is not when he was not," is an almost verbatim denial of the cryptically economic Arian formula *ēn pote hote ouk ēn,* "there was once when he was not." Origen cautioned his readers that, though "the words 'when' or 'never' have a meaning that relates to time," statements concerning Father, Son, and Holy Spirit "are to be understood as transcending all time, all ages, and all eternity" (IV.i.28).

5. Commentary on the Gospel of John, Bk. ii.6.

6. *Against Celsus* v.39.

7. *Theos ēn ho logos,* where the Logos is called *theos,* not *ho theos.* Origen's contention that St. John regularly follows this rule is not borne out by a study of the Greek text. Even in the prologue the anarthrous *theos* is used several times for God, whom Origen defines as "the uncreated cause of all things"; see *para theou* (v. 6), *ek theou* (v. 13), *theon oudeis heōraken pantote* (v. 18). J. H. Bernard has appropriately commented that *ho theos* "would identify the Logos with the totality of divine existence, and would contradict the preceding clause" (*A Critical and Exegetical Commentary on the Gospel according to St. John,* Vol. I [Edinburgh, 1928], p. 2); and C. K. Barrett similarly (*The Gospel according to St. John* [London, 1955], p. 130).

tinction of the Son from the Father, or else deny the divinity of the Son by assigning to him an essence and existence quite separate from the Father, as though he were some other kind of being. Hence his proposal of a distinction between God with the definite article and God without the definite article, or, in other words, between God who is God of himself *(autotheos)* and the Son whose deity is derived from the deity of the Father, with the implication that the deity of Father and Son is identical.[8]

It is evident that Origen's mind was influenced by Alexandrian Logos speculation, which in turn had absorbed notions from the Greek philosophical traditions of Platonic and Stoic thought; Philo, for example, had presented the Logos as a second god and as god without the definite article,[9] though in a sense different from that intended by Origen. Nonetheless, Origen came perilously near to the doctrine of ontological continuity from Creator to creature by extending his concept of derivation or subordination at least to the realm of angelic beings.

The summit of Origen's hierarchical gradation was the Father, whom, he explained, the incarnate Son described as "the only true God" (Jn. 17:3). Next came the Son on the strength of St. Paul's designation of him as "the firstborn of all creation" (Col. 1:15),[10] which Origen claimed as confirmation that the Son was "the first to be with God and to attract to himself divinity," and that he was "a being of more exalted rank than the other gods beside him."[11] Apparently he understood these other gods to be the exalted angelic beings who are the ministers of the divine will.[12] Though he did not intend to equate their divinity with that of the trinitarian Godhead,[13] yet he did not envisage the dignity of their being as absolutely removed from the deity of God himself; it was seen as a power or reality of being bestowed by the God who is the fountain of all deity through the mediation of the Son. Thus he wrote that "it was by the offices of the Firstborn that they became gods, for he drew from God in generous measure that they should be made gods, and he communicated it to them according to his own bounty." They were gods at a distance from the Source, images of him who is himself the Image of God:

8. Origen, Commentary on John, Bk. ii.2.
9. Philo, *Allegorical Interpretation* ii.86; *On Dreams* i.229f.
10. On the interpretation of this designation of Christ see pp. 36ff. above.
11. The reference to "other gods" is based on the opening sentence of Ps. 50, rendered as "The God of gods, the Lord, hath spoken," which reflects the LXX translation of *El Elohim Yahweh*. It is better understood as a threefold appellation of God. Thus A. Cohen, in the Soncino edition of the Psalms (London, 1945), comments that the expression "represents the Deity in three aspects: the Mighty One, the Judge, the Gracious One" (similarly RSV, NEB, NIV).
12. This is not made clear (nor is the Holy Spirit mentioned) in this place; but that this is what Origen meant is apparent elsewhere. Cf. *Against Celsus* viii.3.
13. See *Against Celsus* iv.29. In this place it is apparent that Origen held that men "when made perfect" would attain to the divinity of the angels.

The true God, then, is "The God," and those who are formed after him are gods, images, as it were, of him the prototype. But the archetypal image, again, of all these images is the Word of God, who was in the beginning, and who by being with God is at all times God, not possessing that of himself, but by his being with the Father, and not continuing to be God, if we should think of this, except by remaining always in uninterrupted contemplation of the depths of the Father.[14]

This type of speculation not only ascribes to the Son a status of deity that is secondary and dependent, in such a way that his inferiority places the essential unity and identity of the Godhead in an uncertain light, but also, by including angelic and ultimately human beings within the sphere of deity, obscures the absolute ontological distinction between the Creator and the creature.

The theorizing of Origen regarding the manner of the Son's incarnation was still more open to objection. It can readily be appreciated that the pronouncement that what was needed for redemption was "a being intermediate between all created things and God, that is, a mediator,"[15] could be seized hold of as congenial to the christology of Arianism. It is always perilous to attempt to define a truth that is beyond our finite capacity of comprehension. Of this Origen was aware. Thus he confessed that it surpasses the ability of the human mind to understand "how that mighty power of divine majesty, that very Word of the Father, and that very Wisdom of God in whom all things visible and invisible were created," can have "existed within the limits of that man who appeared in Judea," how "the Wisdom of God can have entered the womb of a woman and been born an infant, uttering the wailing cries of little children," and how he can have been "brought to that death which is accounted the most shameful among men." He should perhaps have heeded his own admonition, that "to utter these things in human ears, and to explain them in words, far surpasses the powers either of our rank or of our intellect and language."[16]

Origen, however, immediately proceeded to offer an explanation of the method of the incarnation which accorded with his theory of the preexistence of the soul.[17] He supposed that a particular soul of absolute purity, destined for the Son from the beginning of creation, became uniquely one with him at the incarnation, and that it was to this soul that Christ referred when he said, "No one shall take my soul from me."[18] Affirming that the substance of a soul was "intermediate between God and the flesh," Origen considered the soul to be the instrument or means apart from which it would be impossible for the nature of God to be conjoined with a body. This soul that was united with flesh

14. Commentary on John, Bk. ii.2.
15. *On First Principles* II.vi.1.
16. Ibid. II.vi.2.
17. See pp. 89ff. above.
18. Jn. 10:18; but Origen gave this statement a sense it could not support, for in this place Jesus was speaking not of his soul as distinct from his body, but of his life, which he was to lay down and to take again.

in Christ was therefore, he said, properly called the Son of God, "either because it was wholly in the Son of God or because it received the Son of God wholly into itself."[19] It was, moreover, a soul that had elected, invincibly, to love righteousness.[20] Thus, as Origen saw it, the soul of the incarnate Son was both the bond and the intervening cushion between his deity and his humanity. It is, indeed, a serious problem in Origen's thought that the soul is something from outside or from beyond which in each human individual is for a time brought into union with a body. The strain of Greek dualism from which his mind seemed never to be wholly freed prevented him from appreciating human nature as in its integral wholeness a harmonious compound of soul and body, or rational personality and corporeity. For him, the body continued to be something of an obstacle and an embarrassment, never a truly congenial home for the spirit. This, together with his hypothesis of subordination within the Godhead, made his doctrine of Christ and the incarnation insecure and, however unintentionally, eased the way for the misconstructions of Arianism, whose adherents would not be slow to claim the support of his writings.

Origen was a controversial figure even in his own day. He was widely admired as a scholar of massive erudition; but there is no question that much of his thinking and many of his biblical interpretations were adversely affected by a residue of Greek philosophical notions and a predilection for allegorization. While still a very young man he had succeeded Clement as head of the catechetical school in Alexandria. Following ordination in Palestine in 230, however, he was synodically deposed, excommunicated, and exiled by Demetrius, bishop of Alexandria, on the ground that his self-mutilation had disqualified him for ordination and also probably because of the heterodoxy of some of his opinions. One of the first patristic authors to write against him was Methodius, who died in the persecution under Diocletian. In the year 394 Epiphanius, bishop of Salamis in Cyprus, wrote to John, bishop of Jerusalem, urging him to "withdraw from the heresy of Origen" and to cease eulogizing "one who is the spiritual father of Arius."[21] Some six years later, in 400, Jerome denied, in a letter sent to Pammachius and Oceanus, two distinguished Romans, that he had ever been an Origenist, even though he had at times expressed admiration of Origen. "I have praised the commentator but not the theologian," he explained, "the man of intellect but not the believer, the philosopher but not the apostle." He insisted that he had always opposed Origen's doctrines and

19. *On First Principles* II.vi.3.
20. Ibid. II.vi.5.
21. An English translation of this letter is given in *St. Jerome: Letters and Select Works* (Nicene and Post-Nicene Fathers, Vol. VI [Oxford and New York, 1893], pp. 83ff.). See also Epiphanius, *Against Heresies* 63 and 64. "Oh horror!" Epiphanius exclaims, "that a man should be so frantic and foolish as to hold that John the Baptist, Peter, the apostle and evangelist John, Isaiah, Jeremiah, and the rest of the prophets, are made coheirs of the devil in the kingdom of heaven!"—referring to Origen's expectation of the restoration of all creatures.

had never been so foolish as to eulogize a system to the extent of endorsing its blasphemy. "His doctrines," he declared, "are poisonous, they are unknown to the Holy Scriptures, nay more, they do them violence."

To the question why Origen had not been named and his teachings specifically condemned at the Council of Nicea Jerome replied that the main purpose of convening the council was to deal with the errors of Arius, not with the errors of all whose teaching might be regarded as suspect; yet he maintained that the bishops then present had "tacitly struck at Origen as the source of the Arian heresy, since in condemning those who deny the Son to be of the substance of the Father they had condemned Origen as much as Arius." Jerome, however, rightly perceived that it was not hostility to the truth but a propensity to indulge in unjustifiable speculation that led Origen into theological error. And so he was careful to temper his judgment with sentiments of commendation such as the following: "It has never been my habit to crow over the mistakes of men whose talents I admire. . . . Does anyone wish to praise Origen? Let him praise him as I do. From his childhood he was a great man and truly a martyr's son. . . . He knew the Scriptures by heart and labored hard day and night to explain their meaning. . . . Which of us can read all that he has written? and who can fail to admire his enthusiasm for the Scriptures? . . . Let us not imitate the faults of one whose virtues we cannot equal."[22]

In a letter written ten years later to another Roman nobleman named Avitus, Jerome complained of "countless things to be abhorred" in Origen's work *On First Principles*. He cited in particular Origen's christology, which makes the Son not merely subordinate but actually inferior to the Father, and the Holy Spirit to the Son; his notion of the preexistence of individual souls, of their association with particular bodies as a punishment associated with their fallenness, and of the transmigration of souls; his disparagement of the body as destined ultimately to pass away and be succeeded by incorporeal existence, which called in question the central doctrine of the resurrection; his conception of a plurality of successive creations; his universalism, which envisaged the eschatological redemption of all men and angels, including the devil; and his blurring of the absolute distinction between the Creator and his creatures in such a manner that angels and men "are in some sort of one essence" with Almighty God.[23] These imaginings also, as we have shown, shrouded the vital issue of the reality of the Son's incarnation with confusion.[24]

22. Jerome, loc. cit. (see preceding note), pp. 175ff.
23. Ibid., pp. 238ff.
24. Origen has not lacked enthusiastic defenders, among whom are numbered the church historians Eusebius and Socrates, and in recent times Charles Bigg, who have attempted to clear his name of the obloquy associated with it. It is not our purpose to discuss the sequence of denunciations and proscriptions with which the writings of Origen have met from the fifth century onward.

CHAPTER 22

Arianism

That the strictures directed against Origen's christological speculations were amply justified must be admitted; but it was Lucian rather than Origen who was the true father of the Arian heresy. Lucian, whose thought is said to have been influenced by the unitarian teaching of Paul of Samosata, was the founder of a theological school in Antioch which has been described as "the alma mater of Arianism."[1] There is, however, some likelihood that he finally turned away from his error and was restored to the fellowship of the church catholic, for he suffered a martyr's death in Nicomedia in 312. Both Arius, from whom Arianism derived its name, and Eusebius of Nicomedia, who became the episcopal leader of the Arian party, had been fellow students in the school of Lucian. There they had heard Lucian propound the teaching that God is one in the unitarian sense and that all other beings are created beings, including the Logos, who, though acknowledged to be a unique heavenly creature, could not be considered coeternal and consubstantial with the Father. To this doctrine was added the concept of adoptionism, according to which Christ had a human body but not a human soul—the place of the soul being supplied by the Logos (an anticipation of the Apollinarian heresy)—and by his constancy progressed until he was received into heavenly glory. Arius, a North African from Libya, received ordination in Alexandria, where he gained a reputation as a preacher and ascetic and developed in his own distinctive fashion the christological theory of Lucian. Apparently the first to have committed the notions of Arianism to writing was Asterius, a native of Cappadocia and another of Lucian's disciples, whom Athanasius disdainfully called "a many-headed sophist," "the unprincipled sophist and patron of this heresy," and "the sacrificer" (because under threat of persecution he had offered pagan sacrifice).[2]

The unorthodox character of the ideas eloquently propagated by Arius and the considerable following he attracted precipitated a new and more intense christological controversy which came to a head in the Council of Nicea in 325. Some five years before the council Arius had written to Alexander, the

1. Adolf Harnack, *History of Dogma,* Vol. III, tr. J. Miller (London, 1897), p. 49.
2. Athanasius, *On Synods* 18; *Orations against the Arians; Defence of the Nicene Definition (De decretis)* 8, 20.

bishop of Alexandria, giving a statement of his theological position. He acknowledged only a unitarian God, who alone was eternal and without origin and the sole ruler of all. The Son he held to have been brought forth by this God "before eternal times" and to have been the agent of creation, himself "God's perfect creature, but not as one of the creatures," "created by the will of God before the times and eons." He professed to have rejected the opinions of the Valentinians, the Manicheans, the Sabellians, and some others regarding the relationship of the Son to the Father, and insisted that there was no identity of being between them.[3] The same views were expressed in a work of Arius known as the *Thalia,* from which Athanasius quoted the following assertions: "God was not always Father," "There was (a time) when God was alone and not yet Father, but afterwards he became also Father," "The Son was not always," "The Word of God himself was made out of nothing," "There was once when he was not,"[4] and "He did not exist before he was made, but he also had a beginning through being created." Arius postulated the existence of "two wisdoms," the one "proper to and coexistent with God," and the other the Son, who was "only named Wisdom and Word" derivatively through participation in the former. He affirmed also that there were "many powers," one power being "by nature proper to God and eternal," but that "Christ is not the true power of God but only one of the so-called powers," and, moreover, that "the Word himself is by nature changeable," so that "being of a changeable nature he is able to change just like us." It was because God foreknew that the Son would choose to be good, so Arius said, that he bestowed on him the glory that he subsequently as a man made his own through virtue.[5]

In Arius's system, then, the Word who is not himself the true and eternal Word "is not authentic God,"[6] for "even though he is called God he is not authentic God, it is only in name, and, like all others, by participation of grace, that he is called God." Further, "as all things are according to their essence[7] foreign and dissimilar from God, so also the Logos is entirely alien and dissimilar from the essence and proper nature of the Father,"[8] since his proper place, according to Arius, was among things created. Arius went on to deny

3. For the text of this letter see A. Grillmeier, *Christ in Christian Tradition,* Vol. I (Atlanta, 1975), pp. 225f.
4. The famous formula, *ēn pote hote ouk ēn.*
5. Athanasius, *Orations against the Arians* i.5. This teaching is identical with that of Asterius. In a manner reminiscent of Origen's interpretation of John 1:1, where the Word is called God without the definite article in the Greek, Asterius argued that because in 1 Cor. 1:24 Christ is called God's power and God's wisdom without the article, therefore he was not *the* power or *the* wisdom of God, but a lesser power and an inferior wisdom (ibid. i.32).
6. *Oude theos alēthinos estin ho Logos.*
7. *Kat' ousian.*
8. "Dissimilar" in this passage is the translation of *anomoios.* This indicates the distinction that developed between the Arians, who denied that the Son was of similar, let alone identical, essence with the Father, and the Semi-Arians, who were willing to affirm that he was of similar essence—*homoiousios,* not *homoousios.*

that the Son could see or know the Father, or know even his own essence, arguing that the essences of the Father and the Son and the Holy Spirit "are by nature separate and estranged and isolated and alien and without mutual participation."[9] Within the Arian perspective to call Christ God and to worship him as God was but a recognition by way of hyperbole of his worth and dignity as a special creature and mediator; it was not an affirmation of ontological reality. Arius adduced the same texts as were cited by Origen in support of his subordinationist doctrine and his designation of the Son as a "second god"; but, as we saw, Origen asserted the coessentiality and coeternity of the Son with the Father, declaring that there never was (a time) when the Son was not existent, which was precisely what Arius would deny.[10]

Origen, too, when he spoke of Christ as "a being intermediate between all created things and God,"[11] did so with reference to the incarnate Son, whereas Arius, though using similar terminology, intended a being *ontologically* intermediate between God and his creatures, that is to say, a being who was neither truly God nor truly man, but something in between the two. The intermediate being of Arianism was proposed as the intervening agent of creation who saved God from direct contact with the material world. Thus the Arians maintained that "when God wished to create the nature that is brought into being and saw that it was unable to partake of the immediate hand of the Father and of his fashioning,[12] he first alone makes and creates one only, and calls him Son and Word, in order that through his mediation all things else might be able to be brought into being." This theory, of course, was no better than a remnant of gnostic dualism. Athanasius records that it had not only been spoken but also actually put down in writing by Eusebius of Nicomedia, Arius, and Asterius.[13]

The Christ devised by Arius was in being as remote from man as he was from God. Sharing neither in man's time nor in God's eternity, he was supposed to serve as a buffer to keep God and matter from direct contact with each other; but then he had to be defined as himself the first creature, before whose begetting God was not the Father, and whose own creation was willed in order that he might become the agent of the creation of all things else. To postulate that he was brought into being nontemporally or pretemporally in no way saved him from being bounded by temporality. The assertion that "there was once when he was not," even though the word "time" is not mentioned, is an inescapably temporal assertion. Estranged from the essential nature and the essential power of God, he cannot in any absolute sense be described as the Son of God and the Divine Word, but only in a reduced deferential sense as a concession to the uniqueness of his intermediate position. Arius's christological state-

9. Athanasius, *Orations against the Arians* i.6.
10. See pp. 260f. above.
11. Origen, *On First Principles* II.vi.1.
12. That is, to have immediate contact with God.
13. Athanasius, *Orations* ii.24; iv.11f.; see also *Defence of the Nicene Definition* 8.

ments define an ontology that is concerned with and controlled by questions of cosmology rather than soteriology; and it was soteriology that was ultimately at issue. The Arian hypothesis incapacitated the Son from acting as the Savior of the world, who as God becoming man in the incarnation, and through his atoning death on the cross, man for man, truly bridged the gulf between sinful man and his holy Creator. Precisely because the gospel itself was at stake the conflict with Arianism was an issue of central importance; it was not an arid wrangle over an abstruse and irrelevant theological theory.

The keyword at the Council of Nicea, at which the errors of Arius were condemned, was the Greek adjective *homoousios,* meaning "coessential" or "identical in being."[14] There is evidence, interestingly enough, that Origen had made use of the term *homoousios* in his definition of christology,[15] and also that he had described the incarnate Son as "God-Man," *Theanthrōpos*[16] (and perhaps was the first to do so). The usage of the word *homoousios* prior to the Council of Nicea, however, had had an uneven history. In the vocabulary of gnosticism the term had signified the affinity that was supposed to exist between "spiritual" individuals and God or between "carnal" or "hylic" individuals and Satan. The condemnation of Paul of Samosata, which took place at a synod held in Antioch in 269, included his manipulation of *homoousios* to comport with his unitarian presuppositions.[17] The term had also been employed by the Sabellians in defining their concept of the Father and the Son as being one and the same, and one of the reasons offered by the Arians for opposing its adoption at Nicea was its association with Sabellianism.[18] The real reason for the hostility of the Arians to this keyword was of course their awareness that to acknowledge the Son to be *homoousios* with the Father would be to destroy their whole system. In a letter read at the Nicene Council Eusebius of Nicomedia declared: "If we say that the Son is true God and uncreated, then we are bound to confess him to be *homoousios* with the Father"; and on hearing this, Ambrose wrote, the fathers there assembled "took the sword which their opponents had drawn to smite off the head of their blasphemous heresy." Indeed, the Arians not only objected to this term but they countered with their own word of the opposite meaning, namely, *heteroousios,* "different in essence," making quite explicit their repudiation of the coessential nature of the Father

14. The rendering of *homoousios* as "consubstantial" has long been in use and is still serviceable provided its significance is properly understood, but is less suitable because of the connotation now widely attached to the term "substance" as descriptive of three-dimensional solidity.

15. See Pamphilus (martyred 309), *Apology of Origen* 5.

16. Homilies on Ezekiel iii.3.

17. See Athanasius, *On Synods* 47. For indications of the gnostic use of the term see Irenaeus, *Against Heresies* I.v.1, 5, 6; II.xvii.2.

18. Ambrose regarded this excuse as a demonstration of their ignorance, since the Sabellians had used the term in a different and in fact impossible sense, "for," he explained, "a being is *homoousios* with another, not with itself" (*On the Christian Faith* iii.15).

and the Son.[19] Arius also expressly averred in his *Thalia* that in his own nature the Son had nothing that was proper to God, and that he was "neither equal to God nor *homoousios* with him."[20]

Historically the council convened at Nicea in Bithynia in 325 was the first general council of the church. Strictly speaking, however, except for the classical credal formula that emanated from it, this council had little right to be described as "general," for the great majority of the 318 bishops in attendance were from the east, many of them uneducated and with little competence to pass judgment on theological issues; and numbered among the many notable leaders of the church who were absent was the bishop of Rome, who was content to be represented by two presbyters. The Arian (or Lucianist) party, some twenty strong, under the leadership of Eusebius of Nicomedia, produced a statement of belief that was rejected by the council. The center party, commonly called Semi-Arian, was led by Eusebius of Caesarea and was the majority party. The third group, with Alexander, bishop of Alexandria, at its head, championed the orthodoxy that prevailed at the council, thanks, in the main, to the theological acuity and persuasiveness of Athanasius, Alexander's deacon and secretary, then a young man of but 27 years. The council had been convened at the behest of Constantine, the Roman emperor, and met under his presidency. His purpose was to put an end to ecclesiastical strife and establish theological harmony. This no doubt was commendable, but he himself was theologically naive and liable to be influenced in his judgment by congenial voices and forceful personalities. As things turned out, Christian orthodoxy carried the day, at least on paper. But the Nicene Council did not succeed in restoring unity to the church. The Arian bishops were deprived and banished; the Semi-Arians subscribed to the creed that was finally approved, but kept their christological reservations and disagreements among themselves; and the youthful Athanasius gained the victory *contra mundum* as the term *homoousios,* safeguarded by other precise definitions, was accorded its place in the statement of belief issued by the council.

The historic document read as follows:

> We believe in one God, the Father Almighty,
>   maker of all things visible and invisible;
> and in one Lord Jesus Christ,
>   the Son of God,
>   the only-begotten of his Father,
>   that is, of the essence *(ousia)* of the Father,
>   God of God, Light of Light, true God of true God,
>   begotten, not made,
>   coessential *(homoousios)* with the Father,
>   by whom all things were made, both in heaven and on earth,

19. Ambrose, loc. cit.
20. Athanasius, *On Synods* 15.

      who for us men and for our salvation came down,
      and was made flesh,
      and became man,
      suffered,
      and rose again on the third day,
      and ascended into heaven,
      coming to judge living and dead;
    and in the Holy Spirit.

This document closed the door firmly on Arianism. The Arian faction would presumably have felt able to put their own private interpretation on the designation of Christ as Son of God and Light of Light, and even God of God and creator of all; but to confess him as being of the essence of the Father, true God of true God, begotten but not created, identical in essence with the Father, and as having been made flesh and become man, required a renunciation of their distinctive teaching. Their exclusion was, however, made doubly sure by the addition of an anathema which specifically condemned their characteristic tenets, as follows:

    Those who say that "There was once when he was not,"
      and "Before he was begotten he was not,"
      and that "He was made of things that were not,"
      or say that he is "of a different substance or essence,"
      or that the Son is a creature or changeable or transformable—
    these persons the holy catholic and apostolic church anathematizes.

Thus the christology of the Arian minority was decisively rejected at Nicea; but it is evident that at the same time the Semi-Arian majority failed to impose its will on the council. The latter party had shown a willingness to adopt a credal formula the terminology of which was sufficiently imprecise for it to be interpreted in an Arian or an orthodox sense, or in a sense between the two. Its leader, Eusebius of Caesarea, was an Origenist who, because of his strongly subordinationist theology, was prepared to speak of Christ as "the created image" and "the second God." But the *homoousios* clause was not to his liking. The concept of the Father as the primal and authentic Deity was a stumbling block in the way of his assigning to the Son an essential identity of nature with the Father. He postulated instead that the Logos who is begotten "had in himself his own entirely divine and rational hypostasis" and was "in every respect similar to the nature of the first and unbegotten and only God."[21] The key phrase here is "similar to," and the addition in the Greek of a mere *iota* (the letter "i") to the controversial adjective would have made it completely acceptable to him: *homoiousios* instead of *homoousios*. It may seem little enough to ask, but it would have introduced a radical change in meaning; "of similar essence" would have replaced "of the same essence." Given his Origenist notion of the Father as "the God" and the Son's divinity as secondary because derivative, he

21. Eusebius, *Demonstration of the Gospel* V.v.10.

suspected that *homoousios* implied a rift or rupture in the singleness of the divine essence, holding as he did that monotheism had its *locus* in the Father, while the Son was always "second," "second God," "second Lord," "second essence," "second cause," and so on.[22] Accordingly, he repeatedly made a distinction, based on his subordinationist interpretation of John 17:3, between "the only true God" and "God the Word" who, as the only-begotten Son of the Father, was "the perfect Word of the supreme God." The Son, he held, "diffuses himself with living power throughout creation" and from his own fulness suffuses all things with "reason, wisdom, light, and every other blessing"; while in this universally intelligent pervasion of all things "he looks upward to his Father and governs this lower creation," which is "inferior and consequent upon himself." The position Eusebius ascribed to the Logos was in fact one of mediation between the Supreme God who is uncreated and the lower world of created entities (and in this respect his own middle stance was on the side of Arianism rather than orthodoxy). "This Word of God," Eusebius wrote, "intermediate, as it were, and attracting the created to the uncreated essence, exists as an unbroken bond between the two, uniting things most widely different by an inseparable tie."[23]

In the thought of Eusebius, therefore, the Son was *ontologically* intermediate. His preexistence was not the same as the eternity of the Supreme God, nor was his generation an eternal generation (and in this he broke away from Origen's christology). "The divine nature can in no sense be divisible into parts," he declared, "since, if compounded, it must be so through the the the agency of another power, and that which is so compounded can never be divine." The essence of God must of necessity be "simple, indivisible, uncompounded." This line of reasoning inevitably placed the Son in a different ontological category from that of the Father, who was seen as the uncaused cause of the Son's being, with the consequence that a certain similarity of essence was the most that could be acknowledged.[24] That is why Eusebius wished only to say that the essence of the Son was *like* that of the Father. The tendency of subordinationism, in fact—depending on how the Son and the Spirit are regarded—is away from trinitarian monotheism and toward either unitarianism or polytheism (tritheism). Eusebius taught that the Holy Spirit was a creature of the Father.

The conduct of Eusebius of Caesarea after the disbandment of the Nicene Council was inexcusably devious. In a letter to his Caesarean church he deliberately twisted the meaning of certain key statements of the creed of Nicea, to which he had subscribed his name, putting forward the explanation that "of

22. See, e.g., *Ecclesiastical History* I.ii.3, 5, 9, 11; *Demonstration of the Gospel* V.prol., 20, 23; iii.9; VI.xx.3, prol., 1; *Preparation of the Gospel* I.vii.9; VII.xv.6, 9; XI.xv.7.

23. *Oration in Praise of the Emperor Constantine* xii.1f. The latter part of this work, written some ten years after the Nicene Council, contains a declaration by Eusebius of his theological position.

24. Ibid. xii.8-11.

the essence of the Father" meant that the Son "has his existence from the Father," that "begotten, not made" meant that "the Son is not a creature like other creatures," and that *homoousios* meant *homoiousios,* "in every way *like*[25] the only Father" by whom he was begotten.[26] Such mental distortions enabled the Semi-Arians not only to survive Nicea but even to continue as the dominant party in the church. Nor, in opposing the orthodox doctrine, were their leaders unwilling to join forces with the Arian bishops, who, but three years after the council, were reinstated and permitted to return to their dioceses—a decision which eloquently reflects the theological uncertainty and incomprehension of Constantine. Prior to the calling of the council Constantine, in a letter addressed to both Alexander and Arius, had rebuked the latter for airing in public abstruse concepts that should have been kept to himself, "buried in profound silence." He assured them that the difference between them was unrelated to "any of the doctrines or precepts of the divine law" or to the appearance of "any new heresy," and that they were "in truth of one and the same judgment." They were contending, he insisted, about "small and very insignificant questions," "some trifling and foolish verbal difference," "points so trivial and altogether inessential," "a slight difference" that "does not affect the validity of the whole," "this truly idle question," "unimportant matters," "subtle disputations on questions of little or no significance," which were causing "profane disunion."[27]

Not surprisingly, Constantine viewed the church with a political rather than a theological eye. He saw no justification for ecclesiastical strife over questions of doctrine. In harmony with the eulogistic character of his *Life of Constantine,* Eusebius leaves his readers with the impression that as the result of the Council of Nicea all were "united as concerning the faith";[28] but this was far from a frank representation of the realities of the situation (as we have already indicated). It is true that Constantine procured the acceptance of the term *homoousios*—and remarkable in view of the fact that the majority of those present looked on it with disfavor; but the emperor was apparently swayed by the advice of Hosius, bishop of Cordova, who had his ear and stood with Athanasius. Constantine's theological gullibility is apparent from the rapid reinstatement of the Arian bishops who had been condemned and banished, and also from the unusual honor with which he treated them in the mistaken belief that peace and unity would now effectively be established in the church. Eusebius of Nicomedia even managed to persuade the emperor to consent to the return of Arius to Alexandria, giving him the assurance that Arius now wholeheartedly embraced the Nicene christology. Thus the stage was prepared, not for peace and goodwill, but for all-out warfare against Athanasius, who succeeded Alexander as bishop of Alexandria in 328.

25. *Homoios.*
26. A translation of this letter is included in *Select Writings and Letters of Athanasius,* pp. 74ff.
27. Eusebius, *Life of Constantine* ii.64ff.
28. Ibid. iii.14.

Athanasius was assailed by wicked slanders of the most scurrilous nature, and the unprincipled fierceness of the hostility increased after the death of Constantine (in 337). Between the years 336 and 366 Athanasius endured no less than five periods of banishment or exile from his diocese. Constantine's son Constantius, at first emperor of the East but after the death of his brother Constans in 350 the sole ruler of the empire, supported and promoted the Arian cause. A series of synods actually repudiated the Nicene formulation and equated an Arian type of christology with catholic orthodoxy. The specious truce of Nicea was thus followed by war, not peace. Reviewing the sequence of events in 379, Jerome observed that Constantine's irenic intentions were fruitless because "wickedness does not long lie hid, and the sore that is healed superficially before the bad humor has been worked off breaks out again." The Nicene faith, he lamented, "stood condemned by acclamation." And then he added his piercing aphorism: "The whole world groaned, and was astonished to find itself Arian."[29]

As for Eusebius of Caesarea's doctrine of the incarnation of the Word, there is sufficient evidence to lead to the conclusion that he started down the road which later in the same century led to the appearance of the Apollinarian heresy.[30] He saw the incarnation as a theophany, the culmination of the theophanies of the Old Testament in which the Word manifested himself to men in human form. Holding that the Son himself was invisible and incorporeal, Eusebius deduced that there was no other way in which he could make himself visible and tangible to men than by taking to himself a human vessel.[31] Eusebius did not develop a full or systematic incarnational theology, but the body assumed by the Logos was, according to his perspective, a body in which the Logos took the place of the human rational soul. The Word, Eusebius said, "procured for himself this body as a thrice-hallowed temple, a sensible habitation of an intellectual power," and by this means "the indwelling Word conversed with and was known to men," but without yielding to human passions or undergoing subjection to the body. Thus the incorporeal Word, uninjured and undefiled by association with our corporeal nature, "performed all his works through the medium of that body which he had assumed for the sake of those who otherwise were incapable of apprehending his divine nature."[32]

In effect, then, the *homoiousios* favored by Eusebius extended not only upward with reference to the association of the Word with the Supreme God but also downward in the incarnation in relation to his association with mankind: the preexistent Word who was only *like* God in nature was in his incarnation only *like* man. There was no full and unequivocal identity in either case. "Assuming a mortal body," Eusebius explained, "he deigned to associate

---

29. Jerome, *Dialogue of a Luciferian and an Orthodox Christian* 19.
30. See pp. 287ff. below.
31. See, e.g., Eusebius, *Ecclesiastical History* I.ii.21ff.; *On the Theophany* iii.39.
32. *Oration in Praise of the Emperor Constantine* xiv.1ff.

and converse with men, desiring through the medium of their own *likeness* to save our mortal race."[33] Furthermore, in a manner reminiscent of docetism, he envisaged the death of Christ as involving a leaving by the Word of that body he had assumed, and the resurrection as a reappropriation of the same body: "Leaving his body for a little while, and delivering it up to death in proof of its mortal nature, he soon redeemed it from death, in vindication of that divine power whereby he has manifested the immortality which he has promised to be utterly beyond the sphere of death."[34]

Eusebius offered three reasons for Christ's "conflict with the power of death." The "first and greatest reason," he said, was that thereby "he proved to his disciples the nothingness of that which is the terror of all mankind and afforded a visible evidence of the reality of that life which he had promised." The second reason was that "by recalling his mortal body to a second life" he gave proof of "his superiority over death." And the third reason was that he was "a victim consecrated for the need of the human race and for the overthrow of the errors of demon worship," by whose sacrifice "the power of impure and unholy spirits was utterly abolished." Though Eusebius spoke of the mortal body of the Word being offered as a ransom for sinners and cited Isaiah 53:5f., his understanding of the atonement was vague and imprecise. The crucifixion is presented as the conquest of the powers of darkness (which it certainly was) rather than as the vicarious offering of the Righteous for the unrighteous (1 Pet. 3:18);[35] and this may be because of his apparent failure to have grasped the necessity for the assumption in the incarnation of the fulness of our humanity in order to redeem our humanity in its fulness—the necessity, in other words, for the Redeemer of mankind to be not only *homoousios* with God in his deity but also *homoousios* with man in his humanity. As a bridge the *homoiousios* of Eusebius was too short, unconnected at both ends, and therefore no bridge at all. The double *homoousios* would receive clear confessional affirmation at Chalcedon in the middle of the next century.

33. Ibid. xiii.16.
34. Ibid. xv.6.
35. Ibid. xv.8ff. The historian Socrates, writing in the next century, drew attention to the reputation of Eusebius for disingenuousness and accused him of "avoiding to specify the causes of these (Egyptian) dissensions because of a determination on his part not to give his sanction to the proceedings at Nicea" (*Ecclesiastical History* i.23). He also complained that Eusebius, in his *Life of Constantine,* "has but slightly treated of matters regarding Arius, being more intent on the rhetorical finish of his composition and the praises of the emperor than on an accurate statement of facts."

CHAPTER 23

The Christology of Athanasius

The complete identity of the human nature which the Son took to himself in the incarnation with our human nature was certainly what was intended by the declaration in the creed of Nicea that he *became man,* which followed immediately after and was explanatory of the assertion that he *was made flesh*—that is to say, "flesh" as in John 1:14, where it stands for our humanity in its wholeness. Athanasius clearly perceived the central importance of this understanding of the incarnation. As he explained later on (in 362) in a letter to the church of Antioch, the incarnation was not an indwelling of the Word in a holy man as had been the case with the prophets of old, but the Word *becoming man for us,* with the consequence that "in him the human race is perfectly and wholly delivered from sin and brought to life from the dead and given access to the kingdom of heaven." And he pointed out further that it was confessed at Nicea that "the Savior did not have a body without a soul, or without sense or intelligence, since it was not possible, when the Lord had become man for us, that his body should be without intelligence, nor was the salvation effected in the Word himself a salvation of body only, but of soul also."[1]

Athanasius, it is true, spoke of the incarnation as the taking of a body by Christ to himself, but with the definite intention that by "body" our humanity is meant in its entirety. It was a body "no different from ours," a body that was clean and pure from sin, which he offered unto death, as "a sacrifice free from any stain," thus annulling the law which was against us and making "a new beginning of life for us by the hope of resurrection which he has given us."[2] The linguistic usage is that of *synecdoche,* in which a part stands for the whole, and it is precisely matched in the New Testament. Indeed, the language used by Athanasius, together with the significance attached to it, is essentially that of Hebrews 10:5-10, where the words of Psalm 40:6ff. are applied to Christ, namely, "a body hast thou prepared for me," and "Lo, I have come to do thy will, O God." "By that will," the author of the Epistle to the Hebrews declares, "we have been sanctified through the offering of the body of Jesus Christ once

---

1. Athanasius, *Tome to the Antiochenes* 7. Likewise in *Orations against the Arians* iii.30 he asserts that the Word "became man, and did not come into man."
2. *On the Incarnation* 8-10.

for all." Similarly St. Paul says that everyone is responsible before God for "what he has done in the body" (2 Cor. 5:10), and what is done in the body corresponds to the life lived "in the flesh" (Gal. 2:20). To say, then, that "the Word became flesh" is, Athanasius wrote, "equivalent to saying that 'the Word has become man'"; and it is by reason of "the Saviour having in very truth become man" that "the salvation of the whole man was brought about"; and from this it follows that "truly our salvation is not merely apparent,[3] nor does it extend to the body only, but the whole man, body and soul alike, has truly obtained salvation in the Word himself."[4]

The incarnation itself remained a profound yet wonderfully true mystery, but nonetheless both a fact of history and an article of faith the understanding of which is necessarily limited by our finitude. That there was a right faith Athanasius was quite certain: it was the faith that is informed and controlled by adherence to the biblical revelation. Moreover, the rightness of the faith is confirmed by the experience of the transforming power of the gospel of Jesus Christ. It was for these reasons that Athanasius was confident of the rightness of the Nicene christology. "Our faith is right, and starts from the teaching of the Apostles and tradition of the fathers, being confirmed by both the New Testament and the Old," he assured Adelphius, bishop of Onuphis in northern Egypt who had been driven into exile by the Arians.[5] In the century after Nicea special care was needed to ward off notions concerning the relationship between the divine nature and the human nature of the incarnate Son which were misguided because they did not do justice to biblical truth—notions which in effect left the humanity diminished or swallowed up by the deity, or the deity by the humanity.

Though there is a true union of the two natures in the single person of Christ, Athanasius always carefully maintained the distinction between the divine and the human. In becoming man "the incorporeal Word made his own the properties of the body, as being his own body." What the human nature suffered the Word himself suffered; it was the conjunction with our passible nature that made possible the suffering of the impassible Word for our redemption. "The Word became flesh," Athanasius wrote, "not by reason of an addition to the Godhead, but in order that the flesh might rise again; nor did the Word proceed from Mary that he might be bettered, but that he might ransom the human race." It is, rather, "to the human body that a great addition has accrued from the fellowship and union of the Word with it," so that from being mortal it becomes immortal, spiritual, and heavenly through its assimilation to the glorified humanity of the risen Lord.[6] Thus Athanasius insisted that "we do not worship a creature." "Far be the thought!" he exclaimed. "For such an error

---

3. "Apparent" is the equivalent of "docetic," that is, in appearance only.
4. Athanasius, Letter 59, to Epictetus (bishop of Corinth), 7f.
5. Letter 60, to Adelphius, 6.
6. Letter 59, 6-9.

belongs to heathens and Arians. But we worship the Lord of creation, incarnate, the Word of God. . . . And we neither divide the body, being such, from the Word and worship it by itself, nor when we wish to worship the Word do we set him apart from the flesh"; for, since we know that "the Word became flesh," "we recognize him as God also after having come in the flesh." The incarnation, therefore, is not the diminution, let alone the setting aside, of the Son's deity, but the glorifying and exaltation of our humanity which has fallen away from God.

> For the flesh did not diminish the glory of the Word: far be the thought! On the contrary, it was glorified by him. Nor, because the Son who was in the form of God took upon him the form of a servant,[7] was he deprived of his Godhead. On the contrary, he thus became the deliverer of all flesh and of all creation. And if God sent his Son brought forth from a woman,[8] the fact causes us no shame but contrariwise glory and great grace. For he has become man that he might deify us in himself, and he has been born of a woman, and begotten of a virgin, in order to transfer to himself our erring generation, and that we may become henceforth a holy race and partakers of the divine nature, as the blessed Peter wrote.[9]

The plain fact, with which all deniers of Christ's deity must be faced, is that "a creature could never be saved by a creature, any more than that creatures were created by a creature."[10]

The essential connection between creation and redemption was repeatedly emphasized by Athanasius, who discerned that the purpose of the incarnation was the restoration not merely of man but of the whole created order, and, indeed, that this was an objective which the Word was uniquely competent to achieve, since it was through him that the world was brought into being. "It will appear not inconsonant for the Father," he said, "to have wrought its salvation in him by whose means he made it."[11] Furthermore, the recovery of what was lost through man's transgression involved not only bringing creation back to its original order and harmony but also bringing it on to the glorious consummation for which it was designed.[12] Only in relation to the origin of all things can there be a proper comprehension of the present and the future. "Inasmuch as he was made out of what is not, man is by nature mortal," Athanasius argued. His rebellion against God carries with it the consequence that he is sinking away from God into that nothingness of nonexistence which preceded his creation.[13]

But a world under judgment presents another problem; for, if the order

7. Phil. 2:6f.
8. Gal. 4:4.
9. 1 Pet. 2:9; 2 Pet. 1:4.
10. Athanasius, Letter 60, 3, 4, 8.
11. *On the Incarnation* 1.
12. *Discourses against the Arians* ii.67.
13. *On the Incarnation* 4.

of creation, brought into existence in accordance with the divine purpose, should end in annihilation, this would mean the failure of God's purpose, which is unthinkable. "It would be unseemly," Athanasius asserted, "that creatures once made rational, and having partaken of the Word, should go to ruin and turn again to non-existence," and "unseemly to the last degree that God's handiwork among men should be done away." Nor is it for a moment thinkable that God, who is the Father of truth, should rescue his creation by simply reversing his word of judgment and thus appearing to be a liar. There is, however, a solution, and it is found in him who is himself the Image after which man was originally created. "His it was once more to bring the corruptible to incorruption and to maintain intact the just claim of the Father upon all; for being the Word of the Father, and above all, he alone by natural fitness was both able to recreate everything and worthy to suffer on behalf of all and to be ambassador for all with the Father."[14]

But this again raised a further question: How was the Son, who is by nature impassible and immortal, to suffer death on our behalf so that we might be liberated from the sentence of death that stands against us? The answer is the incarnation, whereby he took to himself our passible and mortal humanity which he was then able to offer up in death; and this was truly "the offering of an equivalent," man for man.[15] "What was God to do?" Athanasius asked. Was he simply to stand aside and let men be led away from their Creator? But then "what was the use of man having originally been made in God's image?" Plainly, action was needed to effect "the renewing of that which was in God's image, so that by it men might once more be able to know him." Man cannot do this for himself since he is not the image of God, but is made after the image. This was the problem facing men, but it was no problem for God, for whom the remedy of effective action to meet our need was ready to hand in the person of the Son who is the true Image. And so "the Word of God came in his own person, so that, being himself the Image of the Father, he might be able to create man afresh after the image." "None other was sufficient for this need," Athanasius added, "save the Image of the Father."[16] As we have said before, in the incarnation he who is himself the Image of God became one with man who is formed in the image of God, so that the humanity he had taken to himself to redeem might be conformed to that image in which it was made and the purpose of man's creation be fulfilled.

As divine, Christ is the Image of God; as human, he is in the image. But he did not cease to be the former in order to become the latter. His becoming man did not inhibit his cosmic power (Heb. 1:3). His body did not shut him in, as Athanasius puts it: "nor, while present in the body, was he absent elsewhere; nor, while he moved the body, was the universe emptied of his working and

14. Ibid. 6, 7.
15. Ibid. 8-10.
16. Ibid. 13.

providence; but, a thing more marvelous, Word as he was, so far from being contained by anything, he rather contained all things himself." The Word, both as divine and as incarnate, is still the Word of power. "Even while present in the human body and himself quickening it, he was, without inconsistency, quickening the universe as well. . . . And the wonderful thing is this, that at one and the same time as man he was taking part in our daily life and as the Word was quickening all things, and as the Son was dwelling with the Father."[17] Moreover, this was no less true even at the time of his dying on the cross and his burial in the tomb. Athanasius pointed to the phenomena which accompanied Christ's death—the withdrawal of the sun's brightness, the quaking of the earth, the rending of mountains, and the awe of all men—as demonstrating "that Christ on the cross was God, while all creation was his slave, and was witnessing by its fear to its Master's presence."[18]

Athanasius went on to discuss the function of the incarnation more particularly as a means to the death of Christ and the necessity of his death on the cross; but this is a theme to be considered later in this work. As the great champion of Nicene orthodoxy Athanasius had already laid hold of that christological doctrine which would receive fuller expression in the Chalcedonian Definition of 451 (even though in places his language is not as careful as might be wished). The emphasis at Nicea was understandably, in view of the controversy then prevailing, on the full and authentic identity of the Son's essence with that of the Father; but in the years following Nicea it became evident that the full and authentic identity of the humanity assumed by the Son in the incarnation with our own humanity was of no less importance. As we have shown, the significance of the double *homoousios,* intended at Nicea and later affirmed at Chalcedon, was recognized and propounded by Athanasius.

17. Ibid. 17.
18. Ibid. 19. See also *Discourses against the Arians* i.42: "For as he was ever worshipped as being the Word and existing in the form of God, so being what he ever was, though become man and called Jesus, he none the less has the whole creation under foot. . . ." This conclusion is quite naturally inferred from Scripture; there is no need to attribute it, as some do, to the influence of the philosophy of Stoicism.

CHAPTER 24

The "Deification" of Man in Christ

In the passage we quoted above from the letter to Adelphius Athanasius said that the Son became man "that he might deify us in himself."[1] In the treatise on the incarnation he wrote similarly that "he became man in order that we might be made God";[2] and in several other places he expressed himself to the same effect.[3] This is a startling manner of speaking, which might arouse suspicion that his anthropological perspective was influenced by some kind of adoptionist theory which envisaged a transformation of the human into the divine. The quotation from the letter to Adelphius plainly indicates that he had in mind the assurance of 2 Peter 1:4 that Christian believers were to "become partakers of the divine nature."[4] It is true that Athanasius did not always pause to clarify what he intended by his conception of the deification of man, but there are places where he took the trouble to do so, and from these, as well as from the whole tenor of his theology, it is obvious that he was not thinking in terms of an ontological change, but of the reintegration of the divine image of man's creation through the sanctifying work of the Holy Spirit conforming the redeemed into the likeness of Christ, and also of the believer's transition from mortality to immortality so that he is enabled to participate in the eternal bliss and glory of the kingdom of God. Thus he wrote:

> The Word was made flesh in order to offer up this body for all, and that we, partaking of his Spirit, might be deified—a gift which we could not otherwise have gained than by his clothing himself with our created body, for hence we derive our name of "men of God" and "men in Christ." But as we, by receiving the Spirit, do not lose our own proper substance, so the Lord, when made man for us, and bearing a body, was no less God; for he was not lessened by the envelopment of the body, but rather deified it and rendered it immortal.[5]

1. See pp. 278f. above.
2. *On the Incarnation* 54. *Autos gar enēnthrōpēsen hina hēmeis theopoiēthōmen.*
3. See *Defence of the Nicene Definition* iii.14; *Discourses against the Arians* i.39; ii.47, 70; iii.39; On Synods 51; Letter 61, to Maximus, as well as the passages already cited.
4. *Theias koinōnoi physeōs.* The concept is closely related, in the immediately following verses, to the importance of godly living in preparation for "entrance into the eternal kingdom of our Lord and Saviour Jesus Christ."
5. *Defence of the Nicene Definition* 14.

Thus the incarnation itself as the means to the achievement of the destiny designed for mankind was perceived as the deification and immortalization of our humanity. Briefly stated, "he deified what he put on."[6] In the course of a somewhat labored argument Athanasius made his meaning clear, pointing out that for men to be called sons of God did not imply identity with him who is the Son "in nature and truth," or to be called "gods" (Ps. 82:6; Jn. 10:34) did not mean "being made equal to God," something "that is impossible," but that we are sons and gods "by adoption and grace, as partaking of his Spirit" (Rom. 8:15f.), and "by imitation" (Mt. 5:48, etc.), that is, by godly living. When the incarnate Son prays to the Father "that they may be one as we are one" (Jn. 17:11), "the particle 'as' implies neither identity nor equality," but signifies an example or parallel to be copied by us.[7] Had Christ been a creature and not true God, his union with our humanity would never have accomplished its deification.[8] The incarnation of the Son effected the transfer of our origin into himself, "so that we may no longer as mere earth return to earth, but as being joined to the Word from heaven may be carried up to heaven by him." Athanasius even spoke of our flesh being "no longer earthly, but henceforth 'made word,'[9] by reason of God's Word who for our sake 'became flesh,' " bore our sins and our curse, and rose triumphant over death.[10] In Christ we are transported from earth to heaven, from death to life, from shame to glory, to participate everlastingly in the perfection of the new creation. This is what Athanasius meant by "deification." His language is soteriological, not ontological.

This concept of deification was widely held among the fathers of the early church; but it is not our concern here to discuss and illustrate its incidence in the varied writings of other authors of the fourth century and later. A brief investigation of its antecedent occurrence may, however, be useful and interesting. Prior to the time of Athanasius it is found in the works of Origen, Clement, Hippolytus, Irenaeus, Theophilus of Antioch, and Justin Martyr. In Justin, the earliest of these, deification is implied rather than formally expressed. Those who choose what is pleasing to God, he said, are "deemed worthy of incorruption and of fellowship with God" and "of reigning in company with him,"[11] and, on the basis of Psalm 82:6, "of becoming gods and having power to become sons of the Highest."[12] Theophilus wrote more bluntly that the person who kept the commandment of God would receive the reward of immortality and would "become God."[13] In Irenaeus, still in the second century, the main points of the argument of Athanasius are anticipated. "Unless man had

6. *Discourses against the Arians* i.42.
7. Ibid. iii.19-25.
8. Ibid. ii.70.
9. *Logōtheisēs tēs sarkos.*
10. Ibid. iii.33.
11. Justin Martyr, *The First Apology* 10.
12. *Dialogue with Trypho* 124.
13. Theophilus of Antioch, *To Autolycus* ii.27.

been joined to God," he asserted, "he could never have become a partaker of incorruptibility."[14] The admonitory words, "nevertheless you will die like men," which immediately follow the declaration of Psalm 82:6, "You are gods, sons of the Most High," refer, Irenaeus said, to despisers of the incarnation who "defraud man of promotion into God"; and he explained, further, that "it was to this end that the Word of God was made man, and he who was the Son of God became the Son of Man, that man, having been taken into the Word, might become the son of God; for by no other means could he have attained to incorruptibility and immortality, unless he had been united to incorruptibility and immortality."[15] It is evident that Irenaeus, like Athanasius later on, was speaking not of identity of being but of the glory of eternal life in Christ.

Deification is, in fact, associated by Irenaeus with the process of the believer's sanctification. According to him, "being in subjection to God is continuance in immortality, and immortality is the glory of the uncreated One." It is by the gracious working of the Holy Spirit that man "makes progress day by day and ascends towards the perfect, that is, approximates to the uncreated One," until ultimately he is "made after the image and the likeness of God."[16] This conception, it will be noticed, conforms with his interpretation of Genesis 1:26, namely, that man created at first in the image of God is intended to advance to the goal of the likeness of God.[17] That goal is nothing less than the perfection of Christ himself. Accordingly, "our Lord Jesus Christ, through his transcendent love, became what we are that he might bring us to be even what he is himself."[18] Christiformity is the fulfilment of our redemption.

The moralistic emphasis of Theophilus is echoed in the thought of Hippolytus, who advised: "If you are desirous of becoming a god, obey him who has created you."[19] The full fruition of this desire must await the eschatological consummation. Then at last the Christian will "possess a body that is immortal and incorruptible, just like the soul," he will "receive the kingdom of heaven," and he will "be a companion of the Deity and co-heir with Christ"; for, Hippolytus observed, he "will have become a god"—endued with the blessings it is consistent with God's nature to impart, he "will have been deified and begotten to immortality."[20] Here, again, "deification" apparently indicates the enjoyment of the glory, the immortality, and the perfection of harmony with his Creator, that is to say, the full fruition of and attunement to the divine image of his creation which the Christian longs and strives after, but never attains, in this present life.

In his work known as the *Miscellanies* (or *Stromata*) Clement of Alexan-

14. Irenaeus, *Against Heresies* iii.7.
15. Ibid. iii.19.
16. Ibid. iv.38; cf. v. 9.
17. See p. 8.
18. *Against Heresies*, bk. v, preface.
19. Hippolytus, *Refutation of All Heresies* x.29.
20. Ibid. x.30.

dria was intent on instructing pagan readers in the true knowledge *(gnōsis)* as distinct from the false concept of knowledge found in the philosophy of the gnostic sects. There are indeed frequent indications of the continuing influence of Platonic and Stoic ethicism in Clement's formulations. But in asserting that the knowledge necessary for man's advance toward deity is moral as well as intellectual in its demands, he did not omit to emphasize that the true gnosis is inseparable from divine grace and Christian faith. This knowledge, he declared, is itself "a perfecting of man as man"; it is "consummated by acquaintance with divine things" and conformity to the divine Word; through the grace of God it starts from and is developed by faith; and by it faith is perfected. Moreover, "it leads us to the endless and perfect end, teaching us beforehand the future life that we shall lead, according to God, and with gods." The redeemed, "pure in heart" at last and "near to the Lord," who are "destined to sit on thrones with the other gods," will then be called gods. (There is no doubt here an echo of the interpretation of Psalm 82:6 we have already encountered.) Thus transformed and enthroned, they will "gaze on God, face to face, with knowledge and comprehension," and in doing so experience "the perfection of the gnostic soul."[21] This beatific vision of God, the ultimate contemplation, also supposes the maintenance of the distinction between the creature and the Creator. "Being with the Lord" is always being "in immediate subjection to him."[22]

Clement envisaged deification not merely as an eschatological reality but also as a process already operative in the lives of serious Christians, who, as authentic gnostics, "draw God toward them" and in so doing "imperceptibly bring themselves to God," for, he explained, "he who reverences God reverences himself." He held, further, that "man, when deified," is in "a passionless state"[23]—passionless being intended in the Stoic sense. Because believers are described as "the temple of God" (1 Cor. 3:16f.; 6:19), Clement was even prepared to say that "the gnostic," meaning the Christian, is "divine, and already holy, God-bearing and God-borne."[24] Just as a man drugged by the sorceress Circe became a beast, "so he who has spurned the ecclesiastical tradition and darted off to the opinions of heretical men has ceased to be a man of God"; but, on the other hand, "he who has returned from this deception on hearing the Scriptures, and has turned his life to the truth, is, as it were, from being a man made a God."[25] So indissoluble is the link between Christian faith and true gnosis that Clement equated them: "Faith," he wrote, "is, so to speak, a comprehensive knowledge of the essentials."[26] The thrust of Clement's argument must be understood in the light of the controversial and apologetic purpose of the *Miscellanies*.

21. Clement of Alexandria, *Miscellanies* vii.10.
22. Ibid.
23. Ibid. iv.23.
24. Ibid. vii.13.
25. Ibid. vii.16.
26. Ibid. vii.10.

In the mind of Origen, who succeeded Clement as the head of the catecheti-cal school in Alexandria, the notion of deification arose from his distinctive doc-trine of the soul and the function it fulfilled in the incarnation.[27] His conception of the soul as an entity intermediate between God and the flesh carried with it the implication that it had the competence to rise up to God or to sink down to carnality. For it to rise upward was in effect to rise to its original state of angelic and celestial purity. As for the incarnation, it was the intermediary position of the soul that, according to Origen, made this practicable; for the soul of Christ, which from the beginning had committed itself to the love of righteousness, was by nature not only competent to receive God but also to assume a body.[28] And this soul, "along with the Word of God, is made Christ."[29] Origen taught that this had redemptive consequences for sinful man. The disciples of Christ saw, he said, "that the power which had descended into human nature, and into the midst of human miseries, and which had assumed a human soul and body, contributed as the result of believing, together with the more divine qualities, to the salva-tion of believers"; for the incarnation demonstrated that from Christ "the union of the divine with the human nature had its beginning, in order that the human, by communion with the divine, might rise to be divine."[30]

This may well strike us as an incarnational philosophy of salvation that is unrelated to the cross; but it would be a mistake to conclude that Christ's death on the cross held little significance for Origen, even though he does not seem to have fully grasped its profound significance as a vicarious sacrifice. He regarded it as having in some mysterious manner been effective in releas-ing sinful man from the hostile forces of this world. On the basis of the doc-trine of Scripture he did not hesitate to speak of the incarnate Son as the Lamb of God who "became like an innocent sheep being led to the slaughter that he might take away the sin of the world" (cf. Is. 53:5, 7; Jn. 1:29), and "that we might be purified by his death, which is given as a sort of medicine against the opposing power, and also against the sin of those who open their minds to the truth." He explained, further, that "the death of Christ reduced to impotence those powers which war against the human race, and it set free from sin by a power beyond our words the life of each believer."[31] Again, he wrote that "this Lamb has been made, according to certain hidden reasons, a purification of the whole world, for which according to the Father's love to man he submitted to death, purchasing us back by his own blood from him who had got us in his power, sold under sin."[32] That Origen's thought had affinities with the "ran-som" theory of the atonement is readily discernible.[33] He certainly did not wish

27. See pp. 88ff.; 260ff.
28. Origen, *On First Principles* II.vi.3.
29. Ibid. II.vi.4.
30. *Against Celsus* iii.28.
31. Commentary on the Gospel of John, bk. i.37.
32. Ibid., bk. vi.35.
33. See pp. 344ff. below.

to treat the death of Christ as though it were relatively of little importance. On the contrary, he insisted that "it is necessary to the proclamation of Jesus as Christ that he should be proclaimed as crucified."[34] Peter's remonstrance with Jesus over his teaching that it was necessary for him to go to Jerusalem and there to suffer and die was attributable to the fact that "he did not yet know that 'God had set him forth to be a propitiation through faith in his blood'" (Mt. 16:21ff.; Rom. 3:25).[35]

When Athanasius said that the Word of God became incarnate in order that we might be deified he was speaking of the redemptive purpose of the Son's coming, which was not only to set us free from the guilt and power of sin and to reconcile us to the Father but also to exalt us in himself to the glorious perfection of God's everlasting kingdom and to that imperishable life that swallows up our mortality; he was speaking of our transposition from this present frail and fleeting existence to that full and unclouded existence which is bestowed on us by God; he was speaking, in short, of the attainment of that resplendent destiny of harmony with our Creator that was from the beginning intended for us. To enter into the "inheritance which is imperishable, undefiled, and unfading, kept in heaven for us" is to "become partakers of the divine nature" (1 Pet. 1:4; 2 Pet. 1:4). It is not the obliteration of the ontological distinction between Creator and creature but the establishment at last of intimate and uninterrupted personal communion between them.

34. Commentary on the Gospel of Matthew, bk. xii.19.
35. Ibid. 21.

CHAPTER 25

The Christology of Apollinaris

Apollinaris, who was appointed bishop of Laodicea c. 360, was a friend and fellow combatant of Athanasius in the battle against the errors of Arianism. In his own theological formulations, however, his emphasis on the deity was not balanced by a satisfactory doctrine of the humanity of the incarnate Son. Gregory of Nazianzus complained that the proponents of Apollinarian teaching, when accused of advocating unscriptural notions of the person of Christ, "confess indeed the orthodox words but do violence to the sense"—a practice that has ever been characteristic of the propagators of heterodoxy. The source of their error was the assertion that in the humanity assumed by the Son the place of the human mind or rational soul was filled by the Logos. As they conceived it, the presence of the personal Logos and of the human rational soul would imply the presence of two persons in Christ. The solution they proposed was reminiscent of the Greek philosophical distinction between matter and form, or between spirit on the one hand and soul and body on the other—"soul," *psychē*, in this case corresponding to the principle of animal life.[1] Gregory objected that "they bring in the Godhead to supply the soul and reason and mind," and he spoke sharply of "their mindless opinion about his [the incarnate Son's] mind," charging that "it is through want of mind that they mutilate his mind."[2] In his concern to maintain the unity of the person of Christ Apollinaris imagined a unity which was compounded of the divine and the human in such a way as to form by fusion a single unique nature.

What Apollinarianism did in effect was to dehumanize the nature assumed by the Son in the incarnation by reducing it to the level of the irrational beasts—"a mixture of God and flesh," as Gregory described it. Gregory protested further that "they who take away the humanity and the interior image cleanse by their newly invented mask only our outside," and that it was absurd

---

1. Apollinarianism really followed the Platonic trichotomy of body *(sōma)*, soul *(psychē)*, and spirit *(pneuma)*, with 1 Thess. 5:23 as its biblical proof-text. Because "soul" is frequently used as a synonym for "spirit" attention must be paid to the sense in which it is intended. See the immediately following quotation from Gregory above, where "soul," "reason," and "mind" are given as interchangeable terms.

2. Gregory of Nazianzus, Letter 102, the second letter to Cledonius, written a year or two after the Council of Constantinople (381) at which Apollinarianism was condemned.

to claim, as they did, that it was not "a God-bearing man but a flesh-bearing God" that they offered for worship.[3] The statement that "the Word became flesh" (Jn. 1:14) did not, as they averred, support their position, Gregory pointed out, since it is a manner of speaking, namely, synecdoche, in which the part stands for the whole. To interpret this verse in the Apollinarian sense that it was no more than flesh that was joined to God was to "erase the noblest part of man."[4]

The Apollinarian fusion of the divine and the human into one nature led to the conclusion that Christ's Godhead was put to death together with his body, and that therefore the crucified Christ could be described as the "crucified God." Of the two parts of which this single nature was supposedly compounded the divine, because of its superiority to the human, was the governing part. As with Arianism, despite the obvious dogmatic difference, Apollinarianism offered the church a *tertium quid*. Apollinaris, indeed, expressly declared that "in Christ there is a middle-being[5] of God and man, so that he is neither fully man nor God, but a mixture of God and man"; and as examples of the formation of middle beings by the conjunction of the properties of contributing parts he cited the production of a mule from an ass and a horse (!) and of the color grey from the mingling of black and white.[6] If the Godhead took the place of the human intellect, "how does this touch me?" Gregory rightly asked. "Keep the whole man," he insisted, "and with this mingle Godhead, that you may benefit me in my completeness." In accord with the orthodox patristic mind he affirmed that "what needed salvation was also what the Saviour took to himself," and that therefore he assumed the mind as well as the body of man.[7]

It was distressing for those who had found Apollinaris a staunch ally against the Arian heresy and counted him as a friend that they should in his later years have felt compelled to denounce the aberrations he had developed. Basil the Great, bishop of Caesarea, even had to clear himself of charges accusing him, by association rather than on any substantial basis, of having approved the particular teachings of Apollinaris. "I never regarded Apollinaris as an enemy," he wrote, "and for some reasons I even respect him; but I have never so far united myself to him as to take upon me the charges against him; indeed, I have myself some accusations to bring against him after reading some of his books."[8] He spoke of Apollinaris as "a cause of sorrow to the churches" and a man whose literary productivity was uncontrolled.[9] Basil's brother, Gregory of Nyssa, answered the Apollinarian argument that the postulation of two natures meant that there were two Christs or two Lords by insisting that the

3. Ibid.
4. Letter 101 (first letter to Cledonius).
5. *Mesotēs*.
6. Apollinaris, *Syllog.*, frag. 113.
7. Gregory of Nazianzus, Letter 101.
8. Basil, Letter 244, to Patrophilus.
9. Basil, Letter 263, to the Westerns.

duality of natures, divine and human, existed within the unity of the incarnate Word's person, and that this unity of the person was not destroyed by the distinction between the natures. "The Word was in the beginning with God," he explained; "the man was subject to the trial of death; and neither was the human nature from everlasting nor was the divine nature mortal." The natures, however, were not so divided as in effect to constitute two persons. It was the one incarnate Lord, the one Christ, who acted and felt and spoke. The distinction of natures was a distinction in unity: because there was a union of natures, Gregory said, "the proper attributes of each belong to both."[10] This concept of the community or interrelationship of the properties and attributes of the two natures is known in the technical terminology of the theologian as the *communicatio idiomatum*. It would become part of the approved christology of Chalcedon.

The name of Apollinaris and his followers was also connected with eschatological expectations of an extravagant nature which evoked censure from his orthodox contemporaries because they envisaged a millennial period marked by a return to the legalism, the sacrificial system, and the temple worship of the Old Testament—in short, a revival of Judaism. Apollinaris, Basil said, "has written about the resurrection from a mythical, or rather Jewish, point of view, urging that we shall return once more to the worship of the law, be circumcised, keep the Sabbath, abstain from meats, offer sacrifices to God, worship in the temple at Jerusalem, and be altogether turned from Christians into Jews." "What could be more ridiculous?" he asked; "or, rather, what could be more contrary to the doctrines of the gospel?"[11] Gregory of Nazianzus likewise referred to the "gross and carnal" outlook of the Apollinarians with "their second Judaism and their silly thousand years delight in paradise";[12] and his namesake of Nyssa inquired rhetorically: "Do we romance about the resurrection? Do we promise the gluttony of the millennium? Do we declare that the Jewish animal sacrifices will be restored? Do we lower man's hopes again to the Jerusalem below, imagining its rebuilding with stones of a more brilliant material?"[13] Sentiments such as these, which the Cappadocian Fathers condemned without hesitation, were not invented by Apollinaris. They had already been espoused in earlier centuries by Justin Martyr,[14] Irenaeus,[15] Lactantius,[16] and others, including the adherents of aberrant cults like gnosticism and Montanism, and they have continued to circulate right up to the present time.

The christological speculations of Apollinaris were condemned, first of all at synods held in Rome, Alexandria, and Antioch in 377, 378, and 379 re-

10. Gregory of Nyssa, *Against Eunomius* v.5.
11. Basil, Letter 263.
12. Gregory of Nazianzus, Letter 102.
13. Gregory of Nyssa, Letter 17, to Eustathia, Ambrosia, and Basilissa.
14. Justin Martyr, *Dialogue with Trypho* 80.
15. Irenaeus, *Against Heresies* v.33.
16. Lactantius, *Epitome of the Divine Institutes* 72.

spectively, and then, in 381, in Constantinople at what is known as the Second
General Council of the Church, though it was in reality a council only of the
Eastern Church, attended by 150 bishops who professed allegiance to the doc-
trine of Nicea and three dozen heretical, mostly Arian, bishops. The bishop of
Rome was neither invited nor represented, and the bishop who presided,
Meletius of Antioch, was then not in communion with Rome. On the latter's
death, while the council was in session, the presidency passed to Gregory of
Nazianzus. After the death of Constantine the orthodox had suffered much at
the hands of Arian and pagan emperors, until the accession of Gratian in the
West in 375 (who accepted Ambrose as his guide) and Theodosius in the East
in 379 (by whom the Council of Constantinople was summoned). Imperial
preference decisively influenced the course of ecclesiastical affairs throughout
this period, either for good or ill.

The assembly of bishops at Constantinople was marred by bitter factions
and hostilities. At length, hoping to promote peace and weary of all the slanders and recriminations that made a mockery of Christian goodwill and forbearance, Gregory withdrew from the council and at the same time from the bishopric of Constantinople to which he had been appointed but which the bishops
hostile to him contended it was not open to him to accept because he was already the diocesan of another see.[17] On his departure the presidency was taken
over by the prefect of the city, Nectarius, an unbaptized catechumen who had
been selected by Theodosius. Nectarius was forthwith baptized, installed as
chairman, and consecrated bishop of Constantinople.

Despite the discord, the doctrine of Nicea received formal endorsement
at Constantinople, and this was a victory for orthodoxy in that the creed of
Nicea was now officially confirmed for the second time and has ever since remained a standard of theological authenticity. Of the alterations approved at
Constantinople the most important was the expansion of the laconic third
clause, "and in the Holy Spirit," to read as follows:

> And in the Holy Spirit, the Lord, and Giver of life, who proceeds from the
> Father,[18] who with the Father and the Son together is worshipped and glorified,

17. Basil had appointed Gregory bishop of Sasima, a Cappadocian village in which
he never set foot. Instead he had served as his father's suffragan at Nazianzus, and after
his father's death he had lived quietly in Seleucia. In 379 he responded to the invitation
of Theodosius to come to Constantinople and reestablish the Nicene faith. His preaching
there attracted large numbers of hearers. Canon 15 of the Council of Nicea had decreed
that "neither bishop, presbyter, nor deacon shall pass from city to city," only confirming
what had long been the rule. Nevertheless, episcopal translations were not unknown and
at Nicea itself Eusebius of Nicomedia had previously been bishop of Berytus, and Eustathius of Antioch bishop of Berrhoea; and translations continued to take place in the centuries that followed. It would seem to have been in order for a bishop to be appointed to
another sphere of oversight by a superior authority such as an archbishop or a synod; what
was disapproved was for bishops to move themselves from place to place.

18. The *filioque* clause affirming the double procession of the Holy Spirit "from the
Father *and the Son*" was added at the Third Council of Toledo in 589 on the basis of the

who spoke through the prophets; and in one holy catholic and apostolic church. We acknowledge one baptism for the remission of sins; we look for the resurrection of the dead and the life of the world to come.

This formula (sometimes described as Niceno-Constantinopolitan) is, apart from some small variations, identical with what we now know and use as "the Nicene Creed." The expanded third clause was intended to leave no doubt that the Holy Spirit is coessential with the Father and the Son. It betokened no change in the doctrine of the Holy Spirit. Thus in 369 Athanasius explained in his letter to the bishops of Africa that the full deity of the Holy Spirit was implicit in the creed of Nicea:

> For this Synod of Nicea is in truth a proscription of every heresy. It also upsets those who blaspheme the Holy Spirit and call him a creature. For the fathers,[19] after speaking of the faith in the Son, straightway added, "and we believe in the Holy Spirit," in order that by confessing perfectly and fully the faith in the Holy Trinity they might make known the exact form of the faith of Christ and the teaching of the catholic church. For it is made clear among you and among all, and no Christian can have a doubtful mind on the point, that our faith is not in the creature, but in one God, Father Almighty, maker of all things visible and invisible, and in one Lord Jesus Christ, his only-begotten Son, and in one Holy Spirit: one God, known in the holy and perfect Trinity.[20]

The first of the canons promulgated by the Council of Constantinople laid down that the Nicene faith "shall not be set aside but shall remain firm," and also anathematized the teaching of a number of factions by name, including the Anomoeans, as the more extreme Arians were called who rejected *homoiousios* as well as *homoousios,* maintaining that the Son, whom they held to be a creature, was not even to be described as "like" the Father;[21] the Arians, who, while regarding the Son as a special creature, were prepared, at least superficially, to compromise by agreeing that the Son was like[22] the Father; and the Semi-Arians, who disliked the term *homoousios* and interpreted it as meaning *homoiousios,* and who in this canon were also designated *pneumatomachi,* that is, "fighters against the Spirit,"[23] because, like the Arians, they taught that the Holy Spirit was no better than a creature. In his oration on Pentecost, which was probably delivered at the Council of Constantinople on the oc-

---

teaching of the New Testament and was a factor that contributed to the schism between the Eastern and Western Churches.

19. The fathers, that is, of the Council of Nicea.

20. Athanasius, Synodical letter to the bishops of Africa, 11. In his first letter to Serapion Athanasius expounded the coessential deity of the Holy Spirit more fully.

21. The term *anomoean* reflected their view that the Son was *unlike (anomoios)* the Father.

22. *Homoios.*

23. *Pneumatomachoi.*

casion of that festival, Gregory of Nazianzus said that "those who reduce the Holy Spirit to the rank of a creature are blasphemers and wicked servants and worst of the wicked." "The Holy Spirit," this champion of trinitarian orthodoxy asserted, "always existed, and exists, and always will exist. He neither had a beginning, nor will he have an end; but he is everlastingly ranged and numbered with the Father and the Son. For it was not ever fitting that either the Son should be wanting to the Father or the Spirit to the Son."[24] As for the equivocating term *like*, he described it as "a bait to the simple concealing the hook of impiety" and as "a boot fitting either foot."[25] The theological history of this period carries with it the lesson that an inadequate doctrine of the person of Christ (christology) can be expected to lead to a no less, and perhaps an even more, inadequate doctrine of the person of the Holy Spirit (pneumatology).

Also anathematized at Constantinople were the Apollinarians. The christology they proposed tended toward a new form of docetism, even though it was not founded on gnostic premises: its Christ only *seemed* to have become man, for humanity that is without a rational soul is a contradiction in terms. As Gregory of Nazianzus wrote, "man is not a mindless animal."[26] The bishops assembled at the council stated their position on the incarnation in the Synodical Letter subscribed by them as follows: "We preserve unperverted the doctrine of the incarnation of the Lord, holding the tradition that the dispensation of the flesh is neither soulless nor mindless nor imperfect, and knowing full well that God's Word was perfect before the ages and became perfect man in the last days for our salvation."[27] Even so, as we have remarked, most of the bishops in attendance accepted the orthodoxy affirmed at Constantinople with mental reservations. Surveying the church scene as a whole, the prospects for any significant establishment of the theology of Nicea still looked anything but promising. Yet Constantinople in 381, like Nicea in 325, proved to be a milestone in the stormy process of defining the essential christological and trinitarian doctrines and safeguarding the faith against perversions and misunderstandings of biblical truth. The intensity of commitment to this cause so characteristic of Athanasius was impressively displayed also by Gregory of Nazianzus (not to mention others), and perhaps most dramatically on the occasion of his relinquishment both of the presidency of the council and of the bishopric of Constantinople. The oration which announced his decision to withdraw was remarkable for its dignity, its restrained passion, and its wealth of biblical allusion. It was a plea for peace in place of rivalry and for unity in the trinitarian faith in place of heterodoxy.

The worshipers of the Trinity, Gregory declared, were "the perfect suppliants of the perfect Deity." He admonished his audience that "faith, with no other roof but the sky to cover it, is better than impiety rolling in wealth,"

24. Gregory of Nazianzus, Oration 41, §§ 6 and 9.
25. Panegyrical Oration on Athanasius 22.
26. Letter 101.
27. The text of this Synodical Letter is given in Theodoret, *Church History* v.9.

and that "three gathered together in the name of the Lord count for more with God than tens of thousands of those who deny the Godhead," since "nothing is so magnificent in God's sight as pure doctrine and a soul perfect in all dogmas of the truth." Insults and invective were not his weapons in argument, but there could be no compromise when the truth was at stake: "Though peaceable, we do not injure the word of truth by yielding a jot to gain a reputation for reasonableness,[28] for we do not pursue that which is good by ill means." He deplored the silence of those who kept the piety of their faith hidden within themselves, without regard for the need of others to be instructed in the true faith, and he urged such to join the ranks of those who do not consider "that to be salvation which saves themselves alone without bestowing on others the overflow of their blessings."

Appealing to his hearers to "bid farewell to all contentious shiftings and balancings of the truth on either side" and to walk with him "along the royal road which lies between the two extremes,"[29] Gregory summarized his own faith as belief in "the Father, the Son, and the Holy Spirit, of one substance and glory." He dismissed the "scandalous taunts" of contentious persons implying that "our faith depended on terms and not on realities," and he warned against "sophistical mischievous arguments which inquire curiously into the generation and inexpressible procession of God," for these are things, he wisely warned, "which it is beyond the power of language to set forth." He pictured himself as a pilot having not only to control the ship in tempestuous seas but also to cope with uproar among the passengers: "What a struggle I have had, seated at the helm, contending alike with the sea and the passengers, to bring the ship safe to land through this double storm!", he exclaimed. The majority, he was aware, was against him, but it was a majority with whom he was quite unable to associate himself. And now his desire was for respite from his long labors; and so he requested them to release him by appointing another in his place: "Give me my desert, my country life, and my God, whom alone I may have to please and shall please by my simple life."[30]

---

28. The jot he refused to yield was the iota which made the difference between *homoousios* and *homoiousios*.

29. The two extremes, that is, of unitarianism and tritheism.

30. Gregory of Nazianzus, Oration 42.

CHAPTER 26

Nestorius and Nestorianism

The Antiochene theologians were in the forefront of those who denounced the christology of Apollinarianism, and it was to their number that Nestorius belonged. Nestorius, whose native territory was Syria Euphratensis, is believed to have been a student of Theodore of Mopsuestia in Antioch. His outstanding ability as a preacher made his name well known. Theodore, a native of Antioch, had studied (together with John Chrysostom) in the same city under Diodore, another Antiochene by birth. Diodore became bishop of Tarsus in 378 and Theodore bishop of Mopsuestia in Cilicia in 392. Both were authors of numerous important, mainly exegetical, works, and both were held, especially by Cyril of Alexandria who wrote a treatise *Against Diodore and Theodore,* to have anticipated and had a hand, successively, in the formation of the incarnational doctrine of Nestorius, and therefore to be more or less responsible for what was regarded as Nestorian heterodoxy. Theodore, commonly spoken of as "the father of Nestorianism," was condemned posthumously at the council held at Constantinople in 553, and this judgment was largely responsible for the destruction of his writings and those of his teacher Diodore, only fragments of which now remain. Yet in their own day the orthodoxy of these two fathers seems to have been secure, and it is hard not to see some significance in the fact that at the Council of Chalcedon, where the will of Cyril was so dominant, their names were not mentioned censoriously or otherwise. There is the possibility, of course, that Cyril and his colleagues felt that the condemnation of Nestorius at Ephesus in 431 carried with it by implication the condemnation of these two doctors who had preceded him in the school of Antioch; but this is questionable if only because Cyril continued with his polemic in the controversy with Theodoret, the determined champion of Antiochene orthodoxy, who was appointed bishop of Cyrrhus in Syria in 423.

There is a demonstrable kinship between the christology of Diodore and Theodore and that of Nestorius. In the judgment of some, it is true, the incarnational doctrine of Diodore belongs to the "Word-flesh" rather than the "Word-man" category.[1] This judgment is based on the lack of references to the

---

1. E.g., A. Grillmeier in *Das Konzil von Chalkedon* (ed. A. Grillmeier and H. Bacht), Vol. I (Würzburg, 1951), pp. 135ff. The "Word-flesh" christology envisaged the Word as

soul of Christ in the fragments of Diodore's writings that are known to us and also on his description in places of the humanity of Christ as "the flesh" or "the body," whence it has been inferred that the Logos took the place of the rational soul in Diodore's conception of the person of Christ. But this was precisely the position of Apollinarianism, of which Diodore was so persistent an opponent, and it was intrinsically improbable that he would have propounded a view indistinguishable from the system he opposed or, otherwise, that he failed to understand what he professed to oppose. Moreover, to speak of the humanity of the incarnate Son as "flesh" or "body" was not in itself unscriptural. Thus St. John could say that the Word became flesh (Jn. 1:14) and that Jesus Christ had come in the flesh (1 Jn. 4:2; 2 Jn. 7), and St. Paul that the Son was of the seed of David according to the flesh (Rom. 1:3) and was manifested in the flesh (1 Tim. 3:16), and the author of the Epistle to the Hebrews could write of the days of his flesh (Heb. 5:7); St. John, again, spoke of the temple of Christ's body (Jn. 2:21), the author of Hebrews of a body having been prepared for the Son (Heb. 10:5, 10), and St. Paul of his glorified body (Phil. 3:21), and even of his body of flesh (Col. 1:22). In none of these places is there any thought of a diminution or mutilation of the human nature assumed by the Son in the incarnation.

There are, however, passages in which Diodore plainly affirmed the perfection or completeness of the humanity which the Son took to himself. He affirmed, for example, that "the Son of God assumed the son of David, who was perfect from David," and again that "perfect God from perfect God assumed perfect man."[2] What did seem to present itself to Diodore as a problem to be resolved was the question how the Son of God could become man without experiencing change; to say that he *became* man he feared might be taken as implying some essential change in the Son's divine nature, and so he apparently sought to protect the immutability of the divine nature by explaining that "God is called man not because he became (or was made) this, but because he assumed this." How, then, were the perfect Son of God and the perfect son of David unified in the single person of Christ? Diodore's answer, at least in part, was the postulation of the indwelling or inhabitation of the Word in the man as in a temple prepared for himself. He firmly rejected the charge of Apollinarian opponents that he preached two sons, pointing out that he proclaimed neither two natural sons of David nor two natural Sons of God, but the divine Word who is the only Son of God by nature and the son of Mary who is the son of David by nature and the son of God by grace. He insisted, moreover,

---

having taken a body of flesh which, lacking a rational soul, was not completely human, whereas the "Word-man" christology insisted that in the incarnation the Son assumed our human nature in its completeness. For a good critical survey of Grillmeier's opinion see Francis A. Sullivan, *The Christology of Mopsuestia* (Rome, 1956), pp. 181ff. In *Christ in Christian Tradition,* Vol. I (Atlanta, 1975), p. 357, Grillmeier has apparently reconsidered and to some extent modified his assessment of Diodore's christology.

2. See Sullivan, *The Christology of Mopsuestia,* pp. 182f.

that "the two are a single son," but in a way that it was impossible to express in words.[3] The fragmentary and in places questionable nature of such evidence as we have makes any attempt to reconstruct the system of Diodore's thought a precarious exercise. What may with some confidence be said is that Diodore was intent on closing the door securely against Arianism, by asserting the inviolate deity of Christ, and against Apollinarianism, by maintaining the completeness of his humanity.

It may be said, too, that there is every indication that the christological teaching of Diodore was retained and developed by his pupil Theodore of Mopsuestia. That only fragments of Theodore's treatise *On the Incarnation* have been preserved is indeed regrettable, but there is a measure of compensation for this deficiency in the text of his *Commentary on St. John,* which we possess intact. With reference to the statement of John 1:14 that "the Word became flesh and dwelt among us," Theodore wrote that "flesh" stood for "the whole man" and that he became flesh "inasmuch as he dwelt in our nature," specifically rejecting the interpretation of some that "he became flesh" meant that he was *converted* into flesh. That is to say, he understood the meaning of this verse to be that "the Word became flesh and *dwelt in us*" rather than "among us," and, further, that "the Word became flesh" was equivalent to saying "the Word became in man."[4] He obviously wished to counteract any suggestion that the becoming flesh of the Word implied a change or conversion of the essence of deity into the essence of humanity.

Theodore's concept of the incarnation of the Son as his indwelling or inhabitation of our human nature was quite definitely not a new variation of the docetic theory, nor did it imply any affinity with the Apollinarian notion, with which he had no sympathy, that the Word dwelt in man by taking the place of the rational soul. Thus, in a fragment from his work on the incarnation, he insisted that where Scripture assigns the designation of man to Christ it "always denotes the nature of man which was assumed perfect by him for our redemption." While, however, this concept of inhabitation may have been a safeguard against the christological errors of the time, the question must be asked whether it was adequate as a definition of the union of the divine and human natures in the incarnate Son. That Theodore saw God's indwelling of his saints as in some sense a parallel makes it all the more questionable. But it is only fair to acknowledge that he held the Word's inhabitation to have taken place from the moment of Christ's conception in Mary's womb and did not regard it as one and the same with "the common inhabitation," but as a unique and transcendent operation whereby the two natures were united in such a way as to produce the one person.[5]

3. For a careful discussion of Diodore's christology, which includes the passages quoted above, see Sullivan, ibid., pp. 181-96; also Grillmeier, *Christ in Christian Tradition,* pp. 352-60.
4. Sullivan, *The Christology of Mopsuestia,* p. 229.
5. Ibid., pp. 244ff.

Theodore's doctrine of the incarnation is not fully satisfactory. He failed to do justice to the declaration that the Word *became* flesh. Even though he propounded a union of the divine and human natures that was intimate and unique, *indwelling* is less than equivocal with *becoming*. The union seems to be one of close association or conjunction rather than total identification. Yet Theodore was careful to affirm the christological essentials of the full deity and the full humanity of the incarnate Son and their union in the one person of the Redeemer. His christology, as Grillmeier has observed, "falls just short of" the "later understanding of the union of Christ," but still "is open to a unity of person in the Chalcedonian sense";[6] indeed, "he would have seized any opportunity of justifying a 'strict unity' in Christ wherever it was not incompatible with the equally important duality of the natures, but such an opportunity presented itself only when the Council of Chalcedon had made the distinction between nature and person."[7]

Nestorius was appointed bishop of the metropolitan see of Constantinople in 428, the year of Theodore's death. To all appearances, his christology, in its main points, was similar to that of Theodore, emphasizing as it did that the incarnation involved the assumption by the Son of complete manhood, rational human soul as well as human body, that the Son was eternally coessential with the Father and, as incarnate, coessential with man, and that, though in Christ there was a true union of the divine and human natures so that he was constituted a unified person, the divine was absolutely other than the human, and this otherness was apparent in the earthly life of the incarnate Son in which the superhuman or transcendental acts were readily distinguishable from those that were human and mundane.

It was his criticism of the designation of the Virgin Mary as "Mother of God" *(Theotokos)* that the leaders of the campaign against Nestorius seized on as the focal point of their antagonism. They denounced him to the world as a heretic who denied the deity of Christ. There is no evidence that his opponents were in the least concerned to know the grounds for his criticism of this expression. The opposition seems rather to have been fired by Cyril of Alexandria's obsessive jealousy of what he regarded as the rival patriarchate of Constantinople and his distaste for anything emanating from Antioch, covered over of course with the cloak of zeal for orthodoxy. Many of the bishops who joined Cyril in the condemnation of Nestorius did so, it has been said, because the ascendancy of Nestorius as a noted enemy of heterodoxy was threatening to them on account of their own deviations from the faith of Nicea. Be that as it may, the discreditation of the bishop of the imperial capital was pursued with unrelenting intensity, in a manner reminiscent of the heartless unconcern for jus-

6. Grillmeier, *Christ in Christian Tradition*, p. 434.
7. Ibid., pp. 436ff. On the christology of Theodore of Mopsuestia see pp. 421-39; Sullivan, *The Christology of Mopsuestia*, pp. 197-288 and *passim*; and R. A. Norris, *Manhood and Christ: A Study in the Christology of Theodore of Mopsuestia* (Oxford, 1963), pp. 123-262 and *passim*.

tice with which another celebrated preacher and predecessor of Nestorius, John Chrysostom, had been hounded out of the same patriarchate by Theophilus, Cyril's uncle and predecessor in Alexandria, a generation earlier. The church historian Socrates, a native citizen of Constantinople and contemporary of Nestorius, described the latter misleadingly as ignorant and unlearned, mainly, it would appear, on the ground that he showed no awareness that the term *Theotokos* had already been used approvingly by patristic authors. (He cited Eusebius and Origen, whose christological formulations, however, as we have noticed, were less than satisfactory. Socrates, it may be observed, seemed unaware that the title *Theotokos* was also approved and misused in heretical circles, of whose teachings Nestorius was the avowed enemy.) Yet at the same time Socrates admitted that, having himself read the writings of Nestorius, the accusations leveled against him, namely, that he held Christ to be a mere man (psilanthropism) and was a follower of Photinus and Paul of Samosata (unitarianism), were plainly without substance. Nestorius, Socrates testified, "nowhere destroys the proper personality of the Word of God, but on the contrary invariably maintains that he has an essential and distinct personality and existence, nor does he ever deny his subsistence as Photinus and the Samosatan did, and as the Manicheans and followers of Montanus have also dared to do."[8]

Nestorius explained the circumstances which influenced him to question the wisdom of acquiescing in the use of the term *Theotokos* in a letter addressed to the bishop of Rome, Celestine, in 428. He referred to the corruption of orthodox doctrine he had found in Constantinople, of a kind "akin to the festering disease of Apollinaris and Arius," in which a mixture or confusion was made of "the union of the Lord and man in the incarnation." Not only was the birth from Mary asserted to be the first origin of the Word and his consubstantiality with the Father thus openly discountenanced, he said, but Christ's Virgin Mother was being treated "as in some kind of way divine, like God." Associated with this error, he continued, was the practice of calling Mary "Mother of God," whereas "the holy fathers of Nicea" had found it sufficient to state that our Lord Jesus Christ was born of the Virgin Mary, and the Scriptures simply spoke of her as the mother of Christ. The unsuitability of the title "Mother of God" was evident, moreover, from the fact that "a real mother must be of the same substance as that which is born of her"; yet Nestorius was prepared to grant that the application of this designation to Mary was "tolerable on one ground only, namely, that the temple of God the Word[9] which is inseparable from him was derived from her."[10] This makes it perfectly plain that, far from denying, he was intent on affirming the deity of the incarnate Son and on opposing those who denied it. Had this letter, and a number of others, been taken

---

8. Socrates, *Church History* vii.32.
9. That is, the human nature assumed by God the Word.
10. See J. F. Bethune-Baker, *Nestorius and his Teaching* (Cambridge, 1908), pp. 16f.

into account and given due credit, the disruptive and disreputable sequence of events that heaped disgrace on the good name of Nestorius might never have occurred.

The issue was further complicated, however, in that, as he pointed out in his work *The Book of Heracleides,* composed as an autobiographical *apologia* probably shortly before the convening of the Council of Chalcedon in 451,[11] he was also confronted in Constantinople with two conflicting factions of orthodox believers who, on the one side, called Mary the mother of God and, on the other, called her the mother of man. He recounted how, having heard the arguments of the disputants, he perceived that neither the one side nor the other was guilty of heretical doctrine, but that they were concerned to maintain the reality, on the one hand, of Christ's deity and, on the other, of his humanity against false teachers. The problem was solved and peace restored, Nestorius declared, by his proposal that Mary should be referred to neither as mother of God nor as mother of man but as mother of Christ *(Christotokos)*[12]—an appellation designed to imply both the essential deity and the essential humanity of the incarnate Word, Christ being accepted as "the common name of the two natures."[13] His purpose all along was, he protested, to adhere faithfully to the Nicene confession of faith.[14] He, and his chaplain the presbyter Anastasius, might have been better advised, however, to have assailed the heretical abuse of the term *Theotokos* from the pulpit with less flamboyant rhetoric; they ridiculed, for instance, the absurdity of God being confined as an infant wrapped in swaddling clothes. It was the sort of language that lent itself rather readily to being misreported or misinterpreted elsewhere.

During the years 429 and 430 Cyril of Alexandria mounted his assault against Nestorius, canvassing the support of numerous bishops and writing to Celestine, the bishop of Rome, to urge him to take action. The pope, without seriously examining the rights and wrongs of the matter or allowing any weight to the communications received from Nestorius, decided to take the side of Cyril.[15] In August 430 a council held at Rome condemned Nestorius, and

11. This work is commonly known as *The Bazaar of Heracleides,* due apparently to a misrendering from the Greek *(pragmateia* = treatise) in the title of the Syriac version, the only surviving text, which was discovered in the first decade of this century.

12. Nestorius, *The Book of Heracleides* I.iii.151f. For an English translation of this work see *Nestorius: The Bazaar of Heracleides,* tr. G. R. Driver and Leonard Hodgson (Oxford, 1925).

13. F. Loofs, *Nestoriana* (Halle, 1905), p. 175.

14. Ibid., p. 284.

15. Referring to "the interference of the Roman bishop on behalf of Cyril," Harnack expressed the view that "there is not perhaps in the history of dogma a second fact of equal importance which so thoroughly deserves to be pronounced a scandal, nor one which at the same time is so little to the credit of its author," since by this action Celestine "disowned his western view and in the most frivolous fashion condemned Nestorius without having considered his teaching" (*History of Dogma,* tr. E. B. Speirs and James Millar, Vol. IV [London, 1898], p. 183).

Celestine empowered Cyril to execute a sentence of excommunication should Nestorius refuse submission.

Late in 430 an imperial decree announced the plan to hold a general council in Ephesus at Pentecost the following year for the purpose of resolving the dispute and establishing peace in the church—a decision, incidentally, which prevented immediate effect being given to Celestine's sentence of excommunication on Nestorius. The council was duly convened at Whitsuntide in 431. Nestorius was present with ten supporting bishops, a small minority in the company that otherwise was composed of Cyril's men. Neither of the two emperors (Theodosius II and Valentinian III) was present, though Theodosius sent Count Candidianus, an official of the imperial household, to represent him, but not to preside or engage in theological debate. When, however, the determination was made to proceed with the business without waiting for the arrival of John, bishop of Antioch, and a considerable number of other bishops sympathetic to Nestorius whose advent had been delayed by a variety of adverse conditions,[16] Candidianus withdrew under protest, complaining that by holding a council that was incomplete and not properly representative the clear instructions of the emperor were being flouted and his wish for the free expression of the differing points of view and for a peaceful settlement frustrated. With Cyril assuming the right to preside, Nestorius also withdrew from the synod, convinced that there was no hope of his case receiving an impartial hearing. With good reason he complained that Cyril had not only come forward as his accuser, as he was entitled to do, but had also arrogated to himself the position of his judge, something not even the ancient barbarians had dared to do. And in constituting himself "accuser and emperor and judge" Cyril had also assumed dictatorial powers over the whole council. Cyril, Nestorius objected, was "the whole tribunal." His decision was imposed as the decision of all. "Cyril was everything. . . . What need was there for a council," Nestorius asked, "when this man was everything?"[17]

Another deplorable feature of this controversy was the strong-arm tactics to which Cyril was only too ready to resort. The proliferation of monks and hermits provided a handy source of manpower when it was needed for bringing ruffianly pressure to bear on persons who were regarded as uncooperative or inconvenient. Bored by the tedium of their otherwise uneventful existence, many who had rashly chosen solitude were prompt to engage in the diversionary excitement offered by the contact sport of violent intimidation when summoned to action by their patriarch. Cyril did not enjoy a good reputation in this respect. Periodical scenes of mob violence seemed almost endemic in Alexandrian society. As G. L. Prestige remarked, Cyril was "dreadfully accountable" for having roused those monks, several hundreds in num-

16. See *The Book of Heracleides* II.i.371f. for the text of the explanatory letter sent to the emperor by John of Antioch and the bishops accompanying him.

17. Ibid. I.iii.174f.; II.i.195f.

ber, who enthusiastically went into action as his guerillas in "so unnatural a defence and confirmation of the gospel," when it suited his purposes in his own city.[18] Nor was he slow to incite similar activity by the agency of his contacts elsewhere, and not least against Nestorius. Even Cyril's friend Isidore of Pelusium felt constrained to admonish him on this score: "Many of those who were assembled at Ephesus," he wrote, "speak satirically of you as a man bent on pursuing his private animosities, not as one who seeks in correct belief the things of Jesus Christ. 'He is sister's son to Theophilus,' they say, 'and in disposition takes after him; just as the uncle openly expended his fury against the inspired and beloved John (Chrysostom), so also the nephew seeks to set himself up in his turn.' "[19] Nestorius himself complained that in taking action against him Cyril was motivated not by fear of God or concern for the faith but by personal animosity. He accused Cyril of calling up "bands of monks and bishops" to be the agents of his antipathy, and, in league with Memnon, the bishop of Ephesus, of filling that city with "idle and turbulent men" who, armed with offensive weapons, instilled him and the members of his company with terror—so much so that he had to protect himself by posting soldiers around the place of his residence;[20] and he also charged Cyril with descending to bribery in order to secure the favor of persons at court who had the ear of the emperor.[21]

Unlike Cyril, Nestorius was free from envy and self-importance. His personal preference was not for the public power and prominence that attend the life of a metropolitan bishop but for the quiet solitude of his monastic cell in Antioch. Yet he was not without his faults. His mode of theological expression, both spoken and written, tended to be unguarded; and Socrates, who, as we have noticed, judged him to be innocent of christological heresy, wrote of him as an implacable opponent of heretics, whose places of worship he did not scruple to destroy.[22] There is no denying that he had some cause for regarding certain of Cyril's christological formulations as tainted with Apollinarian error, for Cyril, when defining his doctrinal position in the course of the controversy with Nes-

---

18. G. L. Prestige, *Fathers and Heretics* (London, 1954), p. 152.

19. Isidore of Pelusium, Letter 1, 310, cited by J. Stephenson, *Creeds, Councils, and Controversies* (London, 1966), pp. 300f. See also the acerbic letter attributed to Theodoret written on learning of the death of Cyril, which took place in 444: "At last and with difficulty the villain has gone . . . the fellow's malice has been daily growing and doing harm to the body of the church. . . . His survivors are indeed delighted at his departure. The dead, maybe, are sorry. There is some ground of alarm lest they should be so much annoyed at his company as to send him back to us. . . . On seeing the church freed from a plague of this kind I am glad and rejoice; but I am sorry and I mourn when I think that the wretch knew no rest from his crimes, but went on attempting greater and more grievous ones till he died" (Theodoret, Letter 180). Cf. also the strongly critical comments in Letter 150, to John, bishop of Antioch.

20. Nestorius, *The Book of Heracleides* I.iii.155; II.i.198f.; also II.i.367f.

21. Ibid. I.iii.189.

22. Socrates, *Church History* vii.29-31.

torius, actually made use of a number of writings which he supposed to be of orthodox provenance, but which in fact were the compositions of Apollinarian authors. The result was the presence in his own theology of terminology and even argument that could justly be described as distinctively Apollinarian. This does not say much for the perspicacity of Cyril's judgment as a theologian, even when it is conceded that his intention was to adhere to Nicene orthodoxy. Thus he used the characteristically Apollinarian "one nature" formula to describe the unity of the incarnate Son's person. But he, no less than Nestorius, was probing for an acceptable terminology, and the care he took to maintain an absolute distinction between the deity and the humanity of the incarnate Word was entirely in line with the thought of Nestorius: "The flesh is flesh and not deity, even though it has become God's flesh," he wrote; "similarly the Word is God and not flesh, even though he made the flesh his own by way of incarnation." That is to say, the union does not require the confusion or mingling of the divine and the human into some kind of amalgam.[23]

We also find Cyril expressing himself in a way that was virtually indistinguishable from the "two persons" christology of which he had accused Nestorius, and that seemed to leave the reality of the union of the divine and the human in Christ in doubt. In what is known as his second letter to Nestorius (February 430), for example, he asserted that the Word "who is in himself incapable of suffering was in a suffering body," and consequently that it was not the Word but "his own body" that tasted death for every man and was raised from the dead in the resurrection.[24] In his third letter to Nestorius he stated that Christ, "being made one according to nature and not converted into flesh, made his indwelling in such a way as we may say that the soul of man does in his own body."[25] Here the notion of indwelling without being converted into flesh has a distinctly Antiochene ring about it, whereas the analogy of the Word as the soul within the body might have been written by an Apollinarian. That Cyril did not wish to deny a genuine union is apparent in the last of the twelve anathemas that he appended to this letter for Nestorius's subscription: "Any one who does not confess that the Word of God suffered in the flesh, that he was crucified in the flesh, and that likewise in that same flesh he tasted death, and that he became the first-begotten of the dead, for, being God, he is the life and it is he who gives life: let him be anathema."[26] From this language it could be supposed that, contrary to what was said in the earlier letter, the Word was passible and capable of dying. These two letters were received with approval not only by the Council of Ephesus in 431 but also twenty years later by the Council of Chalcedon.

It is evident that, in the case both of Cyril and of Nestorius, incautious

23. Cyril of Alexandria, Letter 45, to Succensus (Migne, *PG*, LXXVII), col. 232; Letter 46, to the same, col. 241.
24. Letter 4, col. 48.
25. Letter 17, col. 112.
26. Ibid., col. 121.

forms of expression were balanced by clearer and more satisfactory statements. The imprecision of Cyril's thought and language in particular places does not justify the conclusion of some authors that his christology was of the Word-flesh rather than the Word-man type, especially as he did not fail to emphasize that it was not merely flesh or an empty body that the Word took to himself in the incarnation but the fulness of our humanity. "We do not say," he wrote in the earlier letter, "that the nature of the Word was changed and became flesh, or that it was converted into a whole man consisting of soul and body, but that the Word, having personally united to himself flesh animated by a rational soul in an ineffable and inconceivable manner, became man." He explained that when "he who had an existence before all ages and is co-eternal with the Father is said to have been born according to the flesh of a woman" this did not mean that "his divine nature received its beginning of existence in the holy Virgin."[27] Again, in another letter, he denied that in the incarnation of the Word "his flesh was changed into the nature of divinity," or that "the nature of the Word of God was laid aside for the nature of flesh," or that "the Word of God dwelt in Christ as in a common man," which would mean that Christ was only "a God-bearing man."[28] But, once more, such teaching was in all essentials the same as that propounded by Nestorius.

The problem, at root, was how to speak of what was confessedly an ineffable mystery without becoming vulnerable to misunderstanding. Language is as finite as it is human. The effable cannot be expected to express fully the ineffable. If Nestorius could speak of two persons, meaning by this two natures, Cyril could speak of one nature, meaning one person; but Nestorius was no more a Nestorian than Cyril was a Eutychean. Hence the protest of Nestorius that he believed the incarnate Son to be "true God by nature and true man by nature,"[29] that the manhood assumed by the Word was manhood in its entirety, possessing "everything which is in the nature of man,"[30] that the two natures, divine and human, "were united by the very union of one person,"[31] and that "the union was not of the persons but of the natures."[32] He explained that if he had spoken of two persons it was with reference to the Son, not as incarnate, but as the eternal person within the tripersonal Godhead, and to man who in his own right is a human person. He did not hold that the incarnate Word was so constituted that there were two sons or two persons.[33] And of the incar-

27. Letter 4, col. 45.
28. Letter 17, col. 112.
29. Nestorius, *The Book of Heracleides* I.i.116.
30. Ibid. I.ii.133.
31. Ibid. II.i.210.
32. Ibid. II.i.229. Grillmeier (*Christ in Christian Tradition,* Vol. I, p. 455) cites the statement made by Nestorius in a sermon preached in 430, "I did not say that the Son was one (person) and God the Word another; I said that God the Word was *by nature* one and the temple *by nature* another, one Son by conjunction," and remarks that "in these words he repudiates the teaching of two sons with which he was so often charged."
33. *The Book of Heracleides* II.i.303f.

nate Son he affirmed: "I predicate one person, one equality, one honor, one authority, one lordship."[34]

The prevailing misunderstandings could and should have been removed in a spirit of Christian forbearance by calm consultation. But Cyril was determined to bring about the humiliation of Nestorius. When John, bishop of Antioch, arrived belatedly in Ephesus his presence was unwelcome to Cyril and he found the churches locked against him. In the meantime Nestorius's followers had set up their own council, which by way of retaliation decreed the deposition of both Cyril and Memnon the Ephesian bishop. Socrates reported that when John appeared on the scene "he pronounced unqualified censure on Cyril as the author of all this confusion, in having so precipitately proceeded to the deposition of Nestorius"; indeed, he recounted that the irenical spirit manifested by Nestorius, who had declared his willingness to accept the term *Theotokos,* struck no answering chord in the heart of Cyril: "When affairs reached this confused condition, Nestorius saw that the contention that had been raised was leading to the destruction of fellowship, . . . and cried out, 'Let Mary be called *Theotokos,* if you will, and let all disputing cease'; . . . but no notice was taken of it."[35]

Affecting a position of neutrality, the emperor gave orders that the mutual depositions were to stand, and both Cyril and Nestorius were committed to prison. By resorting, it was said, to a combination of muscle and money the former devised his escape and return to Alexandria, and the latter was at length granted his wish to retire to the seclusion of his Antiochene monastery. But he was not to be left in peace. Even his friends in Antioch were persuaded reluctantly to accept a concordat with Alexandria, and in 436 Nestorius was transported to Upper Egypt, part of Cyril's domain, where for the remaining fifteen years of his life he suffered the harsh rigors of existence in the inhospitable desert and persecution at the hands of fierce tribal nomads.

It is ironic and, as far as Nestorius was concerned, tragic that the very qualification he had wished to see added to the use of the designation "Mother of God" was approved with enthusiasm by Cyril of Alexandria only a couple of years after the Council of Ephesus and subsequently was incorporated into the Chalcedonian Definition of the Faith. Yet Nestorius himself was ignored; he was not granted a new hearing and his name was ever afterward stained with the disgrace attaching to a heretic. What happened was this: in 433 a conciliatory statement, or symbol of union as it came to be called, was drawn up

---

34. Ibid. II.i.143. Cf. the christological orthodoxy of Augustine in an epigrammatic passage written a few years before Ephesus: "God the truth itself, the Son of God, by assuming man, not by consuming (i.e., doing away with) God *(homine assumpto, non Deo consumpto),* established and founded this faith in order that there might be a way for man to man's God through a God-man *(per hominem Deum).* . . . The only way that is absolutely secured against all errors is when the same person is God and man: God, the goal, man, the way *(quo itur, Deus; qua itur, homo)*" *(The City of God* xi.2).

35. Socrates, *Church History* vii.34.

by Theodoret and submitted by John of Antioch to Cyril, who proclaimed that the middle wall of partition had been broken down.[36] This formulary confessed the Lord Jesus Christ as "the only-begotten Son of God, perfect God and perfect man composed of a rational soul and a body, begotten before the ages from his Father in respect of his divinity, but likewise in these last days for us and our salvation *from the Virgin Mary in respect of his manhood*, coessential *(homoousios)* with the Father in respect of his divinity and at the same time coessential *(homoousios)* with us in respect of his manhood." The statement went on to affirm the union of the two natures and to describe the Virgin as *Theotokos* "because the divine Word became flesh and was made man and from the very conception united to himself the temple taken from her."[37] So also the Chalcedonian Definition of the Faith would affirm the double *homoousios* of Christ in the unity of his person, while declaring that he "was *born from the Virgin Mary, the Theotokos, as touching the manhood.*" Grillmeier rightly speaks of this document of 433 as the link between Ephesus and Chalcedon.[38] Nestorius would have been completely at home with its christology.

Nestorius, moreover, expressed his unanimity with the christological doctrine of Leo (bishop of Rome from 440 to 461) contained in the famous Tome first sent to the notorious "Robber Council" *(Latrocinium)* of Ephesus in 449 and subsequently approved and adopted by the Council of Chalcedon as a model of theological orthodoxy.[39] He wrote that, though he had been urged to seek justice for himself from Leo because of this unanimity, he had declined to do so, not because of silly pride on his part, but because he did not wish association with the name of Nestorius, now commonly connected with error, to prove a hindrance to Leo as he championed the cause of truth. And he added this further reason: "that I, to whom for many years there has not been a moment of repose, might not be suspected of fleeing for security from the contest, through fear of the labors involved; for sufficient are the wrongs that have come upon the world and they are more able than I to make the oppression of the true faith shine forth in the eyes of every man."[40]

Certainly, the serene spirit and deep humility of Nestorius in the midst of adversity shone forth and prevailed. As he saw, like a spectator from a distance, the position he held gaining ground against the fierce opposition that had been stirred up, he was filled neither with bitterness nor with a lust for self-vindication but with gratitude and hope that the truth would triumph, even though his own name should be darkened by obloquy, as the following passage shows:

36. Cyril of Alexandria, Letter 39 (Migne, *PG*, LXXVII), cols. 173ff.
37. Ibid., cols. 176f.
38. Grillmeier, *Christ in Christian Tradition*, Vol. I, p. 484.
39. See, e.g., Nestorius, *The Book of Heracleides* II.ii.466, 513f.
40. Ibid. II.ii.519.

When I was silent, and the authority to speak out was taken away from me, and I was not believed, God raised up men who were believed, when they said the same things as I, which were the truth, without there being any suspicion of their having said these things out of friendship or love for me. And God did not bring these things about on my account. For who is Nestorius? Or what is his life? Or what is his death in the world? But he brought them to pass because of the truth which he has given to the world, and which was suppressed from deceitful causes, while he has also confuted the deceivers. And because they were filled with suspicion about me and did not believe what I was saying, treating me as one who dissembles the truth and represses accurate speech, God appointed for this purpose a preacher who was untouched by this suspicion, Leo, who preached the truth undaunted.[41]

To sum up, in another's words: "Reading his own words, carefully and consecutively, as we can read them now, it is impossible to believe that Nestorius was 'Nestorian.'"[42]

41. Ibid. II.ii.513f.
42. Bethune-Baker, *Nestorius and His Teaching*, p. 198.

CHAPTER 27

On to Chalcedon

During the christological conflict of this period the imperial city of Constantinople seemed to be tragically fated to provide the setting for the defamation and destruction of good men appointed to the office of metropolitan bishop. The ecclesiastical rivalries of the time were frequently marked by a ruthless savageness that was as unchristian as it was uncivilized. The brutal treatment of Chrysostom, who was not only deposed but also driven to death in comfortless climes by his enemies, was in many respects repeated in the experience of Nestorius and Flavian. The controversy that brought about the unrighteous downfall of Flavian, who was made bishop of Constantinople in 446, revolved around the teaching of an elderly monk named Eutyches, the head of a monastery in that city. Once again, the story was one of Alexandrian interference; indeed, but for the domineering intervention of Dioscorus, who in 444 had succeeded Cyril as bishop of Alexandria, matters would have developed very differently. In that he had shown himself strongly hostile to Nestorius, Eutyches could be classified as pro-Alexandrian and perhaps as having established a right to expect Dioscorus to act as a powerful ally. For some time there had been suspicions and complaints regarding views that Eutyches had been expressing, and things came to a head when, in November 448, at a domestic synod of the diocese of Constantinople, one of the bishops, Eusebius of Dorylaeum, brought a charge of heresy against him.

This localized scene provided an opportunity for another exhibition of Alexandrian power politics. The position of Eutyches, as he expounded it to the synod, was that before the union which took place in the incarnation the Lord was "from two natures" but that after the union there was but "one nature"—in other words, the divine and human natures came together to form the single distinct nature of the incarnate Son. Though admitting that the Virgin Mary's nature was coessential with our human nature, he was unwilling to hold that this coessentiality held good for the nature taken from her by the Son, because he considered Christ's body to be the body of God rather than simply a human body. The christology of Eutyches was openly monophysite. The incarnation envisaged by him was invested with an unreal and even docetic character, and it was hardly surprising that the synod condemned him as a follower of Valentinus and Apollinaris. It may well be that he was not consciously or intentionally so, and wished, in his own maladroit fashion, no more than to maintain the unity of the incarnate Son over against the other extreme of a disjointed duality of the type for which Nestorius had been condemned. Be that as it may, Dioscorus in Alexandria sniffed the chance of damaging his rival in Constantinople in a confrontation that promised to be of advantage to his ecclesiastical prestige.

It was perhaps to be expected that the Antiochene see should also become involved in the Eutychian controversy. Theodoret, bishop of Cyrrhus and native of Antioch, who was the friend of Nestorius and advocate of his orthodoxy, had composed at the request of John, bishop of Antioch, a polemical rejoinder to the twelve anathemas which Cyril had published against Nestorius; and his was the theological mind behind the symbol of union to which Cyril had given his cordial approval fifteen years previously.[1] He was also the author of a work called *Eranistes,* in the form of theological dialogues, exposing and refuting the errors of the teaching of Eutyches. The smoldering contention was further revealed by the fact that Eutyches wrote to Leo, bishop of Rome, reporting the recrudescence of Nestorianism, for which he was briefly but warmly thanked by Leo.[2] After the synod in Constantinople had pronounced against him, Eutyches sent another letter to Leo in which he complained that he had not received a fair hearing and that it had been demanded that he should "acknowledge two natures and anathematize those who denied this"—something which, since he considered it to be an addition to the creed of Nicea, he was unwilling to do until Leo had given a ruling on the question. He also professed his antipathy to all heresies right back to Simon Magus.[3]

Flavian, in his capacity of patriarch of Constantinople, also entered into correspondence with Leo. According to him, Eutyches, "for many years a presbyter and abbot," in claiming to hold and promote the right faith was guilty of an empty pretense. He accused him of trying to "revive the old evil dogmas of the blasphemous Valentinus and Apollinaris" and of having disclosed his erratic beliefs when "he openly in our holy synod persisted in saying that our Lord Jesus Christ ought not to be understood by us as having two natures after his incarnation in one substance and in one person, nor yet that the Lord's flesh was of one substance with us."[4] In May of 449 Leo wrote to Flavian that "this man, who has long seemed to be religiously disposed, has expressed himself in the faith otherwise than is right";[5] and the following month he sent Flavian the celebrated letter known as the Tome of Leo, the purpose of which was to provide theological instruction and guidance for those soon to meet in council in Ephesus to consider this issue. In this summary statement of the orthodox faith regarding the incarnation Leo described Eutyches as "very imprudent and

1. See pp. 304f. above.
2. *Letters and Sermons of Leo the Great,* tr. C. L. Feltoe, Vol. XII of Nicene and Post-Nicene Fathers, Second Series (Oxford and New York, 1895), Letter 20, p. 32.
3. Ibid., Letter 21, pp. 32ff.
4. Letter 22, pp. 34ff., and Letter 26, pp. 36ff.
5. Letter 27, p. 38.

exceedingly incompetent," comparing him to the man mentioned by the psalm-ist who "refuses to act wisely so as to do well and devises mischief in his bed" (Ps. 36:3f.) and deploring Eutyches' notion of the incarnation as "absurd," "per-nicious," and "reaching the height of stupidity and blasphemy." Leo counseled, however, that a response of penitence on the part of Eutyches together with the renunciation of his error should meet with mercy and restoration to fellow-ship.[6] Writing to Pulcheria, sister of the emperor Theodosius, Leo offered the opinion that "ignorance rather than ingenuity" was responsible for the error of Eutyches, but that nonetheless the issue was "not about some small portion of our faith on which no very distinct declaration has been made."[7]

Leo in fact was not persuaded of the necessity for a special council to deal with this affair, but pressure from Dioscorus and his party had induced the emperor to approve the holding of one in Ephesus. His own presence at the council, Leo judged, was not required by precedent and for him to leave Rome at this time was not in any case a practical possibility.[8] But he wrote a letter to the company which assembled at Ephesus, commending to them the delegates he had sent as his representatives, demanding the condemnation of the heresy that they had assembled to investigate, and advising the reinstatement of Eu-tyches, "but only on the condition that he embraces the true doctrine and fully and openly with his own voice and signature condemns those heretical opin-ions in which his ignorance has been ensnared."[9]

But what Leo had anticipated as a rather straightforward procedure took an altogether unexpected course. Dioscorus, who enjoyed the smile of the emperor, turned the event into a display of Alexandrian domination. He seized the chairmanship of the council and tyrannically enforced his will on the as-sembled company. Both Leo's Tome and his letter addressed to the council were suppressed. The bishop of Rome might have been nonexistent for all the notice Dioscorus was prepared to give to his communications. The symbol of union of 433 was repudiated. Eutyches was rehabilitated and his one-nature theory of the incarnation pronounced orthodox. Those who had previously passed judgment against Eutyches were prevented from speaking. Theodoret was not even permitted to attend. Flavian was condemned, deprived of his bishopric, and sentenced to exile, as was Theodoret, together with a number of other bishops of whom Dioscorus thought ill. It was a moment of devastat-ing victory for Alexandria and the monophysite teaching that seemed to have an almost irresistible fascination for the Alexandrian mentality. Leo was vir-tually under siege as Dioscorus was now poised to arrogate to himself the posi-tion of supremacy in the Christian world.

There were some 140 bishops at this Ephesian synod, but both Eutyches and Dioscorus brought with them contingents of monks who, with the as-

6. Letter 28, pp. 38, 43.
7. Letter 31, p. 44.
8. Ibid. and Letter 37, to Theodosius, p. 50.
9. Letter 33, p. 47.

sistance of soldiery and a variety of other subsidiaries, formed the shock troops
who were menacingly and noisily at hand whenever the need was apparent to
cow with terror any bishops who showed signs of hesitancy or recalcitrance.
The sessions, accordingly, were punctuated by scenes of anarchy and violence.
Leo complained to the emperor about the disgraceful conduct that had been
tolerated and indeed incited at Ephesus. Had Dioscorus not refused to allow
his letters to be read to the participants, the ignorance and jealousy that were
so much in evidence might have been dispelled; but, Leo wrote, "because private interests were consulted under cover of religion the disloyalty of a few resulted in the wounding of the whole church." If only Dioscorus, "who claimed
for himself the chief place," had followed the course of "priestly moderation,"
permitting freedom of expression and judgment instead of excluding some and
silencing others and intimidating all with threats of violence, the outcome of
the synod might have been beneficial. Leo's appeal now to Theodosius was to
restore proper order and true orthodoxy by summoning a general council to be
held in Italy: "Defend the church in unshaken peace against the heretics," he
pleaded, "that your empire also may be defended by Christ's right hand."[10]

Theodoret, in a letter to Leo, declared his admiring agreement with the
doctrine of the Tome and observed that, far from the waves of controversy
having been stilled at Ephesus, they were now plunged into a yet worse storm.
He, too, complained of the scandalous behavior of Dioscorus, whom he sar-
castically described as "the most righteous prelate of Alexandria," who, "not
satisfied with the illegal and most unrighteous deposition of Flavian, the Lord's
most holy and God-loving bishop of Constantinople," and "his wrath unap-
peased by the similar slaughter of other bishops," had also "murdered him
[Theodoret] with his pen" in his absence, condemning him without a hearing
and driving him from his diocese of 800 churches whose shepherd he had been
for twenty years—and this despite the knowledge of his unflagging opposition
to heretics and unbelievers at whose hands he had suffered stonings and many
other hardships and indignities.[11] Before the end of the year (449) Leo wrote
a letter of encouragement to the clergy and people of the city of Constantinople, expressing his grief at what had recently happened in Ephesus and his
joy because of their own piety and faithfulness. Included in the letter was a
careful statement by Leo of what he held to be sound christological doctrine.[12]
In a later letter to Pulcheria in 451 Leo called the Ephesian gathering a company "not of judges but of robbers";[13] hence the designation "the robber synod"
(latrocinium) by which it has since been known.[14]

Savagely treated, physically as well as verbally, Flavian died in exile not
long after the Robber Council from the injuries he had suffered. There was

10. Letter 44, pp. 53f.
11. Letter 52, pp. 56f.
12. Ibid., Letter 59, pp. 58ff.
13. *Non iudicio sed latrocinio.*
14. Loc. cit., Letter 95, p. 71.

some suspicion that the man whom Theodosius appointed to succeed him as bishop of Constantinople, an Alexandrian priest named Anatolius, had had an interest and a hand in bringing about his death. It was another death, however, that of the emperor Theodosius in July 450, who was suddenly killed when thrown from his horse, that now dramatically changed the whole course of events. His sister Pulcheria, who took his place on the imperial throne, was strongly orthodox in her profession of the Christian faith and at one with Leo in friendship as well as theology. She and Marcian, whom she had taken as her consort and co-ruler, soon showed their willingness to set right the wrongs that had been perpetrated just a year previously in Ephesus. The body of Flavian was brought to Constantinople and interred in the Church of the Apostles in the presence of the grieving people whose chief pastor he had been. Dioscorus's friend Anatolius discreetly protected his position by subscribing his acceptance of the Tome of Leo—though earlier in the year he had supported the power-hungry Dioscorus in proclaiming sentence of excommunication on the bishop of Rome! In April of the following year (451) Leo was able to inform Pulcheria that the clergy who were unjustly expelled from their churches had been restored. "The Christian religion," he said, "requires both that true justice should constrain the obstinate and love not reject the penitent."[15] The spirit of moderation was evident, too, in the instruction he gave to Anatolius to receive back into the communion of the church, after examination in the presence of Leo's delegates, those bishops who now expressed "their sorrow that they did not remain constant against violence and intimidation, but gave their assent to another's crime when terror had so bewildered them that with hasty acquiescence they ministered to the condemnation of the catholic and guiltless bishop (Flavian) and to the acceptance of the detestable heresy (of Eutyches)." Leo also forbade Anatolius to continue reading the names of Dioscorus and certain of his henchmen "at the holy altar," "for," he admonished, "it is very wrong and unbecoming that those who have harassed innocent catholics with their attacks should be mingled indiscriminately with the names of the saints."[16]

Leo seems to have felt that the situation was now sufficiently well settled, both ecclesiastically and theologically; but this view was not shared by Marcian, whose imperial insistence was mainly responsible for summoning another general council for the purpose of establishing harmony by authoritatively defining the orthodox faith. And so upwards of 500 bishops assembled at the beginning of September 451 for what was to be the historic Council of Chalcedon. Actually, it was at Nicea in Bithynia that they came together; but when Marcian, preoccupied with the threat looming from the encroachment of Attila and his Huns, requested them to transfer their meeting to a place nearer to Constantinople to facilitate his being present they moved the venue to Chalcedon, which is situated on the Bosporus. In formulating a new statement

15. Letter 79, p. 65.
16. Letter 80, pp. 65f.

of doctrine they were required by the emperor to accept the Tome of Leo as a basis of christological confession. Aware that his ambitions for personal supremacy were hopelessly shattered, Dioscorus refused to attend the council, and in his absence sentence of condemnation, degradation, and exile was passed against him. Many of the Egyptian bishops who were present abstained from subscribing their acceptance of Leo's Tome on the pretext that it was not proper for them to do so in the absence of their patriarch.

Yet again, as with the preceding general councils, the bishop of Rome did not attend in person. Leo, however, wrote a letter to the council explaining that his presence "was not permitted either by the needs of the times or by any precedent," but asking them to believe that he was present and presiding at their assembly through those he had sent as his representatives. He urged them to "make much of our most merciful prince's piously intentioned council," the design of which was to "destroy the snares of the devil and restore the peace of the church."[17] Theodoret, who had been reinstated sometime previously, was there as a participant with full rights. The rowdy Egyptian faction nonetheless, resenting his defense of Nestorius, caused tumultuous scenes, shouting that Theodoret was no bishop but a fighter against God and demanding that he should anathematize Nestorius; and this at last he reluctantly did, though in fact it was Nestorianism rather than Nestorius that he was willing to denounce.

The Tome of Leo was certainly the most important theological statement so far composed by a scholar or bishop of the Roman see. Though treating of one of the cardinal mysteries of the Christian faith, it is remarkable for its balance and clarity. Taking Holy Scripture as the authority to which he constantly referred and building on the definitions of the Apostles' and Nicene Creeds, Leo affirmed the coessentiality and coeternity of the Son with the Father: "differing in nothing from the Father because he is God from God, . . . not later in point of time, not lower in power, not unlike in glory, not divided in essence." The incarnation did not involve any diminution in the deity of the Son, nor for that matter any increase: "This nativity which took place in time took nothing away from and added nothing to that divine and eternal nativity." The purpose of the incarnation, moreover, was salvific, the redemption of our fallen humanity: it was directed "wholly to the restoration of man who had been deceived; . . . for we should not now be able to overcome the author of sin and death had the Son not taken our nature and made it his own."[18]

Furthermore, the union of the two natures in the incarnate Son implied no loss or alteration on the part of either:

> The property, therefore, of each nature and substance coming together in the one person remained intact, as humility was taken on by majesty, weakness by strength, mortality by eternity; and for the paying off of the debt belonging to our condition inviolable nature was united with passible nature, so that,

17. Letter 93, p. 70.
18. Letter 28, § 2, p. 39.

in a manner appropriate to the remedy we required, one and the same mediator between God and men, the man Christ Jesus, might through the one be able
to die and through the other be unable to die.

The double consubstantiality of the incarnate Son with God and with man is
clearly asserted here and in what follows: "Thus true God was born in the whole
and perfect nature of true man, complete in what is his, complete in what is
ours." Nor did this involve any moral shortfall in the person of the Mediator:
"He did not participate in our faults because he shared in human weaknesses.
He took the form of a slave without stain of sin, increasing the human, not
diminishing the divine." The self-emptying which occurred in the incarnation
was "the bending down of pity, not the failing of power." Again, Leo stressed
that "each nature retains its own proper character without loss" and that the incarnation was a redemptive means for bringing to fulfilment the divine purpose of creation, "the first design of his holy will": "so that man, who was
driven into guilt by the cunning of the devil's wickedness, should not perish
contrary to the purpose of God."[19]

Not only the completeness of each nature but also the distinction between
them must be discerned, in such a way that the divine nature does not cease to
be and act as God even while the human authentically is and acts as man. In a
manner reminiscent of Athanasius, Leo spoke of the Son as "descending from
his heavenly throne and yet not departing from his Father's glory." It is indeed
impossible, when speaking of the incarnation, to avoid using language that is
paradoxical. Thus "he who is invisible in his own nature became visible in
ours," "he whom nothing can contain was willing to be contained," "abiding
before all time he began to be in time," "being God who cannot suffer he did
not disdain to be man who can, and being immortal to subject himself to the
laws of death." Paradox is our necessarily finite and imperfect way of trying
to grasp something of the meaning of the transcendent mystery of the incarnation. The truth of the incarnation hinges upon this one profound reality that "he
who is true God is also true man." That there is indeed the meeting of "the
humility of manhood and the loftiness of deity" is manifested in the life and
ministry of the incarnate Son:

> For as God is not changed by the showing of pity, so man is not swallowed up
> by the dignity. Each form does what is proper to it harmoniously with the
> other,[20] the Word, that is to say, performing what belongs to the Word and the
> flesh carrying out what belongs to the flesh. The one dazzles with miracles,
> the other succumbs to injuries. And as the Word does not depart from the equal-
> ity of the Father's glory, so the flesh does not relinquish the nature of our race.
> For—and this must be said over and over—one and the same is truly the Son
> of God and truly the son of man.[21]

19. Ibid., §§ 3 and 4, pp. 40f.
20. *Cum alterius communione,* the doctrine of the *communicatio idiomatum.*
21. Loc. cit., § 4, pp. 40f.

The dangers in this or any other attempt to define or clarify what took place in the incarnation are inevitable. Statements, if they are lifted from their full context, can appear to be the product of erroneous thinking. For example, to attribute certain words or actions to the divine nature and other words and actions to the human nature can by itself look very much like a division of the person that compromises the true union of the two natures. Hence Leo's emphatic insistence that *"one and the same* is truly the Son of God and truly the son of man."* It is *the one person* of whom we must always speak. It is the one Christ who raises the dead and who dies on the cross. What Jesus does and experiences the Son does and experiences.

The Chalcedonian Definition of the Faith ratified the doctrinal positions of the preceding councils of Ephesus (431), Constantinople (381), and, most particularly, Nicea (325), and specifically repudiated those who taught that Christ was a mere man, or that the incarnation involved a duality of Sons, or that the deity of the Only-Begotten was capable of suffering, or that there was a mixing or confusion of the two natures of Christ, or that the body he assumed as a servant was from heaven or of some substance other than that of our human nature, or that there were two natures before the union but only one after the union. There followed the most famous paragraph of the Definition in which the essentials of christological belief were tersely stated in a memorable manner:

> Following the holy fathers we confess the Son our Lord Jesus Christ to be one and the same, and with one voice we all teach that he is perfect in deity, perfect in manhood, truly God and truly man, with a rational soul and body, co-essential[22] with the Father according to his deity and co-essential[23] with us according to his manhood, in all things like us, apart from sin; begotten of the Father before the ages according to his deity, but in these last days for us and for our salvation born of the Virgin Mary, the Mother of God, according to his manhood, one and the same Christ, Son, Lord, Only-Begotten; acknowledged in two natures unconfusedly, unchangeably, indivisibly, inseparably, without the distinction of the natures being in any way removed because of the union, but rather the property of each nature being preserved and concurring in one person and subsistence, not severed or divided into two persons, but one and the same Son and Only-Begotten, God, the Word, the Lord Jesus Christ, as the prophets from the beginning have taught concerning him, and as the Lord Jesus Christ himself has taught us, and as the creed of the fathers has handed down to us.[24]

22. *Homoousion.*
23. *Homoousion.*
24. For the Greek text of the Chalcedonian Definition see T. H. Bindley, *The Oecumenical Documents of the Faith* (3rd edn. revised; London, 1925), pp. 229ff. An English translation is contained in *The Seven Ecumenical Councils of the Undivided Church*, Vol. XIV of Nicene and Post-Nicene Fathers, Second Series (London and New York, 1890), pp. 262ff.

This confessional statement cut through the root of every christological heresy that had troubled the church from the time of the apostles onward. It struck down the *docetism* of Cerinthus and the gnostics, which, with its dualistic separation of Jesus from Christ, reduced the incarnation to a deceptive appearance; the *adoptionism* of the Ebionites and the exponents of dynamic monarchianism, who held that Christ was a mere man *(psilanthropism)* and therefore denied his preexistence; the *unitarianism* of Simon Magus and the modalistic monarchians (Sabellians), who taught that the designations Father, Son, and Holy Spirit were but modes assumed or parts acted by a unipersonal God, and that therefore it could rightly be said that the Father suffered and died on the cross (patripassianism); *Arianism,* which was an attempt to construct a logical Christ who, as a unique creature, was neither truly God nor truly man, but some kind of intermediate being; *Apollinarianism* with its "one nature" concept of the incarnation, according to which the Logos assumed only a human body without a rational soul; *Nestorianism* with its supposed postulation of two sons or two persons in the incarnate Christ; and *Eutychianism,* which affirmed two natures before but only one, by commingling of the two, after the incarnation (monophysitism). The double *homoousios* is the key to the christology defined at Chalcedon. It is the guarantee of the reality of the incarnation, whereby he who himself is truly God becomes also truly man and truly is the Mediator who bridges the gulf caused by human sin between man and his Creator.

The uneven history of the church in these early centuries, the seemingly chaotic variety of theological speculation, the fierce rivalries, the turbulent confrontations, the imperial interferences, indeed the unpopularity and numerical weakness of those who stood for the orthodox faith—these considerations make it surprising, humanly speaking, that the christology of Nicea and Chalcedon should ever have won acceptance; and they show that the survival and triumph of the truth do not depend on weight of numbers or majority votes or the approval of the powers of this world, but on the inner strength and consistency of the truth itself and on the sovereign control of affairs, both secular and ecclesiastical, by God the Holy Spirit. Chalcedon, however, is not to be regarded as an end point, nor as a new starting point, but rather as a high point in the struggle that is continuously being waged from one generation to another. The formulations of this council and of those that led up to it were necessitated by the appearance of heterodox notions within the church. To guard against false ideas it was important for lines to be drawn which, like the setting up of fences, made a separation between orthodox belief and erroneous theory. It must, however, be stressed that the foundation of orthodoxy is not the credal confessions of the early church but the Holy Scriptures which constitute the Word of God written and which were unanimously accepted by the church fathers as the canon of truth—that is to say, as the standard of right doctrine to which the belief and practice of the church must conform. This is the sacred deposit to be handed down from age to age (1 Cor. 15:3; 1 Tim. 6:20f.; Jude 3f., 17ff.; 2 Pet. 3:2).

Hence the claim that the doctrine concerning Christ given in the Chalcedonian Definition of the Faith is "as the prophets from the beginning have taught concerning him, and as the Lord Jesus Christ himself has taught us, and as the creed of the fathers has handed down to us."

CHAPTER **28**

The Importance of Orthodoxy

We have been advised by certain theologians of our day that orthodoxy is a myth—an illusion of which the Christian mind needs to be disabused. The assurance has been given not only that "modern scholarship has shown that the supposed unchanging set of beliefs is a mirage" but also that "Christianity was from the first very diverse, and has never ceased developing in its diversity," and, further, that "Christianity can only remain honestly believable by being continuously open to the truth,"[1] which must be understood as meaning continuously open to change and alteration. We do not dispute that there has been diversity from the beginning, though not quite in the same sense as these theologians, who wish to persuade us that diversity of belief has ever been authentic and acceptable, whereas we maintain that it was diversity of belief that made theological definition a necessity, and made it so from the beginning. Orthodoxy was for this very reason a matter of constant concern to Jesus himself and his apostles, as the New Testament clearly shows. Urgently and repeatedly Jesus warned his disciples to beware of false prophets and false messiahs who would arise and lead many astray (see, e.g., Mt. 24:4f., 11, 24), and the apostles issued similar warnings (1 Tim. 4:1ff.; Acts 20:29f., etc.). The true faith was being assailed by the presence of many antichrists in the apostolic era (1 Jn. 2:18ff.). Nowhere is it taught that Christian belief is not fixed and must change if it is to be believable. Quite the contrary, for Christ taught that his words would never pass away (Mt. 24:35). Jesus plainly had no misgiving about the orthodoxy of his own teaching. How could it be otherwise with him who declared himself to be the Truth (Jn. 14:6)? Orthodoxy, by definition, is *true teaching* in distinction from erroneous teaching, and Jesus equated his teaching with truth: "If you continue in my word," he said, "you are truly my disciples, and you will know the truth, and the truth will make you free" (Jn. 8:31f.). Truth and life belong together. Error destroys. To reject the truth of Jesus, revealed both in his teaching and in his person, is to bring down judgment on oneself. A person is judged by the very truth he has rejected. "He who rejects me and does not receive my words has a judge," Jesus admonished; "the word that I have spoken will be his judge in the last day" (Jn. 12:48).

1. *The Myth of God Incarnate,* ed. John Hick (Philadelphia, 1977), p. x.

317

Jesus approved as orthodox Simon Peter's confession of him as "the Christ, the Son of the living God," affirming that this truth had been revealed to him not by man but by God (Mt. 16:16f.). But when the same apostle protested against his declaration that he must go to Jerusalem and there suffer and be put to death and on the third day rise from the dead, Jesus rebuked this as satanic heterodoxy (Mt. 16:21-23). No doubt St. Peter's contradiction was well meant, but his perspective at that moment was disastrously wrong. Later on, enlightened by the Holy Spirit, he would lay firm hold of the vital reality and essentiality of the death and resurrection of Jesus (1 Pet. 1:3, 18f.; 2:24; 3:18). Rather than deviate from this orthodoxy, he willingly laid down his life. So, too, St. Paul "kept the faith" to the point of martyrdom (2 Tim. 4:7). And St. Jude appealed to his readers "to contend for the faith which was once for all delivered to the saints" (Jude 3). If this is not the demand for orthodoxy, nothing is.

A major purpose of the writing of the apostolic letters of the New Testament was to establish orthodoxy and dispel heterodoxy. St. Paul's letters to the Christians in Corinth were evoked by the appearance in their midst of erroneous doctrines which were being spread by false apostles. The gospel he had preached to them was not something changeable. Nor was it his invention, for he had faithfully delivered to them what he himself had received. It was this gospel in which they were secure and by which they were saved, *providing they held it fast* (1 Cor. 15:1-3). St. Paul was deeply concerned lest they should be "led astray from a sincere and pure devotion to Christ" by the cunning deceptions of the impostrous prophets who had infiltrated their ranks and were preaching "another Jesus" and "a different gospel" (2 Cor. 11:2-4). He was distressed also to learn that members of the Galatian church were "turning to a different gospel"—"not that there is another gospel," he explained, "but there are some who trouble you and want to pervert the gospel of Christ." This was a matter of such crucial importance that he pronounced an anathema against anyone who should preach to them a gospel contrary to that which they had received (Gal. 1:6-9). St. John, as we have seen, joined issue with those who were propagating the heresy of docetism, denouncing those who denied the truth of the incarnation as deceivers and antichrists (2 Jn. 7); and the letters to the seven churches in chapters 2 and 3 of Revelation, with their warnings and encouragements, were elicited by the various degrees of peril in which they had placed themselves by condoning heterodoxy of one kind or another and the baneful practices that flow from it.

The historic church, likewise, has from the beginning emphasized the essential importance of orthodoxy. This is apparent over and over again in the formulation of creeds and confessions, which are designed to be standards of orthodox belief. Especially significant in this connection is the unanimous insistence of the historic church on Holy Scripture as *canon,* that is, as the rule of faith to which the teaching, the worship, and the practice of the church must conform. "It is from the sacred Scriptures that we confidently proclaim the

authentic faith," Athanasius affirmed.[2] Hence his assertion that "those who
deny the things written in Scripture forthwith deprive themselves of any right
to the name of Christians and should properly be called atheists and enemies
of Christ."[3] And Augustine was equally insistent that "we must not allow even
catholic bishops, if at any time they should be in error, to hold any opinion contrary to the canonical Scriptures of God."[4] Statements to this effect can be mul-
tiplied many times over. They express what was universally agreed: namely,
that the supreme authority of the canonical Scriptures is itself the prime *datum*
of Christian orthodoxy as well as the ground and basis of all that is authentically orthodox in the life of the church.

Orthodoxy, then, was no myth for Christ and his apostles and the historic
church, nor was diversity of belief regarded with complacency. The evidence
is irrefragable. But it is uncongenial to the mind of contemporary rationalism,
which asserts that modern scientific man must be the measure and the arbiter
of all reality, and which has supplanted the canon of the word of God with the
canon of the word of man, claiming that man has now come of age and is self-
sufficient and therefore has no need of help or intervention from beyond. The
modernistic concept of *myth* is the new solvent which has been introduced to
disintegrate the hard evidence. Whatever is awkward or unacceptable has the
label "myth" attached to it and then is eradicated by the bulldozing method of
demythologization. Inconvenient sayings of Jesus can be explained away by
deciding that they were obviously thought up and placed on his lips after his
death by those who had been his devoted disciples. Similarly, his supernatural
deeds can be passed off as imaginative attempts to honor the memory of a
heroic person which also found expression in the christological dogma constructed from the idealistic reflections of the apostles. We are offered a Christ
deprived of his deity and an eviscerated New Testament from which everything that transcends the level of our humanity has been cut away.

We are solemnly advised that in our scientifically enlightened Western
world "supernatural causation or intervention in the affairs of this world has
become, for the majority of people, simply incredible"; and that it is now only
open for us to accept that "there is no room for God as a causal factor in our
international, industrial, or personal lives," since "statistical probabilities and
natural patterns of cause and effect are presupposed in sociology and psychology, in medicine and genetics, as well as all the natural sciences." God no
longer belongs in the picture: "History is to be explained in terms of politics
and personalities, or economics and power-structures. Heavenly powers have
given way to earthly forces."[5] Belief in the incarnation of the Son of God is

2. Athanasius, *Orations against the Arians* i.9.
3. *Defence of the Nicene Definition* 15.
4. Augustine, *On the Unity of the Church* 11.
5. *The Myth of God Incarnate*, p. 31. Cf. J. A. T. Robinson, *The New Reformation?*
(London, 1965), p. 119: "As a factor introduced to make the system work (God) is redundant."

accordingly eliminated. Jesus is idealized as "a man of universal destiny"—but still only a man.[6] He is portrayed as one who was "so powerfully God-conscious that his life vibrated, as it were, to the divine life," and so much so that, had we been in his presence, "we should have felt that we are in the presence of God—not in the sense that the man Jesus literally *is* God, but in the sense that he was so totally conscious of God that we could catch something of that consciousness by spiritual contagion."[7]

But whence is this sentimental concept of Jesus derived? What source of information is there apart from the New Testament whose witness the critical mind has dismissed as incredible and, further, as witness falsely, though it may be amiably, borne. Why believe anything at all when most of what is claimed for him is rejected as unbelievable? And how is it that the church has for so many centuries been so radically deceived in its understanding of Jesus? Why so long after the event should we give credence to the new voice of sophisticated liberalism?[8] When the answer has been given, what is to be gained by reverting to questioning? What advantage does an endless search have over the assurance of discovery?[9] If it is true that "what we have been taught to call 'orthodoxy' was in fact merely the form of Christianity which happened to triumph over the others," this leaves everything in uncertainty in every age, including the new "orthodoxy" of critical unbelief whose exponents wish to persuade us that "the theological task of the modern period" is "that of shifting Christianity from the dogmatic faith of the Christendom period to the critical faith which is to succeed it."[10] Everything then is determined by the shifting forms that happen to triumph from time to time. We are being offered a stone instead of bread.

The advocates of critical skepticism not only depreciate the orthodoxy of the New Testament as the triumph of apostolic theological speculation in the first century but also commonly put down the Chalcedonian Definition of

6. *The Myth of God Incarnate*, p. 56.

7. Ibid., p. 172.

8. The observations of J. B. Lightfoot regarding the assault on historic orthodoxy made by a liberal critic of his day are still very much to the point: "It is strange indeed," he wrote, "that a writer who denounces so strongly the influence of authority as represented by tradition should be anxious to impose on his readers another less honourable yoke. There is at least a presumption (though in individual cases it may prove false on examination) that the historical sense of seventeen or eighteen centuries is larger and truer than the critical insight of a section of men in one late half century. . . . It is comparatively easy to resist the fallacies of past times, but it is most difficult to escape the infection of the intellectual atmosphere in which we live" (*Essays on the Work entitled 'Supernatural Religion'* [London and New York, 1889], p. 23).

9. Cf. Robinson, *The New Reformation?*, pp. 22f.: ". . . there is nothing that will not be questioned . . . [theology which is] a genuinely open-ended search for the truth . . . will carry conviction not by the assurance of its answers but by the integrity of its questioning."

10. *The Myth of God Incarnate*, p. 145.

the Faith as the triumph of Greek philosophy over the Christian mind in the fifth century. Rudolf Bultmann, for instance, while granting (as we would expect) that the New Testament "holds unmistakenly fast to the humanity of Jesus over against all gnostic doctrine," asserted that it did so "with a naiveté for which the problems of 'very God and very man' have not yet arisen" (a sweeping pronouncement hardly supported by the evidence)—problems, he continued, which the ancient church "sought to solve in an inadequate way by means of Greek thought with its objectivizing nature." In any case, he brushed aside the Chalcedonian formula as "now impossible for our thought."[11] Jesus, he allowed, lived and died, but only as an ordinary man. The offense of the gospel, according to Bultmann, was no longer, as in the *kerygma* of the New Testament, the announcement of a Redeemer who, as the incarnate Son of God, died for us sinners and rose again for our justification (Rom. 4:25) but simply this: "that life meets man only in the word addressed to him by a mere man— Jesus of Nazareth . . . a man who claims, without being able to make it credible to the world, that God is encountering the world in him."[12] This "mere man" christology is but the old bare heresy of psilanthropism.

Given his presuppositions, Bultmann was bound to contend that the places in the New Testament which speak of Jesus in divine terms, as God, Lord, and Son of God, were not to be believed as literally true: they were to be understood not as objective definitions but as subjective evaluations; not as ontological statements but as a response evoked from the human existential situation which expressed the significance of Jesus for the apostles and for us; in short, as pronouncements about me rather than pronouncements about him, so that it is not that he helps me because he is the Son of God but that he is the Son of God because he helps me: for me (or the apostles) to call him the Son of God is but an expression of his worth to me (or to them). Accordingly, we are instructed by Bultmann that the profession of St. Peter, "We believe and are sure that thou art the Christ, the Son of the living God" (Jn. 6:69), "would be quite simply just a confession of significance for the 'moment' in which it was uttered, and not a dogmatic pronouncement"[13]—that is, no more than a subjective value-judgment, which is in effect but a repetition of the interpretation proposed by Arius in the fourth century: so much for the assertion of the superiority of the modern scientific mind!

The psilanthropism of the contributors to *The Myth of God Incarnate* finds expression in the demand for "a deabsolutized Jesus," which at the same time is a demand for the deabsolutization of the Christ of Chalcedon. It is even suggested that "Chalcedonian christology could be a remote ancestor of modern unbelief, by beginning the process of shifting the focus of devotion from

11. R. Bultmann, *Essays Philosophical and Theological*, tr. J. C. G. Greig (London, 1955), p. 286.

12. *Theology of the New Testament*, Vol. II, tr. Kendrick Grobel (London, 1955), p. 75.

13. *Essays*, p. 280.

God to man."[14] In other words, to worship Jesus is to worship man, not God—a devotion, however, which began with the apostles, not with the Chalcedonian fathers. And so the orthodoxy of the New Testament, which is also that of Chalcedon, is turned upside down and equated with heterodoxy. Humpty-Dumpty-wise, words are manipulated to mean the opposite of their accepted sense. Historic belief has suddenly become "modern unbelief," and modern belief is disbelief in the doctrine of the incarnation, which, we are told, has had "harmful effects"; and we are counseled to "rethink our ideas of Christ."[15] After approvingly mentioning "two major new adjustments" which were made in the nineteenth century, namely, the acceptance of the emergence of man as a naturalistic development in the evolutionary process and the abandonment of the belief that Scripture is the authoritative word of God, the writers of this book tell us that they are "convinced that another major theological development is called for in this last part of the twentieth century," the recognition, namely, "that Jesus was (as he is presented in Acts 2:21)[16] 'a man approved by God,'" and, further, "that the later conception of him as God incarnate, the Second Person of the Holy Trinity living a human life, is a mythological or poetic way of expressing his significance for us."[17]

Two things must be said about this "major theological development" that is called for in this way. First of all, it is patently disingenuous to cite Acts 2:22 as a proof-text by which it is authoritatively determined that Jesus was merely a man after having denied that the Bible has an authoritative function. To select and brandish a convenient phrase as though it says all that is to be said ontologically about the person of Christ, while suppressing or dismissing as mythological all else that is inconvenient, betrays disreputable and threadbare scholarship. If the Apostle Peter was correct in describing Jesus of Nazareth as a man, why should he not be judged correct in saying that "God did mighty works and wonders through him" (in the same verse of the same sermon), that he "was delivered up according to the definite plan and foreknowledge of God" (in the next verse), that he and his fellow apostles were witnesses of the fact that "God raised up this Jesus" (v. 32), and that Jesus was now "exalted at the right hand of God" (v. 33). But the preconceptions of these authors necessitate the conclusion that only the first of these assertions was prosaic fact and that the rest were expressions of fictional poetry, like St. Peter's confession at Caesarea Philippi that Jesus was "the Christ, the Son of the living God" (Mt. 16:16). Secondly, the deduction from the premise that Jesus was originally regarded as a mere man, speciously authenticated by quoting Acts 2:22, that the designation of him as God incarnate was a "later conception" is open to objections similar to those just mentioned, for, as we have sufficiently shown, it is a

14. *The Myth of God Incarnate,* pp. 141, 143.
15. Ibid., p. 145.
16. *Sic.* This reference should read Acts 2:22.
17. *The Myth of God Incarnate,* p. ix.

conception that belonged without question to the apostolic understanding of the person of Jesus Christ. Thus, even if it were mythological, it cannot honestly be described as later or, for that matter, be blamed on Chalcedon. St. Peter was certainly no psilanthropist.

We have seen that the theologians responsible for *The Myth of God Incarnate* affirm, as a principle fundamental to their position, the constant need for change, in a manner consonant with the "change or perish" principle of evolutionism, if Christianity is to survive and retain its relevance. It is surprising, then, that they deplore the changes, as they wish to view them, that were sanctioned in the christology of the Chalcedonian Definition of Faith, and also that Christianity survived for so many centuries without undergoing credal change; and it is surely interesting that the history of the demand for theological change synchronizes in general with the popularization of the evolutionary hypothesis. Still more surprising, after all this clamor for change, is the claim of these theological professors to have eliminated all the changes of the centuries and to have returned to the original unchanged simplicity of belief of the first Christians—to have "merely come full circle back to the primitive faith of the church," which was supposedly unencumbered by any christology of incarnation.[18] What is this but a claim to have recovered and embraced that orthodoxy which is original and authentic, and an admission that orthodoxy is after all not a myth? And so, if we should believe this, we have been brought back to square one where Jesus is but a man, free from all the supernatural trimmings with which, we are told, he was subsequently invested by apostles and fathers who collaborated to build up an idealized picture of his person and work. Their boast is that now by the alchemy of deabsolutization they have eliminated all change!

If anything should be clear it is that the deabsolutization of Jesus involves a completely radical alteration of the person and the work of the Jesus to whom the New Testament bears witness—and the New Testament is the sole source for our knowledge of Jesus. Moreover, the whole point of the New Testament witness is that in the incarnation, life, death, resurrection, and glorification of Jesus God has personally and concretely intervened in history for the redemption of mankind and the fulfilment of the purpose for which he created all things. To deabsolutize Jesus, therefore, is to rob him of that history which is essential for the right understanding of his person and his work. In all that is most important it is to dehistoricize him. And this is the sabotage of Christianity; for the history of Jesus is divine history as well as human history, and it is divine history before it is human history. Jesus is not just a good and godly man; he is God reconciling the world to himself (2 Cor. 5:18ff.). In the incarnate Son divine history and human history are indissolubly united. The deabsolutization of Jesus divorces the vertical reality from the horizontal and then abolishes the vertical, leaving us with a Jesus who is reduced to the dimensions

18. Ibid., pp. 61f.

of our finite humanity. That is why the radical mind has no place for the New Testament gospel of redemption from sin. By disallowing the incarnation and the resurrection of Jesus it leaves us with one who was and remains dead and buried, and who therefore is powerless to save. The witness of the New Testament is diametrically contrary to this prospect of powerlessness, proclaiming as it does that Jesus is the eternally existent Son who at Bethlehem became our fellowman, at Calvary offered himself to death as our substitute, and on the third day rose victoriously from the dead to die no more. The Christian message is essentially a vital and dynamic message of the power of God's grace to transform lives. If Jesus was a mere man there is no power and no good news.

Far indeed from signaling a return to the original orthodoxy, the deabsolutization of Jesus is the recrudescence of early heterodoxy. In limiting the stature of Jesus to that of a mere man the liberal theologians of our time have attempted to ascribe his continuing influence or relevance to a mystical sort of Christ-idea which in separating Jesus from Christ also separates faith from history. In doing this they are treating as canonical the "ditch" or "chasm" hypothesis which goes back two hundred years to Reimarus, Lessing, and Kant. This separation between faith and history opened the way for them to make their distinction between "the historical Jesus" and "the risen Christ," and also set them off on "the search for the historical Jesus," which continues interminably because, as we have said, they have stripped him of his divine history, the sole master key to the understanding of his human history.

Though starting from different premises, liberal theology has arrived at an end similar to that of docetism by separating the man Jesus from the Christ principle. It is this sort of distinction that lies behind Rudolf Bultmann's notion that, while Jesus, the mere man, remains entombed, a figure of the past, the resurrection becomes a reality in the act of preaching, inviting faith in the risen Lord without any corresponding historical event for it to stand on. The "ditch"-mentality is apparent, too, in the differentiation made by Karl Barth and others between *Historie*, understood as ordinary day-to-day this-worldly history, and *Geschichte*, the equivalent of what Emil Brunner called "superhistory," which is regarded as outside and beyond the sequence of normal history and as the conceptual dimension to which "events" like incarnation and resurrection can be assigned. Dietrich Bonhoeffer rightly objected that "this present-historical *(geschichtliche)* Christ is the same person as the historical *(historische)* Jesus of Nazareth," stressing that if our faith is not to be a vain illusion "there can be no isolation of the so-called historical *(historische)* Jesus from the Christ who is present now"; and he repudiated the position of "liberal theology," which, he said, "stands and falls first of all by the separation of Jesus from the Christ," with the result that "Jesus is the Christ, not in his nature and not in his person, but in his effect on others."[19]

Furthermore, the ancient heterodoxy of the Ebionites and of unitarians

19. D. Bonhoeffer, *Christ the Center* (London and New York, 1966), p. 71.

like Paul of Samosata, whose preconceptions led them to portray Jesus as a divinely inspired man, and thus, in effect, to affirm his *homoousia* with man but to deny his *homoousia* with God, is prototypical of the kind of theologizing which, frequently influenced by the speculations of Friedrich Schleiermacher from the last century, present Jesus as a man with a uniquely developed consciousness of God and an exceptional spirituality, similar to the great prophets of old or the champions of civil rights of our own day, but supremely so.[20] This, too, is an incapacitating reduction of the Redeemer of the New Testament. The modern reductionists have shown that they are well aware that Jesus can be deabsolutized only by deabsolutizing the New Testament. And so they have taken away the authority of Christ and his apostles and left us with no canon save that of existential subjectivism, which varies insecurely from person to person. "We have lost the concept of heresy today because there is no longer a teaching authority," Bonhoeffer complained. "This is a tremendous catastrophe," he continued, for "there can be no confession without saying, 'In the light of Christ, this is true and this is false,'" since "the concept of heresy belongs necessarily and irrevocably with that of the confession."[21] The church's only teaching authority that is fontal and authentic is the teaching authority of Jesus Christ, himself the Truth, communicated through the apostles he instructed in accordance with his assurance that the Holy Spirit would bring back to their remembrance all that he had taught them and lead them into all the truth (Jn. 14:6, 26; 16:13). This authoritative teaching remains available to the world in the doctrine of the New Testament. To deabsolutize the New Testament is to nullify that teaching authority which is essential to the church's existence, indeed survival, and to open the gate to every kind of error and folly. Orthodoxy is not a dispensable commodity.

As for the view, already mentioned, that the Chalcedonian Definition represents the triumph of Greek philosophical thought over other contending forms in the development of christological theory, and became the banner of orthodoxy only by chance, this is another instance of the liberal propensity for standing things on their head. Chalcedon, properly understood, was precisely *the defeat*, not the victory, of the Greek religious mentality. The battle against the infiltration of typically Greek theories was joined right back in the apostolic period with the polemic of St. John and St. Paul against docetism and other early types of gnostic heresy, and it was continued without relaxation on the way to Chalcedon. Greek dualistic thought could not possibly embrace the reality of the incarnation. Greek terms and expressions were employed simply because the Chalcedonian Definition was composed in the Greek language, and it is obvious that those terms and expressions were intended to be interpreted in accordance with the doctrinal thrust and context of the Definition. That is why Bonhoeffer was able to assert: "Against liberalism, it must be said

20. See, e.g., *The Myth of God Incarnate*, pp. 18, 36, 58.
21. Bonhoeffer, *Christ the Center,* p. 78.

that in its own way there is no thought-product less Greek than the Chalcedonian Definition."[22]

No one would wish to suggest that all of the patristic authors succeeded in keeping their minds free from the influence of Greek philosophical concepts or that their writings should be read uncritically. It is true to say, rather, that if there was an attempt to hellenize the christology of the church it was the heretics, not the orthodox, who were to blame. Aloys Grillmeier has given an admirable assessment of the situation. He points out that the *philosophoumena* or virtually technical formulas of the fathers "have a service to perform for the faith of the church."

> They are intended to preserve the Christ of the gospels and the apostolic age for the faith of posterity. In all the christological formulas of the ancient church there is a manifest concern not to allow the total demand made on man's faith by the person of Jesus to be weakened by pseudo-solutions. It must be handed on undiminished to all generations of Christendom. On a closer inspection, the christological "heresies" turn out to be a compromise between the original message of the Bible and the understanding of it in Hellenism and paganism. It is here that we have the real Hellenization of Christianity. . . . Now these formulas clarify only one, albeit the decisive point of belief in Christ: that in Jesus Christ God really entered into human history and thus achieved our salvation. If the picture of Christ is to be illuminated fully, these formulas must always be seen against the whole background of the biblical belief in Christ. They prove the church's desire for an ever more profound *intellectus fidei,* which is not to be a resolution of the *mysterium Christi.* None of the formulas, once framed, should be given up.[23]

The Chalcedonian Definition of the Faith is not the last word any more than it is the first word on the christological question. It is a notable example, as Grillmeier observes, of faith seeking understanding, not the resolution of the mystery of the incarnation. Whatever formulas may be devised, new or old, the mystery continues, because the wonder of the incarnation far transcends the powers of comprehension of the mind of man and the powers of definition of the language of man. The Definition therefore can hardly be expected to be other than a vulnerable document. But the truths to which it bears witness are nonetheless of the utmost importance: especially, that Jesus Christ is truly God

---

22. Ibid., p. 105; cf. also his observation on p. 79 that "the docetic heresy is the typical heresy of Greek thought." Of Athanasius, who is the figure of central significance in the whole history of the christological issue, Adolf Harnack has said: "Athanasius' importance to posterity consisted in this, that he defined Christian faith exclusively as faith in redemption through the God-man who was identical in nature with God, and that thereby he restored to it fixed boundaries and specific contents. Eastern Christendom has been able to add nothing up to the present day . . . but the Western Church also preserved this faith as fundamental. . . . It was the official means of preventing the complete hellenizing and secularization of Christianity" (*History of Dogma* [London, 1897], Vol. III, p. 144).

23. A. Grillmeier, *Christ in Christian Tradition,* pp. 555f.

and truly man, that the divine and the human natures belong to the single unitary person of the incarnate Son, and that the human nature assumed by the Word is our human nature in its completeness.

The fathers at Chalcedon were undoubtedly aware of the absolute ontological difference between the divine and the human, for it is this that makes the formulation of the two-natures doctrine so difficult a task. Their achievement is rightly admired, but the christological statement they produced would have been considerably improved had they but added the explanation that there is no inherent impropriety or incongruity in the conception of the conjunction of the divine and the human in a cooperation of complete harmony. The clue was plainly there in the writings of Athanasius, but it had not been firmly grasped and in the excitement of controversy it had for all practical purposes been overlooked. That clue was the postulation of the particular affinity that exists between the Second Person of the Holy Trinity and God's creature man, established by the fact that the Son who himself is the Image of God is precisely the image in which man was created and to which it is the divine purpose that he should be conformed. Man, in other words, was created to be in harmony with his Creator. The potential of his humanity is only fulfilled by virtue of his oneness with him who is the Image in accordance with which he was constituted. Nothing could be more proper and indeed more natural than for man to exist in union with the Son. The incarnation, the becoming man of the Son in a total harmony of the divine and the human, was the perfect answer to the problem of man's fallenness. And this was clearly perceived and expressed by Athanasius as he insisted that the Son "alone by natural fitness was both able to recreate everything and worthy to suffer on behalf of all and to be ambassador for all with the Father," that "the Word of God came in his own person, so that, being himself the Image of the Father, he might be able to create man afresh after the image," and that "none other was sufficient for this need save the Image of the Father."[24] Unfortunately this key to faith's understanding of the significance of the incarnation seems to have been mislaid *en route* to Chalcedon.

24. See p. 279 above.

CHAPTER 29

The Life of Jesus

We have said that the purpose of Christ's birth at Bethlehem was his death at Calvary, but this is not at all intended to imply that the life that stretched between Bethlehem and Calvary was of little significance. That would indeed be a serious misunderstanding. The life and the death of the incarnate Son are so closely related to each other that they form a coherent whole. This is so because the perfection of his life as our fellowman was essential to the effectiveness of his sacrificial death on our behalf. The "becoming flesh" of the Word (Jn. 1:14) was his becoming the last Adam or the second man (1 Cor. 15:45-47) for the purpose of undoing the curse that was brought upon mankind by the first Adam. The coming of the second Adam was to reintegrate our humanity, which had been shattered in the first. This truth is tersely expressed in the lines of John Henry Newman:

> O loving wisdom of our God!
>   When all was sin and shame,
> A second Adam to the fight
>   And to the rescue came.
>
> O wisest love! that flesh and blood,
>   Which did in Adam fail,
> Should strive afresh against the foe,
>   Should strive and should prevail.

It was not only on the cross but also in his life and ministry which preceded and led up to the cross that Christ strove against the foe and prevailed. The cross was the climax of the lifelong striving of the incarnate Son. Our eternal salvation, it is true, was achieved on the cross, and it is entirely proper that the cross should be the symbol of our redemption and Christ crucified the heart of the gospel message (cf. 1 Cor. 1:18, 23f.; 2:2); but the death of the second Adam could never have had redemptive value had it not been founded on the perfect sinlessness of his life that qualified him to offer himself up, "the righteous for the unrighteous" (1 Pet. 3:18). In speaking of the living Jesus, therefore, we do not wish it to be supposed that his living and his dying can properly be isolated from each other, when in fact they are bound together in the closest possible relationship. The birth at Bethlehem was ever directed toward the death at Calvary. The body prepared for the Son was predestined to be offered up by him in sacrifice to make atonement for our sins (Heb. 10:5-10). The death of Christ was not the end, the last event, of a life, like that of a martyr, but the fulfilment of a coming, as that of a Savior, which opened the gate of eternal life to those who are dead in their sins (Eph. 2:1ff.; Jn. 5:24). His own resurrection was the proof of his power over death and the authentication of his mission now completed.

The splendid destiny that the first Adam forfeited through his sin is restored as a living reality by the reconciling work of the second Adam. There is a distinction between what the first Adam was and what he was intended ultimately to become—and what is said of him holds good for mankind descended from him as protogenitor. That distinction is indicated by the way in which St. Paul compares Adam and Christ. "The first man Adam became a living being," he says, "the last Adam became a life-giving spirit"; and he explains that "the first man was from the earth, a man of dust," whereas "the second man is from heaven" (1 Cor. 15:45, 47). The reference is to the formation of man as described in Genesis 2:7, where we read that "the Lord God formed man of dust from the ground and breathed into his nostrils the breath of life, and man became a living being." Contrasted with this is the coming of "the second man" from above, which is the coming to us of the eternal Son himself. The distinction is made also in the Fourth Gospel: "He who comes from above is above all; he who is of the earth belongs to the earth, and of the earth he speaks" (Jn. 3:31). In the history of human experience it is the earthly that comes first and then the heavenly. Furthermore, the earthly was designed to lead up to and find its true fulfilment in the heavenly. Hence St. Paul's observation that "it is not the spiritual which is first but the psychical, and then the spiritual" (1 Cor. 15:46). The psychical is the *terminus a quo*, the spiritual the *terminus ad quem*.

St. Paul's argument develops from the distinction between soul *(psychē)* and spirit *(pneuma)*, the soul or psyche being the principle of animation which man has in common with the animals, and the spirit the principle of personhood which raised him above the animals to fellowship with his Creator, in whose image he is formed.[1] Man as created was certainly a spiritual being in that he

---

1. The term *psychikos,* "psychical," presents a real difficulty to the translator. In 1 Cor. 2:14, where it is used in contrast to *pneumatikos,* "spiritual" (v. 15), it denotes the person who is unregenerate and therefore unspiritual; and it carries a similar connotation in Jas. 3:15, where it stands together with "earthly" and "demonic," and Jude 19, where it belongs to the description of those who do not have the Spirit *(pneuma mē echontes).* The sense in these places is "brutish," or, negatively, "unspiritual," "unregenerate," with all that those negatives imply in the setting of the New Testament. In 1 Cor. 15:44, 46, however, it applies to regenerate and spiritual persons whose bodies when "sown" in death and burial are "psychical" bodies, but when raised in glory at Christ's parousia will be "spiritual" bodies. The contrast here is between the perishability, humbleness, and weakness of the present body, which is "psychical," and the imperishability, glory, and power of the resurrection body, which will be "spiritual"; the best commentary on this is St. Paul's own declaration in Phil. 3:20f.

enjoyed interpersonal communion with his Creator, but a glory beyond that of his first state as a creature was the destiny to which it was God's purpose to bring him, and at which he would in good time have arrived had he not fallen into sin. That design and that destiny were enacted and illustrated in the single life of the incarnate Son whose psychical body received through Mary was transformed into the spiritual body of his resurrection glory. In his history Christ appears redemptively as the prototype of our history. In his resurrection and transformation he is the firstfruits of the harvest of Christian believers, the firstborn from the dead of the many sons that are being brought to glory (1 Cor. 15:20; Col. 1:18; Heb. 2:10). The death of the Christian is like the sowing of a seed which springs up into new and resplendent life. Hence St. Paul's assurance: "What is sown is perishable, what is raised is imperishable. It is sown in dishonor, it is raised in glory. It is sown in weakness, it is raised in power. It is sown a psychical body, it is raised a spiritual body" (1 Cor. 15:43f.). Notice that the expression "spiritual body" is not a contradiction in terms as it would have been for the Platonist and the gnostic. Just as the resurrection in glory of Jesus was a *bodily* resurrection, so also the consummation awaiting us is a *bodily* consummation, as befits the nature of our humanity; but ours will be the freedom of being clothed with spiritual bodies—still *our* bodies, but bodies transformed into the likeness of the risen Lord's glorious body (Phil. 3:21).

Thus in Christ mankind is redeemed and will be brought to the destiny for which we were always intended. But first the humanity that died in Adam must be created anew and journey afresh toward the goal for which it was originally created. This new beginning is made a reality in the last Adam whose human nature assumed at Bethlehem was the exact equivalent of the first Adam's human nature received from God. St. Luke taught this by tracing the human genealogy of Jesus back to Adam (Lk. 3:23-38), thus affirming his solidarity with our race in its entirety. The author of the Epistle to the Hebrews similarly insists on the authenticity of the incarnate Son's identification with us when he says that "he who sanctifies and those who are sanctified have all one origin," explaining that "since the children share in flesh and blood, he himself partook of the same nature" (Heb. 2:11-14). Moreover, "the second man" entered our world just as did "the first man," without sin and in the freedom of a relationship of direct communion with the Father. The starting point was the same for both.

With the coming of the second Adam there is the coming of new hope for mankind and the prospect of the renewal of creation as the evil work of the first Adam is undone. The way is opened for the reintegration and rehabilitation of man as the grace of God enables him to live in conformity to the divine image which is constitutional to his true being. The Christiformity which is man's true destiny, and which was subverted by the first Adam, is restored and brought to fulfilment in the second, who, himself the Image of God, as the incarnate Son and our fellowman conforms himself to that image. It is in him that the redeemed exchange the image of the man of dust for the image of the man of heaven (1 Cor.

15:49). But first the man of heaven had to establish his own righteousness in mortal conflict with the devil, so that, victorious, he could go to Calvary and cancel our condemnation by bearing our sins in his own body as the spotless Lamb of God (Is. 53:4-7; Jn. 1:29; 1 Pet. 1:18f.; 2:24). The requirements for the second Adam, therefore, were that, like the first Adam, he should be truly man, he should be truly innocent, he should be truly tested, and that, unlike the first Adam, he should be truly victorious in his encounter with the power of evil.

The righteousness of him who "died for sins once for all, the righteous for the unrighteous" (1 Pet. 3:18), was not simply something given and possessed, not a state of being that cost him nothing. It had to be *established;* it had to be *achieved* by conflict and by conflict and conquest. The pioneer of our salvation had to be *made perfect through suffering,* suffering occasioned by the endurance of temptation all the way to the cross, which was the ultimate and the supreme test (Heb. 2:10, 18; 4:15). The obedience of the incarnate Son did not flow from an easy, undemanding disposition; it was costly beyond all calculation; it had to be *learned,* and the learning of it was through suffering. It was in this way that he achieved and established his human perfection: "Although he was a Son, he learned obedience through what he suffered, and being made perfect he became the source of eternal salvation to all who obey him" (Heb. 5:8f.). That obedience necessarily involved obedience "unto death, even death on a cross" (Phil. 2:8). The perfection of Jesus, then, was not just a perfection of being but a perfection of becoming: the former was sustained by the latter, as progressively he consolidated what he was and had to be. But in no sense was the perfecting of Jesus a progress from imperfection to perfection. Had he at any time been imperfect, or had he even momentarily lapsed into disobedience, he would have failed in all that he came to be and do; he would have become as the first Adam became; incompetent then to save others, he would himself have been in need of salvation. The road to his perfection was the road of intense and unremitting struggle, as he joined battle with the devil himself, met the hostility of men with unfaltering love, agonized at Gethsemane, and experienced dereliction on the cross. The incarnation was not a comfortable excursion or an enjoyable interlude. We do not consider sufficiently its extreme costliness in suffering and anguish to him who is the eternal Son of God and the Image after which we are formed; nor do we remind ourselves, as we constantly should, that the perfection of obedience which he established through suffering was not for his but for our sake, "for us men and for our salvation."

A question that has been discussed since the early centuries is whether Jesus was immune to the power of temptation. It would indeed have been calamitous had the incarnate Son fallen into sin, for that, as we have indicated, would have brought about the failure of his redemptive mission. For this reason the Christian believer finds it unthinkable that his Savior *should* at any point have yielded to temptation. But is it unthinkable that he *could* have been conquered by the tempter? Is it right to believe, as some do, that it was *a priori* impossible for Jesus to sin? Those who answer this question affirmatively seem to be concerned to protect the inviolability of the deity in him who is God incarnate. But it was as man, not as God, that Jesus was tempted to commit sin. It is no big step for defenders of his impeccability to slip into error such as that of the Apollinarians, who envisaged the Logos as taking the place of the human reason and will and thus presented Christ as possessing a defective human nature, with the consequence that his battle with temptations is no more than play-acting or make-believe, a docetic display. And this suggestion of falsity immediately creates a difficulty as great as, and not dissimilar from, the difficulty it is intended to remove. If temptations have no force to be withstood and no hope of succeeding, they are deprived of reality and cease to be a threat to be taken seriously. Whatever the appearances, the show of contest must be written off as no contest. That being so, there was no authentic victory of the incarnate Son over temptation, and his being tempted can have no real significance for the Christian.

It will not do, then, to argue that because the person of the incarnate Son is compounded of two natures, of which the divine is incapable either of being tempted or of sinning, therefore there was no possibility that Jesus should have been so tempted as to sin; for it was precisely in our human nature that the Incarnate Son faced and overcame temptation, and in doing so experienced its threatening subtlety and force to the full. Otherwise his effectiveness as the second Adam is overthrown. It was essential that he should face temptation as the first Adam faced it and experience the full threat of its force as the first Adam experienced it. It was essential, moreover, that he should be obedient where the first Adam was disobedient and gain the victory where the first Adam had gone down to defeat. Christ had to face the tempter in the same way as the first Adam faced him, with the same possibility of victory or defeat. His was literally a life-and-death struggle, a true striving against the foe for our salvation. Ours would be no real redemption if it rested on a display of unreal shadow boxing. Since the tempting, which is the testing, of Christ took place not only in the wilderness but constantly and finally, and climactically, at Calvary, it follows logically that if, because of the presence of the divine nature, he was incapable of sinning he was incapable also of suffering and dying, for the divine nature is impassible as well as impeccable; but to approve that logical conclusion would be to bid farewell to the gospel.[2]

2. For a statement of this position see W. G. T. Shedd (*Dogmatic Theology*, Vol. II [Edinburgh, 1889], pp. 330ff.), who certainly had no wish to bid farewell to the gospel. He argued as follows: "The last Adam differs from the first Adam, by reason of his impeccability. He was characterized not only by the posse non peccare, but the non posse peccare. He was not only able to overcome temptation, but he was unable to be overcome by it. . . . A mutable holiness would be incompatible with other divine attributes ascribed to the God-man. . . . The divine nature is both intemptable and impeccable. . . . Should Jesus Christ sin, incarnate God would sin." Shedd asserted that it was "remarkable that a theologian of such soundness and accuracy as the older Hodge should deny the impeccability of the God-man." But Shedd should also have found it unacceptable, by the same reasoning, that Jesus Christ should suffer and die.

To dissociate Jesus from the first Adam in respect of his being vulnerable to temptation is also to remove him from us in this same respect. It is to evacuate of substance, indeed to render untrue, the assurance that "we have not a high priest who is unable to sympathize with our weaknesses, but one who in every respect has been tempted as we are, yet without sinning"; for the whole thrust of this assurance rests on the reality of the temptation he endured, on his temptation being identical in character with that which we endure, and on the authenticity of his victory over that temptation; otherwise his suffering of temptation is of little consequence to us, his "not sinning" has a hollow ring, and so also does the exhortation which immediately follows: "Let us then with confidence draw near to the throne of grace, that we may receive mercy and find grace to help in time of need" (Heb. 4:15f.). The encouragement that, "because he himself has suffered through being tempted,[3] he is able to help those who are tempted" (Heb. 2:18), becomes an empty encouragement. Was there anything false or unreal in the harrowing struggle in the garden against the temptation to avoid the cross and all the horror it involved? What anguish could be more real than that which caused him to sweat drops of blood?—anguish at the prospect not merely of the physical pains of crucifixion, daunting though that was, but of his enduring on the cross our hell and God-forsakenness as the unfathomable price of our redemption. "What shameful softness it would have been," Calvin expostulated, "for Christ to be so tortured by the dread of common death as to sweat blood, and to be able to be revived only at the appearance of angels? What? Does not that prayer, coming from unbelievable bitterness of heart and repeated three times—'Father, if it be possible, let this cup pass from me'—[4] show that Christ had a harsher and more difficult struggle than with common death?"[5] This is the purport, too, of another of the verses of Newman's hymn:

> O generous love! that he, who smote
> In Man for man the foe,
> The double agony in Man
> For man should undergo.

That double agony was the agony both of crucifixion and of our hell.

"Man for man": that is the key to the understanding of all Christ's suffering. The fact that it was as man, as the Son of God incarnate, that he suffered temptation and death does not negate or diminish the truth that it was God the Son who thus suffered for us. What he suffered as our fellow human being was fully suffered by him who is the eternal Word. Nor did the fact that he was the eternal Word made man lessen or alleviate his suffering; on the contrary, it intensified it beyond all calculation, for his self-humiliation was his endurance

---

3. This is the sense of *peponthen autos peirastheis*. Cf. Jerusalem Bible: ". . . because he has himself been through temptation. . . ."
4. Mt. 26:39.
5. J. Calvin, *Institutes* II.xvi.12.

of unimaginable rejection and shame. The victory won at such cost was anything but unreal. The purpose of this, as Irenaeus has said, was "that as our race went down to death through a vanquished man, so we might ascend to life again through a victorious man."[6] And his victory was, from beginning to end, the victory of love: it was love that brought him to us, love that sustained his union with the Father in will and purpose, love that animated all his teaching and manifested itself in deeds of mercy and compassion to all who came to him, and love that took him through every temptation to the final ordeal of the cross for our sakes.

If we wish to know what true manhood is we must fix our attention on Jesus Christ, in whom we see the love of God and man faultlessly displayed and the fulfilment of the inherent potential of our humanity as formed in the image of God. In him alone is the actualization of this amazing potential manifested. The last Adam shows in the life of his own person what the first Adam could and should have been—and all the more strikingly because he does so in the midst of the darkness and disorder occasioned by man's ungodliness. In Jesus Christ we see the concentration of what redeemed humanity will yet be and is even now becoming, in accordance with the purpose of the Creator. The Son is both the Image from which man, created in that image, by his sin fell away and the Image to which man through the power of redeeming grace will be at last conformed, for to be fully Christlike will be to be truly man. While the fall of man is man's self-severance from both his origin and his destiny, his redemption in Christ effects the restoration of both his origin and his destiny. This redemption was accomplished by the atoning death of him whose life had been the perfect life of love. It is to the consideration of his death and its significance that we must now turn.

6. Irenaeus, *Against Heresies* V.xxi.1.

CHAPTER 30

The Death of Jesus

Death is the consequence of sin. It is so because to turn away from God who is the source of life is to choose death instead of life. Turning away from God is the heart of all sin, and while death is rightly understood as divine judgment it is at the same time judgment which sinful man brings down upon himself (Gen. 2:16; Rom. 5:12; 6:23). Jesus was without sin and therefore was not under sentence of death (2 Cor. 5:21; Heb. 4:15; 7:26; 1 Pet. 2:22; 1 Jn. 3:5). Death had no claim on him and was not an inevitability for him. Being himself sinless, his dying was not for his own sins but for the sins of others. The death which he endured, then, was an act of his own free choosing; it was a display of his power, not a proof of his weakness. In dying, contrary to appearances, he was active, laying down his life as a self-offering, not passive, having his life taken from him by others (Jn. 10:11, 15, 17f.). Paradoxically, death is the ultimate weakness, the snuffing out of all power; yet the dying of Jesus, which certainly meant his self-submission to this annihilation of power, was the militant conquest of death through the crushing defeat of the Enemy who wields the power of death (Heb. 2:14; Gen. 3:15).

Although his life was not lived, as our lives are lived, in the shadow of death and judgment (Heb. 9:27), it was precisely to die that the Son took our humanity to himself in the incarnation. Repeatedly he spoke to his disciples of the necessity for him to suffer and die in Jerusalem (Mt. 16:21; 17:12, 22f.; 20:17-19). The ministry he had come to fulfil included, as its climax, the giving of his life as a ransom for many (Mk. 10:45). It was by his being lifted up on the cross that men were to be drawn to him (Jn. 12:32f.). After his resurrection he opened the minds of his apostles to understand that his death was a foreordained necessity which accorded with the teaching of the Scriptures (Lk. 24:44-46). And thereafter it became an indispensable emphasis in the apostolic preaching that Jesus had been delivered up and crucified "in accordance with the definite plan and foreknowledge of God" (Acts 2:23; 3:18; 4:27f.; 13:37). His death, then, was a necessity, not for him, but for us. It was inseparable from the purpose of his coming.

But why death on the cross? Might he not just as well have died in some other way that was less distressing and more dignified? Supposing he had died in childhood, would that not have satisfied the purpose of his coming? But no, for this would have been regarded as a sad mischance rather than as his voluntarily offering up of himself for others; it was important, as we have remarked, for him to come to years of maturity and, before giving himself up to death, to live a life which, by its total victory over the tempter and its unbroken consonance with the will of the Father, would establish the perfection of his love and holiness. Why not, then, some form of death other than the cross as an adult? Might he not have achieved his objective by dying in his bed? or as the result of an accident? or at the hand of an assassin? There was certainly ample opportunity for him to have died in a number of different ways; but it is significant that he studiously avoided any manner of dying other than on the cross. He could have died of starvation in the wilderness (Mt. 4:2); he could have been hurled over a precipice (Lk. 4:29); he could have been stoned to death (Jn. 8:59); he could have been arrested and executed in a prison cell like John the Baptist (Jn. 7:44; 8:20; 10:39; Mk. 6:27); yet every attempt to seize and destroy him in one or other of these ways was frustrated. "No one laid hands on him," St. John tells us, "because his hour had not yet come" (Jn. 7:30).

His coming was for this "hour"; his whole life moved resolutely on to the climax of this "hour"; nothing could be allowed to deflect him from it. When in due course his "hour" arrived the incarnate Son knew it and embraced it as the hour for him to be sacrificed as the passover lamb for the sin of the world (Jn. 1:29; 13:1). It was for him an "hour" both of shame and of glory: of shame because, mocked, scourged, spat upon, and nailed to a cross, he suffered the disgrace of the lowest of criminals; of glory because, notwithstanding all appearances to the contrary, this was his moment of victory over Satan as, fulfilling the grand purpose of his coming, he achieved the redemption of the world. Hence, as he came face to face with this "hour" he told his apostles: "The hour has come for the Son of Man to be glorified," and he prayed earnestly: "Father, the hour has come; glorify thy Son that the Son may glorify thee" (Jn. 12:23; 17:1). This, however, did not make it any the less a bitter hour of indescribable anguish which he was sorely tempted to avoid: "Now is my soul troubled," he cried. "And what shall I say? 'Father, save me from this hour'? No, for this purpose I have come to this hour" (Jn. 12:27). For the joy that was set before him, the joy of the restoration of all things, he endured the cross and absorbed its shame (Heb. 12:2). Only at Calvary were his opponents able to give effect to their homicidal designs.

The point is this: that Christ Jesus came into the world to save sinners (1 Tim. 1:15), and that it should be apparent to the world that he was dying for sinners. This being so, it was appropriate that he should die the death of a criminal, and, what is more, the death of the lowest of criminals, thereby indicating that no sinner, however depraved, is beyond the reach of the love and grace that flow freely from his cross. Crucifixion was exactly such a death. It was the manner of execution reserved for the most degraded of criminals, and it was so abhorrent even to the Romans, who were not renowned for moderation, that it was forbidden for a Roman citizen to suffer the disgrace of being put to death by crucifixion.

It was also necessary, of course, that Jesus should be innocent and free from all offense, not only privately within himself but also publicly before the world. His guiltlessness was plainly attested to all by the perfect consistency of his life of loving and selfless service. But there was need also of a judicial declaration of his innocence, so that it might be inescapably clear that his crucifixion was the execution of an innocent man. Hence the significance of the formal process of his trial before Pontius Pilate and of Pilate's repeated assertions that he found no fault in him (Lk. 23:4, 14, 22; cf. Mt. 27:24)—a verdict strikingly confirmed by the admission of the penitent thief to his fellow malefactor as they suffered on either side of Jesus: "We indeed [have been condemned] justly, for we are receiving the due reward of our deeds; but this man has done nothing wrong" (Lk. 23:41).

The innocence of Jesus was in turn a necessity if he was to suffer and die as a substitute for the guilty. The vicarious role of his person on the cross is essential to a right comprehension of what was taking place there, for it was there that he achieved the objective of the incarnation, namely, "to give his life as a ransom in the place of many" (Mk. 10:45; cf. 1 Tim. 2:6; Tit. 2:14). It is the teaching of St. Paul, who wrote that "while we were yet helpless, at the right time Christ died for the ungodly," and that "God shows his love for us in that while we were yet sinners Christ died for us" (Rom. 5:6, 8); of St. John, who declared that "by this we know love, that he laid down his life for us" (1 Jn. 3:16); and also of St. Peter, who asserted that "Christ died for sins once for all, the righteous for the unrighteous, that he might bring us to God" (1 Pet. 3:18).[1]

The substitutionary function of the death of Jesus was indeed dramatically illustrated in the event itself, for he was nailed to a cross that had been prepared for someone else. Jesus, who had been pronounced innocent, was put to death on the cross to which Barabbas should have been nailed, and Barabbas was a notorious criminal who had been sentenced to death for insurrection and murder. Literally, and for all to see, Christ died at Calvary the innocent for the guilty, the holy one in the place of the unholy sinner. The punishment due to Barabbas was inflicted on Jesus, and Barabbas walked away a free man. This is a paradigm of the deep spiritual significance of the cross of Christ, for the redemptive reality of what took place on that cross is not local and temporary but cosmic and eternal in its dimensions. The blood shed in sacrifice on that cross was not the blood of a brute beast or of a sinful human being, but "the blood of Christ, who through the eternal Spirit offered himself without blemish to God," blood which purifies the conscience of guilty sinners from dead works to serve the living God (Heb. 9:14). It is the perfect atoning sacrifice offered by the perfect high priest once for all. By this "single offering he

1. See also Jn. 10:11, 15; 2 Cor. 5:14f.; Gal. 2:20; Eph. 5:2; 1 Thess. 5:9f.; Heb. 2:9.

has perfected for all time those who are being sanctified" (Heb. 9:26; 10:14). Through the blood of his cross he has made peace and ensured the reconciliation of all things (Col. 1:20). In him, the crucified Lord, we have redemption through his blood, the forgiveness of our trespasses, according to the riches of God's grace which he lavished upon us (Eph. 1:7f.). Thanks to what took place on the cross, "Jesus Christ the righteous . . . is the propitiation for our sins, and not for ours only but also for the sins of the whole world" (1 Jn. 2:1f.).

Christ effectively removed the curse that sinful man had brought on himself by absorbing in his person on the cross the dreadful force of that curse. The marks of the curse were displayed in the thorns with which he was crowned, in the sweat of his ordeal, in the pain and agony of his affliction, and in the last weakness of his dying.[2] Indeed, the very manner of his dying showed that he had made himself accursed for us. "Christ redeemed us from the curse," St. Paul says, "having become a curse for us—for it is written, 'Cursed be every one who hangs on a tree'" (Gal. 3:13; Dt. 21:23). What was taking place on the cross of Christ was of immense significance for our fallen race, for there he who is above all the Blessed One became accursed in our stead.

The grasping of this truth was a life-changing experience for Martin Luther; its wonder and its glory never dimmed for him, and it was at the heart of the gospel he loved to proclaim. He wrote, for example, that

> our most merciful Father, seeing us to be oppressed and overwhelmed with the curse of the law, and so to be holden under the same that we could never be delivered from it by our own power, sent his only Son into the world and laid upon him the sins of all men, saying: Be thou Peter that denier, Paul that persecutor, blasphemer, and cruel oppressor, David that adulterer, that sinner which did eat the apple in Paradise, that thief which hanged upon the cross, and briefly, be thou the person which hath committed the sins of all men.[3]

And likewise John Calvin, who declared that "we shall behold the person of a sinner and evildoer represented in Christ, yet from his shining innocence it will at the same time be obvious that he was burdened with another's sins rather than his own." The conclusion follows inescapably: "This is our acquittal: the guilt that held us liable for punishment has been transferred to the head of the Son of God"—a truth of such central importance that it merits the exhortation: "We must, above all, remember this substitution, lest we tremble and remain anxious throughout life—as if God's righteous vengeance, which the Son of God has taken upon himself, still hung over us."[4]

In the death of Christ substitution and propitiation belong closely together: it is through substitution that propitiation is effected. There has been

2. See Gen. 3:16ff., where thorns, sweat, pain, and death are consequences of the curse.
3. M. Luther, *St. Paul's Epistle to the Galatians*, the 'Middleton' edn. (1807) of the English version of 1575, rev. by P. S. Watson (London, 1953), p. 272 (on 3:13).
4. J. Calvin, *Institutes* II.xvi.5.

much misunderstanding about this. That the Father arbitrarily and for his own pleasure sacrificed his innocent Son is not what is intended, nor that the Son, being well disposed to us, by sacrificing himself propitiated the Father who was ill disposed to us. God cannot be divided, and in no way can the Son be placed at variance with the Father. There are not two conflicting wills and attitudes within the Godhead, for God is one and the divine unity is a unity not only of essence but also of mind and purpose and action. Nor are the love and the justice of God incompatible with each other, as some have wished to persuade us. For God to be loving and merciful to sinners does not require that he should set aside his justice. The coinciding of substitution and propitiation at the cross of Christ is the assurance that divine love and divine justice meet there in perfect unison. The redemption of man restores the *order* of creation. "God is not a God of confusion, but of peace" (1 Cor. 14:33). The design of the cross was not merely to save the sinner but also to deal with sin, and the one could not be accomplished without the other. A God who condoned or ignored the continuing presence of evil in his creation would be neither all-holy nor all-loving. The cross of Christ exhibits God's holy intolerance of sin and disorder as well as his redeeming love for his fallen creatures. If it is not the place of divine judgment it is not the fount of divine love.

No one has insisted more strongly on the *holiness* of God's love than P. T. Forsyth. God's holiness as Judge was the impulse of redemption no less than his love as Creator. Sinful man's great and desperate need was to be justified, to be able to stand before and be accepted by an altogether holy God. Indeed, as Forsyth declared, "the central question in religion" is "How shall I stand before my judge?"[5] God would not be God if he left the issue of sin unresolved. But how could the unholy creature possibly meet the demand of his holy Creator? None but God can meet that requirement, and it was out of pure love for us that he himself satisfied the demand of his holiness in our stead. At Calvary it was not the Son propitiating the Father but God propitiating himself. The vicarious self-sacrifice on the cross was also the self-propitiation of God. Propitiation starts, continues, and ends with God, who "in Christ was reconciling the world to himself" (2 Cor. 5:19).[6] Forsyth has well said that "we live in a saved world only because we live in a judged world,"[7] and that it is God's holiness which gives his love divine value.

5. P. T. Forsyth, *The Cruciality of the Cross* (London, 1909; 2nd edn. 1948), p. 59.
6. C. E. B. Cranfield comments with reference to Rom. 3:25: "We take it that what Paul's statement that God purposed Christ as a propitiatory victim means is that God, because in his mercy he willed to forgive sinful men and, being truly merciful, willed to forgive them righteously, that is, without in any way condoning their sin, purposed to direct against His own very Self in the person of His Son the full weight of that righteous wrath which they deserved" (*The Epistle to the Romans* [new ICC series], Vol. I [Edinburgh, 1975], p. 217). For a fuller discussion of the theme of propitiation see Leon Morris, *The Apostolic Preaching of the Cross* (Grand Rapids, 1955), pp. 125-85.
7. P. T. Forsyth, *Missions in State and Church* (London, 1908), p. 72.

And [he continued] it is meaningless without judgment. The one thing he could not do was simply to wipe the slate and wipe off the loss. He must either inflict punishment or assume it. And he chose the latter course, as honoring the law while saving the guilty. He took his own judgment.[8]

Again, he has written, referring to Schiller's dictum, "The world's history is the world's judgment" (true in a sense though this is):

It is not the world's history, but Christ's history that is the world's judgment. And especially is it Christ's Cross. The Cross, I keep saying, is God's final judgment on the world. It is the eternal moral measure of the world. . . . [Christ] is eternal Judge in his great work as the Crucified, a work historic, yet timeless and final. . . . The absolute and irreversible judgment was passed upon evil. There, too, the judgment of our sins fell once for all on the Holy One and the Just. The judgment Christ exercises stands on the judgment he endured. He assumes judgment because he absorbed it. Salvation and judgment are intertwined.[9]

With similar perception James Denney has written:

The very glory of the Atonement was that it manifested the righteousness of God; it demonstrated God's consistency with His own character, which would have been violated alike by indifference to sinners and by indifference to that universal moral order—that law of God—in which alone eternal life is possible.

And again:

Always, where we have Christian experience to deal with, it is the Christ through whom the divine forgiveness comes to us at the Cross—the Christ of the substitutionary Atonement, who bore all our burden alone, and did a work to which we can for ever recur, but to which we did not and do not and never can contribute at all.[10]

On the cross, then, satisfaction was made for the sin of mankind, and that satisfaction was made not only to God but also by God in the person of the incarnate Son. There the root problem of our fallenness and alienation was dealt with once and forever. The lifeline linking us to our Creator was reconnected. The power to conform ourselves to the divine image of our constitution was recovered. Our true humanity was reestablished. All this was achieved for us by the Son, who humbled himself to the depth of our God-forsakenness so that, by taking it to himself, he might remove it from us. There is no depth lower than that. The incarnate Son's cry of dereliction, "My God, my God, why hast thou forsaken me?" is the most terrible, the most horror-filled cry in the whole of history. It was the cry of his shatteredness as he entered into our hell for us.

8. *The Cruciality of the Cross*, p. 98.
9. *Missions in State and Church*, p. 73.
10. James Denney, *The Atonement and the Modern Mind* (London, 1910), pp. 51 and 116.

His forsakenness opened the way for our acceptance. Such is the awesome mystery of that cross with the Son of God nailed to it in our place. And this was the purpose of the incarnation which made this dreadful self-obliteration possible.

It is true that the Son endured our dereliction in that he was incarnate, that what he suffered was suffered Man for man; but the eternal Son is not in any way to be removed from this suffering. To dissociate the human nature from the divine nature of Christ in such a way as to make them independently functioning entities would disrupt the unity of his person and so resuscitate ancient heresy. The desire to "protect" the deity of Christ from the endurance of the torment of Calvary must be resisted. What was experienced by Christ as our fellow human being and in our place was experienced by the eternal Son of God. It was the Word who is God who became flesh and who gave his flesh for the life of the world (Jn. 1:1, 14; 6:51). It is the Son of God who loved me and gave himself for me (Gal. 2:20). And this means that this was nothing less than *the doing of God.* Jesus in action was God in action. From first to last the work of redemption is the work of God: "All this is from God, who through Christ reconciled us to himself" (2 Cor. 5:18; Col. 1:20). The incarnation was the means to this end, and God was no more insulated from the means than he is from the end. Hence the Apostle's assurance that in the incarnate Savior all the fulness of God was pleased to dwell, and in him to dwell bodily (Col. 1:19; 2:9). By virtue of the incarnation God's putting himself in our place became a reality, even to the extreme of self-alienation. So great a mystery we cannot fathom, but we can and should be grateful for the manifestation of such love and compassion bestowed on us at so incalculable a cost. St. Paul even spoke of God as having purchased his church with his own blood (Acts 20:28);[11] for while the blood shed on the cross was specifically the blood of the incarnate Son, yet it was also in its total setting the blood of God. "Salvation," the redeemed chant in heaven, "belongs to our God who sits upon the throne and to the Lamb" (Rev. 7:10).

---

11. The Greek text reads *tēn ekklēsian tou theou hēn periepoiēsato dia tou haimatos tou idiou.* Some have wished to render this "the church of God which he purchased with the blood of his own," understanding "of his own" to mean "of his own Son"; but, though this might seem to ease what otherwise would be a bold expression, it is awkward and unnatural linguistically. The variant reading *kyriou* for *theou* can claim to be evenly attested, but the likelihood is that it was introduced as a modification by a redactor or scribe who felt it more proper to speak of the Lord (Jesus Christ) as having purchased the church with his own blood. This accordingly is an occasion when the more difficult reading should prevail.

CHAPTER 31

Understanding the Atonement

Differing theories regarding the manner and effect of the atonement have been classified in general as either objective or subjective: if objective, the emphasis is placed on the change in the attitude of God produced by the self-sacrifice of Christ; if subjective, the change in the attitude of man is stressed. This, however, is a generalization which cannot be made to fit every theory that has been advanced. Though the patristic authors in the centuries immediately following the apostolic age may seem, in their concern for christological orthodoxy, to have been preoccupied with the doctrine of the person of Christ, yet, as we have previously observed, this was necessary not only because of the propagation of a great variety of heterodox notions concerning Christ's person which needed refutation, but also because they rightly perceived that false teaching about the person of Christ could only be destructive of a correct understanding of the reconciling work of Christ. The whole purpose of the incarnation was our redemption. The person of Christ receives its full meaning from the work of Christ. Irenaeus, for example, in the second century, asked: "How could he have subdued him who was stronger than men and had not only overcome man but also retained him under his power, and conquered him who had conquered, as he set man free who had been conquered, unless he were greater than man who had thus been conquered?[1] But who is superior to and more eminent than that man who was formed after the likeness of God unless the Son of God after whose image man was made?"[2] It was not alone by his manifestation as the incarnate Word, Irenaeus said, that he revealed and restored us to that image in which we were created, but also by means of his passion: "For doing away with that disobedience of man which at the beginning had taken place in connection with a tree, 'he became obedient unto death, even the death of the cross,'[3] healing that disobedience which had taken place in connection with a tree by that obedience which was on the tree."[4]

We have already seen that Athanasius, in his treatise *On the Incarnation*

1. The allusion is to Lk. 11:21f., where the strong man is Satan and the stronger one is Christ.
2. Irenaeus, *Against Heresies* IV.xxxiii.4.
3. Phil. 2:8.
4. Irenaeus, *Against Heresies* V.xvi.3.

of the Word of God which he wrote as a young man some years before the Council of Nicea, affirmed that the Son, for whom as God death was an impossibility, took to himself in the incarnation a body capable of death, so that he might offer it up in place of us all:[5] "He took, in natural fitness, a mortal body, in order that death might in it once for all be done away and also that men made after the image might once more be renewed. None other but the Image of the Father was sufficient for this need."[6] Thus he confidently declared that "the cross has not been a disaster but a healing of creation."[7] And we find him writing to the same effect some forty years later that, in order to bring man back to his Creator and to replace his mortality with eternal life, God

> sends his own Son, who becomes Son of Man by taking created flesh, so that, since all were under sentence of death, he, being other than them all, might himself for all offer to death his own body, and that henceforth, as if all had died through him, the word of that sentence might be accomplished (for "all died" in Christ),[8] and all through him might thereupon become free from sin and from the curse which came through sin, and might truly abide for ever, risen from the dead and clothed in immortality and incorruption.[9]

We may also cite Augustine to illustrate the patristic recognition of the indissoluble connection between the person of Christ and the work of Christ. The "true sacrifice" which is "due to the one true God . . . cannot be rightly offered," Augustine wrote, "except by a holy and righteous priest"; moreover, this sacrifice must be "received from those for whom it is offered," and must also be "without fault, so that it may be offered for cleansing the faulty." Then, echoing the doctrine of the Epistle to the Hebrews, Augustine affirmed that "the only Son of God" alone was qualified to act as "so holy and righteous a priest," since, being himself free from all sin, "he had no need to purge his own sins by sacrifice"; and, as it was a sacrifice offered for us human beings, "what," he asked, "could be so acceptably offered and taken as the flesh of our sacrifice made the body of our priest?" Our "one and true Mediator," therefore, was by his deity one with him to whom he offered, and by his incarnation one with those for whom he offered, whom also he makes one in himself, while he himself was in one both the offerer and the offering. Thus in the person and work of the incarnate Son, and in him uniquely, what Augustine held to be the four requirements for every sacrifice met together, namely, "to whom it is to be offered, by whom it is to be offered, what is offered, and for whom it is offered."[10] No terser summary of the bond that holds together the person and the work of Christ could be

---

5. *Body* here stands for our humanity in its wholeness, as in Heb. 10:5, 10. See p. 276 above.

6. Athanasius, *On the Incarnation* 9, 13.

7. *Against the Heathen* 1. The *Contra Gentes* and the *De incarnatione* belong together as two parts of a single work.

8. 2 Cor. 5:14f.

9. *Orations against the Arians* ii.69.

10. Augustine, *On the Trinity* iv.14.

desired than that which is enshrined in the christological affirmation of the creed of Nicea: "... very God of very God, ... being of one substance with the Father, ... who for us men and for our salvation came down from heaven, and was incarnate by the Holy Ghost of the Virgin Mary, and was made man, and was crucified also for us under Pontius Pilate...." This declaration of belief has been the recital of the universal church from generation to generation.

A theory that gained some currency in the patristic period maintained that Christ effected our redemption by offering himself as a ransom to the devil. It was intended as an explanation of those passages in the New Testament which describe the work of Christ in terms of a ransom given for mankind. Thus Jesus said of himself that he had come "to give his life as a ransom for many" (Mk. 10:45), and St. Paul stated no less plainly that "Christ Jesus gave himself as a ransom for all" (1 Tim. 2:6). This, too, is the import of 1 Corinthians 6:20 and 7:23, "you were bought with a price," and 1 Peter 1:18f., "you were ransomed with the precious blood of Christ" (cf. 2 Pet. 2:1; Acts 20:28). The emphasis in such passages is on the *costliness* as well as the *substitutionary* aspect of our redemption. To ask the question *to whom* the ransom was paid we can now judge to have been ill advised; but asked it was. Before the end of the second century, Irenaeus had expressed himself in such a way as to imply that man was ransomed by a price paid to the devil, who had unjustly seized control of what was by nature the property of God. The Word of God, however, as Irenaeus saw it, shunning violence and injustice, had recovered what was God's own by means of persuasion, "giving his soul for our souls and his flesh for our flesh," and "attaching man to God by his own incarnation."[11] This certainly indicates some kind of transaction with the devil; but the notion received more explicit formulation during the first half of the following century, when Origen, confronting the inquiry, "To whom did Christ give his life as a ransom for many?", responded that "it was certainly not to God," and suggested that it was paid to the Evil One, who "held us in his power until the ransom for us, namely, the life of Jesus, was given to him." He explained, further, that it was a transaction in which the devil was deceived, since his strength was not sufficient to retain the incarnate Word under the power of death,[12] thus approving the idea of deception.

The fourth century was well advanced when Gregory of Nyssa propounded an elaborate development of this concept. According to Gregory, man had sold himself to the devil and by doing so had become the legal property of the devil, who rightfully held us as his slaves. If God was to regain possession of us, Gregory argued, this could not be achieved by an arbitrary measure, but only in a manner that was "consonant with justice"—that is to say, God was obliged to "make over to the slave's master (Satan) whatever ransom he might agree to accept for the person in his possession." Another factor to be considered was the virtual certainty that the devil would wish to make a profit on the deal: "What would he accept for the thing he held," Gregory asked, "but some-

11. Irenaeus, *Against Heresies* V.i.1.
12. Origen, *Commentary on Matthew* xvi.8; cf. xii.8.

thing assuredly higher and better in the way of ransom, that thus, by receiving a gain in the exchange, he might promote his own special passion of pride?" In view of the wonderful power wielded by Jesus in healing the sick, raising the dead, feeding the multitudes, calming tempests, and so on, the offer of his person in exchange for us appeared to be a most attractive proposition. "The enemy," Gregory explained, "beholding in him such power, saw also in him an opportunity for an advance, in the exchange, on the value of what he held. For this reason he chose him as a ransom for those who were shut up in the prison of death."

Satan, however, was deceived and trapped. He had not realized that the phenomenal power of Jesus belonged not to his human but to his divine nature. In accepting his humanity, therefore, he was not getting the bargain he expected. Christ's deity was "hidden under the veil of our nature," like a hook concealed by the tempting bait; consequently, Gregory concluded, "as with a ravenous fish, the hook of the deity was gulped down with the bait of flesh," and the house of death was penetrated by life and its darkness dispelled by the light of God.[13] If it seems that God, according to this scheme, engaged in a certain amount of deceit to procure our emancipation, Gregory admitted that "some measure of fraud" was involved and was justified not only as a means to a good end, but also because Satan was receiving back some of his own medicine: "By the reasonable rule of justice, he who practiced deception receives in return that very treatment, the seeds of which he had himself sown of his own free will. He who first deceived man by the bait of sensual pleasure is himself deceived by the presentment of the human form." Satan deceived for an evil but God for a noble purpose.[14]

This notion of a pious fraud practiced by God on the devil seemed also to be attractive, at least for a while, to the minds of some of the Latin fathers. Ambrose, for example, saw Christ's imposition of silence on his disciples and on demons regarding his true identity (Mt. 16:20; Lk. 4:35) as designed to conceal his divine nature from the devil who, according to this theory, did not believe that Jesus was the Son of God.[15] The devil's net in which we were ensnared (cf. Ps. 124:7) was broken for us to escape when what seemed to be a more gainful prey was offered to our captor, for, hastening to seize this prey, namely, the body of Christ, the devil was caught in his own net (cf. Ps. 57:6).[16] Augustine argued similarly that in accepting Christ's blood as the price for our deliverance Satan himself was bound instead of enriched,[17] and that it was by the very death of Christ over which he at first exulted that the devil was

13. Gregory of Nyssa, *The Great Catechism* 22-24.
14. Ibid. 26.
15. Ambrose, *Exposition of the Gospel of Luke* ii.3. Ambrose understood Christ's refusal to give proof in the wilderness that he was the Son of God as a concealment from the devil of his divinity—a concealment confirmed, he held, by the evident weakness of the human nature of Jesus there and on the cross (loc. cit. and iv.12). Ambrose actually uses the expression *pia fraus,* "pious fraud" (iv.16).
16. Ibid. iv.12.
17. Augustine, *On the Trinity* xiii.19.

defeated—like a mouse attracted by bait in a trap: "The mousetrap for the devil was the Lord's cross; the bait by which he was caught, the Lord's death; and behold, our Lord Jesus Christ has risen: where now is his death on the tree?"[18] It is a scheme, however, which is not developed and enlarged on by either Ambrose or Augustine. The concentration of their interest is much more on the vicarious character of Christ's death[19] and on the perception that the conqueror of the first Adam who held the human race in thrall has himself been conquered and mankind delivered by him who is the second Adam.[20]

The idea that it was to Satan that Christ offered himself as a ransom was far from being generally approved. Gregory of Nazianzus, writing late in the fourth century, stated that the questions to whom the blood shed for us was offered and why it was shed were "neglected by most people." We were, he granted, "detained in bondage by the evil one, sold under sin" (Rom. 6:16; 7:14), and it was true that ordinarily a ransom was offered to the one who held others in bondage, but he dismissed as outrageous the notion not only that Satan should receive a ransom from God but also that the ransom paid should consist of God himself. Nor would he accept that the ransom was paid to the Father, since it was not by him that we were being oppressed. The question, then, *to whom* the ransom was paid fell away; the death of Christ was simply the price of our redemption and the means of our liberation from the bondage of sin.[21] But Gregory of Nazianzus did not exclude the view that the Deceiver was himself deceived by God: "after he had cheated us with the hope of becoming gods," he said (cf. Gen. 3:5), "he was himself cheated by God's assumption of our nature"; thinking that he was attacking Adam, he really met with God, and thus the old Adam was saved by the new Adam.[22] In similar vein the eighth-century theologian John of Damascus exclaimed: "God forbid that the blood of the Lord should have been offered to the Tyrant!"; but at the same time he asserted that the devil, "swallowing the body as a bait, was transfixed on the hook of divinity," even though he regarded the ransom as received by the Father for us.[23]

That the theory continued to enjoy a measure of popularity into the medieval period is apparent from the rejection by Anselm (d. 1109) of any notion that the devil had a just claim to hold men as his possession and that God had to do business with the devil as it were on an equal footing. Anselm insisted that all the justice was on God's side and none on the devil's, and indeed that the devil no less than man was an apostate creature answerable to his Creator.[24] The symmetry of Irenaeus's conception of recapitulation, in which the disobedience of Adam was counterbalanced by the obedience of Christ, Eve by Mary,

18. Sermon cclxiii.1.
19. See, e.g., Ambrose, *Luke* iv.12; Augustine, *Enchiridion* 41, *Against Faustus the Manichean* xiv.7.
20. E.g., Augustine, *On the Trinity* xiii.23.
21. Gregory of Nazianzus, *Oration 45,* The Second Oration on Easter 22.
22. *Oration 39,* On the Holy Lights 13.
23. John of Damascus, *On the Orthodox Faith* iii.27.
24. Anselm, *Cur Deus Homo? (Why did God become man?)* i.7.

and the tree of the forbidden fruit by the tree of the cross, was strongly attractive to the mind of Anselm,[25] who likewise emphasized the important link between redemption and creation. For the human race, so precious to God, to have utterly perished without any reconciling intervention by God himself would have meant the frustration of the divine purpose of creation (as Athanasius so clearly appreciated); and that would have been anything but fitting: hence the central necessity of redemption in Christ by which the will of the Creator is brought to its destined fulfilment.[26] The alternative to this was unthinkable: "Either God will perfect in human nature that which he began or it is in vain that he made a nature so exalted and capable of so much good." The heart of Anselm's argument is precisely this: that God cannot complete what he designed in human nature "except through an entire satisfaction for sin, which no sinner can make for himself."[27]

The concept of satisfaction is the key to the understanding of Anselm's objective view of the atonement. The sinner, Anselm explained, stands before God as a debtor who is under obligation to repay what he owes. What man is duty bound to pay to his Creator is summed up in the sentence: "The whole will of a rational creature ought to be subject to the will of God"; and sin is not to pay what one owes.[28] Otherwise stated, man owes God his own self in its entirety, with this consequence, that if he sins he has of himself nothing with which to make amends for sin.[29] But Anselm postulated a further problem, contending that the repayment of amends commensurate with the offense required a sum in excess of the equivalent amount, on the ground that the sinner had not only failed to subject himself to God's will but also, thus failing, had deprived God of the honor due to him; and so compensation for the exact amount owing needed to be supplemented by damages for the injury done to the divine dignity.[30] This led to the conclusion that the reparation for sin could be made only by one who was greater than man, indeed, "greater than all that is not God," which meant that it was a reparation which God alone could make. But for God as such to do this would still be no solution of the problem, for if amends were not made by man it could not be said that man had made amends. It followed, then, that "the satisfaction, which God only can and man only should make, must needs be made by one who is both God and man."[31] And this is the logic of the incarnation, whereby the eternal Son, who is God, is enabled, as our fellowman, to pay the debt of our sin for us.

Christ lived his life in complete submission to the Father's will and therefore was altogether free from obligation to forfeit his life in death. "He freely offered to his Father what he would never have been obliged to lose and paid

25. Ibid. i.3; ii.8.
26. Ibid. i.4.
27. Ibid. ii.4.
28. Ibid. i.11.
29. Ibid. i.20.
30. Ibid. i.11, 21.
31. Ibid. ii.6f.

for sinners what on his own account he did not owe." But then, according to Anselm, the Father would have appeared to be unjust had he not recompensed the Son for going beyond what was required of him, that is, by his dying on the cross. But this in turn raised the question as to what recompense could be made to him who had need of nothing and who himself had nothing to be remitted. For him to have remained unrewarded would have made it appear, Anselm argued, that all he had done had been done in vain. Anselm solved this dilemma by explaining that Christ could rightly desire his recompense to be allocated to others of his choice, and that to none could this recompense more fittingly be transferred than "to those for whose salvation he became man and to whom in dying he gave the example of dying for righteousness' sake."[32]

The value of Anselm's theory lies in his insistence, which is thoroughly in line with the teaching of the New Testament, that man is totally incapable of saving himself and therefore that the salvation of mankind is owed entirely to the grace and mercy of God, who is its sole author and perfecter. The defects of the theory, however, are serious. Anselm failed, in the argument offered in his *Cur Deus Homo?*, to penetrate to the heart of what was really taking place on the cross. His thought was unduly influenced by the legal or juridical conventions of his day, and his argumentation was governed in the end by a medieval notion of merit, and in particular surplus merit, which was incompatible with the viewpoint of Scripture. In his logic, the death of Christ became a work of supererogation which made possible the assignment of his surplus merit to us; and this left a big question mark over the cross. Yet, though his doctrine of satisfaction was seriously flawed, satisfaction is an important facet of the truth revealed to us in the living and the dying of the incarnate Son. It is implicit in the strong biblical concept of propitiation and reconciliation, but always with this understanding, that it is God who provides all that is necessary for the satisfaction of his justice and holiness in the person and work of Christ. In postulating a claim of the Son on the Father for a reward on the ground of surplus merit Anselm came perilously, even though unintentionally, close to making a breach in the unity of the Godhead.

The *Cur Deus Homo?*, because of its somewhat theoretical and academic character, should not be accepted as representing the full intensity of the evangelical significance of the atonement for Anselm in his devotional life and pastoral ministry. A surer guide to this is found in the prayer offered at the close of his *Sermon on the Lord's Passion* and his *Admonition to a Dying Man,* from which we now quote.

> Lord Jesus Christ, the Good Shepherd, who condescended to die for your flock, acknowledge me among your sheep and lead me to your pasture. You who drank the bitter cup for me, enable me to share in your glory. Your punishments torture my conscience and your torments my memory: for I feared to drink the potion you drank; the sins you bore were my sins; I, an obstinate

32. Ibid. ii.19, 20.

slave, committed the crimes for which you were flogged; it was my debts that were paid by you; my iniquity was the cause of your death and my misdeeds brought about your wounds. Alas for my sins for which atonement had to be made by so bitter a death. . . . O unspeakable mercy! . . . that when satisfaction for guilt was owed by none but man and none but God was able to provide it, he showed his mercy by becoming man, and, though he owed nothing for himself, paid our debt by dying for us. . . . Behold how God did not spare his own Son but delivered him up for us (Rom. 8:32). O the grace of him who does this! O the holiness of that death! O good Jesus! O holy Jesus! what shall I render to you, what shall I endure for you who endured so often and so much for me? The display of what you have done is the proof of your love. What am I to do who am the unworthy recipient of this love? How can I return this love? Take what is your own; do with your servant what seems good to you. . . . You gave yourself completely for me and my salvation is completely your work. You bought my spirit for yourself, you bought my body for yourself, both are there to serve you. I am yours in spirit and in body. . . . O good Lord, what shall I render to you for such great blessings, I a worthless slave and unprofitable servant? Shall I rejoice or mourn because of your death? Indeed, I will do both. I will rejoice because of the grace of him who delivered you up and because of the love of him who died. But first I will mourn over the cause of that death, that is, because of the consciousness of my sin, and I will mourn with him who dies. If I do not rejoice, I am ungrateful; if I do not mourn, I am unfeeling. . . .[33]

And this is how, as a faithful pastor, he interrogated and gave spiritual counsel to one who was near to death:

Q. Do you confess that your life has been so evil that you deserve eternal punishment?
A. I confess it.
Q. Do you repent of this?
A. I repent. . . .
Q. Do you believe that the Lord Jesus Christ died for you?
A. I believe it.
Q. Are you thankful to him?
A. I am.
Q. Do you believe that you cannot be saved except through his death?
A. I do believe this.
Q. Then do this while the soul remains in you; place your whole trust in this death alone and have no trust in any other thing; commit yourself wholly to this death; cover yourself wholly with it alone; wrap yourself wholly in this death; and if the Lord God should wish to judge you, say: "Lord, I interpose the death of our Lord Jesus Christ between me and your judgment; in no other way do I argue with you." And if he should say to you,

33. Anselm, *Sermo de passione Domini* (Migne, *PL,* CLVIII, cols. 675f.).

"It is because you are a sinner," say: "Lord, I plead the death of our Lord Jesus Christ between you and my sins." If he should say to you, "It is because you deserve condemnation," say: "Lord, I place the death of our Lord Jesus Christ between you and my demerits, and I offer his merit in place of the merit which I owe and do not have." If he should say that he is angry with you, say: "Lord, I place the death of our Lord Jesus Christ between me and your anger. . . ."[34]

Anselm's younger contemporary Peter Abelard (1079-1142) had a very different understanding of the manner in which reconciliation has been made possible through Christ. His thought has been especially influential on many who have embraced a subjective view of the atonement, and there is some justification for seeing him as a forerunner of those who would today be called liberal theologians. Abelard had little time for the idea of original sin and the fallenness of human nature, and the heterodox character of his christological opinions was responsible for his downfall. Indeed, as he presented things, Jesus seemed to differ from the holy men of old only in degree, appearing as an inspiring example of one in whom the true potential of human nature became fully actualized, and through whom atonement is effected as his selfless example evokes on our part the response of our love. "We are justified by the blood of Christ and reconciled to God," Abelard taught, "in that through the singular grace displayed to us by the assumption of our nature, by his instruction of us by word and example, and by his perseverance even to death, he has by love bound us more closely to himself, so that, thanks to the ardor of so great a divine blessing, the true love which is now ours should draw back from no suffering for his sake." Our redemption, then, "is that supreme love in us resulting from Christ's passion, love which not only sets us free from the bondage of sin but also makes real for us the liberty of the children of God." Thus in the thought of Abelard the response of our love to Christ's love for us is to all intents and purposes synonymous with redemption and justification. As Abelard expressed it, "we are now justified by Christ's blood unto salvation, that is to say, through the love which we now have in him, thanks to this supreme grace which he displayed to us by dying for us who hitherto were sinners."[35] It is with good reason that Abelard's theory of the atonement has generally been described as the moral influence theory.

Like Anselm, Abelard also asked the question, "Why did God become man?"[36] He answered it by declaring that the highest and greatest blessing consequent on the taking of flesh by the Wisdom of God from the Virgin was that "he illumined us with his light and displayed to us his love." Like Anselm again,

---

34. Anselm, *Admonitio morienti* (Migne, *PL*, CLVIII, cols. 685-87).
35. Abelard, *Exposition of Paul's Letter to the Romans* (Migne, *PL*, CLXXVIII, cols. 836, 861).
36. *Cur Deus Homo?* is the heading of chapter 28 of his *Epitome theologiae christianae*.

he rejected the idea that the devil had any right to retain man in his power or that Christ's self-offering was a ransom paid to the devil, maintaining, rather, that it was from the bondage of sin that man needed to be set free. This was a distinction of some importance for Abelard if only because it enabled him to move the focus away from the objectivity of the devil (at this point) and to place it on the subjectivity of man. Even though he spoke of the Son as "offering himself as a recompense and pure victim to the Father," the emphasis was on the infusion of his love into us. There was, he contended, no absolute necessity for the incarnation and the cross as the means of our redemption; this method was decided on simply as the best means of achieving the desired end. As a demonstration of the greatness of God's love for man it was designed to inflame man with greater love for God. The Son of God became man, Abelard explained, "in order that as a suitable mediator he might set man free from sin and communicate his love to him"—and he sounded an unwonted vicarious note by adding that Christ accomplished this "by offering to the Father the man he had assumed, that is, by giving as payment man for man."[37] This is an indication that an objective strand was not entirely excluded from the thought of Abelard, even if as a whole his view of the atonement was predominantly subjective and moralistic.

The brilliance of Abelard's mind and the attractiveness of his person won him prominence and a considerable following in the France of his day; but his boldness in propagating opinions of questionable orthodoxy aroused serious concern. In 1121 a council convened at Soissons condemned him as a Sabellian without according him the right to speak in his own defense; and again in 1140 he was summoned to appear in Sens before a synod whose members were more distinguished in their persons and more just in their conduct; but on this occasion, perhaps somewhat surprisingly for one both eloquent and loquacious, he refused to avail himself of the opportunity of explaining his position and instead, condemned by the synod on fourteen counts, he appealed to Rome. Bernard of Clairvaux (1090-1153), Abelard's junior by nineteen years, had played a leading role in the exposure of his theological aberrations. The pope in due course confirmed the synod's condemnation and, imposing silence on Abelard and seclusion in a convent, ordered his books to be burned. It was a sad ending for a man of spectacular gifts whose headstrong propensity for speculation carried him beyond the boundaries defined in the teaching of the New Testament.

In our own century Gustaf Aulén made a plea for the recognition and reinstatement of a third theory of the atonement, supposedly distinct from both subjective and objective theories, which he maintained was the "classic" theory of the patristic period. His lectures propounding this theme, given at the University of Uppsala in 1930, were published under the title *Christus Victor*. The title itself was suggestive of the thrust of the "classic" view, which, according to Aulén, perceived the coming of Christ as God engaging in cosmic warfare with the forces of evil in order to bring about reconciliation between himself

---

37. *Epitome* (Migne, *PL*, CLXXVIII, cols. 1730-32).

and the world. Aulén cited the teaching of Irenaeus as "a thoroughly typical example" of the classic understanding of atonement.[38] There is no question that the theme of conflict between God and evil is prominent in the New Testament, and that in its pages Christ is depicted as having victoriously achieved the purpose of his coming, which was to destroy the works of the devil (see, e.g., 1 Jn. 3:6; Heb. 2:14); and it is no doubt true that this aspect of the atonement has in more recent times suffered from a measure of neglect. But Aulén made too sharp a division. The "classic" view is only one facet of a profoundly rich spectrum. Those whom he regarded as its exponents were not intent, as he imagined, on disallowing "any sort of justification by legal righteousness"[39] or "satisfaction of God's justice."[40] The concepts of satisfaction, propitiation, substitution, and divine justice are clearly important not only in the biblical doctrine of the atonement but also in the mainstream of patristic orthodoxy. They can hardly be depreciated as an idiosyncrasy of the "objective," or, as Aulén called it, the "Latin," type of interpretation, as though they lacked "classic" authenticity. Moreover, for Luther, who, Aulén asserted, "stands out in the history of Christian doctrine as the man who expressed the classic idea of the atonement with greater power than any before him,"[41] the objective understanding of Christ's death was far from being alien and dispensable.[42]

The biblical exposition of the significance of the atonement is by no means monolithic. The merciful love of God manifested at Calvary, the satisfaction of his holy justice in redeeming us from sin, the mortal conflict with the demonic forces of evil, and the moving of our hearts to respond to divine grace are not alternatives, nor are they mutually exclusive. They belong together. To isolate or to exclude the one from the others impoverishes and distorts the truth of our redemption. The dying of the incarnate Son on the cross is indeed the supreme demonstration of God's love for us (Rom. 5:8; 1 Jn. 4:10); but Calvary is at the same time the place where God's justice is satisfied through the offering of Jesus Christ the Righteous as the propitiation for our sins and in our place, the Righteous for the unrighteous (2 Cor. 5:21; 1 Jn. 2:1f.; 1 Pet. 3:18); and it is there that the decisive battle in the war against Satan was fought and won and our liberation from his bondage achieved (Heb. 2:14f.). The divine love is inseparable from the divine justice and conquest. Only this immeasurable love of God for us has the power to awaken the response of love in our cold hearts, so that we are able to say, "We love because he first loved us" (1 Jn. 4:19).

Accordingly, in Augustine, whose doctrine of the atonement is strongly "objective," there is a clear emphasis on the "subjective" response that God's love manifested in Christ should elicit from his human creatures. The purpose of Christ's coming, Augustine taught, was "that man should learn how much

38. Gustaf Aulén, *Christus Victor,* tr. A. G. Hebert (London, 1931), p. 50.
39. Ibid., p. 51.
40. Ibid., p. 163.
41. Ibid., p. 138.
42. See below, pp. 353f.

God loves him . . . to the intent that he might be kindled to the love of him by whom he was first loved, and also might love his neighbor at the command and showing of him who became our neighbor." Nothing, he declared, was more adverse to love than human pride, the primal sin, which is the cause of human misery: "For here is a great misery, proud man! But there is greater mercy, a humble God!" Then there follows an admonition to take this love as the end that is set before us.[43] It would be seriously wrong, however, to conclude that the evocation of love exhausted the meaning and purpose of the atonement in the mind of Augustine. He certainly had no time for the notion that the significance of Christ's suffering was merely exemplary, "that all that the cross does is to provide for us an example for our imitation in contending even to death for the truth," describing this as a supposition which was characteristic of the "natural" or unregenerate man (cf. 1 Cor. 2:14).[44] Fallen man lacks both the will and the power to follow Christ's example. Our very ability to love rises not within ourselves, or by way of imitation, but is received through the bestowal of the grace of God's redeeming love in Christ Jesus. The love of God, as also the grace of God with which it is one, always comes first:

> The love with which God loves is incomprehensible and immutable; for it was not from the time that we were reconciled to him by the blood of his Son that he began to love us; but he did so before the foundation of the world, that we also might be his sons along with his Only-Begotten, before as yet we had any existence of our own.[45]

No more was it the intention of Anselm, for all his "objectivity" in seeking to comprehend the purpose of the incarnation, to separate the justice of God from the merciful love of God, as is evident from the concluding section of his treatise:

> We find that the mercy of God, which seemed to you to vanish away when we were considering God's justice and man's sin, is so great and so much in accord with justice that it would be impossible to imagine anything greater or more just. What indeed could be understood as more merciful than for God the Father to say to the sinner condemned to eternal torments and having no means of redeeming himself, "Receive my only-begotten Son and offer him for yourself," and for the Son himself to say, "Take me and redeem yourself"?[46]

As for Martin Luther, he, no less than Anselm, spoke in the clearest possible manner of the awful holiness of God's justice that was displayed and satisfied by the death of Christ on the cross, as, for example, the following passage shows:

43. Augustine, *On Catechizing the Uninstructed* iv.8.
44. *Tractate on the Gospel of John* xcviii.3.
45. Ibid. cx.6.
46. Anselm, *Cur Deus Homo?* ii.21.

They contemplate Christ's passion aright who view it with a terror-stricken heart and a despairing conscience. This terror must be felt as you witness the stern wrath and the unchanging earnestness with which God looks upon sin and sinners, so much so that he was unwilling to release sinners even for his only and dearest Son without his payment of the severest payment for them. Thus he says in Isaiah 53, "I have chastised him for the transgressions of my people." . . . It must be an inexpressible and unbearable earnestness that forces such a great and infinite person to suffer and to die to appease it. And if you seriously consider that it is God's very own Son, the eternal Wisdom of the Father, who suffers, you will be terrified indeed. . . . For every nail that pierces Christ more than one hundred thousand should in justice pierce you. . . . St. Bernard was so terrified by this that he declared, "I regarded myself secure; I was not aware of the eternal sentence that had been passed on me in heaven until I saw that God's only Son had compassion upon me and offered to bear this sentence for me."[47]

The cross, in other words, proclaims the utter futility of all self-trust and self-security and demonstrates the absolute seriousness of sin and the absolute reality of judgment at the same time as it exhibits the infinite love of God for sinners, for it is both the seat of God's judgment and the source of his grace. As this truth is grasped the penitent and believing sinner "subjectively" finds his terror and hostility and despair replaced by love and peace and gratitude. That "subjectivity" has its proper place side by side with "objectivity" was plain to Luther, who in the same work from which we have just quoted declared, with reference to the suffering Lord:

You must pass beyond that [namely, the terror occasioned by divine judgment] and see his friendly heart and how this heart beats with such love for you that it impels him to bear with pain your conscience and your sin. Then your heart will be filled with love for him, and the confidence of your faith will be strengthened. . . . Thus you will find the divine and kind paternal heart, and, as Christ says, you will be drawn to the Father through him. Then you will understand the words of Christ, "For God so loved the world that he gave his only Son, etc." (Jn. 3:16).[48]

47. M. Luther, *A Meditation on Christ's Passion,* tr. M. H. Bertram, *Luther's Works,* Vol. XLII (Philadelphia, 1969), pp. 8f.
48. Ibid., p. 13. It is of interest that in his first sermon on Genesis 3, preached in 1526, Luther resurrected the theory that God deceived the devil by concealing the hook of Christ's divinity under the bait of his humanity which the devil eagerly swallowed. The imagery was that of a fisherman taking a rod and line and covering over the hook with a worm. Christ appeared to be no more than a poor pitiable worm, as indeed he called himself in Ps. 22:6, a mere man who suffered hunger, thirst, pain, and sorrow, like any other man. Thus tricked, the devil was choked and had to spew Christ forth, so to speak, as the whale did the prophet Jonah, and so it was in fact the devil, not Christ, who was caught (*D. Martin Luthers Werke* [Weimarer Ausgabe], Vol. XX, pp. 334f.).

CHAPTER 32

The Continuing Debate

During the two centuries which followed the Reformation the church, weakened within and assailed from without by deism, moralism, and rationalism, lost its way and its momentum. Many of those who remained nominally within the ranks of Christianity turned away from the historic absolutes of the faith, setting up man as the ultimate arbiter of religious authenticity and applying their energies to works of spiritual demolition rather than edification. The nineteenth century developed as the age of radical criticism in and by the church of its classical standards and foundations. There was indeed in some quarters a reactionary movement away from the frigid mentalism of the Enlightenment to a type of romantic and sentimental subjectivism which emphasized inner warmth and feeling as the center of religious reality; but this could hardly be described as a return to the Christianity of the New Testament. The leading exponent of this position, Friedrich Schleiermacher (1768-1834), regarded feeling as the heart of religion and equated salvation with man's inner awareness of absolute dependence on and oneness with God—a condition, he held, which was fully realized in the person and work of Christ, in contrast to us who are afflicted with a consciousness of sin and imperfection. This predicament of ours is savingly overcome, according to Schleiermacher, as we enter into fellowship with the Redeemer by allowing impulses to flow from him to us so that our lives become more and more filled and formed by his God-consciousness. In this way Christ, reciprocally, "enters into the corporate life of man and sympathetically shares the consciousness of sin, but shares it as something he is to overcome."[1] Schleiermacher took this to be the meaning of those scriptural passages which speak of Christ as being in us and of our being dead to sin and putting on the new in place of the old man. He maintained that we are brought into fellowship with Christ by assent to the influence of his activity which he arouses within us.[2]

Schleiermacher supposed that Christ's priestly office was fulfilled by the suffering of opposition and indifference which was alien to him as the perfectly

---

1. F. Schleiermacher, *The Christian Faith,* ET (Edinburgh, 1960), pp. 425f. The original German edition was published in 1821/22.
2. Ibid., p. 426.

sinless one, but to which he was exposed in the society of sinful mankind, and that through the endurance of this suffering "he had a sympathetic feeling of the world's sin, and thus carried that sin."[3] It was, further, "in virtue of his own perfect fulfilment of the divine will" that Christ, as our high priest, "presents us pure before God"; for, thanks to our sympathetic oneness with him, "the impulse to the fulfilling of that will is also active in us" and "is recognized by God as absolute and eternal," even though it is always less than perfect.[4] While the suffering of Christ has, in Schleiermacher's view, abolished the punishment that is our due, our involvement in the fellowship of his suffering engages us in the work of satisfaction for our and the world's sin, in such a way that "all those who are assumed into the fellowship of Christ's life are called to share the fellowship of his suffering, until the time when sin has been completely overcome and through suffering satisfaction has been made in the corporate life of humanity."[5] The effect of this theory is to substitute the subjectivity of feeling for the objectivity of the cross—indeed, it is impossible to see any real necessity for the cross in Schleiermacher's system—and the end to which it is directed is the universalizing of pious sentiment.

Much the same can be said of the position propounded by Albrecht Ritschl (1822-1889), to whose mind any objective understanding of the atonement had no appeal. As he saw things, it was through his unmerited sufferings that Christ "completely demonstrated his fellowship with sinful humanity, for the purpose of moving them to repentance,"[6] and it was in consequence of "the incalculable and mysterious interaction" between our freedom and the fellowship which is ours by attaching ourselves to the unique lifework of Christ that we become possessors of justification and reconciliation. The ground on which we are justified, that is, admitted in spite of our sins to fellowship with God, is, Ritschl declared, simply "Christ's value for God" and "the determining influence" upon us of his fellowship with God. Faith is described as "the subjective manifestation of fellowship with Christ."[7] Thus "to believe in Christ implies that we accept the value of the divine love, which is manifest in his work, for our reconciliation with God, with that trust which, directed to him, subordinates itself to God as his and our Father," and in this way "we are assured of eternal life and blessedness." Faith in Christ, Ritschl added, "is neither belief in the truth of his history nor assent to a scientific judgment of knowledge such as that presented in the Chalcedonian formula."[8]

We may readily agree that genuine saving faith is something more and deeper than historical knowledge and intellectual assent; but this does not

3. Ibid., p. 453.
4. Ibid., p. 455.
5. Ibid., pp. 458, 461.
6. A. Ritschl, *The Christian Doctrine of Justification and Reconciliation*, ET (Edinburgh, 1900), p. 565. The original German edition was published in 1874.
7. Ibid., pp. 577, 578.
8. Ibid., p. 591.

mean, as the position elaborated by Ritschl seems to imply, that the great acts of God which are the foundation of New Testament faith are not historically true and that the objective absolutes of the Christian creed are dispensable. Like Schleiermacher, Ritschl had no logical place in his system for the cross, except perhaps as an instrument of martyrdom by which Christ consummated the discharge of his suffering vocation. Emphasis on the cross, so central in the teaching of Christ and his apostles, is lacking because there is no intrinsic necessity for the cross in his concept of salvation.[9]

Ritschl's theory of justification and reconciliation became widely influential and enjoyed a dominant position in German theological circles in the generation that followed his death; but, as was to be expected, it aroused critical responses because of the idiosyncratic manner in which he left out of account doctrinal emphases prominent in the historic faith of the church. James Denney, for example, criticized the system of salvation formulated by Ritschl on three main counts. He objected, in the first place, that it was based on an inadequate conception of Christ's person. "Ritschl often speaks of his Godhead," Denney wrote, "but he means by this nothing more than that Jesus in his actual situation was as good as God could have been. He refuses to raise any question whatever—historical, physical, or metaphysical—as to the origin of Christ's person." He asserted, secondly, that Ritschl had an inadequate view of Christ's vocation. This was a consequence of his ill-defined presentation of Christ's person, which placed him in the world exactly on a level with us to face life and death without reference to Easter or Pentecost, let alone his preexistence. Of this attitude Denney said: "In ignoring the Resurrection, which is Christ's real triumph over death, in ignoring the gift and the teaching of the Holy Spirit, which so interpret the life and death of Christ as to make them the foundation of the Christian religion, it seems to me to abandon the New Testament all together." Denney observed, further, that "what Ritschl's theory amounts to is, that Christ redeemed us from death as the debt of nature, by showing how to trust God's love even in that extremity"; whereas "what the apostolic doctrine shows is how Christ redeems us from death by dying *our* death himself, and bearing our sins for us." And this led to his third major criticism, namely, that Ritschl's position "does not treat sin with the seriousness with which it is treated in the New Testament, and it does not put the work of Christ in any precise relation to sin at all."[10]

Denney rightly complained that there was no good news in the formulation offered by Ritschl, no real balm for the sinner who, his conscience weighed down with guilt, is thirsting for forgiveness; and he restated the nature of Christ's redemptive mission in the following terms: "Christ bears our sins; *that*

9. In the summary given by Ritschl of his position (*Justification and Reconciliation,* pp. 607f.), the cross is not even mentioned.
10. James Denney, *Studies in Theology* (9th edn.; London, 1904), pp. 141-43. The chapters in this book were given as lectures in the U.S.A. in 1894.

is the very soul of his vocation; he bears them in his body on the tree; and there is therefore now no condemnation to them that are in him. He does not disillusion us; he ransoms us with his blood. Unto him be glory for ever."[11] In his book *The Death of Christ* Denney again stressed the central importance of the substitutionary and propitiatory character of Christ's death which, as "the key to the whole of the New Testament teaching," "bids us say, as we look at the Cross, *He* bore *our* sins, *He* died *our* death," adding that "it is *so* His love constrains us."[12] It is difficult to see how the doctrine of redemption propounded by Christ and his apostles in the New Testament could lead more clearly to any other conclusion than that expressed by Denney regarding Christ as the propitiation for our sins: "I do not know any word which conveys the truth of this if 'vicarious' or 'substitutionary' does not, nor do I know any interpretation of Christ's death which enables us to regard it as a demonstration of love, if this vicarious or substitutionary character is denied."[13]

Denney's criticisms and conclusions rested on a characteristically careful study of the teaching of the New Testament, but their tenability was denied out of hand by Hastings Rashdall in his Bampton Lectures for 1915 on "The Idea of Atonement in Christian Theology." Rashdall refused to acknowledge Christ's death on the cross as in itself unique or substitutionary, holding to the view that "the death was an incident in a real human life" and that it could be described as necessary only in the relative or incidental sense that "some sort of death . . . was a necessary element in any really human life." The type of death actually suffered by Jesus, he declared, did not come about through his own freedom of will and action, except insofar as it "came to him as the direct and necessary consequence of his faithfulness to his messianic calling." Rashdall even contended that death was not intrinsically indispensable for the fulfilment of that calling. "To the very last," he asserted, "according to the Synoptists, our Lord conceived it as possible that he might accomplish that task without the necessity of dying a violent death."[14]

To say this, however, is disingenuously to fly in the face of the forthright testimony of the Synoptic Gospels, which, as we have seen,[15] report the emphatic and reiterated teaching of Jesus regarding the necessity of his going to Jerusalem to suffer death there and on the third day to rise again. This is further confirmed by St. Luke's account of the instruction given by Jesus to the apostles after his resurrection as he proved from the Scriptures the cardinal significance of his death on the cross (Lk. 24:44-48). Nor does Christ's prayer in the garden of Gethsemane that, if possible according to the Father's will, the suffer-

11. Ibid., p. 145.
12. *The Death of Christ: Its Place and Interpretation in the New Testament* (London, 1902), p. 178.
13. Ibid., p. 176.
14. Hastings Rashdall, *The Idea of Atonement in Christian Theology* (London, 1919), pp. 440f.
15. See p. 335 above.

ing of Calvary might be removed from him provide support for Rashdall's contention; for what happened from then on confirmed beyond dispute the absolute necessity of the cross. It testified, moreover, to the union of the will of the Son with the will of the Father; otherwise the cross would have become a spectacle of paternal cruelty and divine disharmony by which the literally crucial message of the New Testament must forever be falsified. Only by arbitrarily sweeping aside as inadmissible evidence or by attributing to "the belief of the Church" (that is, as a notion or interpretation later devised and imposed on the supposed simplicity of the original events) whatever was incompatible with his preconceptions could Rashdall circumvent facts like these. He could not but grant that the Synoptic Gospels "all contain traces of the common belief of the Church as to the redeeming efficacy of Christ's death" (the implication being that the common belief of the church was other than the belief of Christ); but then without a blush he averred that "in none of them is there any definite theory, substitutionary or other, as to the source of its necessity or the nature of its efficacy." The fact, for example, that both the First and the Second Gospels contain Christ's statement that he had come to give his life as a ransom in place of many was not permitted to be an embarrassment; Rashdall simply denied that it was "a genuine saying of Jesus," with the convenient rider that "it must represent a current formula of the Church."[16]

It was convenient also for Rashdall to leave the Fourth Gospel out of account, on the ground that it is a gospel "which criticism is almost unanimous in repudiating."[17] Thus discredited, the admission that "in the Johannine writings there is a strong underlying sense of some profound necessity for Christ's death" can cease to be a factor to be reckoned with. Even so, Rashdall offered an astonishing piece of special pleading by categorically asserting that, "so far as any actual explanation or formulated doctrine is concerned, there is not a word which necessarily implies a substitutionary sacrifice or, indeed, any literal sacrifice at all: nothing that implies that Christ died for man in any sense other than that which a supreme benefactor of humanity might be said to die for men—though of course he is for the writer much more than a supreme benefactor"; and, further, that "all that is said of the effects of that death may quite well be understood of its subjective effects upon the believer in Christ."[18] And Rashdall wished us to believe that this was the case with St. Paul's as well as St. John's writings. The following opinion suitably summarizes his attitude to the evidence of the New Testament: "After all, the fundamental idea both of St. John and of St. Paul is simply that the death of Christ, the culminating act in a life of self-sacrifice, is the supreme manifestation of Christ's love, and therefore of the love of the Father whom he reveals; and that the contempla-

16. Ibid., p. 174. For Rashdall's argument in defense of this supposition see pp. 29ff and 49ff.

17. Ibid., p. 444.

18. Ibid., pp. 178, 179.

tion of that life and death gives other men the power, as nothing else has done, to overcome temptation and to lead lives like his."[19] This is the subjective theory with a vengeance. It illustrates what is virtually a law in the history of Christian thought, that a subjective attitude to the teaching of the New Testament is commonly associated with a prejudiced and blinkered subjective interpretation of the significance of Christ's death.

There is every justification for describing Rashdall's understanding of the atonement as Abelardian. Abelard was before all others his model. There was no one he quoted more admiringly, though he was, if anything, more radically subjective than Abelard in his appraisal of the significance of Christ's crucifixion. "In Abelard," he wrote, "not only the ransom theory but any kind of substitutionary or expiatory atonement is explicitly denied. We get rid altogether of the notion of a mysterious guilt which, by an abstract necessity of things, required to be extinguished by death or suffering. . . . The efficacy of Christ's death is now quite definitely and explicitly explained by its subjective influence upon the mind of the sinner." And he cited approvingly Abelard's declaration: "I think, therefore, that the purpose and cause of the incarnation was that he might illuminate the world by his wisdom and excite it to the love of himself."[20] Rashdall's sympathies, not surprisingly, were Socinian as well as Abelardian, for Socinus, one of the founding fathers of modern antitrinitarianism, had denied the deity of Christ and rejected the doctrine of his death as a substitutionary sacrifice.[21] Thus he praised Socinus as the one from whom came "the first protest against the immoralities of the traditional doctrine" and expressed his pleasure also with contemporary Unitarianism inasmuch as it, "too, was originally quite as much a protest against the traditional doctrine of the atonement as against the traditional view of the Trinity," adding that "the value of these protests must be acknowledged by all who feel how deeply the traditional views have libelled the view of God's character."[22]

The Bible, however, knows no dichotomy between the love of God and the justice of God, and it does not ask us, as the Socinian does, to choose the God who is loving and reject the God who is just. We can no more live with a God who is unjust than we can live with a God who is unloving. Our own justification before God rests on the solid reality that the fulfilling of God's justice in Christ was at the same time the fulfilling of his love for us. Precisely because he is the propitiation for our sins Jesus Christ the righteous is our advocate in the heavenly sanctuary (1 Jn. 2:1f.). The repudiation of the objectivity of God's reconciling action at Calvary is conducive to the negation of the deity of Christ, since the latter is no longer seen as a necessity for our salvation, and this in turn is conducive to a doctrine of self-salvation inspired by the example

19. Ibid., pp. 184f.
20. Ibid., p. 358.
21. Socinus's book *On the Saviour Jesus Christ,* published in 1578, was antagonistic to the teaching of the Reformers on the person and work of Christ.
22. Rashdall, *Atonement,* p. 438.

of Jesus. But, as P. T. Forsyth came to recognize: "The prime doer in Christ's cross was God. Christ was God reconciling. He was God doing the very best for man, and not man doing his very best before God. The former is evangelical Christianity, the latter is humanist Christianity."[23] Accordingly, in the biblical perspective the cross is seen as "the consummation of God's *judgment* in the central act of mercy." There God assumed our judgment instead of inflicting it on us. There could be no greater demonstration of love than this. But justice is as inseparable from God as is his loving mercy. Neither the one nor the other can be set aside. "There alone do you have the *divine* necessity of the cross in a sinful world—the moral necessity of judgment."[24]

If Rashdall imagined that he had sounded the deathknell of the objective view of the atonement, he was mistaken. Admittedly, this view continues to be summarily dismissed as outmoded and incompatible with the supposedly enlightened state of the mind of modern man by scholars who wish to deliver Christianity from what they regard as its supernatural trappings. The truth of the New Testament, however, is still as powerful today as it has been from the beginning. Far from having uttered its last semirespectable gasp in the theological thought of Rashdall's contemporaries Denney and Forsyth, the objective understanding of the atonement remains alive and well. This is sufficiently demonstrated in the *Church Dogmatics* of Karl Barth, whose position on the atonement was insistently and unashamedly objective. Barth stressed the utter inability of man in his fallenness to redeem himself and therefore his total dependence on the possibility of divine intervention on his behalf as his only hope, and he had no inhibitions about the substitutionary and propitiatory character of Christ's self-sacrifice on the cross. Jesus Christ is "the judge judged in our place."[25] Divine judgment, the justice and righteousness of God, cannot be dissociated from the cross without destroying the Christian doctrine of redemption. "If he were not the judge," Barth wrote, "he would not be the Saviour";[26] and "it is not just any judgment which he exercises and executes, but the judgment of God," and "it is for this reason the ultimate judgment."[27]

> What took place is that the Son of God fulfilled the righteous judgment on us men by himself taking our place as man and in our place undergoing the judgment under which we had passed. That is why he came and was amongst us. . . . Everything happened to us exactly as it had to happen, but because God willed to execute his judgment on us in his Son it all happened in his person, as his accusation and condemnation and destruction. He judged, and it was the Judge who was judged, who let himself be judged. Because he was a

23. P. T. Forsyth, *The Cruciality of the Cross* (London, 1948; 1st edn. 1909), p. 17.
24. Ibid., p. 29.
25. This is the heading of Chapter XIV, p. 59, 2, a section which covers pp. 211-83 in the English translation by G. W. Bromiley of part-volume IV/1 of the *Church Dogmatics* (Edinburgh, 1956).
26. K. Barth, *Church Dogmatics,* IV/1, p. 217.
27. Ibid., p. 219.

man like us, he was able to be judged like us. Because he was the Son of God and himself God, he had the competence and the power to allow this to happen to him. . . . *Cur Deus homo?* In order that God might do and accomplish and achieve and complete all this for us wrong-doers, in order that in this way there might be brought about by him our reconciliation with him and conversion to him.[28]

It was on the basis of this understanding that Barth affirmed that "the mystery of his mercy is also the mystery of his righteousness," that God "did not take the unreconciled state of the world lightly, but in all seriousness," and that "he did not will to overcome it and remove it from without, but from within." Thus it was no "act of arbitrary kindness" that he committed, for that "would have been no help to the world." The purpose of the Word's becoming flesh was "that there might be the judgment of sin in the flesh and the resurrection of the flesh."[29] And, regarding the person of this one who suffered and died on the cross, Barth asserted that "it is the eternal God himself who has given himself in his Son to be man, and as man to take upon himself this human passion"; and, regarding his mission, that "it is the Judge who in this passion takes the place of those who ought to be judged."[30]

The loving God who desires to reconcile his sinful creatures to himself is at the same time the just God whose holiness makes it impossible for him to disregard sin as though it were of no consequence. It is not divine justice and divine love that are antithetical to each other, but the holiness of God's righteousness and the unholiness of our sin, or, still more tersely, godliness and ungodliness, between which there can never be agreement. On the cross we see Jesus, the Holy One, suffering instead of us who are unholy, bearing the punishment due to us, dying our death, and thus meeting the demands of God's, and therefore his own, justice; and this is also and simultaneously the supreme manifestation of divine love. The cross unites the love of God with the suffering of God for our justification. It is the proof that "God himself is righteous," in accordance with his holy justice, "and that he justifies him who has faith in Jesus," in accordance with his holy love (Rom. 3:26). As St. John declares: "In this is love, not that we loved God, but that he loved us and sent his Son to be the propitiation for our sins" (1 Jn. 4:10). The heart of that propitiation is the satisfaction of the divine justice. Its motivation is divine love. Our turning in repentance and faith is the response of our love evoked by the grace of this holy and loving God.

28. Ibid., pp. 222f.
29. Ibid., p. 237.
30. Ibid., p. 246.

CHAPTER 33

The Glorification of Christ

The glorification of the incarnate Son is most obviously associated with his resurrection from the dead and his ascension and enthronement on high. The incarnation, by contrast, was his own voluntary act of condescension and self-humiliation whereby he identified himself with our lowly estate and dwelt among us, his eternal glory veiled by the frailty and finitude of the humanity he had assumed. In this state of humiliation he endured scorn and rejection and bitter shame and suffering and was at last one from whom men hid their faces (Is. 53:2f.). Yet, though his deity was concealed by the human nature he had made his own, his coming was the coming of the true light into the world (Jn. 1:9). His perfect goodness was plain to all. The tragic fact that "men loved darkness rather than light" and stood self-condemned by their hatred of the light was evidence, no less plain, of the deep depravity of man in his fallenness. It was because the light of his goodness exposed the evil of the human heart that the incarnate Son was feared and hated (Jn. 1:10f.; 3:19-21). His very innocence convicted others of their guilt. Rather than face the exposure of their deeds and seek forgiveness they turned their backs on his light, thus intensifying the darkness of their hearts. Nonetheless, his dwelling among men was "full of grace and truth" (Jn. 1:14), as all who received him and believed in his name (Jn. 1:12) thankfully confessed.

Those who through the response of personal faith and self-commitment were Christ's own rejoiced in the glory of him who is the Light of the world (Jn. 8:12). Thus St. John could testify: "We have beheld his glory, glory as of the only Son from the Father" (Jn. 1:14), by which, as we have said,[1] he no doubt referred above all to the unforgettable occasion when he, together with St. James his brother and St. Peter, "saw his glory" displayed in transcendental splendor for a brief while on the Mount of Transfiguration (Lk. 9:32; 2 Pet. 1:16-18). We recall, too, how in a different manner, Christ "manifested his glory" for all to see by the miracles he performed, for these were "signs" that attested his deity (Jn. 2:11; Acts 2:22). The healing of the sick and the maimed, the raising of the dead, the mastery of the elements, and the casting out of demons bore witness to the fact that in Christ God was powerfully and recrea-

---

1. See p. 42 above.

tively active. In all such events there was a display of the glory of God. Thus Jesus said of the illness of Lazarus, whom he would raise from the dead: "it is for the glory of God, so that the Son of God may be glorified by means of it" (Jn. 11:4).

But there was, further, a different and deeper glory which was not so immediately perceptible, and that was Christ's undeviating commitment to the mission he had come into our world to fulfil. The supreme and culminating moment in the achievement of this mission was his offering of himself to death on the cross. To die on a cross was indeed the most inglorious way of dying. No death was more shameful. But, inglorious though it was, that death was at the same time in a hidden way the moment of his glorification; for, as we have previously noticed,[2] it was for *this hour* that he came into the world: the "hour" when he was crucified was specifically the "hour" of the accomplishment of his mission. The cross which looked like his defeat was in fact the place of his victory and of Satan's defeat. It was the attainment of the goal of his coming. Though the cross looked like his disastrous failure, it was in fact the place where we were everlastingly redeemed. That is why, when the time of his terrible ordeal drew near, Jesus was able to declare, "The hour has come for the Son of Man to be glorified" (Jn. 12:23), and could assert with confidence: "Now is the Son of Man glorified, and in him God is glorified; if God is glorified in him, God will also glorify him in himself, and glorify him at once" (Jn. 13:31f.). The fulness of unity and harmony of will between the Father and the Son is evident in the fact that the Son's glorification of the Father is also the Father's glorification of the Son. No greater assurance of the indefectibility of his redemption could be desired by the Christian believer than the words addressed to the Father by the incarnate Son as he delivered himself over to death: "I have glorified thee on earth, having accomplished the work which thou gavest me to do" (Jn. 17:4). The cross, for all its darkness, both real and apparent, is suffused with glory, the glory of the triumph of the reconciling grace of God which flows freely to us from that cross. That is why the redeemed sinner glories in that cross (Gal. 6:14) and glorifies the Savior who steadfastly, "for the joy that was set before him, endured the cross, despising the shame," and is now glorified on high (Heb. 12:2).

The glory of the ascended Christ is his crowning glory. In the words of the author of the Epistle to the Hebrews, "we see Jesus, who for a little while was made lower than the angels, crowned with glory and honor because of the suffering of death" (Heb. 2:9). Having made purification for sins, that is to say, the mission of his incarnation completed, he is now enthroned at the right hand of the Majesty on high (Heb. 1:3; 10:12). Because "he humbled himself and became obedient unto death, even death on a cross, therefore God has highly exalted him and bestowed on him the name which is above every name, that at the name of Jesus every knee should bow, in heaven and on earth and under

2. See p. 336 above.

the earth, and every tongue confess that Jesus Christ is Lord, to the glory of God the Father" (Phil. 2:8-11; cf. Eph. 1:20-23; 1 Pet. 3:22). Thus the Son, still incarnate, has returned to his rightful glory and is glorified as our victorious Redeemer forevermore. In his vision on the isle of Patmos the exiled Apostle was given the privilege of hearing the music of this unceasing praise coming from the myriads of the heavenly hosts as they sang with a loud voice, "Worthy is the Lamb who was slain, to receive power and wealth and wisdom and might and honor and glory and blessing," and the multitudes of God's redeemed creation chanting, "To him who sits upon the throne, even to the Lamb, be blessing and honor and glory and might for ever and ever!" (Rev. 5:11-14).

As Christ's death on the cross (though glorious in that by it he infallibly achieved the purpose of his incarnation) was the lowest depth of his self-abnegation and humiliation for our sakes, so his glorification in the sense of his exaltation began with his resurrection from the dead, continued with his ascension, and will have its consummation in his return to establish the renewed creation from which all hostility and defilement have been completely eliminated. All this takes place in accordance with the divine plan and timetable. St. Peter, for instance, wrote of the prophets as having predicted "the sufferings of Christ and the subsequent glory" (1 Pet. 1:10f., 21), as also in the earliest days of the apostolic church he had informed his audience in Jerusalem: "The God of Abraham and of Isaac and of Jacob, the God of our fathers, glorified his servant Jesus, whom you delivered up" (Acts 3:13).

As we turn our attention now to the first stage of the glorification of Jesus consequent on the completion of his atoning work on the cross, that is, his resurrection from the dead, it must be stated without equivocation that unless it is *bodily* resurrection which is intended we are not speaking about resurrection from the dead at all. This is not to deny that, as with other terms, the word *resurrection* can be employed metaphorically in such a way as to mean something other than a literal rising from the dead. A politician, for example, may speak of the resurrection of national pride and influence or a historian of a resurrection of learning. A person's influence may continue after death through the lives of those he has instructed or through the books he has written or in some other way, but that does not mean that he has risen from the dead; on the contrary, such things are said of one who is known to be dead and buried. No more does the postulation of the continuing existence of a person's soul after death imply the resurrection of that person, for it is the soul of one who is known to be dead and buried. It would very properly be demanded that a claim that a person has risen from the dead must be substantiated by evidence of the return to life from the dead; and that evidence would consist, first of all, in the reappearance of the one who had died, soul and body reunited, and secondly, in the demonstration that there is no longer a corpse in the coffin. In the New Testament, resurrection plainly means *bodily* resurrection, not only with regard to Christ but also with regard to believers who, having died, await the general resurrection at the last day when there will be a reunion of soul and body. In the nature of the case, resurrection that is not bodily is not resurrection from the dead.

This being so, those who deny the possibility of bodily resurrection because, as they suppose, modern scientific man knows that such a thing does not happen (or for any other reason) are faced with the necessity of explaining how the notion that Jesus rose from the dead became current in the apostolic church. Emil Brunner pointed out that "even the unbelieving historian cannot get away from" the fact "that it was the appearances of the Risen Lord which brought the shattered and scattered disciples together again after the catastrophe of Good Friday, and formed the real foundation of the Christian Church"; for, though "he may judge these 'appearances' to be purely subjective," yet, "he cannot shake the actual fact of belief in the Resurrection as the basis of the Christian Church."[3] As we shall see, however, Brunner's own understanding of the resurrection of Jesus was clouded in a fog of equivocation. But first we may observe that the skeptical theologian as well as the unbelieving historian wishes to persuade himself and us that the Easter appearances were no more than subjective experiences. We have been told, for instance, that, whether because of wishful thinking or because of a flash of extra-historical intuition, "the amazing 'truth' dawned" on Peter, "to solve all his problems: Jesus was not dead after all—he had risen again, he was raised to God's right hand in heaven, he would soon return to establish his kingdom in power"; that "Peter's experience was soon told to the others"; and that "so great is the power of hysteria within a small community that in the evening, in the candlelight, with fear of arrest still a force, and hope of resolution budding in them too, it seemed as if the Lord came through the locked door to them, and away again." It was thus, we are asked to believe, through the subjectively real but objectively mistaken experience of the apostles that the magnetism of Jesus reached out and prevailed beyond the grave, and, with the help of later additions and embellishments, provided a basis for the development of Christianity.[4]

Rudolf Bultmann was a theologian who made positive affirmations about the resurrection of Jesus, but his method of demythologization and existential reinterpretation transformed it into an event that was entirely removed from past history. The saving event or complex of the incarnation, crucifixion, and resurrection of Christ became historically real, according to Bultmann, only in the act of proclamation. "The salvation-occurrence," he wrote, "is nowhere present except in the proclaiming, accosting, demanding, and promising word of preaching."[5] Consequently, "the salvation-occurrence is eschatological occurrence just in this fact, that it does not become a fact of the past but constantly takes place anew in the present," since "in the proclamation Christ himself, indeed God himself, encounters the hearer, and the 'Now' in which the

---

3. E. Brunner, *Dogmatics,* Vol. II (Philadelphia, 1952), p. 366.
4. *The Myth of God Incarnate* (Philadelphia, 1977), pp. 59f.
5. This statement was in fact emphasized by Bultmann.

preached word sounds forth is the 'Now' of the eschatological occurrence itself."[6] In this way the historicity of the resurrection is denied to the past and redesigned as the present and private historicity of existential encounter; it is given "a locus in the actual living of men which is true 'history.'"[7]

The importance of the subjective aspect of the believer's encounter with the risen Lord of course should not be minimized; nothing could be more real and moving for the person who experiences the truth of the saving message. But to eliminate the truth of the resurrection of Jesus as a real and pivotal event which took place, objectively, at a particular time and place in the historical sequence is to kick away the foundation of the building. What is subjective reality for the Christian is based on and is the response to objective factuality. Objective falsity cannot be the source of subjective truth. How can belief in an error or a mirage not also itself be an error or a mirage? Bultmann's existentialization is no more than the extension of the subjective experience of the apostles, shorn of objectivity, from past to present, and in particular its realization in my own individual present, since my history is, *ex hypothesi,* the only history that can have any meaning for me. Thus if I think that the existential reality for me of the resurrection validates it as an event of history outside of my own experience I am in effect sharing in the hallucination of the first believers. What, then, am I believing when I profess belief in the resurrection of Jesus from the dead?—not a fact of past history but a floating notion, a personal value-judgment, which holds fast to the term "resurrection" while emptying it of meaning.

To demythologize or dehistoricize the resurrection of Jesus leaves one with nothing except possibly a share in the original mass hysteria which is supposed to have taken hold of the apostolic community. Despite Bultmann's attempts to persuade us that the pronouncements in the New Testament about the deity of Jesus and his being risen from the dead are not to be taken as ontological pronouncements declaring his supernatural nature and power but only as personal existential pronouncements subjectively expressing his worth and significance for the person who makes them, or, in other words, that a christological pronouncement is really a pronouncement about myself,[8] nothing could be plainer from the doctrine of the apostles in the New Testament than that they unhesitatingly believed in Jesus as the incarnate Son of God and affirmed, as witnesses to the fact, the actual, historical, eventful, objective resurrection of Jesus from the dead.

It is no doubt somewhat surprising to find in Friedrich Schleiermacher a defender of the authenticity of this apostolic witness to the literal rising of Jesus from the dead against the skeptical voices of his day; yet, as the following passage shows, he wielded a critical pen to good effect:

6. R. Bultmann, *Theology of the New Testament,* tr. K. Grobel, Vol. II (London, 1952), p. 302.

7. Ibid., p. 305.

8. See, e.g., R. Bultmann, *Essays* (London, 1955), p. 280.

Anyone . . . who, in view of the miraculous element involved, and to avoid accepting the resurrection of Christ as a literal fact, prefers to suppose that the disciples were deceived and took an inward experience for an outward, ascribes to them such weakness of intellect that not only is their whole testimony to Christ thereby rendered unreliable, but also Christ, in choosing for himself such witnesses, cannot have known what is in men. Or, if we suppose that he himself wished or arranged that they should be constrained to regard an inner experience as outward perception, then he himself would be an originator of error, and all oral conceptions would be thrown into confusion if such a higher dignity as his were compatible with this.

But this seemingly detached judgment of Schleiermacher's was in fact based upon his own merely subjective assessment of the reliability of the apostolic authors as reporters of what they said took place. Thus he maintained, with reference to the Scriptures, that "all that can be required of any Protestant Christian is to believe in them so far as they seem to him to be adequately attested," and that what they teach was to be accepted only "in so far as our judgment about the disciples as original reporters reacts upon our judgment about the Redeemer."[9] This can only imply that the belief or unbelief in the apostolic witness is dictated by the subjective decision of each individual, and that the person who on this basis decides that the apostolic report of the resurrection of Jesus is inadequately attested or unacceptable for some other reason can claim to be as correct in his judgment as Schleiermacher was in reaching an opposite conclusion. Individualism of this kind destroys all certainty.

The unsatisfactory consequences of this position are immediately apparent, for Schleiermacher, holding to the same criterion, then went on to pronounce the New Testament testimony to the ascension inadmissible. "With the ascension it is different," he wrote, "so far at least as we have no adequate reason for maintaining that we have before us a direct report from an eyewitness of what actually happened, and least of all from an apostolic eyewitness."[10] Presumably Schleiermacher had in mind the Lucan accounts (Lk. 24:50f. and

9. F. Schleiermacher, *The Christian Faith* (Edinburgh, 1960), p. 420.
10. Ibid. More recently, W. Pannenberg, who holds that "in the age of technology" we can "no longer speak seriously of the descent and ascent of a heavenly divine being" (see pp. 220f. above), has also expressed acceptance of the historical factuality of the resurrection of Jesus. "The Easter appearances are not to be explained from the Easter faith of the disciples," he says; "rather, conversely, the Easter faith of the disciples is to be explained from the appearances" (*Jesus—God and Man*, p. 96). "How could Jesus' disciples in Jerusalem have proclaimed his resurrection if they could be constantly refuted by viewing the grave in which his body was interred?" he asks; and he cites approvingly the judgment of Paul Althaus that the resurrection kerygma "could not have been maintained in Jerusalem for a single day, for a single hour, if the emptiness of the tomb had not been established as a fact for all concerned" (ibid., p. 100). We too regard this judgment as being eminently reasonable, as well as consonant with the belief and doctrine of the apostles; yet the decision reached by Pannenberg is apparently no less subjective than was Schleiermacher's.

Acts 1:9f.), but, while it is true that St. Luke was not one of the Twelve, there is no good reason for overlooking the assurance he gives that he recorded things "just as they were delivered to us by those who from the beginning were eyewitnesses and ministers of the word," and that he did so for the purpose of communicating the truth (Lk. 1:1-4). St. Luke's concern, in other words, was to reproduce faithfully the firsthand facts that had been communicated to him by the apostolic participants in the history he recounts. One may add that Schleiermacher left himself with a risen but unascended Jesus who after his appearances to the apostles and others not only vanished from the scene, or somehow kept himself in concealment, but who also, it must be supposed, finally succumbed to death, as the psilanthropic element in his christology would seem to demand. This would make nonsense of the apostolic proclamation of Christ's resurrection as the proof of his conquest of death and would suggest that all the effort he expended in dying and rising from the dead was after all a waste of time.

The central significance of the resurrection of Jesus in the faith of the apostolic church is clearly indicated in St. Paul's admonition, "If Christ has not been raised, then our preaching is in vain and your faith is in vain . . . and you are still in your sins" (1 Cor. 15:14, 17). With this judgment Emil Brunner, as we have noticed, seemed to be in full agreement. "Without the fact of Easter," he declared further, "the world would scarcely have heard either of a church or of Jesus himself," for "it was the encounter with the Risen Lord which rescued the disciples from their perplexity and hopelessness, restored their broken faith, and more than this, filled them with jubilant certainty of victory, which was, and remained, the vital element in the Primitive Church." Brunner spoke of the resurrection, moreover, as "this historically indubitable fundamental fact" and drew attention to "the absolute unanimity of the New Testament witness to this fundamental tradition."[11] But this very positive attitude to the factuality of the Easter event did not prevent him from postulating a separation of the teaching concerning the resurrection of Jesus from what he described as "the whole problem of the so-called 'Empty Tomb,'" and thereby placing St. Paul, who does not mention the empty tomb, at variance with the writers of the Gospels, who do. Thus he contended that "while in the Gospel narratives the sight of the Empty Tomb is a matter of independent significance, in the mind of Paul it obviously played no part at all."[12]

This conclusion can only be deplored as patently tendentious and intellectually disreputable. It can be explained only on the supposition that in the mind of Brunner, not Paul, the empty tomb obviously played no part at all. For one thing, the mind of St. Paul is not fully revealed in the few brief writings we have from his pen. Silence regarding a particular event does not automatically imply the author's ignorance or rejection of that event. Because St. John

11. Brunner, *Dogmatics*, Vol. II, p. 366.
12. Ibid., p. 367.

alone narrates the washing of the disciples' feet by Jesus it does not follow that in the minds of the other New Testament writers this incident obviously played no part at all. For another thing, and more importantly, there is no logical way in which the resurrection of Jesus can be divorced from the empty tomb. The latter is an essential part of the witness to the "historically indubitable fundamental fact" of the former. If the tomb was not empty, Jesus was not raised from the dead. The consideration that St. Paul did not himself see the empty tomb does not cancel out its significance for him (or for us who also have not seen it); indeed, it would be unreasonable not to conclude that the testimony of eyewitnesses to the emptiness of the tomb in which Jesus had been buried belonged to the evidence *of first importance* which St. Paul received and passed on, namely, "that Christ died for our sins in accordance with the Scriptures, that he was buried, that he was raised on the third day in accordance with the Scriptures, and that he appeared to Cephas, etc." (1 Cor. 15:3f.). The very sequence of Christ's death, burial, and rising on the third day carries the implication that the tomb was left empty, and that this was the necessary and logical preliminary to the appearances that then followed.

Brunner, however, was evidently intent on denying quite categorically the factuality of the empty tomb and limiting the essential reality of Christ's resurrection to his appearances as experienced by different individuals and groups in their encounters with the risen Redeemer. Because it is widely held (though, in view of the absence of hard evidence, by no means established) that 1 Corinthians was written before the Gospels, Brunner argued that Paul was "the earliest and most reliable of the witnesses to the Resurrection," and on this basis decided that it was not the idea of an empty tomb but the risen Lord, "as a spiritual personal reality," that mattered to him. But this again is a piece of specious argumentation. If the first written reference to the resurrection comes from an author who was not an eyewitness of the empty tomb (St. Paul) and another account written some years later comes from one who was an eyewitness (St. John, say), the former is neither absolutely nor, as these things are normally judged, in the most important sense "the earliest and most reliable witness to the resurrection." Besides, leaving aside the question of the tomb's emptiness, the appearances of the risen Lord were experienced first in order of time by the apostles and other disciples to whom the records (including St. Paul's) refer, and only later, at a time after the forty days, by St. Paul. "Last of all, as to one untimely born, he appeared also to me": thus St. Paul recorded (1 Cor. 15:8) that he was *the last* witness of the resurrection, though not for that reason the least reliable! Only as an author could he be supposed to have been the earliest witness *to* the resurrection; there were many who anticipated him in his witness to the resurrection as a preacher. There is no justification for concluding that his literary priority (if such it was) invested his witness with greater reliability or that his understanding of the Easter event varied from that of those who wrote after him but were witnesses by their preaching before him.

Another strand in Brunner's argument *pro* the appearances and *contra* the empty tomb was his contention that, "according to the agreed narrative of all the witnesses, the meeting of the Risen Lord was only granted to those who believed in him." As evidence of this he cited St. Peter's assertion in Acts 10:40f. that "God raised him on the third day and made him manifest, not to all the people, but to witnesses chosen before by God." These postresurrection appearances, Brunner maintained, took place not in Jerusalem but in Galilee, far away from the tomb, thus confirming his contention that "the original testimony to the Resurrection did not contain any reference to the Empty Tomb, but was solely concerned with the appearances of the Risen Lord to his disciples."[13] Brunner, however, left himself wide open to the charge that he read the New Testament selectively, leaving unmentioned passages that did not support his thesis. Matthew, Luke, and John agree in reporting that the first appearances of the risen Savior actually took place in Jerusalem: to Mary Magdalene close by the empty tomb, on two occasions to the apostles, to Simon Peter, and to the two disciples as they walked from Jerusalem to Emmaus (Mt. 28:9f.; Lk. 24:13ff., 34, 36ff.; Jn. 20:11ff., 19ff., 26ff.). In the list of appearances given by St. Paul, Brunner's "earliest and most reliable witness," some are undoubtedly Jerusalem appearances, those, for example, to Cephas and to the Twelve, and probably the appearance "to more than five hundred at one time" (1 Cor. 15:5f.). Others of course took place in Galilee (see Mt. 28:10; Mk. 16:7; Jn. 21:1ff.).

Brunner's concern, however, was not so much to argue over a question of geographical location as to justify his own belief that the tomb of the risen Lord was not empty at all. To distance the appearances from Jerusalem was thought to rule out pointing to the empty tomb as evidence of the resurrection. Brunner argued, further, that, in contrast to the appearances which were private to believers only, the empty tomb would have been a "world-fact," that is, evidence which was public and open to all, whether believers or not. But the empty tomb *was* a "world-fact," which, as St. Matthew records, caused the chief priests and elders to invent and spread the story that the body of Jesus had been secretly stolen by his disciples during the night (Mt. 28:11ff.). In this way they hoped to cover up the real truth to which the empty tomb was a public witness. Brunner apparently failed to see that a tomb that was not empty would have been no less a "world-fact": the dead body still there would have been an unassailable disproof of the resurrection, and therefore a falsification of the apostolic message in which the raising of Jesus from the dead was a central theme.

If, as Brunner asserted, "all questions of 'how' and 'where' the Resurrection took place, including the question of the Empty Tomb and the physical Resurrection, understood in this sense, are secondary," one can but wonder why the discountenancing of the bodily resurrection and the emptiness of the

13. Ibid., p. 368.

tomb was a matter of such importance to him. He actually blamed belief in the bodily resurrection on belief in the emptiness of the tomb, charging that "emphasis upon the Empty Tomb led to the medieval conception of the 'resurrection of the body.'" (The adjective "medieval" seems to be culpably misleading, for Brunner must have known that the doctrine of the resurrection of the body was a component of the church's orthodoxy from the first century on.) It is sheer confusion, then, for him to profess his own belief in the resurrection of the body, understood in his sense, according to which it was no more, evidently, than the survival or revival of personality, not a physical rising; thus he explained that "the resurrection of the body means the continuity of the individual personality on this side, and on that, of death."[14] But this is the torture of terminology, and one must be excused for preferring to let the resurrection of the body mean precisely what it says. It is simply untrue that "the traditional view of the physical Resurrection is not based upon the testimony of the first witnesses, but upon a later, cruder view."[15]

What Brunner offered was a spiritualization or dematerialization of the doctrine of Christ's resurrection, and it was in line with this that he supposed that the incarnation ended on the cross. One can readily agree with his affirmation that "there, on the Cross, the decisive thing happened, for there the Incarnation of the Son of God—paradoxically—reached its climax."[16] But this does not imply, as Brunner seemed to wish, that there was no need or place for a literal bodily or physical resurrection and a tomb that was empty—that the body of Jesus, its purpose fulfilled, was left to rot in the grave. As the apostles soon realized, the extension of the incarnation beyond Good Friday was of essential importance for the consummation of our redemption in Christ (as we shall see). At first, indeed, the apostles were no more disposed than Brunner to believe that Jesus had physically risen from the dead—to believe, that is, in his resurrection. The words of Mary Magdalene and her companions, who brought them the news of the Lord's rising and of the empty tomb early on the morning of Easter Day, "seemed to them an idle tale, and they did not believe them" (Lk. 24:12); and when he appeared to them in the room where they were closeted they thought they were seeing a ghost (Lk. 24:36f.). It was only after Jesus had invited them to touch him and see for themselves that his was truly a physical presence ("See my hands and my feet, that it is I myself; handle me and see; for a spirit has not flesh and bones as you see that I have") and when he joined them in a meal that they were convinced otherwise (Lk. 24:36ff.; Jn. 20:19ff.; cf. Mt. 28:9).

Clearly, then, to declare that "of the 'Resurrection of the flesh'—as the Apostles' Creed expresses it—the New Testament knows nothing," and that, "on the contrary, this concept is in sharp contradiction to the Christian witness,

14. Ibid., p. 372.
15. Ibid., p. 377.
16. Ibid., p. 372.

especially that of Paul,"[17] is a misrepresentation. As for Paul, Brunner cites the assertion of 1 Corinthians 15:50, "flesh and blood cannot inherit the kingdom of God," as a proof-text, observing that "this body of flesh is not destined for eternity, it is destined to be annihilated."[18] In this passage, however, "flesh and blood" is a mode of expression which designates our present mortal and fallen human nature, which, at the resurrection of the last day, is destined to "put on immortality" and to "bear the image of the man from heaven" (1 Cor. 15:53, 49), that is, to be conformed to the image of Christ who was raised physically from the dead with a spiritual body (1 Cor. 15:44; Rom. 8:29; 2 Cor. 3:18; Phil. 3:20f.).

Though from time to time Brunner expressed impatience with theological liberalism, and especially that of the nineteenth century,[19] his own thought was largely in sympathy with the modern liberal mentality; his discontent seems to have been with the more blatantly destructive manifestations of radical criticism and with certain philosophical preconceptions. He claimed, for example, to be committed to acceptance of the overruling authority of Holy Scripture, stating as he did that "the source and norm of all Christian theology is the Bible," that "the God of the Bible is a God who speaks, and the Word of the Bible is the Word of this God," and that "everything that theology avers must remain within this basic structure and everything that contradicts this fundamental presupposition must be rejected and fought against as an un-Biblical and even anti-Biblical error of speculation or doctrinal distortion."[20] But this strong affirmation did not prevent him from postulating a distinction between doctrine and God's Word. Thus he not only defined orthodoxy pejoratively as "objectivism in doctrine" but also charged it with "equating or failing to distinguish between God's Word and doctrine."[21] In this way he opened the door for himself to separate out and discard doctrine in the Bible which in his judgment was erroneous or unoriginal. His christology in particular suffered crippling amputations as doctrines disapproved by him, such as the virgin birth of Jesus and his bodily resurrection, were cut away.

Likewise the ascension was axed. Brunner argued, following the same method he used to discredit the virgin birth, that as St. Luke was the sole New Testament author who recorded the alleged event of the ascension (Lk. 24:50ff.; Acts 1:9ff.), therefore the ascension "plays no part in the teaching of the Apostles," and, further, is a conception "irreconcilable with that of Paul," with this

17. Brunner, *Dogmatics,* Vol. III, tr. D. Cairns and T. H. L. Parker (London, 1962), p. 412.

18. Ibid., pp. 412f. Brunner conveniently left the flesh and bones of the risen Lord (Lk. 24:39) out of account, St. Luke being discredited as an untrustworthy witness.

19. In *The Divine-Human Encounter* (tr. A. W. Loos [London, 1944], p. 332), e.g., Brunner wrote critically of "the Liberal Theology of the nineteenth century" and its "rationalistic immanental theory" respecting Jesus.

20. Ibid., pp. 30, 46.

21. Ibid., p. 123.

consequence, that "once more we stand at a point where theology must have the courage to be ready to abandon the ecclesiastical tradition."[22] Tendentious "reasoning" of this kind shows the mind of Brunner to be in accord (at least at this point) with the mind of nineteenth-century liberalism. It disregards the teaching of St. Paul that "he who descended is he who also ascended far above all the heavens" (Eph. 4:10), that God by his great might both "raised him from the dead and made him sit at his right hand in the heavenly places" (Eph. 1:19f.; cf. Col. 3:1), and that he was "taken up in glory" (1 Tim. 3:16); the words of Jesus in St. John's Gospel about "the Son of Man ascending where he was before" (Jn. 6:62), and his request to Mary Magdalene at the empty tomb: "Do not hold me, for I have not yet ascended to the Father; but go to my brethren and say to them, I am ascending to my Father and your Father, to my God and your God" (Jn. 20:17); the affirmation of St. Peter that the risen Jesus Christ "has gone into heaven and is at the right hand of God" (1 Pet. 3:22); and also the repeated declaration of the author of the Epistle to the Hebrews that "Jesus the Son of God" is our "great high priest who has passed through the heavens" (Heb. 4:14) and "has entered, not into a sanctuary made with hands, . . . but into heaven itself, now to appear in the presence of God on our behalf" (Heb. 9:24; cf. 1:3; 6:20; 7:26; 9:12; 12:2). Such an accumulation of passages indicates that the ascension of Jesus was very definitely an important element of the christology and the *kerygma* of the New Testament, and therefore of the apostolic church.

22. *Dogmatics,* Vol. II, p. 373.

CHAPTER 34

Christology and History

The liberal label must also be attached to Brunner's conception of the relationship between christology and history. The denial of the supernatural birth of Jesus places in question his understanding of the incarnation, and the notion that the incarnation had its terminal point at the cross was congenial to the distinction he posited between "the Jesus of history" and "the Christ of faith."[1] In the development of modern liberalism the postulation of a separation between faith and history can be traced back to Gotthold Lessing (1729-1781), who had contended that "accidental truths of history can never become the proof of necessary truths of reason,"[2] and Immanuel Kant (1724-1804), who similarly had held that objective events of the past were not commensurate with the subjective reality of personal reason and faith. This was also the subsoil of twentieth-century existentialist individualism. Such an outlook could only come to regard events such as the virgin birth and the resurrection of Jesus as irrelevant and therefore dispensable, even if they did occur, and the exponents of the more explicit antisupernaturalism of contemporary liberal theology, which has no place for the possibility of bodily resurrection from the dead, are for that reason unwilling to speak of the risen *Jesus*; hence the now familiar differentiation in their circles between "the historic Jesus" and "the risen Christ."[3] "Jesus" thus becomes a designation limited to the human, corporeal, earthly person who lived and died in Palestine in the first century. It is a theory with docetic overtones.

This distinction raises the whole issue of the Christian understanding of history. With regard to the historicity of the resurrection of Christ Brun-

---

1. See, e.g., *The Mediator,* tr. Olive Wyon (Philadelphia, 1947), p. 184, where Brunner says that "faith presupposes, as a matter of course, *a priori,* that the Jesus of history is not the same as the Christ of faith."

2. Lessing had been influenced by his discovery of the unpublished work *An Apology or Defence on behalf of the Rational Worshippers of God* by Hermann Reimarus (1694-1768).

3. P. T. Forsyth trenchantly observed that "to divide up the personality, to detach the heavenly Christ from the earthly Jesus, is not a feat of criticism so much as a failure of religion, or an intellectual freak and a confession of unfaith" (*The Person and Place of Jesus Christ,* p. 177).

ner claimed as a basis or proof-text for his position, as we have seen, the words of St. Peter recorded in Acts 10:40f.: "Him God raised up the third day and gave him to be manifest, not to all the people, but unto witnesses that were chosen before of God, even to us who ate and drank with him after he rose from the dead." Referring specifically to this statement, Brunner wrote:

> This is the proof that here we are dealing with a history of a different kind from that of the events recorded of the life of Jesus. It is not wrong, but it is at least liable to misunderstanding to designate the event of Easter simply as an "historical event"; for it is not historical in the same way as other events, because the historical event, in the usual sense, is something which, in principle, everyone can perceive. But Easter is *not* an event of this kind. Historically it is for believers only. It is not part of the historical *continuum,* but at this point the Beyond "breaks into" history.[4]

By way of rejoinder, it should be pointed out, first of all, that the antecedent of the pronoun "him" at the beginning of Brunner's proof-text is "Jesus" in verse 38. Thus St. Peter recounted how Jesus of Nazareth, anointed with the Holy Spirit and with power, "went about doing good and healing all that were oppressed by the devil," how he was put to death by crucifixion, and how God raised him on the third day (Acts 10:38-40)—that is to say, Jesus who lived and died also rose from the dead. There is no suggestion of a division between the historic Jesus and the risen Christ; the whole account belongs to the same historical sequence: *Jesus* lived, *Jesus* died, and *Jesus* rose from the dead. That the Apostle was speaking of but one historical *continuum* is confirmed, secondly, by the last part of the proof-text, where he declares that those to whom Jesus appeared "ate and drank with him after he rose from the dead" (v. 41); for the everyday act of eating and drinking, the partaking of such everyday food as fish and bread (Jn. 21:9-14; Lk. 24:41-43), plainly showed that the disciples experienced the personal presence of Jesus on the same historical level and in the same historical sequence after as well as before Easter. The body of the risen Jesus, though now spiritual, was recognizable as the body which was his prior to the resurrection. His presence was not incorporeal: the risen Jesus could eat and drink and be touched, and the wounds of nails and spear were visible and tangible to the disciples (Lk. 24:36ff.; Jn. 20:19f., 27; 1 Jn. 1:1-3).

The attempt that has been made in modern existentialist and dialectical theology to separate faith from history has been perceptively criticized by Wolfhart Pannenberg, who accuses Rudolf Bultmann and Friedrich Gogarten, on the one hand, of "dissolving history into the historicity of existence" (the existence, i.e., of the individual), and Martin Kähler, on the other, of evacuating history of importance by theorizing that "the real content of faith is suprahistorical" (i.e., independent of the sequence of events of which this-

4. *Dogmatics,* Vol. II (Philadelphia, 1952), p. 328.

worldly history is compounded).[5] Both theological positions, he says, "have a common extra-theological motive" and starting point, the presupposition, namely, that "the scientific investigation of events did not seem to leave any more room for redemptive events." Consequently, "the theology of redemptive history fled into a harbor supposedly safe from the critical-historical flood tide, the harbor of superhistory," and "the theology of existence withdrew from the meaningless and godless course of 'objective' history to the experience of the significance of history in the 'historicity' of the individual."[6] The preconception of "a fundamental antithesis between the world views of historical method and the biblical history of God" is responsible for "the anthropocentricity of the historical-critical procedure, which seems apt to exclude all transcendental reality as a matter of course."[7] Predictably, historical relativism is "the consistent end-result of the displacement of God by man as the bearer of history." In this connection Pannenberg draws a line back through Nietzsche and Kierkegaard to Lessing.[8]

Kähler's dictum that "the real Christ is the Christ who is preached" may rightly be seen as seminal in the development of the "kerygma theology" of both the dialectical and the existentialist school, and not least with reference to "the antihistorical front" that kerygma theology "set up against the life-of-Jesus movement of the nineteenth century."[9] It led to "the fatal consequence of making faith rest, in actuality, upon itself instead of . . . being built upon a historical foundation."[10]

> The decisive insight behind this development was that the "Word of God" was not only the written word of the Bible (as the older doctrine of inspiration had it) but primarily the preached word, the Scripture being understood as the written residue of this. . . . All these tendencies flowed into the eruption of the so-called dialectical theology insofar as it wanted to be essentially a "theology of the Word of God." Dialectical theology itself is to be understood as a particular and, in fact, most important manifestation of the man-sided movement of kerygma theology. It is no accident that Barth's doctrine of the Word of God takes the proclamation as the point of departure. Nevertheless, the purest and, so to speak, classical expression of kerygma theology is found in Rudolf Bultmann.[11]

While acknowledging that Kähler had not wished to dispense with the events of history as the foundation of faith, Pannenberg criticizes him for making a distinction between the historical fact and its revelatory value as

5. W. Pannenberg, *Basic Questions in Theology,* tr. George H. Kehm, Vol. I (Philadelphia, 1983), p. 15.
6. Ibid., p. 16.
7. Ibid., p. 39.
8. Ibid., pp. 57, 58.
9. Ibid., p. 81.
10. Ibid., p. 55.
11. Ibid., p. 83.

though the latter were separate from and supplementary to the former. "Does not this argument accept all too uncritically the neo-Kantian distinction between being and value?", he asks. This distinction, as we have previously noticed, is prominent in the system of Bultmann, who contended that christological affirmations, for example ascribing deity to Jesus, were not to be treated as ontological statements but merely as value judgments depicting the existential worth of Jesus to a particular individual. This being so, Pannenberg points out, "the possibility arises that the 'revelatory value' can stand upon itself as witness, and that historical 'fact' whose value it is supposed to refer to would no longer need to have any special interest devoted to it."[12]

Given these premises, Jesus became ever more dim and more distant as a figure of the virtually irretrievable past, and "the quest for the historical Jesus" which was instigated (and still continues) increasingly assumed the relevance of a wild goose chase. The kerygma, as Pannenberg observes, had been rendered "autonomous over against its historical correlate."[13] Pannenberg rightly asserts that "if it really were a matter of indifference for the content of the Christian message whether or not Jesus was a historical person, or what the manner of his historical existence was, then it would be impossible to see why the transmission of this understanding of human existence would have to appeal to Jesus any longer"; and he insists that "since, on the contrary, appeal to Jesus, indeed confession of faith in him, constitutes the fundamental feature of all Christian tradition, its content cannot consist simply in a particular understanding of human existence which is common to the New Testament writings but would itself be independent of the historical Jesus." Of primary importance, he maintains, is "the general maxim that in the realm of history meaning must remain bound to facticity, so that all meaning has its criterion in the fact in which it inheres, even though as meaning it may transcend this fact."[14]

With this vigorous critique we can heartily concur. We have seen how Pannenberg has sought to preserve the historic factuality of Jesus and his resurrection. At the same time, however, we have also seen that he has not succeeded in remaining uninfluenced by the historical-critical temper of the modern age, as is witnessed, for instance, by his contention that the enlightened contemporary individual who cannot affirm belief in the virgin birth and ascension of Jesus may yet join in the corporate credal confession of these articles of belief "without abandoning truthfulness," because this is an act of solidarity with the historic worship and intention of the church. Is he not also guilty of dehistoricizing faith when he holds that such concepts are "mythical" and no longer acceptable "in the age of technology," and that "the figure of a Logos mediating between the transcendent God and the world," which is the biblically historical reality, "no longer belongs to today's scientific perception

12. Ibid., p. 86.
13. Ibid.
14. Ibid., p. 149.

of the world"?[15] Is he not putting a distance between faith and history when he declares that whereas for Luther (let alone the early church) "the literal sense of the Scriptures was identical with their historical content," contrariwise, "for us . . . these two matters have become separated," so that "the picture of Jesus and his history which the various New Testament writers give us cannot, without further qualification, be regarded as identical with the actual course of events"?[16]

Such conflicting statements seem to be indicative of confusion at the center of Pannenberg's thought, welcome though otherwise his attempt to rescue history may be. It still has to be asked what precisely he means when he says that "the understanding of the unity of all reality as history requires taking up the task of understanding all things in relation to the God of the Bible and, thus, to know the biblical God anew as the creator of the world" and therefore as "the God of history";[17] for he appears not to have radically dissociated himself from the anthropocentricity of our time.

It should be a source of great confidence to the Christian believer that the New Testament does not teach that the body of Christ's incarnation was discarded in death, and that it does not in any way limit the use of the name "Jesus," the human name of the incarnate Son, to the period between his birth in Bethlehem and his crucifixion at Calvary, nor refuse to call him by that name after the resurrection, as though there were some ontological difference between "the historic Jesus" and "the risen Christ." Thus the postresurrection appearances were precisely the appearances of *Jesus* (Mt. 28:9, 10, 18; Lk. 24:15, 36; Jn. 20:14ff., 19ff.; 21:1, 4ff.). It was *Jesus* whom the apostles saw ascending heavenward and whose return they were to expect (Acts 1:11). The same *Jesus* who had ministered and died in Palestine, St. Peter testified, was raised from the dead and exalted to glory (Acts 2:22, 23, 32, 36). It was "with great power" that "the apostles gave their testimony to the resurrection of the Lord *Jesus*" (Acts 4:33; 5:30; 13:31ff.; 17:3, 18). The first martyr St. Stephen saw *Jesus* standing at the right hand of God and commended his spirit to him (Acts 7:55, 59). It was *Jesus* who encountered Saul of Tarsus as he journeyed to Damascus (Acts 9:5; 22:8; 26:15). And it is the still incarnate Lord *Jesus* Christ whose reappearance Christians await, and "who will change our lowly body to be like his glorious body, by the power which enables him even to subject all things to himself" (Phil. 3:20f.). In the dynamic message of the apostles the incarnation was not a thing of the past. Our humanity, which he took to himself to redeem, has not been left behind in the tomb. This, as we shall in due course hope to show, is a consideration of real importance for the understanding of the doctrine of our redemption in Christ.

We have noticed Brunner's contention that the resurrection was not a

15. See p. 221 above.
16. Ibid., p. 6.
17. Ibid., p. 14.

historical event, or, insofar as it may be called historical, that it belongs to "history of a different kind from that of the events recorded in the life of Jesus," that is to say, between Bethlehem and Calvary; and we have drawn attention to the fact that this viewpoint does not accord with the experience and judgment of the apostles. Maintaining that "the Gospels were written by faith for faith" and that "their aim is in no way 'historical,'"[18] Brunner postulated a distinction between history and superhistory[19] which is comparable to the distinction favored by Barth between *Historie* and *Geschichte*,[20] and within this framework declared of Christ's resurrection: "It is super-history, eschatological history, hence it is no longer historical at all."[21] On this supposition it was sought to rest the differentiation, the discontinuity on the historical plane, between "the earthly Jesus" and "the risen Lord." But in the biblical perspective, as we have seen, God is constantly active in human history as Creator, Judge, and Redeemer. The hand of God is at work in the affairs of men. Mankind, it is true, has rebelled against his Creator; but God has not for this or for any other reason ceased to be the sovereign Ruler of his creation. All human history is under his control and is ineluctably moving on toward its destined consummation. Because the Son is the agent through whom the world was created, by whom it is redeemed, and whose word of power providentially sustains the universe and carries it on to the glory for which it was designed, Christ is therefore the dynamic key to the understanding of the purpose and destiny of history in its entirety. God's ways are indeed higher than our ways (Is. 55:9), but human history cannot be disengaged from divine history; for Christ, who is the Image of God in which man is created and to which man is redemptively being conformed, is the meeting point of divine history and human history. Unceasingly, it is God "with whom we have to do" (Heb. 4:13). Man is always man before God. The image with which man is stamped at the heart of his being ensures this.

In the infinite power and majesty of his being God is certainly independent of and superior to the world he has created, but it does not follow from this that divine action in relation to our world belongs to a sphere of superhistory which is removed from the daily sequence of events which are the fabric of our history here below. The incarnation which is at the same time the action of God and the central point or fulcrum of world history is proof of this. And this holds good for the resurrection and ascension of Jesus, who is still the incarnate Son, to whose history, both earthly and heavenly, these events belong. That is why St. Paul insisted before King Agrippa that what happened to Jesus, in his life, death, and resurrection, "was not done in a corner" (Acts 26:23, 26).

It is important to understand that what happened to the incarnate Son

18. *The Mediator,* p. 341.
19. Ibid., pp. 369, 389ff.
20. Barth borrowed the distinction between *Historie* and *Geschichte* from Martin Kähler.
21. *The Mediator,* p. 583.

happened to our human nature. For the Son's incarnation to have ended with a corpse in a tomb, and for his resurrection to have been a nonphysical suprahistorical development (which, properly speaking, would not have been resurrection at all but only some kind of "spiritual" continuation after death), would involve a serious diminution of both the christological and the eschatological teaching of the New Testament. Death, the last enemy (1 Cor. 15:26), would have remained undefeated and our humanity which the Son took to himself to heal would have continued unreconciled. His resurrection and his exaltation demonstrate to us that death has been swallowed up in victory, *his* victory, and assure us that God gives us this same victory through our Lord Jesus Christ (1 Cor. 15:54-57).

In him, moreover, our human nature is exalted and brought to perfection. God's purpose is to bring many sons to glory through his incarnate Son, who is the pioneer of their salvation (Heb. 2:10). Splendid as man's beginning was, it was always God's design that his end should be more splendid than his beginning. "Mankind," Athanasius wrote, "is perfected in him, and restored even as it was made at the beginning, or rather is advanced to a higher state of grace; for on rising from the dead we shall no longer fear death but shall ever reign in Christ in the heavens."[22] It is because of his sin that man has sunk lower instead of rising higher than his creation. The Creator's design for his glorification remains firm, however, and achieves fulfilment in Christ; for the attainment of man's restoration and elevation rests not in himself but in his divine-human Redeemer. Accordingly, the author of the Epistle to the Hebrews takes the words of Psalm 8:4ff., spoken of the creation of man, "Thou didst make him for a little while lower than the angels, thou hast crowned him with glory and honor, putting everything in subjection under his feet," and applies them directly to Jesus, who, by virtue of his incarnation, is our fellowman and, by virtue of his perfect holiness, is the only true and faithful man before God (Heb. 2:5ff.). The authentic destiny of man is enacted and realized in Christ, "who for a little while was made lower than the angels . . . so that by the grace of God he might taste death for every one," and is now "crowned with glory and honor" as he is everlastingly made higher than the angels (Heb. 2:9). The purpose of the Creator, therefore, far from being frustrated by the rebellious will of man, is fulfilled in and through the reconciling work of Christ; and that purpose was from the beginning that man should be lower than the angels only *for a little while*, since the consummation of his creation was always that he should be crowned with glory and honor as the master, under God, of the whole created order, including the angels (cf. 1 Cor. 6:2f.). This being so, it is evident that the true way of man is one of *ascent* from creation to glorification.

Even if man had not fallen into sin, his glorification would have been gained by way of intimate relationship with the Son; not, indeed, by way of the Son's incarnation, but through constant conformity to the Son, who, as we

---

22. Athanasius, *Orations against the Arians* ii.67.

have learned, is the Image in which man was created. By such harmonious conformity man would have been true not only to God but also to himself and would have advanced from being lower to being higher than the angels. His being lower than the angels was but "for a little while." As John Donne expressed it: "If we had not sinned in Adam, mortality had not put on immortality (as the Apostle speaks), and corruption had not put on incorruption, but we had had our transmigration from this to the other world, without any mortality, any corruption at all."[23]

The human tragedy is, as we have indicated, that man, far from ascending, has descended from the level of his creation. The bitter consequence of his fighting against the divine image in which he is formed is that he flounders in defeat and has lost the meaning of his existence. He has incapacitated himself to rise to the glorious destiny for which he was created. Marked with failure and futility, he has invited upon himself the judgment of his Creator. But the purpose of God in the forming of man cannot come to nothing (precisely because it is the purpose *of God*); and the Son, who is the image stamped on man's being, is the agent and the guarantor of the fulfilment of that purpose. Thus what Psalm 8 affirms about man generically is attained specifically in Christ Jesus: "We see Jesus, who for a little while was made lower than the angels, crowned with glory and honor" (Heb. 2:9). Humiliation is followed by exaltation. To the same effect it is said, with Psalm 110:1 in mind, that "when he had made purification for sins he sat down at the right hand of the Majesty on high" (Heb. 1:3). In Jesus, the incarnate Son, our flesh-and-blood brother (Heb. 2:11, 14), our human nature has fully and triumphantly completed the course designed for us, and we who by faith are united to him are encouraged to "run with perseverance the race that is set before us," and in doing so to look away from ourselves to "Jesus, the pioneer and perfecter of our faith, who for the joy that was set before him endured the cross, despising the shame, and is seated at the right hand of the throne of God" (Heb. 12:1f.).

The point that must not be missed is this, that Jesus is in absolute reality the alpha and the omega, the beginning and the end, of all God's purposes for mankind and for creation (cf. Rev. 1:8; 21:6; 22:13). What God started in creation he not only started in the Son, who is the Image after whom man is formed, but he also completed in the Son, who is the Image to whom all the redeemed are being conformed (Rom. 8:29; 2 Cor. 3:18). He took our nature to himself not only to redeem it but also to glorify it, that is, to bring it to the destiny that was always intended for it. Our nature, which is compounded of body and spirit, is the nature which by his suffering and death he has redeemed and also the nature which by his resurrection and ascension he has elevated and glorified. The incarnation did not cease with the cross and the tomb; it continues even now in transcendental glory. This means that our salvation from beginning to

23. John Donne, Sermon on Psalm 68:20, preached before the king at Whitehall, 25 February 1630. This was Donne's last sermon.

end is already complete and secure in him who is our crucified and exalted Lord. The destiny of our creation is already achieved in him who, together with our humanity still united to himself, is highly exalted and on whom the name which is above every name has been bestowed (Phil. 2:9-11). The incarnate Son, who for a little while was made lower than the angels and is now crowned with glory and honor, is for that reason the guarantee and gauge to us, who, one with him by grace and faith, are still for a little while lower than the angels, that his present destiny of glory is also our future destiny.

The reality of this destiny is confirmed, moreover, by the witness of the Holy Spirit whom the exalted Lord has sent from above. In Christ, St. Paul assured the Christians in Ephesus, "you also, who have heard the word of truth, the gospel of your salvation, and have believed in him, were sealed with the promised Holy Spirit, who is the surety of our inheritance until we acquire possession of it, to the praise of his glory" (Eph. 1:13f.); and he desired that they might "know what is the hope to which God has called you, what are the riches of his glorious inheritance in the saints, and what is the immeasurable greatness of his power in us who believe, according to the working of his great might which he accomplished in Christ when he raised him from the dead and made him sit at the right hand in heavenly places" (Eph. 1:18-20)—for the same unbounded power which effected the resurrection and ascension of Jesus is at work in the lives of all who are born from above. So also St. Peter rejoiced in the assurance that "by God's great mercy we have been born anew to a living hope through the resurrection of Jesus Christ from the dead, and to an inheritance which is imperishable, undefiled, and unfading, kept in heaven for you" (1 Pet. 1:3f.).

So real is this exaltation of our redeemed human nature in Christ, so complete is the reconciling and glorifying work he has performed for us, so genuine is the union of the believer with the incarnate Lord on high, that there is an authentic identity between the Redeemer and the redeemed. Our baptism signifies to us our death, burial, and resurrection with Christ (Rom. 6:3ff.). Our whole salvation is already a glorious reality in Christ. It is true that we are still occupied with the upward climb of our earthly pilgrimage, but the consummation toward which we are moving is already sealed and settled in that human nature which in Christ is even now redeemed and glorified in heavenly places. Thus even in the present striving of our pilgrimage we gratefully praise God, "who has blessed us in Christ with every spiritual blessing in the heavenly places," and who, "rich in mercy, . . . made us alive together with Christ . . . and raised us up with him, and made us sit with him in the heavenly places, in Christ Jesus" (Eph. 1:3; 2:4-6). This is the language not of pious sentimentality or abstract mysticism but of factual realism.

The key expression in the communication of this truth is that which defines the existence of the believer as being *in Christ,* with its corollary that he is therefore *with Christ*—revitalized with Christ, raised with Christ, enthroned with Christ. Christ has always been the concentration point of God's age-old purposes, before creation, at creation, and in the restoration of all things. Thus God "chose us *in him* before the foundation of the world, that we should be holy and blameless before him"; and now "*in him* we have redemption through his blood, the forgiveness of our trespasses, according to the riches of his grace"; and "the mystery of God's will" for the ultimate consummation has been made known to us, "according to his purpose which he set forth *in Christ,* as a plan for the fulness of time, to unite all things *in him,* things in heaven and things on earth" (Eph. 1:4, 7, 9f.). The regenerate person is no longer *in Adam* but *in Christ* (1 Cor. 15:22; 2 Cor. 5:17). His solidarity in Adam has been annulled and replaced by his solidarity in Christ.

The unique singularity of Christ provides the clue to our collective rehabilitation in him. As he alone is the beloved Son with whom God is well pleased (Mk. 1:11; 9:7), so it is only *in him,* through union with him, that we can become sons of God. As St. Paul told the Galatian believers, "*in Christ Jesus* you are all sons of God" (Gal. 3:26); and to be sons is to be heirs through the same oneness with him who is the sole Heir of eternal glory (Rom. 8:16f.). Likewise the Apostle taught that God's promise to Abraham, that in his seed all the nations would be blessed (Gen. 22:18), received its fulfilment in the single person of Christ, but again with this consequence, that those who would be collectively the seed of Abraham must be *in Christ Jesus,* the true and unique Seed in whom all believers are one and on this basis are constituted "heirs according to promise" (Gal. 3:8, 16, 28f.).

In the teaching of the apostles the resurrection of Jesus is strikingly proclaimed as signalizing the rebirth of our humanity. It is in him, the conqueror of death and Satan, that the new creation comes into being. This does not mean, we repeat, that the first creation is discarded, but that God's plan as Creator, established as it always has been in Christ, is redemptively accomplished as in the incarnate Son our fallenness is cancelled and our humanity is reborn from the dead. This is the force of St. Paul's declaration at Pisidian Antioch that in the resurrection of Jesus God fulfilled the promise implicit in Psalm 2:7, "Thou art my Son, today I have begotten thee" (Acts 13:30-35; cf. Heb. 1:5; 5:5). The rising of Jesus from the dead is the new begetting, the rebirth of sonship in him, and thus the restoration, always in him, of filial harmony and fellowship between us and our Creator. And it is to the same effect that the Apostle affirms that Jesus was "designated the Son of God in power according to the Spirit of holiness by reason of his resurrection from the dead," with momentous consequences for all "who are called to belong to Jesus Christ" (Rom. 1:4-6).

The resurrection of Jesus, then, is the sign to the world (cf. Mt. 12:38-40) that declares the reality of the new beginning of the human race in Christ. The regeneration it proclaims is of such significance that it is described as the new heaven and the new earth (2 Pet. 3:13; Rev. 21:1), which is the restoration of all things (Acts 3:21). As with the original creation, this is the work of God, who in Christ makes all things new (Rev. 21:5; cf. Gen. 1:1). It is the dynamic internalization of the creation principle, for God, who in the original creation said, "Let light shine out of darkness," now dispels the darkness of ungodliness by causing the light of the knowledge of his glory revealed in Christ to shine in the believing heart (2 Cor. 4:6). Hence the description of the person who is in Christ as *a new creation* (2 Cor. 5:17), and the instruction that those who are thus reborn are "God's workmanship, *created in Christ Jesus* for good works, which God prepared beforehand, that we should walk in them" (Eph. 2:10). In this the continuity that relates the new to the original creation is evident, as also in the assertion that "the new man" or "the new humanity" put on by the Christian "is being renewed in knowledge after the image of its Creator" (Col. 3:10), which betokens the recovery of the first principle of man's creation, namely, his formation after the image of God, which, again, is after Christ who is the Image of God. Likeness to Christ, Christiformity, is the whole sum and purpose of man's creation.

The reconciliation of man to God achieves also the reconciliation of all things, the reconciliation not only of man to God but also of man to man and of all creation. Through Christ, St. Paul says, God reconciles to himself "all things, whether on earth or in heaven, having made peace by the blood of his cross" (Col. 1:20). In the crucified, risen, and glorified Savior there is the healing of all enmity and incompatibility, personal, racial, indeed of every kind; for Christ "is our peace, who . . . has broken down the dividing wall of hostility . . . *that he might create in himself one new man* [i.e., one new reborn humanity] . . . in one body through the cross, thereby bringing the hostility to an end" (Eph. 2:13-16). The restoration of harmony between man and God and between man and man inevitably effects the recovery of the harmony of all things. While the focus of the regeneration accomplished through the redeeming work of the incarnate Son is upon man as the head of the created order, the scope of this regeneration is in the end creation-wide. This expectation is altogether logical. Man's fall, apart from its disastrous results for himself, has subjected the creation as a whole to futility—not, however, without hope; for, St. Paul explains, "the creation waits with eager longing for the revealing of the sons of God," when, at the return of the Son himself in glory, "the creation itself will be set free from its bondage to decay and obtain the glorious liberty of the children of God" (Rom. 8:19ff.). Man's rebellion, in Adam, against his Creator led to his rebellious abuse and perversion of the dominion with which he had been entrusted over the earth; but the renewal of man, in Christ, leads to the renewal of the cosmos, and the glorification of man brings with it the glorification of that order of which he is the chief part. The actuality of rebirth which flows from the resurrection of the Crucified One from the dead therefore exerts a regenerative power that is cosmic as well as human in its comprehensiveness, as in Christ, through whom all things were created, the divine purpose in the creation of man and the world is brought to its glorious fulfilment.

CHAPTER 35

Between the Comings

If anything is plain in the pages of the New Testament it is that the apostles, who were witnesses to the first coming of Christ, believed that there was to be a second coming, and that they regarded the interval or period between the two comings as *the last days* or the ultimate age of human history as we presently know it. The author of the Epistle to the Hebrews, for example, declares that God who previously spoke by the prophets has *"in these last days"* spoken to us by his Son, the implication being that the Son through his coming is God's final word to man; and he also instructs his readers that Christ, who "has appeared once for all *at the end of the ages* to put away sin by the sacrifice of himself, . . . will appear a second time, not to deal with sin but to save those who are eagerly waiting for him" (Heb. 1:1f.; 9:26, 28). Similarly, St. Peter assured the scattered believers to whom he was writing that Christ "was destined before the foundation of the world but was made manifest *at the end of the times* for your sake," and encouraged them to be constant in enduring "various trials, so that the genuineness of your faith . . . may redound to praise and glory and honor at the revelation of Jesus Christ" (1 Pet. 1:20, 6f.).

An integral element of this perspective was the apostolic expectation that these last days will terminate in a last day. This last day will be "the great day" of divine wrath against those who impenitently persist in ungodliness (Rev. 6:17; 16:14), and as such "the day of judgment" (Mt. 10:15; 11:22, 24; 12:36; 2 Pet. 2:9; 3:7; Jude 6; 1 Jn. 4:17), "the day when God's righteous judgment will be revealed" (Rom. 2:5), the day appointed by God "on which he will judge the world in righteousness" and "the secrets of men by Christ Jesus" (Acts 17:31; Rom. 2:16). Accordingly, it is also designated "the day of the Lord Jesus Christ" (1 Cor. 1:8; 5:5; 2 Cor. 1:14) or "the day when the Son of Man is revealed" (Lk. 17:24, 30) or simply "the day of the Lord" (1 Thess. 5:2; 2 Pet. 3:10) or "the day of God" (2 Pet. 3:12), which links it with the anticipation in the Old Testament of the Day of the Lord and the ultimate judgment associated with it. Indeed, so uniquely solemn is this day in its finality that it is even referred to without elaboration as "the Day" (1 Cor. 3:13; Heb. 10:25; Rom. 13:12). This day which marks "the close of the age" coincides with the moment of the return of Christ as he comes to purge the creation of all evil and to consummate the work of redemption he accomplished in the humility of his first coming (Mt. 24:3, 30, 37, 44). For the unregenerate it will be a day of terror (Rev. 6:15-17; cf. Is. 2:19, 21; Joel 2:11; Is. 13:6, 9, 13; Zeph. 1:14f.; Mal. 3:2), but for those who are re-created in Christ it is a day to look forward to with joy, since for them it will be the day when they are exalted to the full glory of eternal life (Jn. 5:28f.; 6:40, 44, 54; 11:23-26) and therefore "the day of redemption" for which they are even now sealed by the Holy Spirit (Eph. 4:30; cf. 1:13; Rom. 13:11).

The last day, then, is not only the dread day "when the Lord Jesus is revealed from heaven, . . . inflicting vengeance upon those who do not know God and upon those who do not obey the gospel," but also the day "when he comes to be glorified in his saints and to be marveled at in all who have believed" (2 Thess. 1:7-10). That is why St. Paul could tell the Philippian believers that he was "sure that he who began a good work in you will bring it to completion at the day of Jesus Christ" (Phil. 1:6), and the Christians in Corinth that "as you wait for the revealing of our Lord Jesus Christ" God "will sustain you to the end, guiltless in the day of our Lord Jesus Christ" (1 Cor. 1:7f.). And St. Paul himself, free from all apprehension, was confident that the Lord "is able to guard until that Day what has been entrusted to me" and that "there is laid up for me the crown of righteousness, which the Lord, the righteous Judge, will award me on that Day, and," he added, "not only to me but also to all who have loved his appearing" (2 Tim. 1:12; 4:8).

This period of "the last days," however, which extends between the two comings of Christ, has continued for almost two millennia. The climactic "last day" has still not dawned, and this seems to betoken a considerable delay in the promised return of the Lord, indeed, all the more so as the apostles envisaged the possibility of his second advent taking place in their own lifetime. St. John, for one, warned that it was "the last hour" because of the activity in the world and in the church of "many antichrists" (1 Jn. 2:18), and he urged those he was addressing to purify themselves and to abide in Christ, "so that when he appears we may have confidence and not shrink from him in shame at his coming" (1 Jn. 2:28; 3:2f.). St. Paul, for another, prayed that those to whom he had ministered the gospel might be "pure and blameless for the day of Christ" (Phil. 1:10), and exhorted the members of the church in Rome: "You know what hour it is, how it is full time for you now to awake from sleep. For salvation[1] is nearer to us than when we first believed; the night is far gone, the day is at hand" (Rom. 13:11f.). St. James admonished the Christian dispersion: "Establish your hearts, for the coming of the Lord is at hand; . . . behold, the Judge is standing at the doors" (Jas. 5:8f.). And St. Peter, reminding his readers that the world in its present fallen state is "being kept until the day of judgment and destruction of ungodly men," issued this challenge: "Since all these things are thus to be dissolved, what sort of persons ought you to be in lives of holiness and godliness, waiting for and hastening the coming of the day of God?" (2 Pet. 3:11f.).

---

1. Salvation, that is, as it is brought to completion at Christ's return.

The basis of this apostolic teaching was Christ's own repeated emphasis on the need for faithfulness and vigilance in anticipation of his return at any moment. What could be more urgent than the following admonition to his disciples: "Take heed, watch, for you do not know when the time will come. It is like a man going on a journey, when he leaves home and puts his servants in charge, each with his work, and commands the doorkeeper to be on the watch. Watch therefore—for you do not know when the master of the house will come, in the evening, or at midnight, or at cockcrow, or in the morning—lest he come suddenly and find you asleep. And what I say to you I say to all: Watch!" (Mk. 13:33-37)?

In our own day, certainly, we hear many skeptical voices announcing that both the Master and his apostles were mistaken in thinking that they were living in the last days, and that their expectation of his sudden and early return was a vain imagination. But such critics fail to take into account the emphatic insistence of the New Testament teaching on the unpredictability of the time of this culminating event. It is precisely ignorance in this connection that makes watchfulness so necessary. The day and hour of Christ's appearing may be early or late; the time is known only to the Father (Mk. 13:32ff.). Moreover, delay is acknowledged as a factor in this perspective. It was "as the bridegroom was delayed" that the bridesmaids "slumbered and slept," or, in other words, failed to be watchful (Mt. 25:5). It was "after a long time" that the master of the servants to whom the talents had been entrusted "came and settled accounts with them" (Mt. 25:19). "The faithful and wise servant" diligently fulfils his stewardship and is ready for his master's return; but "the wicked servant says to himself, 'My master is delayed,'" and, neglecting his duty and resorting to injustice and debauchery, is totally unprepared for his master's coming (Mt. 24:45ff.).

As the years went by, St. Paul found it necessary to write to the members of the Thessalonian church for the purpose of assuring them that Christians who had died prior to the Lord's return were not in any way at a disadvantage or excluded from the blessings that would attend his coming (1 Thess. 4:13ff.); and he was constrained to admonish some who had given up working because of their belief that Christ's reappearance was close at hand, and to instruct them to mind their own affairs instead of meddling in the affairs of others and to cease living in idleness, which simply made them a burden to others (1 Thess. 4:11f.; 2 Thess. 3:6ff.). Furthermore, it should not be overlooked that he informed them that certain historical developments must occur before the arrival of the Day of the Lord (2 Thess. 2:1ff.).

St. Peter also addressed this question of delay in order to reassure Christians who were being unsettled by the scornful mockery of unbelievers. They must understand, he wrote, "that scoffers will come in the last days . . . saying, 'Where is the promise of his coming?'" and asserting that "all things have continued as they were from the beginning of creation"—in other words, that divine intervention was a vain hope. Such persons, St. Peter observed, "deliberately ignore" the fact that God, who brought all things into existence, is sovereign over his creation and will not fail to judge those whose lives are ungodly. Moreover, they refuse to heed the testimony of history, which shows that the predictions of God's prophets, though fulfilment may have seemed to be delayed, have not failed to come to pass. A striking illustration of this was the preaching of Noah, whose warning of the coming judgment of the flood fell on deaf ears and who endured the mocking taunts of his scornful generation as he built the ark in preparation for this event; nevertheless, at God's appointed time the world of his day was destroyed by water and those who had scoffed perished though they had derided the deluge as something that would never happen. The word of God regarding final judgment will prove to be just as sure.

Furthermore, it is foolish to measure everything by the yardstick of our finite human experience. God, not man, is the Lord of creation, and as such he controls all things in accordance with his will and purpose. To judge the divine timetable for the future by merely human standards is therefore ill advised. What may seem a very long time to man is as nothing to God, for "with the Lord one day is as a thousand years, and a thousand years as one day." Seen in the perspective of God's eternity any length of time, no matter how small or great to us, is insignificant, and consequently we can speak of delay only in relation to the restricted horizons of man. In any case, "delay" should be interpreted positively, not negatively; for, rightly understood, the apparent delay in the return of Christ is indicative not of weakness or indecision on God's part but rather of his patience and longsuffering as he gives opportunity for the message of the gospel to be proclaimed and responded to throughout the world. "The Lord is not slow about his promise as some count slowness," St. Peter explained, "but is forbearing toward you, not wishing that any should perish, but that all should reach repentance" (2 Pet. 3:3-9). The prolongation of this final age is the prolongation of the day of grace. Those, therefore, who are estranged from God should interpret the "delay" gratefully as a sign of divine goodness which extends to them the opportunity to repent and believe, not scornfully as a sign of divine incompetence.

As watchfulness was enjoined by Christ on his disciples it would have been surprising if the apostles had not seen the return of their Master as an event which could possibly take place in their own lifetime. Being an event whose day and hour was unrevealed, and which therefore could occur at any time, it was meant to be regarded as imminent, and it was this sense of imminence that created the need for watchfulness. In the light of this possibility it was not unrealistic for St. Paul to classify himself with fellow Christians as "we who are alive, who are left until the coming of the Lord," in contrast to those who had "fallen asleep" in death (1 Thess. 4:15; cf. 1 Cor. 15:51). The ardent and unremitting intensity with which he executed his apostleship to the Gentiles was fueled, certainly, by his profound sense of indebtedness—indebtedness, in the first place, to the Lord of all grace whose cause he had previously so fiercely persecuted (1 Tim. 1:12ff.; Gal. 1:11ff.), and indebtedness, in the next place, to the world of mankind whose need of the gospel was as immediate and desperate as his had been (Rom. 1:14; 1 Cor. 9:16); but his zeal was animated, also, by the conviction that the fulfilment of the evangelistic commission was at the same time the hastening of the return of the Redeemer. The task of worldwide evangelization had been entrusted to the apostles by their Master prior to his ascension (Mt. 28:19f.; Acts 1:8); and on an earlier occasion he had said to them: "This gospel of the kingdom will be preached throughout the whole world, as a testimony to all nations, and then the end will come" (Mt. 24:14; cf. Mk. 13:10).

All St. Paul's labors and journeyings were "for the sake of the gospel" (1 Cor. 9:23), and the objective of the missionary enterprise was what he called "the fulness of the Gentiles" (Rom. 11:25; cf. Lk. 21:24-27). It was striving for the realization of the covenant promise given to Abraham that in his seed, who is Christ, all the nations of the earth would be blessed (Gal. 3:6-9, 16). His eagerness to expedite the attainment of the fulness of the Gentiles explains his "ambition to preach the gospel where Christ has not already been named" and also his protestation that he would "not venture to speak of anything except what Christ has wrought through me to win obedience from the Gentiles"; indeed, he felt able to tell his readers in Rome: "From Jerusalem as far round as Illyricum I have fulfilled the gospel of Christ"[2] (Rom. 15:18-20). What is *to fulfil the gospel* in any place if not to advance a stage toward the fulness of the Gentiles, and thereby toward the return of Christ? To this same motivation must be attributed St. Paul's intention of traveling on westward as far as Spain (Rom. 15:24, 28).[3] Again, he spoke of "the divine office" which was given to him "to fulfil the word of God"[4] (Col. 1:25), which is the same as "to fulfil the gospel"; and at last, as his martyrdom drew near, he declared that, despite all the hostility and treachery he had encountered, the Lord had stood by him and given him "strength to fulfil the proclamation [of the gospel], that all the Gentiles might hear"[5] (2 Tim. 4:17).

Thus St. Paul selflessly devoted himself to "fulfilling" the gospel by endeavoring to preach to all the nations. But he did not think of himself as the only one prosecuting this ministry; for it must be remembered that he was but one of the many evangelists who were energetically carrying the Christian message to ever more distant territories. St. John, for example, is reputed to have evangelized in Asia, St. Andrew in Scythia, St. Peter in the provinces of Asia

2. In the Greek, *peplērōkenai to euangelion tou Christou*.
3. Of particular interest in this connection is the statement of Clement of Rome, in a letter written before the close of the first century, that St. Paul "taught righteousness to the whole world and reached the farthest limit of the west," *to terma tēs dyseōs* (*Ep. ad Cor.* 5), which would seem at least to mean that he realized his desire to penetrate into Spain.
4. In the Greek, *plērōsai ton logon tou theou*.
5. In the Greek, *hina . . . to kērygma plērophorēthēi kai akousōsin panta ta ethnē*.

Minor among the Jews of the dispersion, and St. Thomas in Parthia and India.[6] In an ironic and paradoxical manner St. Paul was unwittingly responsible for the beginnings of this outreach at a time prior to his conversion, since one result of the savage persecution he led was the scattering of large numbers of believers from Jerusalem, where the church was first concentrated, and that scattering was in effect the scattering of the good seed of the gospel, for, as St. Luke tells us, "those who were scattered went about preaching the word" (Acts 8:1-4). Thus the wrath of man is turned to the praise of God (Ps. 76:10)! No less remarkable was the transformation of Saul the persecutor into Paul the apostle; and it was in the midst of the dynamic evangelistic activity to which he so totally committed himself that he wrote to the Colossians of his joy that the gospel had come to them, "as indeed in the whole world it is bearing fruit and growing" (Col. 1:6). The hope of completing this grand assignment within the space of a few decades was a tribute to the splendid vision which made the church of Christ in those days a fellowship of such vitality and power.

That the task they had promoted with such earnestness in the face of hardship and persecution was not completed in their lifetime does not mean that the apostles and their fellow workers were mistaken or that they failed. We may well ask what might have been accomplished had the succeeding generations been animated with the same zeal; but, to its shame, during the centuries that followed the church was largely immobilized by lethargy and the loss of the apostolic vision. Nothing is more necessary for the church in every age, including our own, than to recapture the enthusiasm and dynamism of those first days, as recounted in the Acts of the Apostles. God's purposes, however, remain strong and constant; even though nineteen centuries have passed since the apostolic era they have in no respect been incapacitated. The need for watchfulness is just as great now as it was at first. The Day of the Lord is always at hand, his return is always imminent—as it was for the apostles, so also for us. Just as his first coming, though seemingly long delayed, was always imminent and then when God's hour struck took place, so also his second coming. It will happen in God's good time just as certainly as did the first.

Meanwhile what is of abiding importance is its imminence. It is this insistence on imminence that lends force to the ethical emphasis with which the teaching concerning the return of Christ is consistently presented in the New Testament. As with most prophetic utterances there is the inclusion of an element of mystery; certain accompanying signs are mentioned, but the circumstances and magnitude of what is portended will be fully revealed only by the event itself. The theme of Christ's impending return, so prominent throughout the New Testament, was never intended, however, to be pabulum for mystery-

6. See Eusebius, *Ecclesiastical History* III.i.1f. The labors of St. Thomas in India, and his martyrdom there, are not mentioned by Eusebius (who refers to Origen as his source), but occur in another tradition (see the apocryphal *Acts of Thomas the Apostle*) which may well be authentic. He is still venerated as the founder of the Christian church in India by the denomination which bears his name.

mongers and puzzle-solvers, but rather the focus of the Christian hope and, precisely because of its imminence, a daily incentive to godly living. "Take heed, watch!" is the note that is unfailingly struck (Mk. 13:33). "What sort of persons ought you to be in lives of holiness and godliness, waiting for and hastening the coming of the day of God?" (2 Pet. 3:11f.) is the ever-present challenge. From generation to generation as history has unfolded believers have discerned "signs of the times," and not wrong-headedly, for in every age the powers of evil are menacing and the ultimate epiphany of the Son, bringing justice and peace, has rightly been looked for. The imminence has always been there. Thus from the days of the apostles on, the expectation of the Lord's return has been a continual spur to earnest Christian living. The preaching of Girolamo Savonarola provided a striking illustration of this. "The sword of the Lord will come soon and swiftly over the earth," he thundered in 1495 from the pulpit of the Duomo in Florence:

> Believe me that the knife of God will come and soon. And do not laugh at this word "soon," and do not say that it is "soon" as used in the Apocalypse, which takes hundreds of years to come. Believe me that it will be soon. Believing does not harm you at all; as a matter of fact it benefits you, for it makes you turn to repentance and makes you walk in God's way; and do not think that it can harm you rather than benefit you. Therefore believe that it is soon, although the precise time cannot be given, for God does not wish it, so that his elect may remain always in fear, in faith, and in charity, and continually in the love of God.

CHAPTER 36

Between Death and Resurrection

Pending the arrival of the last day, we continue to live in expectation—and to die in expectation. As persons are inexorably carried away by death and generation succeeds generation, it is only natural to ask what happens to the Christian in the interval between death and resurrection. What do we know about what is commonly called the intermediate state? As we seek the answer to this question it must be admitted that the New Testament does not provide much information on the subject; nonetheless, enough is said to enable us to form some positive conceptions. To begin with, death is frequently described as a sleep. When, for example, Jesus told the disciples, "Our friend Lazarus has fallen asleep, but I go to awake him out of sleep," he explained that he meant, "Lazarus is dead" (Jn. 11:11-14; cf. Mt. 27:52; Acts 7:60; 13:36; 1 Cor. 15:6, 51; 1 Thess. 4:13-15; 2 Pet. 3:4). The biblical custom of likening death to a sleep was not intended as a euphemistic disguising of the grim reality of man's mortal finitude. The similitude appropriately served to teach the truth that those who die in the Lord are at rest (as St. John was instructed to write: "Blessed are the dead that die in the Lord henceforth. 'Blessed indeed,' says the Spirit, 'that they may rest from their labors,'" Rev. 14:13), and even more the truth that as sleeping is followed by waking so the Christian believer has the certain knowledge that, though overtaken by death, he will awaken at the resurrection to fulness of life in the presence and likeness of his Redeemer.

There was, however, some controversy in the sixteenth century as to whether, as some Anabaptists maintained, the sleep of death included the soul as well as the body or, as the Reformed theologians contended, the soul continued to be alive and conscious after the death of the body. Calvin's first theological treatise, *De Psychopannychia* (on psychopannychy or soul-sleep), written in 1534, was a refutation of the Anabaptist position; and the 40th of the 42 Articles in 1553 (which were the antecedents of the 39 Articles of Religion of the Church of England) asserted that those who hold "that the souls of such as depart hence do sleep, being without all sense, feeling, or perceiving until the day of judgment, or affirm that the souls die with the bodies, and at the last day shall be raised up with the same, do utterly dissent from the right belief declared to us in Holy Scripture." In the next century, chapter 32 of the Westminster Confession stated this belief in a somewhat fuller formulation: "The bodies of men after death return to dust and see corruption," we read; "but their souls (which neither die nor sleep), having an immortal subsistence, immediately return to God who gave them. The souls of the righteous, being then made perfect in holiness, are received into the highest heavens, where they behold the face of God in light and glory, waiting for the full redemption of their bodies; and the souls of the wicked are cast into hell, where they remain in torments and utter darkness, reserved to the judgment of that great day. Besides these two places for souls separated from their bodies the Scripture acknowledgeth none."[1] The teaching of the death or the sleep of the soul opposed by these definitions implied that there was no personal consciousness and no awareness of any interval between death and resurrection.

But the language used in the Westminster Confession may be overdogmatic. Its authors seem to have been influenced by the details of the story told by Christ of the rich man and Lazarus, and also by the need they saw to eliminate as unscriptural the notion of the entry of souls into a state of purgatory after death. The biblical authors, however, envisage heaven and hell as the final destinations of the redeemed and the unregenerate, and the time between death and the general resurrection as a time of waiting (a view with which the Reformers were in accord). The question is whether the narrative of the rich man and Lazarus conveys, or was intended to convey, teaching about the intermediate state at all. Its main lesson regarding the future is, surely, that it is this present life for which each person is accountable, that at death the irrevocable separation is made, and that hereafter we enter either into rest and security or into anguish and loss (Lk. 16:19ff.). As Calvin says, "our Lord has here drawn a picture which represents the condition of the life to come according to the measure of our capacity," and "the general truth conveyed is that believing souls, when they have left their bodies, lead a joyful and blessed life out of this world, and that for the reprobate there are prepared dreadful torments, which can no more be conceived by our minds than the boundless glory of the heavens."[2] Calvin, it is true, interpreted this passage as descriptive of the intermediate state, though he warned that "the words of Christ give us slender information, and in a manner which is fitted to restrain curiosity"; and so he explained that "this comfort, which the sons of God enjoy, lies in this, that they perceive a crown of glory prepared for them and rest in the joyful expectation of it," whereas "the wicked are tormented by the apprehension of the future judgement which they see coming upon them."[3] In this passage, then, he found disproof of the opinion that at death the soul dies with the body or that it lapses into an unconscious sleep.

In his *Psychopannychia* Calvin adduced a considerable number of bib-

---

1. *The Westminster Confession of Faith* (1646), ch. 32.
2. J. Calvin, *Commentary on a Harmony of the Evangelists Matthew, Mark, and Luke*, tr. William Pringle, Vol. II (Edinburgh, 1845), pp. 188, 189.
3. Ibid., pp. 189, 190.

lical texts to support his contention that between death and resurrection the soul is in a state of consciousness; but when all is said and done no more than a handful of passages may justly be said to have a direct bearing on the question of the intermediate state. One such is the assurance given by Jesus as he hung on the cross to the penitent malefactor: "Truly, I say to you, today you will be with me in Paradise" (Lk. 23:43), which implies the immediate experience of bliss and security after death, and therefore the continued conscious existence of the soul. In Calvin's day some attempted to counter this conclusion by arguing that, according to St. Peter, "with the Lord one day is as a thousand years" (2 Pet. 3:8), and thus thinking to remove any notion of immediacy. This, however, was a sophistry with which Calvin had little difficulty in dealing. More recent is the suggestion that the statement should be rendered, by a simple change in punctuation, as: "Truly, I say to you today, you will be with me in Paradise," which opens the way for relating the assurance of being with Christ to his eschatological return in glory and thereby obviating any reference to the intermediate state. This, it may be granted, is a possible way of rendering the Greek of St. Luke; but it is unacceptable for two reasons: first, because "Truly, I say to you" is by itself a characteristic introductory formula frequently used by Jesus, and this makes it most improbable that "today" belongs to this formula rather than to the assertion it introduces; and, second, because in an earlier statement to St. Peter introduced by the same formula the term "today," used in a similar fashion, clearly belongs to the assertion introduced by the formula—"Truly, I say to you, today, this very night, before the cock crows twice, you will deny me three times" (Mk. 14:30).[4]

The final word from the cross in St. Luke's account, "Father, into thy hands I commit my spirit" (Lk. 23:46; cf. Ps. 31:5), would also appear to favor the continuance of the soul's existence after the death of the body—the terms "soul" and "spirit" being interchangeable within this frame of reference; but otherwise it tells us nothing about the intermediate condition of the soul. St. John's apocalyptic perception of the souls of the martyrs crying out to the Lord for justice and of their being given white robes and being told "to rest a little longer, until the number of their fellow servants and their brethren should be complete" (Rev. 6:9-11), would certainly seem to indicate that between death and resurrection the soul is alive and alert as the consummation is awaited.

---

4. Lk. 23:43 reads, unpunctuated, *Amēn soi legō sēmeron met' emou esēi en tōi paradeisōi*. Mk. 14:30 reads, *Amēn legō soi hoti sy sēmeron tautēi tēi nykti ktl*. Though "today" in the latter place may seem to some to be redundant, the textual evidence for its inclusion is very strong, and for its omission comparatively weak. In the witnesses in which it is omitted there is probably an assimilation to the parallel passage Mt. 26:34, which does not include it. But, as Bruce M. Metzger observes, the pleonastic *sēmeron* is "so typical of Markan style" (*A Textual Commentary on the Greek New Testament* [London and New York, 1971], p. 114). If, perhaps, the word "today" was subconsciously imported from Lk. 23:43, its position in Mk. 14:30 only confirms that it does not belong to the introductory formula.

Moreover, Christ's admonition not to fear "those who kill the body but cannot kill the soul," but to fear rather "him who can destroy both soul and body in hell" (Mt. 10:28), implies that the death of the body does not involve the death of the soul, though the ultimate destruction of hell involves, for the unregenerate, the destruction of both body and soul.

Two places in the letters of St. Paul refer directly to the condition of the Christian after death. In Philippians 1:21-24 he indicates that for the believer the intermediate state is more desirable than continuing in this present earthly existence, for it is a state of *being with Christ*. "For me to live is Christ, and to die is gain," he said; but at the same time he realized that "to remain in the flesh" was "more necessary" for the sake of the ministry with which he had been entrusted. Even so, "My desire," he confessed, "is to depart and be with Christ, for that is far better." He obviously anticipated a personal awareness of the blessed condition of being in the presence of his Redeemer, for there would have been little sense in describing this as "gain" and "far better" if it meant his being unconscious of, and therefore unable to enjoy, this blissful state.

And in 2 Corinthians 5:1-9 St. Paul likens our present bodily existence to an earthly tent-dwelling which is dismantled at death, and contrasts it with the eternal heavenly building, that of the glorious resurrection body, which God has prepared for those who are in Christ. Here, indeed, he discloses a further preference beyond that mentioned in Philippians 1:23, namely, to be still alive at the time of Christ's return, and thus to avoid the experience of an intermediate state of existence. "We groan," he wrote, "and long to put on over [the present earthly dwelling] our dwelling from heaven" (like putting on a topcoat over a suit); and the purpose of this longing was "so that we may not be found naked," that is, divested of our body, for such divestment is disruptive of the integrity of man's true nature, which is bodily as well as spiritual. The Apostle would have preferred not to undergo this experience of "nakedness" which extends from death to resurrection. This demonstrates conclusively that Pythagorean or gnostic notions of the soul needing to be liberated from the body were completely alien to his thought. The sighing while in this present tent-dwelling, he explained, was "not that we would be unclothed," that is, be rid of bodily existence, "but that we would be clothed over," or superinvested, that is, with the glorified body God has prepared for us, "so that what is mortal may be swallowed up by life," that is, by the transformation of the present earthly body into the glorious heavenly body, without passing through death and the intermediate state.[5] But this did not alter his judgment that for the Christian the intermediate state is more desirable than this present existence; for while we are presently "at home in the body" we are, so to speak, "away from the Lord," and, he continued, "we would rather be away from the body and at home with the Lord."

---

5. For a discussion of the terminology of this passage see my commentary on the *Second Epistle to the Corinthians*, ad loc.

This simply means that *being with Christ,* which is the same as being *at home with the Lord,* is better than all that we know in this present life, but also that, beyond that, to be united in the true integrity of our being with Christ in the glorified state is better still than that intermediate condition in which there is the unnatural separation of soul and body. It does not mean, however, that this present existence, whatever its hardships, is deplorable or intolerable for the Christian, for, thanks to the indwelling reality of his Holy Spirit, the Lord is with us and we with him here and now (2 Cor. 5:5). There is a progressive intensity in the believer's experience of closeness to his Lord: first of all in the pilgrimage of this life, then more so in the period of waiting between death and resurrection, and finally most of all when the Lord appears in glory and the human soul is clothed with its resurrection body, thus attaining the full perfection of humanity for which man was all along destined by the Creator. For those who are alive at Christ's return, however, the intermediate stage of soul-nakedness is eliminated.

And so St. Paul declares that "we are always of good courage," never despondent or downhearted. For the present, while "we are at home in the body" and in that sense "away from the Lord," Christ is still everything to us, for "we walk by faith and not by sight" (2 Cor. 5:6-8; cf. 4:16-18); if death overtakes us, we are then "away from the body and at home with the Lord," and that can only be a state of bliss and security; and at last, at his appearing, we who were made in the divine image will be fully conformed to the likeness of him who is the True Image as the destiny of our being is eternally fulfilled, and that is the best of all. God keeps the good wine until last!

CHAPTER 37

Is the Soul Immortal?

Calvin's opposition to the opinion that in physical death the soul dies together with the body and in the intermediate state sleeps a sleep of death was consonant with and indeed required by his belief in the immortality of the human soul. Thus he maintained that his affirmation "that the soul, after the death of the body, still survives, endued with sense and intellect," was identical with the affirmation of "the immortality of the soul."[1] In support of the doctrine of the soul's immortality he cited a number of biblical texts: first of all, Christ's saying in Matthew 10:28, "Do not fear those who kill the body but cannot kill the soul; rather fear him who can destroy both soul and body in hell," on the basis of which he had good reason for concluding that the soul survives the death of the body. But it is difficult to see how he could derive an argument for the immortality of the soul from this saying, since it would seem, quite to the contrary, to imply the soul's mortality: that God can destroy both soul and body must surely mean that the soul is destructible. Nor do other places adduced by Calvin necessarily point to the immortality of the soul, namely, John 2:19, "Destroy this temple, and in three days I will raise it up," which refers, as the Apostle explains, to "the temple of his body"; Luke 23:46, "Father, into thy hands I commit my spirit" (cf. Ps. 31:5), and Acts 7:59, "Lord Jesus, receive my spirit," where Jesus and Stephen respectively, while suffering physical death, entrust their souls to God; John 19:30, Jesus "gave up his spirit," to the same effect; 1 Peter 3:19, which states that Jesus "went and preached to the spirits in prison," but which, as it is one of the most difficult and most widely controverted passages in the New Testament, not least as regards the identity of these "spirits," cannot safely be held to support belief in the soul's immortality; Ecclesiastes 12:7, "The dust returns to the earth as it was, and the spirit returns to God who gave it"; and Luke 16:19ff., which speaks of the state after death of the rich man and Lazarus.

These references are given in Calvin's early work opposing the doctrine of soul-sleep, but there is no indication of any subsequent change of mind on

1. J. Calvin, *Psychopannychia,* in *Tracts,* Vol. III, tr. Henry Beveridge (Edinburgh, 1851), p. 427. The Westminster Confession assigned to the souls of men "an immortal subsistence"—see the quotation above on pp. 393f.

his part. In the *Institutes* some of the same passages of Scripture are cited and man's soul or spirit is defined as "an immortal yet created essence, which is his nobler part." Calvin also argued that in men's fallen state "the light has not been so extinguished in the darkness that they remain untouched by a sense of their own immortality," and, further, that the human conscience "is an undoubted sign of the immortal spirit," indeed that "the very knowledge of God sufficiently proves that souls, which transcend the world, are immortal."[2] There is, however, a strangely Platonic ring to assertions, both in the *Psychopannychia* and in the *Institutes,* about the soul being "freed from the body," about the body "weighing down the soul" and being "the prison of the soul," and about the soul being "set free from this prison" and "loosed from these fetters" when we "put off the load of the body"[3]—even if it is impossible to doubt that Calvin intended this phraseology to be understood in the Pauline context of the conflict in the believer between flesh and spirit (Gal. 5:17), not in the Platonic sense of a radical dualism between soul and body. Commenting on 1 Corinthians 15:43, for example, he observed that "our body is now, indeed, subject to mortality and ignominy, but will then [after the resurrection] be glorious and incorruptible."[4]

The passages quoted by Calvin indicate that the human soul survives physical death, not that it is in itself immortal. The notion of the inherent immortality of the soul, it is true, has been generally accepted in the Christian church, and this is certainly a factor to be taken into account. The question of primary importance, however, is that of its compatibility with the biblical revelation. A consideration that has weighed with many defenders of this notion is the widespread conception of the soul's immortality in numerous different cultures and religions throughout the course of history, or at least the intimation of the continuation of existence beyond the grave. But this suggests an innate awareness that death is not the end of the story, indeed that man is answerable to God who is the source of his life, rather than a proof of personal or collective immortality (cf. Heb. 9:27; 4:12f.). Another argument which has been advanced is that by reason of his creation in the image of God man must participate in the excellencies that are attributed to God of which everlasting existence is not the least; and this has been said therefore to require the postulation of human immortality.[5] Man's formation in the image of God does indeed imply his possession of life in a manner which transcends that of other animate

2. *Institutes* I.xv.2.

3. *Psychopannychia*, pp. 432, 433, 443; *Institutes* I.xv.2. Similarly, Calvin explained the "groaning" mentioned in 2 Cor. 5:4 as arising from the knowledge of Christians that "they are here in a state of exile from their native land" and "shut up in the body as in a prison," with the consequence that "they feel this life to be a 'burden' because in it they cannot enjoy true and perfect blessedness" and "are unable to escape from the bondage of sin otherwise than by death" (*Commentary on 2 Corinthians,* ad loc.).

4. *Commentary on 1 Corinthians,* ad loc.

5. See, e.g., Gregory of Nyssa, *The Great Catechism* 5.

creatures; but it cannot mean the possession of life in the same sense as that in which God possesses it, if only because God possesses life absolutely, from eternity to eternity, whereas man possesses it derivatively and subject to the good pleasure of his Creator. The immortality of man or of the human soul is not then a necessary conclusion from this premise. It has also commonly been argued either *a priori* that the immortality of the soul demands the everlasting punishment of the wicked as well as the everlasting blessedness of the redeemed, or *a posteriori* that the endless punishment of the wicked as well as the endless blessedness of the redeemed demands the immortality of the soul.[6]

What may be deduced from the biblical revelation? First of all, that man as originally created was both potentially immortal and potentially mortal. In close association with this is his having been created potentially sinless, but also potentially sinful. The possibility of his sinning involved the possibility of his dying, just as the possibility of his not sinning involved the possibility of his not dying. As we have remarked earlier, this does not mean that man was originally created in a state of neutrality between righteousness and sinfulness and between living and dying; for, on the contrary, his creation in the divine image, which is the bond of his personal fellowship with his Maker, placed his existence quite positively within the sphere of godliness and life. His loving and grateful concurrence with the will of God, who is the source of his life and blessedness, would have ensured the continuation of his existence in unclouded blessing as he conformed himself to that image in which he is constituted. It was by his rebellion against his Creator that he passed from a positive to a negative relationship and brought the curse upon himself. His death, which is the sum of that curse, is also the evidence that man is not inherently immortal.

To contend that only the human soul is innately immortal is to maintain a position which is nowhere approved in the teaching of Scripture, for in the biblical purview human nature is always seen as integrally compounded of both the spiritual and the bodily. If this were not so, the whole doctrine of the incarnation and of the death and resurrection of the Son would be despoiled of meaning and reality. Man is essentially a corporeal-spiritual entity. God's warning at the beginning, regarding the forbidden tree, "In the day that you eat of it you shall die," was addressed to man as a corporeal-spiritual creature— should he eat of it, it was as such that he would die. There is no suggestion that a part of him was undying and therefore that his dying would be in part only.

The immortality, accordingly, of which the Christian is assured is not inherent in himself or in his soul but is bestowed by God and is the immortality of the whole person in the fulness of his humanity, bodily as well as spiritual. This immortality, unearned by us, has been gained for us by the incarnate Son who, by partaking of our human nature in its fulness, both bodily and spiritual, and by dying our death, nullified the power of the devil and removed from us the fear and the sting of death (Heb. 2:14f.; 1 Cor. 15:55f.). Our new life in

6. See, e.g., Augustine, *The City of God* vi.12.

Christ, which includes our ultimate resurrection to life and immortality, is owed entirely to God and his grace. *It is God who alone has immortality* and thus who alone may properly be described as immortal (1 Tim. 6:15-17; Rom. 1:23). And it is for us to confess, as did the Apostle, that by virtue of God's purpose and grace *"our Savior Jesus Christ has abolished death and brought life and immortality to light through the gospel"* (2 Tim. 1:9f.). The immortality which was potentially ours at creation and was forfeited in the fall is now really ours in Christ, in whom we are created anew and brought to our true destiny.

In his comments on 1 Timothy 6:16 Calvin made it plain that he did not regard immortality as inseparable from human nature or from the essence of the soul. "When it is said that God alone possesses immortality," he wrote, "it is not here denied that he bestows it, as he pleases, on any of his creatures." To say that God alone is immortal is to imply that "he has immortality in his power, so that it does not belong to creatures, except so far as he imparts to them power and vigor." This means, further, that "if you take away the power of God which is communicated to the soul of man it will instantly fade away." Thus Calvin concluded that "strictly speaking, immortality does not subsist in the nature of souls, . . . but comes from another source, namely, the secret inspiration of God."[7] The question that remains unanswered in the position represented by Calvin is this: if it is granted that immortality is a gift imparted by God and, further, that the being to whom it is imparted would "instantly fade away" were God's power to be removed, what grounds are there for concluding that immortality is a permanent gift which will not under any circumstances be removed and accordingly that no rational being will ever relapse into nonexistence, or, in other words, suffer destruction? It is a conclusion which (as we shall see) seems to rest largely on the supposition that the endless bliss of the redeemed requires to be balanced by the endless punishment of the damned.

There is good reason, we believe, for suggesting that the issue of the soul's immortality, in the sense that it is an endowment which will under no circumstances be removed, calls for some reconsideration in the light of biblical truth. We have objected that the survival of the person, or the soul, in the intermediate state between death and resurrection does not necessarily imply its everlasting survival. What God has brought into being he can also destroy. The New Testament foresees "a resurrection of both the just and the unjust" (Acts 24:15; Jn. 5:29), when the latter "will go away into eternal punishment, but the righteous into eternal life" (Mt. 25:46). This final separation will take place "when the Lord Jesus is revealed from heaven"; for it is then that those "who do not know God" and "who do not obey the gospel of our Lord Jesus" will "suffer the punishment of eternal destruction and exclusion from the presence of the Lord and from the glory of his might" (2 Thess. 1:7-9). This punishment is also described as being "thrown into the eternal fire" (Mt. 18:8) or "into hell, where their worm does not die and the fire is not quenched" (Mk. 9:44,

7. *Commentary on 1 Timothy,* ad loc.

47; cf. Mt. 3:12), and as causing weeping and gnashing of teeth to those on whom it comes (Mt. 13:36ff., 49f.; cf. 8:12; 22:13; 24:51; 25:30).

In the Apocalypse of St. John the ultimate doom of the devil, the beast, the false prophet, and all their followers whose names are not found written in the book of life, together with "Death and Hades," is to be cast into the lake burning with fire and brimstone (Rev. 2:11; 19:20; 20:6, 10, 14f.; 21:8). The imagery of this destruction, which is called "the second death," reflects the judgment that overtook Sodom and Gomorrah. It is recorded that "the Lord rained on Sodom and Gomorrah brimstone and fire from the Lord out of heaven, and overthrew those cities, and all the valley, and all the inhabitants of the cities," and that "the smoke of the land went up like the smoke of a furnace" (Gen. 19:24-28). The fate of these cities was seen as a warning and a typification of the final judgment of the wicked. Thus in Revelation 14:10f. it is said that the beast and his worshippers "shall be tormented with fire and brimstone . . . and the smoke of their torment goes up for ever and ever." It was a warning meanwhile of the devastating judgment that was ready to burst upon other civilizations in the course of history—for example, Babylon, regarding which Jeremiah prophesied that "as when God overthrew Sodom and Gomorrah and their neighbor cities, says the Lord, so no man shall dwell there, and no son of man sojourn in her" (Jer. 50:40); and even the people of Israel, whose apostasy, Moses warned, would render "the whole land brimstone and salt, and a burnt-out waste, unsown, and growing nothing, where no grass can sprout, an overthrow like that of Sodom and Gomorrah, Admah and Zeboiim, which the Lord overthrew in his anger and wrath" (Dt. 29:23). And St. Peter gave the admonition that God "by turning the cities of Sodom and Gomorrah to ashes condemned them to extinction and made them an example to those who were to be ungodly" (2 Pet. 2:6).

The terrible fate of the cities of the plain is thus a paradigm not only of the divine retribution which obliterates cities and communities but especially of the final judgment of the world by which the destroyers of the earth will be destroyed and the creation purged of all defilement (Rev. 11:18; 21:8, 27); for "the heavens and earth that now exist have been stored up for fire, being kept until the day of judgment and destruction of ungodly men" (2 Pet. 3:7). Then what cannot be shaken will remain; but meanwhile we must constantly remember the importance of living godly lives, "offering to God acceptable worship, with reverence and awe, for our God is a consuming fire" (Heb. 12:27-29; 2 Pet. 3:11-13).

In St. Jude's brief letter these same cities are said to "serve as an example by undergoing a punishment of eternal fire" (Jude 7). Even though this was not the final judgment, the obliterating fire is described as *eternal* fire. The reason for this, no doubt, is that it was *divine* fire, the fire of judgment sent by the Lord; for obviously in the case of these cities the fire was not eternally endured by their inhabitants. It was fire that struck and left devastation from which no restoration could follow. This consideration may reasonably raise the question whether the eternal and unquenchable fire of the final judgment (Mt. 8:18; Mk. 9:44) will be eternally endured by those who are consigned to it. Is this what is meant by "everlasting punishment" (Mt. 25:46) and by the assertion regarding those who suffer it that "the smoke of their torment goes up for ever and ever" (Rev. 14:11)? Such terminology can certainly bear the inference that the torment of the damned in hell will be endlessly continued; and this inference has been thought, as we mentioned, to provide an appropriate balance for the doctrine of the everlasting life which, as is universally agreed, the redeemed are to enjoy without end or term. It is a balance on which, for example, Augustine insisted. Referring to Matthew 25:41, he exclaimed: "What a fond fancy it is to suppose that eternal punishment means long continued punishment, while eternal life means life without end!" Both destinies, he maintained, "are correlative—on the one hand punishment eternal, on the other hand life eternal"; consequently, to say that "life eternal shall be endless, punishment eternal shall come to an end, is the height of absurdity."[8]

The logic of this interpretation is sound enough so long as it is *punishment* that is spoken of as being endless. But, as we have seen, the ultimate contrast (as was also the original) is between everlasting *life* and everlasting *death,* and this clearly shows that it is not simply synonyms but also antonyms with which we have to reckon. There is no more radical antithesis than that between life and death, for life is the absence of death and death is the absence of life. Confronted with this antithesis, the position of Augustine cannot avoid involvement in the use of contradictory concepts, for the notion of death that is everlastingly endured requires the postulation that the damned be kept endlessly alive to endure it. Thus Augustine was forced to argue that for those in hell "death will not be abolished, but will be eternal," and that "the living bodies of men hereafter will be such as to endure everlasting pain and fire without ever dying";[9] and he depicted the wicked as everlastingly doomed to "drag out a miserable existence in eternal death without the power of dying."[10] It would be hard to imagine a concept more confusing than that of death which means existing endlessly without the power of dying. This, however, is the corner into which Augustine (in company with many others) argued himself.

By way of further illustration we will turn to a famous sermon preached by another notable Christian divine of a more recent period, Jonathan Edwards, who described the endlessness of God's wrath in the following terms:

> It would be dreadful to suffer this fierceness and wrath of Almighty God one moment; but you must suffer it to all eternity. There will be no end to this exquisite horrible misery. When you look forward, you shall see a long forever, a boundless duration before you, . . . and you will absolutely despair of ever having any deliverance, any end, any mitigation, any rest at all. You will know

8. Augustine, *The City of God* xxi.23.
9. Ibid. xxi.3, 5.
10. *Enchiridion* 111.

certainly that you must wear out long ages, millions of millions of ages, in wrestling and conflicting with this almighty merciless vengeance; and then when you have so done, when so many ages have actually been spent by you in this manner, you will know that all is but a point to what remains. So that your punishment will indeed be infinite.[11]

It is only right to point out that, while they firmly believed in the endless torments of hell, Augustine was intent on refuting the notion that future punishment would lead at last to universal restoration (universalism), which was connected with the philosophy of the Platonists and the thought of Origen, and that the purpose of Edwards in this sermon was compassionately to urge his hearers to flee from the wrath to come and all its terrors by taking refuge in the redeeming grace of the gospel.[12]

The difficulty (if such it is) of equating everlasting death with everlasting existence was compounded in the case of Augustine by reason of the fact that he took the unquenchable flames of eternal fire to be meant in a literal sense. In facing the question how it would be possible for resurrected persons of body and soul to be kept from being consumed by these flames he invoked the support of scientific fact, as he thought it to be, that certain lower creatures, and in particular the salamander, "can live in the fire, in burning without being consumed, in pain without dying." It was decidedly shaky support, however, because the naturalists known to him of his own and earlier periods reported this competence of the salamander with skepticism as a traditional or legendary notion. But in any case the supposed ability of the salamander was irrelevant, because it is not a capacity shared by human beings with salamanders, and Augustine had perforce to resort to the hypothesis that in the flames of hell the wicked would in this respect become salamander-like: "Although it is true," he wrote, "that in this world there is no flesh which can suffer pain and yet cannot die, yet in the world to come there will be flesh such as there is not now, as there will also be death such as there is not now."[13]

Augustine, in short, found it necessary to introduce a change in the meaning of *death* if his belief in the endlessness of the torments of hellfire was to be sustained; and this is a necessity for all who understand eternal destruction

11. Jonathan Edwards, Sermon on "Sinners in the Hands of an Angry God," in *Works*, Vol. II (London, 1840), p. 11. The sermon was preached on 8 July 1741.

12. Thus Edwards wrote: "The gospel is to be preached as well as the law, and the law is to be preached only to make way for the gospel, and in order that it may be preached more effectually. The main work of ministers is to preach the gospel. . . . So that a minister would miss it very much if he should insist so much on the terrors of the law as to forget his Lord, and neglect to preach the gospel; but yet the law is very much to be insisted on, and the preaching of the gospel is like to be in vain without it. . . . Some talk of it as an unreasonable thing to fright persons to heaven; but I think it is a reasonable thing to fright persons away from hell. . . . Is it not a reasonable thing to fright a person out of a house on fire?" ("The Distinguishing Marks of a Work of the Spirit of God" i.9 [*Works*, Vol. II, p. 266]).

13. Augustine, *The City of God* xxi.2, 3, 9.

in this way, whether or not they consider the flames of hell to be intended in a literal sense. Such persons can indeed claim to be in good company; but they should be aware that their interpretation is open to serious questioning. Apart from the fact that it involves a drastic change in the meaning of death so that, in this eschatological perspective, it signifies being kept alive to suffer punishment without the power of dying, some other considerations must be taken into account.

First of all, because *life* and *death* are radically antithetical to each other, the qualifying adjective *eternal* or *everlasting* needs to be understood in a manner appropriate to each respectively. Everlasting life is existence that continues without end, and everlasting death is destruction without end, that is, destruction without recall, the destruction of obliteration. Both life and death hereafter will be everlasting in the sense that both will be *irreversible:* from that life there can be no relapse into death, and from that death there can be no return to life. The awful negation and the absolute finality of the second death are unmistakably conveyed by its description as "the punishment of eternal destruction and exclusion from the presence of the Lord" (2 Thess. 1:9).

Secondly, immortality or deathlessness, as we have said, is not inherent in the constitution of man as a corporeal-spiritual creature, though, formed in the image of God, the potential was there. That potential, which was forfeited through sin, has been restored and actualized by Christ, the incarnate Son, who has "abolished death and brought life and immortality to light through the gospel" (2 Tim. 1:10). Since inherent immortality is uniquely the possession and prerogative of God (1 Tim. 6:16), it will be by virtue of his grace and power that when Christ is manifested in glory our mortality, if we are then alive, will be superinvested with immortality and our corruption, if we are then in the grave, will be clothed with incorruption, so that death will at last be swallowed up in victory (1 Cor. 15:51-57; 2 Cor. 5:1-5). And thus at last we shall become truly and fully human as the destiny for which we were created becomes an everlasting reality in him who is the True Image and the True Life. At the same time those who have persisted in ungodliness will discover for themselves the dreadful truth of Christ's warning about fearing God, "who can destroy both body and soul in hell" (Mt. 10:28).

Thirdly, the everlasting existence side by side, so to speak, of heaven and hell would seem to be incompatible with the purpose and effect of the redemption achieved by Christ's coming. Sin with its consequences of suffering and death is foreign to the design of God's creation. The renewal of creation demands the elimination of sin and suffering and death. Accordingly, we are assured that Christ "has appeared once for all at the end of the ages to put away sin by the sacrifice of himself" (Heb. 9:26; 1 Jn. 3:5), that through his appearing death has been abolished (2 Tim. 1:10), and that in the new heaven and the new earth, that is, in the whole realm of the renewed order of creation, there will be no more weeping or suffering, "and death shall be no more" (Rev. 21:4). The conception of the endlessness of the suffering of torment and of the endurance of "living" death in hell stands in contradiction to this teaching. It leaves a part of creation which, unrenewed, everlastingly exists in alienation from the new heaven and the new earth. It means that suffering and death will never be totally abolished from the scene. The inescapable logic of this position was accepted, with shocking candor, by Augustine, who affirmed that "after the resurrection, when the final, universal judgment has been completed, there will be two kingdoms, each with its own distinct boundaries, the one Christ's, the other the devil's, the one consisting of good, the other of bad."[14] To this it must be objected that with the restoration of all things in the new heaven and the new earth, which involves God's reconciliation to himself of *all things,* whether on earth or in heaven (Acts 3:21; Col. 1:20), there will be no place for a second kingdom of darkness and death. Where all is light there can be no darkness; for "the night shall be no more" (Rev. 22:5). When Christ fills all in all and God is everything to everyone (Eph. 1:23; 1 Cor. 15:28), how is it conceivable that there can be a section or realm of creation that does not belong to this fulness and by its very presence contradicts it? The establishment of God's everlasting kingdom of peace and righteousness will see the setting free of the whole created order from its bondage to decay as it participates in the glorious liberty of the children of God (Rom. 8:21).

Fourthly, the glorious appearing of Christ will herald the death of death. By his cross and resurrection Christ has already made the conquest of death, so that for the believer the fear and sting of death have been removed (Heb. 2:14f.; 1 Cor. 15:54-57), the passage from death to life is a present reality (Jn. 5:24), and the resurrection power of Jesus is already at work within him, no matter how severely he may be afflicted and incommoded outwardly (2 Cor. 4:11, 16). We do not yet see everything in subjection to the Son (Heb. 2:8); but nothing is more sure than that every hostile rule and authority and power will finally be destroyed, including death itself. Hence the assurance that "the last enemy to be destroyed is death" (1 Cor. 15:24-26). Without the abolition of death the triumph of life and immortality cannot be complete (2 Tim. 1:10). This is the significance of *the second death:* it will be the abolition not only of sin and the devil and his followers but also of death itself as, in the final judgment, not only will Death and Hades give up their dead for condemnation but Death and Hades themselves will be thrown with them into the lake of fire (Rev. 20:13-15). Hence the clear promise that "death shall be no more" (Rev. 21:4).

Though held by many, it is a hollow contention that if the death sentence pronounced at the final judgment against the unregenerate meant their annihilation the wicked would be getting off lightly and would be encouraged to regard the consequence of their sin without fear. (It may be interposed that far more does the expectation of the never-ending torment of finite creatures raise the question of the purpose that might be served by such retribution.) There is

14. *Enchiridion* 111.

altogether no room for doubting that, first, at the last judgment God will mete out condign punishment in accordance with the absolute holiness of his being, and, second, the Scriptures allow no place whatsoever to the wicked for complacency as they approach that dreadful day when they will stand before the tribunal of their righteous Creator. This ultimate Day of the Lord is depicted as a day of indescribable terror for the ungodly, who will then be confronted with the truth of God's being which they had unrighteously suppressed and experience the divine wrath which previously they had derided. They will then learn at first hand that "it is a fearful thing to fall into the hands of the living God" (Heb. 10:31). There is nothing light or laughable in the terrible scene witnessed by St. John in his apocalyptic vision: "Then the kings of the earth and the great men and the generals and the rich and the strong, and every one, slave and free, hid in the caves and among the rocks of the mountains, calling to the mountains and the rocks, 'Fall on us and hide us from the face of him who is seated on the throne, and from the wrath of the Lamb, for the great day of their wrath has come, and who can stand before it?'" (Rev. 6:15-17).

The horror of everlasting destruction will be compounded, moreover, by the unbearable agony of *exclusion*. To be inexorably excluded from the presence of the Lord and from the glory of his kingdom, to see but to be shut out from the transcendental joy and bliss of the saints as in light eternal they glorify their resplendent Redeemer, to whose likeness they are now fully and forever conformed, to be plunged into the abyss of irreversible destruction, will cause the unregenerate of mankind the bitterest anguish of weeping and wailing and gnashing of teeth. In vain will they have pleaded, "Lord, Lord, open to us!" (Mt. 25:11f.; cf. 7:21-23). Too late will they then wish they had lived and believed differently. The destiny they have fashioned for themselves will cast them without hope into the abyss of obliteration. Their lot, whose names are not written in the Lamb's book of life, is the destruction of the second death. Thus God's creation will be purged of all falsity and defilement, and the ancient promise will be fulfilled that "the former things shall not be remembered or come to mind" as the multitude of the redeemed are glad and rejoice forever in the perfection of the new heaven and the new earth (Is. 65:17f.; Rev. 21:1-4).

CHAPTER 38

The Kingdom

Christ's forerunner John the Baptist proclaimed in the wilderness that the kingdom of heaven was at hand (Mt. 3:2), and this same declaration was made by Jesus as he commenced his ministry in Galilee (Mt. 4:17; Mk. 1:14f.), for the coming of Jesus was the coming of the King. It is not surprising, then, that the kingdom was one of the main focal points of his teaching. He admonished his critics, who wished to dismiss his casting out of demons as a work of the devil, that on the contrary, as any unbiased person should have been willing to acknowledge, it was a clear indication that the kingdom of God had come upon them (Mt. 12:22ff.). By their hostile attitude they were shutting themselves off from "the good news of the kingdom of God" which the incarnate Son had been sent to announce (Lk. 4:43). His coming, in fact, signalized the fulfilment of the ancient prophecies concerning the establishment of an everlasting kingdom of justice and peace (see, e.g., Is. 9:6f.) which the saints of the Most High would possess forever and ever (cf. Dan. 7:18, 27). Hence the assurance given to the Virgin Mary regarding the son she was to bear that "of his kingdom there will be no end" (Lk. 1:33)—a consideration that in itself implied that Christ's kingdom, as he advised Pilate, is not of this world (Jn. 18:36), for the kingdoms of this fallen world are set up and thrown down by force of arms and their decline is more certain than their rising. So, too, the preaching of the apostles could summarily be described as "preaching the kingdom" (Acts 20:25; cf. 28:23, 31; Lk. 9:2, 60) as they obediently followed the example and the instruction of their Master (Mt. 4:23; 9:35).

While the kingdom of the Son is not *of* this world, it is quite certainly *over* this world; and as such it is not really a new development, for he is supreme over all things as the Lord of creation. As St. Paul writes, "in him all things were created, in heaven and on earth, visible and invisible, whether thrones or dominions or principalities or authorities—all things were created through him and for him" (Col. 1:16). Moreover, he is sovereign over the universe because he sustains the whole created order in existence: "he is before all things, and in him all things hold together" (Col. 1:17). It is by his word of power that he providentially bears the cosmos onward to the consummation for which it has from the beginning been destined (Heb. 1:3). Thus it is from and through the Son that the world receives its coherence and its purpose. And yet further, he is supreme over all in his capacity as Redeemer, bringing restoration to man and creation, for "he is the head of the body, the church," which is the community of the twice-born who will inherit the new heaven and the new earth, the reconstituted creation, and "he is the beginning, the firstborn from the dead," through whose resurrection and glorification that inheritance is fully assured, since, "peace having been made by the blood of his cross," it is God's good pleasure "through him to reconcile to himself all things, whether on earth or in heaven." In everything, accordingly, the preeminence belongs to the Son, "for in him all the fulness of God was pleased to dwell" (Col. 1:18-20). If anything should be absolutely beyond peradventure, then, it is this, that, no matter how fiercely the satanic forces of evil may presume to challenge and assail the sovereignty of the Son, his supremacy is from eternity to eternity inviolable and his purpose indefectible. That there are fearsome enemies is not denied. But the inevitability of their defeat and destruction is not open to question: Christ, we are told, "must reign until he has put all enemies under his feet" (1 Cor. 15:25).

This last statement may seem to indicate that the reign of Christ will not after all be everlasting—that it will cease once every hostile power has been subdued by him. And this may appear to be confirmed by the teaching that follows in this passage, for with the coming of Christ on the last of these last days there will be the ingathering of the great harvest of the redeemed (of which, as the firstfruits, he is the guarantee); and "then," we read, "comes the end, when he delivers the kingdom to God the Father after destroying every rule and every authority and power," and "when all things are subjected to him, then the Son himself will also be subjected to him who put all things under him, that God may be everything to every one" (1 Cor. 15:23f., 28). What is described here, however, is the conclusion of the Son's mission rather than the end of his reign. The purpose of the incarnation will then have attained complete fulfilment, and thereby the destiny of creation will simultaneously be realized through the Son who from first to last is the agent of the divine will. God's reconciliation of the world to himself in Christ will then have been actualized (2 Cor. 5:19).

It is as the incarnate Son that Christ, his mission of reconciliation completed, will deliver the kingdom to God the Father. The intention is not that the Son will then cease to reign or will disappear from the scene, but that his reign will be continued evermore within the threefold unity of the Godhead; and so *God* will be all in all—not just God the Father or God the Son or God the Holy Spirit, but God in the perfection of his trinitarian wholeness. Thus in speaking of the Son handing over the kingdom to the Father, the Apostle is teaching not the abdication of the Son but the completion of his redemptive mission and the everlasting rule of God. The moment in view coincides with the announcement in heaven heard by St. John, following the sounding of the trumpet by the seventh angel: "The kingdom of the world has become the kingdom of our Lord and of his Christ, and he shall reign for ever and ever" (Rev. 11:15). It is in the endless era which Jesus called "the regeneration" or "the rebirth,"[1] the renewal of all things, that he will sit "on his glorious throne" (Mt. 19:28). He is indeed already, as St. Peter testified to Cornelius, "Lord of all" (Acts 10:36); but the consummation will come with the subjugation and destruction of every enemy. The appearing of him who is even now "our Lord Jesus Christ" is an event which "will be made manifest at the proper time by the blessed and only Sovereign, the King of kings and Lord of lords" (1 Tim. 6:14f.).

It is as the rightful "heir of all things" that the Son is enthroned "at the right hand of the Majesty of high" (Heb. 1:2, 3); and it is through their union with him who is uniquely the Son with whom the Father is well pleased (Mt. 3:17; 17:5) that Christian believers, having received "the spirit of sonship" and assured by the inner witness of the Holy Spirit that they are children of God, are themselves accepted as "heirs, heirs of God and fellow heirs with Christ," who know that those who suffer with him here will be glorified with him hereafter (Rom. 8:15-18). In Christ they are inheritors of the kingdom of God (Jas. 2:5). God, St. Paul asserts, "has delivered us from the dominion of darkness and transferred us to the kingdom of his beloved Son" (Col. 1:13); and in the light of this truth he charged the Thessalonian Christians "to lead a life worthy of God, who calls you into his kingdom and glory" (1 Thess. 2:11f.). "By God's great mercy," St. Peter writes, "we have been born anew to a living hope through the resurrection of Jesus Christ from the dead, to an inheritance which is imperishable, undefiled, and unfading" (1 Pet. 1:3f.). It follows that those whose lives are given over to vice and violence and unbelief will not inherit the kingdom of God (1 Cor. 6:9; Gal. 5:21; Eph. 5:5). Only those whose lives are animated by the grace of the gospel will hear the King saying to them: "Come, O blessed of my Father, inherit the kingdom prepared for you from the foundation of the world" (Mt. 25:34).

The kingdom of God in the new heaven and the new earth is also the harvest of God, the fruition of all his purposes from the foundation of the world. The realization of man's glorious destiny in Christ is the flowering and fructification not merely of the good seed of the gospel planted in the soil of his heart but also of the good seed of Christlikeness, which is the true significance of his constitution in the image of God, planted in the heart of his being at creation. The purpose of creation is reestablished and achieved in the grace of regeneration. This involves the realization of the cosmic order and harmony of all things—not, however, in a merely static sense, as though it were no more than the recovery of the *status quo ante,* that is, of an original fixity of being, but in accordance with the dynamic and vibrantly progressive will of God which is the energy that interpenetrates the whole of his creation. Eden, ordered and harmonious though it was, was but the beginning, not the full end, of the

---

1. *Hē palingenesia.*

Creator's design for the cosmos. Man, as we have seen, was made lower than the angels only *for a little while;* his true destiny was always intended to be higher than the angels, in union with Christ, the true Image of his being, crowned with glory and honor, "far above all rule and authority and power and dominion," participating in his lordship over all the works of God's hands (Ps. 8:5f.; Heb. 2:5-9; Eph. 1:19-23). Because it is the end toward which creation was always dynamically directed, the paradise regained in Christ is more glorious than the paradise lost in Adam. The end was indeed latent in the beginning, as the oak tree is latent in the acorn; but, as the oak tree is greater and more glorious than the acorn, so the consummation of all things is greater and more glorious than their beginning.

We have endeavored to show how this principle of innate potency and ultimate transcendence has its focus in man who, formed in the image of God, that is, in Christ, himself that Image, by consistently conforming himself to that image should have advanced from glory to glory to the goal of total Christiformity, and by doing so would have promoted the ordered harmony of the world over which, under the Creator, he had been given dominion; how by his fall and the ungodly perversion of his powers man dragged the world down with himself into futility; how by the same token the redemptive restoration of man leads also to the rehabilitation of creation (Rom. 8:19ff.); and how the progressive ascent from glory to glory which at the beginning was the potential planted in man by reason of his constitution in the image of God—which is none other than his constitution in the Son—is now being realized in the same Son, now incarnate, as the Christian believer is being progressively "transformed into the same image from glory to glory" (2 Cor. 3:18). It is the upward advance of our sanctification, and the consummation of total Christiformity will be experienced when Christ appears at the end of the age to establish the new heavens and the new earth in which righteousness dwells (2 Pet. 3:13), for, as St. John says, "we know that when he appears we shall be like him" (1 Jn. 3:2). Then it is that we shall see him, and, fully transformed in his glory, be able to see him, face to face (1 Cor. 13:12).

As we have indicated, however, the designation of the kingdom as the kingdom of God and the kingdom of heaven does not imply that earth will at last be eliminated from the scene. What it does denote is the rule of God over all (cf. 1 Cor. 15:28), earth as well as heaven. It is the bringing of all things to their predestined glory, of the seed to the full harvest of beauty and fruitfulness, of potentiality to actuality. The end must not be disconnected from the beginning, for all that God purposed in the beginning will be achieved in the glory that is yet to be revealed, and is even now infallibly assured in the present sharing of our human nature in the glorification of the incarnate Son. There is a genuine congruence between the end and the beginning. Thus the opening truth of Scripture, that "in the beginning God created the heavens and the earth" (Gen. 1:1), meets with the witness in the closing pages of Scripture of the exiled apostle, "I saw a new heaven and a new earth" (Rev. 21:1),[2] that is, heaven and earth redemptively renewed in accordance with God's immutable purpose for his creation. The life of the world to come, then, is earthly as well as heavenly. Far from being incorporeal, the existence of the redeemed will be the bodily existence of those whose bodies, having been sown in weakness and humiliation, will be raised in power and glory (1 Cor. 15:43), the resplendent harvest springing from the seed of that true image implanted at creation and revivified by redeeming grace.

And the function of the redeemed in heaven will be both the praise and worship of God and also the service of their Creator and Redeemer. Not only will they fall before the throne of God on their faces and adoringly sing, "Amen! Blessing and glory and wisdom and thanksgiving and honor and power and might be to our God for ever and ever! Amen," but they will also "serve him day and night in his temple" (Rev. 7:11f., 15). They will form that "great multitude which no man can number, from every nation, from all tribes and peoples and tongues, . . . who have washed their robes and made them white in the blood of the Lamb" (Rev. 7:9, 14), the authentic seed of Abraham, innumerable, as promised, as the stars of heaven, the sand of the seashore, and the dust of the earth—authentic through their incorporation into the incarnate Son, who is uniquely the seed in whom all the nations of the world are blessed (Gen. 13:16; 14:4f.; 22:15-18; Gal. 3:8f., 16, 29). In the renewed creation they will fulfil and rejoice in the wonderful potential of their humanity as, authentically human at last, in accordance with the divine image of their formation they responsibly and righteously exercise their God-given dominion in the created realm.

As at the beginning man was blessed with the enjoyment of personal friendship and communion with his Creator, after whose image he was made, so in the renewal of creation he will again and forever know the bliss of intimate unclouded personal fellowship with God, purchased by the blood of Christ's cross (Col. 1:20), and, being at peace with God, he will also be at peace with his fellowmen and the whole order of creation. Thus the lonely apostle was assured by the great voice from the throne: "Behold, the dwelling of God is with men. He will dwell with them, and they shall be his people, and God

---

2. The explanatory clause that immediately follows, "for the first heaven and the first earth had passed away," does not mean the destruction or disappearance of the original creation but the passing of creation in its present state of fallenness as the original creation is brought to the glorious destiny for which it was all along designed. It is the regeneration of creation. When, for example, St. Peter speaks of the world of Noah's day being destroyed by the waters of the flood he obviously does not mean the destruction of creation; and when he goes on to say that "by the same word the heavens and earth that now exist have been stored up for fire, being kept until the day of judgment and destruction of ungodly men" (2 Pet. 3:6, 7), he is not predicting the destruction of creation but its purging by the fire of judgment which will overtake all who sinfully oppose themselves to God and his will.

himself will be with them." In the blessed harmony of that existence there will be no more weeping or pain or death, "for the former things have passed away" (Rev. 21:3); and this will be both the recovery of Eden and the fulfilment of the promises of the new covenant through the redemptive work of the incarnate Son (cf. Lev. 26:11f.; Is. 25:8; 35:10; 51:11; 65:17-19; Jer. 24:7; 30:22; 31:33; 32:38; Ezek. 37:26f.; Zech. 8:8; Heb. 8:6ff.; 9:15).

As, moreover, there was a river in Eden bringing life-giving water to the garden (Gen. 2:10), so also St. John was shown in his vision of the heavenly city which is to come (Heb. 11:16; 13:14) "the river of the water of life, flowing from the throne of God and of the Lamb through the middle of the street of the city" (Rev. 22:1f.; cf. Ezek. 47:1ff.), and symbolizing the limitless bounty of the grace of eternal life which we have in Christ Jesus. For, as the psalmist says, "the river of God is full of water" (Ps. 65:9): it is never depleted or diminished; no matter how much we draw from it, it is always full. Never again will there be the forsaking of God, "the fountain of living waters," and the hewing out for ourselves of broken cisterns that can hold no water (Jer. 2:13); for in the new heavens and the new earth the redeemed will evermore realize the truth of the Savior's promise that "whoever drinks of the water that I shall give him will never thirst," and that "the water that I shall give him will become in him a spring of water welling up to eternal life" (Jn. 4:14).

And closely linked to the ceaseless flow of the water of divine grace is the restoration of access to the tree of life which at creation had been "in the midst of the garden" (Gen. 3:3), freely available to man, but the way to which was subsequently blocked by reason of the folly of man's rebellion against his Creator (Gen. 3:24). We have seen how, by turning away from God who is the source of all life, man suicidally turned away from life and brought the sentence of death upon himself (Rom. 6:23). But now, in his preview of the eternal reality, St. John sees, "on either side of the river, the tree of life with its twelve kinds of fruit, yielding its fruit each month," while its leaves are "for the healing of the nations" (Rev. 22:2; cf. Ezek. 47:12)—language which signifies the abundance of life and wholeness, without interruption or cessation, which the redeemed will enjoy in the glory that is to be revealed.

Thus the curse of futility which man through the perverting of his nature brought upon himself and upon the creation over which he had been placed will be removed by virtue of the redeeming work of him who became accursed for us (Gal. 3:13), as at last "creation itself will be set free from its bondage to decay" and will participate in "the glorious liberty of the children of God" (Rom. 8:19-21). As all things were created through Christ and for Christ (that is, with Christ as the omega as well as the alpha), so all things will achieve their ultimate destiny in Christ (Col. 1:15ff.; Rev. 1:8; 21:6; 22:13; Is. 41:4, 6). And man at last will attain the full actualization of the marvelous potential implicit in his beginning as the creature uniquely privileged by being constituted in the image of God, so that his latter will far exceed his former glory as by divine grace he reaches the ever-intended goal of Christiformity and his will becomes one with the Son's will, which is one with the Father's. In this harmony of all things, which is God's kingdom of peace and holiness, the great multitude of the redeemed "will reign for ever and ever" (Rev. 22:5). The glory of heaven will be beyond all imagination. The earth, free from all defilement and disproportion, will be indescribably beautiful. The music of the universe will be without discord. The atmosphere of the new heaven and earth will be totally pervaded by the love of God, who will be all in all. And the willing service of God in his kingdom will be altogether fulfilling and purposeful, free from all doubt and disappointment, for then at last and unfailingly we shall exult in the full power and authenticity of our humanity. We shall be as we were created to be, joyfully conformed to the likeness of the Son who is the True Image of our formation and our being.

> O God, whose blessed Son was manifested, that he might destroy the works of the devil and make us the sons of God and heirs of eternal life, grant us, we beseech thee, that, having this hope, we may purify ourselves, even as he is pure, that, when he shall appear again with power and great glory, we may be made like unto him in his eternal and glorious kingdom, where with thee, O Father, and thee, O Holy Ghost, he liveth and reigneth, ever one God, world without end. Amen.

The English *Book of Common Prayer*

Index of Names and Subjects

Abelard, Peter, 350ff., 360
Adam, the last or second, 24, 27, 60, 62, 129, 134, 156, 217, 328, 329, 330, 332, 334
Adelphius, Bishop of Onuphis, 277, 281
Adoptionism, 209, 249, 259, 315
Albert the Great, 195, 202
Alexander, Bishop of Alexandria, 270, 273
Alexander of Hales, 224
Allison, C. FitzSimons, Bishop of South Carolina, 204, 207
Alogi, 253, 258
Althaus, Paul, 368
Ambrose, Bishop of Milan, 38, 217, 240, 269, 270, 290, 345, 346
Anabaptists, 253, 393
Anastasius, 299
Anatolius, 311
Angels, 74f., 89
Apollinaris, Apollinarianism, 266, 274, 287ff., 295, 296, 298, 301, 302, 307, 308, 315, 332
Aquinas, Thomas, 12, 17, 75, 78, 96, 195, 196, 197, 202
Ariminium (Rimini), Council of, 45
Aristophanes, 20
Aristotle, 83, 195, 196
Arius, Arianism, 15, 36, 37, 38, 44, 201, 248, 255, 260, 261, 263, 264, 265, 266ff., 287, 288, 291, 296, 298, 315, 321
Arminius, Arminianism, 159, 187, 199, 200, 203, 204, 207, 208
Artemas (Artemon), 258
Ascension, 33, 363, 365, 368, 373f., 378, 379, 380
Assurance. See Security
Asterius, 266, 267, 268

Athanasius, Bishop of Alexandria, 16, 37, 87, 158, 219, 257, 266, 267, 268, 269, 270, 273, 276ff., 281, 282, 286, 291, 292, 313, 319, 326, 327, 342, 343, 347, 381
Augustine, Bishop of Hippo, Augustinianism, viii, 9, 11, 16, 17, 22, 51, 53, 65, 75, 77, 78, 86ff., 90, 91, 95, 96, 100, 102, 103, 107, 108, 111, 127, 138, 139, 146, 147, 153, 154, 163, 185, 186ff., 193, 194, 218, 240, 304, 319, 343, 345, 346, 352, 353, 400, 403, 404, 406
Aulén, Gustaf, Bishop of Strängnäs, 351f.
Authority, 61f.

Bach, Johann Sebastian, 63
Bancroft, Richard, Archbishop of Canterbury, 204
Barr, James, 7
Barrett, C. K., 223, 261
Barth, Karl, 18, 19, 20, 21, 101ff., 107, 112, 128, 129, 170, 199, 324, 361, 362, 377, 380
Basil the Great, Bishop of Caesarea, 87, 257, 258, 288, 290
Basilides, 246
Bavinck, Herman, 21, 78
Baxter, Richard, 205
Behm, J., 48
Benedict XV, Bishop of Rome, 202
Bengel, J. A., 43
Berdyaev, Nicolas, 52, 54
Berkouwer, G. C., 21
Bernard of Clairvaux, 187, 202, 351, 354
Bernard, J. H., Archbishop of Dublin, 261
Bethune-Baker, J. F., 298, 306
Bigg, Charles, 265
Bindley, T. H., 314
Bonaventure, Giovanni, 202

Bonhoeffer, Dietrich, 324, 325
Brahms, Johannes, 63
Bready, J. Wesley, 140
Brown, Raymond E., 222
Brunner, Emil, 7, 67, 68, 69, 107ff., 112, 170, 220, 324, 366, 369ff., 375, 376, 379, 380
Buber, Martin, 54
Bultmann, Rudolf, 222, 321, 324, 366, 367, 377, 378

Cabalists, 12
Caesarius, Bishop of Arles, 192
Cairns, David, 68
Callistus, Bishop of Rome, 256, 257
Calvary. See Cross
Calvin, John, 11, 12, 22, 24, 48, 51, 65, 66, 67, 126, 153, 154ff., 166, 173, 176, 177f., 181, 187, 224, 333, 338, 393, 394, 395, 398, 399, 401
Cambridge Platonists, The, 208
Campenhausen, Hans von, 221
Carthage, Council of, 139
Cassian, John, 190f.
Celestine, Bishop of Rome, 298, 299, 300
Celestius, 185, 186
Celsus, 8, 261
Cerdo, 247
Cerinthus, 85, 240, 241, 242, 243, 249, 250, 253, 315
Chadwick, Owen, 187, 191
Chalcedon, Council of, 201, 275, 289, 294, 297, 299, 302, 305, 307ff., 311, 315, 323, 327
Chalcedonian Definition of the Faith, 280, 304, 305, 314f., 316, 320, 321, 322, 323, 325, 326, 356
Christiformity, Christlikeness, ix, 19, 27, 36, 46f., 135, 195, 283, 330, 381, 382, 385, 397, 400, 407, 410, 411, 413f.
Christology, viii, 15, 49, 246, 276ff., 292, 375ff.
Christotokos ("Mother of Christ"), 299
Chrysostom, John, Bishop of Constantinople, 28, 37, 47, 48, 294, 298, 301, 307
Cicero, 11
Clement of Alexandria, 8, 15, 16, 240, 249, 250, 260, 264, 282, 283, 284
Clement, Bishop of Rome, 45, 390
Coessentiality. See Consubstantiality
Cohen, A., 262
Coleridge, Samuel Taylor, 209

Conformity to Christ. See Christiformity
Conscience, 100, 129, 169, 170f., 180, 206
Constans, 274
Constantine, 270, 273, 274, 290
Constantinople, Council of, 290, 291, 314
Constantius, 274
Consubstantiality, 29, 31, 44, 47, 48, 260, 266, 268, 269, 291, 297, 298, 305, 307, 312, 313, 314
Cooperation. See Synergism
Coulton, G. G., 139
Cranfield, C. E. B., 339
Cranmer, Thomas, Archbishop of Canterbury, 204
Creation, 3ff., 14, 16, 24, 26, 27, 28, 33, 42, 51, 56, 60, 61, 80, 83, 84, 102, 106, 109, 164, 213, 214, 216, 232, 237, 246, 347, 381, 382, 405
Creativity, 62ff.
Cross, The, 90, 92, 234, 285, 328, 359, 361, 364, 365, 372
Cullmann, Oscar, 49
Cyril, Bishop of Alexandria, 294, 297, 299, 300, 301, 302, 303, 304, 305, 308

Damasus, Bishop of Rome, 45
Deabsolutization, 200, 210, 321, 323, 324, 325
Death, 32, 116, 119ff., 132, 335ff., 403ff., 413
Deification, 281ff.
Deism, 209, 355
Delitzsch, F., 126
Demetrius, Bishop of Alexandria, 264
Democritus, 239
Demythologization, 200, 209, 319, 366, 367
Denney, James, 340, 357f.
Destiny of man and creation, ix, 9, 27, 28, 36, 56, 60, 102, 113, 114, 157, 158, 171, 213, 217, 232, 246, 282, 329, 330, 334, 347, 380, 381, 382, 383, 397, 405, 409, 410f.
Determinism, 150, 160, 163, 179, 183, 189, 192
Devil, The, 73, 74, 75, 76, 79, 89, 91, 96, 116f., 136, 145, 148, 151, 331
Diocletian, 264
Diodore, Bishop of Tarsus, 294, 295, 296
Dioscorus, Bishop of Alexandria, 307, 308, 309, 310, 311, 312

Docetism, 237ff., 275, 292, 307, 315, 318, 324, 325, 375
Dodd, C. H., 31, 41
Donne, John, 53, 126, 133, 135, 382
Dooyeweerd, Herman, 169
Dryden, John, 11
Dualism, 10, 83ff., 87, 90, 105, 107, 112, 193, 195, 196, 199, 206, 237ff., 250, 264, 268, 315, 325
Duns Scotus, 224

Ebionites, 249, 250, 251, 315, 324
Eddy, Mary Baker, 122
Edwards, Jonathan, 403f.
Election, 103, 106, 158ff., 163, 178ff., 189
Eleutherius, Bishop of Rome, 256
Elizabeth I, 204
Empedocles, 247
Enlightenment, The, 140, 355
Ephesus, Council of, 186, 201, 294, 302, 314
Epigonus, 255
Epiphanius, Bishop of Salamis, 243, 247, 250, 252, 253, 264
Eusebius, Bishop of Caesarea, 38, 248, 249, 250, 251, 258
Eusebius, Bishop of Dorylaeum, 307
Eusebius, Bishop of Nicomedia, 266, 268, 269, 270, 273, 290
Eustathius, Bishop of Antioch, 290
Eutyches, Eutycheanism, 303, 307, 308, 309, 311, 315
Evangelism, 167ff., 172ff.
Evil, 73ff., 76, 86ff., 115, 117, 231
Evolutionism, 90ff., 99ff., 109, 112, 200, 224ff., 322, 323

Faith, 163, 164, 167ff., 182, 184, 188, 192, 262, 379
Fall, Fallenness, 65ff., 73, 88ff., 113, 115ff., 121, 123, 129, 135ff., 141, 143, 148, 155, 160, 185ff., 217, 363
Fatalism. See Determinism
Faustus the Manichean, 86
Fazio, Bartolomeo, 12
Felix Culpa concept, 92, 94, 96, 107, 166, 206
Feuerbach, Ludwig A., 210
Ficino, Marsilio, 12
Filioque clause, 290f.
Firstborn, 35ff.

Flavian, Bishop of Constantinople, 307, 308, 309, 310, 311
Foreknowledge, 152ff.
Foreordination. See Predestination
Form (morphē), 47ff.
Forsyth, P. T., 339, 361, 375
Freedom, of man, 98, 143ff.; of God, 148ff.
Fromm, Erich, 136

Glory, Glorification, 42ff., 363ff., 381, 383, 411
Gnostics, Gnosticism, 44, 85, 86, 237, 239, 240, 241, 243ff., 268, 269, 284, 315, 325, 396
Gogarten, Friedrich, 376
Gore, Charles, Bishop of Oxford, 224, 225, 226f.
Grace, 163ff., 182, 184, 188, 190, 191, 192, 364
Gratian, 290
Gregory of Nazianzus, 75, 287, 288, 289, 290, 292, 293, 346
Gregory of Nyssa, 11, 18, 37, 87, 88, 257, 288, 289, 344, 345, 399
Grillmeier, Aloys, 234, 267, 294, 295, 296, 297, 303, 305, 326

Hadrian, 246
Haeckel, Ernst, 109
Harnack, Adolf, 187, 266, 299, 326
Hegel, G. W. F., Hegelianism, 96ff., 99, 112, 199
Heidegger, Martin, 106
Heraclitus, 41
Hermas, 249
Hilary, Bishop of Poitiers, 257
Hippolytus, 4, 239, 240, 247, 248, 250, 251, 253, 255, 256, 257, 258, 282, 283
History, 375ff.
Hodge, Charles, 186, 332
Holy Spirit, The, 33, 291, 383
Homer, 40
Hooker, Richard, 204
Hosius, Bishop of Cordove, 273
Huxley, Julian, 210
Hypercalvinsim, 209

Iamblichus, 239
Ignatius, Bishop of Antioch, 216, 221
Illingworth, J. R., 225ff.
Image, 3ff., 26ff., and passim

Immortality, 398ff.

Incarnation, 12, 13, 20, 29, 33, 46, 47, 85, 90, 92, 100, 195, 213ff., 237, 249, 253, 263, 264, 279, 280, 282, 296, 297, 303, 307, 308f., 313, 314, 315, 322, 325, 327, 331, 341, 360, 364, 365, 372, 379, 380, 381

Infantilism, 110, 111, 112

Intermediate State, 393ff., 398

Irenaeus, Bishop of Lyons, 4, 8, 9, 13, 35, 67, 85, 111, 195, 201, 237, 238, 240, 241, 243, 245, 246, 247, 249, 260, 282, 283, 289, 334, 342, 344, 346, 352

Isidore of Pelusium, 40, 301

Isocrates, 239

James I, 204

Jerome, 218, 252, 264, 265, 274

Jewel, John, Bishop of Salisbury, 9, 22

John, Bishop of Antioch, 300, 301, 304, 305, 308

John of Damascus, 75, 127, 346

John, Bishop of Jerusalem, 264

Judge, Judgment, 69, 216, 231, 361, 362, 382, 402, 406f.

Julian of Eclanum, 185

Justin Martyr, 38, 201, 238, 260, 282, 289

Kähler, Martin, 376, 377, 380

Kant, Immanuel, 110, 111, 199, 324, 375

Keats, John, 120

Keil, C. F., 126

Kenosis, 232ff., 363

Kierkegaard, Søren, 377

Kingdom, The, 408ff.

Kittel, Gerhard, 25

Kuhn, Helmut, 104

Lactantius, 289

Latimer, Hugh, Bishop of Worcester, 21, 22

Laud, William, Archbishop of Canterbury, 208

Law, 59, 115ff.

Lecky, W. E. H., 137, 139, 140

Leibniz, G. W., 93ff., 102, 106, 112

Leo the Great, Bishop of Rome, 305, 308, 309, 310, 311, 312, 313

Leo XIII, Bishop of Rome, 202

Leo, Tome of, 305, 308, 309, 310, 311, 312f.

Lessing, Gotthold, 199, 324, 375, 377

Lightfoot, J. B., Bishop of Durham, 28, 38, 48, 245, 320

Likeness, 7, 8, 9, 10, 11, 13, 194f., 197, 283

Loewenich, W. von, 203

Logos. See Word

Lombard, Peter, 16, 22

Loofs, F., 299

Lucian of Antioch, 266

Lucidus, 192

Luther, Martin, 7, 105, 338, 352, 353f., 379

Machen, J. Gresham, 223

Manetti, Bartolomeo, 12

Manicheans, Manicheism, 85, 102, 107, 267, 298

Marcian, 311

Marcion, 85, 247

Mariology, 201ff.

Martin, R. P., 49

Mary Tudor, 204

Mascall, Eric, 228

Maximilla, 251, 252

Mayor, J. B., 43

McLachlan, H. John, 208

McTaggart, J. McT. E., 98, 99

Melchizedekians, 250f.

Meletius, Bishop of Antioch, 290

Memnon, Bishop of Ephesus, 301, 304

Menander, 246

Merit, 188, 190, 191, 197, 198, 201

Metempsychosis. See Transmigration of Souls

Methodius, 264

Metzger, Bruce M., 395

Michelangelo, 63

Miegge, Giovanni, 203

Monarchianism, Dynamic, 258f., 260, 315

Monarchianism, Modalistic, 254, 256, 260, 315

Monergism, 210

Monet, Claude, 63

Monophysitism, 309, 315

Montanus, Montanism, 251ff., 298

Moral Influence (subjective) Theory, 350ff.

Morality, 59ff.

Morris, Leon, 339

Mozart, W. A., 63

Murray, John, 131

Nectarius, Bishop of Constantinople, 290
Neoorthodoxy, 107ff.
Nestorius, Nestorianism, 294ff., 307, 308, 312, 315
Newman, John Henry, 141, 142, 225, 328, 333
Nicea, Council of, 38, 265, 266, 269, 270, 272, 273, 314, 343
Nicea, Creed of, 270f., 291, 315, 344
Niebuhr, Reinhold, 120f.
Nietzsche, F. W., 210, 377
Noetus, 255ff.
Norris, R. A., 297
Nothingness, 101ff.

Orange (Arausiacum), Second Council of, 192, 193
Origen, 8, 16, 28, 45, 75, 87, 88ff., 91, 112, 249, 251, 260ff., 266, 267, 268, 269, 272, 282, 285, 298, 344, 404
Original Sin, 125ff., 194, 197, 205, 207
Orr, James, 46
Orthodoxy, 317ff., 373
Osiander, Andreas, 11, 12, 16, 224
Owen, John, 205, 208

Pannenberg, Wolfhart, 220f., 368, 376ff.
Patripassianism, 253, 315
Paul of Samosata, 258f., 266, 269, 298, 325
Pelagius, Pelagianism, 92, 101, 102, 110, 121, 153, 185, 186, 187, 196, 197, 202, 205, 209
Perkins, William, 161
Person, Personhood, 5, 30, 40, 51ff., 119, 159, 169, 178, 182, 195, 218, 329f.
Phidias, 63
Philo, 10, 12, 15, 16, 20, 34, 45, 239, 262
Photinus, 298
Pico della Mirandola, 12, 224
Pighius, 177
Pious Fraud (pia fraus), 244, 345
Pius X, Bishop of Rome, 202
Pius XI, Bishop of Rome, 202
Pius XII, Bishop of Rome, 202
Plato, Platonism, 20, 40, 41, 83, 84, 86, 90, 93, 196, 239, 248, 262, 284, 404
Pneumatomachi, 291
Point of Contact, 168ff.
Polycarp, Bishop of Smyrna, 240, 247
Praxeas, 253ff.
Predestination, 152ff., 183, 189, 200

Prestige, G. L., 300, 301
Priscilla (Prisca), 251, 252
Privation, 86ff., 107f.
Propertius, 120
Propitiation, 338ff., 348, 352, 358, 360, 361, 362
Prosper of Aquitaine, 191
Psilanthropism, 201, 249, 250, 253, 256, 258, 260, 298, 314, 315, 321, 322, 323, 324, 369
Psychopannychy. See Soul-Sleep
Pulcheria, 309, 310, 311
Pythagoras, Pythagoreanism, 83, 84, 239, 248, 396

Qumran, 251

Rad, Gerhard von, 12
Rahner, Karl, ix
Ramsey, A. M., Archbishop of Canterbury, 25, 46
Ransom Theory, 285, 344ff., 360
Rashdall, Hastings, 358ff.
Rationality, 40, 41, 57f., 82, 196, 207
Reconciliation, 14, 348, 362, 385
Re-creation, 14, 24, 27, 33, 75, 164, 384, 410
Redemption, 9, 14, 16, 24, 27, 104, 157, 246, 347, 361, 364, 379, 405, 411
Reimarus, Hermann, 199, 324, 375
Rembrandt, 63
Resurrection, 32, 33, 165, 362, 363, 365, 366, 367, 369ff., 375, 379, 380, 381, 384, 385, 393
Return of Christ. See Second Coming
Ritschl, Albrecht, 126, 356f.
Robber Council (Latrocinium), 305, 310
Robinson, J. A. T., 210, 319, 320

Sabellius, Sabellianism, 252, 257f., 267, 269, 315, 351
Sartre, Jean-Paul, 106
Satan. See Devil
Satisfaction, 340, 347ff., 352, 362
Saturninus, 246
Savonarola, Girolamo, 392
Schleiermacher, Friedrich, 219f., 325, 355f., 357, 367f., 369
Schmidt, K. L., 39
Scholem, Gershom G., 13
Schubert, Franz, 63

Second Coming, 32, 110, 365, 379, 386, 388ff.
Second Death, 123, 131, 402, 405, 406, 407
Security in Christ, 182ff., 189, 198
Semi-Arianism, 270, 271, 273, 291
Semipelagians, Semipelagianism, 9, 185, 187, 189, 193ff., 200
Sethian-Ophites, 35
Servetus, Michael, 224
Shaw, George Bernard, 231
Shedd, W. G. T., 332
Shelley, Percy Bysshe, 120
Simon Magus, 85, 237ff., 242, 243, 246, 247, 254, 308, 315
Socinus, Socinianism, 61, 207, 208, 209, 360
Socrates, 84
Socrates (church historian), 265, 275, 298, 301, 304
Solzhenitsyn, Aleksandr, 54
Son, 3, 17, 19, 29ff.
Soul, 398ff.
Soul-Sleep, 393f., 398
Sovereignty, 38, 81f., 143f., 150, 153, 159, 160, 162, 176, 178ff., 190, 194, 195, 203, 231, 315, 389, 408ff.
Spicq, Ceslas, 25, 49
Spirituality, 55f.
Stamp, 15, 45ff.
Stephenson, J., 301
Stoicism, 262, 284
Subordinationism, 260, 261, 264, 271, 272
Substitution, 333, 337ff., 344, 352, 358, 360, 361, 362
Suetonius, 137
Synergism, 9, 187, 198, 200ff.

Taylor, Jeremy, Bishop of Down and Dromore, 205ff.
Teilhard de Chardin, Pierre, 229ff.
Tennant, F. R., 99ff.
Tertullian, 46, 137, 138, 201, 239, 247, 248, 249, 250, 251, 252, 253, 254, 255
Theanthropic Person of Christ, 214, 216, 218, 235ff., 269
Theodore, Bishop of Mopsuestia, 39, 294, 296, 297
Theodoret, Bishop of Cyrrhus, 39, 40, 45, 46, 250, 258, 292, 294, 301, 305, 308, 309, 310, 312
Theodosius I, 290

Theodosius II, 300, 309, 310, 311
Theodotians, 251, 258
Theodotus (the leather merchant), 249, 250, 251, 256
Theodotus (the banker), 250, 251, 256
Theophilus, Bishop of Alexandria, 298, 301
Theophilus, Bishop of Antioch, 111, 282, 283
Theotokos ("Mother of God"), 201, 297, 298, 299, 304, 305, 314
Thomas Aquinas. See Aquinas
Thornton, Lionel, 227f.
Tillich, Paul, 210
Transmigration of Souls, 84f.
Trent, Council of, 187, 197, 198
Trevor-Roper, Hugh, 208
Trinity, 17, 30
Tyack, Nicholas, 204
Tyndale, William, 21

Unitarians, Unitarianism, 249ff., 261, 266, 267, 269, 272, 298, 315, 324, 360
Universalism, 174, 265, 404

Valentinian III, 300
Valentinus, 239, 247, 248, 249, 254, 255, 267, 307
Van Til, Cornelius, 170
Vatican Council, The Second, 203
Victor, Bishop of Rome, 249, 256
Vincent of Lérins, 191f.
Virgin Birth, The, 165, 214ff., 373, 375, 378
Vitz, Paul, 54

Wallace, Dewey, 204
Warfield, B. B., 222
Weber, Otto, 123
Wesley, John and Charles, 140
Westcott, B. F., Bishop of Durham, 13
Whitefield, George, 140
Whittaker, Sir Edmund, 58
Will, The, 86f., 88, 115, 143ff., 157, 160, 169, 179, 188, 189, 190, 191, 192, 193, 197, 199, 207
Williams, N. P., 90ff., 100, 112
Williamson, R., 45

Zephyrinus, Bishop of Rome, 250, 256
Zoroaster, Zoroastrianism, 85, 239
Zwickau Prophets, 253

Index of Biblical References

GENESIS
1	57
1:1	384, 411
1:2	103, 104
1:3	26
1:3-5	75
1:21ff.	19
1:24	4
1:26	7, 8, 9, 10, 12, 16, 49, 67, 194, 197, 283
1:26f.	3, 13, 49, 57
1:27	7, 8, 18, 20, 21, 34
1:28	61
1:31	104, 113
1:31–2:2	13
2	34
2:7	34, 329
2:10	413
2:16	335
2:17	122
2:19f.	6
2:23	131
2:24	19
3	34
3:1-5	116
3:3	413
3:5	50, 55, 79, 346
3:6	79
3:14-19	136
3:15	118, 127, 128, 216, 335
3:16ff.	338
3:17ff.	127
3:19	27
3:24	413
4:1	127
4:25	128
5:1	7
5:3	7, 27, 29
5:6-32	128
6:5	128
8:8ff.	136
9:3	6
9:6	6
12:3	162
13:16	412
14:4f.	412
15:6	164
18:18	162
19:24-28	402
22:1-19	165
22:15-18	412
22:18	162, 219, 384
25:23	89, 162
25:29ff.	39
42:11	34
45:7f.	81
50:20	81

EXODUS
3:14	150
4:22	35, 39
9:16	81
20:5f.	126

LEVITICUS
11:44f.	59
18:5	59, 116
19:2	59, 78
20:7	59, 78
20:26	59
26:11f.	413

DEUTERONOMY
6:13	55
18:15	250
21:23	338
25:16	156
29:23	402
30:15-20	172
32:4	183
32:15	183

JOSHUA
21:4	150

1 SAMUEL
2:2	183

2 SAMUEL
7:12ff.	219
7:28	41
22:3	183
22:32	183
22:47	183

1 KINGS
17:17ff.	36

2 KINGS
4:18ff.	36

NEHEMIAH
9	150
9:8	150

9:29	59, 116

JOB

35:7	148
38:4-7	75
38:7	75
40:4	149
41:11	148

PSALMS

2:1f.	82
2:7	384
5:4	159
8	382
8:1	56
8:4	33, 381
8:5	27
8:5f.	411
8:6	61
14:1	125
19:1-4	57
19:7f.	149
22:6	354
31:5	395, 398
33:6	42
36:3f.	309
36:6	153
38:4	133
40:6ff.	276
40:7f.	146
50:1	262
51:3-5	127
51:5	217
57:6	345
65:9	413
76:10	81, 391
82:6	282, 283, 284
89:3f.	31, 219
89:20	219
89:26f.	39
89:27	35
89:28f.	219
89:35-37	31
92:5	153
103:20f.	74
104:1	56
104:24	56
104:33	56
110:1	382

110:4	250
111:10	168
116:7	89
119:105	149
119:160	41
124:7	345
139:5	21
143:10	180
147:5	153

PROVERBS

1:7	168
12:22	156
15:9	156
15:26	156
15:33	77
18:12	77

ECCLESIASTES

12:7	398

ISAIAH

2:19	387
2:21	387
5:20	117
7:9	viii
7:14	44, 250
9:6f.	31, 219, 408
10:22	163
11:9	62
13:6	387
13:9	387
13:13	387
14:12ff.	79
25:8	413
28:16	181
29:14	244
35:10	413
40:8	42, 150
40:13	138
40:17	148
40:28	153
41:4	413
41:6	413
42:1	181
44:6-8	150
46:8-11	150
51:11	413

52:3	134
53	50, 354
53:2	29, 216
53:2f.	363
53:4-7	331
53:5	285
53:5f.	275
53:7	285
55:8f.	148
55:9	380
55:11	42, 150
61:1f.	181
64:4	56
65:1-3	175
65:17f.	407
65:17ff.	113
65:17-19	413

JEREMIAH

2:5	175
2:11	175
2:13	175, 413
2:17	175
2:19	175
3:12	175
3:13	175
3:22	175
5:25	175
9:23	183
9:23f.	164
23:6	28
24:7	413
30:22	413
31:33	413
32:17	148
32:27	148
32:38	413
50:40	402

EZEKIEL

18:4	116
18:20	125
18:23	159
18:30-32	172
18:31	186
18:32	159
18:33	160
20:11	59, 116
20:13	59, 116

20:21   59, 116
33:11   159, 172, 179
36:26   186
37:9f.   167
37:26f.   413
38:2   148
47:1ff.   413
47:12   413

DANIEL
3:19   49
4:35   150
7   31
7:13   31
7:18   408
7:27   408

HOSEA
1:10   163
2:23   163
11:9   148

JOEL
2:11   387
2:32   167, 179

JONAH
1:1f.   176
3:4-10   176
3:10   177
4:1f.   176

HABAKKUK
2:14   62

ZEPHANIAH
1:14f.   387

ZECHARIAH
8:8   413

MALACHI
1:2   89

1:2f.   161
3:2   387

MATTHEW
1:1   218
1:21   184
1:22f.   234
1:23   44, 250
3:2   408
3:12   402
3:17   29, 180, 410
4:1ff.   60
4:2   336
4:8-11   55
4:17   408
4:23   408
5:43-48   162
5:48   29, 78, 113,
           185, 282
6:28   64
7:21   145
7:21-23   407
7:24-27   183
8:5ff.   190
8:12   402
8:18   403
8:27   236
9:6   31
9:35   408
9:36   159
10:15   386
10:18   78
10:23   31
10:27   32, 162
10:28   396, 398, 405
11:22   386
11:24   386
12:8   31
12:22ff.   408
12:24ff.   74
12:28   236
12:31   236
12:36   386
12:38-40   384
12:39f.   32
13:36ff.   402
13:49f.   402
14:14   159
14:33   236
15:24   184

15:25   189
16:16   322
16:16f.   318
16:20   345
16:21   32, 335
16:21-23   318
16:25   54
16:26   56
16:27f.   31
17:1ff.   236
17:5   180, 410
17:12   32, 335
17:22f.   32, 335
18:3   110
18:8   401
19:4-6   19
19:14   110
19:16f.   59
19:17   116
19:25f.   200
19:26   148
19:28   31, 410
20:17-19   335
20:18f.   32
20:28   32, 223
20:34   159
22:13   402
22:15-20   46
23:12   77
23:35   42
23:37   159
24:3   387
24:4f.   317
24:11   317
24:14   390
24:24   317
24:30   387
24:30-31   42
24:35   317
24:37   387
24:37f.   31
24:44   387
24:45ff.   388
24:51   402
25:5   388
25:11   407
25:19   388
25:30   402
25:31   31, 42
25:34   410
25:41   403

25:46	401, 403	14:30	395	18:8	31
26:2	32	14:41	32	18:14	77
26:24	32, 152	14:62	31	18:31	152
26:34	395	16:7	371	18:31-33	32
26:39	333	16:16	167	19:10	32, 171
26:45	32			20:24	24
26:54	32, 152			21:24-27	390
26:56	32, 152	**LUKE**		21:27f.	31
26:64	31	1:1-4	369	20:34-36	18
27:24	337	1:31-35	165	21:36	31
27:46	123	1:32f.	219	22:24	32
27:52	393	1:33	408	22:48	32
28:9	372, 379	1:35	214, 218	22:69	31
28:9f.	371	1:47	202, 218	22:69f.	34
28:10	371, 379	1:54f.	219	23:4	337
28:11ff.	371	1:69f.	219	23:14	337
28:18	32, 62, 371	1:73-75	219	23:22	337
28:19f.	167, 390	2:7	35	23:35	181
		2:32	43	23:41	337
		3:23-38	330	23:43	395
MARK		4:16-21	181	23:46	395, 398
1:1	218	4:29	336	24:6	32
1:11	30, 384	4:35	345	24:12	372
1:14f.	408	4:43	408	24:13ff.	371
1:41	159	5:24	31	24:15	379
2:10	31	6:5	31	24:26	42
2:28	31	7:11ff.	36	24:34	371
3:22-27	75	9:2	408	24:36	379
4:41	236	9:22	32	24:36f.	372
5:35ff.	36	9:26	31, 42	24:36ff.	371, 372, 376
6:27	336	9:28ff.	236	24:39	373
8:31	32	9:29	363	24:41-43	376
8:38	31, 42	9:32	363	24:44-46	335
9:2ff.	236	9:35	184	24:44-48	358
9:7	30, 384	9:44	32	24:45f.	152
9:31	32	9:58	32	24:50ff.	373
9:44	401, 403	9:60	408		
9:47	401	10:17f.	74		
10:33f.	32	10:22	32	**JOHN**	
10:45	14, 32, 216,	11:15ff.	74	1:1	34, 40, 41,
	219, 223, 234,	11:21f.	342		216, 218, 223,
	335, 337, 344	11:30	32		235, 261, 341
12:13-17	46	12:8f.	31	1:1-3	151, 241
12:25	217	14:11	77	1:3	42, 75
12:27	122	14:22f.	173	1:4f.	200
13:10	390	14:26	161	1:5	41, 42
13:26	31, 42	16:19ff.	394, 398	1:9	363
13:32ff.	388	17:22-25	32	1:10f.	363
13:33	392	17:24	386	1:12	363
13:33-37	388	17:24ff.	231	1:14	29, 30, 34, 40,
14:21	32	17:30	31, 386		41, 42, 44,

	216, 218, 223, 235, 241, 276, 288, 295, 296, 341, 363	6:62	374	14:26	251, 325
		6:69	241, 321	14:30	55, 75, 195
		7:30	336	15:17	151
		7:44	336	15:26	251
1:16	245	8:12	41, 43, 363	16:7	251
1:17	242	8:16	30	16:11	55, 75, 195
1:18	30	8:20	336	16:13	251, 325
1:29	285, 331, 336	8:24	123	16:32	30
1:34	241	8:29	30	17:1	336
1:41f.	241	8:31f.	317	17:3	262, 272
1:49	241	8:31-36	147	17:4	364
1:51	241	8:34	145	17:5	30, 42, 236, 242
2:11	236, 363	8:35	149		
2:19	398	8:36	146	17:11	282
2:21	295	8:38	195	17:17	41
3:13	32, 223	8:40	250	17:24	30, 42
3:16	157, 171, 354	8:41	195	17:26	31
3:16-19	180	8:41f.	223	18:36	408
3:17	14, 147	8:44	74, 79, 195	19:30	398
3:17f.	171	8:56	165	20:11ff.	371
3:19f.	117	8:58	223, 242	20:14ff.	379
3:19-21	149, 363	8:59	336	20:17	374
3:21	42	9:22	32	20:19f.	376
3:31	223, 329	9:25	169	20:19ff.	371, 372, 379
3:34	173	9:44	32	20:22	167
3:35	30	9:58	32	20:26ff.	371
3:36	131, 175, 180, 244	10:11	151, 335, 337	20:27	376
		10:15	335, 337	20:31	167, 241
4:1-3	242	10:17f.	233, 335	21:1	379
4:14	413	10:18	263	21:1ff.	371
4:24	55, 80	10:30	30, 241	21:4ff.	379
4:34	147, 180	10:34	282	21:9-14	376
5:23	216	10:39	336		
5:24	119, 123, 131, 216, 329, 406	11:1ff.	36		
		11:4	364	**ACTS**	
5:25-27	34	11:11	393	1:8	167, 390
5:27	31	11:14	393	1:8ff.	33
5:28f.	387	11:23-26	387	1:9f.	369, 373
5:29	401	11:27	241, 336	1:11	379
5:30	147, 216	12:23	233, 336, 364	1:22	239
5:37	216	12:27f.	233	2	252
6:27	32	12:31	55, 75, 195	2:22	322, 363, 379
6:33	32	12:32f.	335	2:23	82, 152, 335, 379
6:35	32	12:46f.	171		
6:37	179	12:47	14	2:32	379
6:38	32, 147, 216, 223	12:48	171, 317	2:32f.	167, 322
		13:1	336	2:36	379
6:40	387	13:1f.	364	2:47	179
6:44	146, 179, 387	14:6	41, 317, 325	3:13	365
6:51	32, 341	14:16	251	3:18	335
6:54	387	14:16-18	33	3:21	151, 384, 406

4:24-28	82	1:23	401	8:14-17	36
4:27f.	152, 335	1:23-25	26	8:15f.	282
4:33	379	1:25	55, 145	8:15-17	184
5:30	379	2:5	134	8:15-18	410
7:55	43, 379	2:11	158	8:16f.	384
7:55f.	33	2:16	180, 386	8:18-42	42, 152
7:58	170	3:8	94	8:19ff.	385, 411
7:59	379, 398	3:9	168	8:19-21	81, 413
7:60	393	3:9ff.	202	8:21	406
8:1-4	391	3:9-12	116, 125	8:28	151, 152
8:5ff.	238	3:19f.	125	8:28-30	81, 182
8:9ff.	85	3:19-28	182	8:29	22, 27, 36,
8:18-24	238	3:21-23	151		373, 382
9:5	184, 379	3:22f.	116, 125, 167	8:29f.	152, 183
10:34	158	3:23	59, 130, 202	8:31-39	152
10:36	410	3:25	339	8:32	151, 184, 349
10:38	376	3:26	161, 362	9:6ff.	162
10:38-40	376	3:28	198	9:11	162
10:40f.	371, 376	4:16-22	164	9:11-13	89
10:41	376	4:17	164	9:13	161
13:30-35	384	4:25	321	9:16	162
13:31ff.	379	5:1	198	9:17	81
13:36	393	5:2	42	9:24-26	163
13:37	335	5:5	162	9:27ff.	163
13:46	175	5:6	166, 200, 337	9:30-33	163
16:30f.	167	5:8	157, 161, 337,	10:5	59, 116
17:3	379		352	10:12f.	167, 171
17:18	379	5:10	160, 200	10:13	179
17:30f.	172	5:12	115, 130, 174,	10:14	167
17:31	180, 386		335	11:5f.	163
20:25	408	5:12ff.	129, 174	11:17-23	163
20:28	341, 344	5:12-21	128ff.	11:25	390
20:29f.	317	5:15ff.	134	11:33	153
22:8	379	5:17	175	11:33-36	148
24:15	401	5:18	174	12:2	117
26:14	170	5:20	173	13:11	387
26:15	379	6:1	94	13:11f.	387
26:23	380	6:3ff.	383	13:12	386
26:26	380	6:6-11	168	13:14	135
28:23	408	6:16	346	14:12	60
28:31	408	6:17-19	168	15:7-12	163
		6:20	145	15:18-20	390
		6:22	146	15:24	390
ROMANS		6:23	59, 116, 122,	15:28	390
1:3	218, 295		166, 335, 413	16:13	181
1:4	165	7:10	116	16:14	249
1:14	390	7:12	59, 116		
1:16	175	7:13	59		
1:19-21	55	7:14	59, 116, 346	**1 CORINTHIANS**	
1:21f.	200, 255	8:1	180	1:5	243
1:22	244	8:2	147	1:7f.	387

1:8	386	15:6	393	5:14f.	337, 343	
1:14	245	15:8	370	5:17	28, 127, 245,	
1:18	328	15:14	369		384, 385	
1:18ff.	244	15:17	369	5:18	341	
1:23f.	328	15:20	36, 330	5:18f.	151, 323	
1:24	260	15:21f.	130	5:18ff.	171	
1:25	244	15:23	36	5:18-21	182, 183	
1:26-31	182	15:23f.	409	5:19	134, 180, 218,	
1:27ff.	216	15:24-26	406		233, 339, 409	
1:28-31	183	15:25	409	5:20	175	
1:29-31	164	15:28	406, 409	5:21	123, 134, 202,	
1:30	28	15:43	399, 412		352	
2:2	328	15:43f.	330	6:1-10	173	
2:8	44	15:44	329	8:9	233	
2:9	56	15:45	24, 110, 329	10:4f.	169	
2:12-15	244	15:45-47	328	10:17	183	
2:14	146, 170, 329,	15:46	329	11:2-4	318	
	353	15:47	329	11:23-29	173	
2:15	329	15:49	16, 27, 29, 330	12:7	148	
3:1-3	244	15:51	389, 393			
3:13	386	15:51-57	405			
3:16f.	284	15:54	119	**GALATIANS**		
3:21	183, 184	15:54-57	123, 381, 406	1:6-9	318	
3:21-23	151	15:55f.	400	1:11ff.	390	
4:6f.	55			2:20	277, 337, 341	
4:7	184			3:6-9	390	
5:1ff.	138	**2 CORINTHIANS**		3:8	219, 384	
5:5	386	1:9	200	3:8f.	412	
6:2f.	381	1:14	386	3:12	59, 116	
6:9	410	1:20	150, 162, 165	3:13	338, 413	
6:9-11	170	3:7	116	3:16	162, 165, 219,	
6:19	284	3:7ff.	26, 59		384, 390, 412	
6:20	344	3:9	116	3:26	384	
7:23	344	3:18	26, 27, 28, 45,	3:28f.	384	
8:1-3	243		113, 198, 373,	3:29	412	
9:16	173, 390		382, 411	4:4	34, 216, 218,	
9:22	173	4:4	3, 17, 22, 26,		278	
9:23	390		42, 55, 75, 195	4:23	216	
10:31	147	4:4-6	26, 200	4:24	216	
11	23	4:6	385	4:29	216	
11:7	16, 17, 22, 24	4:11	406	5:17	399	
11:17ff.	139	4:16	406	5:19-24	244	
13:2	243	4:16-18	397	5:21	245, 410	
13:9	252	4:17	42	6:14	364	
13:12	82, 148, 243,	5:1-5	405			
	252, 411	5:1-9	396			
14:33	339	5:4	399	**EPHESIANS**		
15:1-3	318	5:5	397	1:3	383	
15:3	315	5:6-8	397	1:3-5	181	
15:3f.	370	5:10	277	1:4	384	
15:5f.	371	5:14	130	1:5	179	

1:7	384	1:23	396	3:9f.	135
1:7f.	338	2:5ff.	49	3:10	16, 27, 385
1:9f.	151, 384	2:5-11	234		
1:11	118, 151, 152	2:6	49		
1:13	387	2:6f.	278	**1 THESSALONIANS**	
1:13f.	383	2:7	34, 216	2:11f.	410
1:17	43	2:7f.	233	4:11f.	388
1:18-20	383	2:8	234, 331, 342	4:13ff.	388
1:19f.	166, 374	2:8-11	365	4:13-15	393
1:19-23	411	2:9ff.	27	4:15	389
1:20ff.	27	2:9-11	32, 383	5:2	386
1:20-22	32	2:13	180	5:9f.	337
1:20-23	365	3:8	243	5:23	287
1:23	234, 406	3:20	373		
2:1	122	3:20f.	329, 379		
2:1ff.	329	3:21	27, 295, 330	**2 THESSALONIANS**	
2:1-5	145, 200	4:8	64	1:7-10	231, 387
2:2	55, 75			1:9	405
2:3	126, 195			2:1ff.	388
2:4f.	166	**COLOSSIANS**		3:6ff.	388
2:4-6	62, 383	1:6	391		
2:4-10	182	1:13	13, 410		
2:8f.	166	1:15	3, 16, 17, 22,	**1 TIMOTHY**	
2:8-10	182		25, 28, 36, 38,	1:12ff.	390
2:10	127, 385		39, 40, 260,	1:15	216, 219, 336
2:13-16	385		262	1:18	156
3:18f.	234	1:15ff.	413	2:1-4	173
3:19	245	1:15-17	213	2:4	243
4:9f.	223	1:15-20	35	2:5	34
4:10	374	1:16	37, 75, 151,	2:6	337, 344
4:12f.	113		408	3:6	79
4:12-14	28	1:16f.	28	3:16	42, 295, 374
4:13	ix, 245	1:17	13, 151, 408	4:1ff.	317
4:17f.	118	1:18	36, 39, 330	4:10	174
4:22-24	135	1:18-20	409	6:14f.	410
4:23f.	118	1:19	245, 341	6:15	152
4:30	387	1:20	151, 338, 341,	6:15-17	401
5:2	337		385, 406, 412	6:16	400, 405
5:5	410	1:21	200	6:20	238
5:14	200	1:22	295	6:20f.	315
5:22ff.	23	1:25	390		
6:9	158	1:27	44		
6:10ff.	156	1:28	244	**2 TIMOTHY**	
6:12	75	2:2f.	244	1:9	182
		2:9	25, 218, 237,	1:9f.	400
			245, 341	1:10	405, 406
PHILIPPIANS		2:9f.	234	1:12	387
1:6	150, 166, 182,	2:17	25	2:3	156
	387	3:1	374	2:10	42
1:10	387	3:1-4	62	3:1-4	231
1:21-24	396	3:4	42	3:12f.	231

4:7	318	5:5	384	**1 PETER**	
4:8	387	5:7	295	1:3	318
4:17	390	5:8f.	331	1:3f.	383, 410
		6:20	374	1:4	286
		7:26	202, 335, 374	1:10f.	365
		7:27	206	1:15f.	59, 78
TITUS		8:6ff.	413	1:18f.	318, 331, 344
2:13	43, 48	9:12	374	1:21	365
2:13f.	182	9:14	200, 337	1:23-25	42
2:14	337	9:15	413	1:25	150
3:4-6	182	9:24	374	2:2	202
3:13	42	9:26	338, 386, 405	2:6	181
		9:27	123, 335, 399	2:9	278
		9:28	386	2:22	335
		10:1	24, 25	2:24	116, 234, 318,
HEBREWS		10:5	29, 295, 343		331
1:1f.	386	10:5-10	276, 329	3:11f.	387
1:2	42, 410	10:7	180, 216	3:15	168
1:2f.	151, 213	10:7-10	146	3:18	14, 116, 202,
1:3	29, 44, 45,	10:9	216		234, 275, 318,
	233, 279, 364,	10:10	29, 295, 343		328, 331, 337,
	374, 382, 408,	10:12	364		352
	410	10:14	337	3:19	398
1:5	384	10:22	200	3:22	365, 374
1:6	36	10:25	386	4:5	60
1:7	75	10:31	407	4:13	42
1:14	74	11:3	42	5:8f.	156
2:5ff.	27, 381	11:13	165	5:10	113
2:5-9	411	11:16	413		
2:6ff.	33, 62	11:17-19	165		
2:8	406	11:35	36	**2 PETER**	
2:9	14, 337, 364,	12:1f.	382	1:4	278, 281, 286
	381, 382	12:2	166, 336, 364,	1:6f.	386
2:10	330, 331, 381		374	1:7	43
2:11	382	12:16	35	1:16-18	42, 236, 263
2:11ff.	36	12:16f.	39	1:17	42
2:11-14	330	12:23	36, 39	1:20	386
2:14	218, 335, 352,	12:27-29	402	2:1	344
	382, 400	13:8	81	2:6	402
2:14f.	14, 75, 96,	13:14	413	2:9	386
	123, 146, 352,			2:19	145
	406			3:2	315
2:15	145			3:3-9	389
2:18	331, 333	**JAMES**		3:4	393
3:17-19	137	1:13f.	78	3:5	42
4:12	42, 150	1:17	78	3:6	412
4:12f.	123, 399	2:1	43	3:7	402, 412
4:13	60, 380	2:5	410	3:8	395
4:14	374	3:15	329	3:9	161, 173
4:15	202, 331, 335	4:7	156	3:10	386
4:15f.	333	5:8f.	387	3:11f.	392

3:11-13	402	5:12	255	7:14	412	
3:13	231, 384, 411	5:19	180	7:15	412	
		5:20	41, 242	11:15	410	
				11:18	402	
				12:7ff.	74, 156	
1 JOHN		**2 JOHN**		12:9	74	
1:1-3	242, 376	7	242, 295, 318	14:10f.	402	
1:5	41			14:11	403	
2:1f.	242, 338, 352,			14:13	393	
	360	**JUDE**		14:14	33	
2:2	174	3	318	16:14	156, 386	
2:17	145	3f.	315	19:11	156	
2:18	242, 387	6	386	19:20	402	
2:18ff.	317	7	402	20:2	74	
2:19	242	17ff.	315	20:6	123, 402	
2:22	242	24	44, 113	20:10	75, 402	
2:28	387			20:11-15	123	
2:29	156			20:13-15	406	
3:2	36, 411			20:14f.	402	
3:3f.	113, 387	**REVELATION**		21:1	231, 384, 412	
3:5	156, 202, 335,	1:5	36	21:1ff.	114	
	405	1:8	150, 382, 413	21:1-4	102, 407	
3:5-10	96	1:13-16	33	21:3	45, 413	
3:6	352	1:16	171	21:4	405, 406	
3:8	79	1:18	119	21:5	36, 384	
3:9	156	2:11	402	21:6	382, 413	
3:16	337	2:12	171	21:8	156, 402	
4:1-3	242	2:16	171	21:23	43	
4:2	295	4:11	56	21:27	156, 402	
4:9f.	157, 166	5:11-14	365	22:1f.	413	
4:10	352, 362	6:9-11	395	22:2	115, 413	
4:15	242	6:15-17	387, 407	22:3-5	42	
4:16	162	6:17	386	22:5	43, 406, 414	
4:17	386	7:9	412	22:13	34, 150, 382,	
4:19	352	7:9ff.	183		413	
5:1	242	7:10	341	22:14	115	
5:6	242	7:11f.	412	22:17	179	